W9-CIE-617

1808
The Flight of the Emperor

King João VI in 1818

1808
The Flight of the Emperor

HOW A WEAK PRINCE, A MAD QUEEN, AND THE BRITISH NAVY
TRICKED NAPOLEON AND CHANGED THE NEW WORLD

LAURENTINO GOMES

TRANSLATED FROM THE PORTUGUESE
BY ANDREW NEVINS

LYONS PRESS
Guilford, Connecticut
An imprint of Globe Pequot Press

To Carmen, my wife and companion on this journey

First published in Brazil in 2007 by Editora Planeta do Brasil as *1808: Como uma rainha louca, um príncipe medroso e uma corte corrupta enganaram Napoleão e mudaram a História de Portugal e do Brasil.* First published in the United States of America in 2013 by Lyons Press, an imprint of Globe Pequot Press.

Frontispiece portrait by José Leandro de Carvalho.

"One Hundred Days between Sea and Sky" map on page vi by Andréia Caires, courtesy of Editora Planeta do Brasil. Map on page vii by Melissa Baker © Morris Book Publishing, LLC.

Project editor: Meredith Dias
Layout: Mary Ballachino

Library of Congress Cataloging-in-Publication Data

Gomes, Laurentino, 1956-
  [1808. English]
  1808 : the flight of the emperor : how a weak prince, a mad queen, and the British navy tricked Napoleon and changed the new world / Laurentino Gomes : translated from the Portuguese by Andrew Nevins.
      pages cm
  Originally published in Portuguese under the title: 1808 : como uma rainha louca, um príncipe medroso e uma corte corrupta enganaram Napoleão e mudaram a história de Portugal e do Brasil. São Paulo : Editora Planeta do Brasil, 2007.
  Includes bibliographical references and index.
  ISBN 978-0-7627-8796-8
  1. Peninsular War, 1807-1814—Portugal. 2. Portugal—History—Maria I, 1777-1816. 3. Portugal—History—John VI, 1816-1826. 4. Brazil—History—1763-1822. 5. Monarchy—Portugal—History—19th century. 6. Napoleon I, Emperor of the French, 1769-1821—Relations with Latin Americans. I. Nevins, Andrew, translator. II. Title.
  DP644.G6613 2013
  946.9'034—dc23

                                                    2013016667

Printed in the United States of America

10 9 8 7 6 5 4 3 2 1

"He was the only one who tricked me."
—NAPOLEON BONAPARTE ON JOÃO VI

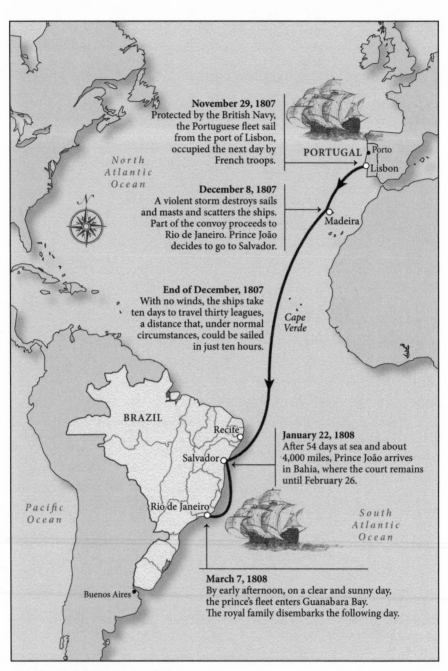

November 29, 1807
Protected by the British Navy, the Portuguese fleet sail from the port of Lisbon, occupied the next day by French troops.

December 8, 1807
A violent storm destroys sails and masts and scatters the ships. Part of the convoy proceeds to Rio de Janeiro. Prince João decides to go to Salvador.

End of December, 1807
With no winds, the ships take ten days to travel thirty leagues, a distance that, under normal circumstances, could be sailed in just ten hours.

January 22, 1808
After 54 days at sea and about 4,000 miles, Prince João arrives in Bahia, where the court remains until February 26.

March 7, 1808
By early afternoon, on a clear and sunny day, the prince's fleet enters Guanabara Bay. The royal family disembarks the following day.

North Atlantic Ocean

South Atlantic Ocean

Pacific Ocean

PORTUGAL   Porto
Lisbon

Madeira

Cape Verde

BRAZIL

Recife

Salvador

Rio de Janeiro

Buenos Aires

A hundred days between sea and sky
It took the Portuguese court almost three and a half months to make their way to Rio de Janeiro, with a five-week stop in Salvador.

CONTENTS

Introduction x

PART ONE: THE FLIGHT OF THE EMPEROR

    I   Flight from Lisbon 3
    II   The Era of Deranged Monarchs 8
   III The Plan 15
   IV The Declining Empire 23
    V   Departure 31
   VI The Royal Archivist 40
  VII The Voyage 46
 VIII Salvador 57
   IX The Colony 68
    X   Tree Frog, the Reporter 84
   XI A Letter 96

PART TWO: THE RISE OF BRAZIL

   XII Rio de Janeiro 101
  XIII Dom João 115
  XIV Carlota Joaquina 125
   XV Hands in the Coffers 132
  XVI A New Court 138
 XVII Empress of the Seas 144
XVIII Transformation 151
  XIX The Chief of Police 162
   XX Slavery 169
  XXI The Travelers 184
 XXII Napoleon's Downfall 196
XXIII The Republic of Pernambuco 203
XXIV Tropical Versailles 210

PART THREE: THE RETURN OF THE MONARCH

XXV Portugal Abandoned 221
XXVI The Return 230
XXVII A New Brazil 235
XXVIII The Conversion of dos Santos Marrocos. 242
XXIX The Secret 249

Acknowledgments 253
Notes 255
Bibliography 296
Index 310

INTRODUCTION

In 1784, five scant years before the French Revolution began, Bernardino da Motta Botelho had put his cattle to graze in Monte Santo, one of the most arid regions in the backlands of the state of Bahia, Brazil, when a rock different from any other in the middle of the pasture attracted the boy's attention. It was smooth and dark and was a discovery that soon became famous. In 1810, scientists from the Royal Society of London concluded that it was a meteorite, a rock that, after traveling millions of miles through the darkness of the universe, had crashed into Earth's surface. At just over six feet in diameter and weighing five tons, the Bendegó meteorite—the largest ever found in South America—today stands proudly on display in the lobby of the National Museum in Rio de Janeiro.

Situated in the Quinta da Boa Vista gardens a few hundred yards from Maracaná stadium, with a view of the Mangueira favela, it is one of the strangest museums in Brazil. In addition to the meteorite, its collection features stuffed birds and the traditional clothing of indigenous tribes, all housed in glass cases that resemble the storefront window displays of rural cities. The pieces appear randomly, without any apparent criteria for organization or identification. The National Museum is even stranger for what it hides than for what it displays, though. The building that houses it, the Palace of São Cristovão, supplied the setting for one of the most extraordinary events in Brazilian history.

There lived the only European sovereign ever to set foot in the New World in over four centuries. Dom João VI, king of Brazil and Portugal, received his subjects, ministers, diplomats, and foreign visitors in that building over the course of more than a decade. The transformation of Brazil into an independent nation also took place there. Despite its historical importance, however, virtually nothing in the São Cristovão Palace recalls the Portuguese court that thrived in Rio de Janeiro. This three-story rectangular building, which Dom João received as a present from one of the city's slave traffickers when he arrived in Brazil in 1808, stands today neglected and forgotten. No plaques indicate where the royal bedrooms, kitchens, or stables once lay. It is as if history had vanished deliberately from the place.

The same negligence repeats itself in the center of Rio de Janeiro, where another building ought to serve as a place of remembrance for this period. In the Plaza 15th of November, in front of the docks where ferries cross the Bay of Guanabara toward the city of Niterói, lies the ancient Imperial Palace, a two-story seventeenth-century mansion. This was the official seat of the government of Dom João in Brazil from 1808 to 1821, but today you might pass in front of it without discovering any such information. An unidentified old-timey wooden carriage sits against the window to the right of the main entrance, but otherwise nothing makes reference to the building's past. On the wall next to the carriage, a map in high-relief shows the buildings and skyscrapers of modern Rio de Janeiro—an anachronistic curiosity. A map of the colonial city when the Portuguese court first arrived would be more in keeping. This is the Imperial Palace after all.

The otherwise empty rooms sporadically host events often either ignorant or devoid of context. On the upper floor in November 2005, the throne room where João VI once dispatched his ministers contained an art exhibition in which rosaries on the floor simulated male genitalia. It is the province of art to surprise and challenge common sense, but the exhibition of these objects in a place that for so many years housed one of the most pious courts in Europe amounted to little more than provocation for provocation's sake.

But then disdain for historical monuments was never a novelty in Brazil. In the case of João VI, however, an additional factor heightens the seemingly deliberate amnesia surrounding him. Modern caricatures represent the king and his court in books, theater, television, and film. Take for one example, among many, the film *Carlota Joaquina, Princess of Brazil,* by Carla Camurati. The queen, who gives her name to the film, appears as a hysterical and treacherous nymphomaniac, and João as a bumbling, gluttonous ruler incapable of making a single decision.

The present book attempts to recapture the history of the Portuguese court in Brazil from the relative oblivion into which it has sunk and to develop its protagonists and the roles they played two centuries ago in the most accurate dimensions possible. As you will see, these people at times behaved unbelievably cartoonishly, as have many of the rulers who have followed them—including many of the present day. The flight of the royal family to Rio de Janeiro occurred during one of the most passionate and revolutionary periods of world history, in which monarchists, republicans, federalists, separatists, abolitionists, traffickers, and slave-masters opposed each other in a power struggle that radically changed the history not only of Brazil and Portugal but eventually the world. These clashing interests explain in part the abandonment of the locales frequented by the royal family as much as the weight of prejudice that still accompanies the works depicting them.

Equally important as the first objective, this book also aims to make this central thread of Brazilian history more accessible to readers interested in the past but unaccustomed or disinclined to decipher the elaborate academic language that permeates many existing works on 1808 and its consequences. The most important book about this period is *D. João VI in Brazil* by diplomat and historian Manuel de Oliveira Lima. Published in 1908, it is both erudite and fundamental, a study unequalled in the depth of its content. De Oliveira Lima's dry style, however, makes it tiring even for readers familiar with the peculiar language of postgraduate dissertations. Curiously the two most recent and accessible books on the topic appeared in English: *Empire Adrift* by Australian journalist Patrick Wilcken and *Tropical Versailles* by historian Kirsten Schulz.[1]

Aside from their typically academic language, historians who examine this period often present a semantic question: Did the Portuguese court *move* or *flee* to Brazil? Which term more properly defines what happened between November 1807 and July 1821, the dates of João VI's departure from and return to Portugal? They never have reached agreement on this point. De Oliveira Lima refers to the "translocation of the court." Luiz Norton calls it a "voluntary transfer" and a "transposition of the Portuguese seat." Ângelo Pereira speaks of "the removal of the royal family to Brazil." Tobias Monteiro treats it as a "transplant." Others use expressions like "transmigration" or "moving," all of them either seeking to minimize—or doing so unknowingly—the military influence of a certain general from Corsica. I refer to the event as a *flight* in the wake of historians Pereira da Silva, Jurandir Malerba, and Lília Moritz Schwarcz, among others.[2]

Although transferring the court to Brazil was an old plan in Portugal, in 1807 the prince regent had little choice: Flee or be apprehended and deposed as happened a few months later with the Spanish monarchy. If no alternative presented itself, then no justification exists for the use of semantic acrobatics to downplay or disguise what happened: a pure and simple fugue, disorderly, rushed, and subject to improvisation and errors. So great was the commotion of departure that hundreds of crates of the Church's silver and thousands of precious volumes of the Royal Library, among other items, lay forgotten on the docks of Belém in Lisbon. The French invaders melted down the silver, which the English recovered some months later. The books arrived in Brazil only in 1811.

While the events of the past remain immutable, their interpretation depends on the tireless investigations of researchers and also on the judgment of future readers. In the case of João VI and the flight of the court, even if two centuries have elapsed, new facts have emerged. Among the important contributions recorded in recent years are the complete transcriptions of the onboard diaries of the British ships accompanying the royal family to Brazil, completed in 1995 by Kenneth H. Light. This work helps resolve some previously nebulous points regarding the crossing of the Atlantic. Equally relevant are the interpretations of historian Jurandir Malerba, author of *The Court in Exile*, which show how the pomp and ritual of the Portuguese court in Rio helped legitimize and consolidate their power in the tropics.

The work of historians such as Mary Karasch, Leila Mezan Algranti, Manolo Garcia Florentino, and João Luis Ribeiro Fragoso stand out for their decisive contributions to more specific themes such as slave trafficking and the accumulation of wealth in João VI's Brazil. In this same line, the research of architect Nireu Cavalcanti and historian Jean Marcel Carvalho França enrich our understanding of colonial Rio de Janeiro. All of these scholars have dedicated themselves to the patient, difficult work of investigating primary sources, such as official documents, diplomatic correspondences, post-mortem inventories, and letters and diaries stored in the National Archive in Rio de Janeiro, the National Archive of the Torro do Tombo in Lisbon, and other institutions. This mining of the past has decisively improved our knowledge of the facts of the time and corrected erroneous interpretations previously dominant.

This book, a journalistic endeavour, builds on the work of these and countless other researchers in order to describe what happened in Brazil two hundred years ago. All of the information contained here derives from historical documents and reports, exhaustively selected and verified. Even so, as with any book, it cannot be immune to potential errors of fact or interpretation that may and indeed should be corrected in the future. With the objective of facilitating reading and comprehension, the text of letters, documents, and personal registers from earlier historical periods has been adapted in the translation to contemporary language.

As a final disclaimer, it's worth saying that I have attempted in a few places to provide contemporary equivalents for some of the prices and monetary amounts from two hundred years ago. As every serious researcher knows, this can be a dangerous exercise. Attempting to update monetary amounts from a period so long ago and with a currency as unstable as Brazil's risks much imprecision. In this case, nonetheless, my objective is to give readers a sense, even if approximate, of the prices and amounts of the era—for example, what a slave or a house in Rio de Janeiro cost in 1807. For those interested in these pursuits, both the British Parliament and a joint project of the University of Illinois and Miami University offer Internet services with currency translators of reasonable precision. Both of these appear in the electronic sources section of the bibliography at the end of this work.[3]

PART ONE
THE FLIGHT OF THE EMPEROR

I

Flight from Lisbon

I magine waking up one morning to the news that the president of the United States has fled to Guam under the protection of the Canadian Air Force. With him have departed all of the country's diplomats, senior judges, elected representatives, and leaders of industry. Furthermore, at this very moment, troops from Mexico are marching overland and in a matter of hours will reach Washington, D.C. Abandoned by the government and without any form of leadership, the nation lies at the mercy of invaders ready to plunder anything they encounter and poised to assume control over the country for an indefinite period.

Facing such unexpected news, one might feel overwhelming abandonment and betrayal, followed immediately by fear and revolt. This was how the Portuguese reacted on the morning of November 29, 1807, when information circulated that the queen, the prince regent, and the entire court were fleeing to Brazil under the protection of the British navy. Nothing like it had ever happened in Europe. In times of war, kings and queens had perished or taken refuge in foreign territories, but none had ever gone so far as crossing an ocean to rule from the other side of the world. Although the kingdoms of Europe maintained immense colonies on widespread continents, until that moment no monarch had ever set foot in an overseas colony even for a simple visit—much less to live and govern. It was, therefore, an event without precedent as much for the Portuguese, orphaned by their monarchy overnight, as for the Brazilians, until then little more than an export colony.

In the case of the Portuguese, another factor aggravated their sense of abandonment. The political idea that power emanates from the people to be exercised in their name, the fundamental principle of democracy, didn't yet exist. Remember, the French Revolution—toppling the House of Bourbon, which ruled by the divine right of kings—had begun fewer than twenty years earlier. In our time, if, through unexpected circumstances, all our political leaders fled the country, the people would gather to elect a new president, senators, and representatives to reconstitute the state and its government. Businesses, too, after a period of uncertainty, given the absence of owners and directors, would likewise reorganize and carry on.

But Portugal in 1807 offered a different story. Without a monarch, the country entered an aimless void. Everything depended on that central ruler: all of the country's economic activity, the survival of its citizens, national autonomy, and the very reason for the existence of a Portuguese state. Complicating this situation even more, Portugal was one of the more backward countries in Europe in terms of political reform. Unlike Great Britain and Holland, where royalty had been giving way gradually to popular representation in parliaments, the regime of absolute monarchy held steadfast in Portugal. The monarch had complete power.[1] It fell upon the central ruler not only to create laws but also to execute and interpret them in the most adequate form. Judges and municipal councils functioned merely as helping hands to the monarch, who could negate their opinions and decisions at any moment.

This context frames the sense of abandonment and irreparable loss that the Portuguese felt in the streets of Lisbon that cold morning at the end of autumn. With the flight of the monarchy, Portugal itself, an independent country with its own government, ceased to exist as all had known it. It had become an empty territory, without identity, its inhabitants unwittingly delivered to the interests and greed of any adventurer who could invade its cities and seize the throne.

So why then did the monarchy flee?

First things first: The throne of Portugal was occupied not by a king but by a prince regent. Dom João reigned in the name of his mother, Dona

Maria I, the nation's first sovereign queen. But having been declared insane and incapable of governing in 1792, she lived in virtual imprisonment in the Palace of Queluz, outside Lisbon. Furthermore, as the second son of this mad queen, Dom João hadn't grown up to direct the destiny of the country. His older brother, Dom José, heir apparent, had died unexpectedly of small-pox in 1788 at the age of twenty-seven.[2] Besides being unprepared to reign, Dom João, a naturally solitary person, was enduring serious marital prob-lems. By 1807 he and his wife—Princess Carlota Joaquina, an ill-tempered and bossy Spaniard, with whom he had had nine children—already had been separated for three years. The couple hated each other intensely. Not only did they sleep in separate beds, but they lived in separate palaces far away from each other. Carlota lived in Queluz with the mad queen while Dom João resided in Mafra in the company of hundreds of friars and monks who lived at the expense of the Portuguese court.

About twenty miles from Lisbon, the Palace of Mafra—iconic of the era of abundance and glory of the Portuguese empire—contained a mix of palace, church, and convent, with an 865-foot façade, 5,200 portals and windows, 114 bells, and a dining hall 330 feet long. Construction of the palace took thirty-four years and required the work of some 45,000 men. The marble came from Italy, the wood from Brazil, and it was completed in 1750 during the height of gold and diamond mining in the state of Minas Gerais in Brazil. In addition to serving as the residence of the court and its servants, it included three hundred monastic cells that housed hundreds of friars.[3] In this gigantic, somber structure, Dom João passed his days, far from his family, dividing his time among government meetings and prayer, mass, and religious chants.

The principal trait of the timid, superstitious, and ugly prince regent's personality, reflected on all of his work, was his indecision. When squeezed between groups of conflicting opinions, he always hesitated to make deci-sions until the last minute. The most elementary measures of governance tormented and anguished him beyond limits. As a result, he delegated much to the ministers who surrounded him. But in November of 1807, Dom João, up against the wall, had to make the most important decision of his life. The flight to Brazil resulted from the irresistible pressure exercised by the greatest military genius the Western world had seen since the age of the Caesars: Napoleon Bonaparte.

In 1807, Napoleon, who had by now crowned himself emperor of the French, ruled as absolute lord of Europe. His armies had brought every king and queen on the continent to their knees in a succession of brilliant and surprising victories. Only Great Britain he hadn't succeeded in subjugating—yet—and not for lack of desire. Protected by the English Channel, the British had avoided direct confrontation with Napoleon's armies, having consolidated their role as masters of the seas in the Battle of Trafalgar in 1805 when Admiral Nelson destroyed the combined fleets of France and Spain.[4] Napoleon reacted by decreeing a continental blockade, a measure that closed all European ports under either his control or influence to British goods. Every country immediately obeyed—with one exception: small, unprotected Portugal. Pressured by England, Portugal's traditional ally, Dom João remained reluctant to surrender to the emperor's demands. So in November 1807, French troops marched toward Portugal, ready to invade and dethrone the prince regent.

Suddenly corralled between the two greatest economic and military powers of the era, Dom João found himself confronted by two mutually exclusive and bitter alternatives. The first: Cede to Napoleon and conform to the blockade; the second: Accept the highly unorthodox offer of his British allies and embark to Brazil, taking with him the entire royal family, the nobility, treasures, and apparatus of the state. On the surface, it seemed a generous offer on the part of Britain, but in practice it was blackmail. If Dom João opted for the first alternative and caved to Napoleon's demands, Britain would repeat in Portugal what they had done months earlier in the similarly reluctant Denmark. On the morning of September 1, 1807, Copenhagen awoke to a barrage of cannon fire from British ships docked in their harbor. The bombardment lasted four days and four nights, during which some two thousand people perished. On September 7, Copenhagen surrendered. The British seized their ships, materials, and munitions, thereby leaving the city defenseless.[5]

In Portugal, the consequences could be even worse. If the prince regent yielded to Napoleon, the British not only would bombard Lisbon and capture the Portuguese fleet, but they would quite likely seize their colonies as well, upon which Portugal depended for economic survival. With the support of Britain, Brazil—the largest and richest of these colonies—would no doubt declare its independence, following the example of the United States of America and its neighboring Spanish territories. Without Brazil, Portugal would falter.

But a third alternative remained, one that Dom João considered: Remain in Portugal, face Napoleon, and fight alongside the British in defense of his country. That move ran the considerable risk of losing the throne and the crown, but later analysis shows that there was a decent chance of success in this case. In 1807, however, the insecure and fearful prince regent, incapable of resisting and facing an enemy he and many others judged as far too powerful, decided to flee. "Preferring to abandon Europe, Dom João proceeded with precise self-knowledge," writes historian Tobias Monteiro. "Knowing himself to be incapable of heroism, he chose the peaceful solution of spearheading an exodus, and searching within the dull torpor of the tropics that tranquility and inactivity for which he was born."[6]

II

The Era of Deranged Monarchs

The dawn of the nineteenth century offered a time of nightmares and terror for Europe's kings and queens. Two of them recently had gone mad. In England, King George III had been seen wearing a nightgown in palace corridors, his head wrapped in a pillowcase, as he cradled a pillow rolled up in the form of a newborn baby, which he claimed to be a prince named Octavius. At the same time in Portugal, demons were chasing Queen Maria I. In the cold and foggy early mornings, her screams of terror echoed throughout the Palace of Queluz. During these increasingly frequent bouts of madness, she reported seeing the image of her father, Dom José I—dead since 1777—as "a calcified mass of ashes atop of a pedestal of blackened and horrific molten iron, all the time ravaged by a phantasmagoric horde," according to the marquis of Angeja, one of her ministers.[1]

Two explanations might account for these patterns of bizarre behavior. The first and most obvious is that the two sovereigns suffered from severe mental disturbances, the nature of which doctors and scientists have not yet deciphered. Recent research suggests that they both had an illness called mixed porphyria, a hereditary disease with symptoms similar to schizophrenia and manic-depressive disorder. Descriptions of their behavior fit this diagnosis.

Psychotic outbreaks periodically interrupted the sixty years during which George III reigned over Great Britain. In one of them, he spent seventy-two hours awake, talking nonstop for sixty of them. On another occasion, he gathered the court to announce that he had conceived a new doctrine of the divine trinity, composed of 1) God, 2) his own private doctor, and 3) the countess of Pembroke, the maid of honor of his wife, Queen Charlotte. "Our king is mad," declared Dr. Richard Warren in 1788. In the final stages of his illness, George III fell under the care of the doctor and priest Francis Willis, who used shock treatment and a straitjacket and chair to immobilize him during bouts of madness.

Trained at Oxford University and a pioneer of a science until then unknown—psychiatry—Willis was enticed to Portugal in 1792 to care for Dona Maria I with an honorarium of £20,000, equivalent today to $1.7 million.[2] But it was all in vain. George III spent the final years of his life imprisoned in an isolated wing of Windsor Castle amid bouts of dementia each tragically more intense than the last. Maria I grew equally incapable of making decisions by 1799, when the regency of Portugal passed to her son, the future King João VI.[3]

The second interpretation of the monarchs' madness is more symbolic. Besides dementia and a political alliance, George III and Maria I had another peculiarity in common. Both belonged to a species condemned to extinction in the Europe of 1807: enthroned monarchs. Never had European rulers lived through times as turbulent and tormented. Kings and queens were persecuted, rendered destitute, imprisoned, exiled, deported, and even executed in public squares.

Napoleon Bonaparte stood at the height of his power in 1807. Three years earlier he had declared himself the emperor of France. "I am not the heir to King Louis XIV," he had written to his minister of external relations, Charles Maurice de Talleyrand, "I am the heir to Charlemagne."[4] The comparison reveals the heights of his pretensions. Louis XIV, the Sun King, had been one of the most powerful kings of France, but Charlemagne, founder of the Holy Roman Empire, controlled territory that covered the vast majority of Western Europe. In other words, for Napoleon, France was not enough; he wanted to be emperor of Europe. In practice, he already was. One year later, in 1808, he practically doubled the original territory of France with the virtual annexation of Spain and Portugal. His territory also extended over

Belgium, Holland, Germany, and Italy to say nothing of the surrounding nations that he controlled more indirectly.

Over the course of a decade, Napoleon led innumerable battles against the most powerful armies of Europe without facing a single defeat. He repeatedly trounced a dynasty of kings considered unbeatable, the Habsburgs of the Austro-Hungarian Empire. He subdued the Russians and the Germans in Austerlitz and Jena, two of the most memorable battles of the Napoleonic wars. Kings, queens, princes, dukes, and nobles had fallen from their thrones, and Napoleon installed upon them members of the Bonaparte family.

"If we were to cast our eyes over Europe in 1807, we would see an extraordinary spectacle," writes historian Manuel de Oliveira Lima.

The King of Spain, on French soil, begging for Napoleon's protection, the King of Prussia ousted from his capital after the invasion of French soldiers, the . . . would-be King of Holland taking refuge in London, the ruler of the Kingdom of the Two Sicilies exiled from his beloved Naples; the dynasties of Tuscany and Parma, vagrant; . . . Scandinavia ready to beg for an heir among Bonaparte's marshals; the Emperor of the Holy Roman Empire and the Papal States obliged to abandon the thrones that they said were eternal and untouchable.[5]

The triumph of Napoleon ended the age of European history known as the Ancien Régime, in which monarchs dominated their countries with absolute power. France had once stood as the paradigm of this system. Louis XIV, the most exuberant of all monarchs in this epoch, ruled for more than seventy years and became known for the phrase "L'état, c'est moi" (I am the State). The Sun King also fought interminable wars. As a result, at the end of his rule, the French monarchy was broke. At that point, France's national debt equaled seventeen times the operating budget of the French government. The court at Versailles supported more than 200,000 people.[6]

Louis XV continued his predecessor's lavish spending, and on the eve of the French Revolution many criticized Marie Antoinette for her expenditures on jewels, clothing, and all-night gambling binges with her friends.

Her enemies called her Madame Deficit, as if she held total blame for the chronic financial problems of the government. These problems drastically worsened over time under the rule of her husband, Louis XVI, during the French involvement in the American Revolution. Supplying arms and funds to the army of General George Washington would help expel the English from North America, but it also left France in financial ruin. To cover its expenses, the government had to raise taxes, generating enormous discontent among the bourgeoisie, the emerging merchant class that had grown rich without direct dependence on the goodwill or favor of the king.

This combination of poor financial management and lack of individual rights resulted in the French Revolution of 1789. The people, incited by the bourgeoisie, occupied the streets, dethroned the monarchy, and installed a new regime—an act unheard of in modern times—which promoted justice and popular participation in government under the motto "Liberty, Equality, Brotherhood." What nobody could have imagined was that to implement these ideas still more bloodshed had to take place. Within a short time, the Revolution escaped the control of its leaders and the Reign of Terror spread through France. In 1793, King Louis XVI and his queen, Marie Antoinette, were decapitated at the guillotine. Chaos overwhelmed the country. A young Corsican official named Napoleon Bonaparte assumed command of the army in 1796 with two objectives: to restore order at home and to stand against the other European monarchies at war with revolutionary France.

Thereafter an incredible series of events radically altered the map of Europe. Napoleon created the most powerful war machine known to modern man and managed devastating victories over opponents stronger both in force and numbers. Regimes that had maintained relatively stable power for centuries began to fall, one after another. The long respected privileges of the nobility ceased to exist virtually overnight. The Napoleonic wars, which lasted some two and a half decades, left millions dead across countless battlefields and changed the course of world history.

In the last two centuries, more books have been written about Napoleon than any other individual in history except for Jesus. More than 600,000 works refer to him directly or indirectly.[7] His immeasurable ambition and vanity stood inversely proportional to his minimal stature of 5'5". Napoleon liked to call himself the Son of the Revolution, and, a military genius by nature, it was the Revolution that gave him the opportunity to demonstrate his talent on the battlefield. He was, therefore, the right man in the right place at the right time—depending of course on how one views the situation. Born in 1769, he was the scion of a family of the petty nobility. During military school, he gained a reputation as a republican and established links with future revolutionary leaders. At sixteen years old, still an adolescent, he became a lieutenant in the French army.

Those revolutionary links placed him in 1793 at the frontlines of the artillery in the Battle of Toulon, a rebel city defended by the English. So decisive was his participation that in the following eight weeks he rocketed from captain to general at a mere twenty-four years old. Three years later he was army commander in Italy, where he distinguished himself for bravery and the boldness of his military maneuvers. Three years after that he became the first consul of France, a position that granted him unrestricted powers. In 1804 he proclaimed himself emperor, at the tender age of thirty-five.

Napoleon transformed the art of war. His armies moved with more rapidity and agility than any other. He always took the offensive and assumed the most advantageous positions on the battlefield, surprising the enemy who quite often withdrew or surrendered without firing a single shot. In December 1805 on the eve of his most memorable victory at the Battle of Austerlitz, a squad of his troops traversed more than sixty miles in just two days—when there were no trucks, tanks, airplanes, or helicopters to transport personnel and equipment. This tremendous mobility allowed his armies to surprise their enemies with unexpected maneuvers in battles that sometimes seemed lost before they even began. Such unpredictable tactics were devastating to his opponents, accustomed to slower, conventional maneuvers.

Before Napoleon, it took months and sometimes years to recruit, train, and mobilize troops for a battle.[8] "In the century before the French Revolution wars had become formal affairs, pursued with limited means for limited objectives by highly trained and brutally disciplined professional armies, commanded, especially in the higher ranks, by an aristocratic cousinage," writes Gunther Rothenberg, military specialist at the Smithsonian Institute and author of *The Napoleonic Wars*. "Battles were avoided because heavy casualties, coupled with desertions, proved too costly for victors and vanquished alike. Wars commonly ended with the exhaustion of finances and manpower rather than with a decisive battle."

Two factors contributed to this change of scene. First, new agricultural techniques increased the yield of food supplies at the end of the eighteenth century and produced a drastic demographic change in Europe. In just a few decades, the population of the continent nearly doubled. France, which had 18 million inhabitants in the middle of the eighteenth century, increased to 26 million by 1792, thereby becoming the second most populous country in Europe (if you count Russia, which had a population of 44 million). More people of course meant more soldiers for the armies involved in the Napoleonic wars. At the same time, the Industrial Revolution, the second factor, allowed for mass production that increased the yield of iron for cannons and rifles, textiles for uniforms, and other equipment necessary for military campaigns.

Napoleon boasted of being able to replace losses on the battlefield at a rate of 30,000 soldiers per month. In 1794, France counted 750,000 men who were trained, equipped, and highly motivated to defend the ideals of the Revolution. This gave him an army on a scale not seen since the Roman Empire. But what mattered to the emperor—a practical, methodical, and cold general—was the result of his combined forces and not the individual destiny of soldiers who fell by the wayside. He planned battles meticulously and shared command with nobody: "In war, one lousy general is better than two good ones," he said.[9] But he was also charismatic and capable of rapidly rousing the spirits of his officials and soldiers. "Morale and the army's attitude are half the battle," he claimed.

Important achievements on various fronts marked his rule, including the hygiene of public finance, the adoption of the metric system, a new constitution, and the Napoleonic Code, which still forms the basis of the judicial systems of France and many other countries to this day. He also began changing the urban landscape of Paris, opening new, wide avenues and inaugurating parks, public squares, and monuments—efforts later continued famously by Georges Haussmann.[10] In 1814, exiled to Elba and isolated from the continent by the Mediterranean after the failed invasion of Russia, Napoleon began drawing up plans to improve education, agricultural production, fishing, and living conditions on the island.

At the height of his power, Bonaparte roused fear and admiration as much in his enemies as in his supporters. Lord Wellington, who defeated him definitively at Waterloo in 1815, once said that on the battlefield Napoleon by himself was worth 50,000 soldiers. The writer François René de Chateaubriand, his adversary, described Napoleon as "the mightiest breath of life which ever animated human clay."

This was the man whom the indecisive and fearful Dom João, prince regent of Portugal, was about to confront in 1807.

III

The Plan

While the imminent invasion of Portugal by Napoleon's troops forced the prince regent to flee, the plan to move to Brazil was an idea almost as old as the Portuguese Empire itself. Based on sound geopolitical logic, it arose every time Portugal's neighbors threatened its independence. Despite having launched the Age of Discovery, Portugal still remained a small country with few resources. Squeezed and constantly threatened by the interests of its more powerful neighbors, it had neither the reach nor the army to defend itself in Europe, much less to colonize and protect its overseas territories fully. Brazil offered more natural resources, a larger workforce, and better chances of defense against would-be invaders. "It was a well-ripened proposal, invariably considered throughout all difficult moments," observes historian Manuel de Oliveira Lima.[1]

At the beginning of the nineteenth century, Portugal depended completely on Brazil. The gold, tobacco, and sugarcane produced in the colony constituted the axis of its commercial relations. The volume of goods and commodities imported from the colony exceeded the amount exported to it by almost double. The commercial balance therefore tipped more favorably to Brazil at a proportion of two to one.[2] Some 61 percent of Portuguese exports to England, its principal commercial partner at the time, originated in Brazil.[3] Of the three hundred ships moored each year in Lisbon's port, one third traded exclusively with Brazil. After observing the vigor of its colonial economy, English traveler Arthur William Costigan wrote that the very existence of the Portuguese as a people "and the immediate support of the throne" depended on Brazil.[4]

This dependence had grown gradually since Vasco da Gama opened the route to the East Indies and Pedro Álvares Cabral landed his fleet in the Brazilian port of Bahia. At the same time, threats to the wealth and autonomy of the Portuguese throne had increased. In 1580, less than a century after the discovery of Brazil, King Phillip II of Spain assumed the Portuguese throne, left vacant two years earlier after the disappearance of King Sebastião during his crusade against the moors in Morocco. For the following sixty years, Spain governed Portugal during the period known as the Iberian Union. It was during this time that the first documents record the proposal to move the court to the Americas.[5]

A few decades later, in 1736, the ambassador in Paris, Luiz da Cunha, wrote in a secret memorandum to Dom João V that Portugal was no more than "a finger's worth of land" where the king "could no longer sleep in peace and security." Da Cunha suggested moving the court to Brazil, where João V would assume the title of emperor of the Occident and appoint a viceroy to govern Portugal.[6] Da Cunha further suggested that the eventual loss of Portugal and the Algarve to Spain could be compensated with the annexation of part of Argentina and Chile to Brazil's territory.

In 1762, facing another threat of invasion, the marquis of Pombal proposed that King José I take "the necessary measures for his voyage to Brazil." With Europe occupied by Napoleon Bonaparte in 1801, this age-old plan took on a heightened sense of urgency. That year, Spanish troops aided by France invaded and defeated the country in an episode known as the War of the Oranges. Frightened by the fragility of the kingdom, Dom Pedro de Almeida Portugal, marquis of Alorna, wrote the following recommendation to Prince Regent Dom João: "Your Royal Highness has a grand empire in Brazil. . . . It is necessary to order with urgency that all of your warships are armed and that all of your transport ships find their way to the Port of Lisbon, where you board the ships with the Princess, your children, and all of your treasures."[7] Two years later, in 1803, the head of the Royal Treasury,

Dom Rodrigo de Sousa Coutinho, completed an account of the political situation in Europe. In his evaluation, the future of the Portuguese monarchy lay in danger, and it would prove impossible to maintain the politics of neutrality between England and France for much longer. The solution? Sail for Brazil.

"Portugal is neither the best part of the monarchy, nor the most essential," wrote Dom Rodrigo. "After the devastation of a long and barbarous war, the remains of the Sovereignty and its people will create a powerful empire in Brazil." The new empire in the Americas could serve as the basis from which Dom João could later recover "all that he had lost in Europe" and still punish "the cruel enemy." According to Dom Rodrigo, "whatever the dangers might be that accompany such a noble and resolute determination, they are much smaller than those that would certainly follow from the entrance of the French in the ports of the Kingdom."[8] Dom Rodrigo's proposal was rejected in 1803, but four years later, with Napoleon's troops at the border, this extraordinary plan of relocation went into action.

The prior existence of so many plans with so much history behind them explains why the relocation of the court to Brazil succeeded in 1807. It was indeed a flight but it was neither rushed nor improvised. The decision already had been made and analyzed by various kings, ministers, and advisors over the course of three centuries. "There would be no other way to explain how a classical country of improvidence and languor, shortly after the announcement of French troops within the national borders, could manage to embark an entire court, with all of its furniture, tableware, paintings, books, and jewels," observes de Oliveira Lima.[9]

But the months preceding the departure were tense and unsettling. In 1807, two groups attempted to influence the actions of the ever indecisive prince regent. The "French party," led by the minister of external relations, Antonio de Araújo e Azevedo, favored joining with Napoleon and his Spanish allies. The "English party," which ultimately triumphed, had Dom Rodrigo as its principal advocate. The godson of the marquis of Pombal and minister of marine commerce and overseas territories, Dom Rodrigo had a long-term vision. He had ambitious plans for Brazil and believed that the future survival of the Portuguese monarchy depended on its New

World colony. In 1790, as the minister of foreign affairs, he approached the Brazilian elite and sponsored trips for Brazilian students to the University of Coimbra in Portugal, then the main academic center of the Portuguese Empire. (Among these students was José Bonifácio de Andrada e Silva, the future patriarch of the Brazilian Independence movement.)

On August 19, 1807, the Council of State met at the Palace of Mafra to discuss the political crisis. The nine closest counselors to the prince regent, including his master of wardrobe and private doctor, the council constituted the most important body of advisers to the monarchy, responsible for proposing large-scale governing measures in times of war and peace.[10] Dom João read out the terms of Bonaparte's intimidation: Portugal had to adhere to the Continental Blockade, declare war on Britain, withdraw their ambassador—Dom Domingos de Sousa Coutinho, Dom Rodrigo's brother—from London, expel the British ambassador from Lisbon, and close the ports of Portugal to British ships. They also had to imprison any English citizens inside Portugal and confiscate their property. The terrified council immediately approved Napoleon's conditions with two reservations: They wouldn't imprison English citizens nor confiscate their property. On August 26, a second meeting took place at the Palace of Mafra, during which the terms of the response to Napoleon were approved and the correspondence immediately sent to Paris.[11]

This was all, however, a clever ruse and a dangerous game in which Portugal was bluffing both France and Britain at the same time. While pretending to accept France's ultimatum, they negotiated a different solution to the impasse with Britain. "In the war between France and Britain, Portugal played the role of a clam caught in the battle of the tide and rocks," writes historian Tobias Monteiro.[12] Shortly after the meeting, Britain's representative in Lisbon, Percy Smythe, Viscount Strangford, wrote to his minister of foreign affairs, George Canning, offering a version of events quite different from the letter to Napoleon. According to Strangford, Portugal was trying to buy time with an "ostensible approach of hostility." War with Britain would be officially declared but only as a decoy. In the meantime, the Portuguese government requested that the British neither invade their colonies nor attack their merchant ships.

Squeezed between two powerful rivals, Portugal nonetheless had in its favor the precariousness of communication and transportation. In 1807, the delivery of a letter from Lisbon to Paris took close to two weeks. The post traveled along roads pockmarked by holes and practically impassable during rainy weather. A round trip took a month, sometimes more. From Lisbon to London by sea took at least seven days.[13] This sluggishness allowed Portugal to buy time while they attempted an escape both honorable and acceptable to its fragile kingdom. Upon receiving the terms of the Portuguese counter-proposal, Napoleon reacted as predicted; he sent warning that, if Dom João did not comply, Portugal would be invaded and the Bragança dynasty would be dethroned.

On September 30, gathered at the Palace of Ajuda in Lisbon, the Council of State finally recommended that the prince regent prepare his ships for departure.[14] At the beginning, it was thought that only the prince of Beira, the oldest son of Dom João, should go to Brazil. Young Dom Pedro—just eight years old but destined to become emperor of Brazil—was the natural heir to the Portuguese throne. On October 2, 1807, Dom João issued a proclamation to the Brazilian people, requesting that they receive and defend the young prince.[15] The plan rapidly evolved, however, into something more ambitious: transferring the whole of the court with its rulers, functionaries, and state apparatus—the entire Portuguese elite.

By the middle of October, the definitive decision to transfer the court to Brazil began in earnest. Through the mediation of his ambassador in London, Dom João signed a secret agreement with Britain through which, in exchange for naval protection during the voyage to Rio de Janeiro, he would open the ports of Brazil to commerce with other nations. Up until that point, only Portuguese ships had authorization to buy or sell goods in the colony.

But while the ink of his secret agreement with allied England was drying, Dom João persisted in his game of make-believe with the French. On the eve of his departure, he announced the prohibition on British ships entering Portuguese ports and the imprisonment and the confiscation of property of all British residents in Lisbon. At the same time, he sent an ambassador to Paris, the marquis of Marialva, who swore total surrender to the French. To mollify Napoleon, the diplomat brought a box full of diamonds as a gift. He also suggested that Dom Pedro, the oldest son of Dom João, marry a princess from Bonaparte's family. Though Marialva was held prisoner, his actions singularly allowed Dom João to deceive Napoleon, who believed on the eve of Dom João's departure that Portugal had surrendered to his orders.

On November 1, the post from Paris arrived in Lisbon with another frightening message from Napoleon: "If Portugal does not do what I want, the House of Bragança will no longer have a throne in Europe within two months." At that moment, the French army was already crossing the Pyrenees and heading toward Portugal. On November 5, the Portuguese government finally ordered the imprisonment of Englishmen residing in Lisbon and the confiscation of their property. Faithful to their double-crossing, they had warned Lord Strangford to protect himself. As part of the ruse, even the count of Barca, leader of the French Party in the Portuguese court, proposed the confiscation of British goods in Portugal, but behind closed doors he had negotiated with the British the reparations for eventual victims of this measure.[16]

On November 6, the British fleet appeared at the mouth of the Tagus River, some seven thousand men strong. Their commander, Admiral Sir Sidney Smith—the same official who had bombarded Copenhagen two months earlier—had two seemingly contradictory orders. The first, and his priority, was to protect the royal family as they boarded the ships and to escort them all the way to Brazil. The second, in case the first did not succeed, was to bombard Lisbon.

It was a game of marked cards, in which no party had any illusion about the outcome. Convinced that Portugal had aligned with Britain, the governments of Spain and France had divided Portuguese territory among themselves already. The Treaty of Fontainebleau, signed by the two sides on October 27, 1807, split the tiny nation into three parts. The Northern region, consisting of the provinces of Entre-Douro and Minho, called the kingdom of Northern Lusitania, would go to the reigning queen of Etruria, Maria Luisa of Spain. Next, Alentejo and Algarve, in the Southern region, would pass to Don Manoel de Godoy, the most powerful minister of Spain, also known as the prince of peace. Finally, France would take over the central and richest part of the country, composed of the regions of Beira, Trás-os-Montes, and Estremadura.[17] To the great humiliation of the Portuguese, this piece of land was offered to Napoleon's youngest brother, Lucien, who turned it down. "At a time in which the most voracious of rulers went unchecked . . . nobody wanted little Portugal," writes de Oliveira Lima. "Above all, not without that which constituted its importance . . . its colonial empire."[18]

Some 50,000 French and Spanish soldiers invaded Portugal.[19] If he had wanted, Dom João could have resisted and with a good chance of winning. The soldiers whom Napoleon sent were mostly rookies and members of the foreign legion who had no interest in defending the ambitions of the French emperor.[20] Their commander, General Jean-Andoche Junot, was a second-rate official: a brave combatant but a terrible strategist. Due to lack of planning and the last-minute nature of the invasion, the troops arrived at the border famished and in tatters. Half of the horses had died along the way. Only six cannons arrived. Of the 25,000 soldiers who left France, 700 of

The French enter Lisbon: famished soldiers in tatters, whom Prince João could have defeated with British help—if only he had the courage.
Engraving by Louis Gudin, 1820

them had already died before entering combat.[21] A quarter of the infantry had disappeared because, in the despair of searching for food, the soldiers had become separated from the main column and gotten lost.[22]

In her memoirs, the duchess of Abrantes, wife of General Junot, said that her husband entered Portugal "more as a fugitive than as an emissary who was sent to announce overtaking the country."[23] On arrival at the port of Lisbon, the soldiers were so weak they could barely stand. Many forced the Portuguese to carry their weapons for them. "We were in a situation that was hard to believe," wrote Baron Paul Thiebault, who participated in the invasion as Junot's division general. "Our uniforms had lost their form and color. My toes poked out of my boots."[24]

"Without cavalry, artillery, cartridges, shoes or food, stumbling with fatigue, the troop resembled 'the evacuation of a hospital more than an army triumphantly marching to the conquest of a kingdom,'" notes English historian Alan Manchester, describing the invasion of Portugal.[25] "There is certainly no example in history of a kingdom conquered in so few days and with such small trouble as was Portugal in 1807," says Sir Charles Oman, author of *A History of the Peninsular War,* the most important work written about Napoleon's campaign in the Iberian peninsula. "That a nation of three million souls, which in earlier days had repeatedly defended itself with success against numbers far greater than those now employed against it, should yield without firing a single shot was astonishing. It is a testimony not only to the timidity of the Portuguese Government, but to the numbing power of Napoleon's name."[26]

IV

The Declining Empire

I t seemed that human imagination had no limits in 1807. In England, steam propelled an empire. This new technology, invented by James Watt in 1769, gave birth to the mechanical loom, the driving force of the Industrial Revolution, to the locomotive, to the steam ship, and to the steam-powered printing press, among other mechanical novelties.

Throughout Europe, salons, cafés, theaters, museums, and galleries incubated innovative ideas and creations that definitively marked the history of culture and arts. In Germany, writer and poet Johann von Goethe finished the first part of *Faust,* his masterpiece. In Vienna, Ludwig van Beethoven composed his *Fifth Symphony.* The American Revolution of 1776 echoed across the globe, and the French Revolution of 1789 had redrawn the map of Europe.

Few periods in history brimmed with so many adventures, inventions, and conquests—including political convulsions and ruptures—but curiously none of this seemed to affect the Portuguese. Three centuries after inaugurating the great era of navigation and discovery, Portugal lay far from even remembering the vibrant times of Vasco de Gama and Pedro Álvares Cabral. The signs of decline appeared everywhere. Lisbon, the capital of the empire, had long fallen behind its European neighbors as a radiating center of ideas and innovation. The call to enterprise, of curiosity, of the search for the unknown somehow had slipped away from the Portuguese spirit. The age of glory had passed.

What had happened? Two theories offer explanations. The first is demographic and economic. With a relatively small total population of just three million inhabitants, Portugal had neither the people nor the resources to protect, maintain, and develop its immense colonial empire. It depended on slave labor, a demand that kept increasing in order to exploit gold and diamond mines and an industry of sugarcane, cotton, coffee, and tobacco farming.[1] With an essentially import and mercantile economy, the capital faced shortages. Although ships continued to arrive from all parts of the world, the Portuguese metropolis remained a relatively poor locale because the riches didn't stay there. Lisbon functioned as little more than a commercial waystation. From there, gold, wood, and agricultural products from Brazil proceeded directly to Britain, Portugal's main trade partner, while the New World diamonds headed for Amsterdam and Antwerp.

A sovereign of the seas two centuries earlier, Portugal no longer could defend itself on its own. Its formerly powerful navy had shrunk to thirty ships, of which six or seven were unfit for sailing. It was an insignificant fleet when compared with the British Navy, which at that time dominated the world's oceans with 880 combat ships.[2] As a result of its weakness, the French had captured more than two hundred Portuguese merchant navy ships between 1793 and 1796.[3] Attacks by French pirates between 1794 and 1801 also affected the kingdom's commerce to the tune of more than 200 million francs, almost all of it cargo loaded in Brazil.[4] Today that loss would amount to about $550 million.[5]

The second explanation for the decline comes from the realms of politics and religion. Of all the countries in Europe at the beginning of the nineteenth century, Portugal remained the most resolutely Catholic, conservative, and averse to the libertarian ideas that germinated revolutions and more peaceful transformations in other countries. It is difficult to overestimate the enormous power of the Church. Close to 300,000 Portuguese—10 percent of the total population—belonged to a religious order or remained in some way dependent on monastic institutions. Lisbon alone, a relatively small city of 200,000 inhabitants, contained 180 monasteries. Virtually every ostentatious building in the country was a church or convent.[6] For three centuries, the Church held control over the people, nobles, and royalty. Because of religious scruples, science and medicine were backward or practically unknown. Dom José, heir apparent to the throne (older brother to Dom João), had died of smallpox because their mother, Maria I, had prohibited doctors from vaccinating him. The queen grimly believed that the decision between life and death lay in the hands of God. For her, it did not fall to science to interfere in this divine process.[7]

Processions, masses, and other religious ceremonies guided social life. The Church both determined and monitored individual and collective behavior. In the middle of the eighteenth century, elaborate wooden screens divided the interior of all churches in Lisbon to hinder contact between men and women during liturgical services.[8] Portugal was the last European country to abolish the autos-da-fé of the Inquisition, in which people who might dare criticize or oppose the doctrine of the Church, including infidels, heretics, Jews, Moors, Protestants, and women suspected of witchcraft, were judged and condemned to death by burning at the stake. Until 1761, less than half a century before the transfer of the court to Brazil, public executions of this type still occurred in Lisbon, attracting thousands of devotees and onlookers.

"We left a society of lively men who moved through fresh air, and entered into a timid, almost sepulchral enclosure, with a turbid atmosphere of the dust of old books, inhabited by the ghosts of doctors," lamented the poet and writer Antero de Quental, analyzing the desolate situation of Portugal and its mightier neighbor, Spain, in the eighteenth century. "The last two centuries on the Iberian Peninsula have not produced a single outstanding man who could be put alongside the great creators of modern science. From the Peninsula has not emerged even one of the great intellectual discoveries, which are the great work and highest honor of the modern spirit."[9] Although Quental included Spain on his roster of backwardness, between the two countries Portugal was by far the more decadent (in the stricter, etymological sense) and averse to modernization of traditions and ideas.

The combination of these two factors—the scarcity of demographic and financial resources and the backwardness of political ideas and of traditional customs—had transformed Portugal into a land of nostalgia held hostage to the past and incapable of facing the challenges of the future. With a small population disproportionate to the vastness of its empire, it had no means to defend or even propel its colonial economy. It was a sedentary, obese animal with a weakened heart, lacking the force to advance the parts of its monumental body, its limbs stretching across three continents and two oceans, from South America, through Africa, to the limits of Asia. "The immense colonial empire, as vast as it was vulnerable, was in the most complete disagreement with the means of action deployed by the metropolis to defend and maintain it," observed de Oliveira Lima.[10]

The wealth of Portugal came from easy money, like the profits of inheritance, casinos, and lotteries, none of which demand sacrifice, creative effort, innovation, long-term investment in education, or the establishment of lasting institutions. During a period when the Industrial Revolution in Britain and America began to redefine economic relations and the future of nations, the Portuguese still existed as prisoners of an extractive economy on which they had constructed their ephemeral prosperity three centuries earlier. The economy persisted on the pure and simple exploitation of its colonies, without any investment in their infrastructure or strictly unnecessary improvements of any kind. "It was a wealth that did not beget wealth," writes historian Lília Schwarcz. "Portugal contented itself in draining its colonies in a very parasitic manner."[11] Sérgio Buarque de Holanda, author of *The Roots of Brazil*, shows how in Brazil the colonists had an aversion to hard work. They aimed to exploit all available wealth as quickly as possible with the least effort and without any commitment to the future: "What the Portuguese came to Brazil in search of was without a doubt wealth, but wealth that required audacity, and not work."[12]

Following the chain of missed economic opportunities, this dependence on resource extraction meant that manufacturing never developed in Portugal. Everything was bought from abroad. "The tendency for an abundance of natural resources to weaken institutions and undermine the development sustained by its nations is almost a curse," Dr. Eliana Cardoso, professor at the Getúlio Vargas Foundation in São Paulo, points out. "Countries with economies based principally on the trade of raw materials are driven to commit a series of errors and negligences that impede the modernization of society."[13]

The five principal products of Portuguese colonies—gold, diamonds, tobacco, sugar, and slaves—constituted the commercial axis of the South Atlantic. Those commodities were simultaneously the salvation and damnation of Portugal. "They lacked manufacturing, and failed to produce foodstuffs or clothing in sufficient quantity to meet the minimum necessities of the population, but nonetheless lived in an ostentatious manner, bankrolled by the gold that flowed nonstop from the Americas," writes Lília Schwarcz. "The capital of the Portuguese empire was like that, completely rife with contrasts, where the luxury of the court, living off precious metals from the tropics, cohabited alongside lack of provisions and financial dependence."[14]

The first shipment of gold from Brazil arrived in Portugal in 1699. That first half ton of ore grew to twenty-five tons by 1720. In total, an estimated one thousand to three thousand tons of gold sailed from Brazil into the imperial Iberian capital.[15] Historian Pandiá Calógeras calculates the value of gold shipped to Portugal between 1700 and 1801 as amounting to £135 million—the contemporary equivalent of $11.8 billion. One fifth of this amount went directly into the coffers of the king in the form of taxes.[16] Another historian, Tobias Monteiro, estimates that from the Brazilian state of Minas Gerais alone, some 535 tons of gold were sent between 1695 and 1817, to the tune of 54 million pounds sterling at that time, or $4.7 billion in today's equivalent. Monteiro calculates that another 330,000 pounds of gold were illegally smuggled in the same period.[17] The flow of wealth to Lisbon grew even more with the discovery of diamond deposits in the colony in 1729. Pandiá Calógeras estimates that approximately 3 million carats—1,355 pounds of diamonds—were extracted from Brazil between the middle of the eighteenth century and the beginning of the nineteenth, counting stones traded legally and smuggled.[18]

The prosperity and pageantry generated by this commerce resulted neither in culture nor sophistication. The last to end the Inquisition, Portugal was also last to abolish slave trafficking and to guarantee freedom of expression and individual rights. "In Portugal, there was no science, nor politics, nor economy, nor nobility, nor a court," wrote the Portuguese diplomat José da Cunha Brochado, disturbed by the comparison that he himself made between the habits of the Portuguese court and those of other monarchies in Europe. "Knowledge is in exile; in the convents, all that is known is how to pray the Divine Office."[19]

Then in 1755, a massive natural catastrophe aggravated the economic decadence and further reduced the Portuguese national self-esteem. On the morning of November 1, All Saints' Day, a devastating earthquake detonated off the southwest coast of the country, killing between 15,000 and 20,000 people in Lisbon alone. An enormous tsunami followed as did a conflagration that burned for six days. Churches, homes, palaces, markets, public buildings, and theaters all fell to cinders and ash. Rubble blocked two-thirds of all roads. Only 3,000 homes remained habitable of 200,000. Of the forty churches in the city, thirty-five collapsed. Only eleven of the sixty-five convents that existed before the earthquake remained standing afterwards. The famous Royal Library—70,000 volumes maintained with diligence and pride since the fourteenth century—turned to smoke and had to be entirely reconstructed.[20]

Curiously the tragedy resulted in the one brief surge of modernity in Portugal, though. Sebastião de Carvalho e Melo, the marquis of Pombal, all-powerful minister to King José I since 1750, received orders to reconstruct Lisbon. Atop the ruins, his government redesigned the city with promenades and wide avenues, plazas, fountains, and new buildings. Roads were to be illuminated and cleaned, gardens well-maintained, construction efficiently organized. Pombal saw to this with an iron fist. Reconstructing the capital, he ended up reforming the empire itself. He subdued the nobility and drastically reduced the power of the Church. He expelled the Jesuits from the country and its colonies. He also reorganized education, which until then the Church had controlled.

With Pombal's government began a late entry in the Age of Enlightened Despotism in Europe, in which the monarch and his trusted associates kept the nobility under control and wielded the power to reform not only the state but also the customs of the people and the very landscape of royal rule. It was a period of progressive reforms, though quite far from being liberal. Censorship continued to maintain rigorous control over the publication of books and periodicals, for example. Before Pombal, this role lay in the hands of the Church and the Inquisition. Afterward, it passed to the state. No work could be published or sold without having passed through the winnow of the Royal Censorial Court, its members appointed by the government.

This spate of reforms ended abruptly on February 24, 1777, with the death of José I, a weak king who had delegated governing to Pombal. His daughter and successor, Maria I, the first sovereign woman to occupy the throne in the history of Portugal, restored power to the more conservative, pious, and backward sectors of nobility. The queen was "the most sanctimonious product of Jesuit education in the course of nearly three centuries," according to historian Oliveira Martins. "All around were whispered rosaries, saints were placed in all corners, in every oratory and niche, as candles and lamps blazed alight."[21] Pombal was ostracized. On August 16, 1781, royal decree prohibited him from coming near the court. According to the law, Pombal had to maintain a minimum distance of seventy miles from the queen.[22] The objective of this royal restraining order was to keep him away from the center of power—and it succeeded.

With the fall of Pombal and the spirit of his reforms, Portugal once again fell prisoner to the destiny of its past: a small, rural country incapable of breaking with centuries-old vices and traditions, dependent on slave labor, intoxicated by easy money, and lacking a clear plan for the future of its colonies. As a result, the nation soon became a pawn on the chessboard of Europe. Like the proverbial ostrich that buries its head in the sand to escape danger, it futilely sought to maintain political neutrality among its richer and more powerful neighbors. If the country involved itself as little as possible in conflicts, the theory went, it would avoid counter-attacks and ensure the uninterrupted flow of wealth that arrived from overseas territories. The theory failed miserably.[23]

As with Spain and Switzerland in the course of the twentieth century, the politics of neutrality are never as neutral as they seem. Portugal always had Britain as a preferred business partner and with good reason. The ancient alliance derived from the very origins of the Portuguese monarchy itself. English crusaders on their way to the Holy Land to fight the Second Crusade in 1147 helped the young Afonso de Borgonha, first king of Portugal, to expel the Moors and conquer the port near the mouth of the Tagus River that became Lisbon.[24] The first trade alliance between Portugal and England came into effect in 1308.[25] In 1387, the Anglo-Portuguese alliance further consolidated in the form of the marriage of Dom João I, the Master of Aviz, to Phillipa of Lancaster. Thanks to English aid, Dom João I, illegitimate son of King Pedro I, secured his position as the king of the new Aviz dynasty and wrested from Spain the recognition of an independent Portugal in 1414.[26] One of the sons of João and Phillipa, Henry the Navigator, receives credit for the development of long-distance seafaring that enabled the great discoveries and formation of the Portuguese colonial empire—though ironically he himself never sailed.

Constantly threatened by neighboring Spain and France, Portugal would have ceased to exist many centuries earlier if not for the strategic alliance with England. The partnership provided mutual benefits, however, of which England also availed itself in moments of necessity. With the aid of Portugal, England conquered the Rock of Gibraltar—still part of its dominion today—from Spain in 1704. That crucial position at the mouth of the Mediterranean has played a decisive role in all major conflicts involving the British for the last three centuries.[27] In 1799, during Napoleon's Egyptian Campaign, the Portuguese squadron lent its services to the commander of the British fleet, Admiral Nelson, in blocking Malta.[28] Two years later, in 1801, when Spanish troops invaded Portugal, Britain reciprocated with monetary aid and troops.

It was this ancient alliance that Prince Regent Dom João invoked in 1807, when Bonaparte once again imperiled the future of his small and fragile nation.

V

Departure

The day of November 29, 1807, broke in Lisbon full of sunshine. A light breeze blew from the east. The sky shone blue, but the roads still roiled in mud from the rains of the previous day.[1] Near the port, confusion reigned. An unprecedented spectacle was unfolding over the calm waters of the Tagus River: The queen, princes, and princesses, and all the nobility were abandoning their country. Incredulous, the people gathered at the edge of the docks to behold the departure.

At 7 a.m., the *Royal Prince* billowed its sails and began to glide toward the Atlantic. It carried the mad queen Maria, Prince Regent João, and his two heirs, princes Pedro and Miguel. The rest of the royal family sailed on three other ships. The *Afonso de Albuquerque* transported Princess Carlota Joaquina, wife of the prince regent, and four of her six daughters. Her other two daughters, Maria Francisca and Isabel Maria, traveled on the *Queen of Portugal.* João's aunt and sister-in-law followed on the *Prince of Brazil.*[2] Four dozen more boats took up position behind the royal squadron.[3]

It was an impressive scene, but it didn't come close to recalling the heroic departure from these same docks of the fleet of Vasco de Gama, sailing out to navigate seas unknown and to discover distant territory. Instead, in 1807, the spirit of adventure gave way to fear. Rather than seeking conquests or glory, the Portuguese elite were fleeing without any attempt to resist the

French invaders. "Three centuries earlier, Portugal embarked for India, full of hope and lust; in 1807, a funereal entourage left for Brazil," records Portuguese historian Oliveira Martins.[4]

Between 10,000 and 15,000 people accompanied the prince regent on his voyage to Brazil—a huge number considering that Lisbon had close to 200,000 inhabitants.[5] The group included nobles, advisors, soldiers, judges, lawyers, merchants, and their families. Doctors, bishops, priests, handmaidens, valets, pages, cooks, and stable grooms also set sail with the court. Because of the obvious urgency of the boarding, the vast majority of travelers was not registered or catalogued. The figure for the number of passengers comes from reports and estimates from this period. The few existing official lists record 536 people, but the actual total certainly stood many times larger if only because alongside these names appear imprecise descriptions such as "the Viscount of Barbacena with his family," as historian Lília Schwarcz observes.[6]

At the beginning of the nineteenth century, maritime voyages made for a risky adventure. They demanded careful and protracted preparation. A voyage from Lisbon to Rio de Janeiro took two and a half months and encountered storms, doldrums, and surprise attacks by the pirates who infested the Atlantic. Disease, shipwrecks, and marauders took a heavy toll on the few voyagers who risked traveling so far. The dangers were so great that the British Navy—the most skilled, organized, and well-equipped naval force in the world at the time—considered a rate of one death per thirty sailors acceptable on long maritime journeys.[7] Voyagers normally took great care in organizing their affairs and saying farewell to relatives and friends. The chances of never returning were enormous.

But in 1807 nobody had time to prepare or organize a thing. Although the plan to flee to Brazil was old, the decision to enact it came at the last minute. Up to one week prior to the largely improvised departure, hope still circulated in Dom João's court of a possible reconciliation with Napoleon that would thwart an invasion. But that hope fell flat on November 24, when the latest edition of the Parisian newspaper *Le Moniteur*, Napoleon's official publishing arm, arrived in Lisbon, announcing that "the House of Bragança has ceased to reign in Europe."[8] The news caused an uproar in the court and finally prevailed over the prince regent's chronic indecision. There was no alternative: Either the royal family fled to Brazil, or Bonaparte would dethrone them. It was time to go.

At midnight, a messenger awoke Joaquim de Azevedo, court official and the future viscount of Rio Seco, and summoned him to the Royal Palace. De Azevedo found the state advisors assembled there as he received personal orders from Dom João to organize the departure. Before heading to the port, Azevedo guaranteed a place onboard for himself and his family, and then he went to work. Azevedo had fewer than three days to handle all of the necessary preparations, and counter-winds and strong rains conspired to postpone the departure to the morning of the 29th.[9]

The royal palaces at Mafra and Queluz were evacuated with haste. Valets and pages worked through the night to remove carpets, paintings, and wall ornaments. Hundreds of trunks containing clothing, dishes, cutlery, jewels, and personal effects made their way to the docks. The caravan totaled more than seven hundred wagons.[10] Pack mules drew the Church's silver and the 60,000 volumes of the (reconstituted) Royal Library in fourteen carts. Gold, diamonds, and the currency of the royal treasury were packed in crates and escorted to the wharf, ready to make their ironic trip back across the Atlantic Ocean.

During those three days, the people of Lisbon watched the movements of horses, carriages, and government employees without exactly understanding what was happening. The official explanation asserted that the Portuguese fleet was undergoing repairs. The rich and well-informed, however, knew perfectly well what was happening. Pedro Gomes, a prosperous merchant, wrote to his mother-in-law: "We don't yet have a vessel, and I'm not sure we will, as there are many who want to go, and few ships. What we will do is prepare ourselves to leave the capital, to wherever it must be, at the first indication of danger. . . . The ships continue to be prepared with great haste, and all of the patterns point towards boarding."[11] No surviving reports indicate whether Gomes and his family found a place aboard one of the ships.

When news of the royal departure finally spread, the populace reacted with understandable indignation. In the streets, tears flowed alongside demonstrations of despair and revolt. Stones pelted the carriage and injured the coachman of Antonio de Araújo, the count of Barca, when he tried to make his way through the multitudes to the frigate *Medusa*. Araújo, João's minister of foreign relations, sympathized with the French and was viewed with suspicion in Portugal.[12] "The highly noble and ever-loyal people of Lisbon could not become comfortable with the idea of their king departing for overseas territories," wrote de Azevedo, himself called a traitor by the infuriated crowds. "Wandering through the plazas and streets, without believing their eyes, shedding tears and curses . . . everything to them was shock, heartbreak, and longing."[13] "The capital found itself in a state of gloom too somber to describe," reported Lord Strangford, the British envoy to Lisbon in charge of negotiating the transfer of the royal family to Brazil. "Bands of unknown armed men were seen roaming the streets, in the most complete silence. . . . Everything seemed to indicate that the departure of the Prince, if not carried out immediately, would be delayed by public outbursts rendering it impossible to leave before the arrival of the French army."[14]

Amid the confusion, a five-year-old boy looked on in fright. José Trazimundo, future marquis of Fronteira, stood in the company of his uncle, the count of Ega, who at the last minute attempted to board his family on one of the ships of the fleet. They couldn't make their way through the mob quickly enough, so when finally he arrived at the quay the ships had already weighed anchor. Many years later, Trazimundo recorded his memories of that day: "I will never forget the tears that were shed, as many of them by the populace as by the servants of the royal residences and by the soldiers that were on the banks of Belém." Unable to secure a place on a ship, the Trazimundo family took refuge in the house of the count of Ribeira in anticipation of the arrival of General Junot's troops. "The halls were filled with relatives who had faced the same luck, not even having said their last goodbyes to the emigrés," he wrote of those who managed to depart.[15]

Other people of importance had to return home after unsuccessfully attempting to make it to the ships. Such was the case of the apostolic delegate Dom Lourenço de Caleppi. Days before, the sixty-seven-year-old showed up at the Palace of Ajuda, and João invited him on the voyage. Thereafter, he sought the minister of the Navy, the viscount of Anadia, who, to be on the safe side, had reserved him a place on both the ships *Martim de Freitas* and the *Medusa*. On one or the other, de Caleppi would travel with his private secretary, Camilo Luis Rossi. On the arranged day, however, the two arrived at the docks only to find both ships completely full. The apostolic delegate eventually arrived in Brazil in September 1808, almost a year after the departure of the royal family.[16]

Information about how Dom João boarded is imprecise. In one version, to avoid protests, he traveled to the port in a closed carriage, without a convoy, accompanied by only one servant and Dom Pedro Carlos, *infante* of both Portugal and Spain and his preferred nephew. Despite technically belonging to the Spanish House of Bourbon, the boy came to live in Lisbon after the death of his parents, both of whom had fallen victim to smallpox in 1788. On arriving at the port with no one to greet him, João waded over the mud atop badly positioned planks of wood supported by police cables.[17] In the report of Portuguese historian Luiz Norton, the prince and his nephew crossed these planks "with the help of the people," and had embarked "after a cold and funereal kiss upon the hand."[18] In the version of events by French general Maximilien Foy, Dom João, after descending from his carriage, had trouble walking. "His limbs trembled under him," the general writes. "With his hand he put aside the people who clung round his knees. Tears trickled from his eyes, and his countenance told plainly enough how woe-begone and perplexed was his heart."[19]

A farewell speech was impossible under the circumstances, so Dom João ordered a decree posted in the streets of Lisbon, explaining the reasons for his departure. It said that French troops were marching toward Lisbon and that resisting them would spill blood needlessly. In addition, despite all his efforts, he couldn't uphold the peace for his beloved subjects. Therefore, he was moving to Rio de Janeiro until the situation calmed down. He also left instructions in writing for how the Portuguese should treat the invaders: The troops of General Junot would receive the welcome of the Royal Assembly, a council of governors appointed by the prince. The Assembly had guidelines for cooperating with the French general and for offering shelter to his soldiers.[20]

Princess Carlota Joaquina's carriage arrived at the port shortly after the prince regent, along with three of her eight children: Pedro, future emperor of Brazil, eight years old; Miguel, six years old; and Ana de Jesus Maria, eleven months old. The rest of the family arrived in separate carriages: the adolescent Maria Teresa and her sisters Maria Isabel, ten years old; Maria Francisca, seven years old; Isabel Maria, six years old; and Maria da Assunção, two years old. Finally came Queen Maria I, now seventy-three years old. For the people gathered on the wharf watching the departure, the presence of the queen offered a great novelty. Because of her bouts of madness, the queen had lived for sixteen years as a recluse in the Palace of Queluz, not seen in the streets of Lisbon during all that time. As her coach darted toward the port, she shouted to the coachman, "Slow down! They'll think we're fleeing!"[21] On arriving, she refused to descend from the carriage, forcing the captain of the royal fleet to carry her to the ship in his arms. Dom João's sister-in-law Maria Benedita, sixty-one years old, and her aunt Maria Ana, seventy-one years old, brought up the rear.[22]

To guarantee the future of the monarchy in the event of a disaster, planners considered it prudent to avoid putting all the heirs to the throne on the same ship. But in the haste of departing, this precaution was forgotten. Carlota Joaquina herself took charge of distributing the family across the ships. Their sons Pedro and Miguel, the two direct heirs to the throne, boarded the *Royal Prince* along with their father and their grandmother. It was a risky decision. In the event of a fatal shipwreck, this vessel could bring three generations of the Bragança dynasty to the bottom of the ocean. Carlota Joaquina and four daughters—Maria Teresa, Maria Isabel, Maria da Assunção, and Ana de Jesus—remained on the *Afonso de Albuquerque,* commanded by Inácio da Costa Quintela, along with the counts of Caparica and Cavalheiros, their families, and servants, yielding a total of around 1,058 people. The other two children traveled with the marquis of Lavradio on the *Queen of Portugal.*[23]

Before embarking, João scraped clean the royal coffers, a measure he repeated when leaving Rio de Janeiro to return to Lisbon. In 1807, they departed with a royal treasury of 80 million cruzados, nearly half of the currency in circulation in Portugal, along with a huge quantity of diamonds extracted from Minas Gerais that rather unexpectedly were returning to Brazil.[24] The royal baggage also included all of the archives of the Portuguese monarchy. A new printing press, recently purchased in London, was loaded onboard the *Medusa* just as it had arrived from England, its original packing still intact.[25] It was yet another instance of ironic cargo: To prevent the spread of potentially revolutionary ideas in the colony, the Portuguese government expressly had prohibited printing presses in Brazil. (To escape censorship, Brazilian journalist Hipólito da Costa published the *Correio Braziliense*, Brazil's first newspaper, in London in 1808.)

Two days of strong winds blew toward the continent, but on the morning of November 29 the wind finally changed direction, the rain stopped, and the sun emerged. At 7 a.m., the order to depart was issued.[26] Lord Strangford withdrew to board the *Hibernia*, writing to Lord Canning, prime minister of Britain:

> *I have the honor of communicating that the Prince Regent of Portugal has decided on the noble and magnanimous plan of withdrawing from a kingdom that no longer can maintain itself as anything but a vassal of France, and that His Royal Highness and family, accompanied by the majority of warships and by a throng of loyal defenders and supportive subjects, departed Lisbon today, and are on their way to Brazil under the guard of the English navy.*[27]

The commander of the British fleet, Admiral Sidney Smith, described the moment of departure as follows:

> *At 7am on this memorable day, the morning was marvelous, as a light breeze propelled the Portuguese ships towards the mouth of the Tagus river. The signal was made by two sailors, and then repeated by three ships, as the Portuguese colors were flown. The spectacle was impressive for all onlookers (except the French, in the mountains), held by the most vivid gratitude to Providence for having witnessed that there was still a power on earth capable of protecting the oppressed.*[28]

Commanding the fleet stationed in Lisbon, Smith's presence gives an idea of the importance that the British conferred on the operation. He had participated in some of the most decisive events in modern Western history: He fought in the American Revolution, faced Napoleon, and battled the tsar of Russia. He also had worked with one of the most important inventors of all time, Robert Fulton, father of the submarine and the steamboat. He had retired to Bath, in the English countryside, when in the autumn of 1807 he was called to return as admiral specifically to take part in the events in Portugal.[29]

At around three in the afternoon, young José Trazimundo was dining in the company of his father and two brothers when he heard the distant rumble of cannons. A volley of twenty-one shots by the English fleet saluted the Royal Pavilion of the ship carrying the prince regent, who at that moment was leaving the shoals of the Tagus for the Atlantic Ocean. Portuguese ships were still visible on the horizon when French troops entered Lisbon. Only sadness and desolation remained behind. "Even though at my young age, I could not give due importance to the crisis that the country was in, and especially the capital, which had the French army two leagues from its borders, nonetheless I remember being amazed by my relatives' expressions, and those of the people around us," wrote Trazimundo.[30]

The logbooks of the British ships, collected by historian Kenneth Light, reveal that as they accompanied the flight from Lisbon, the English weren't as friendly as many contemporaneous reports would have us believe. Tension and anticipation hung in the air. Without exception, all the English commanders recorded in their diaries that, upon catching sight of the Portuguese ships leaving the port of Lisbon between 8 and 9 in the morning on November 29, they ordered their ships to prepare for action and form a line of combat.[31]

Apparently, all of them were operating under the supposition that the Portuguese in fact had surrendered to the demands of Napoleon and at that instant might try to break the stronghold of the British naval blockade. This brief moment of uncertainty dissipated when the Portuguese fleet crossed the shoals of the Tagus. In an open and friendly move, the *Royal Prince* approached the HMS *Hibernia,* the captain's ship of the British fleet. To reaffirm peaceful intentions, the two exchanged salutes conforming to protocol: twenty-one cannon shots on each side, first the English, then the

Portuguese. "Until recently, Portugal and England had been at war, and Sidney Smith did not want to run any risks," wrote Light. "Only after friendly dialogue was there an exchange of volleys."[32]

Left to its own devices, Portugal was about to live through the worst years of its history. In the next seven years, more than half a million citizens left the country, perished of hunger, or fell on the battlefield during a series of confrontations that became known as the Peninsular War.[33] On that bright morning in November 1807, hundreds of trunks remained scattered on the wharf in Lisbon, forgotten in the commotion of the departure. Among them were crates of the Church's silver and the books of the Royal Library. The French invaders confiscated and melted the silver. The books of the Royal Library—which included a first edition of Camões's *Os Lusíadas*, Portugal's national epic poem; ancient manuscript copies of the Bible; and maps drawn on parchment—arrived in Brazil later, in three consecutive voyages: the first in 1810 and the other two in 1811.

On one of these voyages came the royal archivist, Luiz dos Santos Marrocos. The events of 1807 were about to change his life radically.

VI

The Royal Archivist

At the end of October 1807, while Emperor Napoleon's troops approached the Portuguese border, the life of archivist Luiz dos Santos Marrocos hung suspended between two cities, one from the past and the other in the future. A twenty-six-year-old bachelor, he lived with his family in the Belém neighborhood in Lisbon, the capital of the vast colonial Portuguese empire, an exotic, thriving place replete with traders from China, India, Arabia, and Africa. In three years, he would be in Rio de Janeiro, the capital of colonial Brazil, a city teeming with novelties, a port of replenishment, and an obligatory stop for ships bearing toward distant lands, including the recently discovered Oceania.

In Lisbon, dos Santos Marrocos and his father, Francisco, worked for the prince regent in the Royal Library, one of the most extraordinary in Europe. Situated in a pavilion in the Palace of Ajuda, it housed 60,000 volumes. It was ten times larger than the collection of Thomas Jefferson's books that became the Library of Congress.[1] In the Royal Library, the two dos Santos Maroccos translated foreign works and catalogued and cared for rare books and documents.

This steady routine of silent dedication to books suffered an abrupt interruption in the final week of November, however, when dos Santos Marrocos received orders to pack the entire collection in crates as fast as possible and to dispatch them to the docks of Belém, where the ships of the Portuguese fleet awaited the royal family to embark for Brazil. In these hours of uncertainty and anguish and with the assistance of colleagues and court officials, dos Santos Marrocos packed all 60,000 volumes and sent them to the port in carts drawn by mules and horses, tussling through the narrow streets of Lisbon, vying among hundreds of other carriages all headed for the same destination. The rush turned out to be futile, though. In the chaos of the departure, every single crate packed with books was forgotten on the docks, left amid the mud and sludge from the previous day's rain.

Two and a half years later, in March 1811, dos Santos Marrocos himself left for Brazil to oversee the second of three shipments of books. He arrived in Rio de Janeiro on June 17, a few days before his thirtieth birthday. In the ten years that followed, he maintained a regular correspondence with his father, Francisco, and his sister, Bernardina. These 186 unassuming letters, housed today in the archives of the Ajuda Library, transformed the archivist into an important character in the history of Brazil and Portugal. This one-way correspondence—we don't have the responses that Luiz received in Rio de Janeiro—has become one of the most cherished primary sources for researchers studying this period of Brazilian history. The simple reports by a common citizen tell of the enormous transformations that the Portuguese and Brazilians experienced during the thirteen years in which the royal family ruled from the New World. Court intrigues, petty bureaucracy, and the harsh reality of slavery appear in raw form in dos Santos Marrocos's letters, like an instant photograph, free from retouching and without the filtering of documents or official reports.

He penned the first letter while still on the high seas, aboard the frigate *Princess Carlota*. It is dated April 12, 1811 (Good Friday), 10 p.m., in the vicinity of Cape Verde, off the coast of Africa. The last letter bears the date March 26, 1821, one month before the return of King João VI to Lisbon.[2] Some of these letters discuss historical events, such as the death of Queen Maria I, the coronation of João VI, and the arrival and departure of ships in the port of Rio de Janeiro. Others slide into pure and simple gossip, as on May 19, 1812, when dos Santos Marrocos criticizes the sexual affairs of João de Almeida de Melo e Castro, count of Gâlvea and minister of naval affairs and overseas territories. Without offering many details, the archivist suggests that the count maintained homosexual relations with vagabonds in the center of Rio de Janeiro, around the docklands. "It is frightening and disgusting, the age-old, filthy vice of this man," he writes. "A married man, he completely ignores his wife, nourishing his frailty with rascals and shameful parasites."[3]

In Portugal, the dos Santos Marrocos family belonged to an elite class of bureaucrats affiliated with institutions of culture and knowledge. Francisco, strict, educated, and authoritarian, was a professor of philosophy in Belém. In 1797, he had ordered the reprinting, in the office of Simão Ferreiro in Lisbon, of a bibliographic jewel: *A History of the Discovery and Conquest of the Indians by the Portuguese*, written in 1559 by Fernão Lopez de Castanheda.[4] In 1811, the Royal Press published Francisco's own book, *An Alphabetized Map of the Settlements of Portugal*. Luiz, a graduate of the University of Coimbra, followed in his father's footsteps as a literary custodian, translator, and author. He worked as an assistant in the royal libraries in 1802. In 1807, he finished translating, by royal order, the five-volume, 2,500-page *Treatise on Legal Medicine and Public Hygiene* by French doctor F. E. Foderé.[5] He had also written his own book, *An Inoculation of Understanding*. Neither of these two works saw publication, though. The originals of the former remained forgotten on the docks of Lisbon in the commotion preceding the court's departure to Brazil, never to be seen again. The latter is known only through the letters that Luiz wrote to his father.[6]

The Lisbon of the dos Santos Marrocos family was a conservative city, profoundly religious and based on antiquated customs. Its homes featured Eastern tapestries, and quilts from India covered its verandas. Historian Oliveira Martins calls it the most oriental of European capitals.[7] Other chroniclers and travelers of the time describe it as a medieval city: dirty, dark, and dangerous. The burial of corpses in cemeteries became obligatory only in 1771. Until then, they had been abandoned, cremated, or laid to rest in improvised graves on the periphery of the city. Those who had wealth or power were buried in churches.

Lack of hygiene was a chronic problem. "Dirty water, dishwater, urine, and excrement were tossed out of windows with no advance notice at any hour of night or day," wrote Frenchman J. B. F. Carrère, a resident of Lisbon at the end of the eighteenth century. "One who walked through the city streets was always at risk of being soaked and covered with filth."[8]

"This great city had no illumination at night, as a result of which it frequently occurred that a person would become lost at night, running the risk of being soiled in the squalor that was unloaded from windows onto the streets, as houses did not have latrines," wrote French traveler Jácome Ratton.[9] "Everyone is supposed to bring their waste to the river, and there is a great quantity of blacks who perform this service, but this law is not exactly followed, especially by the masses." Another traveler, William Beckford, spoke of the ravenous and stray dogs that wandered the street, scavenging in the garbage for scraps of food. "Of all the capitals in which I have lived, Lisbon is the most infested by packs of these famished animals, who at least provide the service of cleaning the streets of a bit of its aromatic waste."[10]

The absence of collective good hygiene brought on the spread of plague and disease, not limited to the common people of course. Such problems affected the royal family as well. We can gather some idea of the fragility of life in the court through a letter that Prince João wrote in 1786 to his sister Mariana Vitória, who had moved to Madrid after marrying the Spanish infante. In the letter, the prince conveys that Carlota Joaquina, his wife for just a year at this point, had to cut her hair due to an infestation by lice. "The Infanta is getting better, but her head still itches a lot," he writes. "You know quite well that skin irritations don't give up easily. I cannot explain to you the lice she has. It's like a plague. After cutting her hair, her head became even drier. But she left a forelock, which seems to be the hiding-place of all the lice, and you can believe how she suffered, but nonetheless she took it all in stride, as if she were a thirty-year-old woman."[11] At the time, Carlota Joaquina was just eleven years old.

As employees of the Royal Library, the dos Santos Marrocos had a close familiarity with the prince regent's court and with the palaces frequented by the nobility. The suffocating presence of the Church and its numerous religious rituals dominated the grim and depressing atmosphere. Travelers and diplomats found surprising the lack of parties, dinners, balls, or receptions in the Portuguese court, in marked contrast with the animated palaces of

Paris and Madrid, where music, dance, and the colors of culture predominated. In Lisbon, "a decadent court surrounded a half-insane queen and an obese prince royal who suffered from a chronic case of indecision," writes historian Alan Manchester.[12] Another scholar, Pedro Calmon, described the Portuguese court as "one of the most frail and sickly in Europe" at the end of the eighteenth century. "The inbred marriages, the morbid legacy, the melancholy of its mystic, apathetic court, stunned by undefined fears, gave it the visage of an aged, crumbling lineage."[13]

In this repressive, holier-than-thou atmosphere, the effects of the French Revolution of 1789 reverberated and terrified the nobility. The superintendent of police, Diogo da Pina Manique, rigorously battled the revolution's influence. Combining the roles of magistrate, customs inspector, and administrator of pavements and public illumination, da Pina Manique blocked the entry of books considered dangerous and ordered the closure of Masonic lodges, suspected of promoting the spread of revolutionary ideas.[14] He ordered the arrest of subscribers to Diderot's and Voltaire's encyclopedias and deported writers sympathetic to the French Revolution.[15] Among his oppressed was Manuel Maria Barbosa du Bocage, one of Portugal's greatest writers and poets.

On discovering the establishment of a Masonic lodge on the island of Madeira, some six hundred miles southwest of Lisbon, da Pina Manique sent a police magistrate there with the following instructions:

> *Whoever you see with pointed, shiny shoes, suspenders on their leggings, a necktie up to their beard, a collar up to their ears, hair cut close to the neck and coiffed up to their fontanel, and sideburns down to the corners of their mouth—apprehend him immediately and lock him up in an ironclad jail until a ship can take him to Limoeiro prison: he's either a follower of the Enlightenment or a freemason.*[16]

Manique's persecutions were so intolerable for the French and the followers of the ideas of the revolution that, under pressure from Napoleon Bonaparte, the prince regent fired him.

In this Lisbon, where culture and science had long since fallen into decline, the mere existence of the Royal Library represented a particular eccentricity. It showed that the Portuguese court pretended to be more learned that it actually was, according to historian Lília Schwarcz, author of the most authoritative book written about the library. Portuguese kings had cultivated its fabled collection since the fourteenth century.[17] It was there that dos Santos Marrocos, father and son, passed their days cataloguing, copying, filing, and preserving books and documents. The Royal Library wasn't just a means of livelihood for the family—it was their very reason for existing.

In the months following the departure of the royal family, thousands of Portuguese citizens raised arms to resist the French invasion. Luiz dos Santos Marrocos stood among them. Before embarking for Rio de Janeiro in 1811, he served on the battlefields and fought on the barricades erected around the entrance of the Portuguese capital. His good service raised him to the rank of captain in the Portuguese army.[18] Like all of the Portuguese in this period, though, his family went through great tribulations. With the departure of the court and the virtual paralysis of the Portuguese government, the salaries of public servants, including the dos Santos Marrocos family, remained overdue for more than a year. Prices tripled. Citizens lacked basic necessities and starved.

Involuntarily swept up in the gale of history, the royal archivist himself became a symbol of the great transformations that profoundly affected Brazilians and Portuguese on both sides of the Atlantic during the court's years in Rio de Janeiro. For Luiz, however, a journey of great changes was just beginning, as we will see in greater detail in the final chapters of this book.

VII

The Voyage

Designed to prevent seawater infiltration and to survive the most violent ocean storms, Portuguese ships two centuries ago resembled hermetically sealed wooden compartments with small hatches that remained shut most of the time. The atmosphere inside, lacking ventilation, was asphyxiating. During the day, under the equatorial sun, they became floating saunas. The ships had neither running water nor toilets. To attend to bodily necessities, mariners and passengers alike used cloacas—platforms tied to the bow, suspended over the gunwales of the ships, through which they defecated directly into the sea.[1]

The menu consisted of biscuits, lentils, olive oil, sour cabbage, and salted pork or cod. But in the suffocating heat of the tropics, rats, cockroaches, and weevils infested the stored rations. Contaminated by bacteria and fungus, water putrefied quickly. For just this reason, the regular beverage on British ships was beer. On Portuguese, Spanish, and French ships, the seafarers drank wine of poor quality. The lack of fruits and fresh foods caused one of the greatest threats on long voyages: scurvy, a fatal disease caused by a vitamin C deficiency. Its weakened victims burned with fever and suffered excruciating pain. Gums became gangrenous, and even a gentle touch could knock teeth clear of a jaw. By coincidence, 1808 was the first year that the young navy of the fledgling United States of America distributed doses of vitamin C among its crews to prevent the disease. In tropical regions, other threats included dysentery and typhoid, caused by lack of proper hygiene and contamination of food and water.[2] "The water supply was insufficient, food ran short, and plague beset the *émigrés* in the crowded and unhygienic quarters," records historian Alan Manchester of the Portuguese fleet.[3]

Shortly after arriving in Rio de Janeiro in 1811, Luiz dos Santos Marrocos wrote his father a letter that provides an idea of the discomfort involved in sailing across the Atlantic. Cramped and bumpy, the ship was thrown from one side to the other by the waves:

> *My dearest father and master of my heart,*
>   *It merits serious consideration, the discomfort suffered by one not used to sailing, especially if he has threatening illnesses requiring care, and must restrain himself from coughing, sneezing, or blowing his nose. . . . It is injurious, and of greatest consequences, to expose oneself to the seasickness that wrenches one's entrails and bursts one's veins, a torment lasting days, weeks, and sometimes even the whole trip. Besides this, the shock of the sea, thunderstorms and downpours, the rocking and dipping of the ship are no laughing matter for anyone who is refined.*[4]

To avoid disease and the spread of plague, commanding officers required linens and the ships themselves always to be clean through rigorous discipline. In this regard, the British Navy serves as a paragon. In times of war, Britain stationed more than 60,000 men aboard its gigantic fleet—a number equal to the entire population of Rio de Janeiro in 1808. For these sailors, life at sea began early, often before adolescence. At seventeen, they already had become trained professionals. But a steadily substandard diet and grueling work, without breaks or comfort of any kind, shortened their careers to a maximum of ten to fifteen years. Life expectancy didn't extend much beyond age forty except for the very lucky.[5]

Aboard British ships, sleeping on duty, disrespecting a superior, or attending to bodily necessities on deck instead of using the rudimentary cloacas represented grave misdeeds. The punishments for putting the crew in danger, which included failing to respect the rules of hygiene and cleanliness, came down hard and severe. In such cases, sailors could be flogged. In more grave cases, the captain had the authority to have them hanged. Such punishment, always on public display, served as an example for other members of the crew.

The logbooks of the British ships accompanying the Portuguese royal family to Brazil, published in 1995 by historian Kenneth Light, reveal the harsh routine of onboard discipline:

Diary onboard the HMS Bedford:

"5 December 1807: James Tacey, 48 lashes for negligence of duty;

14 December: John Legg, 12 lashes for negligence;

24 December: Hugh Davis, 24 lashes for negligence and disrespect; Neal McDougal, 24 lashes for negligence and attempting to incite mutiny; Thos Mirrins, 3 lashes for negligence."

Diary onboard the corvette HMS Confiance:

"23 November: Got Horp, 36 lashes for desertion; Mcdougold, 36 for insolent behavior; Staith, 18 more for negligence."[6]

In 1807, it took the Portuguese fleet nearly two months to cross the Atlantic Ocean. The reports of the trip are incomplete and confused, but the voyage clearly teemed with malady and suffering. Antiquated and badly equipped, the vessels and frigates from Portugal heaved with crowds. The captain's ship, the *Royal Prince,* which conveyed Prince João and Queen Maria I across the troubled waters, carried 1,054 people.[7] We can imagine the disarray. Even with three quarterdecks for the battery of eighty-four cannons and a cellar full of cargo, at 220 feet long and 55 feet wide, the ship simply didn't have space for all her passengers.[8] Many slept on deck in the open air.

On the first days of the voyage, while the ships still sailed the waters of the northern hemisphere, strong waves pitched cold water onto the overloaded quarterdecks, where sailors worked in thick fog and cold gusts of wind. Hulls leaked, and the boats filled with water relentlessly. Many sails and ropes had rotted. Timbers groaned under the waves and wind, spreading panic among passengers unused to the roughness of the seas. Nausea overtook every ship.

The haste of departure and the miserable state of the Portuguese Navy further increased the journey's discomfort. A third of the ships that Prince João had at his disposal before setting sail were left abandoned in the port of Lisbon at the mercy of the French invaders. They were useless.[9] "The fleet left the Tagus in such haste that very few of the merchant ships had rations or water for more than three weeks to a month," wrote Lord Strangford. "Many warships found themselves in the same state, and Sir Sidney Smith is of the opinion that most of the convoy should head towards England in order to stock up on provisions."[10]

On the eve of departure, a report summarized the startling shortcomings of the Portuguese fleet:

Queen of Portugal: in need of 27 tanks of water, all are empty

Frigate Minerva: has only 60 tanks of water

Count Henrique: has 6 empty tanks, needs apothecary

Golphinho: has 6 empty tanks, lacks apothecary, hens, and firewood

Urânia: lacks firewood

Vingança: lacks water and firewood

Royal Prince: needs an apothecary, hens, cables, wax, 20 tanks of water, cleats, a chip log, and firewood

Flyer: lacks three tanks of water

Prince of Brazil: lacks olive oil, wax, cables, thirty tanks of water, firewood, and a chip log[11]

At the end of the afternoon of the first day of travel, after performing the protocol of trading volleys of cannon fire, the combined fleet remained stationed near the Portuguese coast for the final inspections before crossing the Atlantic. At around 4 p.m., Lord Strangford and Admiral Sidney Smith visited Prince João aboard the *Royal Prince*. Both Britons considered the conditions far short of the needs of the prince regent. The atmosphere was grim and depressing, as Strangford recorded in one of his dispatches to London. "It is impossible to describe the situation of these distinguished persons, their discomfort, the patience and resignation with which they have tolerated the deprivations and difficulties resulting from the transfer of the capital."[12] Smith offered to convey the prince regent on the *Hibernia,* lead ship of the English fleet, a new and more comfortable vessel. But João refused. The Portuguese court already felt more than sufficiently beholden to and dependent upon Britain. Traveling as a guest of the British commander would send a politically heavy and undesirable message.

The meeting among Strangford, Smith, and the prince lasted nearly three hours, during which they discussed the final details of the voyage. In case of any unexpected event while crossing, a contingency plan directed that all ships head toward the island of São Tiago in the archipelago of Cape Verde, where the fleet would regroup before proceeding to Rio de Janeiro. The only exception was the *Medusa,* which, bearing the ministers Antonio de Araújo, José Egydio, and Thomaz Antonio, would sail directly to Bahia.[13]

The meeting had barely ended when an abrupt change of weather took the passengers and crew by surprise. The wind—until then pushing the ships further into the ocean—changed course and blew strongly on a diagonal, perpendicular to the direction from which they embarked and directly opposite to the planned course. By nightfall, the wind had gathered the force of a storm that threatened to push the entire fleet back to the Portuguese coast, already occupied by French troops. After much anguish and tension, the commanding officers decided to take advantage of the windstorm and navigated northwest, as if heading toward Canada. This change of course would keep the ships at high sea, preventing them from being pushed back to shore. Only on the fourth day, having traversed more than 160 nautical miles, could they finally correct their sails and head southwest toward Brazil.[14]

At this point, at a safe distance from the Portuguese coast, the ships gathered one more time for inspections. One small warship, considered too fragile to cross the ocean, was sent back to Lisbon, where French troops immediately apprehended it. British officials also deemed a second ship inadequate for such a long voyage, but the Portuguese decided to risk it. Luckily, no vessels suffered shipwreck, although some arrived at Brazil in a pitiful state.

On December 5, approximately midway between Lisbon and Funchal, on the island of Madeira, the British fleet divided itself in half. One part, under the command of Admiral Smith, changed course and, after a farewell exchange of volleys with the Portuguese fleet, returned to the now occupied Lisbon blockade. The other half, composed of the *Marlborough, London, Bedford,* and *Monarch,* under the command of Captain Graham Moore, continued escorting the Portuguese fleet to Brazil.[15] Lord Strangford, the architect of the flight of the royal family, also returned to England. A few months later, he and Smith would meet again with Prince João in Rio de Janeiro.

A little more than week after the departure, on December 8, just before approaching the Madeira archipelago, a thick fog enveloped everything. "It was so heavy that we could not see beyond a distance equal to three lengths of the ship," wrote Captain James Walker aboard the HMS *Bedford,* a seventy-four-cannon vessel that began plying the world's waters in 1775.[16] But the worst hadn't arrived yet. As soon as darkness fell, a violent storm further tormented the ships. Powerful winds whipped the decaying sails as the crew desperately tried to keep them fixed to the masts.

The danger lay not on the ships themselves, but deep within the black of night blanketed by fog. A point known as the Eight Rocks, north of Porto Santo in the Madeira archipelago, posed a mortal pitfall for less experienced sailors. The partially submerged rocks had caused the wrecks of innumerable ships. To avoid this risk, the commanders of the fleet decided to wait for the weather to improve.[17] The result surprised everyone: By dawn the next day, some of the ships had disappeared. Winds had dispersed the fleet during the night, and no one had noticed. "In the light of day, not a ship is in sight," recorded James Walker in his captain's log in the early hours of December 9.

The storm continued for two days without respite. In the early morning of the 10th, the sail of the main mast of the *Bedford* was destroyed. While the crew tried to repair the damage, a violent gust of wind flung a sailor named George Green into the sea. A small rescue boat was sent to save him. After various attempts amid strong waves, the rescue party saved Green from death and brought him back aboard—to the relief of the entire crew.[18]

On the Portuguese ships the damage was even greater. The main mast of the *Medusa*, which, according to the contingency plan, was making for Bahia, broke into pieces and came crashing down. Shortly thereafter, the third mast snapped, leaving the ship adrift in a choppy sea. "The great mast went without sails and collapsed because it was completely rotten," witnessed Antonio de Araújo e Azevedo, future count of Barca. "The corporals are furious. Everything has contributed to putting our lives in danger and owes much to the activity and intelligence of the command of a few officials."[19]

The hours following the storm swarmed with confusion and uncertainty. Dispersed by the winds, the fleet followed different routes. Half the ships, including the *Royal Prince* and the *Afonso de Albuquerque,* sailed northwest. The rest of the fleet maintained a southwesterly course, in the direction of the agreed meeting place, the Cape Verde archipelago. The *Queen of Portugal,* damaged and transporting two of the prince's daughters, began to lose track of the rest of the convoy but arrived in Cape Verde, where it underwent repairs before continuing on.

After the seas had calmed, Princess Carlota Joaquina and her daughters decided to visit Prince João and Queen Maria I aboard the *Royal Prince.* They achieved this visit by means of a small boat hoisted by sailors over the gunwales and onto the ship. It was the royal family's last contact before arriving in Brazil five weeks later. It was also the point at which Prince João decided to make for Bahia instead of Rio de Janeiro as planned.

The two fleets, Portuguese and British, had no further communication between them. Until recently, historians believed that they strayed from one another to the point of losing line of sight. But records aboard the British ships reveal, however, that the two convoys followed a parallel course, quite close to one another, until reaching the coast of Brazil. On the morning of January 2, 1808, the commander of the *Bedford*, Captain James Walker, who protected the convoy of Prince João heading to Bahia, recorded in his ship's log having seen three vessels at a distance. He preferred not to approach them, though, so as not to lose contact with the rest of the group. The last point of contact between the two flotillas took place via a bright and wondrous signal in the dark night. That night, Captain Walker ordered a blue light installed atop the mast. Around 11:15 p.m., the commander of the *Marlborough*, Captain Graham Moore, who accompanied the convoy headed to Rio de Janeiro, remarks in his diary that he sighted a blue light on the horizon.[20]

After several weeks' travel, the cold of Europe's winter gave way to unbearable heat, aggravated by the infamous doldrums of the Atlantic. Nearing the Equator, the ships of the fleet heading toward Salvador (Bahia) entered a calm zone, the same that had frightened Portuguese navigators since the Age of Discovery and which, in the official version, obligated Pedro Álvares Cabral to change course three centuries earlier, landing in Brazil while en route to India. Here the ships of the prince regent and princess took ten days to cover just thirty leagues, a distance that under normal circumstances required only ten hours.[21]

We can only imagine the torment of the hundreds crowded on deck: ten days under the equatorial sun, where the temperature reached 95 degrees Fahrenheit in December, without even the waft of a miserable breeze to alleviate their suffering. The dense throng of passengers and the lack of hygiene and sanitation favored the proliferation of disease. On the *Afonso de Albuquerque*, aboard which Princess Carlota Joaquina sailed, an infestation of lice forced the women to shave their heads and toss their wigs into the sea. They dusted their tormented scalps with antiseptic powder and then smeared them with pig lard.[22]

In total, sixteen British warships took part, directly or indirectly, in the transfer of the royal family from Lisbon to Brazil. These were wide, comfortable ships, well-organized and with highly professional, disciplined crews. Some were already legendary, having participated in memorable campaigns and battles. The largest, the HMS *Hibernia,* sailed under the command of Captain John Conn, one of the officials who massacred the French and Spanish squadrons in the Battle of Trafalgar alongside Lord Nelson two years earlier. Launched in November 1804 as a first-class ship of the Royal British Navy, the *Hibernia* had 110 cannons, stretched 203 feet long, and weighed 2,530 tons.[23]

Traveling aboard the HMS *London* was First Lieutenant Thomas O'Neill, an Irishman who soon became fundamental in the history of the flight of the royal family to Brazil. O'Neill witnessed the embarkation of the Portuguese court in Lisbon and every event that marked the voyage to Rio de Janeiro. After the court's arrival, he remained in the city for sixteen months before being recalled for another mission for the Royal Navy. In 1810, he wrote and published in London an eighty-nine-page book that describes the court's voyage to Brazil.[24] His lively reports contain much emotion and dramatic detail. One characteristic passage describes the discomfort of noblewomen aboard the Portuguese ships and frigates:

> *Females of Royal and most dignified birth, nourished in the bosom of rank and affluence . . . compelled to encounter November colds, and tempests through unknown seas, and exposed to inclement skies, deprived of all the delicacies and most of the necessaries of life, without a change of raiment or even beds to lie on—constrained to huddle promiscuously together onboard shipping totally unprepared for their reception.*[25]

In another passage, O'Neill records the testimony of a Portuguese official who accompanied the part of the fleet that moored in Bahia with Prince João:

> *So great was the number of people . . . and so crowded were all of the ships, that there was barely space to sit on the decks. The women*

. . . lacked any apparel aside from that which they were wearing. As the ships had very few provisions, it soon became necessary to ask the British Admiral to house some passengers aboard his ships. And (for these people) it was tremendous luck, as those which stayed behind were the object of pity from Lisbon to Bahia. The majority slept on the quarterdeck, without beds or blankets. Water was the main article which begged our attention: the amount they received was minimal and the food of the worst quality, so deficient that life itself became a burden. Our situation was so horrible that I wish nobody should have to experience nor witness it. Men, women and children all formed the most devastating scene.[26]

Despite their historical importance, O'Neill's reports aren't universally worthy of our credence. Obvious exaggeration and even fantasy pervade some of the scenes and situations that he describes. Relating the departure of the court from Lisbon, for example, he claims that some "ladies of distinction" drowned during the desperate attempt to gain a place aboard the ships.[27] But no corroborating evidence exists that this really happened. O'Neill also claims that, before departing, Dom João met with General Junot, commander of the invading French troops, a story similarly unconfirmed by any other source.[28] These exaggerations aside, however, his reports constitute some of the earliest coverage of these events.

Extremely battered, the *Medusa* moored in Recife, Brazil, on January 13, where, after undergoing repairs, she continued to Salvador, her original destination. On January 22, after fifty-four days at sea and approximately four thousand miles, the prince regent also landed in Salvador. The rest of the convoy had made port in Rio de Janeiro a week earlier, on January 17. Despite many dangers and hardships, the voyage brought on no deaths nor fatal accidents. The only known victim of the ocean crossing was Dom Miguel Álvares Pereira de Melo, duke of Cadaval, already ill when he departed Lisbon aboard the *D. João de Castro,* the most storm-battered of all of the ships. Separated from the rest of the fleet and sailing without its main mast, the ship docked in Paraíba completely smashed up and without water or provisions.[29] After rescue and assistance, the crew continued to Bahia, but Álvares Pereira de Melo, in his weakened state, could no longer withstand the journey. He died shortly after arriving in Salvador.[30]

Bahia, which three hundred years earlier had seen the arrival of Cabral and his fleet, now witnessed an event that forever changed the lives of Brazilians—and profoundly so. With the arrival of the court in the Bay of All Saints, the colonial era of Brazil concluded, and the first stage of an independent Brazil had begun.

VIII

Salvador

Prince João's layover in Salvador in 1808 remains a poorly under-stood episode in the history of the flight to Brazil. In the original plan, traced in Lisbon on the date of departure, the entire fleet was to maintain a consistently southwest course, heading straight for Rio de Janeiro. In case of unplanned diversions, the arranged meeting place was the Cape Verde archipelago off the coast of Africa, part of the Portuguese colonial empire, where ships could undergo repairs, take on provisions, and continue thereafter on the previously planned route. But the prince regent suddenly changed this plan during the third week of the voyage. Nothing seems to explain this decision. Why make an unplanned stop in Salvador, running unnecessary risks on an already complicated journey, when main-taining the original plan of sailing directly for Rio de Janeiro was not only easier but more prudent?

Until recently, the most widely accepted hypothesis by historians cent-ers on the storm that dispersed the fleet from December 8 to 10, near the Madeira archipelago. Amid the storm, the ships lost sight of one another. Part of the convoy—including the ships on which Queen Maria I, Prince Regent João, and Princess Carlota Joaquina traveled—drifted northwest, while the rest of the fleet continued on the original route, first toward Cape Verde and then to Rio de Janeiro. At a certain point, the story goes, discovering that

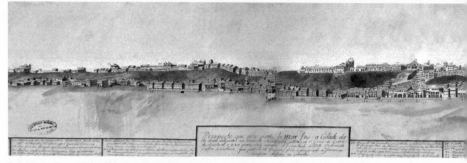

Salvador in the mid-eighteenth century, one of the most beautiful cities of the Portuguese Empire.

they were nearing the Bahian coast, Prince João ordered the ships to dock in Salvador.[1] According to this explanation, the prince regent landed in Bahia basically by accident.

This questionable explanation began to fall from grace with the discoveries of historian Kenneth Light. A retired cigarette company executive, Light immersed himself in the archives of the British Navy, which stores the onboard logs of every one of its ships as well as letters and reports that its respective commanders sent to the admiral's headquarters in London. This trove of correspondence explains some of the most important decisions made during the crossing, including the stop in Bahia. In meticulously analyzing these documents, Light reached two surprising conclusions. First, the hypothesis that part of the fleet went to Salvador after drifting in the storm made no sense. Second, Prince João went to Bahia deliberately, uninfluenced by any climatic accident on the high seas.

Two hundred years ago, both the Portuguese and the British intimately understood the navigation routes of the South Atlantic. The logs of the British commanders prove that they knew perfectly well the coordinates of their ships at every hour of every day along the entire voyage. They were never lost. Furthermore, they easily could have corrected their route after the storm and proceeded to the agreed-upon rendezvous before departing again for Brazil. No, the decision to stop in Salvador had already taken place in the third week of the journey before duly being transmitted to the other ships.

Prospecto que pella parte do mar faz a cidade da Bahia, drawing of Salvador in about 1756 from Luis do Santos Vilhena's book, *Notícias soteropolitanas e brasílicas* (Salvadoran and Brasilian News), 1801. Fundação Biblioteca Nacional, Rio de Janeiro

According to the documents collected by Light, on December 21, 1807, the prince regent communicated to Captain James Walker, commander of the *Bedford,* that he had decided to sail to Salvador instead of carrying out the planned route. This was eleven days after the storm. On this same occasion, the frigate *Minerva* was dispatched to São Tiago in Cape Verde, where it communicated Dom João's change in plans to the rest of the ships.[2] This intermediate mission further proves that the Portuguese and British commanders knew the locations of their own ships and of the rest of the fleet. But if the change in destination wasn't accidental, what compelled the prince to make for Salvador?

Arriving in Bahia fulfilled a political point of strategy. As we will see in more detail, the political and administrative units in the Brazilian colony two hundred years ago were quite shaky. More than ever Prince João needed a Brazil unified in favor of the Portuguese crown, and the success of his plans in 1808 depended on the financial and political support of *all* of the provinces. Almost half a century earlier, in 1763, Salvador had lost its status as first capital of the colony. It remained an important center for commerce and colonial decisions, true, but its residents profoundly resented the transfer of the capital to Rio de Janeiro. An attempt at secession took place ten years earlier, in the 1798 Tailors' Revolt, and signals of discontent still floated in the air.

Arriving in Salvador, therefore, providentially and diplomatically ensured the loyalty of the Bahians and the northern and northeastern provinces in a moment of great difficulty. João not only stopped there, but later, in Rio de Janeiro, he appointed as Bahia's governor the count of Arcos, previously the viceroy of the entire colony. In Salvador, the prince also announced the most important of all the measures he undertook during his thirteen years in Brazil: the opening of the ports to foreign trade. Thus did he demonstrate Bahia's significance within the political landscape of the monarchy's New World interlude.

This newer theory—that the prince planned the Bahian layover rather than drifting into it by accident—significantly changes interpretations about the transfer of the court to Brazil, starting with the image of the prince regent himself. Few dispute the characterization of Dom João as fearful and indecisive in Portugal, preferring escape to facing the French troops, even if it did seem the most sensible decision, given Napoleon's power. Upon arriving in Brazil, however, João's actions took on a more insightful and resolute character. Choosing Salvador made for a skilled political maneuver at a moment when the weakened and impoverished Portuguese court needed all the support it could get—and that was exactly what happened.

When notice of the voyage reached the colony, the governor of Pernambuco, Caetano Pinto de Miranda Montenegro, sent to sea the brigantine *Three Hearts*, a small ship with two masts that, in the absence of wind, could also be oared.[3] Carrying a load of cashews, pitanga cherries, and other fruits and refreshments, it had the mission of trying to locate the prince regent in the vicinity in which they calculated the Portuguese to be.

Three days after leaving the port of Recife—and sailing blind—the *Three Hearts* amazingly managed to locate the Portuguese ships in one of the most extraordinary naval feats during the royal family's trip to Brazil.[4] In a time without radio, GPS, or satellite communications, imagine a small boat fewer than thirty feet long finding another ship at high sea without any precise information about its location. For the passengers and crew of Dom João's fleet, the brigantine came as a welcome relief. After almost two months' voyage, subsisting on a diet of salted meat, dry biscuits, wine gone bad, and contaminated water, they could finally enjoy fresh fruit and other nutritious fare. Even better, these tropical species were of an appearance, consistency, and flavor never before experienced in Portugal. Thus did Brazil present itself in the fruits of its exuberant and prodigious nature to Prince João and his court, fugitives of the torments of war in Europe.

Relief gave way to uncertainty shortly after arriving in Salvador, however. At 11 a.m. on January 22, 1808, the ships weighed anchor in the shoals—near where today the Mercado Modelo and the Lacerda Elevator stand—and found . . . not a soul in sight. It was as if Bahia was ignoring the arrival of the royal family. For the passengers and crew, this lack of any kind of response came as a great surprise. After all, news of their voyage had arrived in Brazil two weeks earlier, brought by different sources. On January 14, the brig *Flyer*—a small sailing vessel much faster than heavy transport ships—entered the port of Rio de Janeiro with the mission of informing the viceroy that the prince regent was approaching. Shortly thereafter, the frigate *Medusa*, battered by the storms around Madeira, docked in Recife with three of João's ministers aboard. Another ship, the *Martim de Freitas*, arrived on the 10th, also on the Northeast coast. Some ships of the royal retinue itself, carrying two of Prince João's aunts and two of his daughters, landed in Rio on the 17th. During its stopover in Cape Verde, the frigate *Minerva* had already informed this group, part of the fleet that left Lisbon on November 29, that the prince had decided to sail for Bahia.

In those days, the Brazilian coast made use of a paltry communication network based on seaside forts, villages, and lighthouses to transmit urgent information. An integral part of the defense system of the colony, it allowed governors and captains general from diverse provinces to alert their neighbors of pirate attacks, invasions, rebellions, or other threats to Portuguese-owned territory. Given certain specific information, each of these posts had the responsibility of retransmitting it to its next neighbor as fast as possible. What news could be more important than the arrival of the monarchy?

But even breaking news traveled slowly in this glorified mode of mouth-to-mouth communication. It took weeks to traverse the thousands of miles of coastline.[5] Even if the authorities of Salvador had known that the royal court was coming to Brazil, the city still wouldn't have had time to prepare a grand reception properly.

The collective anxiety dissipated, though, when Governor João de Saldanha da Gama, count of Ponte, arrived to greet Dom João.

"Are the locals not on their way to greet me?" asked the surprised prince regent.

"Sir," said the governor, "the entire city did not come immediately because I specified that nobody should approach until I received orders from Your Royal Highness."

"Let the people come as they please," the prince replied, "since they want to see me."[6]

After the governor came the archbishop, José da Santa Escolastica, to greet Prince João. But no festivities took place that day. The great reception feast would wait another day. Exhausted by the ocean crossing, the royal family slept one last night aboard the ships, surrounded by the calm waters of the Bay of All Saints and under the protection of the cannons of Fort Gamboa that presided over the entrance to the city.[7]

The prince disembarked on the morning of January 23.[8] This time, multitudes swarmed the docks of the bay. Cannon shots and salutations mixed with the incessant tolling of bells in the numerous churches of the Bahian capital. After reaching solid ground, the royal family entered the carriages waiting for them and proceeded along the Rua da Preguiça and the Ladeira da Gameleira until reaching the Largo do Teatro (today, Castro Alves Square). There, representatives of the City Council welcomed the prince and his retinue and invited them to continue on foot, under a purple canopy, to the Sé Church, where the archbishop performed a *Te Deum Laudamus* in gratitude for the success of the ocean crossing. Along the way, rows of soldiers saluted, while the bells of every church continued to chime. At night, the royal party met at the governor's palace. There followed an entire week of music, dance, performances in the streets, and extended ceremonies of hand-kissing, in which the prince regent patiently received endless queues of subjects. Farmers, merchants, millers, priests, public servants, soldiers—all had come to pay homage to the sovereign.

Its churches sparkling with gold and baroque carvings, white houses spread across the hillsides, and imposing mansions cresting the mountains, Salvador, one of the most beautiful cities of the Portuguese empire, dazzled visitors from abroad, as we can see from this description by one Maria Graham, who arrived on October 17, 1821:

> *This morning, at day-break, my eyes opened on one of the finest scenes they ever beheld. A city, magnificent in appearance from the sea, is placed along the ridge and on the declivity of a very high and steep hill: the richest vegetation breaks through the white houses at intervals, and beyond the city, reaches along to the outer point of land on which the picturesque church and convent of Sant Antonio da Barre is placed. Here and there the bright red soil shows itself in harmony with the tiling of the houses. The tracery of forts, the bustle of shipping, hills melting in the distance, and the very form of the bay, with its promontories and islands, altogether finish this charming picture; then the fresh sea-breeze gives spirit to enjoy it, notwithstanding its tropical climate.*[9]

Despite its bustling port and its political and economic importance, Salvador remained a relatively small city of about 46,000 inhabitants, slightly smaller than Rio de Janeiro, which had 60,000 at the time.[10] Salvador's location—elevated terrain sloping down to the sea—matched Lisbon and Porto in Portugal, Luanda in Angola, Macau in China, and Rio de Janeiro and Olinda in Brazil.[11] All followed the same model: churches, convents, public buildings, and residences of wealthy families all took their place in the high part of the city. In the low part, on a strip near the sea, lay the commercial quarter with its warehouses, stores, workshops, and the wharves of the port. "There is nothing in the low city but merchants," described the painter Johann Moritz Rugendas, who visited Salvador some years earlier. "The rich, and notably foreigners, also have country homes and vast gardens on the heights, outside the city limits. The slave market, the stock exchange, the traders' shops, the arsenal, and the workshops of maritime construction remain in the lower city."[12]

Ramps, paths, and narrow alleys connected these two sectors but made wheeled transport between them largely impossible. For this reason, city planners installed a great reel to hoist heavy merchandise up the hills. A century and a half later, the electric-powered Lacerda Elevator replaced this fragile system of mechanical tension and remains one of the postcard icons of the Bahian capital. Slaves and pack animals also transported merchandise, ascending and descending the ramps in long, slow-moving queues. The same slaves also carried visitors and distinguished residents up and down the hill in sedans and chairs suspended from hitching-posts.[13]

The churches, almost all constructed between 1650 and 1750, before the transfer of the colonial capital to Rio de Janeiro, decorated the landscape and enchanted visitors from abroad. Mansions in the upper city commonly had two stories, with primary residences, including rooms with verandas, parlors, and dining rooms, on the second floor. Ground floor spaces housed slaves and stored heavy merchandise.[14] By and large, Salvador represented a "typical Portuguese city, medieval in its lack of planning and in its haphazard growth, forming a strong contrast to the methodically laid out Spanish-American towns," according to English historian Charles Boxer.[15]

The dazzling landscape, however, gave way to disappointment when visitors entered the city. Maria Graham found everything dirty and falling apart. "The street into which we proceeded through the arsenal gate, forms, at this place, the breadth of the whole lower town of Bahia, and is, without any exception, the filthiest place I ever was in," she observed.

> It is extremely narrow, yet all the working artificers bring their benches, and tools into the street: in the interstices between them, along the walls, are fruit-sellers, venders of sausages, black-puddings, fried fish, oil and sugar cakes, negroes plaiting hats or mats, caderas, (a kind of sedan chair) with their bearers, dogs, pigs, and poultry, without partition or distinction; and as the gutter runs in the middle of the street, every thing is thrown there from the different stalls, as well as from the windows and there the animals live and feed![16]

Her negative impression continued inside the city's homes.

> For the most part, they are disgustingly dirty. The lower story usually consists of cells for the slaves, stabling, etc.; the staircases are narrow and

dark and, at more than one house, we waited in a passage while the servants ran to open the doors and windows of the sitting-rooms, and to call their mistresses, who were enjoying their undress in their own apartments. When they appeared, I could scarcely believe that one half were gentlewomen. As they wear neither stay nor bodice, the figure becomes almost indecently slovenly.[17]

Already in those days, the city had a reputation for processions and religious festivals that mixed rituals both sacred and profane. A traveler in 1718 observed the viceroy dancing around in front of the high altar, in honor of Saint Gonçalo do Amarante. "He rattled around in a wild manner that suited neither his age nor his standing," wrote the Frenchman, who signed his name Le Gentil de la Barinais.[18] Charles Boxer detailed that fathers and husbands in Salvador often kept their women and children confined at home to avoid their exposure to the loose morality of the city.

The frequency of slave prostitution and of other obstacles in the way of a sound family life, such as the double standard of chastity as between husbands and wives, all made for a great deal of casual miscegenation between white men and coloured women. This in turn produced many unwanted children, who, if they lived to grow up, became criminals and vagrants living on their wits in the margins of the city.[19]

He also refers to the shameful "practice of lady owners living on the immoral earnings of their female slaves, who were not merely encouraged but forced into a life of prostitution."[20]

Prince João spent a month in Bahia, day after day passing in countless parties, celebrations, and strolls, while he was making important decisions that changed Brazil's destiny. He and his mother, Queen Maria I, stayed in the palace of the governor. Princess Carlota Joaquina did not. After landing, she remained aboard the *Afonso de Albuquerque* for five days. Thereafter, she took up residence in the Palace of Justice in the center of the city.[21] On January 28, just one week after docking in Salvador and after one more *Te Deum*, the prince regent went to the Municipal Council to sign his most famous legislation issued on Brazilian territory: the royal decree opening Brazilian ports to commercial trade with all friendly nations. From this date onward, imports were allowed "of all and any kind of materials and merchandise transported on foreign ships of those powers that keep peace and harmony with the Royal Crown."[22]

Two myths about the opening of Brazilian ports still persist. The first attributes the decision to the Bahian public servant José da Silva Lisboa, future viscount of Cairu. A disciple of Adam Smith—author of *The Wealth of Nations* and father of modern capitalism—da Silva Lisboa supposedly presented a study to the prince regent on the advantages of opening up commerce in Brazil as a way of stimulating economic development in the colony. The second myth holds that Prince João intended it as a symbolic gesture to liberate the beleaguered Brazilians from the Portuguese monopoly and commercial isolation at last.

The opening of the ports without a doubt benefited Brazil and did coincide with the liberal opinions of da Silva Lisboa. But in practice it was an inevitable measure. With all of Portugal occupied by the French, commerce among the territories of the empire was grinding to a halt. Opening the Brazilian ports, therefore, made sound economic sense for the entire empire— not just Brazil—and the prince owed a debt of gratitude on that count to Britain. It was the price that he paid for protection against Napoleon; the move had been negotiated in London in October 1807 by the Portuguese ambassador, Domingos de Sousa Coutinho. The agreement provided not only for the opening of the ports but also for the authorization of a British naval base on Madeira.[23] "The opening of the ports of Brazil to the commerce of the world meant, in reality, that, as far as Europe was concerned, they were opened only to the commerce of England as long as the war lasted on the continent," writes Alan Manchester, as England ruled the seas and itself helmed a vast international trading empire.[24]

Historian Melo Moraes records that, on the eve of the departure from Lisbon, Lord Strangford met with minister Antonio de Araújo and warned that Admiral Smith would lift the naval blockade and permit the Portuguese fleet to leave only under the following conditions: "The opening of Brazilian ports, with free market competition reserved for England, which would immediately be based on a tariff of insignificant commercial rights. Moreover, one of the ports in Brazil (that of Santa Catarina) should be handed over to England." De Araújo may have bristled, but, with the exception of the exclusive port in Santa Catarina, the crown met all of these demands after landing in Brazil.[25]

In Salvador, the prince regent also approved the creation of the first school of medicine in Brazil and the bylaws of the first underwriting company, christened as Maritime Commerce. He authorized the construction of a glass factory and a gunpowder factory, devolved power to the governor to establish the production and milling of wheat, ordered the opening of roads, and drew up a plan for the defense and fortification of Bahia, which included twenty-five new cannon boats, two cavalry squads, and an artillery.

The Bahian interlude featured many indulgences, pleasure trips, and popular celebrations. On February 11, the prince regent visited the Itaparica island, bringing with him the prince of Beira, Pedro, the future emperor of Brazil. On their return, a storm caught them by surprise, and they had to spend the night in the home of an island resident.[26] On another occasion, João went out into the streets and threw gold coins to a clamoring mob. The Bahians tried not surprisingly, but in vain, to convince him to stay. Representatives of the provincial council promised to raise funds to build a luxurious palace and to underwrite the expenses of the court. The prince regent diplomatically refused the offer, however. Salvador lay more vulnerable to potential attack by the French than the well-protected, more distant Rio de Janeiro.[27] It was to Rio that he set sail on February 26, completing the last step of the memorable journey to Brazil.

IX

The Colony

Two hundred years ago, Brazil didn't exist—at least not the Brazil that exists today: an integrated country with well-defined borders and residents who define their identity as Brazilian, root for the same national football team, carry the same documents, travel to nearby cities and states for pleasure or work, attend schools with unified curricula, and buy and sell products and services from each other.

On the eve of Prince João's arrival in Rio de Janeiro, Brazil consisted of a jumble of more or less autonomous regions without commerce or any other form of relations between them, having in common only the Portuguese language and the crown in Lisbon on the other side of the Atlantic. "Each captaincy had its own government, small militia and small treasury; communication between them was precarious, as each generally ignored the existence of the other," recorded French naturalist August Saint-Hilaire, who traversed the country from north to south between 1816 and 1822. "There was no Brazil with a common center. It was an immense circle, whose rays converged very far from its circumference."[1]

Not even the word *brasileiro* (Brazilian) adequately referred to people born in Brazil. Pamphlets and articles published at the beginning of the nineteenth century discussed whether the right term was *brasileiro, brasiliense,* or *brasiliano.* Journalist Hipólito da Costa, owner of the *Correio Braziliense* newspaper, published in London, believed that Europeans born in Brazil should be called *brasilienses*.[2] In his opinion, a *brasileiro* was a Portuguese or foreigner who moved to the country, while a *brasiliano* was an indigenous person.[3] "Brazil was nothing more than a geographic unit formed by provinces deeply estranged from one other," according to historian Manuel de Oliveira Lima. All of this changed, though, with the arrival of the prince regent. "These provinces would incorporate into a real political unit, finding their natural axis in the capital, Rio de Janeiro, where the King, court, and cabinet would come to reside," added de Oliveira Lima.[4]

The map of Brazil in 1808 looked very much as it does in the present day with the exception of the state of Acre, bought from Bolivia in 1903. During João VI's reign a small change in the southern borders also took place. The Cisplatina Province was annexed to Brazil in 1817 but then declared its independence eleven years later, becoming modern-day Uruguay. The Treaty of Madrid in 1750 had cancelled the older Treaty of Tordesillas and refashioned the Portuguese and Spanish colonial borders on the basis of *uti possidetis*, the concept of effective possession of territory.[5] Occupying territory guaranteed its integrity. "Without Brazil, Portugal is an insignificant power; Brazil without force is a precious territory left to whoever wants to occupy it," wrote Martinho de Mello e Castro, secretary of the Navy and overseas territories, in 1779 in a letter to the viceroy of Brazil, Luís de Vasconcelos e Sousa.[6]

De Mello e Castro meant that the future of Portugal depended on the occupation and defense of Brazil. For this reason, the forces of the Portuguese administration concentrated on this task. Explorers and cartographers had charted almost all the major Amazonian rivers by 1808. Forts marked and protected the most strategic points. In Tabatinga, on the border with Peru and Colombia, the marquis of Pombal had ordered the construction of a commercial warehouse and a fort, the cannons of which controlled access to the Solimões River.[7] It stood as the most advanced post within Portuguese territory and the Spanish colonies to the west. Expeditions had reached all the way to the Oiapoque River, near present-day French Guiana, and had mapped the source of the Trombetas River, near present day Guyana.

In its immense virgin territory, Brazil had slightly more than 3 million inhabitants—less than 2 percent of its present-day population.[8] One in

Vila Velha (interior of Bahia), engraving from *Travels in Brazil* by Johann Baptist von Spix and C. Philipp von Martius, London, 1824, Lucia M. Loeb/Biblioteca Guita e José Mindlin

three inhabitants was a slave. The indigenous population was estimated at 800,000. The splotch of settlements was concentrated on the shore, with some cities in the interior of the regions of São Paulo, Minas Gerais, Goiás, Mato Grosso, and along the Amazon River. The village of Itu, sixty miles from São Paulo, the last urban agglomeration offering comfort and regular communication with other regions, represented "the gateway to the backlands," an early point of departure for Paulista trailblazers heading toward the deserted interior of the country. From there inward, the country offered little more than a green desert inhabited by natives, diamond prospectors, and scant cattle ranches, a territory of contraband activity, its goods typically sold in Buenos Aires. Minas Gerais was the most populous province with more than 600,000 inhabitants. Next came Rio de Janeiro with a population of half a million, then Bahia and Pernambuco in third and fourth place respectively.[9]

When the court arrived in Rio de Janeiro, the colony had just experienced a population boom. In little more than a century, the number of inhabitants had increased tenfold. Prospectors had discovered gold and diamond deposits at the end of the seventeenth century. The rush for new mining areas, including Vila Rica (modern-day Ouro Preto), Tijuco in Minas Gerais, and Cuiabá in Mato Grosso led to the first great wave of migration from Europe to the interior. From Portugal alone, between 500,000 and 800,000 people moved to Brazil between 1700 and 1800. At the same time, slave traffic accelerated heavily. Nearly two million captive blacks were forced to work the mines and plantations in Brazil during the seventeenth century in one of the largest forced migrations in all of human history. As a result, the population of the colony, estimated at around 300,000 people in the last decade of the seventeenth century, shot up to more than 3 million by 1800.[10]

This population was largely illiterate, poor, and needy, though. In the city of São Paulo in 1818, during King João VI's reign, only 2.5 percent of school-aged free males knew how to read and write.[11] Health conditions were precarious at best. "Even in the most important centers along the coast it was impossible to find a doctor who had completed regular training," recounts de Oliveira Lima, based on the reports of English merchant John Luccock, who lived for ten years in Rio de Janeiro, beginning in 1808. "The simplest procedures were practiced by bloodletting barbers, and for the more difficult procedures one resorted to boastful individuals who were nonetheless generally equally ignorant of anatomy and pathology."[12] Authorization to perform surgery and clinical work was granted only in audience of a judge, himself ignorant of medicine. Candidates could do so only if they could prove a minimum of four years experience in a pharmacy or hospital. Put simply, first you practiced medicine, then you obtained authorization to perform it.

Due to the fragility of communication with the interior of the colony, news of the death of King José I in 1777 took three and a half months to reach São Paulo.[13] Two and a half decades later, the province of São Pedro do Rio Grande (the present-day state of Rio Grande do Sul) waited three months and thirteen days to learn that Portugal and Spain were at war. When the news arrived on June 15, 1801, it had already been nine days since the conflict ended with the defeat of Portugal. Without knowing of the truce, the captain at arms of Rio Grande, Sebastião da Veiga Cabral da Camara, immediately declared war on his Spanish neighbors and, commanding Portuguese troops, conquered a vast area from the territory of Missões in the west of the captaincy to Rio Jaguarão in the south. This failure of communication ended up winning the Portuguese crown a dispute in Brazil that it had lost in Europe, as told by Jorge Caldeira in *Mauá: Entrepreneur of the Empire*, which recounts the story of the Viscount of Mauá in the Second Empire.[14]

This mutual isolation and ignorance resulted from a deliberate policy of the Portuguese government, which maintained Brazil as the jewel in the crown of an extractive economy, without its own will, out of sight, and far from the avarice of foreigners. It was a policy as old as the colony itself. In 1548, on assuming the post of governor general, the first in that position, Tomé de Sousa received twelve orders from the Portuguese crown on how to conduct business in Brazil. One of them, the ninth, determined that the governor should "Impede communication from one captaincy to another through the backlands, unless it is duly authorized."[15] A law in 1733 prohibited the opening of roads in order to block the contraband trade of gold and diamonds and enable surveillance by Portuguese employees charged with collecting the tax called the royal fifth on production of precious metals and minerals from the colony. The few roads that did exist ran over paths already cut by natives before the European discovery of Brazil, which the first colonists reused.[16]

Portugal's intention to keep Brazil closed to the world became manifest in its July 1808 order to imprison German baron, naturalist, and geographer Alexander von Humboldt, who had traversed the Amazon region in search of new flora and fauna. Ignoring the scientific merit of the expedition, the Portuguese government considered his presence detrimental to the interests of the crown because of the dangerous ideas that he could disseminate in the colony.[17] A letter from the minister Rodrigo de Sousa Coutinho to his brother Francisco, then governor of Grão-Pará province, alerted him that Humboldt's voyage was "suspect" because he could, "under specious pretexts . . . tempt the souls of the populace with new ideas based on false and wily principles." Similar orders went out to the governors of Maranhão and Paraíba.[18] Kept isolated in backwardness and ignorance for three centuries, the colony consisted of administrative islands, sparsely inhabited and cultivated, distant and unfamiliar each to one another.

A cassava flour plantation, part of Brazil's rudimentary economy later transformed by the opening of the ports.
Mandioca, the farm of Mr. Langsdorff (at the foot of the Serra de Estrela, an extension of the Órgãos Mountains, Rio de Janeiro, on the way to Villa Rica), engraving from *Travels in Brazil* by Johann Baptist von Spix and C. Philipp von Martius, London, 1824, Lucia M. Loeb/Biblioteca Guita e José Mindlin

Rio Grande do Sul produced wheat and cattle, the latter used also in the production of leather, jerky, tallow, and horns. Its farms were enormous. One of the greatest cattlemen of the region, José dos Anjos, slaughtered 50,000 cattle per year. In 1808, the port of Rio Grande—which contained some 500 homes of 2,000 inhabitants—received 150 ships per year, triple that of neighboring Montevideo.[19] They exported goods to the rest of the country as well as Portugal, Africa, and the Portuguese dominions in the Indies. In turn, they imported cassava, cotton, rice, rum, sugar, sweets, and tobacco from other regions in the colony, while from Portugal they imported glass, ink, machetes, munitions, oil, olives, rifles, rope, wine, and English goods such as iron, textiles, and hats.[20] Porto Alegre, promoted to capital of the province in 1773, had been until then a tranquil village of 6,035 inhabitants.[21]

With nearly 3,000 inhabitants, the island of Santa Catarina—where the modern-day city of Florianopolis lies—dazzled visitors at the time with its beauty and organization.[22] "These houses are well built, have two or three stories, with boarded floors, and are provided with neat gardens, well stocked with excellent vegetables and flowers," noted John Mawe in 1807 during a trip through the south of Brazil. "It affords an agreeable retirement to merchants who have discontinued business, masters of ships who have left off going to sea, and other persons who, having secured an independence, seek only leisure to enjoy it."[23] Florianopolis maintains this role even today as a favored destination for executives and retired professionals. Mawe also passed through Curitiba, at that time a pastoral region with few residents, dedicated to raising oxen and mules to supply the markets of São Paulo and Rio de Janeiro. "More to the Westward it is dangerous to travel, since in that direction live the Anthropophagi [cannibals], who were driven from these boundaries a few years ago," he advises. "The country to the North is very full of wood."[24]

São Paulo, today the largest metropolis in South America, then was a small town of 20,000 inhabitants, including slaves.[25] At the junction of various commercial routes between the coast and the interior and between the south and the rest of the country, it can also be considered the most indigenous and most Brazilian of all of the great colonial cities, according to journalist Roberto Pompeu de Toledo, author of *The Capital of Solitude,* an excellent book about the history of the *paulista* capital. Tupi, a native language, was the most widely spoken language in São Paulo, even by Europeans, until the eighteenth century, when Portuguese became the dominant language. The majority of the population slept in hammocks, a tradition inherited from the natives, until the middle of the nineteenth century, when beds finally replaced them. Homes were little more than adaptations of *ocas,* traditional indigenous dwellings. During the first two centuries of the colony, "the diet of the Indians was followed, weapons of the Indian were used, and *Nheengatu,* the *lingua-geral,* or indigenous-based lingua franca, was spoken as much as or even more than Portuguese," recounts Pompeu de Toledo.[26]

The drawings of Austrian artist Thomas Ender, who reached Brazil in 1817 with Princess Leopoldina (recently married by proxy in Vienna to the future emperor Pedro I), show *paulista* men and women wearing dark cotton jackets and trousers and gray felt hats with wide brims tied with cords below the chin. They secured their loose boots of raw leather, dyed black, below the knee with straps and buckles. Men kept long knives with silver handles in their belts or upright in their boots, to use as weapons or as cutlery during meals. During trips to the interior by horse or by caravan of mules, they protected themselves against the cold using long, wide, blue ponchos. This apparel was so common in São Paulo that for many years it was called *paulista*, until falling into disuse with the disappearance of the troopers, and became typical of the *gaúchos* of Rio Grande do Sul.[27]

One peculiarity caught the attention of almost all visitors from abroad passing through São Paulo at the time: the large number of prostitutes in the streets at night on the heels of troopers. They used wide wool mantles to cover their shoulders and part of their faces. Governors of the captaincy at various times had prohibited these cloaks, called *baetas*, in vain attempts to contain prostitution. In 1775, Martim Lopes Lobo instituted fines and threats of jail for whoever used them. In August 1810, Captain General Franca e Horta ruled that slaves caught with baetas must not only pay a fine but be beaten with a paddle. The fines went toward the lepers' hospital, but none of these measures had any lasting effect. Thomas Ender and his botanical colleague Karl von Martius described the very same scenes in the streets of São Paulo a decade later.[28]

The economic heart of the colony beat in the triangle formed by São Paulo, Rio de Janeiro, and Minas Gerais. The axis of development moved to this region in the beginning of the eighteenth century after the end of the sugarcane boom in the Northeast and the discovery of gold and diamonds in Minas.[29] In his travel notebooks, the botanist von Martius, who also arrived in Princess Leopoldina's retinue, described the incessant movement of mule troopers between São Paulo and Minas Gerais in 1817:

Each troop consists of 20-50 mules, conducted by a muleteer on horseback, in charge of the general direction of the convoy. It is he who gives the orders to depart, rest, spend the night, rebalance the cargo, assesses the state of the yokes and the conditions of the animals, whether they are injured or unshod. Under his orders the carters travel by foot, each

Muleteers supplied a colony awash in ignorance and isolation.
Troperos or Muleteers, engraving from *Views and Costumes of the City and Neighbourhood of Rio de Janeiro* by Henry Chamberlain, London, 1822, Lucia M. Loeb/Biblioteca Guita e José Mindlin

one of them in charge of seven mules, who they have to load and unload with cargo, lead to pasture, and cook for themselves and the other travelers. The muleteer, generally a freed mulatto, also takes care of buying and selling goods in the city, representing the commission of the owner of the troop. The carters are mostly black, and who seek such work as they find the wandering and adventurous life preferable to laboring in the mines or on the farms.[30]

On the troops' route lay waystations and outposts that served as shelter and restocking points for the men and their animals. "It is a custom of these travelers not to carry food," noted von Martius. "As in every place they find shops providing rations and ingredients ready to be prepared." These meals generally consisted of beans cooked with lard, accompanied by dried meat

A sugarcane mill.

A Sugar Mill, engraving from *Travels in Brazil* by Henry Koster, London, 1816, Lucia M. Loeb/Biblioteca Guita e José Mindlin

and a dessert of cheese and banana. At night they slept under a mantle made of ox hide, extended over a grating supported by small pieces of wood stuck into the soil.[31]

Arriving in Rio de Janeiro in 1808, the Englishman John Luccock immediately identified the problem of a lack of currency. Simply put, no money circulated in Brazil. Under the Portuguese dominion, the colony essentially subsisted on bartering, which greatly restricted the opportunities that new merchants could exploit in a country recently opened to international trade. "The commerce between Rio de Janeiro and Minas Gerais consists principally in negroes, iron, salt, woollens, hats, printed cottons, hard-ware, arms, and some fancy articles, a little wine and oil, salt-fish, and butter," related John Mawe. "Few luxuries enter these remote parts, the inhabitants seeking for little beyond mere necessities." [32] Mawe also speaks of the dietary habits in Minas Gerais:

The master, his steward, and the overseers, sit down to a breakfast of kidney beans of a black colour, boiled, which they mix with the flour of Indian corn, and eat with a little dry pork fried or boiled. The dinner generally consists, also, of a bit of pork or bacon boiled, the water from which is poured upon a dish of the flour above-mentioned, thus forming a stiff pudding. A large quantity (about half a peck) of this food is poured in a heap on the table, and a great dish of boiled beans set upon it: each person helps himself in the readiest way, there being only one knife, which is very often dispensed with. A plate or two of colewort or cabbage-leaves complete the repast. The food is commonly served up in the earthen vessels used for cooking it; sometimes on pewter dishes. The general beverage is water. At supper nothing is seen but large quantities of boiled greens, with a little bit of poor bacon to flavour them. On any festive occasion, or when strangers appear, the dinner or supper is improved by the addition of a stewed fowl.[33]

As a result of the gold and diamonds springing forth from the ground, the population of Minas exploded in the eighteenth century. At the height of its prosperity, Vila Rica was the largest city in Brazil with 100,000 inhabitants. Tijuco, modern-day Diamantina, had 40,000 people in the era of Chica da Silva, the famous slave who became rich after she won the heart of a rich Portuguese diamond mine owner.[34] But when the royal court docked in Brazil, the cycle of gold already had reached its end. The German geologist Wilhelm von Eschwege calculates that, at the beginning of the nineteenth century, 555 gold and diamond mines still existed in the colony, directly employing 6,662 laborers, of which only 169 were free men; the remaining 6,493 being slaves of course.[35] Prospecting and mining activity devastated vast swaths of land. "On all sides, we had before our eyes the afflicting vestiges of panning, vast regions of earth stirred up, and mountains of pebbles," wrote botanist Augustin de Saint-Hilaire while traveling through the interior of Minas Gerais. "As far as the eye can see, there is earth overturned by human hands, from so many dreams of profit spurring the will to work."[36]

The control over mining was rigorous. By the laws of the Portuguese government, gold extracted from mines and alluvia had to be delivered to the foundry houses in each district, where the rights of the crown were charged. One fifth of the mineral dust was reserved for the king. Another 18 percent went to the coining houses.[37] The rest stayed with the prospectors and miners in the form of bars marked with weight, carat, number, and the king's coat of arms, along with a certificate allowing them to enter into circulation. To facilitate commerce, the circulation of gold dust was also authorized in small quantities and used for day-to-day purchases. Aside from the severe control of foundry houses, surveillance posts dotted the roads, especially between the mines and the coast, where a military garrison composed of a lieutenant and fifty soldiers had the right to inspect anyone passing through. The punishment for smuggling was drastic: imprisonment, confiscation of all goods, and deportation to Africa.

Still, smuggling dominated the majority of commercial activity in the colony despite all attempts to prevent it. Precious stones and metals flowed along the Rio da Prata in the direction of Buenos Aires. From there, they proceeded to Europe without paying tax to the Portuguese crown. Historian Francisco de Varnhagen calculates that 40 percent of the total gold was diverted illegally.[38] Mawe describes the imprisonment of a smuggler in the village of Conceição, in the interior of Minas:

About a week previous to my arrival, this village was the scene of a somewhat remarkable adventure. A tropeiro going to Rio de Janeiro with some loaded mules was overtaken by two cavalry soldiers who ordered him to surrender his fowling-piece; which being done, they bored the butt-end with a gimblet, and finding it hollow, took off the iron from the end, where they found a cavity containing about three hundred carats of diamonds, which they immediately seized.

The trooper went to prison in Tijuco and the diamonds were confiscated. "The fate of this man," judged Mawe, "is a dreadful instance of the rigour of the existing laws: he will forfeit all his property, and be confined, probably, for the remainder of his days in a loathsome prison, among felons and murderers."[39]

Despite an isolationist policy and the stiff control of the Portuguese government, the colony was still more dynamic and creative than the decaying and stagnant metropolis in Portugal, not only in economic terms but also in the arts and sciences. Between 1772 and 1800, a total of 527 Brazilians graduated from the University of Coimbra, at the time the most respected university in the Portuguese empire and a center for the formation of an intellectual elite that constituted what Sérgio Buarque de Holanda called "the Brazilian ruling class." A quarter of the graduates came from the captaincy of Rio de Janeiro, 64 percent of them trained in law, which offered the most professional opportunities at the time, especially in the public sector.[40]

One of the Brazilians trained in Coimbra was José Bonifácio de Andrada e Silva, the future Father of Independence. A mineralogist of international renown, de Andrada e Silva also wrote the first treatise for the Royal Academy of Sciences in Lisbon on the improvement of whaling techniques.[41] He had traveled through all of Europe, observed the French Revolution in Paris, and participated in the offensive in Portugal against Napoleon's troops, organized by the British after the court's flight.[42] He was probably more experienced and prepared than any other Portuguese statesman or intellectual of his time.

The very existence of this small intellectual elite represented a feat in a colony in which everything was either prohibited or censored. Books and newspapers were prohibited from free circulation. A letter in 1798 from Rodrigo de Sousa Coutinho to Fernando de Portugal, governor of Bahia, recommended severe vigilance over the circulation of books, as there was evidence in the court that the prominent citizens of Salvador were found "infected with abominable French principles."[43] Anyone heard publicly expressing opinions contrary to the mode of thought in the Portuguese court ran the risk of being arrested, put on trial, and eventually deported. Printing such opinions, therefore, was unthinkable.[44] Even meetings to discuss ideas were illegal.

Created in 1786 with the support of the viceroy, Luís de Vasconcelos e Sousa, the Literary Society of Rio de Janeiro counted among its members important figures in the capital, including doctors, lawyers, writers, and poets. In weekly meetings, they discussed diverse topics such as astronomy, literature, philosophy, physics, and politics in Europe and America. It was the era of the French Revolution, American Independence, and the *Conjuração Mineira*—the independence movement in Minas Gerais that transformed the ensign Joaquim da Silva Xavier, better known as Tiradentes, into a national hero. Out of fear that the Literary Society would incontrollably allow for the fermentation of such ideas, the next viceroy, the count of Rezende, successor to de Vasconcelos e Sousa, decided to shut it down in 1794. Eleven people suspected of an alleged conspiracy against the monarchy were imprisoned in the Conceição Fortress in Rio de Janeiro, where they remained until 1797.[45]

To escape censorship, the *Correio Braziliense,* the first Brazilian newspaper, was published in London. Its founder, journalist Hipólito José da Costa, was born in Rio Grande do Sul and left Brazil at sixteen. He graduated from Coimbra and lived for two years in America. He returned to Lisbon and was arrested in 1803 for being a freemason. Put on trial by the Inquisition, he fled to England in 1805, where he had started the *Correio* three years earlier. "Hipólito José was no more and no less than an English whig," wrote historian Roderick Barman, referring to the liberals of British parliament who defended individual rights and limited the power of the king. "He believed in a balanced constitution, a strong legislature, freedom of religion and the press, and liberty—respect for the rights of the individual."[46]

The same Hipólito José who defended freedom of expression and liberal ideas ended up inaugurating a system of promiscuous relations between the press and the government in Brazil, however. In a secret agreement, Prince João subsidized da Costa in England and guaranteed the purchase of a specified number of copies of the *Correio Braziliense* with the objective of preventing the radicalization of opinions expressed in the newspaper. According to Barman, through this agreement, negotiated by the Portuguese ambassador in London, Domingos de Sousa Coutinho, da Costa received an annual stipend in exchange for more temperate criticism of the prince regent, an assiduous reader of its articles and editorials.[47] "The public never learned of the arrangement," affirms the historian. In any event, da Costa showed himself sympathetic to the crown even before negotiating this subsidy. "He always treated D. João with the utmost respect, never questioning his beneficence," records Barman.[48]

In the Portuguese Americas in 1808, an additional factor aggravated political tensions: slavery. For more than two hundred years, the ceaseless trafficking of Africans sustained the prosperity of the colonial economy. Slaves fueled the engine of the cotton, tobacco, and sugarcane plantations as well the gold and silver mines that siphoned riches to the metropolis. The number of slaves, along with the freed blacks, mulattos, and mestizos—their natural allies among the poor at the margins of colonial society—formed more than two-thirds of the population, leaving whites in the minority.[49]

This at best tenuous situation yielded an unsustainable and potentially explosive situation. The dread of a slave revolt kept white, wealthy, educated families sleepless at night. In a letter of February 13, 1799, Fernando de Portugal affirmed:

> *What has always created fear in the colonies is slavery, because of its conditions, and because the majority of its inhabitants, not being as settled as employed and established men who have possessions and property, wish to participate in a conspiracy or attempt that would yield dire consequences, leaving men to be exposed to assassinations by their own slaves.*[50]

In 1791, a slave rebellion led by Toussaint Louverture resulted in a bloodbath in the French Antilles, present-day Haiti. Could this potentially occur in Brazil? Definitely. In the so-called Tailors' Conspiracy, which took place in Salvador in the middle of 1798, the rebels promulgated manifestos in public places, demanding "the end of the detestable metropolitan yoke of Portugal," the abolition of slavery, and equality for all citizens, "especially mulattos and negroes."[51] The most radical called for the hanging of part of the white elite in Salvador. The repression by the Portuguese government came down harsh and immediate. Some forty-seven suspects were arrested, of which nine were slaves. Four of them, all free mulattos, were decapitated and quartered. Their limbs were impaled on stakes in the streets of the capital, where they remained until they had decomposed completely. Of the suspects, sixteen prisoners were released, the rest exiled to Africa.[52]

A drooping lip, fine hands, small feet, and a slight frame gave João a grotesque appearance.

Retrato de D. João VI by Jean-Baptiste Debret, Museu Histórico Nacional, Rio de Janeiro

The coronation of Napoleon, "the mightiest breath of life which ever animated human clay."
Le Sacre de Napoléon by Jacques-Louis David, 1806–7

In the haste of departure, 60,000 books from the Royal Library and the Church's silver were forgotten on the docks.

Embarque de D. João, Ministério das Relações Exteriores, Rio de Janeiro

While preparations for the flight were made on the eve of departure, the plan for the court's transfer to Brazil was an ancient one. *Embarque de D. João, príncipe regente de Portugal, para o Brasil, em 27 de novembro de 1807,* painting by Nicolas Lowis Albert Delerive, 1807–1818, Museu Nacional dos Coches, Lisbon

The allegory of Prince João's arrival in Rio de Janeiro: For the first time, a European sovereign sets foot on American soil.

Alegoria da chegada da família de D. João VI by Domingos António Sequeira, Coleção duque de Palmela, Lisbon

João and Carlota Joaquina had a marriage of crisis, due to his indecision and her conspiracies.

Retrato de D. João VI e D. Carlota Joaquina by Manuel Dias de Oliveira, early 1800s, Museu Histórico Nacional, Rio de Janeiro

Judicial penance, as this type of punishment was known, had the objective of serving as an example and as an affirmation of the power of the king over his subjects. This extreme form of atonement for serious crimes by means of bodily mutilation or even burning of the guilty had been used in Portugal since the Middle Ages, becoming gruesomely popular in the autos-da-fé of the Inquisition. An extreme case was the Tavora Affair, in which a noble family, accused of weaving a plot against King José in 1758, were executed, their corpses mutilated and burned in the public square in Lisbon. Their ashes were thrown into the sea.[53] Transported to the Brazilian colony, the judicial penance included mutilation, branding with hot irons, lashing, and quartering.[54] It was applied without pity or piety whenever there was a good reason—from the point of view of the Portuguese crown of course. It was used against Tiradentes in the Conjuração Mineira, against the leaders of the Tailors' Conspiracy in Bahia, and in countless other regional rebellions.

Instead of threats and coercion, however, Prince João used another attribute of the monarchy to govern: the image of a benign king who provided for, cared for, and protected all. The prince would pass into history as a good-natured monarch, relaxed and paternal, who patiently received his subjects each night at the Palace of São Cristovão for the hand-kissing ceremony, in which even the most humble people, including natives and slaves, had the right to make entreaties and pay homage. "The court and its power fascinated us like a veritable messianic attraction: it bore the hope of succor from a father who came to cure the wounds of his children," noted historian Maria Odila Leite da Silva Dias.[55]

X

Tree Frog, the Reporter

Prince João, the Portuguese royal family, and their fleet entered Guanabara Bay in the early afternoon of March 7, 1808. The sun shone bright in the cloudlessly blue sky. A strong wind blew off the ocean, alleviating the suffocating heat of the end of the *carioca* summer. After three months and one week of traveling—including the respite in Salvador—hundreds of noblemen and other illustrious passengers pressed themselves to the gunwales of the ships to contemplate the superb spectacle unfolding before their eyes: a small city of white houses along a strip of beach, extending around the margins of a bay of calm waters, itself framed by towering granite mountains covered with luxuriant, dark green forests. They had seen nothing like it before in Portugal.

Those on land enjoyed their own moment of celebration and rejoicing. Standing among the thousands of anxious people squeezed along the docks to watch the arrival of the Portuguese ships, a reporter recorded the scene:

> *It was two minutes to three o'clock in the afternoon, a refreshing, beautiful, and delightful hour. . . . Since sunrise we had been told of this most auspicious day for Brazil: not a single cloud obstructed the sun's radiance, whose heat was mitigated by the freshness of a strong and constant breeze. It seemed like a brilliant star, deviating from every*

obstacle, as if rejoicing the triumphant entrance of the first sovereign of Europe in the most serendipitous city in the New World, and wanting to participate in the jubilation and applause of a people giddy with the most intense delight.[1]

The author, Luis Gonçalves dos Santos, was not a journalist by trade but rather a chronicler by calling. At age forty, versed in Greek, Latin, and philosophy, he served as the canon of the Catholic Church in Rio de Janeiro.[2] He also had a funny nickname: *Padre Perereca*—Father Tree Frog—because of his short, scrawny frame and bulging eyes.[3] Even then, irreverence and humor formed part of the carioca personality, sparing no one. Father Gonçalves dos Santos recorded everything he saw and defended his ideas passionately. As such, he remains the best and most detailed reporter of events between 1808 and 1821. In 1825, he published two volumes of his book *Memoirs of the History of the Reign in Brazil, Divided in Three Eras of Happiness, Honor, and Glory, Written in the Court of Rio de Janeiro in 1821, and Offered to His Majesty the King D. João VI.* While laudatory and replete with flattery and wonder, the details of the work reflect the diligence of an attentive and curious observer.

Gonçalves dos Santos's texts capture the encounter of two worlds previously unfamiliar and distant to each other. On one side: a European nobility attired in powdered wigs, golden epaulets, velvet coats, silk socks, and buckled shoes, all of their clothes far too dark and heavy for the blistering sun of the tropics. On the other side: a colonial, almost African city, two-thirds of its population composed of blacks, mestizos, and mulattos, full of great adventurers,[4] slave traffickers, troopers, diamond and gold traders, sailors, and merchants from the Indies.

On January 14, having learned that the brig *Flyer* had arrived in Rio de Janeiro carrying news that Napoleon's troops had invaded Portugal and that the royal family was en route to Brazil, Father Gonçalves dos Santos recorded:

Never before has there been news more sad, and at the same time, more agreeable. I cannot explain the astonishment, the consternation, and the sentiments that we all have about the disgraceful events in our mother

View of Rio de Janeiro from Guanabara Bay in 1822, an obligatory stop for ships crossing the oceans and the site of the largest slave market in the Americas.

country. Tears streak down the faces of everyone, and many cannot utter a single word or bear to hear more calamitous news. However great the motives of grief and sorrow, however, they are no greater than the causes for consolation and delight: a new order will take shape in this part of the southern hemisphere. The Empire of Brazil is already within sight, and we anxiously await for the mighty hand of our lord the Prince Regent to cast the first stone towards future grandeur, prosperity, and power in the new empire.[5]

View of the City of Rio de Janeiro, Taken from the Anchorage, engraving from *Views and Costumes of the City and Neighbourhood of Rio de Janeiro* by Henry Chamberlain, London, 1822, Lucia M. Loeb/Biblioteca Guita e José Mindlin.

The news brought by the *Flyer* caused a frenzy in Rio de Janeiro. Not knowing of the prince regent's decision to stop in Bahia first, the capital city had few weeks to prepare. Charged with organizing the reception, the viceroy, the count of Arcos, moved out of his home, a modest two-story structure in front of the docks of the port, where today the Plaza 15th of November stands. This building, known as the Palace of Viceroys, also functioned as the Court of Relations with colonial Brazil. Here the prince regent and his family would live. There was no time for a proper

renovation, but the building was whitewashed on the outside. Its interior was repainted and lined with silks of many colors. Such decoration was all that the urgency of the moment would permit. The count also ordered the governors of the neighboring provinces, São Paulo and Minas Gerais, to send along bananas, beans, beef, cassava, corn, fowl, grapes, guava, lamb, peaches, pork, potatoes, and sweet-potatoes—provisions all crucial to satisfy the hunger and nutritional wants of a court arriving famished and weakened by the long ocean crossing.[6]

Two days later, on January 16, the Senate of the Chamber—a kind of council of aldermen in the era of colonial Brazil, composed of esteemed

representatives of society—gathered to organize the reception of the royal family. The festivities would include civic and religious ceremonies, dances, and popular fanfare. Along the entire path, houses were to be lit up and their windows decorated. Music in grandstands would spread throughout the streets. Bells would toll in every church, and the roar of cannons on the shoals of Guanabara Bay would crown the grandiloquent event. Despite the haste, everything went as planned, according to the reports of Father Gonçalves dos Santos.

But these plans had barely come into being when, on the afternoon of January 17, seven Portuguese ships and three English ships entered the

Guanabara Bay. It was the part of the convoy that had separated from the royal entourage near Madeira and arrived in Rio de Janeiro after a stopover in Cape Verde. The ships carried the two sisters of Queen Maria I, the princesses Maria Benedita and Maria Ana, as well as the princesses Maria Francisca and Isabel Maria, daughters of Prince João and Carlota Joaquina. Invited to disembark by the count of Arcos, the princesses preferred to stay aboard until receiving confirmation that the rest of the family had arrived safely in Bahia. They received word a month later, on February 22; only then did they agree to disembark.[7] Two weeks later, on March 7, the rest of the fleet anchored in front of the Palace Square. As arranged by the viceroy, cannon fire from forts and warships stationed in the bay and bells in churches and monasteries saluted them.

Gonçalves dos Santos reports:

Rio de Janeiro, O happiest of cities of the New World! Rio de Janeiro, you have your august Queen and eminent Prince with his royal family, the first majesty that the southern hemisphere has ever seen or known. These are your sovereigns and lords, descendents and heirs of those great rulers who discovered you, populated you, and aggrandized you, such that now you are the Princess of all America and are the court of the lord rulers of Portugal. Fill yourself with joy, let loose in delight, decorate yourselves with your richest clothes, go out to greet your sovereigns, and receive the auspicious Prince with respect, worship, and love, as he comes in the name of the Lord to visit his people.[8]

The royal family again stayed aboard this first day, receiving innumerable courtesans who extended their welcome: a commission of the Chamber of Senate, magistrates, priests and bishops, and army officials, all accompanied by the viceroy. First they greeted João on the *Royal Prince* and then Princess Carlota Joaquina on the *Afonso de Albuquerque*.[9] Father Gonçalves dos Santos recorded nightfall on March 7: "It has just barely gotten dark, and the entire city has lit up so much that the sun could be extinguished, as there is no house, not even of the poorest families, that does not demonstrate through its lights the interior happiness of its residents."[10] The royal family alighted the next day, on March 8, around four in the afternoon. A scarlet and gold brigantine covered by a purple canopy transported João from the *Royal Prince* to solid ground. Everyone disembarked except for Queen Maria I, who stayed aboard for two more days.

A certain air of disappointment inevitably descended upon the colonial Brazilians on seeing a court of fugitives suffering from the vagaries of a long journey. A European monarch had never before set foot on American soil. Until then, *brasileiros* had seen the prince regent only on the coins and engravings that arrived from the metropolis: a sovereign with a resolute look and a proud bearing, robed with purple mantle and noble scepter. The man who disembarked the red and gold brigantine differed quite drastically from the handsome prince of the official portraits. He was "a very fat man, very fatigued, very simple, with chestnut sideburns streaking down a red face, a lagging gait due to hereditary erysipelas, and wearing a brown coat smudged with stains," according to the report of the historian Pedro Calmon.[11] In the description of another historian, Tobias Monteiro, "João wore a long jacket with a high collar, an embroidered white vest, satin stockings, short boots, epaulets, a giant bicorn hat decorated with ermine, and a sword tucked in his belt, hanging from gold threads and tassels." At the Prince's side, "walking with difficulty," came his wife. "Thin, bony, restless eyes, closed mouth, fine lips, a long, stern, and wilful chin, she did not hide her contempt at finding herself in a land of people that she would always detest," writes Tobias Monteiro.[12]

Carlota, her daughter, and the other ladies of the court had all arrived with shaved heads or short hair, protected by turbans, due to the infestation of lice that had attacked the ships during the voyage. Monteiro recounts that, on seeing the peculiar headdresses of the princesses, the women of Rio de Janeiro thought this the latest fashion in Europe. Within a short time, almost all began cutting their hair short and using turbans to imitate the Portuguese noblewomen.[13]

Despite the disappointment of this first sight of the court's appearance, the people of Rio de Janeiro paid homage from their greatest depths. The crowd that gathered on the ramps of the dock included aldermen, canons, magistrates, nobles, priests, and troops bearing the Portuguese flag. Priests blessed the royal family with holy water, amid copious prayers and burning incense. Prince João kissed the cross and received the blessings of the bishop. Afterward, they seated him under a canopy of red silk and golden posts to protect him from the sun. A pageant then formed, composed of the receiving party and the arriving party, slowly walking in the direction of the Rosario Church, then the city's cathedral. Hastily constructed triumphal arches marked their path. The streets were covered with "fine white sand, leaves, aromatic herbs, and flowers," according to priest-reporter Gonçalves dos Santos. The facades of houses were draped with "curtains of carmine damask, and the windows, with rich and showy tapestries of various pretty colors; some of damask, others satin, and others even more precious silk."[14] Music poured into the streets.

Before the pageant went the authorities of Rio de Janeiro: military officials and judges, together with priests, monks, and seminarians from the numerous convents. Immediately behind them "followed the banner of the Chamber, carried by a citizen dressed in black silk, a cape of the same color, a vest and stockings of white silk, a large-brimmed hat with white feathers, and suspenders decorated with precious stones and richly embroidered silk."[15] He was flanked by two long rows of men dressed in the same manner, who formed the "banner guard."[16] At the rear of the pageant procession went the canopy under which the royal family marched. Eight men bore the poles of this canopy, among them Amaro Velho da Silva, one of Brazil's major slave-traffickers at the time.[17]

The *Te Deum* was observed in the cathedral, a celebration of gratitude for the success of the voyage. Thereafter followed a hand-kissing ceremony, in which the participants of the pageant prostrated themselves before Prince João to kiss his hand in a gesture that simultaneously represented obedience and submission by the subjects of the colony to the prince regent. This curious ritual of the Portuguese monarchy, already practiced by the viceroys of the colony, marked the entire period in which the court stayed in Brazil. It was already dark when the royal family proceeded by carriage to the viceroy's palace, now the Royal Palace. Exhausted, everyone went to bed. In the streets nearby, however, festivities continued all night, with fireworks, music, and poetry recitations in honor of the occasion.

Queen Maria I, the mad queen, disembarked on March 10. An armchair carried by royal servants transported the seventy-four-year-old queen, demented and debilitated by the voyage, to the palace. "The poor queen proceeded all the way to her room carried in an armchair, with an uncertain look of idiocy and senility, surrounded by the infanta D. Mariana and by all of her granddaughters and servants, who came to receive her with tenderness and love," describes chronicler Luiz Norton, based on the reports of Father Gonçalves dos Santos.[18] The festivities lasted until March 15, officially closing with yet another ceremony of gratitude in the Rosario Church and a hand-kissing ceremony in the Royal Palace.

In these first days, João, Carlota Joaquina, and their children lived in the Royal Palace, the converted residence of the viceroy—but it was only a temporary arrangement. Within a short time, the prince regent would move to a much more spacious and agreeable palace in the present-day neighborhood of São Cristovão, near the Mangueira favela and Maracanã Stadium. Princess Carlota Joaquina moved to an estate near Botafogo beach. Queen Maria I stayed in a Carmelite convent, connected to the Royal Palace by an improvised passageway over the Rua Direita, today's 1st of May Avenue. The devout who had lived in this convent hastily moved to the seminary in the neighborhood of Lapa. The convent also housed the kitchen, workshops, and Royal Pantry, where the court's victuals were stored. To the side of the convent lay the Church of Carmo, soon transformed into the Royal Chapel. The neighboring Chamber Headquarters and public jail were also annexed to the Royal Palace by a passageway and provided accommodations for the royal servants.[19]

It was understandably complicated finding housing for the thousands of courtiers and their attendants newly arrived in a still relatively small city of just 60,000 inhabitants. By order of the count of Arcos, a notorious system of "pensions" began, under which houses were solicited for the use of nobility. The addresses that were selected were marked on the door with the initials PR, for *príncipe regente,* which the population immediately recast as *Ponha-se na Rua*—Put yourself in the Street. Hipólito da Costa, editor of *Correio Braziliense,* described the system of pensions as a "medieval" ordinance, which "could not but make the new government in Brazil odious to its people."[20] The new residents of the pensions, however, not only complained of the price of rent but also complained that the homes were badly constructed and uncomfortable.

The arrogance and presumptuousness of those who arrived from overseas resulted in various abuses of the pension system. The count of Belmont seized a recently constructed but not yet occupied house belonging to the chief overseer of the port. The count lived there for a decade, rent-free, while the owner and his large family stayed in a small dwelling erected next to the count's new mansion. The count even commandeered the port overseer's slaves without explanation. The duchess of Cadaval, whose husband had died during the interlude in Salvador, took over a country house belonging to the colonel of the militia, Manoel Alvas da Costa, and lived there without paying a penny. When Alvas da Costa decided to take back the house, his noble tenant responded that she had no other place to live and offered an annual rent of 600,000 reís, equivalent today to $20,000. Alvas da Costa thought this too little and refused. The duchess pretended not to hear him and remained until 1821, when she returned to Portugal in the company of the king, dispatching a bank deposit of 600,000 reís for each year that she stayed—but without thanks or even a word of explanation to the colonel.[21]

Rents in the city at large doubled according to a residents' petition kept in the National Archives. For a ground-level house outside the city, the diplomat Colonel Maler, consul from France, paid 800,000 reís (today $28,000). An excursion in a mule-drawn carriage to the Santa Cruz plantation, fewer than sixty miles from the capital, cost almost 400 francs, equivalent to $2,400. On this plantation the prince regent spent his summers. But on one occasion, because he hadn't yet received his salary, the French consul had to decline the prince's invitation to accompany him there because he couldn't afford to hire a coach. "There is no corner of the universe with worse food and worse accommodation for such excessive prices," wrote Maler.[22]

All of these aggravations contributed to the quick dissipation of the enthusiasm of those first days of the court's arrival. The Brazilian colony gained much from the prince's presence, including its eventual independence, but the royal family's early years in Rio de Janeiro brought enormous problems and costs. They needed to feed and pay the expenses of an idle, corrupt, and wasteful court, which they did in two ways. The first was by lists of voluntary donations, for which the rich and powerful in the colony signed up quite willingly with the certainty of obtaining favors and generous advantages in exchange. The second was the indiscriminate raising of taxes and duties, which the entire populace paid with no ability to evaluate the immediacy or efficacy of the benefits they received in exchange. Their resulting dissatisfaction would eventually prove ungovernable.

XI

A Letter

Plunged into darkness in the Atlantic Ocean, on April 12, 1811, a
Good Friday, at 10 p.m. the frigate *Princess Carlota* prevailed over
the waves near Cape Verde, off the coast of Africa, en route to Rio de
Janeiro. In its cellars lay the final shipment of books from the precious Royal
Library, abandoned on the docks of Belém three and a half years earlier
during the flight of the royal family to Brazil.[1] Alone in his cabin with the
faltering flame of an oil lamp, archivist Luiz dos Santos Marrocos wrote the
following letter to his father, Francisco, in Lisbon:

> *My father and master of my heart,*
> *This [letter] is composed between sky and sea, over thousands of
> anguishes, discontents and labors that I never thought I would suffer;
> but having left the shoals of Lisbon with favorable winds, we barely
> arrived at high seas when a cross-wind hit us, impelling us toward the
> coast of Africa. I have suffered great discomfort in my throat, mouth,
> and eyes, to the point of taking medication. I had no seasickness when
> we left Lisbon, but nevertheless felt great compassion for the widespread
> number of people vomiting aboard the frigate, as among 550 people
> here, few have been spared from nausea. At night I cannot sleep for
> more than an hour, as I spend the rest thinking of the present and future*

risks of my life. On the eighth day of the voyage, our water rations were already spoiled and rotten, and we had to cast off the bugs in order to drink it. We have had to dump many barrels of rotten salted-meat into the sea. In sum, everything here is in disarray, due to the general lack of preparations. All of the ropes of the frigate are rotting. . . . All of the sailings are rotting, and they are torn with any breeze. The crew is inadequate. In a similar manner, we will be lost if, through some misfortune, we are stricken by any intense weather. There is not enough apothecary for the sick, as there are not more than a half-dozen herbs here, and the maladies are in abundance. There are neither chickens or fresh meat. To conclude, and say it all at once, if I knew of the state that the Frigate Princess Carlota was in, I would have been repulsed to place myself and the Library aboard.

P.S.: I long for Mana and Ignez, and still have so much to say, and with such haste that I must lift my pen now, reserving this for the calm of Rio, if God allows me to reach there.[2]

PART TWO
THE RISE OF BRAZIL

XII

Río de Janeiro

The city that welcomed the Portuguese royal family in 1808 represented for transatlantic maritime routes what the Frankfurt airport does today for intercontinental flights. It was a world hub, at which practically every ship leaving from Europe or America would stop before proceeding to Asia, Africa, and the recently discovered lands of the South Pacific. Protected from wind and storms by the mountains, the calm waters of Guanabara Bay served as ideal shelter for repairing ships and restocking potable water, jerky, sugar, rum, tobacco, and firewood. "No colonial port in the World is so well situated for general commerce as Rio de Janeiro," observed John Mawe. "It enjoys, beyond any other, an equal convenience of intercourse with Europe, America, Africa, the East Indies, and the South Sea islands, and seems formed by nature as a grand link to connect the trade of those great portions of the globe."[1]

It offered a crucial stopover on long and drawn-out navigations around the world. At the beginning of the nineteenth century, a journey from London to Rio took between 55 and 80 days. Rio to Capetown took 30 to 50 days. To India, between 105 and 150 days. To China, 120 to 180 days. To Australia, between 70 and 90 days.[2] The strategic importance of Rio de Janeiro on these routes ranked so high that, after the arrival of the royal family in Brazil, the city became the headquarters of the British Royal Navy in South America, under the command of Vice-Admiral Sidney Smith, the same who escorted the Portuguese fleet during its departure from Lisbon in November 1807.[3]

For crews and passengers, arrival in Rio de Janeiro in the middle of a perilous and monotonous voyage always made for a pleasing and surprising event. All reports refer to the grand scenery, imposing mountains, and spectacular vegetation everywhere. Passing through Rio de Janeiro aboard the *Beagle* in April 1832, Charles Darwin used an unbelievable sequence of adjectives to describe what he saw before his eyes:

> *Sublime, picturesque, intense colors, blue prevailing tint, large plantations of sugar rustling and coffee, Mimosa natural veil, Forests like but more glorious than those in the engraving; gleams of sunshine; parasitical plants; bananas; large leaves; sun sultry. All still, but large and brilliant butterflies; Much water . . . the banks teeming with wood and beautiful flowers.*[4]

The most detailed records of the landscape and customs of Rio de Janeiro during the court's presence come from an Englishman, John Luccock. A merchant from Yorkshire, he disembarked in Rio de Janeiro in June 1808, three months after the arrival of the royal family. "Churches and monasteries, forts and country-houses, glittering in whiteness, crown every hillock, and decorate the sides of its fanciful and symmetrical heights, backed by a screen of woods, which overshadow the whole," he noted.[5] He lived in Brazil for ten years, during which time he also traveled to São Paulo, Santa Catarina, Rio Grande do Sul, Minas Gerais, and Bahia. He had an insatiable curiosity. Intelligent and discerning, he recorded everything he saw and did in Brazil. In addition to his travel reports, he compiled a dictionary of the Tupi-Guarani language. In 1820, he published a book in England that became famous in Brazil for the lively testimony it offered of a country in rapid transformation.[6] In the introduction, Luccock says that he aims to give "the reader an impartial opinion of the practices and customs of the people, of the political events, and of the social landscape of an immense and unknown country."

He relates that shortly after setting foot on solid ground, he learned that the population of Rio de Janeiro consisted of 80,000 inhabitants. He thought the figure inflated and recalculated it on his own. According to him, the city had 4,000 homes, with an average of 15 residents in each. This totaled 60,000 inhabitants, a figure that most historians consider quite precise. The detail-oriented Luccock divided the population as follows:

16,000 foreigners

1,000 people associated with the court

1,000 public servants

1,000 who reside in the city but make their living in neighboring regions or on ships

700 priests

500 lawyers

200 professionals practicing medicine

40 regular merchants

2,000 retailers

4,000 cashiers, apprentices, and store servants

1,250 mechanics

100 publicans, "vulgarly called grocers"

300 fishermen

1,000 soldiers

1,000 sailors

1,000 freed blacks

12,000 slaves

4,000 housewives

29,000 children, almost half the city's total population[7]

After the occupation of Lisbon by the French, Rio de Janeiro became the most important naval and commercial center in the empire. More than a third of all exports and imports in the colony passed through its port, well ahead of Salvador, which, despite its importance in sugar production in the Northeast, at this time was responsible for only a fourth of external Brazilian commerce. Rio was also the largest slave market in the Americas. Slave ships that had crossed the Atlantic from Africa congested its port. According to the calculations of historian Manolo Garcia Florentino, no fewer than 850,000 African slaves had passed through the Port of Rio in the eighteenth century, slightly less than half the total number of captive blacks brought to Brazil in this period.[8]

Observed from the sea while ships approached the port, it was a tranquil little city, with a bucolic appearance, perfectly integrated with the splendor of nature encircling it. Up close, though, this impression changed rapidly. It suffered from excessive humidity, filth, and the lack of good hygiene among residents. On a visit in 1803, James Tuckey, a British navy official remarking on the houses, relates that from the outside they had "all the apparent neatness of our best English villages. But too soon we find, on entering them that this is the mere effect of white-wash, and that within they are the habitations of sloth and nastiness. . . . The streets, though straight and regular, are narrow and dirty, the projecting balconies sometimes nearly meeting each other."[9]

"The cleaning of the city was entrusted to the vultures," wrote historian de Oliveira Lima.[10] The number of rats infesting the city and its environs shocked Alexander Caldcleugh, who visited Brazil between 1819 and 1821: "Many of the first houses are so full of them that during dinner it is by no means an unusual circumstance to see them playing about the room."[11] Because of the height of the water table, constructing septic tanks was prohibited.[12] Urine and feces were collected at night and transported and poured into the sea in the morning by slaves carrying barrels of sewage on their backs. En route, these barrels, full of ammonia and urea, sloshed on their skin, and, with the passage of time, left white streaks down their black backs. As a result, these slaves were known as tigers. In the absence of a system of sewage collection, these "tigers" worked in Rio de Janeiro until

A Market Stall, engraving from *Views and Costumes of the City and Neighbourhood of Rio de Janeiro* by Henry Chamberlain, London, 1822, Lucia M. Loeb/Biblioteca Guita e José Mindlin

1860 and in Recife until 1882. Sociologist Gilberto Freyre writes that the easy availability of these tigers and their low cost held back the creation of sanitation networks in coastal Brazilian cities for decades.[13]

The habits of the residents themselves didn't improve this state of affairs. In the humid heat of the tropics, sluggishness reigned, as did a lack of elegance in the manner of dress and habits. Emanuel Pohl, a naturalist who accompanied Princess Leopoldina to Brazil, observed that men wore slippers, light trousers, and jackets of low-grade cotton. Women, wrapped in rosaries with little saints as pendants, spent the majority of the day in simple shirts and short skirts. "In a blissful state of *far niente* (do-nothing), they used to sit on a mat near the window, legs crossed, the whole day long," noted Pohl.[14] James Tuckey left a curious record about carioca women: "Their black eyes, large, full and sparkling, give a degree of brilliance to their dark complexion, and throw some expression into their countenances; but it is too generally the mere expression of animal vivacity untempered by the soft chastising power of

A typical family in Rio de Janeiro—a rich and prosperous though unrefined city—during the time of João VI. *A Brazilian Family,* engraving from *Views and Costumes of the City and Neighbourhood of Rio de Janeiro* by Henry Chamberlain, London, 1822, Lucia M. Loeb/Biblioteca Guita e José Mindlin

tender sensibility." Tuckey, however, had one significant reservation: "Among other habits of the Brazilian ladies, which, separately considered, form a powerful opposition to the empire of female charms, is that of constantly spitting, without regard either to manner, time, or place."[15]

Luccock painted an amusing portrait of the habits of cariocas. According to him, families generally spent their time in rooms toward the back of the house. Women sat in a circle and sewed, making stockings, lace, embroidery, and other stitchwork. There they also all gathered to take their meals, using a board set upon an easel in the middle of the sitting room for a table. "The chief meal is a dinner at noon, at which the master, mistress, and children occasionally sit round the table; more frequently it is taken on the floor, in which case the lady's mat is sacred, and none approach it to sit down but acknowledged favourites," recorded Luccock. "Knives are only used by the

Life in Rio de Janeiro, as depicted in this carioca scene, remained provincial despite the presence of the court.

Uma História—Gossiping, engraving from *Views and Costumes of the City and Neighbourhood of Rio de Janeiro* by Henry Chamberlain, London, 1822, Lucia M. Loeb/Biblioteca Guita e José Mindlin

men; women and children employ their fingers. The female slaves eat at the same time, in different parts of the room; and sometimes are favoured with a mess from the hands of their mistress. If there be a dessert, it consists of oranges, bananas, and a few other different kinds of fruit."[16]

Invited to one of these dinners by a rich family, Luccock surprisingly found that everyone was supposed to show up with his own knife, "usually broad, sharp-pointed, and mounted in silver." At the table he observed that "the fingers, too, are as often used as the fork." Moreover, he notes, they often ate from the plate of someone sitting next to them with their own hands. "It is accounted a mark of strong attachment for a man to eat off his neighbour's plate: so that the hands of both are not unfrequently dipped into it at the same time." The meal also featured "a weak sort of red wine" drunk from cups rather than glasses. Due to the effect of alcohol, toward the end of the meal, all of the diners became noisy. "Their common gesticulation in talking is increased, and they throw their arms about, with their knives and forks, in such a way that a stranger feels no little surprise, how eyes, noses, and cheeks, escape from injury," observed the Englishman. "When the knives and forks are at rest, one is grasped in either hand, and held upright on the table, resting on the end of its haft; and when they are no longer wanted the knife is deliberately wiped upon the cloth, and returned to its sheath, which is placed in the girdle behind the loins."[17]

The painter Jean-Baptiste Debret, who arrived at the French Artistic Mission in Brazil in 1816, also found shocking the lack of good table manners among the rich:

> *The man of the house eats with his elbows jutting on the table; the lady with the plate on her knees, seated on her settee, in oriental fashion; the children, lying or squatting on mats, gladly smearing themselves with the food in their hands. If they are wealthier, the merchant might add a loin of grilled or boiled fish with a spring of parsley, a quarter of an onion, and three or four tomatoes. But to make it more appetizing, they would dip every mouthful in spicy sauce. Bananas and oranges would complete the meal. Only water was drunk. Women and children used neither fork nor knife—they all ate with their hands.*[18]

Fresh meat was a rarity. It came from afar, sometimes six hundred miles away. Many of the oxen driven along substandard roads from Minas Gerais or the Paraíba Valley died along the way from hunger or exhaustion. "Those of which held out to the end arrived in a most miserable condition, at a public Slaughter-house," recounts Luccock. Situated near the center of Rio, the slaughterhouse was "highly distressing, and always of the filthiest description." The condition of the animals, including how they had been slaughtered and transported, turned the meat so bad that "nothing but dire necessity, or the perpetual sight of it in the same wretched condition, could induce a person of the least delicacy to taste it." Pork also was sold "in a very diseased state." For these reasons, dried meat from far away—salted and cured in the sun—was more widely consumed.[19]

Despite the rarity of freshly slaughtered meat, the population of Rio de Janeiro had a rich and varied diet. It consisted of many fruits, such as bananas, oranges, passion fruits, pineapples, and guava, as well as fish, fowl, vegetables, and legumes. Bread baked from wheat flour proved rare and very expensive. Flour made from cassava root or corn flour was used throughout the colony. Together with dried meat and beans it completed the basic pyramid of the Brazilian diet.

In 1808, Rio de Janeiro had only seventy-five public spaces or areas of usage, composed of forty-six roads, four alleyways, six backstreets, and nineteen fields or plazas.[20] The names of the roads help explain their purpose: Praia do Sapateiro: Shoemaker's Beach, today Flamengo Beach; Rua dos Ferradores: Blacksmiths' Street, today Alfandega; Rua dos Pescadores: Fishermen's Street, today Visconde de Inhaúma; and Rua dos Latoeiros: Tinsmiths' Street, today Gonçalves Dias. The main street was Rua Direita, today 1st of May Avenue, featuring the house of the governor, the customs house, and later the Carmo Convent, the mint, and the Royal Palace itself.

During the week, the bustling, noisy streets of the city teemed with mules and four-oxen carriages carrying construction materials, the friction of their wheels and axles making a noise like iron-cutting. Historian Jurandir Malerba recounts that the largely forgotten language of church bells measured and announced the rhythms of life. Nine clangings announced the birth of a boy, seven the birth of a girl. The incessant roar of cannons on the numerous ships and forts protecting the city shocked visitors. "In homage to the King, every ship entering the port would fire off 21 shots, responded in turn by the forts on shore—a custom unknown to any other part of the world," writes Malerba.[21] In 1808, 855 ships entered the port of Rio de Janeiro, an average of three per day.[22] If each fired 21 shots, followed by a response of equal number from the forts, then each day by nightfall each carioca heard no fewer than 126 rounds of cannon fire.

In fact, depending on the ship, this number could reach much higher. In 1818, Henry Brackenridge, a naval official from America, entered Guanabara aboard the frigate *Congress* on an official mission. The protocol of salute involved an exchange of no fewer than seventy-two cannon shots. First, the American frigate discharged twenty-one shots saluting the king, immediately

Slaves and freed black merchants selling coal, corn, hay, and milk.

echoed by twenty-one more from one of the forts guarding the bay, followed by fifteen more shots in salute of the admiral, who responded in equal proportion. Only thereafter could the *Congress* dock in port. "The Portuguese appear to be extremely fond of expending their powder," remarked a surprised Brackenridge. "Hardly an hour of the day passed without the sound of cannon in some direction or other."[23]

Another aspect of the city that piqued visitors' curiosity was the number of blacks, mulattos, and mestizos in the streets. Slaves undertook every type of manual labor. Among other activities, they were barbers, shoemakers, couriers, basket makers, and merchants selling hay, refreshments, sweets, cornmeal, and coffee. They also carried around people and goods.[24] In the morning, hundreds of them fetched water from the fountain in the Carioca aqueduct, transporting it in barrels similar to those used to carry sewage to the beach in the afternoons.[25]

Negros vendedores de carvão e vendedorias de milho and *Vendedores de leite e capim,* engravings by Jean-Baptiste Debret
from *Voyage pittoresque et historique au Brésil,* Paris, 1834–1839, as in *Rio de Janeiro, cidade mestiça,* Companhia das
Letras, 2001

"The racket is incessant," complained Ernst Ebel, a German visitor
describing the noise of slaves in the streets transporting merchandise.

*A mob of half-naked slaves carrying sacks of coffee on their heads, led
forward by one who sings and dances to the rhythm of a cowbell or
beating two shackles in the lilt of a droning stanza which the rest of
them repeat, two more carrying on their shoulders a heavy barrel of
wine, suspended on a long pole, intoning a melancholy ditty at every
step; further ahead, a second group carrying bales of salt, wearing nothing more than a loincloth, indifferent to their burden and to the heat,
race around shouting at the top of their lungs. Chained to one another,
six more appear yonder with buckets of water on their heads. They are
criminals employed as public servants.*[26]

Slaves dominated the landscape on holidays and weekends as well. Wearing colorful clothes, ornaments, and turbans, they gathered in the Santana Fields, in the suburbs of the city, where they sang and danced, clapping in large circles. "On every Saturday and holiday, which are called festival days, masses of negroes travel there, reaching a total of ten or fifteen thousand," described two visitors. "It is quite curious recreation, and offers a unique spectacle of happiness, tumult, and confusion, which is probably not possible to see on the same scale anywhere besides Africa itself."[27]

In addition to discomfort, the combination of heat and lack of hygiene generated massive health problems. "The people are very subject to fevers, to bilious complaints, and what are called diseases of the liver, to dysentery, and elephantiasis, and to other disorders of a similar, and probably connected, kind, which are often violent and fatal," observed John Luccock. "The small pox, too, when it makes its appearance, carries off multitudes; but lately its ravages have been checked by vaccination."[28] In 1798, the Chamber of Rio de Janeiro proposed to a group of doctors a program to combat epidemics and eradicate the endemic maladies of the city. The plan included a survey of these illnesses. The report, completed by Army doctor Bernardino Antonio Gomes, is frightening:

According to an observation of nearly two years in Rio de Janeiro, I have counted that the endemic maladies of the city include scabies, erysipelas, mycoses, yaws, morphea, elephantiasis, pruritus, tungiasis, leg oedema, hydrocoeles, sarcoceles, roundworms, hernias, leuchorrea, dysmenorrhea, haemorrhoids, dyspepsia, various convulsions, hepatitis, and different types of intermittent and recurring fever.[29]

Aided by the medical report, the aldermen raised the suspicion that the primary source of these epidemic illnesses—especially scabies, erysipelas, pox, and tuberculosis—lay with the recently arrived blacks from Africa. The councilmen suggested transferring the slave market from the Plaza 15th of November to some location further away. Seeing their business interests threatened, slave traffickers sued the Municipal Chamber. A legal dispute dragged on, ending only when the viceroy, the marquis of Lavradio, sided with the aldermen and ordered the transfer of the slave market to the Valongo region, where it remained when Prince João arrived in Brazil.[30]

But even more difficult than diagnosing the cause of various diseases was fighting them. As was the case everywhere in the colony, no university-trained doctors lived in Rio de Janeiro. Hearkening back to the Middle Ages, barbers practiced a rudimentary form of medicine. Thomas O'Neill, a lieutenant of the British Navy who accompanied the prince regent, noted with intrigue the number of barbers and the purposes that they fulfilled: "The barbers shops are singular, as they are designated by the sign of a basin; and the barber unites in himself the three professions of a surgeon, dentist, and shaver."[31]

Carioca researcher Nireu Cavalcanti found documents in the Brazilian National Archives that give a sense of the state of health and medical care in Rio in the time of King João VI. The post-mortem inventories of doctors, they record possessions left behind. One of them, of the head surgeon Antonio José Pinto, who died in 1709, includes the following startling list of "surgical instruments": a large hand-saw, a small hand-saw, a ratchet, two straight knives, two pairs of pliers, an eagle's claw, two tourniquets, a spanner wrench, and a large pair of scissors. An inventory of Antonio Pereira Ferreira, a pharmacist who died in the same year, gives an idea of the assortment of drugs available at the time. The list includes compresses, fungus, minerals, oils, peels, roots, seeds, and a curious item listed as "animals and their parts" with "human oil," "lizard sandpaper," "raw salamander eyes," "deer antler shavings," and "wild boar teeth."[32]

The arrival of the royal family in Rio de Janeiro soon effected a revolution in architecture, the arts, culture, customs, health, and sanitation, everything changing for the better—at least for the white elite who frequented the court. Between 1808 and 1822 the city tripled in size with the creation of new neighborhoods and parishes.[33] The population grew 30 percent, while the number of slaves tripled from 12,000 to 36,182.[34] Animal and coach traffic grew so intense that laws and regulations had to restrain it. Rua Direita became, starting in 1824, the first road in the city with numbered addresses and traffic organized in a two-way street with separate lanes.

Despite the rapid growth, in 1817, nine years after the royal family's arrival, Austrian naturalist Thomas Ender registered the presence of a group of natives in São Lourenço, one of the entrances to Guanabara Bay, not far from the Palace of São Cristovão, where King João VI lived. It was doubtless the last indigenous stronghold close to the capital of a Brazil still desolate and unexplored.

XIII

Dom João

João, prince regent and, after 1816, king of Portugal and Brazil, had a crippling fear of crustaceans and thunder. During the frequent tropical storms in Rio de Janeiro, he took refuge in his rooms in the company of his favorite valet, Matias Antonio Lobato. With a candle lit, the two prayed to Santa Barbara and San Jeronimo until the thunder ceased.[1] On another occasion, a tick bit him while he visited the ranch at Santa Cruz where he spent his summers. The wound became inflamed, and he developed a fever. Doctors recommended a bath in the ocean. Terrified of being attacked by crustaceans, he ordered the construction of a wooden box in which he bathed in the waters of Caju Beach near the Palace of São Cristovão. Essentially a portable bathtub, the box had two crosswise poles and holes in the sides through which seawater entered. The king remained inside for a few minutes, the box submerged and held tight by slaves, as the marine salt helped the wound form a scab.[2]

These improvised washings on Caju Beach, under medical advice, remain the only evidence of any baths that the prince took during his thirteen years in Brazil. Almost all historians describe him as unkempt and averse to bathing. "He was very dirty, a bad habit he shared with the rest of the family and the rest of the nation," affirms Oliveira Martins. "Neither he, nor D. Carlota, despite hating each other, differed on the rule of not bathing."[3] The

Despite his defects of personality, King João VI, here with royal scepter, crown, and mantle, knew how to delegate power and weather geopolitical turbulence.

O rei D. João VI, engraving by Jean-Baptiste Debret from *Voyage pittoresque et historique au Brésil,* Paris, 1834–1839, Lucia M. Loeb/Biblioteca Guita e José Mindlin reluctance of the Portuguese court to bathe contrasted sharply with the Brazilian colony, where attention to personal cleanliness caught the attention of nearly every visitor. "Despite certain habits that come close to savagery among the Brazilians of lower classes, it must be remarked that whatever their race, every one of them is notably attentive to bodily cleanliness," wrote Henry Koster, who lived in Recife from 1809 to 1820.[4]

João Maria José Francisco Xavier de Paula Luis Antonio Domingos Rafael de Bragança was the last absolute monarch of Portugal and both first and last ruler of the United Kingdom of Portugal, Brazil, and the Algarves, which existed barely longer than five years. Born on May 13, 1767, he died on March 10, 1826, two months before his fifty-ninth birthday. Paintings of him reveal, in the words of historian Ângelo Pereira:

A high forehead, disproportional to his face, sharply defined eyebrows, sagging cheeks and jowls, rather buggy eyes, a fine nose, thick lips, a half-opened mouth, short and fat legs, tiny feet, a protuberant belly, chubby hands with dimples at the knuckles, sagging shoulders, and a short neck. His eyes were small, dark, frightened, distrustful, and insecure, as if asking permission for his actions.[5]

Descriptions of him penned by historians usually disparage him.

According to Luiz Norton: "He was physically grotesque and his sickly obesity gave him the air of a peaceful dullard."[6] According to Pandiá Calógeras:

He was darling, but also lovingly and tolerantly dismissed for his weakness and cowardice. Nobody paid attention to his opinion, and this led him to hide his feelings, seeking victory by postponing solutions, inciting his advisors against each other, ministers thus opposing their colleagues. He achieved the realization of his intentions through tremendous apathy and procrastination. He triumphed by tiring his adversaries.[7]

According to Lília Schwarcz: "He was lackluster and had no active voice."[8] According to Oliveira Martins: "He had attacks of vertigo and attacks of melancholy because he suffered from hemorrhoids. His ill health yellowed his flaccid visage, from which hung that famous lifeless pout, peculiar to the Bourbons."[9] According to de Oliveira Lima, he was: "Short, fat . . . [with] the small hands and feet of the aristocracy, overly vulgar thighs and legs much too thick for his body, and above all a round face lacking majesty or any distinction, from which loomed the thick and dangling lower lip of the Habsburgs."[10]

He ascended to power accidentally after his mother, Queen Maria I, went mad and his older brother, José, heir presumptive, died of smallpox. In 1792, when it was confirmed that his mother was incurably mad, he assumed power provisionally with the support of the State Assembly, composed of nobles, military leaders, and representatives of the Church. In 1799, he became prince regent, which made him a king without a crown. His ascension took place in 1816, a year after his mother died and eight years after arriving in Rio de Janeiro. With his infamously indecisive and fearful personality, he governed Portugal during one of the most turbulent periods in the history of European monarchies.

Despite—or perhaps because of—the turbulence, João suffered periods of deep depression. In the first major bout, recorded in 1805, he distanced himself completely from public life and from participation in the court. People thought that he had gone mad like his mother. "He had no wish to hunt or to ride horses, and turned to a completely sedentary existence," writes Ângelo Pereira. "His neurological condition facilitated a nervous breakdown, at this time poorly understood, which was confused with an attack of alienation. He had vertigo and outbursts of extreme anxiety." He moved from the Palace of Queluz, where he lived with his family, to the Palace of Mafra, in the company of friars. Thereafter he isolated himself even further, moving to the royal family's manor in Vila Viçosa, in the region of Alentejo. Thinking her husband demented, Princess Carlota tried to have him removed from power and assume control of the state herself. Alerted by his doctor, Domingos Vandelli, João returned to Lisbon in time to block the coup. From then on, husband and wife lived separately.[11]

Responsible for his education since childhood, priests surrounded the prince regent in the Palace of Mafra. He adored sacred music and detested physical activity. "He was brought up far away from active, happy, strong and sanguine men, who loved to live life," writes Pedro Calmon.[12] Profoundly religious and influenced by the Church, the prince attended mass every day. General Junot, commander of the French troops who invaded Portugal, described him to Charles de Talleyrand, French minister of foreign relations, as "a weak man, suspicious of everyone and everything, conscientious of his authority but unable to command respect. He is dominated by priests, and can only act under the coercion of fear."[13]

The prince's love life was mediocre at best. He married Carlota Joaquina under dynastic obligation. They had nine children, with whom he lived very briefly under the same roof. His only true love lingers in the history books as an obscure tragedy. At age twenty-five, living in Portugal and already married, Prince João became enamored of Eugênia José de Menezes, one of his wife's maids of honor.[14] Eugênia was granddaughter of Pedro, fourth marquis of Marialva, and daughter of Rodrigo José Antonio de Menezes, first count of Cavaleiros and Princess Carlota's head steward. Eugênia was born in 1781 when her father was governor of Minas Gerais. In May 1803, still unmarried, she became pregnant. Suspicions understandably fell on the prince regent, who had had amorous encounters with her through the combined machinations of a court priest and Dr. João Francisco de Oliveira, head physician of the army, himself married with children.

After discovering that Eugênia was pregnant, Oliveira quickly decided to sacrifice his own reputation to save the prince regent: He left his wife and children in Lisbon and fled with Eugênia to Spain, abandoning her in Cádiz. The nuns of the Conceição de Puerto de Santa Maria convent took her under their wing and helped her give birth to her daughter. From there, Eugênia moved to two other religious convents, dying in Portalegre on January 21, 1818, after the prince regent had been crowned king in Rio de Janeiro. During this entire period, João paid all of her expenses. Dr. Oliveira, after leaving Eugênia in Spain, fled to America and then to England where, according to Portuguese historian Alberto Pimentel, he reunited at last with the family he had abandoned in Portugal. In 1820, King João granted Dr. Oliveira the distinction of the Order of Christ and named him the head of Portuguese affairs in London.[15]

It remains João's only known extramarital affair. In Brazil, he proved himself an even more solitary monarch than he had been in Portugal. His marriage to Carlota Joaquina, already unraveling since 1805, became an explicit separation in Rio de Janeiro. While D. João went to live in the Quinta de Boa Vista, Carlota preferred to live on an estate near Botafogo. They interacted with each other only according to protocol, in public ceremonies, masses, and concerts in the Royal Chapel.

Few historians risk entering into the details of João's personal life. Two of them, Tobias Monteiro and Patrick Wilcken, point to evidence that, in the absence of his wife, he maintained homosexual relations—more out of convenience than from conviction—with Francisco Rufino de Sousa Lobato, one of the royal valets. Monteiro suggests that Rufino's duties included regularly masturbating the king. A friar who is identified only as Father Miguel had observed, against his intentions, intimate scenes between the king and his servant on the Santa Cruz ranch at the Summer Palace. After this episode, the friar was transferred to Angola, but before leaving he left written testimony of what he had witnessed.[16] It is possible that much of this resulted from palace intrigues, but Rufino received generous sums of money and promotions on various occasions in gratitude for his services. At the end of the Portuguese court's interlude in Brazil, Rufino had become: viscount of Vila Nova da Rainha, royal councilor, chamberlain, the king's personal treasurer, secretary of the Casa do Infantado, deputy secretary of the Mesa de Conscienca e Ordens in Brazil, and governor of Fortaleza de Santa Cruz.[17]

Francisco Rufino was the third of four brothers of the Sousa Lobato family that accompanied João to Brazil in 1808. The others were Matias Antonio, Joaquim José and Bernardo Antonio. All four served as valets and personal assistants to the prince. Two also took part in the State Assembly, the highest advisory body to the king. Their relationship with the prince regent caused much gossip in Rio de Janeiro. Carlota Joaquina attributed to them "the disgraces of Portugal" during her husband's government, her secretary José Presas recounts. "The Prince always gives himself over to his favorites and courtiers, and he has done no more than aggrandize them, to the detriment of the kingdom and general discontent, as is the case today with the Lobatos," she said to him.[18]

Historian Vieira Fazenda recounts that Matias Antonio, given the title of baron and later viscount of Magé, lived in the City Palace, next to the São José Church, in a room contiguous to João's. He helped the king undress and accompanied him in the reading of the breviary before going to sleep. He stood by the king's side during nights of thunder and lightning.[19] Prussian traveler Theodor von Leithold, arriving in Brazil in 1819, confirmed João's fear of thunder. "If the King does not feel well, if he nods off or if there comes to pass a storm, which produces a strong reaction in him, he shuts himself in his chambers and receives no one," he wrote, explaining the cancelation of a ceremony at the Palace of São Cristovão.[20]

João referred to himself always in the third person: "Your Majesty wants to eat," "Your Majesty wants to go for a walk," "Your Majesty wants to sleep."[21] A methodical man, he obsessively and rigorously repeated his daily routines. "D. João VI was a man of habits," related the painter Manuel Porto Alegre. "If he slept once in a certain place, he would never want to sleep in another, taking things to the point where he would not allow that the bed remained more or less near the wall—it had to be right up against it. Any small change that was attempted would make him suspicious and irksome with whoever made it."[22]

This extreme aversion to change included his own apparel. In contrast to the showy kings of France and Spain who preceded him, João dressed badly. He wore the same clothes every day and refused to change them even when he stained or ripped them. "His usual outfit was a broad, greasy jacket made of old corduroy, threadbare at the elbows," according to Pedro Calmon. In the pocket of this jacket, the king carried grilled and buttered boneless chickens that he devoured between meals.[23] "Horrified of new clothes, the King stuffed himself in the same ones from the evening before, which each day withstood less and less the pressure of his startlingly chubby thighs and buttocks," adds Tobias Monteiro. "The servants noticed the rips, but nobody dared to tell him. They took advantage of his siestas, and sewed his pants while he slept in them."[24]

Three men played a fundamental and abiding role in João's life. During different points in his life, in addition to helping him overcome fear, timidity, insecurity, and depression, they advised him on the decisions that marked his reign. Rodrigo de Sousa Coutinho, count of Linhares, heir and godson of the marquis of Pombal and leader of the "English faction" in the court, acted as the main player responsible for the transfer of the royal family to Brazil. He "picked up where Pombal left off and promoted the Prime Minister's plan to counter Portugal's political weakness within Europe by developing the territories of Portuguese America," affirms historian Kirsten Schultz.[25] His death in 1814 left a lacuna in the government that the prince regent never filled.

The second, Antonio de Araújo e Azevedo, count of Barca, succeeded de Sousa Coutinho in the Ministry of War and Foreign Affairs. De Araújo e Azevedo didn't have the same stature as a statesman as de Sousa Coutinho but was considered one of the most illustrious intellectuals in Brazil. In 1807 he brought in his luggage the English printing presses that initiated the Brazilian press. He was also responsible for important advances in science and culture, including the arrangement of the French Artistic Mission, which arrived in 1816. He died in 1817, one year before João's coronation.

The last of the three key men was Thomaz Villa Nova Portugal, successor to these first two in the same ministry. During the final phase of his government in Brazil, João, aging and tired, blindly confided in Villa Nova Portugal. "D. João did not even bother to think," wrote Tobias Monteiro. "However insignificant the decision to be taken was, it fell to Tomas Antonio to resolve it."[26] The correspondence between the two reveals João's ongoing timidity and insecurity in exercising power. In notes to the minister on January 24, 1821, about an audience that day, the king wrote: "O.C. is coming today, tell me what I should say to him." João depended on Villa Nova Portugal even for conversations with his own son. "Until this moment, I have not yet spoken with my son, and I want you to tell me if you are of the same opinion; tell me what I should say to him, and if he should have a reply, how I should respond," the king wrote on January 31, 1821, with respect to the decision about whether to return to Portugal or remain in Brazil. "I have just received my son's vote, now tell me your judgment," he prompted on February 4, dealing with the same subject.[27]

These three men helped save King João VI's reign and to a large extent his biography, otherwise doomed to failure on the merits of his own personality.[28] Thanks to them, João went down in history as a relatively successful sovereign, especially when compared with his peers of the era—dethroned, exiled, imprisoned, and even executed. "The truth is, in spite of the period of unparalleled upheavals during which he ruled, D. João lived and died as king, while the majority of crowned heads in Europe fell before Napoleon," Jurandir Malerba observes.[29] Pedro Calmon defined him as a sovereign who was "troubled and clever, who reigned until his death, in spite of Spain and France, a devilish wife, Napoleon, wars, revolutions, and conspiracies."[30] De Oliveira Lima writes that, although he was no great sovereign capable of military feats or brash administrative coups, João knew how to combine good will, intelligence, and common sense to efficient result. "He was gentle and discerning, ingratiating and prudent, affable and persistent."[31] In the opinion of de Oliveira Lima, thanks to these attributes, "D. João VI, without a doubt, was and is a popular king in Brazil."[32]

Queen Carlota Joaquina—ugly, Machiavellian, and unhappy but not demonstrably unfaithful.

A rainha D. Carlota Joaquina, engraving by Jean-Baptiste Debret from *Voyage pittoresque et historique au Brésil,* Paris, 1834–1839, Lucia M. Loeb/Biblioteca Guita e José Mindlin

XIV

Carlota Joaquina

I n the books and films that she has inspired, Princess Carlota Joaquina appears as an unfaithful wife and an ugly, unhappy, Machiavellian woman. While suspicions remain, no hard proof exists that she was ever unfaithful. Ugly, unhappy, and Machiavellian, however, she was indeed. No other individual from that time and place etched a portrait in history with such a caricatured and debated image. Quarrelsome, intelligent, and vindictive, she has merited diametrically opposed depictions through the ages. In Carla Camurati's film *Carlota Joaquina, Princess of Brazil*, she is a depraved and promiscuous queen. In the official Portuguese history, she appears as a pious and ultraconservative sovereign.[1] Her unbridled ambition and thirst for power remains undeniable, however, and led her to participate in numerous conspiracies and coup attempts, some of them against her own husband. All of them failed.

She had powerful black eyes and a wide, capricious mouth, with thin lips over which presided dark, pronounced whiskers. Straight, virile lines shaped her face. Thin, dark-haired, and short, she had skin mottled by scars from smallpox during her childhood.[2] The duchess of Abrantes, wife of General Junot, commander of the invading French troops, described her as "small, hobbling on one leg, cross-eyed, a purplish nose, and all too disagreeable given the legends of love affairs that accompanied her."[3] The hobble came after falling from a horse in childhood.[4] "The manly, crude features of her face, the nature of her worries, her very impudence, meant that the only feminine part of Carlota Joaquina was the exterior wrapping," wrote de Oliveira Lima, who also defined her as "one of the major, if not the greatest encumbrances in D. João VI's life."[5]

Daughter of Carlos IV and sister of Fernando VII, both kings of Spain, she was born in 1775 and died in 1830, at fifty-four years old. According to the history books, she participated in at least five conspiracies. In the first, in 1805, she tried to dethrone her husband and assume control of Portugal. The prince regent discovered the coup in time, punished those involved, and separated from her. Later, in the Americas, Carlota attempted to assume the throne of the Spanish colonies in America after Napoleon deposed her brother. Again João blocked her plans, preventing her from traveling to Buenos Aires, where she had planned to be named princess regent in place of her brother. In 1821, now back in Portugal, she refused to sign the Portuguese Liberal Constitution, opposing the demands of the Cortes and the advice of her husband. As a result, she was confined to the Palace of Ramalhão, far from Lisbon and far from power. In 1824, even while in isolation, she conspired to install her favorite son, Miguel, as king of Portugal in what became known as the April Revolt. Leader of a traditionalist party, Miguel, backed by troops, imprisoned his father and attempted to assume the throne. This coup also went awry, and Miguel ended up in exile like his mother. Some still suspect Carlota Joaquina's hand in her husband's death. João VI died in 1826 amid bouts of nausea and vomiting. Rumors at the time mentioned poisoning ordered by the queen. After João's death, she once again tried to install Miguel and displace her daughter Isabel Maria, whom João had appointed as regent. Carlota Joaquina failed yet again.[6]

The queen contrasted sharply with her husband. Pedro Calmon wrote that "no other princess of the century seemed less appropriate as the wife of calm D. João."[7] Few other couples could so differ in their preferences and behavior. João, obese, lethargic, and good-natured, hated riding horses, and a simple walk of a few feet exhausted him. He yawned during feasts and official receptions. But he loved Gregorian chant and ceremonies in the company of priests and monks.[8] Carlota Joaquina, on the other hand, lively, hyperactive, and talkative, rode horses better than most men of her era—even with her hobble. Her jaunts on horseback through the outskirts of Rio de Janeiro became famous. She loved feasts and was handy with cannons.[9]

She demanded—and even threatened—that people pay homage when she passed through the streets of Rio de Janeiro. According to protocol, men had to remove their hats and kneel in front of the royal family as a sign of respect. This requirement caused a series of diplomatic incidents because a large number of foreign visitors refused to enact the ritual. Thomas Sumpter—American envoy to the royal court, a dyed-in-the-wool Republican, and Carlota's neighbor near Botafogo—was out riding when the queen's retinue approached him galloping. The minister greeted them politely but without removing his hat or kneeling. Carlota, dissatisfied, demanded that her guards force him to dismount and fulfill the protocol. The soldiers surrounded Sumpter and threatened a whipping. Irritated, Sumpter drew a pistol in each hand and warned the soldiers that he might kill them if they raised a whip against him. Afterward, he pressed charges against D. João. In another incident, one of Carlota Joaquina's stablemen whipped Lord Strangford, the British envoy to the court. So many complaints accrued that João finally decided to exempt all foreigners from gestures of deference to the Portuguese royal family.[10]

João and Carlota Joaquina were married by proxy, as was the custom in the European courts at the time. She met her husband for the first time a month after the wedding. She was ten years old, he seventeen. The destinies of these two children fulfilled key roles in the game of power in the era. Marriage was one of the most practical means of maintaining stability on the Iberian peninsula and avoiding the countless wars that had imposed so many sacrifices on Spain and Portugal in preceding centuries. Young Carlota arrived in Portugal in May 1785. Out of courtesy, João received her at the border, but the misunderstandings between them—a result of her indomitable character—didn't take long to manifest themselves. On the night of June 9, during a feast in the Palace of Vila Viçosa, Carlota bit her husband's ear and bashed him over the head with a candlestick.[11] They had been married for only two months.

The pair consummated the marriage six years later, after the princess had turned fifteen. While not allowed to share the same bed as her husband, Carlota spent her days playing patty-cake in the Palace of Queluz under the care of Queen Maria I, whose signs of madness had already begun to show.[12] The couple had nine children in the span of thirteen years:

- Maria Teresa, born April 29, 1793, one year after João assumed control of the throne

- Antonio, born March 25, 1795 (died June 11, 1801, six years old)

- Maria Isabel, born May 10, 1797, married to King Fernando VII of Spain but died shortly thereafter on December 2, 1818

- Pedro, born October 12, 1798, future emperor of Brazil as Pedro I and king of Portugal as Pedro IV

- Maria Francisca, born April 22, 1800, married to the infante Carlos of Spain, brother of Fernando VII

- Isabel Maria, born June 4, 1801, princess regent of Portugal from 1826 to 1828

- Miguel, born October 22, 1802, king of Portugal from 1828 to 1834, lost the throne to his brother Pedro, who had abdicated the throne of Brazil; fled on an English ship to Germany, where he died in 1866

- Maria da Assunção, born June 25, 1805, died January 1834

- Ana Maria de Jesus, born December 23, 1806, the first infanta of Portugal to marry a man not of royal rank since the Middle Ages

Some historians raise the suspicion that some of these children issued not from Prince João but rather from Carlota's extramarital affairs. De Oliveira Lima writes that João "was not wholly certain of the paternity of the last children" and that Carlota Joaquina was "a traitor of a spouse, a conspirer of a princess, constantly and forever disloyal."[13] No solid evidence proves her infidelity, but suspicions linger. In October 1820, rifle shots killed Gertrudes

Carneiro Leão, baroness of São Salvador de Campos do Goitacazes, as she alighted from her carriage in front of her house in the Catete neighborhood in Rio de Janeiro. The crime occurred one year before the royal family's return to Lisbon and gave rise to a wave of rumors, according to which Carlota Joaquina ordered the killing because she had an amorous relationship with Fernando Carneiro Leão, Gertrudes's husband, count of Vila-Nova de São José, and director of the Bank of Brazil.[14]

Another insinuation of infidelity involved the commander of the British fleet in Rio de Janeiro, Admiral Sidney Smith. In a polemic, José Presas, the Catalunian former private secretary of Carlota Joaquina, claims that the princess had a rendezvous with the admiral in the outskirts of Rio de Janeiro. Presas doesn't explain the nature of this encounter, but Carlota and Smith had allied themselves politically in the so-called River Plate Question of the period, in which the princess fought to assume power over the Spanish colonies against the will both of her husband and Lord Strangford. According to Presas, she presented the admiral with a jewel-studded sword along with a note that read: "In gratitude from the Princess of Brazil for the services of Sir Sidney Smith."[15]

While it seems possible, the problem is that the greatest suspect in this story is not Carlota Joaquina but Presas himself. One of the most colorful personalities of this era, Presas became well known as the author of an explicit case of literary blackmail. Born in Catalunia, he moved as a boy to Argentina, where an uncle trained in law cared for him. In 1806, when England invaded Buenos Aires in reprisal for the Spanish alliance with Napoleon, Presas immediately adhered to the "English party," believing British victory inevitable. He miscalculated. Argentina defeated and expelled the English from the River Plate region. Pursued for treason, Presas fled to Rio de Janeiro, where he joined the employ of Carlota Joaquina as her personal secretary on the recommendation of Sidney Smith himself, who knew him from Buenos Aires. More than just a secretary, he became her man of confidence, co-conspirator, and, some suspect, her lover.[16]

With the return of the royal family to Portugal, Presas obtained a position in the court of Spain, thanks to her influence. He fell into disgrace, though, after writing pamphlets against monarchic absolutism. Threatened with imprisonment, he fled to France, where he wrote a book entitled *The Secret Memoirs of D. Carlota Joaquina,* replete with intrigues, gossip, and insinuations, and revenge for the nonpayment of a pension that the queen had promised him. In the book, Presas insinuates possessing Carlota Joaquina's correspondence—which he calls her "confessions," containing compromising information about her life and actions. He gives the impression that he could use this information if he doesn't receive the money promised to him. "Meditate deeply upon the fatal consequences that could befall you, if the Prince himself (D. João) were to have in hand the confessions that you involuntarily—having forgotten them—left with me," he writes openly to the princess. In the end, he makes his mercenary point: "A brief response, accompanied by a bill of exchange for a modest amount, would be sufficient to hush me."

Presas wasted ink, paper, and money in vain, though. Carlota Joaquina died at the beginning of 1830, when the book was still being printed in Bordeaux, France. She never had a chance to read the disloyalties of her ungrateful and treacherous secretary. Even if she had read the book, Presas's blackmail might not have had any effect. At the time that he wrote it, she, already a widow, was living ostracized in Portugal and drowning in debts.

Carlota Joaquina detested Brazil. In 1807, she resisted leaving Portugal as much as she could. "In this country nothing lasts," she wrote after arriving in Rio de Janeiro. "Even salted meat does not keep, and rots quickly."[17] Upon embarking to return to Portugal in 1821, she removed her sandals and beat them against one of the cannons on the gunwale of the ship. "I have knocked the last dust of Brazil from my feet," she said.[18] "At last, I am going back to civilization!"[19]

Back in Portugal, she refused to swear to the Constitution, as the Cortes had demanded. As a result, she lost all of her political rights and the title of queen. She spent the rest of her days imprisoned in the Quinta do Ramalhão, the summer estate near Sintra. In a letter to the king, she explains that she wouldn't swear the oath simply because she had said she wouldn't. Her position, she said, came not from pride nor contempt for the Cortes, but because "a decent person does not retract." She added: "I shall be more free in my banishment than you in your palace. At least I have my liberty to keep me company. My soul was never enslaved nor humiliated by those rebellious vassals, who dare to impose laws upon you and struggle to compel me to take an oath that my conscience repels."[20] This was Carlota Joaquina in the role that she performed her whole life: stubborn, headstrong, obstinate, and inflexible.

Even her death was controversial. In the official version, she died of a malady of the uterus, probably cancer. The rumors of the era, however, maintained that she brought on her own end by drinking tea laced with arsenic. In her final days, she was "a tattered individual" according to historian Alberto Pimentel. She lived in complete abandonment. "She went around badly dressed, filthy, with a jacket of common cotton and a muslin turban on her head."[21] Two years before dying she wrote a will. She was poor—nearly bankrupt actually—but she still had enough money to order that 1,200 masses be said, 100 of them for the soul of her husband, King João VI, who had died four years earlier. It was, according to the historian Raimundo Magalhães Jr., "a last minute reconciliation."

XV

Hands in the Coffers

The court arrived in Brazil impoverished, destitute, and in need of everything. It was already nearing bankruptcy when leaving Lisbon, but the situation deteriorated even further in Rio de Janeiro. Between 10,000 and 15,000 people crossed the Atlantic along with the prince regent. By way of comparison, when President John Adams moved the US capital from Philadelphia to Washington, D.C., in 1800, he transferred approximately 1,000 employees. The bureaucratic machine of the Portuguese court in Brazil, in other words, was 10 to 15 times more bloated than that of the United States. Every one of the people who sailed to Brazil depended on the royal exchequer or awaited some benefit from João in exchange for the "sacrifice" of the journey.[1] "A swarm of needy and unprincipled adventurers had come over with the royal family," wrote historian John Armitage. "The newcomers were but little interested in the welfare of the country. They regarded their absence from Portugal as temporary and were far more anxious to enrich themselves at the expense of the state than to administer justice or benefit the public."[2]

Historian Luiz Felipe Alencastro recounts that, along with the royal family, 276 noblemen and royal dignitaries received royal funding for their presence, paid in gold coins or silver taken from the royal treasury in Rio. Based on the reports of John Luccock, Alencastro adds 2,000 more royal employees and individuals exercising functions related to the crown: 700 priests, 500 lawyers, 200 medical practitioners, and between 4,000 and 5,000 soldiers.[3] One of these priests received a fixed annual salary of 250,000 reís— equivalent today to $9,500—just for taking the queen's confession.[4] "Few European courts, comparatively speaking, have so many persons attached to them as the Brazilian, consisting of *fidalgos* [noblemen], ecclesiastics, and numerous attendants," wrote British consul James Henderson.[5] On visiting the stables of the Quinta da Boa Vista where João lived, Henderson took surprised note of the number of animals and, more so, the number of people employed there. The stables contained three hundred mules and horses and enlisted "double the number of persons to look after them that would have been deemed necessary in England."[6]

It was an expensive, wasteful, and ravenous court. In 1820, just prior to the return to Portugal, they consumed 513 hens, chickens, pigeons, and turkeys and 1,080 eggs *per day*. This gluttony totaled 200,000 fowl and 396,000 eggs per year, costing approximately 900 million réis or $31.5 million today. The demand became so great that, by order of the administrator of the Royal Pantry, the department responsible for the court's food supply, the sale of all hens in Rio de Janeiro was prioritized for agents of the king. The decision provoked a market shortage of fowl and revolt among city residents. In an open letter to the king, they complained of the lack of hens as well as the behavior of the employees of the Royal Pantry, who sold the hens in a gray market at higher prices.[7]

During the thirteen years that the court remained in Brazil, the expenses of the corrupt and badly administered Royal Pantry more than tripled. The deficit grew nonstop. In the final year, 1821, the budget gap had grown more than twenty times—from 10 million réis to 239 million.[8] Yet the court continued to finance everyone without worrying overmuch about the sustainability of doing so. "Everyone, without exception, received rations, according to their place and worth," explains historian Jurandir Malerba. "Nobles and also hired artists, such as Italian singers and musicians, French painters and architects, Austrian naturalists, ambassadors and employees of each department received quotas financed by the Royal Pantry, a practice that finally ended in the austere government of D. Pedro I."[9]

Where did they find the money to sustain so many people? The first solution came in the form of a loan of £600,000 from Britain. This amount, lent in 1809 to cover the expenses of the journey and the initial costs of setting up the court in Rio de Janeiro, eventually comprised part of the £2 million debt that Brazil inherited from Portugal with its independence.[10] Another measure taken, also not sustainable in the long term, was the creation of a state bank to mint coins. The sad, brief history of the first Bank of Brazil, created by the prince regent seven months after arriving, stands as an example of the cronyism between the monarchy and a caste of privileged merchants, ranchers, and slave traffickers starting in 1808.

By royal fiat in October 1808, the Bank of Brazil started with a capital of 1,200 stocks with a total unit value of 1 million réis. To stimulate the purchase of these stocks, the court established a politics of give-and-take. Stockholders received titles, knighthoods, and appointments to the Royal Board of Governors of Commerce in addition to promises of dividends much higher than the results that the institution generated. In return, the prince regent had at his disposal a bank to print at will as many notes as the recently arrived court needed.[11] As a result, rich commoners became nobility.[12] The already rich and noble became even richer. The magic lasted for a little over ten years.

By 1820, the bank was falling into ruins. Its gold deposits, which served as a guarantee for issuing money, represented only 20 percent of the currency in circulation.[13] In other words, 80 percent of the money in circulation had no foundation or corresponded to rotten assets. The royal family made 90 percent of all withdrawals. To make a bad situation even worse, upon returning to Portugal in 1821, João took with him every gold bar and diamond that the crown maintained in the bank's coffers, thereby definitively overturning its credibility. Bankrupt and with zero chance of recovering, the institution went into liquidation in 1829. Another version of the bank came to life in 1853 during Pedro II's reign. The current Bank of Brazil derives from a continuation of this second incarnation and itself had many moments similar to its predecessor in providing unsecured loans to bankrupt plantation owners, politicians, and factory proprietors.

Another practice in effect at the time was a "kitty" on kickbacks and payments to public servants. De Oliveira Lima, citing Luccock's reports, observes that a commission of 17 percent was charged on all payments or withdrawals from the public treasury. It was a veiled from of extortion: If the paying party didn't comply with the "commission," the transaction simply halted.[14] "The era of D. João was destined to go down in history for its administration, full of corruption and embezzlement," asserts Lima.[15] "Corruption thrived scandalously, and just as much as it contributed to increasing their spending, it also contributed to smuggling, which in turn diminished their income."[16]

In Rio, the Portuguese court consisted of the following six large administrative sectors, called partitions.[17] The Royal Scullery handled all matters related to the royal family's table, including the supply and washing of tableware and napkins. To the Royal Wardrobe fell the management of all of the family's clothing. The Livery took care of the animals of the cavalcade, the traction of the royal coaches and chaises, and the mules used to transport goods. The Royal Pantry and Buttery dispensed the food and drink. The Royal Warren administered the royal forests and thickets. Finally, the Head Steward organized everything with funds from the Royal Exchequer and its administrative arm, the Bank of Brazil.

Those responsible for these partitions passed into history as symbols of illegal enrichment and monkey business. Joaquim José de Azevedo—the same who in November 1807 was hastily invited to the Palace of Queluz to organize the departure of the court—administered the area in which purchases were stocked in the royal home. Bento Maria Targini headed the royal treasury. Close to João and Carlota Joaquina, these two enjoyed intimate companionship with the royal family, who gave them power and influence to go far beyond their normal tasks. Their departments oversaw meals, transportation, comfort, and all of the benefits that supported the thousands of court dependents. Their friends enjoyed everything, their enemies nothing.

In Brazil, de Azevedo prospered so quickly, his image so linked to spectacular robbery, that during the king's return in 1821 the Portuguese Courts prevented him from disembarking in Lisbon. Still, this prohibition didn't stop his successful career. On the contrary, his family continued getting wealthier after independence. In May 1823, English traveler Maria Graham was invited for a night of gala performances to celebrate the first constitution of an independent Brazil. On arriving at the theater, she headed toward the box seats of de Azevedo's wife, a friend, and took surprised note of what she saw. The hostess was glistering with diamonds worth around £150,000 in Graham's estimate—the equivalent today of $2 million. According to Graham, Madame de Azevedo also gloated that she had left an equal amount of jewels in the strong box at home.[18]

Targini hailed from a modest family of Italian origins in Santa Catarina. He entered public service as a bookkeeper, a relatively low function within the bureaucracy of the colonial government. Intelligent and disciplined, he became a clerk in the treasury and quickly rose to the highest position in this department. With the arrival of the royal family in Brazil, he gained power and distinction. Responsible for administering public finances, which included all of the contracts and payments of the court, he quickly prospered. At the end of João's time in Brazil, Targini's house, with its two stories and an attic, situated at the corner of Rua dos Invalidos and Riachuelo, was one of the largest in Rio de Janeiro.[19] Amid the constitutional revolution of March 1821, he was imprisoned and his possessions were confiscated. Two weeks later, he was released. He, too, couldn't return to Portugal with King João VI, but he continued to live a relaxed and comfortable life in Brazil nevertheless.[20]

The power of Azevedo and Targini grew so great that, in recognition of their services, João raised them both from barons to viscounts. The first became viscount of Rio Seco, the second viscount of São Lourenço. The elevation of these two corrupt characters led the cariocas, true to their tendency of satirizing even their own misfortunes, to compose popular verse catapulting these scandalous robbers into infamy:

> He who steals little is a thief.
> He who steals a lot, a chief.
> Go steal more, and hide out.
> You'll pass from chief to viscount.[21]

In one letter, Royal Archivist Luiz dos Santos Marrocos recorded the following popular ditty about them:

As Azevedo robs the Palace
And Targini robs the Treasury
The ailing people carry
A heavy cross to Calvary.[22]

XVI

A New Court

The two worlds that collided in Rio de Janeiro had advantages and necessities that complemented each other. On one side stood a court that viewed itself with a divine right to rule, govern, and distribute privileges and favors—but had the disadvantage of not having any money. On the other side stood a colony richer in many ways than its old world masters—but with no education, refinement, or nobility. Three centuries after its discovery, Brazil remained a land of tremendous opportunities, typical of the new American frontiers where fortunes grew overnight from nothing.

Historian João Luis Ribeiro Fragoso tells of an immigrant who left Portugal poor, became a merchant in Rio, and by the time the court arrived in Brazil had amassed a fortune great enough to make the majority of nobility accompanying the prince regent envious. Braz Carneiro Leão was born on September 3, 1723, in Porto, to a family of peasants. At sixteen years old, he emigrated to Rio de Janeiro, where he began to work as a cashier in a Portuguese home in exchange for room and board. He soon opened his own business, a consignment house for imports and exports, and in 1799, he appeared on a list of the most important merchants drawn up by the viceroy, the count of Rezende. At his death in 1808, he owned six sugarcane mills near Campos and had a net worth of 1.5 billion réis, a figure 25 percent more than the initial capital used to found the Bank of Brazil.[1]

João needed the financial and political support of this elite class of men rich in assets but destitute in prestige and cultivation. To cultivate them, he began distributing titles and distinctions of nobility, a system that lasted until his return to Portugal in 1821. In the first eight years alone, he bestowed more titles than his forebears had given during the previous three centuries. Since its liberation from the Muslims in the Reconquista in the twelfth century until the end of the eighteenth, Portugal had a total of sixteen marquises, twenty-six counts, eight viscounts, and four barons. Upon arriving in Brazil, João created twenty-eight new marquises, eight new counts, sixteen new viscounts, and four new barons. According to Sérgio Buarque de Holanda, João also distributed 4,048 insignias of knights, commanders, and grand crosses of the Order of Christ, 1,422 commanders of the Military Order of Aviz, and 590 commanders of the Order of Santiago.[2] "In Portugal, to become a count took 500 years; in Brazil, it took 500 million (réis)," wrote Pedro Calmon.[3] "Individuals who had never buckled on a spur were dubbed Knights; while others, in utter ignorance of even the primary doctrines of their missals, were created 'commendadores' of the Order of Christ," added John Armitage.[4]

In 1809 a resident of Vila Rica, modern-day Ouro Preto, offered the prince regent 100 cruzados, and in exchange he became a commander of the Order of Christ and a fidalgo of His Majesty's House. His two sons, cadets in the cavalry regiment, immediately rose to the rank of ensign.[5] *Paulista* merchant Manuel Rodrigues Jordão received a knighthood of the Order of Christ in 1808 "for having contributed a large sum to top up the funds of the Bank of Brazil, so that the State may reap the extensive and precious advantages of this useful and important establishment," according to the decree, signed by the prince, granting him his title.[6]

It fell to this new nobility to help João in his financial troubles. Some became stockholders in the Bank of Brazil. Others signed the countless "lists of voluntary subscriptions" that circulated in Rio de Janeiro after the court's arrival. These donation lists raised funds to cover the crown's expenses. Historian Jurandir Malerba calculated a total of approximately 1,500 subscribers. Of this number, 160 made contributions greater than 150,000 réis, an amount sufficient to purchase a slave between the ages of ten and fifteen.

"The rich that supported the King sought and received distinction, honor, social prestige, conferrals of nobility, titles, privileges, exemptions, liberties, and concessions, as well as favors of material return, such as posts in administration and tax auctions."[7]

On the first list of subscriptions, in 1808, half of the contributors were slave traffickers.[8] One of them, José Inacio Vaz Vieira, was singlehandedly responsible for 33 percent of the traffic catalogued between 1813 and 1822. He received the Order of Christ in 1811. Amaro Velho da Silva, the trafficker who in 1808 held up one of the poles of the canopy mounted during João's arrival on the docks of Rio de Janeiro, also appeared on the list of great donors to the court. He was royally compensated for his services. On August 28, 1812, the prince regent signed a decree naming Amaro and his brother Manuel as official advisors of the prince, with the following justification:

After having shown ample proof of their zeal and patriotism on different occasions of State importance and supplying my Royal Exchequer with great sums, they have recently made the unsolicited donation of fifty thousand cruzados, for me to make use of as I please, thereby showing their honorable sentiments and the greatest zeal for my Royal Service and the public good.[9]

Aside from becoming a royal counselor, Amaro also received the titles of first viscount of Macaé, avowed knight of the Order of Christ, fidalgo of the Royal House, and nobleman-at-arms.[10]

This new nobility created in Brazil now possessed money, titles, and power but few signs of taste or sophistication. All the chroniclers and travelers of the era refer to Rio as a prosperous city lacking refinement. "One perceives the demonstration of plenty, perhaps as a form of self-affirmation of the new elite," posits historian Jurandir Malerba. On arriving in Brazil in 1817 as the minister of foreign affairs and war, the count of Palmela found everything quite strange. "There is a dearth of white people, luxury, and good roads; in sum they lack many things that will come with time," he wrote to his wife, who stayed in Portugal.[11] "Despite all of this expense, there is no appearance of splendor or elegance," wrote James Henderson, the English consul, referring to the wasteful character of the court.[12] The American naval official Henry Brackenridge noted with intrigue the number of people in the streets of Rio de Janeiro wearing ribbons, bows, medals, and decorations to distinguish themselves from others. This group included nobles, merchants, and public servants as well as slaves, who also wore ribbons and other decorations:

> *It is not the custom in this country to lay aside any insignia of distinction, to be used only on days of ceremony or parade. Nothing surprised me more than the number of persons I saw in the street with decorations of one kind or other; I could not but think that in becoming so common and being so frequently exhibited, they must cease to impart dignity or importance to the wearers.*[13]

The meeting of the rich and newly noble with the poor and established nobility took place in the countless rituals surrounding the royal family, which included concerts, processions, masses, and other religious ceremonies. Nothing, however, compared to the hand-kissing ceremony. The prince and the entire royal family opened the portals of the royal palace so that subjects could kiss his hands, pay homage, and directly make any request or complaint they had. While this ancient ritual had fallen into disuse for quite some time in the rest of the courts of Europe, it remained an active practice in Portugal and by the viceroys of colonial Brazil.

One of the most detailed descriptions of the ceremony comes from an anonymous and mysterious author who signed his texts and illustrations with the abbreviation APDG. His identity was never revealed, although apparently he was an English official who lived closely alongside the nobility in Lisbon and Rio. His caricatures and reports satirize the antiquated and pious customs of the time—and thereby explaining his anonymity. APDG describes the ritual as follows:

> *The signal being given for the opening of the royal saloon, the court band of music, in their rich antique costume, begin to play; and the whole scene assumes an imposing appearance. The nobles file into the*

throne room, one after the other at a slow pace, and when at a few steps from the throne make a profound inclination, then advance, kneel and kiss the hand of the sovereign, who extends it to all his subjects with a look truly paternal. This being done, they perform the same homage precisely towards Her Majesty and each of the royal family. They then file out in the same order through the other door at the same end of the room whence they entered.[14]

Some ceremonies lasted up to seven hours, "to the great fatigue of the princes and princesses, who are standing all the time." Another witness, English consul James Henderson, wrote that the hand-kissing took place every night in the Palace of São Cristóvão, around eight o'clock, with the exception of Sundays and holidays. "The roads that came from Cidade Nova, Catumbi and Mata Porcas are covered, on those occasions, with officers, and numerous persons in cabriolets, on horseback, and on foot, pressing forwards towards the palace, consisting of those who have some object to carry with his Majesty," he relates. "When the door is opened there is a promiscuous rushing forward, and a mulatto will be seen treading upon the heels of a general. They advance in single rank up one side of the room to the upper part, where his Majesty is seated, attended by his fidalgos in waiting."[15]

Everyone had the right to kiss the king's hand, even those who were neither noble nor fidalgos. "It was a ceremony that put the monarch in direct contact with the vassal, who presented his dutiful bows and pleaded for mercy," explains Malerba. "It reinforced the paternal authority of the sovereign protector of the nation."[16] In 1816, a dispatch by the superintendent of police, Paulo Fernandes Viana, makes reference to a group of natives who wanted to participate in the ceremony. Viana requested that the commander of the Royal Guard "send an inferior of the cavalry to the Superintendence, to go by land to the Rio Doce though the Vila de Campos and the Captaincy of Espirito Santo, and to accompany a certain group of Indians who wish to have the honor of kissing the hand of His Majesty." Viana recommended that the official should "treat them with humanity and thoughtfulness."[17]

Viana's recommendation was surprising when one takes into account the manner in which the Portuguese were accustomed to treating Brazilian

Indians up until then. It is estimated that at the time of the Portuguese arrival in Brazil in 1500, the indigenous population totalled 5 million. In 1808, at the time of the court's arrival in Rio de Janeiro, this had been reduced to 800,000 indigenous people, almost all of them living in remote areas far from the coast, following the expulsion from their lands and massacres at the hands of the Portuguese colonizers.

XVII

Empress of the Seas

On June 25, 1808, five months before the signature of the royal letter opening the Brazilian ports, 113 English merchants gathered in a London pub. The brother of a powerful man in Dom João's new ministry in Rio de Janeiro, Domingos de Sousa Coutinho, the Portuguese ambassador in England, had invited them there. Three weeks earlier, he had published in the London newspapers a notice urging the assembly of all businessmen interested in getting the first crack at the untapped Brazilian market.[1] The opportunities, de Sousa Coutinho assured, were enormous. Brazil—for three centuries a mysterious land prohibited to outsiders—was opening to the world. Its ports, until then restricted to ships from Portugal alone, could finally receive shipments from and load them for other countries.

In practice, the outlook for the English promised to be even better than the ambassador assured. With all of Europe occupied by Napoleon's armies, at that moment no other European country had the means to conduct commerce with Brazil. Lord Nelson's fleet had trounced the combined forces of France and Spain during the Battle of Trafalgar in 1805, making Britain the only power with free transit on the seas. Britain therefore became the greatest beneficiary of the opening of Brazilian ports, as the months ahead attested. The businessmen gathered in the London pub had to seize this once-in-a-lifetime chance immediately. During the meeting, reported in the pages of the *Correio Braziliense,* 113 merchants founded the Society of English Merchants Trading in Brazil under the presidency of John Prinsep.[2] From that point on, Brazilian ports grew cluttered with English products on a scale never before imagined.

Everything made its way to Brazil, much of it practical and useful, such as cotton fabric, rope, nails, hammers, saws, saddle buckles, and hardware. But eccentricities also crossed the seas, such as ice skates and heavy woollen shawls, objects of wonder in the humid and sweltering heat of the tropics. English factories dispatched some products in monumental quantities and at low prices, thanks to new production techniques developed during the Industrial Revolution of the late eighteenth century. Because of the Continental Blockade, Britain lacked access to the European market and sent these products to Brazil and other South American countries at bargain prices. The goods caused quite a sensation among inhabitants who were used to shortages and the low quality of the crude, handmade products that circulated in the colonies of the Americas.

In 1808, Britain was extending to the four corners of the Earth the second incarnation of its empire, the largest that world had ever known. At its apogee, a few decades after the sixty-year reign of Queen Victoria—the longest in the history of England—the British proudly said that the sun never set on their dominions. The empire began easternmost in recently discovered Oceania, passing through Asia, Africa, and the islands of the Caribbean, and finally terminating in the icy vastness of Canada, which remained loyal to the British crown after American independence. British cannons forcibly protecting British commerce had subjugated India, one of the most ancient civilizations, which regained its independence only in the middle of the twentieth century. Britain even stuck its elbows into millennial China; their enclave in Hong Kong finally returned to the Chinese only in 1997.

The power and influence of this new supremacy reverberated across the entire planet. With over a million inhabitants, London was the largest city on earth at the time.[3] Its countless chimneys released endless clouds of soot that covered the roofs of the city, earning it the nickname of The Big Smoke. Thanks to revolutionizing inventions such as the steam engine, fortunes multiplied. In this creative, dynamic atmosphere, ideas circulated freely—in contrast to the patriotic, even authoritarian ardor of Napoleonic France, where books and culture were subject to the whims of the emperor.

At the beginning of the nineteenth century, 278 newspapers circulated in London alone. This number included English periodicals, such as the venerable *Times,* as well as a plethora of foreign language newspapers, published there to evade censorship and persecution in their countries of origin, as was the case of the *Correio Braziliense.* The city hosted debate, research, and innovation, attracting scientists, thinkers, writers, and poets. Some of the masterpieces of the greatest names in English literature—Lord Byron, Percy Shelley, Jane Austen—were published there. Throngs gathered to attend the lectures, expositions, and debates in countless societies dedicated to research in anthropology, astronomy, geography, and geology, among many other areas of science.[4]

As a result of the Industrial Revolution, combined with dominion over the oceans and commercial expansion, Britain's national wealth doubled between 1712 and 1792.[5] In under a century, the volume of commerce in London's ports tripled. By 1800, the Thames, flowing through the capital, had become a thicket of ships' masts. Every day between two thousand and three thousand merchant boats lay at anchor, awaiting their turn to load or unload goods. Tea and silk arrived from China. Tobacco, corn, and wheat came from America. From Brazil ships carried sugar, wood, coffee, and minerals. From Africa, ivory and minerals arrived.[6] Between 1800 and 1830, cotton consumption by the textile industries in the Liverpool region jumped from 5 million pounds to 220 million—a growth of 4,400 percent in just three decades.[7]

The 880 warships that the Royal British Navy maintained around the world protected this monumental volume of commerce. It comprised the most powerful and efficient naval force of its era, 147 times larger than that of the recently independent United States of America, which had a naval fleet of no more than six ships.[8] Over a period of two centuries, the British had won every naval battle in which they engaged.[9] The British Navy's ships were equipped and organized in exemplary form, its crews capable of rigging and lowering sails and loading and firing cannons in less time than any other navy of the era. They also kept their ships extremely clean and orderly, thereby reducing the threat of disease and epidemics on board.

In 1808, the recently opened Brazilian market became a natural target for the interests of this flourishing world power. After escaping from Napoleon under the protection of the British Navy, João owed a huge debt of gratitude to Britain. His dependence on the British was so great that, during the stage of the voyage between Salvador and Rio de Janeiro, he entrusted Captain James Walker, commander of the *Bedford*, with eighty-four safes of the Royal Treasury being transported from Lisbon.[10] Later, in Rio de Janeiro, he presented Vice-Admiral Sidney Smith, commander of the British fleet, with a country estate on Santa Luzia beach, in appreciation for his services. The property included a country house, fields, and slaves to cultivate them.[11]

The English government recognized the fragility of the Portuguese monarchy and how to take advantage of the situation. After coordinating João's departure for Brazil in 1807, Lord Strangford returned to England, where he remained for four months. He arrived in Rio de Janeiro on April 17, 1808, with very precise instructions with respect to the treaty to be negotiated with the exiled court. These instructions, discovered by Alan Manchester while researching the correspondence between Strangford and Lord Canning, the British minister of Foreign Affairs, show that while the Portuguese court was trying to save its neck by fleeing to Rio de Janeiro, Britain maintained complete control of the situation and knew exactly how to negotiate in order to secure its political and commercial interests in the region. One of the instructions from Canning to Strangford orders the negotiation of an agreement to "induce the British merchants to make the Brazils an emporium for the British Manufactures destined for consumption of the whole of South America." In other words, Brazil was becoming part of a larger commercial strategy, in which English interests extended throughout the entire continent.[12]

The plan worked perfectly. In the commercial sphere, the privileges conceded to Britain were greater than even those that Lisbon would have enjoyed there. The opening of Brazilian ports, decreed during the Bahia interlude, was just the beginning. Two years later, a treaty making Britain the preferential trading partner of this colony-turned-nation further amplified the benefits of the arrangement. By 1810, not even the Portuguese could compete with English products in the Brazilian market. In the new treaty, customs duties on British goods in Brazilian ports shrank to 15 percent of the import value, as opposed to the 16 percent paid for Portuguese goods.[13]

Aside from commercial advantages, the treaty of 1808 gave the British special prerogatives, including the right to enter and exit the country as they pleased, set up residences, acquire property, and maintain a system of parallel justice. By Article 10, the most controversial of all, Britain reaffirmed in Brazil a privilege that it had held in Portugal since 1564: to appoint special magistrates to judge cases involving British citizens. The English residents in Brazil elected these judges themselves, and the Portuguese government could remove them only with the approval of the English representative in Brazil. In practice, two judicial systems came to exist in Brazil: one for Portuguese and all foreigners, and another only for the English, untouchable by local laws.[14]

The English also received the guaranteed right to religious freedom. In a decision without precedent in the Portuguese Americas, English Protestants gained authorization to construct religious meeting houses—as long as these churches and chapels resembled private homes and didn't signal services with bells.[15] This article of the treaty naturally encountered ferocious opposition from the apostolic delegate of Rio de Janeiro, Lourenço Caleppi, who threatened Prince João with excommunication if he accepted the English demands, which of course ultimately prevailed.

As repayment for the protection of the English fleet during the voyage to Brazil, João conceded to the British the privilege of cutting timber in the Brazilian forests for the construction of warships. Moreover, British warships could enter any port of Portuguese dominion, without limits, in times of war or peace. The final articles stipulated that the treaty would have an unlimited duration and that the express conditions and obligations would be "perpetual and immutable."[16] Twelve years later, when Pedro I sought Britain's recognition of Brazilian independence, part of the price he paid was Brazilian ratification of the clauses of the treaty of 1810.[17]

The agreement was signed under the false appearances of reciprocity. In reality, the situation was quite different. In Brazil, the English had the right to elect judges and hold special trials, but this right didn't extend to the

Portuguese in England, for whom the contract guaranteed only the benefits of "the acknowledged excellence of the British jurisprudence." The treaty represented no more than a concession of power, pure and simple, to England, which guaranteed the Portuguese monarchy's survival with its troops, arms, munitions, and ships. "These benefits were so great and essential that in the actual state of affairs, without them, the Portuguese would cease to be even nominally a nation," wrote Alan Manchester.[18]

The consequences of the opening of Brazilian ports and of the treaty of 1810 can be quantified. In 1808, 90 foreign ships entered the port, constituting 10 percent of the overall total; the other 90 percent were Portuguese shipments. Two years later, the number of foreign ships grew five times, to 422, nearly all English, while the Portuguese numbers diminished.[19] In 1809, one year after the ports opened, more than 100 British commercial enterprises existed in Rio de Janeiro.[20] In 1812, Brazil sold £700,000 of merchandise, while in the other direction five years later the English exported to Brazil nearly double that amount. British exports to Brazil were 25 percent greater than all of its sales to Asia and half of what it exported to America, a former colony. Three quarters of the pounds sterling exported to South America came through Brazil.[21]

More impressive than the number of shipments and vessels was the variety of products entering Brazil. "It is natural to suppose that the market would be almost instantly overstocked," recorded the English mineralogist John Mawe.

> So great and so unexpected was the influx of manufactures into Rio de Janeiro, within a few days after the arrival of the Prince, that the rent of houses to put them into became enormously dear. The bay was covered with ships, and the custom-house soon overflowed with goods: even salt, casks of ironmongery, and nails, salt-fish, hogsheads of cheese, hats, together with an immense quantity of crates and hogsheads of earthen and glass ware, cordage, bottled and barrelled porter, paints, gums, resin, tar, etc. were exposed, not only to the sun and rain, but to general depredation . . . one speculator, of wonderful foresight, sent large invoices of stays for ladies, who had never heard of such armour;

another sent skates, for the use of a people who are totally uninformed that water can be ice; a third sent out a considerable assortment of the most elegant coffin furniture, not knowing that coffins are never used by the Brazilians.[22]

Another witness of the era, a French visitor, confirmed having seen the unloading of ice skates in Rio de Janeiro, aside from other "strange merchandise," including heavy wool shawls and copper warming-pans to heat beds.[23]

These products had nothing to do with the climate and local necessities of course, but they arrived in Brazil practically without import taxes and ended up fulfilling uses never envisioned for them. The same French traveler recounts that the wool shawls were used more effectively in place of ox leather and to pan gravel in gold mines. The perforated copper basins became giant skimmers in the sugarcane mills. The ice skates transformed into knives, horseshoes, and other metallic objects. The traveler even saw a doorknob in Minas Gerais made of ice skates.

But lest we mistakenly think that only the English benefited from this arrangement, many Brazilians and Portuguese also became rich—some through dishonest means. Travelers' reports brim with stories of foreigners tricked by local merchants who foisted off goods and products of low quality as if they were something else. "Tourmalines were sold for emeralds, crystals for topazes, and both common stones and vitreous paste have been bought as diamonds to a considerable amount," recounts John Mawe. "The brass pans purchased of the English were filed, and mixed with the gold in the proportion of from five to ten percent."[24] Cheap wood from the forests of Rio de Janeiro was dyed red and sold as Brazilwood, an extremely valuable hardwood the trade of which was rigorously controlled in Pernambuco. Brazilian trickery was in the midst of performing yet another spectacle on the pages of history.

XVIII

Transformation

With the hubbub of the royal arrival over, it was time to get to work. The plans were grandiose, and there was everything to be done. Among other lacunae, the colony lacked banks, commerce, courts, currency, factories, hospitals, libraries, roads, schools, a press, and efficient communication. Most importantly, it needed an organized government that could take charge of all of these deficiencies. "It was a vast virgin territory in which the new extrinsic and impoverished government had to create everything from scratch and improvise," wrote historian Pedro Calmon, and Prince João lost no time.[1] On March 10, 1808, just forty-eight hours after disembarking in Rio de Janeiro, he organized his new cabinet as follows:

- Minister of Foreign Affairs and War: Rodrigo de Sousa Coutinho, future count of Linhares

- Minister of Royal Affairs: Fernando José de Portugal, future marquis of Aguiar

- Minister of Naval and Overseas Affairs: João Rodrigues de Sá e Menezes, viscount of Anadia.

This cabinet had to create a country from nothing on two fronts of action. The first, internal, included the numerous administrative decisions João made shortly after arriving: to improve communications between provinces, to encourage settlement, and to profit from the wealth of the colony. The second front, external, aimed at widening Brazil's borders in an effort to increase Portuguese influence in the Americas. It also took aim at Portugal's European adversaries by occupying their territories and threatening their colonial American interests.

At the end of 1808, a troop of five hundred Brazilian and Portuguese soldiers escorted by a small naval force—in retaliation for the invasion of Portugal by Napoleon's troops—invaded French Guiana and besieged the capital, Cayenne, which they vanquished without facing resistance on January 12 of the following year.[2] A second offensive annexed the so-called Eastern Strip of the Rio de la Plata, forming modern-day Uruguay, in revenge for Spain's alliance with Napoleonic France. Both were short-lived conquests. The Treaty of Vienna, which redrew the map of Europe after the fall of Napoleon, returned French Guiana to France eight years later, and Uruguay, occupied by King João's troops in 1817, gained its independence in 1828.

With plans of territorial expansion scuppered, it fell to João to concentrate on the first and more ambitious of his tasks: advancing Brazil so that the dream of a Portuguese Empire in America could rise from the tropics. To this end, new improvements occurred at a maddening pace, having a great impact on the future of the country. During the Salvador stopover, João opened Brazilian ports. On arriving in Rio de Janeiro, he granted the freedom of manufacturing and industrial commerce. This measure, announced on April 1, revoked a charter of 1785 that prohibited the manufacturing of any products in the colony. These two acts effectively ended the colonial system. The "weak" prince had freed Brazil from three centuries of Portuguese monopoly and integrated it into a system of international production and commerce as an autonomous entity.[3]

Free of prohibitions, countless industries sprang up on Brazilian soil. The first iron factory appeared in 1811 in the city of Congonhas do Campo, created by then-governor of Minas Gerais Francisco de Assis Mascarenhas. Three years later, now as governor of the province of São Paulo, de Assis

Mascarenhas helped construct a steelworks factory in Sorocaba, the Royal Factory of São João de Ipanema.[4] In other regions wheat mills sprouted as well as factories producing gunpowder, boats, fabric, and rope.

The opening of new roads, authorized by the prince regent while in Salvador, helped break the isolation that until then had prevailed among the provinces. Their construction officially had been prohibited since 1733, with the excuse of combating the smuggling of gold and precious stones. In 1809, a road of 121 leagues (nearly 500 miles) opened between Goiás and the Northern region of the country. Following a route similar to today's Belém-Brasília highway, it facilitated communication with French Guiana after the Portuguese occupation of Cayenne. New roads also stretched among the provinces of Minas Gerais, Bahia, Espirito Santo, and north of the present-day state of Rio de Janeiro. The Commerce Road, linking the cities of the Valley of Paraíba, cut in half the distance that troopers had to traverse between São Paulo and the south of Minas.[5]

Explorers mapped Brazil's most distant regions. Marine cartographers drew up new nautical charts of the provinces of Pará and Maranhão. Goiás saw the creation of its first navigation company. Expeditions traversed the tributaries of the Amazon all the way to their sources and established riverboat communication between Mato Grosso and São Paulo.[6] Steam navigation came in 1818 by way of Felisberto Caldeira Brant, the future marquis of Barbacena and the future first Brazilian ambassador to Great Britain. João granted Brant the privilege of a monopoly for fourteen years, a decision that journalist Hipólito da Costa criticized for its lack of competition that inhibited the expansion of this valuable new means of transportation.[7]

Another novelty was the introduction of secular and higher education. Before the arrival of the court, religious institutions handled all education—limited to primary school—in colonial Brazil. Exams often took place inside churches, with an audience observing the students' performance.[8] In contrast to its colonial Spanish neighbors, who already had inaugurated their first universities, Brazil didn't have a single facility of higher learning. João changed this, creating a medical college, an agricultural college, a laboratory for chemical analysis and studies, and the Royal Military Academy, which included among its functions teaching civil engineering and mining. He also established the Superior Military Court, the General Superintendence of the Court Police (a mixture of city hall and a department of public safety), the royal exchequer, the Finance Council, and the Corps of the Royal Guard. Later came the National Library, National Museum, Botanical Gardens, and Royal Theatre of São João.[9]

The *Rio de Janeiro Gazette,* the first newspaper published on Brazilian soil, began circulation on September 10, 1808, printed by machines brought over still packed in the crates originating from England. The paper had one restriction: to print only news favorable to the government. "To have judged of Brazil by its only journal, it must certainly have been deemed a terrestrial paradise, where no word of complaint had ever yet found utterance," observed historian John Armitage.[10] Hipólito da Costa, who launched the *Correio Braziliense* in London three months before the premiere of the *Gazette* in Rio de Janeiro, complained of their "wasting such high quality paper in printing such awful material" which "would be put to better use in wrapping butter."[11]

The transformations reached their culmination on November 16, 1815. On this day, the eve of the eighty-first birthday of Queen Maria I, Prince João elevated Brazil to kingdom status and into a united kingdom with Portugal and the Algarves, raising Rio de Janeiro to the official seat of the court. This measure had two objectives. First, it paid homage to the Brazilians who had hosted him during the 1808 arrival. Second, it reinforced the role of the Portuguese monarchy during the negotiations of the Treaty of Vienna, in which the powers victorious over Napoleon discussed the future of Europe. With Brazil raised to the status of a kingdom in union with Portugal, the court in Rio de Janeiro gained a voice and the right to vote, despite lying thousands of miles from Lisbon, the only Portuguese seat that other European rulers recognized until then.

Alongside these grandiose initiatives, the prince also adopted parochial measures, including the order to change the facades of houses in Rio de Janeiro. When the court arrived, the majority of carioca residences had windows in the Moorish style, known as trellises or lattices. Wooden trellises—with a span in the lower part through which residents could observe activity in the streets without themselves being seen—protected openings in house walls. These wooden gratings blocked the sun, though, and kept interiors dark and suffocating. João detested this architectural feature and ordered the immediate removal of the trellises, to be replaced by windowpanes "within a term of eight days," according to an announcement signed on June 11, 1809.[12]

In another quaint decision, he officially declared war on the Botocudo Indians, who made life hell for the ranchers and settlers in the province of Espirito Santo. According to the report of Englishman John Mawe,

> *A proclamation has been issued by the Prince Regent, in which they are invited to live in villages, and become Christians, under a promise that, if they come to terms of peace and amity with the Portugueze, their rights shall be acknowledged, and they shall enjoy, in common with other subjects, the protection of the state; but, if they persist in their barbarous and inhuman practices, the soldiers of his royal highness are ordered to carry on a war of extermination against them.*[13]

From London, Hipólito da Costa ironically lampooned João's measure in a *Correio Braziliense* editorial: "It is quite a while that I have not read such a celebrated document, and I will publish it when I receive the response of His Excellency, the Secretary of State of Foreign Affairs and War of the Botocudo Nation."[14]

The effort to transform Brazil stretched beyond the administrative arena. While he ordered the opening of roads, the construction of schools and factories, and the organization of government infrastructure, Prince João also dedicated himself to what historian Jurandir Malerba called "civilizing projects." In other words, he promoted the arts and culture, attempting to infuse a degree of refinement and good taste in the backward habits of the colony. The greatest such initiative involved contracting the famous French Artistic Mission from Paris. Headed by Joachim Lebreton, the permanent secretary of the fine arts section of the Institute of France, this mission arrived in Brazil in 1816, consisting of some of the most renowned artists of the era: Jean-Baptiste Debret, a disciple of Jacques-Louis David, Napoleon's favorite painter; Nicolas Taunay, landscape painter; his brother

Auguste Taunay, sculptor; Grandjean de Montigny, architect; Simon Pradier, engraver and carver; Francisco Ovide, professor of applied mechanics; and Sigismund von Neukomm, musician and disciple of Austrian composer Franz Joseph Haydn. The mission also included two leather tanners, an iron-smith, three carriage mechanics, and a master of hardware.[15] João paid their travel expenses and guaranteed all of them generous pensions on the condition that they remained in Brazil for at least six years.[16]

On paper, the official principal objective of the French Artistic Mission was to create an academy of arts and sciences in Brazil.[17] In actuality, the French spent their time pampering the king and court, which guaranteed their livelihood in the tropics. It fell to the mission to organize and decorate the grand celebrations that the monarchy held in Brazil during the four years before their return to Lisbon, including the wedding of Prince Pedro and Princess Leopoldina, and João's birthday, accession, and coronation. For these occasions, the French erected monumental arches in the streets of Rio de Janeiro, organized plays and concerts, and commissioned famous paintings. Insomuch as the mission served this purpose it proved useful. After the celebrations, however, the project fell apart. The death in 1817 of its principal patron, Antonio de Araújo e Azevedo, the count of Barca, also dealt a severe blow to the mission. Joachim Lebreton fell into ostracism and retired to a house on Flamengo beach, where he died in 1819.[18] "The artists had the greatest disappointment," observed historian Tobias Monteiro. "With the exception of music, the court was not interested in fine arts. Neither the fidalgos nor the wealthy owned paintings."

Despite these difficulties, Debret stayed in Brazil for fifteen years. The most well known of all of these French artists and responsible for the best and widest range of imagery from this era, he created paintings, engravings, and notes that meticulously register the landscape, locals, and customs of Rio de Janeiro and its environs; the royal family, including the most famous portraits of João VI; the rituals of the court; and the coronation of Pedro I. His images lend a luster and sophistication to a European monarchy who were little more than a ragtag hodgepodge of regal hillbillies bereft of any real sense of culture. Debret also documented slavery in the Brazilian plantations and cities. In this case as well, he paints sterile, academic scenes that portray black men and women with curvilinear Greek profiles, clean clothes, and uniformly good posture. At no moment do his works reflect on the cruelty and brutality of the mistreatment and beatings that the slaves endured.

Among the arts, the Portuguese court in Rio de Janeiro preferred music by far. Debret estimates that in 1815, Prince João spent 300,000 francs ($3 million today) per year on the maintenance of the Royal Chapel and its company of artists, which included "fifty singers, among them magnificent Italian *virtuosi*, some of which were famous *castrati*, and additionally 100 excellent performers, directed by two masters of the chapel."[19] In 1811, the most famous Portuguese musician, Marcos Antonio Portugal, arrived in Rio de Janeiro. From his arrival until the court's departure in 1821, he composed numerous pieces of sacred music in homage to the crown and the grand events it hosted.

Concerts took place in the Royal Chapel and in the then-recently inaugurated São João Theatre, with 112 loges and seats for 1,020 people in the general audience. Theodor von Leithold, captain of the Prussian cavalry, visited Rio de Janeiro in 1819 and described these spectacles as follows:

> *There are four or five weekly presentations, which vary among comedies, dramas, and tragedies in Portuguese, and Italian operas accompanied by ballets. The Italian operas are performed in an extremely particular manner. During my stay, the opera Tancredo was performed many times, but I barely recognized it, as it was mangled and mutilated by a terrible orchestra. Madame Sabini and Demoiselle Faschiotti, the sister of one of the castrati of the Royal Chapel, sung passably, largely helped by their physical endowments. The orchestra was greatly reduced in size, and in a word, miserable: only one flautist—a Frenchman—and a cellist caught my attention. The violinists, in fact, are below criticism.[20]*

Rio de Janeiro certainly resisted comparison with London or Paris, but the new habits and rituals imported by the court quickly altered the behavior of its inhabitants. "The opening of the ports and the new dignity of Rio de Janeiro as capital of the entire Portuguese empire attracted businessmen, adventurers, and artists to the city," relates Jurandir Malerba.[21] A former combatant in the Prussian army in the war against Napoleon, the naturalist Prince Alexander zu Wied-Neuwied arrived in Rio in 1815, expecting to find a sleepy colonial village among the tropical jungle. What he found surprised him: "Improvements of every type have been achieved in the capital. She has lost much of her originality, having turned similar to European cities."[22]

Three years later, American Navy official Henry Brackenridge had a similar surprise upon entering Guanabara Bay aboard the frigate *Congress*. "The number of vessels continually entering and leaving the harbor, gave us a high opinion of the commercial importance of the city we were about to visit," he noted in his diary.

> *As we entered the harbor, a most magnificent scene opened upon us. The noble basin scarcely surpassed by any in the world, resembling a large lake rather than a harbor, expanded majestically, bordered by high woody mountains, interspersed with rocky peaks and precipices; their ridges or spurs sloping down to the water's edge, in some places terminating abruptly, in others leaving narrow vallies and a thousand beautiful coves or recesses, with sandy beaches. The ridges, or broken grounds, below the mountains, are covered with convents, churches and beautiful gardens, while the little indents or sandy bays are occupied by elegant country seats; a great many of them constructed by Portuguese noblemen, since the establishment of the court at this place, or by English merchants who have grown rich since the opening of trade.*[23]

The advertisements published in the *Rio de Janeiro Gazette* from 1808 onward provide one of the most entertaining ways to observe the evolution of the sophistication of the habits of carioca society. In the beginning, they offer simple products and services, the domain of a closed colonial society importing few objects and producing almost everything it consumed. These first advertisements cover the hiring of horses and carriages, sales of homes and lots, and basic services such as lessons in catechism, Portuguese, history, and geography.[24] Here are two examples of announcements published in 1808:

Whoever wants to buy a residence of multi-story houses facing Santa Rita, talk to Anna Joaquina da Silva, who lives in these houses, or with Captain Francisco Pereira de Mesquita, who has orders to sell them.

For sale: a good horse, a carriage leader. If you have an intention to buy, look for Francisco Borges Mendes, who lives above a shop on the corner of João Baptista alley.[25]

From 1810, however, the tone and content of these announcements change radically. Instead of horses, houses, and slaves, they offer books, champagne, cologne, fans, gloves, linen, paintings, pianos, porcelain vases, silk sheets, watches, and countless other imported merchandise. "I can't even begin to explain the abundance and surfeit of French fabrics and bric-a-brac which have flooded the city," wrote Royal Archivist Luiz dos Santos Marrocos to his sister in Lisbon in 1816. "One no longer sees English fabrics that have all been abandoned, as everyone goes adorned in the French style, except me, as I am of Old Portugal, and no one shall tear me from this fixation."[26] In the March 2, 1816, edition of the *Gazette*, a Frenchman named Girard announces himself as "the hairdresser of Her Royal Highness Lady D. Carlota, Princess of Brazil, of her Royal Highness the Princess of Wales, and of her Royal Highness the Duchess of Angoulême" and offers the following services: "To provide hairstyles in the latest fashions of Paris and London, to cut men and ladies' hair, to coif men and women's hair, to dye with the ultimate perfection hair, eyebrows, and sideburns, without causing any damage to skin or clothing; and to provide a pomade that makes one's hair grow and thicken." On November 13 of the same year, on 8 Rua do Ouvidor [Ombudsman's Road], House of Bellard advertises having received "a new assortment of real and fake jewelry, ladies' hats, French books, dresses and adornments for modern women, scents of all varieties, pendulums, shotguns, and fans."

Despite the flood of British goods, in time the French influence left its mark. The stores of Rio teemed with novelties from Paris. In the June 26, 1817, edition of the *Gazette*, merchant Carlos Durante advertises to his clients that he has moved from 28 Rua do Ouvidor to 9 Rua Direita, where he offered,

Scents, colognes, pomades, diverse vinegars and essences for the bathroom and dining room, gloves, suspenders, soap, fans of all varieties, brushes and combs of every quality, shoes, slippers for men and women, vests of silk and morocco leather, all from Paris, tobacco boxes of all kinds, necessary for men, sewing-boxes for women, candles, clarified oil for lamps. Straw hats and beaver hats for men and boys; straw hats for women, decorated and non-decorated; silk hats, plumes, ribbons, tulle embroidered with gold and silver, artificial flowers, cashmeres, gloves, veils, twine, raw silk, etc; tables, bathroom mirrors, mirrors of every size with frames and without, prints, precious panels; real and fake jewelry, such as necklaces, earrings, rings, and ornaments; pendulums, pocket watches and music for men and women, champagne at 480 a bottle, a portable grain mill for one slave alone to grind; an assortment of French books, and much other merchandise at comfortable prices.[27]

In 1824, three years after the court's departure, chronicler Ernst Ebel visited a store called "Vivienne" on Rua do Ouvidor, which made him feel as if he was in Paris:

Behind a well-polished table sits a Madame or Mademoiselle, elegantly posed, attended by a half-dozen negro women, dressed with care and chosen for their physique, employed to sew. . . . Everything is on demand that the most elegant lady could wish for; naturally, at a high price. In the salon of the maître-coiffeur, if you want to cut your hair, you will be directed to a fanciful parlor, decorated with mirrors, where you can be done up à la française or à l'anglaise and with huile antique, to your heart's content, at a price left to your discretion; it will be, however, unseemly to give less than a thousand réis.[28]

The apparel and new habits transplanted by the court appeared in the evenings during performances in the São João Theatre or at Sunday masses. On these occasions, the number of accompanying slaves and servants reigned as an undisputed status symbol. The most rich and powerful had the largest retinues and made a point of exhibiting them as an indication of their social importance. The Prussian traveler von Leithold remarked that even the first-class harlots, "of which there were many," proudly displayed their escorts in the streets. Whoever didn't have private servants hired them for masses or events on saint days. "It is a point of honor to present oneself with a numerous entourage. They walk ceremoniously through the streets, at measured steps."

"It is on Sundays and feast days that all the wealth and magnificence of a Brazilian family is exhibited," related British traveler Alexander Caldcleugh, who visited Rio de Janeiro between 1819 and 1821.

At an early hour the household prepares for church, and marches, almost without exception, in the following order: first, the master, with cocked hat, white trousers, blue linen jacket, shoes and buckles, and a gold headed cane; next follows the mistress in white muslin, with jewels, a large white fan in her hand, white shoes and stockings; flowers ornament her dark hair; then follow the sons and daughters; afterwards a favorite mulatto girl of the lady, with white shoes and stockings, perhaps two or three of the same rank; next, a black môrdomo, or steward, with cocked hat, breeches and buckles; next blacks of both sexes, with shoes and no stockings, and several others without either; and two or three black boys, little encumbered with clothes, bring up the rear.[29]

Of course, appearances can deceive. Despite the effort and rapidity of the changes put in place by the prince regent, transforming Brazil proved a much more arduous task than could be seen by observing shops or the pomp of families in the streets of the new seat of the Portuguese court.

XIX

The Chief of Police

The population of Rio de Janeiro exploded during the thirteen years that the Portuguese court relocated to Brazil. The number of inhabitants, 60,000 in 1808, doubled by 1821. Only São Paulo—which transformed into the largest metropolis in South America during the industrialization in the first half of the twentieth century—saw such accelerated growth. Rio de Janeiro had an additional factor: half the population were slaves.[1] We can only imagine what such rapid growth meant for a city already short on space, infrastructure, and services that would receive thousands of new residents from Lisbon.

Crime reached record highs. Robberies and assassinations became commonplace. Pirates targeted ships in port. Gangs of hooligans roamed the streets, attacking with knives and stilettos. Prostitution and gambling, while officially prohibited, took place in broad daylight. "In this city and its environs we have been quite affronted by thieves," relates Royal Archivist Luiz dos Santos Marrocos to his father in Lisbon. "In five days, 22 murders were counted within a small boundary, and one night in front of my door, a thief murdered two people and left a third gravely wounded."[2] Dos Santos Marrocos also complained of too many blacks and beggars in the streets of Rio de Janeiro, noting that most were shamefully dressed.

The task of imposing order on the chaos went to the magistrate and court commissioner Paulo Fernandes Viana. Born in Rio de Janeiro and trained at the University of Coimbra, Viana became superintendent of police by charter in 1808, a post that he held until 1821, the year of his death. He had a role equivalent to both mayor and secretary of public safety. More than this, however, he acted as a "civilizing agent" in Rio de Janeiro.[3] It was his job to transform a colonial, provincial, uncultured, dirty, dangerous village into a European-style capital worthy of hosting the Portuguese monarchy. His mission included filling swamps, organizing the water supply, arranging rubbish and sewage collection, paving roads and illuminating them with whale-oil streetlamps, and constructing thoroughfares, bridges, aqueducts, fountains, passageways, and public squares. He also oversaw policing the streets, issuing passports, observing foreigners, monitoring the sanitary conditions of slave warehouses, and arranging accommodation for the new inhabitants that the city received with the arrival of the court.[4]

One of the most influential assistants to the prince regent, he had an audience with him every other day.[5] He claimed it "a duty of the police to keep the people busy and to promote love and respect for the sovereign and his royal dynasty."[6] Furnished with broad powers, he meddled in practically everything. Squabbles among families and among neighbors, arguments between slaves and masters, the organization of festivals and public spectacles, the distribution of foreign books and newspapers, individuals' behavior inside and beyond their homes—nothing escaped his scrutiny. In an official letter to the police commander in January 1816, he ordered that all stray dogs be killed, "as they make this city unbearable, and tolerating them in this sweltering weather may lead to maladies, as they lunge at, bite, and frazzle the populace."[7] In another such letter, he ordered the military guard to curb "whistling, shouting, foot-stomping, and other uncivil behavior practiced by the populace" during theater performances.[8]

In his new and thankless role, Viana had as one of his first tasks to change the very architecture of the city. He had to execute João's orders to replace the austere wood window trellises with windowpanes. "Being now a court, Rio de Janeiro needed properties of another order, that ennoble and beautify it," registered one official.[9] But the measure was enacted not just for aesthetic reasons: Windows hidden by trellises could be used in ambushes against the Portuguese court.

The crusade to change local customs met obstacles given the massive presence of slaves in the city, creating a permanent source of social tension especially after the revolts in 1791 by captive blacks in St. Domingue—Haiti today—resulted in bloodbaths among the white settlers. "Slaves are forever natural enemies of their masters: they are kept in place by force and violence," wrote José Antonio de Miranda in a pamphlet that circulated in Rio de Janeiro in 1821 analyzing the political situation in Brazil and Portugal. "Everywhere that whites are outnumbered by slaves and wherever there are many castes, disruption of the status quo . . . may lead to a death sentence and bloodbath for the whites, as was in the case in St. Domingue, and this may happen anywhere that slaves are greater in force and numbers than free men."[10]

Viana favored slavery but didn't think it looked good on display in a city inhabited by a European court. Blacks, dressed in rags, congregated in the streets and squares on Sundays and holidays to play sports; practice *capoeira*, a Brazilian martial art accompanied by music; and hold drum circles. When they committed any wrongdoing, their owners reserved the right to have them whipped in the public square. A report of the superintendent in 1821 reveals that one third of all slave prison sentences punished "crimes against public order." Recorded in police bulletins under the generic banner of "disorder," this category included fights, drinking binges, forbidden sports—such as capoeira—and physical aggression.[11] Petty thievery and possessing weapons, including razorblades, were met with severe punishment. A slave often received two hundred to three hundred lashes for having a razor or practicing capoeira.[12]

"Capoeira was a symbol of African culture, which slaves proudly displayed in the streets of Rio de Janeiro," relates historian Leila Mezan Algranti. It also served as a means of self-defense, feared by the police who patrolled the city. Blacks could be arrested simply for whistling the rhythm of capoeira, wearing caps with yellow and scarlet ribbons—a symbol of capoeira matches—and even carrying musical instruments used in these events. A police report of April 15, 1818, reveals that "José Rebolo, a slave of Alexandre Pinheiro, was arrested for using a headpiece with red and yellow ribbons." He had a knife in his possession as well. His punishment was three hundred lashes and three months in prison.[13]

In Viana's opinion, none of this stood in keeping with the new elegance and refinement that Rio de Janeiro ought to display in the presence of the royal family. According to the superintendent, in a city hosting a court, whipping slaves in a public square was "truly indecent." Above all, though, it could provoke unnecessary revolts.[14] As a result, his countermeasures included the prohibition of meetings among slaves in public places. Whippings continued—but in closed quarters under the supervision of the superintendent general of police, far from the eyes of the nobility and foreigners who moved through the streets.

In Rio de Janeiro during the Portuguese court's interlude, most people went around armed. English consul James Henderson took note of the number of people who carried knives hidden in the sleeves of their cloaks, "which they throw and use with great dexterity."[15] Few people ventured into the streets alone after dark. Stone-throwing was a common type of attack. Many slaves were arrested for throwing stones and injuring people simply passing by. In October 1817, the wife of American ambassador Thomas Sumpter was hit in the eye by a stone while driving through the Rua do Ouvidor in her carriage. In another case, the superintendent reprimanded the commander of the court guards after a concert in São João Theatre when a well-aimed stone hit actor Manuel Alves and brought the show to an abrupt and unexpected end.

Subversion and threats to the dominant social order constantly preoccupied Viana. In 1816, alarmed by the news of the slave revolt in Haiti and the dissemination of French ideas in the Americas, he organized a counterespionage unit inside the Superintendence of Police. According to Viana, it was necessary to be cautious with foreigners, especially the French, "a race which had revealed themselves to be quite harmful." In a memorandum, he recommended that "foreigners be observed without oppression" by trustworthy spies "who knew their languages, frequented their dinners, and followed them in the theaters, passageways, and at public entertainment."[16] He also ordered a report of the inhabitants and their occupations in every part of the city "to discover which people were suspicious and lacked professions."[17]

Viana also took an equal concern in the rapid changes in customs in Rio. In 1820, a recently arrived composer requested whether he could present a theatrical performance during Lent. Viana refused the request, asserting that, while it appeared innocent, it represented a strong break with colonial traditions of modesty, piety, and prayer during that holy time of sacrifice. "As the people of Brazil are not accustomed to seeing anything besides the Stations of the Cross, it is imperative to ensure that nobody will say that the arrival of the court abolished the customs of silence and abstinence during Lent."[18]

The superintendent often complained of a lack of resources to combat crime and to fulfill the great tasks entrusted to him. His police force, which should have had 218 men, had only 75.[19] They didn't patrol openly, as police do today, but rather went on concealed rounds, hidden in the darkness of alleys and roads, lying in wait for wrongdoers. The regulations prescribed that these watchmen had to "hide in discreet sites, and in complete silence, to be able to hear the slightest din or mutiny and suddenly pounce on the site of disorder."[20] As a result of their stealth in carrying out their duties, Viana's men earned the nickname "the bats."

The most famous of his truculent and merciless agents was Major Miguel Nunes Vidigal. Second commander of the new Royal Guard, Vidigal became the terror of carioca scofflaws. He waited in ambush on street corners or suddenly swooped down on capoeira matches or drum circles where slaves gathered, drinking cachaça until late at night. Without heeding legal procedure, he ordered his men to arrest and pummel any participant in these activities, whether a legitimate delinquent or merely an ordinary citizen out having fun. In place of military sabers, Vidigal's troops used whips with strips of raw leather on the end and long and heavy handles. The major personally commanded various attacks on *quilombos*—Maroon settlements— established by runaway slaves in the forests surrounding Rio de Janeiro.[21] As a reward for his services, Vidigal received a plot of land at the foot of the Hill of Two Brothers in Rio, a present from Benedectine monks. They donated the land to Vidigal in return for what they judged to be the chief of police's excellent services in maintaining public safety in Rio de Janeiro.

Invaded by shanties in the 1940s, this land today has become the Vidigal favela, with its spectacular views of the beaches of Ipanema and Leblon.

Two doctors who doubled as royal counselors inspired many of Superintendent Viana's urban reforms. The first, Domingos Ribeiro dos Guimarães Peixoto, surgeon of the king's chamber, propounded a radical policy of municipal sanitation. He proposed not only constructing sewers and grids of water treatment but also the demolition of certain hills, filling swamps with earth, and overhauling a landscape that, in his opinion, despite being beautiful, proved noxious to public health. He said that the air in Rio de Janeiro, due to high temperatures, low circulation of winds, and stagnant water in the swamps and mangroves, harmed human respiration because it resulted in "lowly oxygenated blood" and favorably allowed the proliferation of disease.[22]

The second counselor doctor, Manuel Vieira da Silva, author of the first medical treatise published in Brazil, also advocated filling the swamps with landfill, establishing water drainage systems, widening roads, and regulating markets where meat and other foodstuffs were sold. He had a particular concern with the age-old custom of burying the dead inside churches—according to him a major source of disease propagation. "Burials inside churches have received the condemnation of all enlightened societies, and they particularly warrant such condemnation in this city, owing to its atmospheric standards," he said. "They bury corpses in the Church of Compassion, leaving them essentially exposed to heat and open air, where they freely release their life-suffocating gases." The doctor proposed instead the creation of cemeteries "where both rich and poor would be buried, while still retaining the differences necessary to maintain social distinctions."[23]

A stone was lodged in the two doctors' sanitation improvement plans, however—or rather, a mountain: the Morro do Castelo (Castle Mountain). In the middle of the city, near the Royal Palace, this mountain rendered the circulation of air and free flow of water difficult in their opinion and therefore proved hazardous to the health of cariocas. Referring to the mountains of Rio de Janeiro, dos Guimarães Peixoto called Castle Mountain "the most inconvenient of all of them," adding that "Not only does it obstruct the elegance of the view, it also blocks the city from being bathed in the most constant and healthy of breezes, and moreover holds rainwater at its base for a long time."[24] Vieira da Silva asked the superintendent, "Shouldn't its demolition enter into the plan of the Rio de Janeiro police?"[25]

In the intervening centuries, the city has been flattened, packed with landfill, deforested, perforated, and thinned out to such an extent that its coastal outline is almost unrecognizable when compared with maps drawn at the time of the court's arrival in Brazil. The target of years of constant attacks, Castle Mountain lasted only another century. In 1922, engineer Carlos Sampaio, then mayor of the Federal District, decreed its end as dos Guimarães Peixoto and Vieira da Silva had wanted all along. Its earth filled the regions of Urca, the Rodrigo de Freitas lagoon, the Botanical Gardens, and other low areas around Guanabara Bay.

On retiring from his position in 1821, Viana recorded his deeds in a *res gestae*:

> *I filled the immense swamps of the city, through which they became more salutary. . . . I built sidewalks on Rua do Sabão and Rua de S. Pedro, in the new city: on the Rua dos Inválidos . . . I built the Valongo pier . . . as there was not an abundance of water for public use, I managed . . . to conduct drinking water to it from a distance of one league. . . . I created and continued increasing the system of illumination in the city.*[26]

As we can see, though, these projects—all easy to plan and execute—affected only the face of the city.[27] A quite different force was stirring changes among the habits and customs of the people.

XX

Slavery

While Rio de Janeiro has many monuments and historic sites from João VI's epoch that have been abandoned or poorly maintained, nothing compares with what has happened with the Valongo Market. The largest slave warehouse in the Americas disappeared seemingly without a trace, as if it had never existed. Maps and tourist guides ignore its location. The old Rua do Valongo, situated among the neighborhoods of Gamboa, Saúde, and Santo Cristo, has even changed its name. Today it's the Rua do Camerino. At its end, toward Mauá beach, a slope called Valongo Hill—with no sign, monument, or explanation—remains the only geographic reference to the old warehouse. The city has tried to forget the old slave market and the stain that it made on Brazilian history. Such willful amnesia is futile, however, because nearby lies the Sambadrome, where each year at Carnaval one of the samba school performances persists in remembering slavery as part of the history of Brazil.

In 1996, the history of Valongo abruptly emerged from underground. A couple living at 36 Rua Pedro Ernesto in the Gamboa neighborhood was remodeling their house, built at the beginning of the eighteenth century. During the excavations, they found hundreds of bone fragments mixed with ceramic and glass shards in the rubble. These were the remnants of the *Pretos Novos* (New Blacks) Cemetery. On this spot, two hundred years earlier, recently arrived slaves from Africa were buried if they died before being sold. As of the beginning of 2007, archaeologists had gathered 5,563 bone fragments belonging to twenty-eight corpses of young males between the ages of eighteen and twenty-five. All of them showed signs of cremation. It revealed a telling disparity: in the Rio de Janeiro of King João VI, only whites had the privilege of church burials—close to God and celestial paradise, according to the prevailing beliefs of the time. The bodies of slaves were thrown onto barren land or in ditches, set on fire, and afterward covered by a layer of quicklime.[1]

When the Portuguese court arrived in Brazil, slave ships coming from the coast of Africa unloaded 18,000 to 22,000 men, women, and children each year at the Valongo Market.[2] They were held in quarantine, to be treated for disease and fattened. Once they acquired a healthier appearance, they went to market in the same way that livestock did at the hands of cattle drivers and ranchers negotiating the sale of animals for slaughter. But in 1808 this human "merchandise" fed not the people of Rio but rather the gold and diamond mines, sugarcane mills, and cotton, coffee, tobacco, and other plantations that sustained the Brazilian economy. Slavery had been abolished in Portugal in 1761, as a result of the decision of the marquis of Pombal, the all-powerful minister of King José I, but in Brazil the practice continued unabated until nearly the end of the nineteenth century, in 1888.

The unloading, selling, and buying of slaves comprised part of the normal routine of colonial Brazil for nearly three centuries. For the foreign visitors authorized for the first time to visit Brazil following the court's arrival, it made for a shocking sight. Visiting Valongo in 1823, Maria Graham, an English traveler and friend of Empress Leopoldina, recorded in her diary:

> *I have this day seen the Val Longo; it is the slave-market of Rio. Almost every house in this very long street is a depôt for slaves. On passing by the doors this evening, I saw in most of them long benches placed near the walls, on which rows of young creatures were sitting, their heads shaved, their bodies emaciated, and the marks of recent itch upon their skins. In some places the poor creatures were lying on mats, evidently too sick to sit up.[3]*

The Slave Market, engraving from *Views and Costumes of the City and Neighbourhood of Rio de Janeiro* by Henry Chamberlain, London, 1822, Lucia M. Loeb/Biblioteca Guita e José Mindlin

English consul James Henderson, describing the disembarkation of slaves, observed that

> *The slave-ships arriving at the Brazil present a terrible picture of human wretchedness, the decks being crowded with beings as closely stowed as it is possible, whose melancholy black faces, and gaunt naked bodies, are of themselves sufficient to transfix with horror an individual unused to such scenes, independently of the painful reflections connected with a consideration of the debasing circumstances and condition of this portion of mankind. A great many of them, as they are seen proceeding from the ships to the warehouses where they are to be exposed for sale, actually appear like walking skeletons, particularly the children; and the skin, which scarcely seems adequate to keep the bones together, is covered with a loathsome disease, which the Portuguese call sarna, but may more properly be denominated the scurvy.*[4]

A third report comes from English diplomat Henry Chamberlain, who tells what it was like to buy a slave at Valongo:

When a person is desirous of making a purchase, he visits the different depots, going from one house to another, until he sees such as please him, who, upon being called out, undergo the operations of being felt and handled in various parts of the body and limbs, precisely in the manner of Cattle in a Market. They are made to walk, to run, to stretch their arms and legs violently, to speak and to show their tongue and teeth; which latter are considered as the surest marks whereby to discover their age and judge of their health.[5]

Between the sixteenth and nineteenth centuries, the Americas absorbed approximately 10 million African slaves. Brazil, the largest importer on the southern continent, received nearly 40 percent of this total, somewhere between 3.6 and 4 million slaves, according to the estimates accepted by the majority of researchers.[6] Historian Manolo Garcia Florentino estimates that 850,000 slaves disembarked in Rio de Janeiro during the eighteenth century, about half the total number brought to all of Brazil during this period. With the arrival of the court and the acceleration of commerce in the colony, slave traffic increased exponentially. The number of slaves unloaded in Rio jumped from 9,689 in 1807 to 23,230 in 1811—more than a two-fold increase in four years. The annual average of slave ships docked in the port also increased from twenty-one in the period before 1805 to fifty-one after 1809.[7] "By 1807 slave labor in Brazil had become an economic god with the slave trade as its strong right arm. To attempt to suppress the traffic, which was an essential adjunct to slavery itself, by simply passing statues and signing treaties was a futile performance," writes Alan Manchester.[8]

A gigantic business, slave trafficking mobilized hundreds of ships and thousands of people on both sides of the Atlantic, including agents on the coast of Africa, exporters, arms suppliers, ship owners, transporters, insurers, and wholesalers who resold merchandise in Rio to hundreds of regional traffickers—known as conveyors—who in turn redistributed it to the cities, plantations, and mines in the interior of the country. In 1812, half of the thirty largest enterprises in Rio de Janeiro were slave traffickers, and the profits of this business proved astronomical.[9] In 1810, a slave purchased in Luanda, Angola, for 70,000 réis was resold in the Diamond District of Minas Gerais for up to 240,000 réis, more than three times the price paid in Africa. An ideal buyer had another slave serve as collateral in case of non-payment of the debt.[10] In taxes alone, the state made the equivalent of £80,000 per year on the slave trade, the equivalent today of $11.3 million.[11]

Despite its enormous profits, trafficking in slaves made for a very risky business. The mortality rate of the enterprise was extremely high. About 80 percent of the captives came from the Congo, Angola, or Mozambique. In Africa, slaves first arrived into the hands of a local merchant, generally as prisoners of war or offered as payment in tribute to a local chief. This merchant brought the slaves to the coast, where agents of the Portuguese traffickers bought them. Until the beginning of the eighteenth century, these purchases were made with contraband gold bars. In 1703, the crown prohibited the use of precious metals in these transactions and punished offenders with confiscation of property and deportation for six years to São Tomé off the coast of Africa. From then on, slaves were bartered with products from the colony, in particular fabric, tobacco, sugar, cachaça, gunpowder, and firearms.[12]

In Africa, nearly 40 percent of slaves died on the way from the capture zones to the coast. Another 15 percent died crossing the Atlantic due to abominable sanitary conditions in the slave ships. Vessels coming from Mozambique and other regions on the east side of Africa lost even more. From the Atlantic coast, a voyage to Brazil took between thirty-three and forty-three days, while from Mozambique, in the Indian Ocean, up to seventy-six days.[13] On reaching Rio, between 10 and 12 percent of the slaves remained in warehouses like the Valongo Market before being sold. Of one hundred blacks captured in Africa, only forty-five arrived at their final destination alive. Which means that for the 10 million slaves transported to the Americas, another 10 million or more died along the way. It remains one of the largest and least documented genocides in human history.[14]

Shipwreck and pirates in the South Atlantic also imperiled the enterprise. Of the forty-three ships that transported slaves to the Company of

Grão-Pará and Maranhão during the second half of the eighteenth century, fourteen—just over a third—were shipwrecked. In the 1820s, Rio de Janeiro newspapers recorded sixteen pirate attacks on slave ships, many by corsairs from North America. One of these ships, the *Star of the Sea,* was robbed while still in the port of Malembo, Angola, losing all 213 of the slaves aboard before even setting sail.[15]

Slaves aboard these ships were considered and treated as a cargo like any other. On September 6, 1781, the English ship *Zong,* sailing from Liverpool, headed to Jamaica with an excess of slaves on board. On November 29, in the middle of the Atlantic, sixty blacks had already died from disease and lack of food and water. "Chained two by two, right leg and left leg, right hand and left hand, each slave had less room than a man in a coffin," writes F. O. Shyllon, author of *Black Slaves in Britain.*[16] Afraid of losing all of his cargo before arriving at his destination, Captain Luke Collingwood decided to throw all ill and malnourished slaves into the sea. Over the course of three days, 133 negroes were pitched from the gunwales alive. Only one managed to climb aboard again. The ship's owner, James Gregson, requested indemnity from his underwriters for the lost cargo. The insurance company in London appealed to the courts. According to English law, if a slave died onboard from maltreatment, hunger, or thirst, responsibility fell to the captain of the ship. If the slave fell in the sea, the insurer paid. In the case of the *Zong,* the courts decided in favor of the underwriters; that is, the captain was held responsible for their deaths. The case opened Britain's eyes to the cruelty of the slave trade and became a flashpoint for the abolitionist movement around the world.[17]

In Rio de Janeiro, slave traders—prominent businessmen, respected and revered—had much influence in society and government affairs. In the Portuguese court, they took pride of place among the greatest donors, duly compensated with distinctions and titles of nobility. A native of Porto, Elias Antonio Lopes, a trafficker, arrived in Brazil at the end of the eighteenth century. In 1808 he already had received a knighthood in the Order of Christ and the title of notary and scribe of the village of Paraty in return for the "noteworthy generosity and demonstration of loyal subjecthood in tribute of my Royal Person." That year he offered the prince regent a palace on the

São Cristovão ranch. Also that same year, the prince granted him the post of deputy of the Royal Council of Commerce. In 1810, he was consecrated a knight of the Royal House and graced as permanent captain-general and lord of the village of São José Del Rei, a district of Rio de Janeiro. He also became a broker and trustee of the House of Insurance of the Court Square, and in time he received responsibility for levying taxes in various locales. At his death in 1815, he owned 110 slaves and a fortune of 236 million réis ($7.5 million) in palaces, plantations, shares of the Bank of Brazil, and slave ships.[18]

Unloaded by the thousands in Rio, slaves were a relatively affordable possession even for the middle class. James Tuckey, a British navy official, relates that in 1803 an adult slave sold for £40, the equivalent today of $6,300, less than half of the price of a mid-range car.[19] Women cost a bit less, around £32, and boys £20. Blacks who had survived smallpox cost more since they developed an immunity to the disease and therefore had a chance of living longer.[20] "I bought a negro for 93,600 réis," wrote Luiz dos Santos Marrocos to his father on July 21, 1811, after his arrival in Rio de Janeiro.[21] This amount corresponds to a little more than 20 pounds sterling ($3,200) at the time, the price of an adolescent slave. In another letter, dos Santos Marrocos refers to the slave as "my little urchin."[22]

A common way of evaluating the price of a slave was comparing him to a pack animal. From the point of view of their owners, this comparison made sense: Both were destined for the same activity. A century earlier, the reports of Jesuit priest Father João Antonio Andreoni—author of *Culture and Opulence in Brazil through Its Drugs and Mines,* a classic of Brazilian history—had established the equation. Writing under the pseudonym André João Antonil, Andreoni relates that in 1711, "a well-built, brave, and wily negro" cost 300 eighths of gold, equal to three times the price of "a riding horse."[23] In the time of the Portugese court, a tame beast of burden cost approximately 28,000 réis, the price that Austrian botanist Karl von Martius paid for an animal in 1817, according to historian Almeida Prado.[24] Therefore, dos Santos Marrocos paid for his slave the equivalent of three pack mules, curiously maintaining an exact parity of price between slave and animal a hundred years later.

In Rio de Janeiro, anyone with social standing owned slaves. Spanish traveler Juan Francisco de Aguirre records in 1782 that the thirty monks of the convent of São Bento—the richest in Brazil at the time—lived on income acquired from "four sugarcane mills employing 1,200 slaves and from some houses for rent distributed throughout the city." Benedictine monks and Jesuit priests also kept slaves according to de Aguirre.[25] Some landowners had more slaves than necessary for their activities and leased the excess slaves to third parties for yet more profit. There were even brokers who specialized as intermediaries in this type of negotiation—a system not unlike today's real estate agents or car rental agencies. "Those who can acquire half a dozen slaves, live in idleness upon the ways of their labour, and stroll the streets in all the solemnity of self-importance," wrote Englishman James Tuckey in 1803.[26] "As such, anyone with a whiff of nobility could reap income from more humble labor without degrading themselves or callusing their hands," observed historian Sérgio Buarque de Holanda.[27]

German traveler Ernst Ebel recounts that upon arriving in Rio de Janeiro in 1824 he hired a slave for 700 réis per day, a little less than $18 in today's currency. Unsatisfied with the man's service, he fired him and after some time advertised in the *Fluminense Daily* for "a negress that knows how to wash and iron." He hired a sixteen-year-old "blacky"—his description—named Delfina, who cost 11,000 réis per month: 6,000 in cash and the rest in food and other daily necessities. For this amount, equivalent to about half of contemporary minimum wage, Ebel wrote, "I make use of someone who not only washes my clothes and sews them, but in case of necessity, knows her way around the kitchen, staying in the house more and more, to my own greater safety."[28]

Another variation of slavery developed in the form of moonlighting "for-profit" slaves. These slaves, after finishing their work in the houses of their owners, went into the streets in search of supplementary activity. They sold their labor piecemeal to diverse clients, offering services from a few hours' duration to a full day. It became such a popular system that commercial houses specialized in renting them. Moonlighting slaves did everything: fetched water, did the shopping, removed garbage, delivered and collected messages, and accompanied women to church. John Luccock recounts that

Exploited by their owners, slaves moonlight for profit as itinerant vendors in the streets of Rio de Janeiro. *Pretos de ganho,* engraving from *Views and Costumes of the City and Neighbourhood of Rio de Janeiro* by Henry Chamberlain, London, 1822, Lucia M. Loeb/Biblioteca Guita e José Mindlin

some were even hired to say Ave Marias for their temporary employers in the many oratories in the city.[29]

At the end of each day, the moonlighting slaves passed part of their earnings to their owners, a previously determined figure. A slave who surpassed this amount kept the difference. "This form of work was equally as convenient for the owner as for the slave," writes historian Leila Mezan Algranti, an authority on the subject. "The master did not bother with the occupation of his workers, nor with controlling them. The negroes, in turn, lived free in the streets, enjoying a liberty never dreamed of by their counterparts in the countryside." According to Algranti, the system proved profitable: Some masters lived solely on the labor of one or two "profit-blacks." At the same time, some moonlighting slaves not only paid the agreed rental price to their owners but even managed to make enough money to buy their freedom.[30] If a slave didn't reach the target amount, however, he was punished.

Colonial period museums teem with horrifying instruments of punishment and torture used on slaves. As classified by historian Artur Ramos, various categories of punishment existed in Brazil. The first involved punishment with instruments of capture and restraint, including: chains, iron collars, handcuffs, fetters and shackles (for feet and hands), in addition to the pillory and the *viramundo,* a smaller pillory made of iron. A tinplate mask prevented a slave from eating sugarcane or brown sugar or from swallowing precious stones or gold nuggets. Pilliwinks—iron rings to crush the thumbs—obtained confessions. Thrashings made use of a paddle or a "codfish," a whip with a short handle of gold or wood and five points of twisted leather. Hot irons branded a slave with his or her owners' initials or the letter F for fugitive. The *libambo* consisted of an iron hoop fastened around the neck, from which a long iron stem or stems protruded and bent down to the top to the slave's head, sometimes with rattles at the tips.

The three instruments used with the most regularity were the whip, the pillory, and shackles. The most common punishment was lashing, either on the back or buttocks, for when a slave tried to escape or committed a crime or some great fault on the job. At the beginning of the seventeenth century, Italian friar Jorge Benci recommended that whippings not surpass forty per day to avoid mutilating the slave.[31] But travelers' and chroniclers' reports reference two hundred, three hundred, and even up to six hundred lashes. That mind-boggling amount of whipping left the back or buttocks completely shredded. At a time without antibiotics, the risk of death by infection, gangrene, or sepsis was great, so the punished slave would be bathed in an excruciating mix of salt, vinegar, or chili pepper in an attempt to stave off any infection.[32]

Painter Jean-Baptiste Debret recounts that in Rio de Janeiro slaves accused of grave misconduct such as escape or theft received punishments of fifty to two hundred lashes. The master had to report "the name of the delinquent and the number of lashings he was to receive" to the jail authorized by the police superintendent. The tormentor charged with executing the punishment received one *pataca,* a silver coin worth 320 réis, for every one hundred lashes applied. "Every day between nine and ten in the morning, one can see the queue of negroes waiting to be punished," wrote Debret.

They are chained at the arm, two by two, and escorted by the police to the place designated for their punishment. To this end pillories are erected in every major public square, with the intention of displaying the punished. . . . After being released from the pillory, the negro is laid on the ground face down to avoid blood loss. The sores hidden below their shirttails thus escape the bites of the swarms of insects seeking this horrible repast. Finally, the beating complete, the condemned adjust their trousers and return to prison, two by two, with the same escort that brought them. . . . Back in prison, the victim is subjected to a second trial, no less painful: washing the sores with vinegar and chili pepper, a sanitary procedure with the intention of preventing infection.[33]

A key difference between urban and rural slavery was the administration of punishment. On plantations and in gold and diamond mines, overseers or masters punished slaves directly. In the city, this task fell to the police. Slave owners who didn't want to punish a slave personally could appeal to their services—for a fee of course. Blacks were punished in the prisons and pillories around the cities. Consul James Henderson witnessed one of these punishments in Rio de Janeiro:

A gentleman obtained an order for the flagellation of one of his runaway slaves, with two hundred lashes. On his name being called several times, he appeared at the door of a dungeon, where the negroes seemed to be promiscuously confined together. A rope was put round his neck, and he was led to a large post, in the adjoining yard; around which his arms and feet were bound, while a rope secured his body in like manner, and another, firmly fastened round his thighs, rendered the movement of a single member wholly impossible. The black degradado set to work very mechanically, and at every stroke, which appeared to cut part of the flesh away, he gave a singular whistle. The stripes were repeated always upon the same part, and the negro bore the one hundred lashes he received at this time with the most determined resolution. On receiving the first and second strokes he called out "Jesus" but afterwards laid his head against the side of the post, not uttering a syllable, or asking for mercy.[34]

With the exception of homicide, the most grave misconduct a slave could attempt was escape. Nearly 16 percent of the total arrests by the court police between 1808 and 1822 were of runaway slaves. It was an age-old conflict. Nearly a century earlier, in March 1741, responding to a request by the miners of Minas Gerais, the crown ordered that all runaway slaves found on quilombos, "if they were there voluntarily," should be branded with an F, for fugitive, on their upper backs. Repeat offenders had one of their ears cut off, and if caught a third time they were sentenced to death. Despite these measures, escapes continued in great numbers. In 1755, the City Council of Mariana, in Minas Gerais, proposed that captured fugitives have their Achilles tendons cut so they could no longer run but remain able to work limping. The court found this measure overly inhumane and unchristian and denied the request.[35]

The surrounding areas of Rio de Janeiro, replete with forests and mountains, offered refuge for hundreds of runaway slaves. The Tijuca Forest, Santa Teresa Mountain, and the regions of Niteroi and the present-day Rodrigo de Freitas lagoon became famous for sheltering quilombos. Their inhabitants foraged in the forest, collecting fruit and root vegetables, and hunted small animals and rodents. Their principal sustenance, however, came from neighboring farms that they frequently raided. At times the runaway slaves even managed to sell stolen goods in the city.[36]

In contrast to what we might imagine, however, most runaway slaves took refuge not in the forests or solitary rural locales but the city itself. Given the many freed slaves and mulattos in the urban environment, runaway slaves blended easily with the crowds. It was practically impossible for the police to verify the identity and status of every black slave in the streets of Rio de Janeiro. As a result, newspapers brimmed with announcements describing runaway slaves and offering rewards for their capture, a practice that continued almost up to abolition in 1888. Here is an example of one such announcement at the time:

A slave named Lourenço escaped two months ago from the farm of Francisco de Moraes Campos of the parish of Belém, municipality of Jundiaí, province of São Paulo. . . . He has the following traits: about

30 years old, average height, long face, handsome features, shaggy hair,
a refined nose, mouth and lips quite regular, with the lower lip thicker
and redder, good teeth, very dark skin color, a thin beard, a fine frame,
the crown of his head worn bald from carrying objects, thin legs, reedy,
feet jutting outwards, he is very wily. He is a ploughman, and a very
good muleteer. I will handsomely reward anyone who catches him and
pay all expenses incurred up until his delivery.[37]

Woodsmen often had the task of capturing runaway slaves, their work similar to bounty hunters of the American Wild West. Armed with lasso and harness, they traversed forests and rural areas in search of fugitives. They used announcements published in newspapers or nailed on posts along road-sides or in public squares as clues. When they recaptured slaves, they tied them with ropes and forced them to walk on foot behind their horses. Some woodsmen even had pillories at home to hold recaptured slaves while nego-tiating rewards with their owners. "The woodsmen were armed, but only used their weapons if they met with resistance," according to Theodor von Leithold. "Negroes killed in skirmishes with the police had their heads cut off and staked atop poles on the corner of the main roads as warnings."[38] In general, the sum paid to woodsmen amounted to around 15 to 20 percent of the total estimated price of the slave and included the bounty for the capture, reimbursement for food, and a fee for guarding the slave until his return to his owner.[39]

Rio de Janeiro had hundreds of manumitted or freed slaves, called forros. Luccock estimated their number at around one thousand in 1808. A slave could gain his freedom in many ways. He could purchase it at a previously negotiated amount, generally equal to what the owner had paid for him. The slave accumulated this money himself, earned it by doing piecemeal work for others, or received it through the help of family members or a brother-hood. Owners could grant freedom outright, and some manumissions had deadlines. For example, a slave might have to remain captive and in service until the owner's death, after which he was legally free, as stipulated in his owner's will. The government could also intervene in cases of abandonment, illness, or maltreatment.[40]

The law also outlined special conditions that authorized manumission. A slave who found a diamond of twenty carats or more, for example, gained his freedom, and in this case the owner received an indemnity of 400,000 réis, enough to buy four more slaves. Englishman John Mawe describes this system of manumission by reward in the diamond mines of Cerro Frio in Minas Gerais, which he visited in 1810:

> *When a negro is so fortunate as to find a diamond of the weight of an octavo (17½ carats), much ceremony takes place; he is crowned with a wreath of flowers and carried in procession to the administrator, who gives him his freedom, by paying his owner for it. He also receives a present of new clothes, and is permitted to work on his own account. When a stone of eight or ten carats is found, the negro receives two new shirts, a complete new suit, with a hat and a handsome knife.*[41]

A slave who denounced his master for smuggling also legally received his freedom. In this case, the slave himself received a reward of 200,000 réis.[42]

Many forros, having become rich enough to acquire land and other property, became slave owners themselves. These cases were rare, but they add a surprising element to the landscape of slavery in Brazil. The most famous case concerns the mulatta Francisca da Silva de Oliveira, known as Chica da Silva, of the Tijuco diamond district in Minas Gerais. Chica was born a slave but gained her liberty in 1753, granted by the diamond miner João Fernandes de Oliveira who bought her from Manuel Pires Sardinha, a Portuguese doctor. While they never legally married, she and de Oliveira had a seventeen-year relationship during which they had thirteen children. Among Chica da Silva's possessions was a "sizeable pack of slaves," according to historian Ronaldo Vainfas.[43]

The power brokers of Brazil, who considered slavery an economic institution to be preserved, didn't view manumission kindly. Historian Leila Mezan Algranti cites the case of the forra Clara Maria de Jesus, who requested of Dom João the freeing of her son Jorge Pardo, slave of the priest João da Cruz Moura e Camara. She claimed that Jorge was the son of a free man, the lieutenant colonel of the line troops in Angola, conceived while she was still in captivity. Clara Maria was willing to pay 200,000 réis for the manumission of her son, but the priest refused the deal. The superintendent general of police, Paulo Fernandes Viana, denied her request. According to him, "nobody should be forced to sell their property" because "a good slave is a good find, and precious property." Viana advised against manumission because the country couldn't afford the risk of a large population of freed blacks. "The evils that we await from blacks are even greater when they are free than when captive," he warned, concluding ominously that he couldn't grant Clara Maria's request because "there are more powerful political motives at large in this country."[44]

Freedom didn't always mean a better quality of life, however. With a certain degree of rigor, the law regulated the possession and maintenance of slaves. Masters had to feed, house, and provide minimum requirements for the survival of their slaves. Legislation maintained that, in the case of proven maltreatment, the slave master could lose his property, thereby causing financial detriment. Once freed, however, the forros were on their own, completely marginalized from any system of legal or social protection. In many cases, manumission meant plunging into the ocean of poverty composed of forros, mulattos, and mestizos pushed to the margins of opportunities such as education, health, housing, and public safety—problems that, 125 years after the official abolition of slavery, Brazil still hasn't fully resolved.

XXI

The Travelers

Thanks to João VI, foreigners discovered Brazil—albeit after a delay of three centuries. Researcher Rubens Borba de Moraes catalogued a total of 266 travelers who had written about the people, geography, and riches of Brazil as of 1949. The vast majority visited the country in the decades immediately following the opening of the ports.[1] These travelers recorded their impressions in letters, official reports, and books, making this one of the best-documented periods in Brazilian history. Their work includes descriptions of cities, landscapes, people, customs, and scientific discoveries. Their reports register astonishment, all of them surprised by the beauties of an idyllic, untouched land. "In Rio I encountered an entirely new world, compelling me to reproduce what I saw day and night, until I was exhausted," recounted Austrian painter Thomas Ender, who arrived in Brazil in 1817 along with the scientific mission accompanying Princess Leopoldina.[2] "Every object of nature is here on the boldest and most magnificent scale," noted American Naval official Henry Brackenridge the following year on entering Guanabara Bay.[3]

At the beginning of the nineteenth century, the Brazilian colony remained the last major tropical part of the planet left unexplored by non-Portuguese Europeans. The English, Dutch, and Spanish already knew Africa, India, and China well, after intense commercial rivalry had established direct contact with these regions by the sixteenth century. The same was happening with the rest of North America, including America, Canada, and the Spanish colonies, but the Spanish didn't impose significant restrictions on the entry of foreigners into their territories. Japan and Oceania of course remained remote points of difficult access, with Australia being the last major landmass colonized by Europeans. But nothing compared to Brazil, until then kept closed and isolated from the rest of the world. The Dutch and French had occupied swaths along the coast of Pernambuco and Rio de Janeiro respectively for short periods, but the interior of the country remained a vast terra incognita. The prohibition of access imposed by the Portuguese made the colony even more mysterious, prompting rumors in Europe of immense hidden underground mineral deposits, boundless tropical forests teeming with exotic flora and fauna, and natives still living as they had in the Stone Age. The arrival of the court and the opening of the ports suddenly changed all this, resulting in a foreign invasion without precedent.

The first travel reporter of the era, English mineralogist John Mawe, wrote *Travels in the Interior of Brazil,* published in London in 1812 to instant success. In the following years, nine more editions followed, published in different languages, including Russian, German, Italian, and Swedish.[4] Born in Derbyshire, Mawe was forty-one years old in 1805 when he departed from Cádiz to Montevideo, where officials arrested him on suspicions of being a spy. He languished in jail there for a year. In 1806, after General William Beresford took the South American city, Mawe was released, then passed through Buenos Aires, chartered a boat, and set sail for Brazil. After he visited Santa Catarina, Paraná and São Paulo, Prince Regent João welcomed him in Rio de Janeiro. Over little more than two years, he traversed almost every region in Brazil, becoming the first foreigner authorized to visit the diamond mines of Minas Gerais.

Mawe had an insatiable curiosity. He described gold and diamond prospecting, plants, fruits, insects, snails, landscapes, people, clothing, dietary habits, and architecture. He noted everything that entered his gaze in meticulous and riveting detail. He also played a part in an episode involving a false diamond that an ex-slave from Minas Gerais had given to Prince João as a present. After a voyage of twenty-eight days, the freed slave, escorted by two

View of Negroes Washing for Diamonds at Mandango on the River Jequitinhonha in Cerro do Frio, Brazil, engraving from
Travels in Interior of Brazil, Particularly in the Gold and Diamond Districts by John Mawe, London, Lucia M. Loeb/
Biblioteca Guita e José Mindlin

soldiers, personally delivered the stone to the prince. An inch and a half in diameter, it weighed a full pound. João believed it the largest diamond on earth and ordered it stored in a safe in Rio de Janeiro. Mawe, a specialist in precious minerals, knocked the wind out of everyone's sails, though, after identifying the stone as a simple quartz rock with no commercial value. The former slave, who had hoped to receive a reward, had to return home empty-handed and on foot—a distance of nine hundred miles from Rio de Janeiro.

Travelers in Brazil at the time of the Portuguese court fall into five classifications: The first, of merchants, miners, and businessmen, included John Mawe and John Luccock. The second consisted of noblemen, diplomats, military men, and government officials who resided in or passed through the country on official missions, as was the case of Henry Brackenridge and the British consuls James Henderson and Henry Chamberlain. Scientists—part of the countless expeditions traveling the country—comprised the third category, the most famous of their number being botanists Augustin de Saint-Hilaire, Karl von Martius, and Johann Baptist von Spix. The fourth group included painters and landscape artists, such as Frenchman Jean-Baptiste Debret and Austrian Johann Moritz Rugendas. The fifth and final group consisted of adventurers, onlookers, and people who arrived in the country almost by accident. This last category, a curious group, included two women, Rose de Freycinet from France and Maria Graham from England.

Rose de Freycinet ended up in Brazil through a life of romance and adventure straight out of the movies. In 1817—at twenty-five years old and married to naturalist and French navy official Louis de Soulces de Freycinet—she learned that her husband had been sent on a mission that would take him away from home for two years. Commanding the corvette *Uranie,* de Soulces de Freycinet was to travel around the world, leading a scientific mission to explore South America, the South Pacific islands, India, and the coast of Africa. Unhappy with the news, Rose made a bold move: She cut her hair, bound her breasts, and clandestinely boarded the ship on the eve of its departure disguised as a man. It was a very risky decision.

At the time, women were forbidden on French navy ships, so she ran the risk of arrest and deportation at the ship's first docking. Luckily for her, all turned out well in the end. The next day, already at high sea, she revealed herself to her husband, who had no choice but to summon the ship's commanders and communicate her presence. Instead of being chastised, however, she was roundly greeted and welcomed. She and her husband arrived in Rio de Janeiro in December of that year. They found the city very beautiful and the climate agreeable—despite the blistering summer heat—but recorded devastating comments about the Portuguese and Brazilians in their diaries. "It is a pity that such a beautiful country was not colonized by an active and intelligent nation," she wrote, referring to Portugal, and in another passage: "Brazilians emphasize abundance much more than they do elegance in service."[5]

The de Freycinets left Brazil in 1818 and returned in 1820, after a trip around the world. On July 16, King João and the entire royal family welcomed them with a feast at São Cristovão Palace. Rose's notes depict a court that, despite all efforts to the contrary, continued to behave as inelegant bumpkins. "The King is likeable, though of little majesty," she observed. "The Prince (future Emperor Pedro I) has a handsome figure, but his manners are quite bad and his air is common. He wears a brown jacket and nankeen trousers, which seem to me a little ridiculous at eight in the evening during a great feast given to the public." She also criticized Princess Leopoldina, Pedro's wife:

I could not see in the manners of the royal Princess the noble and ceremonious appearance of a lady from the court of Austria. Here she does not care for her toilette nor for the natural elegance of her figure. For this feast . . . our poor Austrian dressed in a gray riding suit, made of ordinary cloth, wearing a pleated blouse, her hair in disarray and held up by a tortoiseshell comb. She is not ugly. I think that if well dressed she could be quite nice. The other princesses wore satin clothes, with flowers and plumes in their hair.[6]

Maria Graham also visited Brazil in the company of her husband aboard a naval ship, but in her case the journey ended tragically. Born in a village in the English countryside near the Scottish border, the daughter of Vice-Admiral George Dundas, commissioner of the British admiralty, she had a first-rate education, specialized in arts and literature, and wrote and drew quite well. She had already visited India and Italy when she arrived in Brazil in 1821 aboard the frigate *Doris*, commanded by her husband, Captain Thomas Graham. They went to Olinda, Recife, and Salvador, arriving in Rio de Janeiro a short while after the Portuguese court had returned to Lisbon, landing in time to witness the famous Dia do Fico ("The day that I stay") on January 9, 1822, during which King João's son Pedro, then prince regent, decided to remain in Brazil, refusing to comply with the orders of the Portuguese Cortes to return to Lisbon. In the region of Pernambuco, Graham witnessed a rebellion in which her husband had to negotiate with insurgents in the city of Goiania. From Brazil, the couple proceeded to Chile, but Captain Graham died shortly after passing through the Straits of Magellan. Widowed at thirty-six years old, Maria continued alone to Santiago, where destiny carried her to Admiral Thomas Cochrane, a fascinating character.

A Scottish lord, member of Parliament, and a hero of the Napoleonic Wars, Cochrane at forty-nine years old had become a legend of the seas. Contracted as a mercenary in South America, he helped the independence movements of Chile, Peru, and Brazil, fighting against the Spanish and Portuguese naval forces. Graham met Cochrane when he was commander-in-chief of the Chilean navy. Shortly thereafter, Emperor Pedro I invited him to organize the Brazilian navy. While Cochrane and Graham never admitted publicly to an amorous relationship, some biographies of the admiral argue that this was the case.[7] In any event, the relationship between the two was profound and long-lasting. Maria returned to Rio de Janeiro with him, where she befriended and became the confidante of Empress Leopoldina and tutor to Princess Maria da Gloria. After returning to England, Graham married a renowned painter, Sir Augustus Callcott, and wrote books on art history. Her accounts of Brazil appeared in 1824 under the title *Journal of a Voyage to Brazil, and Residence There, during Parts of the Years 1821, 1822, 1823*. Historians consider it one of the most valuable documents from this period.[8]

Born in Portugal to an English family, the traveler Henry Koster arrived in Brazil in 1809 and journeyed through the cities and backlands of the Northeast for eleven years, dying in Recife in 1820. Brazilian folklorist Luis da Camara Cascudo translated into Portuguese Koster's account of his journey, *Travels in Brazil*, originally published in London in 1816. "Koster's testimony is the first, chronologically, to deal with the traditional ethnography and psychology of the Northeast, the Backlanders in their setting," writes da Camara Cascudo. "Before him, no foreigner had ever crossed the backlands of the Northeast, from Recife to Fortaleza in the dry season, traveling by convoy, drinking water from a rubber flask, eating roasted meat, and sleeping under the trees, so completely adapted to the world in which he chose to live."[9]

Koster adored living among the Northeastern people and participating in their festivals and religious celebrations. "I missed no festivals," he wrote proudly in his diary. "Amongst others, I went to that of St. Amaro, the healer of wounds, at whose chapel are sold bits of ribbon as charms, which many individuals of the lower orders of people tie round their naked ankles or their wrists, and preserve until they wear out, and drop off." In the interior of Rio Grande do Norte, he noted the isolation of the Backlanders there. They had outside contact only with the priests who traveled the region performing masses, weddings, and baptisms in exchange for offerings and contributions from its inhabitants.

"Certain priests obtain a license from the Bishop of Pernambuco and travel through these regions with a small altar constructed for the purpose; of a size to be placed upon one side of a pack-saddle, and they have with them all their apparatus for saying mass," wrote Koster.

These men make in the course of the year between 150 and 200 pounds—a large income in Brazil, but hardly earned, if the inconveniences and privations which they must undergo to obtain it are taken into consideration. They stop and erect the altar wherever a sufficient number of persons who are willing to pay for the mass is collected. This will sometimes be said for three or four shillings, but at other times, if a rich man takes a fancy to a priest, or has a fit of extreme devotion upon him, he will give eight or ten mil réis, two or three pounds, and it does happen, that one hundred mil réis are received for saying a mass, but this is very rare—at times an ox or an horse, or two or three, are given.

Koster left a detailed description of the way of life in the Northeastern interior: "The *Sertanejo* is very jealous, and more murders are committed, and more quarrels entered into on this score, by tenfold, than on any other," he related.

> *These people are revengeful; an offence is seldom pardoned, and in default of law, of which there is scarcely any, each man takes it into his own hands. . . . Robbery in the Sertão is scarcely known; the land is in favorable years too plentiful to afford temptation, and in seasons of distress for food, every man is for the most part equally in want. . . . They are extremely ignorant, few of them possessing even the commonest rudiments of knowledge. . . . The Sertanejos are courageous, generous, sincere, and hospitable: if a favor is begged, they know not how to deny it; but if you trade with them either for cattle, or aught else, the character changes, and then they wish to outwit you, conceiving success to be a piece of cleverness of which they may boast.*

Certain images recur in the numerous accounts of foreigners who visited Brazil at the beginning of the nineteenth century. The first is of a carefree and sluggish colony with no inclination to work, dependent for three centuries on the proceeds of an extractive economy. Englishman Thomas Lindley, who traveled along the coast near Porto Seguro, in Bahia, took surprised note that the abundance of natural resources in Brazil failed to result in significant wealth, cultural development, or material comfort for the Brazilians. "In a country which, with cultivation and industry, would abound with the blessings of nature to excess, the greater part of the people exist in want and poverty, while even the small remainder know not those enjoyments which make life desirable."[10]

John Mawe had much the same reaction upon encountering cheese production in a region near Vila Rica and Mariana in Minas Gerais. "Its taste was sometimes so extremely rancid and disagreeable, as to be utterly unwholesome, and from this circumstance I judged that there must be great mismanagement in the preparation of it," he related.

All the farms which I had occasion to visit on my journey to Villa Rica, [and from thence to this place], fully confirmed my opinion; for, miserable as was the condition of every department belonging to them, that of the dairy was still worse. In the few places where they pretended to prepare milk for cheese, not only were the various utensils in an extremely filthy condition, but the rennet was so putrid as to be in the last degree sickening.

Mawe relates how he tried time and again to teach the farmers more hygienic production techniques for the production of cheese and butter, but he knew his efforts were in vain. "The people seemed highly satisfied with the success of the process; but I had strong doubts that they would not pursue it after my departure, as they must naturally dislike the trouble and care which it required."[11]

Another theme that arises frequently in these travelers' accounts is illiteracy and the paucity of education and culture. "Brazil is not the seat of literature," remarked James Henderson. "In fact, its total absence is marked by the prohibition of books generally, and the want of any single medium through which its inhabitants can attain even to a knowledge of the existing state of the world, or what is passing in it. The inhabitants are principally involved in great ignorance and pride, its usual consequence."[12] Henderson, departing from London on March 11, 1819, aboard the *Echo*, stands as one of the later voyagers of João's time in Brazil. Henderson's travel diaries include a map of the country and eight engravings portraying landscapes and types of Brazilian people. "In this illiterate country, one does not meet anyone with an intimate knowledge of science," observed English botanist William Burchell, who traveled through the country later, between 1825 and 1830, after the court had already returned to Portugal. "Nature has done many things here—but man, nothing. Here, nature offers many themes for study and admiration, while men continue to vegetate in the darkness of ignorance and extreme poverty, a consequence of indolence alone."[13]

The opening of the ports and the end of prohibited access to Brazil represented a quantum leap for scientific advancement there. The country, suddenly thrown open to geographers, geologists, botanists, ethnographers, and more, offered an immense laboratory, rich and abounding with new discoveries. Augustin de Saint-Hilaire, born in Orléans, France, ten years before the French Revolution, lived in Brazil between 1816 and 1822. He visited the regions of Goiás, São Paulo, Rio Grande do Sul, Minas Gerais, and Espirito Santo, traversing a total of approximately nine thousand miles. A professor of botany at the Muséum National d'Histoire Naturelle in Paris, he arrived in the company of the duke of Piney, Charles Emmanuelle Sigismond de Montmorency-Luxembourg, whom King Louis XVIII appointed as ambassador to the court in Rio de Janeiro in 1816. In the following years, Saint-Hilaire collected more than 15,000 species of plants and animals, from the northern region of Goiás—where today the state of Tocantins is located—to Rio Grande do Sul. He discovered two new botanical families, the Paronychiae and the Tamariscinae, and more than one thousand previously unknown species. Upon returning to France, he published fourteen volumes, including travel memoirs, botanical descriptions, and agricultural reports.[14]

Saint-Hilaire arrived in São Paulo carrying eighteen suitcases and stayed in a country estate where the neighborhood of Brás is located today.[15] He found the region agreeable but the mess and filth of the shops in the city center astounding. "One should not expect to find these shops clean and orderly," he observed. "The lard, cereals, and meat are thrown about every which way, mixed one with the other, and the shopkeepers are still quite far from possessing the arts of our merchants in Paris, who know how to give an appetizing appearance to even the most crude provisions." The streetwalkers also surprised him. "In no part of the world that I have traversed did I see such a large number of prostitutes. They were of every color; the sidewalks were covered, so to speak, with women of that low station. They pass leisurely from one side to the other or wait on the corners for customers," he wrote, adding unsurprisingly that "nothing is more widespread in this region than venereal diseases."

The most famous scientific expedition of this period arrived with Princess Leopoldina in 1817, directed by the twenty-three-year old Bavarian botanist Karl von Martius, and including painter Thomas Ender and botanist Johann Baptist von Spix. Responsible for studying plants, animals, minerals,

Rancho near the Serra do Caraça (Minas Gerais), engraving from *Travels in Brazil* by Johann Baptist von Spix and C. Philipp von Martius, London, 1824, Lucia M. Loeb/Biblioteca Guita e José Mindlin

and natives, von Martius and von Spix covered more than six thousand miles in the interior of Brazil between 1817 and 1820, making the expedition one of the largest scientific explorations of the nineteenth century. Traveling by mule troop and canoe, the two researchers began in Rio—passing through the regions of São Paulo, Minas Gerais, Bahia, Pernambuco, Piauí, Maranhão, Pará, and finally the modern-day state of Amazonas—and went all the way to the border with Colombia. At the trip's end they brought 85 species of mammals, 350 species of birds, 130 species of amphibians, 116 species of fish, 2,700 species of insects, 80 species of arachnids and crustaceans, and 6,500 species of plants to Munich.[16] The result of this research, published in Germany in three volumes between 1823 and 1831, still holds pride of place as an important reference work of the natural sciences.

In the upper stretches of the Japurá River, a tributary of the Solimões River, almost at the border with Colombia, von Martius and von Spix met a picturesque individual: João Manoel, an emperor of the wilderness. Chief of the Miranhas, a native group with a population estimated at six thousand

Dom João: an ugly and insecure prince, who lived apart from his wife and feared thunder and crabs.
Vista da Praça do Palácio, engraving by Jean-Baptiste Debret from *Voyage pittoresque et historique au Brésil,* Paris, 1834–1839, Lucia M. Loeb / Biblioteca Guita e José Mindlin

Palace Square in Rio de Janeiro, with the palace at the left. Painter Johann Moritz Rugendas called it a "vast and irregular edifice, of the worst type of architecture." *Vista da Praça do Palácio,* engraving by Jean-Baptiste Debret from *Voyage pittoresque et historique au Brésil,* Paris, 1834–1839, Lucia M. Loeb / Biblioteca Guita e José Mindlin

The hand-kissing ceremony, according to APDG. The corrupt and wasteful court thrived on the exchange of favors.
Court day at Rio, engraving from *Sketches of Portuguese Life Manners and Costume and Character* by APDG, London, 1826. Lucia M. Loeb / Biblioteca Guita e José Mindlin

Coaches and sedans transported the rich and the nobility. Only commoners walked. *The Chege and Cadeira,* engraving from *Views and Costumes of the City and Neighbourhood of Rio de Janeiro* by Henry Chamberlain, London, 1822, Lucia M. Loeb / Biblioteca Guita e José Mindlin

A hammock with poles carried by slaves was a common means of transport during longer voyages in the interior of the country. *The Rede or Net,* engraving from *Views and Costumes of the City and Neighbourhood of Rio de Janeiro* by Henry Chamberlain, London, 1822, Lucia M. Loeb / Biblioteca Guita e José Mindlin

William Carr Beresford, the British governor of Portugal during João's absence, his left eye blinded by a musket shot.

William Carr Beresford, *Viscount Beresford* by Sir William Beechey, 1814–15, National Portrait Gallery, London

The infamous massacre of Spaniards resisting French troops during the Peninsular War. *El 3 de mayo de 1808 en Madrid: los fusilamientos en la montaña del Príncipe Pío* by Francisco de Goya y Lucientes, 1814, Museo del Prado, Madrid

The return of the court from Rio de Janeiro to Lisbon in 1821. If it were solely up to him, King João VI would have remained in Brazil. *A partida da corte do Rio,* engraving by Jean-Baptiste Debret from *Voyage pittoresque et historique au Brésil,* Paris, 1834–1839, as in Rio de Janeiro, cidade mestiça, Companhia das Letras, 2001

The coronation of Emperor Pedro I: Within thirteen years, the colony of Brazil transformed into an independent nation. *Coroação de D. Pedro,* engraving by Jean-Baptiste Debret from V*oyage pittoresque et historique au Brésil,* Paris, 1834–1839, as in Rio de Janeiro, cidade mestiça, Companhia das Letras, 2001 by the researchers, Manoel had enslaved a neighboring tribe. His power extended over an area two and a half times larger than the modern state of Sergipe. Manoel didn't speak Portuguese, so they communicated in the *lingua-geral*, a common idiom among the majority of indigenous tribes of Brazil at this time. Manoel wore cotton shirts and trousers like the Portuguese colonizers, ate from china dishes, wore a hat, and shaved daily.

The botanists observed an unusual means of communication developed by the natives of the upper Solimões. Beating a hollow wooden log called a *trocano*, the Natives emitted signals, like a primitive telegraph, to communicate with neighboring villages. Depending on the signal, messages conveyed, for example, that two white men had just visited a tribe or that at a certain moment a village was sleeping or eating. Because of these signals, the day after their arrival in the village of the Miranhas, von Martius and von Spix received a visit from hundreds of neighboring natives, curious to investigate for themselves these strangers who had suddenly appeared from nowhere.[17]

This moment demonstrated the transformations in progress at the time. From the point of view of European civilization, the upper Solimões was a heart of darkness: an isolated location lost in time and space. Von Martius and von Spix came from Vienna, one of the most cultured and educated cities of its era, where at that time Ludwig van Beethoven was composing his *Fifth Symphony*. Trekking through the Amazonian wilderness, they had gone further than any other traveler in the Brazilian interior. Once there, they came face to face with a tribal society that nonetheless had a rudimentary system of communication sufficient to announce the biggest news of João VI's Brazil: The foreigners were coming.

XXII

Napoleon's Downfall

One of the most popular works in the Prado Museum in Madrid, Francisco Goya's *Los Fusilamientos del Tres de Mayo* portrays a startling scene that occurred on May 3, 1808, on Príncipe Pío Hill, in the Spanish capital. On the right, shrouded in heavy, dark tones, a firing squad aims at a group kneeling on the left. In the center, a square lantern on the ground throws phantasmagorical light across a man in a white shirt and beige trousers, who lifts his arms in the direction of the firing squad. Is he begging for mercy, attempting some explanation, performing a last act of protest? The moment of pure fear and despair stands frozen in Goya's painting. At the feet of the man in the white shirt lie three or four stacked and bloodstained corpses. At his side, other prisoners await their fatal bullet. Some cover their eyes, while others hang their heads in resignation.

Goya's painting silently but powerfully witnesses the tragic events that rocked the Iberian peninsula in the year that the Portuguese royal family arrived in Brazil. On the eve of those mass executions, the Spanish rebelled against the French invasion and the removal of Carlos IV from the throne. The French reacted with ruthless violence. Between the afternoon of May 2 and the night of May 3, hundreds of rebels were shot in the suburbs of Madrid. Two of the most bloody conflicts of the Napoleonic wars started there and had profound consequences for both sides.

Between 1807 and 1814, Portugal and Spain represented for Napoleon what Vietnam did for America a century and a half later. Many years afterward, in exile on Saint Helena, Napoleon reflected in his memoirs: "It was the Peninsular War that destroyed me. All of my disasters had their origin in this fatal knot." He added a rationale much abused by countless leaders and governments throughout history: "What I tried to do in Spain was for their own good, but the people didn't understand. As a result, I failed."[1]

The Peninsular War, seizing these two countries between 1807 and 1813, involved a series of non-conventional clashes including guerrilla skirmishes and ambushes. Not unlike the English Redcoats in colonial America several decades prior, the disciplined, regimental French troops were unaccustomed to this style of martial engagement. Master of the battlefield, Napoleon based his military strategy on massive concentrations of troops, with the objective of deciding battles as quickly as possible and forcing his enemies to accept his terms of surrender. In these meticulously planned conflicts, fought in open fields under the control of generals, the strengths and weaknesses of each side quickly became apparent. In Spain and Portugal, however, the French faced bands of men armed with scythes, tridents, sticks, and even rocks, who ambushed them on difficult and mountainous terrain.

The errors of judgement that Napoleon committed on the Iberian peninsula—which sealed his destiny—began with the choice of the man responsible for commanding the invasion of Portugal. Despite being an old friend of the French emperor, General Jean-Andoche Junot was far from a first-rate official. He had enjoyed a mediocre career when compared with Napoleon's other great generals, such as Louis Davoust, André Masséna, and Nicolas Soult. Before invading Portugal, he hadn't commanded any large military expeditions. "Junot was one of Napoleon's most active and vigorous officers, but not a great strategist after the style of Masséna, Soult, or Davoust," wrote Sir Charles Oman, author of *A History of the Peninsular War*. "He was a good fighting man, but a mediocre general."[2]

Bonaparte apparently chose Junot for three reasons. First, they were old comrades in arms. They became acquainted at the beginning of both of their military careers in the famous Siege of Toulon in 1793, in which the future French emperor distinguished himself with his courage and cleverness in defeating the English. Thereafter, Junot fought alongside Napoleon in Italy, Egypt, Palestine, and in the Battle of Austerlitz. He was a little over thirty years old when he received the order to invade Portugal. Nicknamed "The Storm" on account of his ferocious, irascible temperament, Junot had a face marked by the various battles in which he had fought. One side featured a deep scar from top to bottom, the result of a saber wound received during a campaign in Italy.[3]

Second, Junot had served as French ambassador in Lisbon for a brief period between 1804 and 1805. He married the duchess of Abrantes, who went down in history as the author of the most stinging and irreverent comments about the customs of the Portuguese court. Recorded in her personal diary, the duchess's criticisms still delight historians and students of this era. (It's hard to forget her account of Princess Carlota Joaquina as small, hobbling, cross-eyed, and disagreeable.)

Third, Portugal's obvious unpreparedness convinced Bonaparte—and soon Junot himself—not to expect any resistance on the part of the Portuguese, who, at first sight, didn't seem to warrant the presence of a top-of-the-line general. Junot, despite his limitations, seemed able to handle the errand. In 1808, weeks after occupying Lisbon, he wrote in his diary: "This people is easily managed. I am better obeyed here, and more expeditiously, than ever the Prince Regent was."[4]

But he was terribly mistaken. As the following years showed, despite their poverty and meager resources, the Portuguese and Spanish mounted an obstinate resistance that proved fatal to the destinies of Junot and even Bonaparte himself. Of the 29,000 soldiers who invaded Portugal, only 22,000 would return home.[5] The other 7,000—nearly a quarter of the total—died on forced marches, in battle, or during ambushes led by the Portuguese.[6] As a result of his failure in the Iberian peninsula, Junot was court-martialed. Although Bonaparte ultimately pardoned him, Junot's career was ruined. In 1813, the general jumped to his death from a window in Paris during a bout of insanity.

Countless acts of resistance took place in Portugal. The venerable University of Coimbra, a citadel of knowledge and training of the Portuguese elite, became a military arsenal. The chemistry lab turned into a gunpowder factory. A metallurgy professor oversaw the manufacture of bullets, cartridges, and other weaponry. On June 24, 1808, forty students leading two thousand countrymen surrounded a French garrison tasked with monitoring the Santa Catarina fort in the city of Figueira de Foz. Caught by surprise and without sufficient provisions to hold out long enough to await reinforcements, the soldiers surrendered three days later, brought as prisoners in triumph to the university campus.[7]

The French reacted with severe repression. Organized in various cities and villages, firing squads attempted to eliminate the rebels. General Loison's troops massacred the inhabitants of the historic city of Evora in the Alentejo region after they futilely tried to resist his military advances. French troops mercilessly hunted men, women, children, and the elderly in blood-soaked streets that in some cases witnessed the deaths of more than two thousand people in a single afternoon. General Loison's cruelty branded him odiously into Portuguese history, a feeling that still lingers there today. Injured in battle, Loison had part of one arm amputated and thus became known as "One-Arm." In 1808, entering Porto to demand its surrender, General Maximilien Foy was nearly lynched by the populace, who mistook him for One-Arm. Foy saved his own skin by lifting up both arms to the crowd—though he was still arrested. Released a few weeks later, General Foy later became one of the main historians of Napoleon's campaigns in Portugal and Spain.

Of the 110,000 soldiers who participated in the Peninsular War under Bonaparte, only 34,000 belonged to the regular French army. The other 76,000 were badly trained recruits or foreign legionnaires, a reserve force that the emperor maintained in the French countryside while employing his best soldiers in the memorable campaigns against the Austrians, Prussians, and Russians.[8] The catastrophic results that took place in Iberia changed the course of history after more than a decade of uninterrupted victories in Europe. They demonstrated that the French armies were not invincible and gave redoubled spirit to the Corsican's enemies.

"On the Iberian Peninsula, the Emperor embarked on a venture that ultimately proved to be a major cause of his downfall," wrote David Gates, author of *The Spanish Ulcer: A History of the Peninsular War.* "It was evidence of his greed and ambition and his failure to correctly grasp the situation." In

Portugal and Spain, the French emperor saw the rise of the man who decisively defeated him on the battlefields of Waterloo in 1815. Born in Dublin, Sir Arthur Wellesley, future duke of Wellington, then thirty-nine years old, took charge of organizing the defense of Portugal after the royal family had departed for Brazil. A master of planning marches and troop supply, he rarely took the offensive in battles—in contrast to Napoleon. Wellesley preferred a cautious, studied defense systematically prepared and detailed. He had in his favor another decisive factor: the extraordinary capacity of British industry to supply arms and other vital equipment for the troops on the battlefield. Riding the wave of the first Industrial Revolution, British factories had reached a height of production in 1808, English gunpowder was considered the best in the world, and their rifles incomparable.[9]

The Peninsular War consisted of two great campaigns. The first began in October 1807, when Napoleon pressured the Spanish government to support the 25,000 soldiers who had crossed the Pyrenees under General Junot's command, ready to attack small and insolent Portugal. Spain cooperated, but the march proved difficult and cost the French heavily. Junot arrived in Lisbon on December 1, 1807, two days after the royal family set sail for Brazil. Some four hundred miles from the French border with no steady line of communication and supplies, Junot had marched too far away from France to ensure the safety and survival of his troops.

In the meantime, Bonaparte betrayed the subservient Spanish monarchy. At the beginning of 1808, a second line of French forces, under the command of General Murat, invaded Spain. In a few weeks, Murat occupied every fort in the north and center of the country and, leading 82,000 men, entered Madrid on March 14. Foreseeing this maneuver, King Carlos IV attempted a final, desperate measure: Taking a page from Prince João's book, he ordered his minister Manuel de Godoy to prepare ships in order to transport the Spanish royal family to the Americas. They didn't make it, however. Surprised in Seville by French troops before embarking, the king and his heir, Prince Fernando, unwillingly abdicated in favor of Joseph Bonaparte—Napoleon's brother and king of Naples at the time—who reigned as José I.

In the beginning, the Spanish resisted minimally, but the deposing of their king and the brutality of the French forces in Spain created hugely unpopular sentiment, which exploded in the May revolt in Madrid that was so brutally repressed, as seen in Goya's painting. In the interior of the country, the people resisted more fiercely. On July 20, in the city of Bailén, 20,000 French troops were surrounded and forced to surrender. The seemingly impossible news of this defeat sent a shockwave through Europe. In Portugal, the resistance, organized by the English, also surfaced much more strongly than imagined. On August 1, 1808, an army of 15,000 English soldiers commanded by General Wellesley disembarked on the Portuguese coast and three weeks later defeated Junot in the city of Vimeiro.

The second phase of the Peninsular War involved the personal intervention of Napoleon, who sent his best generals to the front lines of resistance in Spain and Portugal. In December 1808, the emperor himself entered Madrid, commanding a monumental army of 305,000 men. His triumph proved short-lived. Shortly thereafter, concerned with news of conspiracies in Paris and the reorganization of Austrian forces, he returned to France— just as the momentum leading to his definitive fall began to swell in Spain. His defeat in the first phase of the Peninsular War landed a blow to the confidence of the French troops and reinforced the courage of the Spanish and Portuguese. Moreover, it gave the English time to get a foot in the door and reorganize the dismantled Spanish and Portuguese armies. Under the command of General William Carr Beresford between 1809 and 1812, the Portuguese army, consisting of some 40,000 soldiers, became more professional and more dangerous for the French.

In May 1809, while Napoleon was trying to defeat the Austrians once more in the Battle of Wagram, Sir Arthur Wellesley, who had retired to England at the end of the first phase of the Peninsular War, returned to Portugal with a reinforced army. In the four years that followed, he expelled the French from the continent using a combination of guerrilla tactics, conventional battles, and ingenious bids. In October 1809, British engineers and Portuguese laborers began constructing one of the great wonders of modern military history: the Lines of Torres Vedras, a sequence of one hundred fortifications built in strategic positions, beginning at the edge of the Tagus River and extending to the Atlantic Ocean, forming a ring of thirty miles around Lisbon.

The towers, which served simultaneously as lookouts and as defense posts in case of attack, proved impassable. In July 1810, André Masséna, one of Napoleon's most experienced generals, tried to cross them with a force of 70,000 men and 126 cannons. He failed. Forced to retreat, Masséna opened the way for Lord Wellington to proceed all the way to the French border. In the meantime, Napoleon had lost 250,000 soldiers in his infamous attempt to invade Russia. Bonaparte's final defeat at Waterloo was only a matter of time.

The Republic of Pernambuco

I n May 1817, a mysterious individual was roaming the streets, battered by the brisk spring winds of Philadelphia. Antonio Gonçalves Cruz—a merchant known as Cabugá and the secret agent of a conspiracy brewing in the province of Pernambuco in Northeast Brazil—carried $800,000 in his luggage, a staggering amount now and even more so then. In today's currency, that would have amounted to $12 million.[1] Cabugá arrived in America with three missions. He was to purchase arms to fight King João VI's troops; he was to convince the American government to support the creation of an independent republic in the Northeast of Brazil; and, third and most spectacular of his objectives, he was to recruit old French revolutionaries exiled in America so that with their help he could liberate Napoleon Bonaparte, imprisoned by the English on Saint Helena in the South Atlantic after his defeat in the Battle of Waterloo. According to Cabugá's plan, Napoleon would travel from the island in the still of the night to Recife, capital of Pernambuco, where he would command the Pernambucan revolution, after which he would return to Paris and reassume the throne as emperor of France.[2]

Cruz Cabugá today names one of the main thoroughfares running through the neighborhood of Santo Amaro in Recife. Every day, thousands drive along it in a rush, on their way to the city of Olinda or downtown Recife, most with no idea about the source of the road's name. In 1817, Cabugá had spectacular plans, but they were doomed to failure before he even began implementing them. By the time he arrived in America with funds collected from the masters of sugarcane plantations, cotton producers, and merchants favorable to a republic, troops loyal to the Portuguese crown had already besieged the Pernambucan rebels. Surrender was inevitable. Unaware of this turn of events, however, Cabugá successfully recruited four veterans of Bonaparte's armies: Count Pontelécoulant, Colonel Latapie, an orderly named Artong, and a soldier named Roulet. They arrived in Brazil long after the suppression of the uprising, and all were arrested even before disembarking.[3]

Even in defeat, the Pernambucan revolt bore a high cost for the plans of the Portuguese court in Brazil. While the rebels held onto power for less than three months, they struck a blow to the confidence behind João's dream of building an American empire. They also accelerated the process of Brazilian independence. "Although the crisis of 1817 produced no immediate visible consequences in Brazil or Portugal, it had in reality shaken the existing system to its foundations," writes historian Roderick Barman.[4] "The structure of authority had collapsed under assault, and the elements in society most identified with the Crown had actively collaborated with the rebel regime." For this reason, according to Barman, the crown never again felt sure that its subjects could resist contamination by the ideas responsible for the subversion of the old order in Europe. Brazilian historian Manuel de Oliveira Lima considered the 1817 rebellion as "the first genuinely republican movement in Brazil" and also "the most spontaneous, the least disorganized, and the most congenial of our numerous revolutions."[5]

At the beginning of the nineteenth century, Olinda and Recife, the two largest cities in Pernambuco, together had 40,000 inhabitants. This was a large population, considering that Rio de Janeiro, capital of the colony, had 60,000. Recife, which had one of the busiest ports in Brazil, directed the outward flow of sugar from the hundreds of cane mills of the Zona da Mata, a humid strip on the Northeastern coast running from Bahia up to Rio Grande do Norte. After sugar, the second most exported product was cotton.

Aside from their political and economic importance, the Pernambucans earned a measure of fame for their freedom struggles. First and most importantly, they expelled the Dutch in 1654. Half a century later, during the Mascate War, a conflict between rival traders, the possibility of proclaiming the independence of Olinda arose.[6] "Pernambuco was the captaincy where the most pronounced and deep-rooted rivalries lay between colonists born in Brazil and colonists born in Portugal," wrote historian Francisco Adolfo Varnhagen.[7]

While rebellion broke into the open in Pernambuco, it reflected the discontent of all of the provinces with the rise in taxes to finance the expenses of the Portuguese court in Rio. A sentiment of dissatisfaction hung in the air, especially in the provinces of the North and Northeast affected by the fiscal voracity of King João VI. "A tax is paid at Pernambuco for lighting the streets of the Rio de Janeiro, whilst those of Recife remain in total darkness," wrote Englishman Henry Koster, who lived in Recife at the time of the rebellion. Koster also counted the salaries of many public servants as too low, barely sustaining their families. "Consequently, peculation, bribery, and other crimes of the same description . . . become so frequent as to escape all punishment or even notice."[8]

"The people of Recife, and its immediate neighborhood, had imbibed some of the notions of democratical government from their former masters, the Dutch," wrote Maria Graham, another foreign visitor, who visited Pernambuco in 1821.

> *They remembered, besides, that their own exertions, without any assistance from the government, had driven out those masters, and had restored to the crown the northern part of its richest domain. They were, therefore, disposed to be particularly jealous of the provinces of the south, especially of Rio, which they considered as more favored than themselves, and they were disgusted at the payments of taxes and contributions, by which they never profited, and which only served to enrich the creatures of the court, while great abuses existed.[9]*

Aside from the rise in taxes, Pernambuco in particular had a difficult time with the conjunction of three other factors that profoundly affected its economy. First, sugar production increased dramatically worldwide during the eighteenth century. This spike in supply caused a global fall in the price of Pernambuco's principal export. At the same time, the growing pressure of abolitionists in Europe created gradual restrictions on slave traffic, making the cost of labor increasingly more expensive. Slavery fueled the engine of the entire Pernambucan agricultural economy at this time. Last, contributing greatly to aggravating the situation, a devastating drought hit the northeastern backlands in 1816.[10]

The economic crisis and the discontent with the Portuguese administration provided fertile ground for liberal French and American ideas. A prosperous merchant and avid reader of works of French philosophy, Cruz Cabugá became an activist for liberal and republican ideals. Sent to America in the earliest days of the Pernambuco revolt, he returned practically empty-handed. He did meet with Secretary of State Richard Rush, from whom he solicited the dispatch of troops and arms for the revolution.[11] He managed only to secure a commitment that the United States would authorize the entry of Pernambucan ships in American waters during the rebellion, even against the will of King João VI. They also agreed to give asylum or shelter to refugees in case the movement failed.

The first great republic of the modern age, America at this time still wanted to sign commercial agreements with Portugal and Britain, the latter newly its ally after the War of 1812. As a result, Americans didn't want to involve themselves with the republican cause in Brazil so as not to displease either crown. America repeated this same behavior seven years later, refusing to help the rebels in the Confederation of the Equator, a movement led by a Carmelite friar known as Brother Mug.[12] "We are not in search of proselytes to republicanism," observed Henry Brackenridge—rather ironically considering future history—who between 1817 and 1818 served in Brazil as a special envoy of the American government. "It is enough for us to know that our own institutions are the best."[13]

The rebels occupied Recife on March 6, 1817. In the artillery regiment situated in the neighborhood of Santo Antonio, one of the leaders of the conspiracy, Captain José de Barros Lima, known as the Crowned Lion, resisted arrest and killed Commander Barbosa de Castro with a sword. Thereafter, in the company of other rebel soldiers, he took over the barracks and dug trenches around it to impede the advance of any troops loyal to the monarchy. The governor, Caetano Pinto de Miranda Montenegro—a weak figure disinclined to work—took refuge in the Brum Fort at the port. Once surrounded, he surrendered.[14]

With the imprisonment of de Miranda Montenegro, the rebels established a provisional government, seized the treasury, and proclaimed a republic. After three weeks, on March 29, they announced the convocation of a constituent assembly, formed by elected representatives from every district of the province. A new "organic law" established the separation between executive, legislative, and judicial powers. Catholicism continued as the official religion, but the new republic would tolerate other Christian denominations. Finally, they proclaimed freedom of the press, a great novelty in Brazil, where ideas, the publication of books, and the right to free opinion hadn't circulated freely for three centuries. Slavery also continued so as not to affect the interests of the masters of the sugarcane mills who supported the movement. The republic abolished duties on commerce and raised soldiers' pay. Those who had participated in the rebellion received lightning promotions. Domingos Teotonio, one of the chiefs of the new junta, promoted himself from captain to colonel.[15]

They designed a new flag that, on its upper half, had a rainbow with a star above it and the sun below it, representing the union of all Pernambucans. In the lower half, a red cross on a white background symbolized faith in justice and understanding. Although the revolution failed, Governor Manoel Pereira Borba officially adopted it as the flag of the state in 1917.

Aside from these republican measures, the revolutionary council made a few other equally colorful decisions. They abolished all pronouns indicating hierarchy or authority of one person over another, such as the commonly used "your excellence" or "your lordship," the word "patriot" replacing "lord."[16] Historian Tobias Monteiro recounts that the chief rebel Domingos José Martins and his wife invited Pernambucan women to cut their hair, considered a "vain ornament," as a symbol of adhesion to the republic. As a result, any women with long hair in Recife or Olinda fell under suspicion.[17] Measures like these revealed the lingering influence of the French Revolution, under the impetus of which, aside from adopting a new system of weights and measures, the names of the months changed under the short-lived French Republican Calendar.

The new republican government remained in power until May 20. During this period, all attempts to obtain support from neighboring provinces failed. In Bahia, the envoy of the revolution, José Inacio Ribeiro de Abreu e Lima, known as Padre Roma, was arrested upon disembarking his ship and immediately shot by order of the governor, the count of Arcos. In Rio Grande do Norte, the movement gained the support of André de Albuquerque Maranhão, proprietor of a large sugarcane mill. After arresting the governor, José Inacio Borges, and sending him by escort to Recife, de Albuquerque Maranhão occupied the village of Natal and formed a junta government, though it stirred absolutely no public interest. He fell from power in a few days.

In England, the revolutionaries tried to obtain the support of the journalist Hipólito José da Costa, founder of the *Correio Braziliense,* offering him the role of minister plenipotentiary of the new republic. Da Costa refused.[18] As we have seen, the Portuguese court had signed an agreement with the owner of the *Correio* in 1812, unbeknownst to the Pernambucans, that provided for the purchase of a specified number of copies of the newspaper and a stipend for da Costa himself in exchange for moderation in criticism of the monarchy. In an official dispatch from London, the Portuguese ambassador, Domingos de Sousa Coutinho, evaluated the results of this agreement: "I have restrained him here, in part with the promise of the subscription that he requested. I know of no other way to keep him quiet."[19] Historian de Oliveira Lima, evaluating this secret relation, relates da Costa, "if not downright venal, was certainly not incorruptible, as he began to moderate the barbs of his discourse in exchange for distinctions, considerations, and official sponsorship."[20]

The Portuguese reaction to the rebellion came down fast and hard. From Bahia, troops sent by the count of Arcos advanced through the Pernambucan backlands, while a naval force dispatched from Rio de Janeiro blocked the port of Recife. In a few days, a total of eight thousand men surrounded the rebel province. In the backlands, the decisive battle took place in the region of Ipojuca, today the municipality that hosts the famous Porto de Galinhas beach resort. Defeated, the revolutionaries retreated toward Recife, Brother Mug, future leader of the Confederation of the Equator, among them.

On May 19, two months after the start of the rebellion, Portuguese troops entered Recife. They found the city abandoned and defenseless. The isolated provisional government surrendered the next day. The repression, as always, was ruthless. The sentence against the rebels ordered that "after killing them . . . their hands shall be cut off, their heads decapitated and staked atop posts . . . and the rest of their cadavers tied to horses and dragged to the cemetery."[21] As an additional punishment, the captaincy of Pernambuco lost the district of Alagoas, the rural landowners of which had remained loyal to the crown. As a reward, they became an autonomous province.[22]

The events in Pernambuco caused great apprehension in Rio de Janeiro and forced King João to change the timetable of some of the more grandiose acts he had planned for his Brazilian stay. One was his own official consecration as king of the united kingdom of Portugal, Brazil, and the Algarves. In the original plans, the coronation was to occur after one year of mourning for Queen Maria I, who died in March 1816. After the Pernambucan revolt, King João VI decided to postpone the ceremony for another year. He didn't want to display to the world an image of a king being crowned amid a power struggle. For the same reason, he considered postponing the wedding of his son Pedro. This step didn't occur only because, by the time the news of the Pernambucan agitation had reached Europe, Princess Leopoldina had already married the heir to the throne by proxy and set sail for Brazil.

With the rebellion choked, it was time to celebrate. On February 6, 1818, a royal decree ended investigations into the rebellion. Four revolutionary leaders had been executed, but the rest received amnesty in a gesture of magnanimity by the new sovereign. Among those pardoned by the king was Cabugá, the agent of the revolutionaries in the United States. Thereafter began the most glorious and festive stage of the thirteen years during which the Portuguese court lived in Brazil. Two full years of celebrations, pomp, and displays of power followed, the likes of which Rio de Janeiro had never seen before.

XXIV

Tropical Versailles

1818 saw the pinnacle of King João VI's stay in Brazil. Despite financial difficulties, the kingdom was at peace, the monarchy enjoyed good health, Carlota Joaquina's conspiracies had been defeated, the colony was prospering, and in Europe the threat of Napoleon had become a distant memory. Defeated by Lord Wellington in the Battle of Waterloo in 1815, the French emperor had been imprisoned for three years on Saint Helena, a remote volcanic island in the south Atlantic. Despite being impoverished, the Portuguese court celebrated and enjoyed the amenable and tranquil climate of Rio de Janeiro. Dom João's dream, to reconstruct his empire in the tropics, finally seemed to have a chance.[1] It was an illusion, however. Within two years, unexpected events on both sides of the Atlantic obliged him to change his plans and resume the role that destiny had chosen for him—that of a king forced always to act on the defensive, pressured by events beyond his control.

The brief period of festivities of the Portuguese court in Brazil began in 1817, the year of the arrival of Princess Leopoldina from Austria, and proceeded with the acclamation, coronation, and birthday of King João VI the following year. The death of Queen Maria I, at eighty-two years old, changed little. João had already ruled Portuguese dominions for more than two decades, ever since his mother had been deemed incapable of governing. Nonetheless, he made it a point to ascend to the throne officially, with much pomp and circumstance. Beforehand, he had to quell the Pernambucan revolution and marry off three children, including his firstborn and the heir to the throne, Dom Pedro. The coronation took place on February 6, 1818, making it the first and only acclamation of a European sovereign in the Americas. "From the arrival of Dona Leopoldina up until the birthday of D. João, the court in Rio de Janeiro was, so to speak, a nonstop party," according to Jurandir Malerba. "During these grandiose days of the monarchy, Rio became the amphitheater where the royal family represented with splendor the highest moments of their voyage to Brazil."[2]

The form with which these rituals took place clearly demonstrates that King João VI wasn't concerned with the opinion of his Brazilian subjects. He wanted to impress his counterparts in Europe. Outcast from his own capital, Lisbon, and exiled to distant territory, exploited and oppressed by more powerful neighbors, and submitted to humiliation by fleeing in haste, the king nonetheless tried to maintain his poise. It was no accident, then, that the largest demonstration of pomp and richness of the Portuguese court in Brazil occurred in Vienna, more than six thousand miles away. In the Austrian capital, countless ceremonies took place between February and June 1817 to mark the proxy wedding between Princess Leopoldina and the future Emperor Pedro I.

The Portuguese ambassador, the marquis of Marialva, in charge of negotiating the wedding and signing the papers in the name of the king, starred in one of the most grandiose and expensive spectacles that the Austro-Hungarian empire had ever seen. As Malerba describes it,

> On February 17th 1817, Marialva entered Vienna with a retinue of
> 41 carriages [each] pulled by six horses, accompanied by servants on
> both sides, dressed in rich liveries. The entourage was composed of 77
> people, including pages, servants, and officials, on horse and on foot.
> They followed the imperial coaches, flanked by their footmen and fur-
> ther escorted by servicemen following behind. At the rear of the pageant
> were the carriages of the ambassadors of England, France, and Spain.
> On June 1st, there was a ball for 2,000 people in salons specially con-
> structed in the gardens of Augarten park. The Imperial Austrian family

was present, as were the diplomatic corps and the entire nobility. The ball began at 8 o'clock. At 11 o'clock, supper was served, with forty pieces of cutlery at each plate. The Emperor and family ate from serving sets made of gold and the other guests all had serving sets of silver. The cost was 1 million florins, or 1.5 million francs.[3]

Adjusting for inflation in the last two hundred years, this would be the equivalent today of $11 million, a staggering amount that represents approximately $5,400 per person.[4]

Aside from sponsoring a monumental feast, Marialva brought presents to distribute in the Austrian court: 167 diamonds worth a total of $10,532 at the time, 17 gold bars worth $1,700, and decorations studded with precious jewels and stones worth $8,800. The prince of Metternich, who signed the agreement and gave the bride away to the ambassador, received a total of $5,500 in presents, including a medallion, a box engraved with the likeness of King João VI, the Great Cross of Christ, and a diamond-encrusted plaque. The priest who officiated the wedding ceremony received a breastplate cross of precious stones worth $1,800.[5]

This exhibition of luxury in Vienna contrasted sharply with the difficulties that the royalty in Brazil were experiencing. In Rio de Janeiro, feasts and balls also took place, but the king became progressively indebted and depended on issuing new currency through the Bank of Brazil and through the list of volunteer donations from the wealthy in exchange for favors, privileges, and titles. On a daily basis, the court had nothing of delicacy or refinement, as the reports of diplomats and travelers who saw them in person can attest. The old seat of the monarchy, in the center of the city, became the Imperial Palace, modest compared with a royal residence. "It is a vast and irregular edifice, of the worst type of architecture," evaluated painter Johann Moritz Rugendas.[6] "A mansion with no architectural merit," confirmed Ernst Ebel.[7] Luccock found the palace of Quinta da Boa Vista, a gift from the slave trafficker Elias Antonio Lopes, "small and formal, ill-contrived and wretchedly furnished."[8]

The poverty of architectural style reflected in the habits of the court. Jacques Arago, a French chronicler on the corvette *Uranie*, commanded by

Captain Louis Claude de Fraycinet, made two stopovers in Rio de Janeiro between 1817 and 1820 and recorded a terrible impression of Queen Carlota Joaquina in a reception at the Palace of São Cristovão. "She dressed like a gypsy, wearing a kind of nightgown pinned with lapels," he wrote. "Her hair unkempt in a rage, a stranger to any comb, attested to the absence of a hairdresser in the palace, or any diligent chamberlain."[9] The German ambassador, count von Flemming, confirmed this impression in a diplomatic report in 1817:

> *With the exception of the half-asian court of Constantinople, there is probably no other as strange as this one. Despite having been established in America not long ago, it may be considered totally alien to European habits, and completely exotic. No other court has so many servants, wardrobe attendants, assistants, domestic staff, and coachmen. This tendency towards orientalism in no way corresponds to luxury.*[10]

The celebrations of 1817, initiated in Vienna, continued with the arrival of Princess Leopoldina in Rio de Janeiro. The superintendent-general of police, Paulo Fernandes Viana, organized the preparations. The beaches, ordinarily an open-air sewage depository, were sanitized. The streets were swept and washed, covered with a fine layer of white sand, and topped with aromatic flowers. Lace and damask quilts decorated the windows of mansions. In the streets to be traversed by the court three triumphal arches, designed by the French Artistic Mission, were constructed. For three nights in a row the city burned brightly.[11]

Princess Leopoldina arrived on November 5, 1817. On descending from her ship, she unexpectedly kneeled before her mother-in-law, Queen Carlota Joaquina, hugging her feet and kissing her hands. Then she repeated the same gestures with the king. Next she hugged and kissed her brothers-in-law and sisters-in-law. After this exchange of greetings and courtesies, she returned to her ship and remained until two in the afternoon the next day, when the official disembarking began.

Arm in arm with her new husband, Leopoldina descended to the docks accompanied by the entire royal family. She wore a cloak of white silk, embroidered with gold and silver. A thin veil covered her face. The instant she stepped on solid ground, cannon volleys rang out from the surrounding forts and ships anchored in port. The bells of every church in town chimed in unison. Jubilantly applauded by the crowds gathered in the streets, the retinue proceeded toward the Royal Chapel, on the Rua Direita, near the Royal Palace. Nearly one hundred carriages paraded along, accompanied by formally dressed servants. A coach bore the king, queen, prince, and princess. "Behind one of the triumphal arches, one could see the carriage, yoked with eight horses decorated with white plumes and saddled with gold-embroidered velvet," noted painter Jean-Baptiste Debret.[12] After a ceremony of thanksgiving and a gala dinner, the couple greeted the public from the window of the palace. At eleven o'clock that night, everyone returned to the Palace of São Cristóvão, where Pedro and Leopoldina spent the first night of their honeymoon.

For the coronation of the king, the painters, sculptors, and architects of the French Artistic Mission went even further in their preparations. The timid Palace Square suddenly turned into an imperial plaza with allegories to the greatest civilizations that humanity had witnessed in the preceding two millennia. In a reference to the Roman Empire, Grandjean de Montigny constructed at the edge of the docks a reproduction of the Temple of Minerva, goddess of war. Earlier, Jean-Baptiste Debret designed a copy of the Arc de Triomphe—the monument that Bonaparte ordered to celebrate his military victories—to be placed alongside the square's fountain. But this copy of the triumphal arch had a double meaning. In 1810, as the French arch was being built, Napoleon had a full-size wooden replica of it built on the spot and proceeded through it with his second wife, Archduchess Maria Luisa of Austria—Princess Leopoldina's sister. In the center of the square stood an Egyptian obelisk designed by Auguste Taunay. "It created an agreeable sensation of simultaneously viewing these Greek, Roman, and Egyptian monuments, not only due to the beautiful illumination with which they decorated it, but also by the good taste of its architecture, which could only be appreciated and understood by intelligent people," wrote Father Luis Gonçalves dos Santos (Father Tree Frog).[13]

Henry Brackenridge arrived right in the middle of these great court celebrations. When the frigate *Congress* arrived in Guanabara Bay in January

1818, Princess Leopoldina had already disembarked, and the preparations for the king's coronation for February 6 were moving ahead. On descending from the ship, Breckenridge found all the streets decorated for the event: "Rows of columns formed of boards covered with canvas, painted to resemble marble, an obelisk, triumphal arches of the same, and a Grecian temple supported on pillars of like durable materials, were the most conspicuous among the preparations for the important event." Brackenridge also observed that some of these monuments, erected for the princess's arrival and to be used also for the king's coronation, were already dissolving under the force of the rain and wind. "I saw part of a splendid entablature literally in rags," he noted.[14]

These artificial monuments proved short-lived. This imitation of marble, bronze, and granite mirrored the precarious and illusory character of a weakened and exiled European monarchy celebrating in the tropics, thousands of miles from home. "The secret was to act on two fronts," observed historian Lília Schwarcz in *The Long Voyage of the King's Library.* "On one side, the event was decorated with monuments as fragile as the political moment itself. One the other, classical allegories and references to the past conferred on the celebration the tradition that they lacked and the history that they needed."[15]

On Coronation Day, King João VI wore a scarlet velvet cloak covered with gold embroidery. As he had when he arrived in 1808, he promenaded from the palace to the Royal Chapel accompanied by the members of the nobility and foreign ambassadors. After the oath, he donned the imperial crown and wielded the scepter for the first time. The princes extended their hands over the prayer book and promised him obedience. Lively crowds concentrated in front of the Royal Palace followed the ceremony, along with cannon fire and the uninterrupted chimes of churchbells. Popular festivals, bull runs, military parades, musical spectacles, and dances dominated the city for the entire week.

Brackenridge, who observed all from the docks in front of the Royal Palace, recounts an amusing episode involving the commander of his ship. At dawn on Coronation Day, he tells us, all the forts and ships began firing their cannons in homage to the king, the ships decked with various

Surrounded by numerous attendants, João drives his own carriage through the outskirts of Rio de Janeiro, a scene of serene and tranquil life in the tropics. The king distributed more titles of nobility in Brazil than had been done in three centuries in Portugal.

D. João VI, king of Portugal and Brazil, and his attendants at Rio de Janeiro from History of Brazil; comprising its geography, commerce, colonization, aboriginal inhabitants by James Henderson, London, 1821, Lucia M. Loeb/ Bibioteca Guita e José Mindlin

flags of the nations of the world. As a mark of respect, the American frigate joined the celebrations and fired its cannons as well—until the commander noticed that none of the other ships was flying the American colors. On discovering this glaring absence, the captain ordered his crew to halt their firing and to limit themselves to observing the festivities, without taking part in them.[16]

Aside from these moments of celebration, King João VI lived a placid, tranquil life in Rio de Janeiro. He woke at 6 a.m., dressed with the help of his chamberlain, Matias Antonio Lobato, and went to pray at oratory. He ate chicken with toast during his morning audiences, during which he received the most obsequious and intimate fidalgos of the court. His most frequent interlocutor was Viana, the superintendent-general of the police, whom he received three times a day to discuss urban improvements and security issues in Rio de Janeiro. He took his main meals together with his children. At dessert, a small hand-washing ceremony took place: Pedro, the eldest son, held a silver basin, while the youngest, Miguel, poured water for the king to wash the grease from his hands. After lunch, the king slept for one or two hours and then in the late afternoon went for a ride, sometimes driving a small mule-drawn carriage on his own.[17]

Historian Tobias Monteiro adds a picturesque detail to these rides. In front of the retinue went a cavalry boy, called the "broadener"—perhaps because he opened space for the king to pass or perhaps because he wore enormous sleeves. This vassal rode along with two saddlebags at his sides. In one were the king's snacks; in the other a chamber pot and a three-piece structure that functioned as a portable toilet bowl, to be used in the open country. During the ride, the king would murmur a certain order, and the boy descended from his mule and set up the equipment.

> *Then the King descended from his carriage and the chamberlain would approach him, and unbutton and lower his trousers. Right in front of the officials and others in the retinue, including his favorite daughter Princess Maria Teresa, if present, he would beatifically sit down, as if no-one was around. Having taken care of his need, a particular servant came to clean him and the chamberlain arrived again, to help him get dressed.*[18]

Having completed this ritual, the king continued the excursion until snack time arrived. Aside from the food stored in the saddlebags of the cavalry boy, João also carried an extra supply of roast, boneless chickens in the grubby pouch of his jacket, nibbling at them while contemplating the scenery or stopping to chat with people who saluted him along the road. At night, he received his subjects for the hand-kissing ceremony before going to bed at 11 p.m.[19]

Monteiro offers more curious information about the private matters of the king. He recounts that João's quarters in the São Cristóvão Palace opened onto a veranda. João VI slept alone in one of these rooms. In an adjacent hall, which led to the interior of the building, he received visits and dispatched ministers and government officials. This meeting hall was the only means of access to the king's room, so palace servants also had to pass through it when they needed to empty the royal chamber pots in the morning. Depending on the timing, this task sometimes took place while the monarch was receiving guests. To avoid embarrassment, these chamber pots were covered with a wooden lid framed with a fringe of crimson velvet. "But the seal was imperfect, and let volatile elements escape, betraying the contents," Monteiro recounts indiscreetly.[20]

Indeed not everything smelled of roses in the court of Rio de Janeiro, but imperfectly sealed chamber pots weren't the greatest of their problems by far.

PART THREE
THE RETURN OF THE MONARCH

XXV

Portugal Abandoned

I f you can contain the reality of an entire nation in a work of art, the Portuguese Empire in 1820 would fit perfectly into a painting found in London's National Portrait Gallery. William Carr Beresford, an Irishman by birth and a general in the British Army, governed Portugal on behalf of the Portuguese while the court remained in Brazil. A portrait in oil by Sir William Beechey depicts a severe man who inspires both fear and respect. Tall, corpulent, and bald, with tufts of hair rising above his ears, Beresford sports a dark jacket covered in decorations with a high collar. The left side of his face reveals a sinister and enigmatic detail. Blinded by a musket shot years earlier, his left eye appears languid, deflated, and lifeless, forming a startling contrast with his right and giving him the appearance of having two simultaneous and antagonistic personalities. His left side is inert, inexpressive, moribund; his right is agile, vivacious, scanning the horizon for what the future holds.

The same dichotomy held for Portugal and its overseas dominions on the eve of João VI's return to Lisbon. On one side of the Atlantic, anchored in a land exhausted by war, lay a metropolis left amorphous, impoverished, and humiliated by the long absence of its king. On the other lay a former colony that, in the same period and for the same reason, had changed, prospered, and was contemplating the future with optimism and hope. They were irreconcilable realities. Within two years, Brazil became an independent nation. Portugal, by contrast, continued in a whirlpool of conspiracies and political revolts for much longer. The venerable colonial empire thereby ended its glory days with frayed nerves, paying a high price for the choices made in the tumultuous days of 1807 and 1808.

The thirteen years during which João VI lived in Brazil saw much hunger and immense suffering for the people of Portugal. On the morning of November 30, 1807, the day after the royal family fled, the sails of their fleet hadn't even disappeared over the horizon as panic overtook Lisbon. A small earthquake hit the city, interpreted by some as an omen—rightly, as it happened.[1] Knowing that the French would attack them first, farmers abandoned their properties and fled to the capital. There they and everyone else in the city scrambled like never before to purchase and hoard rations, locking themselves in at home. "Each, while he shed tears for the royal family, had first wept for his own fate," wrote General Foy, one of the French officials who participated in the invasion of Portugal. "Other reflections now took their place: the Prince no longer made common cause with his people; the nation was conquered without having been vanquished. Priests, nobles, soldiers, plebeians, all turned their thoughts sadly inwards; all began to think of their own safety."[2]

Before occupying Lisbon, General Junot futilely tried to pacify the Portuguese with a proclamation in which he promised to protect them and preserve their rights. "My army will enter your city," declared the French general.

I came to save your port and your prince from the malign influence of England. But your prince, while respectable for his virtues, let himself be dragged by treacherous advisors . . . to be handed over to his enemies. Residents of Lisbon, remain calm. You have nothing to fear from my army or me. The beloved, mighty Napoleon has sent me to protect you, and protect you, I shall.[3]

As you might imagine, that's not quite what happened. When Junot's exhausted and ill-equipped troops entered the capital, the streets stood deserted. On arriving at the docks, the men caught sight only of a solitary cargo ship. Cannon shots fired from the Tower of Belém forced the commander of the ship to return to port. Thereafter began the sack of the city. The crates and suitcases left behind on the docks during the haste of the departure were confiscated. Shops and homes were ransacked. The price of food skyrocketed. The currency devalued by 60 percent. Money changers closed up shop due to the lack of cash in circulation.[4]

Tricked by the court's flight to Brazil, Bonaparte imposed severe punishments on Portugal. First, he announced war reparations in the amount of 100 million francs, an astronomical figure, equivalent today to approximately $500 million, which the country, in its penurious situation, could never repay.[5] French troops confiscated the property of anyone who had left with the prince regent, including royal palaces and land. The silver of the church, forgotten in the haste of flight on the docks, was melted down. Part of the Portuguese army, totaling about 40,000 soldiers, amalgamated into the French forces and marched off to Germany, where many died in 1812 during Napoleon's failed attempt to invade Russia. The provisional government appointed by Prince João on the day of departure was dissolved and replaced with an administrative council subordinate to General Junot. Finally, as the French emperor had promised months before in *Le Moniteur*, the Bragança dynasty was declared extinct.[6]

In these days of fear and uncertainty, two diametrically opposed attitudes formed in Portugal. With privileges and property to safeguard, the nobility quickly adhered to the conquerors. The prince regent had barely left for Brazil when a large delegation of elite Portuguese traveled to Bayonne, France, to pay homage to Napoleon. The group included four marquises, a count, a viscount, the head inquisitor, and the bishop of Coimbra. This same delegation published a manifesto in Lisbon, in which they urged the Portuguese to accept the French dominion "under the magnanimous protection of a world hero, the arbiter of kings and people," such that the Portuguese nation could "one day form part of the great family of which His Majesty (Napoleon) was the beneficent father."[7] Satisfied with this development, Junot attended the opera the first night after the invasion and promised to respect all of the property and rights of the nobility—with the exception of those who had fled to Brazil of course.

But the common Portuguese people had everything to lose and nothing to gain from the French invasion. Without the option to flee as their prince had or the ability to curry meaningful favor, as the remaining elite did, the Portuguese ignored the proclamations of General Junot and the manifesto of the nobility and resisted the invaders. Trouble began on December 13, two weeks after the royal family's departure. General Junot had ordered the Portuguese flag lowered from São Jorge Castle, where it dominated the view of the city above the neighborhood of Alfama, and the French colors raised in its stead. That same day, Junot ordered six thousand soldiers to parade through Rossio Square to the beat of a military march. This demonstration of force, unexpected and unnecessary, provoked a popular insurrection, promptly suppressed by the general. In the following days, conflicts spread throughout the nation.[8] In the bishopric of Coimbra, the terrorized inhabitants fled to the mountains, where French soldiers followed and surrounded them. Some managed to save their hides in exchange for gold, jewels, or cash. The rest were shot dead on the spot. Nearly three thousand people were killed, and more than one thousand homes were burned.[9]

Between 1807 and 1814, Portugal lost half a million inhabitants. One sixth of the population perished of hunger, battle, or simply fled the country.[10] Never in its history had the country lost so much of its population in such a short period. In May 1808, the Portuguese ambassador in London, Domingos de Sousa Coutinho, wrote to Prince João in Rio de Janeiro that the number of Portuguese refugees in England was enormous. "Every walk of life has come, in numbers I don't even know how to convey," recounted the diplomat. "The majority of them are almost naked, in need of everything."[11] The Portuguese court was bankrupt, however, so de Sousa Coutinho had to ask the English government for financial assistance to shelter the refugees. In the meantime, the rich bribed Junot in exchange for permission to embark on ships leaving Lisbon.

"Portugal indeed was in a dismal state," wrote English historian Sir Charles Oman.

Her ports were blocked and her wines could not be sold to her old customers in England, nor her manufactures to her Brazilian colonists. The

working classes in Lisbon were thrown out of employment, and starved,
or migrated in bands into the interior. Foy and other good witnesses
from the French side speak of the capital as "looking like a desert, with
no vehicles, and hardly a foot-passenger in the streets, save 20,000 per-
sons reduced to beggary and trying vainly to live on alms."[12]

Thanks to the fierce resistance of the Portuguese and Spanish, Britain finally penetrated the Continental Blockade and initiated a series of victorious campaigns in the Peninsular War that set in motion the definitive fall of the French emperor at Waterloo. But in their conflict, the two great European powers—Britain and France—treated the Portuguese almost as sideline participants. A demonstration of this treatment occurred soon after the first great English victory over the French in Vimeiro, Portugal, on August 21, 1808. It was such a decisive battle that General Junot preferred surrender, leaving Portugal to British control. This agreement, known as the Convention of Cintra, after the city where it was negotiated, stipulated that the French withdraw immediately from the forts and military outputs and hand over all possessions, supplies, munitions, horses, and other means of transport taken from the Portuguese. In exchange, British forces would protect them on their return to France.

The possessions that the French had plundered weren't returning to their original owners, the victims of the invasion, but rather going to the new occupiers, the English. These goods included $60,000 worth of the Church's silver, already melted down and ready to be transported; $40,000 confiscated from the Portuguese treasury; and another $25,000 worth of merchandise stolen from public warehouses. The agreement caused a general revolt in Portugal, prompting the British parliament, who deemed it excessively unjust to the Portuguese, to revoke it in part.[13]

In the absence of the court, Portugal essentially became a British protectorate. Marshal Beresford, charged with commanding and restructuring the battered Portuguese army, took over the governing of the country de facto between 1809 and 1820—and he did so with an iron fist. In 1817, on discovering a military conspiracy that planned to overthrow him, the marshal reacted with alarming cruelty. The leader of the rebellion, General

Gomes Freire de Andrade, and another twelve rebels were hanged. Some of them, including Gomes Freire, were then decapitated, burned, and their ashes thrown into the sea.

Even though it was quelled, the rebellion served as a warning signal for those in the coming years. Gomes Freire had an extensive record of conspiracy attempts. In 1805, he participated in the failed coup d'état led by Princess Carlota against her husband. Now a pariah to the Portuguese army, he turned his allegiance to Bonaparte. In 1808, he actively collaborated with the French invaders. After Napoleon's defeat, he returned to Portugal imbued with liberal ideas. His shifting allegiances foretold not only the end of the English protectorate but also the end of absolute monarchy. Some of the more extreme revolutionaries even proposed the overthrow of the Bragança dynasty and the replacement of João VI with the duke of Cadaval.[14]

Signs of discontent appeared everywhere. Assessing the failed movement led by General Gomes Freire, Portuguese governors loyal to João VI alerted the king to the rising climate of dissatisfaction in Lisbon and the risk that he ran by staying in Brazil. "Our lord, abiding by our honor and obligation, we should not hide from Your Majesty the discontent of all of your loyal vassals that Your Majesty has stayed so long in the Kingdom of Brazil, after the extraordinary sacrifices they have carried out to ensure the salvation of the Monarchy," they wrote. "This discontent has now grown in the city, and will continue to increase in all the lands of the Kingdoms."[15]

This dissatisfaction resulted less from the humiliations that the country had suffered in the war than from the growing privileges that João VI guaranteed to the English and Brazilians after having transferred the court to Rio de Janeiro. From the perspective of the Portuguese, the situation was unsustainable. They bore the entire burden of the court transfer, while all the benefits went to Brazil and England. The opening of the Brazilian ports in 1808 and the special commercial treaty with the English in 1810 landed hard blows on Portuguese merchants, who nearly went bankrupt. The extraordinary duties imposed by the court to finance the struggle against Napoleon continued even after the end of the war, overburdening merchants and urban workers, especially in Lisbon and Porto.[16]

Harmed by British competition, Portugal's trade with Brazil plummeted. The exports to the colony, totalling 94 million cruzados between 1796 and 1807, fell to just 2 million in the following ten years. In the other direction, exports from Brazil to Portugal reduced by half, from 353 million cruzados to 189 million.[17] In 1810, 1,214 Portuguese ships entered the port of Rio de Janeiro. Ten years later, in 1820, no more than 212 entered, and of these only 57 came from Lisbon. The rest came from India, Africa, or other South American ports.[18] "The widespread hunger, the lack of basic foodstuffs, and the disorganization of wine and olive oil production amounted to paralysis in the ports, initially closed by Junot and afterwards debilitated and at a standstill due to the treaty of 1810," observed historian Maria Odila Leite da Silva Dias.[19]

We can find an example of Rio's favor by looking at this new system in the redistribution of gunpowder in the Portuguese Empire. Before the arrival of the court in Brazil, the sale of this product fell under the absolute monopoly of the ancient Royal Gunpowder Factory in Portugal. It supplied Lisbon and all of the colonies with no competitors. After 1808, the situation reversed. The new factory installed by João in Rio de Janeiro received the privilege of selling gunpowder to the most attractive and lucrative parts of the market, including Pernambuco, Bahia, São Paulo, Rio Grande do Sul, the ports off the coast of Africa, and the court itself. In the meantime, the old factory received the scraps of the marginal and secondary markets: the Azores, Madeira, Cape Verde, and the Brazilian provinces of Maranhão, Pará, and Ceará.[20]

The Portuguese eagerly consumed the hope that when the war ended the treaty would be revoked and the court would return to Lisbon. Neither eventuality happened. The terms of the treaty continued vigorously for much longer, and João VI simply didn't wish to return yet. Strictly speaking, after 1810 he had no real reason to stay in Brazil. By then, Britain had expelled the last French troops. From then on, the Peninsular War continued in Spain, where it lasted three more years. If he had wanted, the prince regent could have returned to Lisbon without a hitch just two years after he left. But João learned in those two years that, if the Portuguese Empire had a future, its chances of survival lay in Brazil more than in Portugal. He resisted pressure to return for as long as he could. In 1814, even the English government tried to bring him back, sending to Rio de Janeiro a fleet commanded by Admiral John Beresford, brother of the marshal governing Portugal, with the mission of transporting the royal family. The British government feared that if the court didn't return, the climate of dissatisfaction in Portugal would grow uncontrollable. History soon confirmed their fears.[21] The specter of revolution quashed in 1817 resurged in Porto three years later.

On the morning of August 24, 1820, rebel troops gathered in the Santo Ovidio fields of Porto and declared themselves against the English dominion. In the manifesto they distributed, they lamented the penurious situation in which the country found itself and the absence of the king: "As the height of this misfortune, our beloved Sovereign has abandoned living among us. People of Portugal! Since that fateful day, we can count the disgraces as our orphanage continues. We have lost everything!"[22] Three weeks later, on September 15, the revolt reached Lisbon, where various popular protests called for the end of absolute monarchy.[23] On the 27th, the Provisional Preparatory Board of the Cortes convened in Alcobaça with the task of drafting a new liberal constitution. The Cortes, a council of state, hadn't met since 1698. Their very convocation, after such a long absence on the Portuguese political scene, indicated how much the king's power was under threat. The rebels decided to spare the Bragança dynasty, but the return of the king to Portugal became a point of honor.

On October 10, Marshal Beresford, who had traveled to Rio de Janeiro to seek more resources and power from João VI to counter the rebellion, was blocked from disembarking in Lisbon and stripped of his functions. In his place, a new Board of Governors was formed, composed of representatives of the gentry, nobility, clerics, and military men, under the leadership of Sinédrio, a secret organization created in Porto on January 22, 1818, its ideas and expression fundamental to the success of the Liberal Revolution.[24]

Gathered in February 1821, the Cortes had an extensive docket of work to accomplish: freedom of the press, elaboration of a new civil and criminal code, ending the Inquisition, reducing the number of religious orders, granting amnesty to political prisoners, and installing a bank in Portugal, among other measures. The principal demand, however, was returning the king to Portugal. In Rio, the return of the monarch also became a campaign point of the so-called Portuguese Party, composed of highly privileged military men, public servants, and merchants interested in reestablishing the ancient colonial system.[25]

We can see the climate of resentment among the Portuguese in relation to Brazil in the pamphlet signed by Manuel Fernandes Tomas, one of the chief revolutionaries of 1820, in which he attacks the Brazilians with outright prejudice. Tomas defines Brazil as "a veritable giant, without arms or legs, speechless in its burning, unhealthy climate . . . reduced to a few hordes of blackies, caught off the coasts of Africa, the only ones able to withstand the scalding rays of this seething land." The pamphlet, which provoked indignation in Rio de Janeiro, asked of King João whether he should choose to reside "in the land of monkeys, blacks, and snakes, or in a nation of white people, of civilized people, who love their Sovereign." The pamphlet ended with "Let us turn our eyes away from that savage and uncouth country, towards this land of civilization, to Portugal!"[26]

Upon hearing the rebels' demands, which arrived in Rio de Janeiro on October 17, 1820, with the brig *Providence*, João VI faced an unsolvable dilemma, which questioned the very future of the Portuguese Empire. If he returned to Portugal, he could lose Brazil, which might follow the path of its neighboring Spanish colonies and declare independence. If, on the other hand, he remained in Rio de Janeiro, he could lose Portugal, where revolutionary winds produced by the resentment accumulated over a decade and a half could topple him from supremacy there. From the start, João VI considered sending his heir, Pedro, to Portugal, while he himself stayed in Brazil. It would satisfy the Cortes's demands and appease the revolutionaries. But Pedro didn't want to go for two reasons. First, he felt more at home in Brazil, where he had arrived when he was only ten years old, and where all of his friends and advisors lived. Second, Pedro's wife, Princess Leopoldina, was in the last weeks of her pregnancy and could give birth at sea, a highly risky situation in those days. Worse still, some of the ministers wanted Pedro to travel to Portugal alone, leaving his wife behind in Rio de Janeiro, a suggestion that the princess desperately fought for weeks. After many discussions, João VI surprised his ministers with the following utterance: "Well, then, if my son does not wish to go, I shall be the one."[27]

It was an unexpectedly courageous move for a king who had always shown himself to be insecure, fearful, and indecisive.

XXVI

The Return

A funereal entourage crossed the streets of Rio de Janeiro in silence. They were transporting the remains of Queen Maria I, who had died in 1816, and those of the infante D. Pedro Carlos—both nephew and son-in-law to the king and victim of tuberculosis in 1812—into the stifling chamber of a frigate anchored at port. On the night of April 24, 1821, João VI accompanied the procession by torchlight, behind two caskets, the first removed from the Convent of Ajuda, the other from the Convent of San Antonio. It was the final act of the Portuguese court in Brazil.

Two days later, the king departed from Rio de Janeiro against his will and without knowing what awaited him in Portugal. He left behind a vastly changed country that had welcomed him with such happiness thirteen years earlier. Its independence was already inevitable. A few hours before the grim ceremony of the night of April 24, João called his elder son and heir to the crown, then twenty-two years old, for a last recommendation: "Pedro, if Brazil separates, better that it happens under you, who will respect me, than under these adventurers."[1]

The tense weeks leading up to the departure churned with distress. The echoes of the Porto revolution had arrived in Brazil in mid-October of the preceding year, and it only took a few weeks for them to ignite the spirit of the Brazilians and Portuguese surrounding the court. On the morning of

November 26, a crowd gathered at Rocio Square, today Tiradentes Plaza, demanding the presence of the king in the center of Rio de Janeiro and the signing of the liberal constitution. On hearing the news, a few miles away, João, quite startled, ordered all the windows of São Cristovão Palace shut, just as he did on stormy nights.

"How should I treat the rebels?" he asked the count of Palmela, minister of foreign affairs and war.

"Unfortunately, sir," the count responded, "there is nothing to deliberate; it is necessary to meet all of their requests."[2]

Shortly thereafter arrived Prince Pedro, who spent the wee hours of the morning conversing with the rebels. He fetched the king as the mob had demanded, but João, recalling recent scenes from the French Revolution, took fright. Thousands had surrounded the Palace of Versailles, captured King Louis XVI and Queen Marie Antoinette, and carried them off to Paris, where, after an escape attempt, they were summarily tried and guillotined. Despite the fear that this episode stirred in him, João entered the carriage that awaited him and proceeded to the city center. On the way, however, he noticed that, instead of shouts of protest and offences, the crowd was cheering him. As much as the French mob had hated Louis XVI, so did the Brazilian people love João VI. After half an hour's journey, he appeared, tremulous, on the balcony of the Royal Palace. He could barely mumble the words dictated to him, which Pedro had to repeat for him aloud, much to the delight of the crowds. João VI, the last absolute monarch of Portugal and Brazil, had agreed to swear to and sign the very constitution that stripped some of his powers.[3]

The euphoria of February 26 quickly gave way to new agitation, though. The more radical leaders thought the constitutional reforms insufficient. They wanted the king to cede even more ground. As a result, a second popular demonstration was scheduled for April 21, a date that marked the anniversary of the 1792 hanging of Tiradentes, the rebel leader of the Conjuração Mineira. To shouts of "It is the people who give the orders!" and "There will be revolution!" the crowd, gathered at the Plaza of Commerce, demanded that João swear to the Spanish constitution—an even more radical document than the first—adopted in Cádiz in 1812 during the uprisings of the Peninsular War, which had become an inspiration for the Portuguese rebels in 1820. They also wanted the king to remain in Brazil, defying the decision of the Portuguese Cortes. But this time the demonstration ended in tragedy, violently repressed by troops commanded by Prince Pedro. Thirty people were killed, and dozens wounded. Dawn broke on the façade of the elegant building designed by Grandjean de Montigny in the Plaza of Commerce scrawled with the graffiti, "Butchery of the Braganças."[4]

João departed Rio de Janeiro on April 26, five days after the massacre at the Plaza of Commerce. His retinue included approximately four thousand Portuguese—a third of the total who had accompanied him southwest across the Atlantic thirteen years earlier.[5] It is said that the king embarked in tears. If it were up to only him, he would have stayed in Brazil forever. Nonetheless, once more, this fat, good-natured, tranquil, solitary, indecisive, and often fearful king hunkered down under the responsibility put upon him by history.

Hard evidence that the king didn't want to return exists in a pamphlet that circulated in Rio de Janeiro and major Brazilian cities in January 1821. Written by Francisco Cailhé de Geine, the French text defends the notion that João VI should remain in Brazil. It argues that Brazil could live without Portugal—but not vice versa. It warns further that the departure of the king would bring independence, which in fact happened the following year. "The king should not abandon the country while the revolutionary storm threatens and while he is needed more than ever here."[6] The proof lies in the document's origins. Under the order of Thomaz Villa Nova Portugal, minister and private advisor to João VI, the Royal Press printed the leaflet in 1820. Historian Tobias Monteiro uncovered evidence that João not only knew of the text but authorized its propagation.[7] The document therefore defended ideas shared by the king and his principal assistant.

The departure of the court left Brazil indigent on the eve of its independence. On embarking, João VI scraped clean the coffers of the Bank of Brazil and withdrew all that remained of the royal treasury brought to the colony in 1808. "The royalty, which lived in corruption, carried out a veritable raid on the Brazilian treasury," wrote de Oliveira Lima.[8] Eyewitness Maria Graham recounts that "the treasury was left so poor" that Pedro had to delay the increase of military pay promised before the king's departure, which further heightened the discontent and uncertainty in Brazil. "The funds for carrying on several branches of industry, and several works of public utility were destroyed by this great and sudden drain," she wrote, "and thereby much that had been begun after the arrival of the court, and which it was hoped would have been of the greatest benefit to the country, was stopped."[9]

The withdrawal of treasury funds had dramatic consequences on the Brazilian economy and in practice "amounted to bankruptcy, even if not declared" in the evaluation of historian Pereira da Silva.

Gold is no longer found in circulation. Silver has raised to a 7 or 8 percent premium. The discredit of bank notes has paralyzed, tormented, damaged, and dragged commerce to a slow liquidation. It has suspended the regular whirl of commerce. Many things have failed. A hideous crisis has formed. A panic of terror has seized everyone's spirits. The price of basic necessities has raised, and this fact has powerfully influenced everyone and everything, multiplying the disasters resulting from the restless spirits, anarchic ideas, and general disorder in which the society is plunged.[10]

João VI arrived in Lisbon on July 3 after sixty-eight days of travel, as vulnerable as when he had left. When he departed in 1807 he was a hostage to England and a fugitive from Napoleon. Now he was again a hostage, this time of the Portuguese Cortes. According to historian Oliveira Martins, even before setting foot on solid ground, the king was "insulted and humiliated."[11] While still aboard his ship, he was obliged to swear to the new Constitution, developed without consulting him. José Honório Rodrigues recounts that "D. João swore the oath in a hushed voice, mumbling with the cowardice that was his alone."[12]

The king had to accept certain impositions that in the epoch of absolute monarchy were unimaginable. One prohibited a number of his companions, accused of corruption and robbery in the administration of the public treasury, from disembarkation in Portugal. Among the blacklisted was Joaquim de Azevedo, count of Rio Seco, the official invited to the Palace of Queluz in

November 1807 to organize the voyage to Brazil in the first place. In Rio de Janeiro, where he served as head treasurer in the royal exchequer, he became one of the richest men in the former colony and new kingdom. In addition, Bento Maria Targini, viscount of São Lourenço, and the Lobato brothers, chamberlains and private advisors to the king, couldn't enter Lisbon either.[13]

For the Portuguese, who for so many years anxiously awaited the return of the royal family, the arrival of João VI on the docks of Lisbon was a spectacle to behold, just as much as it had been for the Brazilians thirteen years earlier. Oliveira Martins captures the moment vividly:

> By then old, overweight, filthy, greasy, ugly, obese, with a dead look in his eyes, a fallen, sunburned face, a sagging pout, hunched over on swollen knees, he hung like a sagging load between the velvet pillows of aged golden coaches . . . and was followed by a gaunt cavalry—for those who beheld this scene on the rocky streets of Lisbon, he was a grotesque apparition.[14]

XXVII

A New Brazil

I n May 1821, while João VI's fleet was sailing northeast to Lisbon, thousands of miles to the east, on the solitary rocks of Saint Helena, Napoleon Bonaparte breathed his last—in Chateaubriand's words: "He gave up to God the mightiest breath of life that ever animated human clay." This mighty Corsican, responsible for the Portuguese court's flight to Brazil and for virtually all the torments of João's life, died on the morning of May 4 in the company of his private doctor, amid attacks of vomiting blood and bouts of delirium in which he called after his son, the king of Rome, a scrawny boy of ten years, known officially as the duke of Reichstadt, at that moment prisoner of the Austrian court in Schönbrunn Palace, Vienna. The cause of the French emperor's death remained a subject of controversy for many years. At the outset, some suspected arsenic poisoning. More recent research suggests the more probable cause of stomach cancer. While imprisoned on Saint Helena, Bonaparte dictated his memoirs, in which he weighed in the balance his life and military career, his victories and defeats. For João VI, he reserved a single laconic phrase: "He was the only one who tricked me."[1]

These two men, whose destinies crossed for the last time in the waters of the South Atlantic, left behind legacies that profoundly affected the future of millions. Napoleon's legacy, already well tilled by historians and enthusiasts, included redrawing the map of Europe. Within twenty years, the old regime that had dominated the continent for centuries collapsed and gave way to a world stirred by revolutions that continuously cast doubt on the authority and legitimacy of its own governments. João VI's legacy still remains a matter of controversy. Some view the downfall of the Portuguese monarchy and the colonial empire itself as the result of his timid and fearful personality. Others consider him a political strategist who successfully faced Napoleon's forces without recourse to armed conflict and managed not only to preserve the interests of Portugal but also to leave behind a bigger and better Brazil than he found upon arriving in 1808.

No other period of Brazilian history has witnessed such profound, decisive, and rapid changes as those thirteen years in which the Portuguese court resided in Rio de Janeiro. Within that span, Brazil transformed from a closed and backward colony into an independent nation. For this reason, most view João VI in a positive light, despite all his weaknesses. For historian de Oliveira Lima, he was "the real founder of Brazilian nationhood" for two reasons: He secured its territorial integrity, and he put in place a ruling class responsible for constructing the new country.[2] "In effect, he began the process of decolonization," claimed writer and literary critic Wilson Martins, "not only by the act of elevating Brazil to a kingdom, but by having so quickly provided the structures that constitute a nation."[3]

One way of evaluating João VI's legacy is to approach the question in reverse: What would Brazil be today if the court *hadn't* arrived? Despite their reluctance to engage in such conjectures, most historians agree that the country simply wouldn't exist in its present state. In the most likely hypothesis, independence and the republic might have come sooner, but the old Portuguese colony would have fragmented into a patchwork of small autonomous countries resembling their Spanish American neighbors and with little affinity beyond a shared language. We can envision the chief consequence of this separation: This Brazil in pieces wouldn't even come close to having the power and influence that it exerts over Latin America today. In the absence of a large, integrated Brazil, this role would fall probably to Argentina, the second largest country on the continent.

We should not underestimate the role of João VI in constructing the identity of today's Brazilians. Remember that two centuries ago the political and territorial unity of Brazil looked quite delicate. Evidence of this fragility lies in the Brazilian delegation sent to Portugal to participate in the elections of the Cortes between 1821 and 1822. While Brazil had the right to sixty-five representatives, only forty-six showed up in Lisbon, which left them squarely in the minority compared with the Portuguese representation, composed of one hundred delegates.[4] Their numbers aside, the Brazilians were divided in their voting as well. The delegates of the provinces of Pará, Maranhão, Piauí, and Bahia remained loyal to the Portuguese crown and systematically voted against the interests of other regions.[5] Nor did these northern and northeastern provinces adhere to independence in 1822. Pedro I had to resort to military force to convince them to break away from Portugal. Even after doing so, the Brazilian political atmosphere remained unstable for many decades, subject to numerous rebellions and regional separatist movements.

Based on these regional divergences, Roderick Barman, author of *Brazil: The Forging of a Nation*, posits a few hypotheses about the destiny of the Portuguese territories in America had the court not arrived. Barman believes that Brazil could have disintegrated into three different countries. The first, which he calls the Republic of Brazil, would encompass the current South and Southwest regions, including the provinces of Minas Gerais, Rio de Janeiro, Espirito Santo, São Paulo, Santa Catarina, Rio Grande do Sul, Goiás, and Mato Grosso (Paraná at this time constituting part of the province of São Paulo). These provinces encircled the region where the Conjuração Mineira of Tiradentes took place in the late eighteenth century. A repeat episode, in Barman's opinion, would potentially hit all of them along a single axis, thereby consolidating a single independent republic.

The second country, Barman conjectures, would be called the Republic of the Equator, formed in the Northeast, including Bahia, Sergipe, Alagoas, Pernambuco, Paraíba, Rio Grande do Norte, and Ceará. Three large insurrections agitated this region in less than three decades. First came the Tailors' Conspiracy of 1798 in Bahia, then the Pernambucan Revolt in 1817, and finally the Confederation of the Equator, again in Pernambuco, in 1824. It would have made a strong candidate for autonomy had a central government in Rio de Janeiro not sufficiently controlled those rebellions.

The third country would form in the North, encompassing Maranhão, Grão-Pará, and the Province of Rio Negro, in the modern-day state of Amazonas. These provinces, already an autonomous territory enjoying direct relations with Lisbon in the colonial period, would probably detach last from Portugal. The state of Piauí, Barman postulates, would act as a wild card: It could just as easily become part of the Republic of the Equator as it could remain loyal to the Portuguese Crown and align with the northern provinces.[6]

When viewed from this hypothetical perspective, the preservation of territorial integrity therefore made for a great royal victory. Without the transfer of the Portuguese court, regional conflicts would have deepened to the point where separation between the provinces would have become inevitable. "These colonies would indeed no longer belong to the metropolis if D. João did not migrate to Brazil," claimed Admiral Sidney Smith, commander of the fleet who brought the court to Rio de Janeiro, in his memoirs. "The English would have occupied them under the pretext of defending them, and if this did not come to pass, the Independence of Portuguese America would have been realized at the same time, and with much less resistance, than that of Spanish America."[7]

But thanks to João VI, Brazil maintained itself as a country of continental proportions—larger than Australia—and today the chief heir of Portuguese culture and language. "D. João VI came to create, and indeed founded an empire in America; this is how his act of giving the status of nationhood to an immense, amorphous colony deserves to be seen," wrote de Oliveira Lima.[8] But ironically neither João himself nor Lisbon enjoyed the fruits of this legacy. "While he himself would return less of a king than when he arrived," adds de Oliveira Lima, "nonetheless he left Brazil larger than he found it." In other words, by improving Brazil he lost it forever. Independence, the direct result, came in 1822. "The doors shut for three hundred years were thrown open, and the colony passed beyond the control of the mother country," writes historian Alan Manchester. "Contact with the outside world awakened the torpid colony; new people, new capital, and new ideas entered. As a consequence of the new importance of the colony, the Brazilians felt their destiny to be larger and more important."[9]

But Brazilian independence resulted less from a desire for separation on the part of the Brazilians than from the divisions among the Portuguese themselves. Historian Sérgio Buarque de Holanda defined Brazilian independence as "a civil war among the Portuguese," triggered by the Porto Revolution rather than the mobilization of the colony in defense of their common interests against Lisbon.[10] "The Porto Revolution of 1820 was an anti-Brazilian movement, an explosion of resentment, of wounded pride," writes historian José Honório Rodrigues. The result, according to him, contrasted sharply with the hopes of the Cortes, as it "strengthened Brazil, its conscience, its national sentiment, its unity, and its indivisibility."[11]

In no way did this mean that the country was ready, however. On the contrary, poor, illiterate, and dependent on slave labor, the new Brazil left behind by King João to his son Emperor Pedro I continued the three anesthetized centuries of colonial exploitation inhibiting its sense of initiative and entrepreneurial spirit. The debates surrounding independence foretold of the enormous challenges that the country faced—and which, two hundred years later, still remain in many ways. Brazil at the beginning of the nineteenth century constituted a dangerous, unruly place where whites, blacks, natives, mestizos, masters, and slaves lived alongside one another precariously, without any clearly defined vision of society or even a cohesive nation. "Amalgamation of so much heterogeneous metal will be difficult indeed . . . in forging a solid political body," wrote the patriarch of independence, José Bonifácio de Andrada e Silva, in 1813 to Domingos de Sousa Coutinho, the Portuguese ambassador in England.[12]

In the view of José Bonifacio and other leaders of the era, if independence seemed inevitable, it was necessary to block Brazil from becoming a republic at all costs. In this case, they believed, the conflicts of interest in such a heterogeneous society could prove uncontrollable. "The white race will end up hostage to other castes and the province of Bahia will disappear from the civilized world," claimed Francisco de Sierra y Mariscal in 1823 on analyzing the independence movement in Northeast Brazil.[13]

In 1821, a pamphlet by José Antonio de Miranda circulated in Rio de Janeiro, asking,

How is it possible to form a republic in a vast country, still largely unknown, full of infinite forests, without citizenry, without civilization, without art, without streets, without mutually necessary relations, with opposing interests and with a multitude of slaves, without customs, with neither civil nor religious education and full of vices and antisocial habits?[14]

The proposed solution, which in the end triumphed, was to maintain a centralized, powerful monarchy capable of quelling popular insurrections and separatist movements. "Brazil, still in its infancy, made up of many huge, distant and uninhabited provinces, needs to grow out from a center of power, where measures can be taken vigorously, forcefully, and with promptness," argued an anonymous pamphlet published in Lisbon in 1822. "Well, there is no government more vigorous than a monarchy. . . . The general character of the Nation clearly excludes the possibility of a republic."[15]

Fearful sentiments of this type catalyzed political force, maintaining the country under the crown at a moment in which regionalists and diverse interests could have divided it. According to historian Maria Odila Leite da Silva Dias,

Under complete political separation, the prospects of the colony to transform itself into a nation would not seem promising for the men of the Independence generation. . . . They were quite conscious of internal tensions, social and racial, of fragmentation, regionalism, and lack of unity, which did not yield the conditions for a national conscience capable of supporting a revolutionary movement to reconstruct society.[16]

We should view the events of 1822, therefore, as a controlled break, threatened by internal divisions and by the sea of poverty and marginalization left by three centuries of slavery and colonial exploitation. When regional rebellions appeared, the new crown immediately suppresed them. As a result, the path chosen in 1822 represented neither republican nor genuinely revolutionary aims. It was simply conciliatory. Instead of being faced and resolved, long-lived social tensions were damped and postponed.

In the interests of maintaining the colonial elite, slavery remained as a festering wound in Brazilian society until its total abolition in 1888 under the Golden Law, signed by Princess Isabel, a great-granddaughter of João VI. Regional divisions violently reappeared from time to time, as in the Confederation of the Equator in 1824, the War of the Ragamuffins in 1835, and the Constitutionalist Revolution of 1932. Popular participation in government decisions persisted largely as an idea. In 1881, when the Saraiva Law established direct election of certain legislative posts for the first time, only 1.5 percent of the population had this right to vote. Only prominent merchants and rural proprietors could participate, excluding an enormous disenfranchised mass composed of women, blacks, the poor, the illiterate, and the destitute.[17] Legacies barely resolved in 1822, these problems remained for the following two hundred years, haunting the future of Brazilian society like the phantom of an unburied corpse.

XXVIII

The Conversion of dos Santos Marrocos

Royal Archivist Luiz dos Santos Marrocos was one of the thousands of Portuguese associated with the court who remained in Brazil after the royal family's return to Lisbon. Exactly one month before the king's departure, he wrote the last of the 186 letters he sent to his father, Francisco, and sister Bernardina since arriving in Rio de Janeiro in 1811. The letter drips with lamentation and farewells: "Feeling myself to be totally abandoned in your memories, without knowing the reason for such an extraordinary occurrence, I will be suspending my correspondence for a while, seeing that it is useless."[1]

Relations between the archivist and his family had been unraveling for some time. In the first three years after his arrival in Rio de Janeiro, the exchange of messages is intense, friendly, and affectionate. Little by little, however, the correspondence from Lisbon begins to thin out. "Five successive ships have arrived and Your Mercy has not given me the pleasure of receiving any news," complains dos Santos Marrocos to his father on April 1, 1814. "Nor has my sister remembered to write me."[2] Four months later, another eleven ships had arrived with no news. Marrocos feels himself "estranged by everyone's silence . . . as if I no longer existed."[3]

The fissures in their relationship coincide with the archivist's changes in attitude toward Brazil and its people. Dos Santos Marrocos arrived in Brazil criticizing the climate, landscape, and habits and customs of the Brazilians, deploring everything and everyone. Gradually, his tone began to change, though. A decade later, he had become passionate about the city, the country, and the people. Moreover, he decided to stay in Brazil and support independence against the will of his Portuguese countrymen and crucially his own family. His personal transformation coincides with the geopolitical changes that Brazil and Portugal witnessed in that notable period of history. As a result, our archivist becomes a paradigm of a European colonizer caught up in the maelstrom of history at the beginning of the nineteenth century, who, surprised by events at first, attempts to react against them but later adapts to them and undergoes a sea change.

As indicated when he first appears in this present book, the surviving communication is one-way: We have only the letters that he sent to Lisbon, which were preserved by his father in the Royal Library at Ajuda. Either the son didn't do the same, or the vagaries of history destroyed them. We don't know the exact wording of the responses that he received, but we can indirectly grasp their content from excerpts in Luiz's own correspondence. It's also worth noting that, evidently no longer writing to each other after 1821, the father still kept all of his son's letters, preserving them and thereby transforming them into invaluable historical documents.[4]

In the earliest letters sent to Portugal, between 1811 and 1813, dos Santos Marrocos describes Brazil as the worst place on earth, full of disease, filth, vagabonds, and ignorant and immodest people. "They are undignified, arrogant, vain, and libertine; the animals are ugly and poisonous," he declares.[5]

I do not like being trapped in this land, and feel myself in exile. . . . I am so shocked by this place that I want nothing from it, and when I leave, I shall not forget to clean my boots on the edge of the docks so as to not bring back any trace of this place. . . . When the topic is the shortcomings of Brazil, it makes for vast material of aversion and loathing . . . and I am sure that I even curse it in my sleep.[6]

From 1814 onward, though, he changes his tune. Brazil becomes a beautiful, welcoming place, with hard-working and friendly people. In a letter sent on November 1 of that year, dos Santos Marrocos gives thanks to God for the benefits of his new life in Rio de Janeiro. "I live in peace, in abundance, with all of the comforts that I need, with a good house, well-equipped and organized, with slaves and other conveniences," he explains.[7] "An aversion to this country . . . is a great error, which I consider to have said farewell to long ago," he writes, correcting himself, after referring to the "good character of the situation with which God has favored me."[8]

His change of heart had a name: Anna Maria de São Thiago Souza, a twenty-two-year-old carioca whom he met and began dating two years after arriving in Brazil. The daughter of a rich Portuguese merchant and a Brazilian woman, she came from a family that, according to Marrocos, was "clean, honest, and wealthy."[9] In his letters to his father, he describes her as "a saint of a woman," serious and dedicated, of a kind unequalled even in Portugal. According to him, thanks to her mother's supervision, Anna Maria had escaped the laziness and ignorance that, in his opinion, characterized the daughters of Brazilians. "In spite of being a Brazilian, she is better than many Portuguese women," he wrote.[10] "Her sole defect is that she is a carioca," he offered as a reservation in another letter.[11]

The couple married on September 22, 1814, the news only communicated to his family two months later. They had three children: Luiz Francisco, born on September 8, 1816, died a week later of a navel infection known in those days as "the seven-day disease." A year and a half later on March 7, 1818, Maria Tereza was born. Finally, Maria Luiz entered the world on August 13, 1819.[12] As we will see, however, the correspondence that conveyed these milestones of life concealed a secret kept for two hundred years.

After the birth of his first daughter, Maria Tereza, Luiz tells his father of refusing to hire a black wet nurse, the custom among the elite in Rio de Janeiro. "It seems to be more natural and decent that she is cared for by her mother than by negroes, for whom I feel repulsion and disgust," he explains.[13] A little before the birth of his second daughter, however, dos Santos Maroccos has changed his position radically. "I have just purchased a wet-nurse to do the breastfeeding, at a price of 179,200 réis," he wrote his sister. He also tells of having brought home a newborn boy from the orphanage with the aim of ensuring that the slave wet nurse's breastmilk would be ready by the time his wife gave birth.[14]

In a letter of July 21, 1811, which we saw earlier, he tells his father that he has bought a black slave for 93,600 réis. This slave reappears nine months later in one of his longer correspondences. The archivist tells his father of using a paddle to punish the slave only once. "It took a dozen hand-bashings for stubbornness," he writes. "But I broke him of the vice." Thereafter, Luiz describes him in a congenial manner:

He is one of my good friends, as much as I am one of his. He is very skilled and shows a lot of prudence. He serves very well at the table. He takes good care of the cleanliness of my clothing and shoes, always brushing them. He is very capricious in going around elegantly and owns lots of clothes. He is very loyal, wholesome, and sound in force.[15]

Before closing the letter, Luiz makes two odd observations about the slave: the first that he "had a great rancor for women and cats," and the second his habit of watching over the archivist to prevent mosquitoes from attacking while he slept. "He has the unique ability to act as the sentinel at my feet while I am taking a siesta, with the only goal of shooing away flies so that they do not wake me." Luiz hopes that "he will come to be a good slave, without the need for thrashings, being driven only by valor and friendship."[16]

In addition to his rich family life, dos Santos Marrocos became wealthy in Rio de Janeiro. His connections with the nobility and with the prince regent himself had become closer, giving him higher social standing than he had enjoyed in Lisbon. In his letters, he relates to his father that, owing to the importance of his work in the library, he frequented the Royal Palace and kissed the prince's hand every day. Prince João frequently visited the library to consult works of arts and science.

Thanks to this proximity, in 1811 dos Santos Marrocos suggested to the prince regent that he create a library in Salvador containing duplicates of the books in the Rio de Janeiro library. The plan resolved two problems: to provide the Bahians with access to literacy and at the same time to provide a destination for the books that had remained in crates since arriving from Lisbon, "all of them mined by termites, and the tapestries reduced to powder." Preoccupied with more urgent matters, the prince ignored the suggestion, but seven years later the archivist renewed the proposal. This time, the newly crowned King João VI agreed and ordered thirty-eight crates of books shipped to Salvador. As a result, the Bahian library, founded in 1811, nearly doubled its holdings.[17]

An episode involving the British ambassador, Lord Strangford, demonstrates the importance of the Rio de Janeiro library to the Portuguese crown. In 1815, on returning to London after a sojourn of six years in Brazil, Strangford declined a present of twelve gold bars offered by the prince regent. João didn't take offense at Strangford's refusal, but he bristled when he found out that the ambassador had forgotten to return two old books borrowed from the Royal Library. Taking this act personally, Prince João made a formal complaint to the English government and sent his ambassador in London, Cipriano Ribeiro Freire, to retrieve them.[18]

In 1813, two years after arriving in Brazil, dos Santos Marrocos supervised the Crown Manuscripts, a collection of six thousand codices that, by order of the prince regent, the archivist would catalog and organize. These papers, their preservation highly valued by the crown, included originals of letters, reports, diplomatic dispatches, and other official documents dating to the beginning of the Portuguese Empire. In 1821, this collection of manuscripts returned to Lisbon with the court. The rest of the holdings of the old Royal Library remained in Brazil, later bought from Portugal by Emperor Pedro I to form the foundation of the National Library of Rio de Janeiro. The price paid for these books, 800 million réis (approximately $23 million today), corresponded to 12.5 percent of the indemnities demanded by the Portuguese government for recognizing Brazilian independence.[19]

In September 1817, Luiz ceased working at the library. Thomaz Antonio Villa Nova Portugal, the prime minister and king's advisor, had appointed him as an official in the Ministry of State Affairs of the Kingdom. He debuted his uniform in this new post on February 6, 1818, the day of João VI's acclamation ceremony. He returned to a more bookish routine on March 22, 1821—just weeks before the king's return to Portugal—in the loftier post of "directorate and arrangement" of the Royal Libraries, with an annual salary of 500,000 réis, taking over from Brother Gregorio José Viegas, himself newly appointed bishop of Pernambuco.[20]

After independence, dos Santos Marrocos became a high-ranking official in the government of Emperor Pedro I. In 1824, he cut ties with the library to assume the post of chief official of the Ministry of Imperial Affairs, which he occupied until his death. His name appears at the bottom of two important texts of independent Brazil: the first imperial constitution of 1824 and the first patent law, signed in 1830. His signature doesn't mean that he authored these documents, only that he was the scribe, drafting the texts in the bureaucratic and legal language that was his specialty, in addition to handling the protocol and promotion in the official press.

In the letters written on the eve of João VI's return to Lisbon, Luiz tried to convince his family to move to Rio de Janeiro as well. Francisco declined his son's suggestion. But Luiz insists, trying to understand the reasons behind his father's refusal. "Is it the motherland?" he asks, referring to Portugal. "Aside from being a frivolous pretext of the senile and worrisome, the Portuguese motherland has been highly ungrateful for all of your devotion, and the fruits of your studies and labors since your earliest years."

In the same letter, the longest of all the 186 we have, dos Santos Marrocos insists for the last time:

> My father, now is the moment to decide. This is a matter of the utmost importance, and of the future survival of our family, amidst thousands of amenities. The first steps of this project seem appalling and difficult . . . but they are merely temporary. The circumstances offered are all favorable and concomitant with this end. . . . Leave this disgraceful lethargy in which you have lived and moaned for so many years. Leave a land that is no longer prosperous for you and has made you recede in your career, and come enjoy more relaxed and happy days, delighting in everything within reach of the appetite of your genius.[21]

Though a private letter to his father, this exhortation encapsulated the two kingdoms and their people at that decisive moment. Portugal was the past: ancient ideas, the colonial system, and decadence. Brazil was new: the future, wealth, prosperity, and transformation. The end of their correspondence marked the separation of the dos Santos Marrocos family between these two worlds. "Founding a family in Rio de Janeiro resulted in a transformation of son into father that paralleled Brazil's own transformation from colony into the center of empire," observes Kirsten Schulz.[22]

Luiz dos Santos Marrocos died on December 17, 1838, news laconically recorded in the next day's edition of the *Journal of Commerce:* "Luiz Joaquim dos Santos Marrocos, chief official of the Secretary of State of Imperial Affairs, passed away yesterday." Buried in catacomb 85 of the Church of São Francisco da Paula in Rio de Janeiro, he was fifty-seven years old.[23]

A piece of Portugal that had crossed the Atlantic with João's original court had died, never to return. The royal archivist had brought with him the heavy cultural baggage that characterized the Portuguese of preceding centuries. He was conservative, bureaucratic, superstitious, prejudiced, and fearful of the changes awaiting him on the other side of the world in an adverse tropical climate among uncouth, illiterate, poor people. At his death, nearly three decades later, he was a man transformed. He had involved himself in politics, cast off his fear of living with uncertainty, and discovered love, prosperity, and hope for the future. His transformation represents a perfect, detailed, and complete portrait of the new nation born then and there, its roots deeply entwined in Portugal—yet distinct.

XXIX

The Secret

For most readers, this book came to an end—or should have done so—in the preceding chapter. What follows will interest historians because it reveals previously unknown details of the life of Royal Archivist Luiz dos Santos Marrocos. In the grander context of the transfer of the Portuguese court to Brazil, it will reveal minor details. Nevertheless, those details will reinforce the fascinating and transitory nature of investigating the lives of people that even two hundred years later may continue to change.

On June 15, 1814, a child named Joaquinna dos Santos Maroccos was born in Rio de Janeiro. She is the daughter born to Luiz and Anna Maria de São Thiago Souza before their marriage, her existence maintained in secrecy in all the letters he sent to his family in Lisbon. At four months old, on November 22, Joaquinna was baptized in the Brotherhood of the Blessed Sacrament of the Sé.

Her birth certificate and baptismal certificate endure on microfilm in a database of more than a billion names, stored in Salt Lake City, Utah, at the headquarters of the Church of Jesus Christ of Latter-Day Saints. You can find them on the Internet via FamilySearch.org, a service maintained and provided by the Mormons and considered one of the largest and most complete genealogy services in the world. The Mormons constructed this giant database because they believe that the dead can be redeemed and saved through baptism, even after death. For such purposes, it's necessary only that they be correctly identified. In this genealogy database, Joaquinna appears as the daughter of Luis Joaquim dos Santos Marrocos and Anna Roza de São-Tiago. Setting aside the common exchange of an "s" for a "z," the spelling of the father's name exactly matches that of the royal archivist. The main difference we face is the mother's middle name: Roza instead of Maria.

This difference represents nothing more than a slip of the pen. Two centuries ago, church scribes and notaries commonly erred in the transcription of names on birth and baptismal certificates. Statistically it's also virtually impossible that in a city of only 60,000 inhabitants, of which fewer than half were white, another couple with the same names left no other details in the historical record.

The discovery of the birth of their daughter three months before the wedding clarifies several mysteries that subsequent researchers hadn't yet been able to decipher. First is the coldness and near-hostility with which the family received the news of the marriage. Dos Santos Marrocos communicated the news to his father in a letter of November 12, 1815, two months after the ceremony took place in Rio de Janeiro. Francisco reacted violently to the news. He accused Luiz of lacking respect for him, acting "like a stupid African and a presumptuous American" in having married without notifying him in advance or asking his permission, behavior that he considered "vile and incivil." His sister Bernardina criticized him for having married "in the stealth of night, as if the populace were blind and deaf."[1]

The second enigma regards an apparent misunderstanding in the exchange of letters in the period before the wedding. Luiz rebuts the criticisms of his family, saying that he had indeed notified them in advance of his intention to marry. He maintains that he had mentioned it in two letters, one to his father and the other to his sister, both dated December 23, 1813, nine months before the ceremony. The family claimed that this correspondence never reached them. In November 1815, Luiz defends himself, saying that it wasn't his fault that the letters went astray. Curiously, of the 186 letters in the Ajuda Library, these are the only two that are copies. The whereabouts of the originals remain unknown.

If the family's allegations are correct—in other words, that neither father nor sister were notified in advance of the wedding—what would have led Luiz and Anna to have married in near secrecy, without respecting protocol? Joaquinna's birth and baptismal certificates suggest that the marriage probably was decided in haste following an unexpected pregnancy. The estrangement from his family coincides with Joaquinna's date of birth.

The third mystery, which reinforces the first and second, concerns a letter of November 1814, at which point the girl would have been four months old. In this correspondence, dos Santos Marrocos warns his sister to pay no attention to the gossip and rumors about him spreading in Rio de Janeiro that could arrive in Lisbon. "I am laughing at the blindness of these silly people, diligently fraternizing with me with the worthless intention of discovering my secret, a satisfaction I will give no-one."[2]

What gossip could possibly evoke this kind of reaction from a thirty-three-year-old archivist and bureaucrat to the king, conservative to the roots of his hair? The explanation appears with Joaquinna, born in June of that year. In those days, pregnancy out of wedlock was reason for scandal. It also explains his sister's phrase "as if the populace were blind and deaf." Blind and deaf to what? The evidence suggests that in Lisbon the family might have had knowledge, via other people, of the information that Luiz deliberately tried to hide in his letters.

So what happened to Joaquinna, the mysterious baby born in 1814? Aside from her birth and baptismal certificates, the Mormon database contains no other reference to her fate. We have no news of whether she was abandoned, whether she survived, died, married, or had children. But the key to these questions lies in documents archived in Salt Lake City. The microfilm containing the birth and baptismal certificates for Joaquinna dos Santos Marrocos forms part of a set of documents called batch C032065 of the International Genealogical Index. It consists of names of 1,855 girls born in Rio de Janeiro between 1812 and 1816, with a few exceptions from the end of the eighteenth century.

The majority of these children appear with only a first name. It records hundreds of girls named Justina, Honorata, Inocencia, or Jezuina, with no reference to genealogy or family name. Others have generic surnames associated with religious societies, dates, or events, such as "of the Holy Spirit," "of the Conception," "of the Rosary," or "of the Gospel." The only point in common among all of them is that all were baptized at the Blessed Sacrament of the Sé—which explains the entire mystery. Blessed Sacrament was one of the oldest religious orders in colonial Brazil. Maintained by laymen of high social distinction, it counted among its responsibilities sheltering and providing assistance to the orphans of single mothers from wealthy families. This was the case of dos Santos Marrocos's fiancée: Anna Maria de São Thiago Souza came from a rich, socially well-connected family of legitimate Portuguese lineage.

The obvious conclusion is that, surprised by the pregnancy, Luiz and Anna Maria preferred to deliver the newborn baby to the care of a religious order rather than expose themselves to an inevitable scandal in presence of the court. Today, children born outside of wedlock are a normal phenomenon of life, accepted by society. Two hundred years ago, it was quite different. In the court of João VI, the news of a child born out of wedlock would be unacceptable. For the parents, it was better to hide the child and deliver her for adoption than to compromise the families' reputations.

The delivery of unwanted children for adoption was a widely spread habit in Rio de Janeiro. Orphanages and certain convents had a "foundling wheel," an institution imported from Portugal, in which it was possible to leave a newborn without being identified. In 1823, Maria Graham visited a shelter in Rio de Janeiro the foundling wheel of which had received 10,000 orphan children in nine years. The majority died before finding a home to take them.[3]

In the case of Joaquinna dos Santos Marrocos, despite all the risks involved, her parents nevertheless registered the unwanted child with her own surname. Identified as number 587 in batch C032065 of the Mormon record, Joaquinna is one of the rare children in this set of documents who appears with both a first name and a family name. It's as if they left a silent clue to their secrets buried for posterity.[4]

Acknowledgments

This book stands as the result of ten years of journalistic investigation. It also pays homage to three people whose support, encouragement, and guidance proved indispensable to what I have written. First is Tales Alvarenga, my friend and editor colleague, who passed away prematurely in 2006. Second is the professor and historian Maria Odila Leite da Silva Dias. Third is the academic and bibliophile José Mindlin.

In 1997, Tales Alvarenga was editor in chief of the magazine *Veja,* and I was his head editor. Inspired by a successful experience during the centennial celebration of the Proclamation of the Republic, Tales commissioned me to do a special series of historical pieces to be distributed with the regular edition of *Veja* as a freebie to subscribers and newsstand buyers. The project would include the discovery of Brazil, the flight of the Portuguese royal family, and Brazilian independence. Of these three, only the first was ever published, in 2000, and distributed in Brazil and Portugal bundled with the magazines *Veja* and *Visão* under the title *The Adventure of Discovery.*

As for the special piece on Dom João's flight from Lisbon, Tales decided to cancel it as there was no "hook"—an expression which in editorial parlance refers to a particular reason or opportunity for an article to be published. While the plan had changed, I continued working, moved by the enthusiasm that the topic and the historical figures had stirred in me. During these ten years, I read and researched over 150 books, printed sources, and electronic sources on the subject, in places as varied as the José Mindlin libraries, libraries in São Paulo and Rio de Janeiro, the Ajuda Library in Lisbon, and the Library of Congress in Washington, D.C.

In the initial phase of research, Professor Maria Odila Leite da Silva Dias acted as my advisor. My neighbor in Higienopolis, a district of São Paulo, she suggested the first of the books I consulted: the classic *Dom João VI in Brazil* by Manuel de Oliveira Lima, which I read in 1997. A PhD of the University of São Paulo and a professor at the Pontifical Catholic University of São Paulo, Maria Odila is the author of numerous books and articles on Brazilian history. The most recent, *A interiorização da metrópole (The Internalization of the Metropolis*), published in 2005, has become a reference work in studies of the factors leading to independence. Maria Odila is also considered a major authority on the work of historian Sérgio Buarque de Holanda. As of mid-2007, her curriculum vitae on the website of the National Council for Scientific and Technological Development listed that she has supervised over eighty PhD and master's theses.

To the bibliophile José Mindlin, elected to the Brazilian Academy of Letters in 2006, I am indebted for access to his extraordinary library. Situated in the neighborhood of Brooklin, São Paulo, it holds the largest private collection of books in Brazil, with more than 38,000 rare or antique titles including a first edition of *Os Lusíadas* by Luis de Camões (1572). With the supervision and support of the librarians Cristina Antunes, Elisa Nazarian, and Rosa Gonçalves, responsible for the collection, I spent many unforgettable mornings conducting research and had the opportunity to consult, among other rarities, the first treatise on medicine published in Brazil in 1808, written by Manuel Vieira da Silva, as well as the original edition of Lieutenant Thomas O'Neill's *A concise and accurate account of the proceedings of the squadron under the command of Admiral Sir William Sidney Smith in effecting the escape of the Royal Family of Portugal to Brazil on November 29, 1807, and also the suffering of the royal fugitives during their voyage from Lisbon to Rio de Janeiro with a variety of other interesting and authentic facts* (1810). Both of these appear in the bibliography that follows.

The English-language edition of *1808* has been made possible thanks to the efforts of three professionals. I am indebted to Andrew Nevins, professor of linguistics at University College London, for the patient and careful work of translating the original text into English, a task replete with traps and challenges that could be overcome only with his profound knowledge of the subtleties of the Portuguese language. Jonah Straus, my literary agent in New York, took charge of the extremely important task of identifying Lyons Press, a division of Globe Pequot Press, as the publisher for the American market. Finally, it was the work of James Jayo in meticulously editing the final text which, besides greatly enriching the content of this work, made it more accessible for the background of an Anglophone readership.

NOTES

1 Worth mentioning in the same category of highly readable books written in accessible language is *A longa viagem da biblioteca dos reis: do terremoto de Lisboa à Independência do Brasil* by historian Lília Moritz Schwarcz, professor at the University of São Paulo.

2 J. M. Pereira da Silva, *História da fundação*, Volume 1, p. 5.

3 During the thirteen years in which the Portuguese court ruled from Brazil, the value of the pound sterling, the standard currency for international trade, oscillated between 3,000 and 5,000 réis, according to the report of the Ambassador Joaquim de Souza Leão Filho, translator and annotator of Ernst Ebel's book *O Rio de Janeiro e seus arredores em 1824*, p. 14. With this reference as a guide, it is possible to have an approximate notion of the currency values of this period. The British Parliament offers a website in which one can calculate the equivalent of monetary amounts with their present-day value for the last three centuries. Through such a calculation, £1 in 1808 is equivalent today to £56. This means that goods sold in Rio de Janeiro at this time for 4,000 réis (approximately £1) would be worth today $100. Created by professors at the University of Miami and Illinois, the Economic History Service is a free site that provides conversions for older currencies: MeasuringWorth.com. GlobalFinancialData.com offers similar and even more detailed information but is not free. For historical information on the value of the pound sterling, see Robert Twigger, *Inflation*, available at www.parliament.uk.

I

THE FLIGHT FROM LISBON

1 For more detailed information about the power of monarchs during absolutist regimes, see Albert Sorel, *Europe Under the Old Regime*, and Geoffrey Bruun, *The Enlightened Despots*.

2 In the era during which Prince José died, the smallpox vaccine was already in wide use across Europe. Queen Maria I, however, didn't authorize her eldest son and heir to the throne to be vaccinated "out of religious scruples," according to historian Pedro Calmon in *O rei do Brasil,* p. 34. Later, under the regency of Prince João, the entire royal family received the vaccine.

3 For a description of Mafra Palace, see Lília Moritz Schwarcz, *A longa viagem da biblioteca dos reis,* p. 62, and Tobias Monteiro, *História do Império,* p. 168.

4 In 2005, the BBC created a website called *British History: Empire and Sea Power* to commemorate the 200th anniversary of the Battle of Trafalgar. For an insightful analysis of the consequences of Lord Nelson's victory over the French and Spanish fleets, see Nam Rodger, *Trafalgar: The Long-Term Impact,* on the same website.

5 Tobias Monteiro, *História do Império,* pp. 20–21.

6 Ibid, p. 55.

II

THE ERA OF DERANGED MONARCHS

1 For more information about this illness and about the behavior of George III and Maria I, see Christopher Hibbert, *George III;* Marcus Cheke, *Carlota Joaquina;* and Vivian Green, *A loucura dos reis.*

2 Patrick Wilcken, *Empire Adrift,* p. 57. The equivalence conversion derives from Robert Twigger, *Inflation.*

3 "Queen Maria I for a long time had been showing signs of psychological disturbance and was abruptly affected by a serious attack of madness while attending a performance at the theater in the Palace of Salvaterra on Feburary 2, 1792," writes historian Ângelo Pereira in *D. João VI,* p. 57.

4 Cited in H. A. L. Fisher, *Napoleon.*

5 Manuel de Oliveira Lima, D. *João VI no Brasil,* p. 49.

6 Information about the size of the French debt after Louis XIV's reign and the

number of individuals in the court of Versailles comes from Winston Churchill, *The Age of Revolution.*

7 This figure comes from Alistair Horne, in the audiobook *The Age of Napoleon.* Cameron Reilly, in *Napoleon 101,* a podcast available at Napoleon. ThePodcastNetwork.com, claims that there are 300,000 books in which Napoleon is the main character.

8 For a detailed analysis of Napoleon's military strategy and his capacity to mobilize troops, see Gunther Rothenberg, *The Napoleonic Wars,* pp. 18–47.

9 Alexandre Dumas, *Napoleão,* p. 37.

10 Alistair Horne, *The Age of Napoleon* (audiobook).

III

THE PLAN

1 Manuel de Oliveira Lima, *D. João VI no Brasil,* p. 43.

2 J. M. Pereira da Silva, in *História da fundação,* pp. 79–80, says that in 1806 Portugal imported from Brasil 14,153,752,891 réis and exported to the colony only 8,426,097,899 réis.

3 Thomas E. Skidmore, *Brazil,* p. 23.

4 The total number of ships used for commerce with Brazil and Costigan's commentary come from Kenneth Maxwell, *Conflicts and Conspiracies,* p. 5.

5 In 1640, a group of royal adivsors, worried by the constant threats to Portugal's autonomy, including Jesuit priest Father Antonio Vieira, proposed the creation of an empire in the Americas, to which the seat of the monarchy would be transferred. Vieira had a messianic vision of the idea. According to him, Portugal was destined to recreate in the Americas the "Fifth Empire," a biblical kingdom predicted by the prophet Daniel in the Old Testament. For defending such ideas, he was investigated by the Inquistion and later censured by the pope. For more information, see Kirsten Schultz, *Tropical Versailles,* p. 17.

6 Kenneth Maxwell, *Conflicts and Conspiracies,* p. 6.

7 Manuel de Oliveira Lima, *D. João VI no Brasil*, p. 45.

8 Letter to the prince regent of August 16, 1803, reproduced in Ângelo Pereira, *D. João Príncipe e Rei*, pp. 127–136.

9 Manuel de Oliveira Lima, *D. João VI no Brasil*, p. 16.

10 In 1807, the Council of State consisted of Antonio de Araújo de Azevedo, Rodrigo de Souza Coutinho, João de Almeida de Melo e Castro, José Egídio Alves de Almeida (head of the cabinet), João Diogo de Barros (secretary of the infantado), Tomás Antônio Vilanova Portugal (treasurer of the Aerarium), Manuel Vieira da Silva (D. João's personal physician and the author of the first medical treatise published in Brazil, in 1808), and the brothers Francisco José e Matias Antônio de Sousa Lobato (chamberlains and personal valets to the prince). For more details, see Lília Schwarcz, *A longa viagem da biblioteca*, p. 65.

11 Lília Schwarcz, *A longa viagem da biblioteca*, p. 199.

12 Tobias Monteiro, *História do império*, p. 23.

13 Lília Schwarcz, *A longa viagem da biblioteca*, p. 204.

14 Manuel de Oliveira Lima, *D. João VI no Brasil*, p. 47.

15 Alexandre José de Melo Moraes, *História da transladação*, p. 50.

16 Manuel de Oliveira Lima, *D. João VI no Brasil*, pp. 51–52.

17 Ibid, p. 37.

18 Ibid, p. 40.

19 According to René Chartrand, *Vimeiro 1808*, p. 17.

20 For a description of the indigence of the French army and the errors made during the invasion of Portugal, see René Chartrand, *Vimeiro 1808;* Charles Esdaile, *The Peninsular War;* General Maximilien Foy, *Junot's Invasion of Portugal;* David Gates, *The Spanish Ulcer;* Charles Oman, *A History of the Peninsular War;* and Gunther E. Rothenberg, *The Napoleonic Wars.*

21 General Maximilien Foy, *Junot's Invasion*, p. 57.

22 Charles Oman, *A History of the Peninsular War*, p. 28.

23 Cited in Tobias Monteiro, *História do Império*, p. 59.

24 Charles Oman, *A History of the Peninsular War*, p. 27.

25 Alan Manchester, *British Preeminence in Brazil*, p. 67, quoting Albert Sorel, *Europe and the French Revolution.*

26 Charles Oman, *A History of the Peninsular War*, p. 26.

IV

THE DECLINING EMPIRE

1 Júlio Bandeira, "O barroco de açúcar e de ouro," in the introduction to *Viagem ao Brasil* by Thomas Ender, p. 26.

2 Kenneth Light, "Com os pés no mar," pp. 48–53.

3 Joaquim Pedro de Oliveira Martins, *História de Portugal*, p. 519.

4 Manuel de Oliveira Lima, *D. João VI no Brasil*, p. 25.

5 Converted according to the inflation of the past two hundred years, a French franc in 1808 would be worth 4.07 euros today, according to GlobalFinancialData.com.

6 This data comes from Marcus Cheke, *Carlota Joaquina*. Pereira da Silva, in *História da fundação*, p. 77, claims based on the statistics of 1801 that the population of Portugal was 2,951,930 residents, including 30,000 bishops, priests, nuns, and seminarists cloistered in 393 monasteries or convents.

7 Pedro Calmon, *O rei do Brasil*, p. 34.

8 Maria Antonia Lopes, *Mulheres, Espaço e Sociabilidade*, 1989, cited in Francisca L. Nogueira de Azevedo, *Carlota Joaquina na Corte do Brasil*, p. 54.

9 Cited in Luis Edmundo, *Recordações do Rio Antigo*, p. 68.

10 Manuel de Oliveira Lima, *D. João VI no Brasil*, p. 23.

11 Lília Schwarcz, *A longa viagem da biblioteca*, p. 86.

12 Sérgio Buarque de Holanda, *Raízes do Brasil*, p. 49.

13 Interview in *Veja* magazine, volume 1967, August 2, 2006, p. 11.

14 Lília Schwarcz, *A longa viagem da biblioteca,* p. 39.

15 Ibid, p. 86.

16 Pandiá Calógeras, *Formação histórica do Brasil,* p. 60. The conversion to present-day equivalents derives from Robert Twigger, *Inflation.*

17 In *História do Império,* pp. 499–500, Tobias Monteiro calculates the amount of gold sent from Minas Gerais to Portugal as 35,687 *arrobas* or 590 tons.

18 Pandiá Calógeras, *Formação histórica do Brasil,* p. 60.

19 Cited in Lília Schwarcz, *A longa viagem da biblioteca,* p. 87.

20 For a description of the damage caused by the Lisbon earthquake, see Lília Schwarcz, *A longa viagem da biblioteca,* chapter 1.

21 Oliveira Martins, *História de Portugal,* pp. 494–496.

22 Lília Schwarcz, *A longa viagem da biblioteca,* p. 161.

23 The policy of neutrality and noninterference in extradomestic matters held so strong in Portugal that, directly inherited, it characterized the relationship between Brazil and the rest of the world after independence. Even today it forms an important thread within Brazilian foreign policy.

24 Alan Manchester, *British Preeminence in Brazil,* p. 2.

25 Oliveira Martins, *História de Portugal,* p. 575.

26 Alan Manchester, *British Preeminence in Brazil,* p. 2.

27 Winston Churchill, *The Age of Revolution* (audiobook).

28 Manuel de Oliveira Lima, *D. João VI no Brasil,* p. 29.

V

DEPARTURE

1 Descriptions of the weather in Lisbon on the day of departure come from the lieutenant of the British Navy Thomas O'Neill in *A concise and accurate account of the proceedings*, p. 22, and from Portuguese historian Ângelo Pereira in *Os filhos d'El-Rei D. João VI*, p. 113.

2 Thomas O'Neill, *A concise and accurate account*, p. 16.

3 The information about the number of ships that accompanied the Portuguese royal family to Brazil remains a matter of dispute. Based on onboard diaries, historian Kenneth Light affirms that on the first day of the voyage the commander of the English vessel *Hibernia* counted a total of fifty-six ships. These would have been thirty-one warships, thirteen of them English and eighteen Portuguese, plus twenty-five merchant vessels. In his memoirs, Admiral Sidney Smith speaks of "a multitude of large armored merchant ships." In Lord Strangford's version, they would have been "numerous brigs, armed corvettes and sloops, and some other ships from Brazil," totalling "nearly 36 ships in all." Historian Alexandre de Melo Moraes reports eight large ships (*Príncipe Real, Martim de Freitas, Príncipe do Brasil, D. João de Castro, D. Henrique, Afonso de Albuquerque, Rainha de Portugal*, and *Meduza*), four frigates (*Minerva, Urânia, Golphinho*, and *Thelis*), three brigs (*Lebre, Voador*, and *Vingança*) and a schooner (*Carioca*) and numerous merchant vessels, besides the British ships.

4 Oliveira Martins, *História de Portugal*, p. 516.

5 The number of individuals who accompanied D. João also remains a matter of dispute. Some historians speak of up to 15,000 people. Carioca architect Nireu Cavalcanti, author of *O Rio de Janeiro setecentista*, considers this figure an exaggeration. Based on the list of passengers who disembarked in the port of Rio de Janeiro between 1808 and 1809, he calculates that there were only 444. Historian Kenneth Light disagrees. In his calculations, the *Príncipe Real* alone carried 1,054 individuals. In his opinion, it would be reasonable to estimate a total between 10,000 and 15,000 people. The problem is that, since there was no official list of passengers, it's practically impossible to know how many people actually made the journey. Moreover, not all of them disembarked in Rio de Janeiro. Some ships docked in Paraíba, Recife, Salvador, and other coastal cities. The comparison between the number of passengers and the population of Lisbon comes from Patrick Wilcken, *Empire Adrift*, p. 30.

6 Lília Schwarcz, *A longa viagem da biblioteca,* p. 217.

7 This information comes from Robert Hughes, *The Fatal Shore,* cited in Patrick Wilcken, *Empire Adrift,* p. 266.

8 Alan Manchester, *British Preeminence in Brazil,* p. 65.

9 Patrick Wilcken, *Empire Adrift,* p. 21.

10 Thomas O'Neill, *A concise and accurate account,* p. 10.

11 Patrick Wilcken, *Empire Adrift,* p. 14.

12 Ibid, p. 23.

13 Oliveira Lima, *D. João VI no Brasil,* p. 53.

14 Cited in Francisca L. Nogueira de Azevedo, *Carlota Joaquina,* p. 60.

15 Patrick Wilcken, *Empire Adrift,* pp. 26–27.

16 Lília Schwarcz, *A longa viagem da biblioteca,* pp. 213, 451.

17 This report comes from the duchess of Abrantes, the wife of General Junot, whom the Pernambucan historian considers not an entirely trustworthy source. Cited in Manuel de Oliveira Lima, *D. João VI no Brasil,* p. 53.

18 Luiz Norton, *A Corte de Portugal no Brasil,* p. 35.

19 Maximilien Foy, *Junot's Invasion of Portugal,* p. 47.

20 Ibid, p. 46; and Melo Moraes, *História da transladação,* pp. 55–56.

21 Oliveira Martins, *História de Portugal,* p. 517.

22 Patrick Wilcken, *Empire Adrift,* p. 25.

23 Francisca L. Nogueira de Azevedo, *Carlota Joaquina,* p. 65.

24 Jurandir Malerba, *A Corte no exílio,* pp. 20, 224. Tobias Monteiro, in *História do Império,* note 13 to chapter 3, p. 65, cites the US envoy in Lisbon, who reports that the diamonds taken by the court were worth $100 million and the money and silver $30 million.

25 Manuel de Oliveira Lima, *D. João VI no Brasil,* p. 16.

26 Kirsten Schultz, *Tropical Versailles,* p. 69.

27 Melo Moraes, *História da transladação,* p. 62.

28 Richard Bentley, *Memoirs of Admiral Sidney Smith,* cited in Francisca L. Nogueira de Azevedo, *Carlota Joaquina,* p. 65.

29 Patrick Wilcken, *Empire Adrift,* p. 10.

30 Ibid, p. 28.

31 Kenneth Light, *The Migration of the Royal Family* (no page numbers).

32 Kenneth Light, "Com os pés no mar," pp. 48–53.

33 The data on the reduction of Portugal's population during the Peninsular War, described in more detail in chapter 25 of this book, comes from Oliveira Martins, *História de Portugal,* p. 527.

VI

THE ROYAL ARCHIVIST

1 The library contained just three thousand volumes in August 1814, when British troops burned the US capitol during the War of 1812. Jefferson offered his personal library, containing some six thousand titles, to replace it. The comparison between the two libraries comes from Robert Stevenson, "A Neglected Johannes de Garlandia Manuscript (1486) in South America," at JSTOR.org.

2 Information about the life of Luiz dos Santos Marrocos in Portugal and his work at the Royal Library derive from Rodolfo Garcia's introduction to *Cartas de Luiz Joaquim dos Santos Marrocos.*

3 Luiz dos Santos Marrocos, *Cartas,* p. 78.

4 The book by Fernão Lopez de Castanheda can be found in the online catalog of the library of the University of Navarra, Humanities, Fondo Antiguo, at www.unav.es/biblioteca.

5 Besides the work of F. E. Foderé, Marrocos translated the two volumes of Barbier's *Tratado de higiene aplicada à terapia* from the French. Later, while in Brazil, he translated Foderé's *Tratado da polícia de saúde, terrestre e marítima, ou Higiene militar e naval.*

6 Rodolfo Garcia in Luiz dos Santos Marrocos, *Cartas,* pp. 7–8.

7 Oliveira Martins, *História de Portugal,* p. 498.

8 Cited in Jurandir Malerba, *A Corte no exílio,* p. 130.

9 *O comentário de Ratton é de 1755,* cited in Lília Schwarcz, *A longa viagem da biblioteca,* p. 45.

10 Cited in Lília Schwarcz, *A longa viagem da biblioteca,* p. 165.

11 Ângelo Pereira, *D João VI, Príncipe e Rei,* p. 48.

12 Alan Manchester, *British Preeminence in Brazil,* p. 54.

13 Pedro Calmon, *O rei do Brasil,* p. 8.

14 Oliveira Martins, *História de Portugal,* p. 494.

15 *Dicionário Histórico de Portugal,* at www.arqnet.pt/dicionario.

16 Oliveira Martins, *História de Portugal,* p. 514.

17 For detailed information on the origins of the Royal Library and its symbolic character for the Portuguese monarchy, see Lília Schwarcz, *A longa viagem da biblioteca,* chapters 1 and 2.

18 Rodolfo Garcia in Luiz dos Santos Marrocos, *Cartas,* p. 7.

VII

THE VOYAGE

1 Patrick Wilcken, *Empire Adrift,* p. 39.

2 For more on the fight against scurvy and the precariousness of maritime travel in the eighteenth and nineteenth centuries, see Stephen R. Bown, *The Age of Scurvy.*

3 Alan Manchester, *British Preeminence in Brazil,* p. 69.

4 Luiz dos Santos Marrocos, *Cartas,* p. 38.

5 On the history and organization of the British navy, see David Howarth, *British Sea Power;* Brian Lavery, *Nelson's Navy;* Niall Ferguson, *Empire.*

6 Kenneth Light, *The Migration,* (no page numbers).

7 As with the majority of statistics from this era, the number of passengers on board each ship in the fleet poses some controversy. The number 1,054 comes from Kenneth Light, based on a letter that Captain James Walker, commander of the British *Bedford,* wrote from Salvador to William Wellesley-Pole, secretary of the Admiralty, in London, on January 31, 1808. According to Light, the handling of the ropes and anchors alone required a crew of 385 men.

8 Patrick Wilcken, *Empire Adrift,* p. 50.

9 This inventory was made by Admiral Sidney Smith, commander of the English fleet, in a letter to the Admiralty in London written on December 1, 1807, and cited by Maria Graham in *Journal of a Voyage to Brazil.*

10 Patrick Wilcken, *Empire Adrift,* p. 35.

11 Melo Moraes, *História da transladação,* p. 59.

12 Patrick Wilcken, *Empire Adrift,* p. 31.

13 Melo Moraes, *História da transladação,* p. 62.

14 Kenneth Light, "Com os pés no mar," pp. 48–53.

15 Kenneth Light, "A viagem da família real para o Brasil."

16 Letter from James Walker of January 6, 1808, to William Wellesley-Pole, secretary of the Admirality, transcribed in Kenneth Light, *The Migration* (no page numbers).

17 Kenneth Light, "A viagem da família real para o Brasil."

18 Information about the scattering of the fleet during the storm and the accident involving George Green come from the onboard diaries of Captain James Walker, transcribed by Kenneth Light, in *The Migration* (no page numbers).

19 Letter to the prince regent, transcribed by Ângelo Pereira, *D. João VI,* pp. 183–185.

20 Kenneth Light, *The Migration* (no page numbers).

21 Kenneth Light, "A viagem da família real para o Brasil."

22 Tobias Monteiro, *História do império,* p. 67.

23 J. J. Colledge, *Ships of the Royal Navy.*

24 The original edition of Thomas O'Neill's book is one of the greatest rarities in the book world. One of the few copies can be found in the Mindlin Library in São Paulo.

25 Thomas O'Neill, *A concise and accurate account,* pp. 11–12.

26 Ibid, pp. 60–61.

27 Ibid, p. 14.

28 Ibid, pp. 17–20.

29 Ângelo Pereira, *Os filhos d'El-Rei D. João VI,* p. 113.

30 Historian Ângelo Pereira argues that, if the duke of Cadaval had not traveled to Brazil, he would have been appointed president of the regency, in charge of administrative affairs in Portugal and negotiations with French troops following the court's departure. The duke preferred to accompany João and hence embarked on the *D. João de Castro,* during which time he "suffered all of the deprivations imaginable of clothing and rations," according to Pereira. "He spent the entire journey sick, and he perished in Bahia, thereby forever providing an example of solid character and devotion to his ruler" (*Os filhos d'El-Rei* p. 115).

VIII

SALVADOR

1 This is the version according to Melo Moraes, *História da transladação,* pp. 66–67.

2 Kenneth Light, "A viagem da família real para o Brasil."

3 Brigantines were small, rapid ships used by the Portuguese for coastal reconnaisance and tactical transportations between docks and deep water ships anchored farther out. They had between ten and nineteen rowing benches and could be equipped with one or two masts. They were used also for ceremonial

transportation. One was used in just such a way during João's arrival in Brazil in 1808 and is on display today at the Maritime Museum in Rio de Janeiro. For more information about vessels used in the Portuguese colonial period, see Fernando Gomes Pedrosa (editor), *Navios, Marinheiros, e Arte de Navegar. 1139–1499*, pp. 63–65.

4 Ângelo Pereira, *D. João VI*, p. 113.

5 As the following chapter discusses, communication in the interior of the colony proved even slower and more unreliable. Information sent from Lisbon took months to reach São Paulo or Rio Grande do Sul.

6 Melo Moraes, *História da transladação*, p. 67.

7 For a detailed description of their arrival and reception in Salvador, see Melo Moraes, *História da transladação*, p. 67, and Pedro Calmon, *O rei do Brasil*, pp. 123–129.

8 That Dom João disembarked in the morning comes from Pedro Calmon. Melo Moraes argues that he disembarked between 4 p.m. and 5 p.m.

9 Maria Graham, *Journal of a Voyage to Brazil*, p. 132.

10 This data comes from Nireu Cavalcanti, *O Rio de Janeiro setecentista*, p. 258, based on a list of the thirty largest cities in the world at the beginning of the nineteenth century as compiled by historian A. H. Oliveira Marques.

11 For a description of Salvador and the strategic aspects of its location, see Charles Boxer, *The Golden Age of Brazil*, pp. 127–128.

12 Johann Moritz Rugendas, *Viagem pitoresca pelo Brasil*, p. 52.

13 Charles Boxer, *The Golden Age of Brazil*, p. 128.

14 Ibid, p. 130.

15 Ibid, p. 128.

16 Maria Graham, *Journal of a Voyage to Brazil*, pp. 132–133.

17 Ibid, p. 135.

18 Cited in Charles Boxer, *The Golden Age of Brazil*, p. 129.

19 Ibid, p. 140.

20 Ibid, p. 138.

21 Patrick Wilcken, *Empire Adrift*, p. 66.

22 Lília Schwarcz, *A longa viagem da biblioteca*, pp. 229–230.

23 Nelson Werneck Sodré, *As razões da Independência*, p. 139.

24 Alan Manchester, *British Preeminence in Brazil*, p. 71.

25 Melo Moraes, *História da transladação*, p. 59.

26 Ibid, p. 74.

27 Patrick Wilcken, *Empire Adrift*, p. 68.

IX

THE COLONY

1 Cited in J. F. de Almeida Prado, *D. João VI e o início*, p. 134.

2 *Correio Braziliense* is written with a "z" and not an "s," maintaining the orthographic standard of the era. For the same reason, the word portuguêz was often written with a "z" according to Adriano da Gama Cury, *Correio Braziliense: ortografia e linguagem, artigo para o site Observatório da Imprensa*, at Observatorio, at UltimoSegundo.ig.com.br.

3 José Honório Rodrigues, *Independência*, p. 52.

4 Manuel de Oliveira Lima, *D. João VI no Brasil*, pp. 55–56.

5 Pandiá Calógeras, *Formação histórica do Brasil*, p. 76.

6 Magazine of the Instituto Histórico e Geográfico Brasileiro, 1861, cited in Silvia Hunold Lara, *Campos da Violência*.

7 Alcide D'Orbigny, *Viagem pitoresca através do Brasil*, p. 43.

8 Fernando Novais, *História da Vida Privada*, volume 2, p. 20, based on data collected by Dauril Auden.

9 The census of 1819, the first conducted by João VI's government, calculated the population of Brazil at 3,596,132 inhabitants, not taking into account nearly 800,000 indigenous people. There were 1,107,389 slaves. Minas Gerais, the most populous province, had 631,885 inhabitants, including 168,543 slaves. Rio de Janeiro came in second with 510,000 inhabitants, of which 23 percent were slaves, then Bahia and Pernambuco with 477,912 and 371,465 inhabitants respectively. Pandiá Calógeras, *Formação histórica do Brasil,* pp. 63–64.

10 Nelson Werneck Sodré, *Formação Histórica do Brasil,* p. 158. Fernando Novais, in *História da Vida Privada,* volume 2, p. 20, gives the precise figure of 2,931,000 for the population of Portugal in 1801, which means that the kingdom and the colony had a comparable number of inhabitants at the turn of the century.

11 Thomas Skidmore, *Brazil,* p. 18.

12 Manuel de Oliveira Lima, *D. João VI no Brasil,* p. 160.

13 Roberto Pompeu de Toledo, *A capital da solidão,* p. 247.

14 Jorge Caldeira, *Mauá,* p. 36.

15 Mara Ziravello, *Brasil 500 Anos,* p. 91.

16 Alcir Lenharo, *As tropas da moderação,* p. 58.

17 Sérgio Buarque de Holanda, *Raízes do Brasil,* p. 12.

18 Francisco Adolfo de Varnhagen, *História geral do Brasil,* volume V, p. 82.

19 Manuel de Oliveira Lima, *D. João VI no Brasil,* p. 91; and Jorge Caldeira, *Mauá,* p. 41 and 46.

20 John Mawe, *Travels in the Interior of Brazil,* p. 212.

21 Francisco Aldolfo de Varnhagen, *História geral do Brasil,* volume V, p. 79.

22 Manuel de Oliveira Lima, *D. João VI no Brasil,* p. 94.

23 John Mawe, *Travels in the Interior of Brazil,* pp. 47–48. For more information about Mawe, see chapter 21.

24 John Mawe, *Travels in the Interior of Brazil,* p. 57.

25 In the 1798 census, São Paulo had 21,304 inhabitants. Even considering the recent separation of the city of Atibaia, this was nearly the same as the result of the

1765 census: 20,873 inhabitants, including slaves. Roberto Pompeu de Toledo, *A capital da solidão,* pp. 239, 256.

26 Roberto Pompeu de Toledo, *A capital da solidão,* p. 136.

27 The text in this paragraph comes from J. F. de Almeida Prado, *Tomas Ender,* p. 35.

28 Ibid, p. 67.

29 For a description of commerce in Rio de Janeiro during D. João VI's era, see Alcir Lenharo, *Tropas da moderação,* p. 25ff.

30 J. F. de Almeida Prado, *Tomas Ender,* p. 240.

31 Ibid, p. 240.

32 John Mawe, *Travels in the Interior of Brazil,* p. 240.

33 John Mawe, *Travels in the Interior of Brazil,* pp. 195–196.

34 Pandiá Calógeras, *Formação Histórica do Brasil,* p. 60.

35 Ibid, p. 60.

36 Cited in Warren Dean, *A ferro e fogo,* p. 114.

37 Alcide D'Orbigny, *Viagem pitoresca através do Brasil,* p. 145.

38 Francisco Aldolfo de Varnhagen, *História geral do Brasil,* volume V, p. 61.

39 John Mawe, *Travels in the Interior of Brazil,* p. 211.

40 Nireu Cavalcanti, *O Rio de Janeiro setecentista,* p. 169.

41 Maria Odila da Silva Dias, *A interiorização da metrópole,* pp. 42–43.

42 Jorge Caldeira, *Mauá,* p. 140.

43 Francisco Aldolfo de Varnhagen, *História geral do Brasil,* volume V, p. 23.

44 On censorship in colonial Brazil, see Isabel Lustosa, "Insultos impressos: o nascimento da imprensa no Brasil" in *A Independência brasileira,* p. 242.

45 Ronaldo Vainfas, *Dicionário do Brasil colonial,* pp. 139–140.

46 Roderick Barman, *Brazil,* p. 51.

47 Ibid, p. 52. That D. João avidly read the Correio comes from Manuel de Oliveira Lima, *D. João VI no Brasil*, p. 166.

48 Roderick Barman, *Brazil*, p. 52.

49 Jurandir Malerba, *A Corte no exílio*, p. 26.

50 Silvia Hunold Lara, *Campos da violência*, p. 35.

51 Thomas Skidmore, *Brazil*, pp. 27–28.

52 On the punishments for those involved in the Minas Gerais Conspiracy of 1789 and those guilty of participating in the Tailors' Conspiracy, see Kenneth Maxwell, *Conflicts and Conspiracies*.

53 For the history of the Tavora Affair, see Silvia Hunold Lara, *Campos da violência*, p. 92, and Lília Schwarcz, *A longa viagem da biblioteca*, pp. 100–101.

54 Thomas H. Holloway, *Polícia no Rio de Janeiro*, p. 44.

55 Maria Odila Leite da Silva Dias, *A interiorização da metrópole*, p. 27.

X

TREE FROG, THE REPORTER

1 Luis Gonçalves dos Santos, *Memórias*, pp. 18–19.

2 Luis Gonçalves dos Santos was born in 1767 and died in 1844. Aside from his records of the court's presence in Rio de Janeiro, he argued in favor of independence, penned works on mysticism, and locked horns in a long debate with Father Diogo Feijó about the question of celibacy in the clergy, according to *A vida na Corte* at Camara.gov.br.

3 The explanation comes from Lília Schwarcz, *A longa viagem da biblioteca*, p. 240.

4 This specific phrase comes from João Luís Ribeiro Fragoso, *Homens de Grossa Aventura*.

5 Luis Gonçalves dos Santos, *Memórias*, pp. 4–5.

6 Lília Schwarcz, *A longa viagem da biblioteca,* pp. 236–237.

7 Ibid, pp. 238–239.

8 Luis Gonçalves dos Santos, *Memórias,* p. 16.

9 Ibid, pp. 18–19.

10 Ibid, p. 21.

11 Pedro Calmon, *O rei do Brasil,* p. 131.

12 Tobias Monteiro, *História do Império,* pp. 82–83.

13 "Having observed them arrive sheared, all of the fairer sex of Rio de Janeiro underwent the procedure dictated by fashion, and within a short time the plentiful locks of carioca women fell one by one to the scissors." Tobias Monteiro, *História do Império,* p. 67.

14 Luis Gonçalves dos Santos, *Memórias,* p. 25.

15 Ibid, p. 24.

16 Tobias Monteiro, *História do Império,* p. 83.

17 That Amaro Velho da Silva bore one of the canopy poles comes from Padre Gonçalves dos Santos, *Memórias,* p. 26. That Amaro was a major slave trafficker comes from João Luis Fragoso, *Homens de Grossa Aventura,* pp. 182, 258–259. According to Fragoso, the post-mortem inventory of Amaro's estate valued his fortune at 948,934,770 réis, making him one of Brazil's wealthiest individuals. The inventory of his wife, Leonarda Maria da Silva, in 1825, totaled 61,620 pounds sterling, 254 slaves, and two planatations in the city of Campos, north of Rio de Janeiro.

18 Luiz Norton, *A corte de Portugal no Brasil.*

19 Jurandir Malerba, *A Corte no exílio,* p. 233.

20 Cited in Kirsten Schultz, *Tropical Versailles,* p. 106.

21 Alexandre de Melo Moraes, *História da transladação,* p. 95.

22 Cited in Manuel de Oliveira Lima, *D. João VI no Brasil,* p. 79. De Oliveira Lima cites all values in either réis or francs. Monetary conversions derive from the system available through the British Parliament, listed in the electronic bibliography.

XI
A LETTER

1 Rodolfo Garcia, in the introduction to Luiz dos Santos Marrocos, *Cartas.*

2 Luiz dos Santos Marrocos, *Cartas,* p. 29. To facilitate readability, the text of the letter has been edited.

XII
RIO DE JANEIRO

1 John Mawe, *Travels in the Interior of Brazil,* p. 100.

2 These calculations derive from the report of naturalist George Gardner and traveler Rudy Bauss, cited in Luciana de Lima Martins, *O Rio de Janeiro dos viajantes,* p. 70.

3 Luciana de Lima Martins, *O Rio de Janeiro dos viajantes,* p. 71.

4 *Charles Darwin's Beagle Diary,* cited in Luciana de Lima Martins, *O Rio de Janeiro dos viajantes,* p. 126.

5 John Luccock, *Notes on Rio de Janeiro,* p. 33.

6 John Luccock's book is *Notes on Rio de Janeiro and Southern Parts of Brazil.*

7 John Luccock, *Notes on Rio de Janeiro,* p. 41.

8 Manolo Garcia Florentino, *Em costas negras,* p. 31ff.

9 James Tuckey, *An Account of a Voyage,* pp. 44–45.

10 Manuel de Oliveira Lima, *D. João VI no Brasil,* p., 78.

11 Alexander Caldcleugh, *Travels in South America,* p. 36.

12 Jurandir Malerba, *A Corte no exílio,* p. 129.

13 Cited by Luiz Felipe Alencastro, "Vida Privada e Ordem Privada no Império" in *História da Vida Privada no Brasil,* volume 2, p. 67.

14 Cited in Jurandir Malerba, *A Corte no exílio*, p. 152.

15 James Tuckey, *An Account of a Voyage*, pp. 60–61.

16 John Luccock, *Notes on Rio de Janeiro*, p. 121.

17 Ibid, pp. 123–125.

18 Cited in Eduardo Dias, *Memórias de forasteiros*, p. 114.

19 John Luccock, *Notes on Rio de Janeiro*, pp. 42–44.

20 Gastão Cruls, *Aparência do Rio de Janeiro*.

21 Jurandir Malerba, *A Corte no exílio*, p. 132.

22 Rubens Borba de Moraes, in the Brazilian introduction to John Luccock's *Notes on Rio de Janeiro*, citing data from the *Gazeta Extraordinária do Rio de Janeiro* of February 25, 1811.

23 Henry Brackenridge, *Voyage to South America*, volume 1, p. 116.

24 Leila Mezan Algranti, *O feitor ausente*, p. 144.

25 John Mawe, *Travels in the Interior of Brazil*, p. 98.

26 Ernest Ebel, *O Rio de Janeiro e seus arredores em 1824*, p. 13.

27 J. Parrish Robertson and William Parrish, *Letters on Paraguay; comprising an account of a four years residence in that republic under the government of the Dictator Francia*. Cited in Leila Mezan Algranti, *O feitor ausente*, p. 144.

28 John Luccock, *Notes on Rio de Janeiro*, pp. 50–51.

29 Melo Moraes, *A história da transladação*, p. 441.

30 Nireu Cavalcanti, *O Rio de Janeiro setecentista*, p. 193.

31 Thomas O'Neill, *A concise and accurate account*, pp. 61–62.

32 Nireu Cavalcanti, *O Rio de Janeiro setecentista*, pp. 420–422.

33 Leila Mezan Algranti, *O feitor ausente*, p. 26.

34 Ibid, p. 30, based on reports by John Luccock and the 1821 census.

XIII
DOM JOÃO

1 This story is related by Vieira Fazenda in *Antiqualhas,* volume II, pp. 307–308, and cited by Magalhães Jr. in the notes to José Presas, *Memórias Secretas.*

2 James Henderson, *A History of Brazil,* p. 75, and Tobias Monteiro, *História do Império,* p. 91.

3 Oliveira Martins, *História de Portugal,* p. 536.

4 Cited in Tobias Monteiro, *História do Império,* p. 91.

5 Ângelo Pereira, *D. João Príncipe e Rei,* p. 157, based on Pellegrini's painting of 1805, in the collection of the Museu de Arte Antiga de Portugal.

6 Luiz Norton, *A corte de Portugal no Brasil,* p. 124.

7 Pandiá Calógeras, *Formação histórica do Brasil,* p. 84.

8 Lília Schwarcz, *A longa viagem da biblioteca,* p. 189.

9 Oliveira Martins, *História de Portugal,* p. 536.

10 Manuel de Oliveira Lima, *D. João VI no Brasil,* p. 578.

11 Ângelo Pereira, *D. João VI Príncipe e Rei,* p. 91.

12 Pedro Calmon, *O rei do Brasil,* p. 21.

13 Letter of August 13, 1805, cited in Varnhagen, *História geral do Brasil,* volume V, p. 91.

14 On the history of João's affair with Eugênia José de Menezes, see Tobias Monteiro, *História do Império,* pp. 96–103.

15 Alberto Pimental, *A última corte do absolutismo,* p. 64, Cited in Tobias Monteiro, *História do Império,* p. 100.

16 Patrick Wilcken, *Empire Adrift,* pp. 173–174; Tobias Monteiro, *História do Império,* p. 97.

17 Vieira Fazenda, *Antiqualhas,* volume II, pp. 307–308, cited by Magalhães Jr.

18 José Presas, *Memórias Secretas.*

19 Vieira Fazenda, *Antiqualhas,* volume II, p. 307–308, cited by Magalhães Jr.

20 Theodor von Leithold, Ludwig von Rango, *O Rio de Janeiro.*

21 Oliveira Martins, *História de Portugal,* p. 536.

22 Cited in Almeida Prado, *D. João VI,* p. 79.

23 Pedro Calmon, *O rei do Brasil,* pp. 76–77.

24 Tobias Monteiro, *História do Império,* p. 91.

25 Kirsten Schultz, *Tropical Versailles,* p. 25.

26 Tobias Monteiro, *História do Império,* p. 231.

27 Ibid.

28 For more details on the roles of the count of Linhares, the count of Barca, and Thomaz Antônio in João's government, see Manuel de Oliveira Lima, *D. João VI no Brasil,* pp. 150–152.

29 Jurandir Malerba, *A Corte no exílio,* p. 204.

30 Pedro Calmon, *O rei do Brasil.*

31 Manuel de Oliveira Lima, *D. João VI no Brasil,* p. 577.

32 Ibid, p. 31.

XIV

CARLOTA JOAQUINA

1 Ronaldo Vainfas, *Dicionário do Brasil colonial,* p. 102.

2 This description is based on Pedro Calmon, *O rei do Brasil,* p. 28. The information about her smallpox scars comes from Marcus Cheke, *Carlota Joaquina, Queen of Portugal,* p. 2.

3 Cited in Pedro Calmon, *O rei do Brasil,* p. 29.

4 Tobias Monteiro, *História do Império,* p. 86.

5 Manuel de Oliveira Lima, *D. João VI no Brasil,* p. 177.

6 Ronaldo Vainfas, *Dicionário,* p. 103.

7 Pedro Calmon, *O rei do Brasil,* p. 30.

8 Marcus Cheke, *Carlota,* p. 2.

9 Lília Schwarcz, *A longa viagem da biblioteca,* p. 193

10 Henry Brackenridge, *Voyage to South America,* pp. 131–133.

11 Pedro Calmon, *O rei do Brasil,* p. 32.

12 R. Magalhães Jr. in the notes to José Presas, *Memórias secretas.*

13 Manuel de Oliveira Lima, *D. João VI no Brasil,* p. 23, 74.

14 J. F. de Almeida Prado, *D. João VI,* p. 157; Tobias Monteiro, *História do Império,* p. 94.

15 José Presas, *Memórias secretas,* pp. 55–62.

16 For more background on José Presas, see R. Magalhães Jr. in the preface to *Memórias secretas.*

17 Correspondence in the archives of the Castelo do Conde D'Eu, transcribed in Tobias Monteiro, *História do Império,* p. 216.

18 Marcus Cheke, *Carlot Joaquina,* p. 81.

19 Manuel de Oliveira Lima, *D. João VI no Brasil,* p. 692.

20 Tobias Monteiro, *História do Império,* p. 106.

21 R. Magalhães Jr. in the notes to José Presas, *Memórias secretas.*

XV

HANDS IN THE COFFERS

1 Luiz Felipe Alencastro, "Vida Privada e Ordem Privada no Império" in *História da vida privada no Brasil,* volume 2, p. 12.

2 John Armitage, *The History of Brazil,* volume 1, pp. 14–15.

3 Luiz Felipe Alencastro, "Vida Privada," p. 12.

4 Jurandir Malerba, *A Corte no exílio,* p. 236.

5 James Henderson, *A History of Brazil,* p. 82.

6 Ibid, p. 63.

7 Santiago Silva de Andrade, "Pondo Ordem na Casa."

8 Ibid.

9 Jurandir Malerba, *A Corte no exílio,* p. 240.

10 Lília Schwarcz, *A longa viagem da biblioteca,* pp. 387–423.

11 Lenira Menezes Martinho and Riva Gorenstein, *Negociantes e caixeiros na sociedade da independência,* p. 148.

12 Fernando Carlos Cerqueira Lima and Elisa Muller, *Moeda e Crédito no Brasil.*

13 In 1820, deposits of precious metals totaled 1,315 *contos de réis,* while bills in circulation amounted to 8,070 *contos.* In 1821, the Bank of Brazil's balance revealed a negative balance of 6,016 contos according to Carlos Manuel Peláez and Wilson Suzigan, *História Monetária do Brasil,* p. 12.

14 Cited in Nelson Werneck Sodré, *As razões da Independência,* p. 149.

15 Manuel de Oliveira Lima, *D. João VI no Brasil,* p. 84.

16 Cited in Nelson Werneck Sodré, *As razões,* p. 148.

17 Santiago Silva de Andrade, "Pondo Ordem na Casa."

18 Maria Graham, *Journal of a Voyage to Brazil,* p. 244.

19 Tobias Monteiro, *História do Império,* p. 274.

20 Ibid, p. 309.

21 Ibid, p. 273.

22 Cited in Nelson Werneck Sodré, *As razões,* p. 150.

XVI
A NEW COURT

1 João Luis Ribeiro Fragoso, *Homens de grossa aventura,* pp. 288, 294.

2 Jurandir Malerba, *A Corte no exílio,* p. 216.

3 Pedro Calmon, *O rei do Brasil,* p. 149.

4 John Armitage, *The History of Brazil,* volume 1, p. 16.

5 Anonymous, *Relação das festas que se fizeram,* p. 15.

6 Jurandir Malerba, *A Corte no exílio,* p. 278.

7 Ibid, pp. 231–232.

8 Ibid, p. 249.

9 Ibid, p. 280.

10 João Luis Ribeiro Fragoso, *Homens de grossa aventura,* p. 288.

11 Cited in Tobias Monteiro, *História do Império,* p. 245.

12 James Henderson, *A History of Brazil,* p. 82.

13 Henry Brackenridge, *Voyage to South America,* p. 122.

14 APDG, *Sketches of Portuguese Life,* p. 176.

15 James Henderson, *A History of Brazil,* p. 64.

16 Jurandir Malerba, *A Corte no exílio,* p. 184.

17 Ibid, p. 186.

XVII
EMPRESS OF THE SEAS

1 Alan Manchester, *British Preeminence in Brazil,* p. 70.

2 Cited by Rubens Borba de Moraes in the Brazilian introduction to John Luccock, *Notes on Rio de Janeiro* (p. 8).

3 Nireu Cavalcanti, *O Rio de Janeiro setecentista,* p. 258.

4 Peter Ackroyd, *London: The Biography* (audiobook).

5 Gunther E. Ruthenberg, *The Napoleonic Wars,* p. 25.

6 Peter Ackroyd, *London: The Biography* (audiobook).

7 Jorge Caldeira, *Mauá,* p. 160.

8 Kenneth Light, "Com os pés no mar," pp. 48–53. That the American Navy had six ships comes from Richard Zacks, *The Pirate Coast* (audiobook).

9 British History—*Empire and Sea Power,* at www.bbc.co.uk.

10 Kenneth Light, "A viagem da família real para o Brasil."

11 José Presas, *Memórias Secreta.*

12 Alan Manchester, *British Preeminence in Brazil,* p. 78.

13 Ibid, pp. 88–89.

14 Ibid, pp. 79, 87–88.

15 Ibid, p. 88.

16 Ibid, p. 108.

17 Ibid, p. 103.

18 Ibid, pp. 79, 94.

19 Rubens Borba de Moraes in the Brazilian introduction to John Luccock, *Notes on Rio de Janeiro,* citing data from the *Gazeta Extraordinária do Rio de Janeiro* of February 25, 1811.

20 Kirsten Schultz, *Tropical Versailles,* p. 210.

21 Alan Manchester, *British Preeminence in Brazil,* p. 98.

22 John Mawe, *Travels in the Interior of Brazil,* pp. 324–325. J. J. E. Roy, *L'Empire du Brésil—Souvenirs de Voyage,* cited by Rubens Barbosa de Morais in the introduction to John Luccock, *Notes on Rio de Janeiro.*

23 John Mawe, *Travels in the Interior of Brazil,* p. 218.

24 Ibid, p. 328.

XVIII

TRANSFORMATION

1 Pedro Calmon, *O rei do Brasil.*

2 Francisco Aldolfo de Varnhagen, *História geral do Brasil,* volume 5, p. 112.

3 Jorge Miguel Pereira, "Economia e política na explicação da independência do Brasil" in *A Independência brasileira—Novas Dimensões,* pp. 77–84.

4 Maria Odila Leite da Silva Dias, *A interiorização da metrópole,* p. 87.

5 Alcir Lenharo, *Tropas da moderação,* pp. 59–60.

6 Maria Odila Leite da Silva Dias, *A interiorização da metrópole,* p. 36.

7 Ibid, p. 86.

8 Manuel de Oliveira Lima, *D. João VI no Brasil,* p. 174.

9 Warren Dean, *A ferro e fogo,* p. 140.

10 John Armitage, *The History of Brazil,* volume 1, p. 21.

11 Cited in Lília Schwarcz, *A longa viagem da biblioteca,* p. 253.

12 Jurandir Malerba, *A Corte no exílio,* p. 145.

13 John Mawe, *Travels in the Interior of Brazil,* p. 192.

14 Cited in Francisco Aldolfo de Varnhagen, *História geral do Brasil,* volume 5, p. 99.

15 Tobias Monteiro, *História do Império,* p. 221.

16 Manuel de Oliveira Lima, *D. João VI no Brasil,* p. 170.

17 The building designed by Grandjean de Montigny to host the academy took ten years to be ready, inaugurated in 1826 during the reign of Pedro I.

18 Manuel de Oliveira Lima, *D. João VI no Brasil*, p. 171.

19 Cited in Luiz Norton, *A corte de Portugal no Brasil*, p. 145.

20 Teodor von Leithold and Ludwig von Rango, *O Rio de Janeiro*.

21 Jurandir Malerba, *A Corte no exílio*, p. 226.

22 Cited in Leila Mezan Algranti, *D. João VI*, p. 39.

23 Henry Brackenridge, *Voyage to South America*, volume 1, pp. 113–115.

24 For a description of the changes in Rio de Janeiro following the court's arrival, see Jurandir Malerba, *A Corte no exílio*, p. 165ff; on the effects of the changes and the announcements in the *Gazeta do Rio de Janeiro*, see Delso Renault, *O Rio antigo nos anúncios de jornais*.

25 Francisco Gracioso; J. Roberto Whitaker Penteado, *Propaganda brasileira*.

26 Luiz dos Santos Marrocos, *Cartas*, p. 444.

27 Jurandir Malerba, *A Corte no exílio*, pp. 167–168.

28 Ernst Ebel, *O Rio de Janeiro e seus arredores*, p. 71.

29 Alexander Caldcleugh, *Travels in South America*, p. 64.

XIX

THE CHIEF OF POLICE

1 As with all statistics from this period, the figures remain controversial. Manuel de Oliveira Lima calculates a population of 110,000 in 1817. James Henderson estimates 150,000 in 1821, which Kirsten Schultz reduces to 80,000.

2 Luiz dos Santos Marrocos, *Cartas*, p. 163.

3 This expression comes from Francis Albert Cotta, "Polícia para quem precisa" in *Revista de História* of the National Library, December 2006, p. 65.

4 For a description of Paulo Fernandes Viana's duties, see Kirsten Schultz, *Tropical Versailles*, p. 105; and Thomas Holloway, *Polícia no Rio de Janeiro*, pp. 46–47.

5 Jurandir Malerba, *A Corte no exílio*, p. 264.

6 Oliveira Lima, *D. João VI no Brasil*, p. 156.

7 Jurandir Malerba, *A Corte no exílio*, p. 132.

8 Ibid, p. 137.

9 Cited in Kirsten Schultz, *Tropical Versailles*, p. 106.

10 Cited in Maria Odila Leite da Silva Dias, *A interiorização da metrópole*, p. 134.

11 Leila Mezan Algrantri, *O feitor ausente*, p. 168.

12 Jurandir Malerba, *A Corte no exílio*, p. 134.

13 Leila Mezan Algranti, *O feitor ausente*, p. 169.

14 Kirsten Schultz, *Tropical Versailles*, p. 125.

15 James Henderson, *A History of Brazil*, p. 77.

16 Kirsten Schultz, *Tropical Versailles*, p. 111.

17 Leila Mezan Algranti, *O feitor ausente*, p. 76.

18 Kirsten Schultz, *Tropical Versailles*, p. 109.

19 Ibid, p. 108.

20 Cited in Leila Mezan Alegranti, *O feitor ausente*, p. 39.

21 Thomas Holloway, *Polícia no Rio de Janeiro*, pp. 48–49.

22 Domingos Ribeiro dos Guimarães Peixoto, *Aos sereníssimos príncipes reais*, p. 2.

23 Manuel Vieira da Silva, *Reflexões sobre alguns dos meios*, p. 12.

24 Guimarães Peixoto, *Aos sereníssimos príncipes reais*, p. 2. (The text has been modified to faciliate ease of reading.)

25 Manuel Vieira da Silva, *Reflexões sobre alguns dos meios*, p. 8.

26 Paulo Fenandes Viana, *Abreviada demonstração dos trabalhos da polícia*. Cited in Leila Mezan Alegranti, *O feitor ausente*, p. 37.

27 The urban reforms that Viana put into motion in Rio de Janeiro came nearly half a century later than similar initiatives in European capitals. In 1785, London, for example, already had a system of streetlamps, police stations, and a squad of sixty-eight men who patrolled the city on foot each night. See J. J. Tobias, *Crime and Industrial Society in the Nineteenth Century.*

XX

SLAVERY

1 For more information about the Valongo Slave Market and the archeological research in the Gamboa district, see PretosNovos.com.br.

2 The estimate comes from Sir Henry Chamberlain, *Views and Costumes of the City and Neighbourhood of Rio de Janeiro,* the chapter entitled "The Slave Market" (no page number). Mary Karash, in *A vida dos escravos no Rio de Janeiro: 1808– 1850,* catalogued 225,047 who disembarked between 1800 and 1816, which gives an annual average of 14,000.

3 Maria Graham, *Journal of a Voyage to Brazil,* p. 227.

4 James Henderson, *A History of Brazil,* p. 74.

5 Henry Chamberlain, *Views and Costumes,* "The Slave Market" (caption to slide 11).

6 Ronaldo Vainfas, in *Dicionário do Brasil colonial,* p. 555, warns that figures on slave traffic in Brazil often vary, ranging from 3.3 million to 8 million. Robert Conrad, in *Tumbeiros: o tráfico de escravos para o Brasil,* estimates 5.6 million, distributed as follows: 100,000 in the sixteenth century, 2 million in the seventeenth, another 2 million in the eighteenth, and 1.5 million in the nineteenth. João Luis Ribeiro Fragoso, in *Homens de grossa aventura,* p. 181, says that between 1811 and 1830, 1,181 slave ships arrived in Rio de Janeiro from Africa, transporting 489,950 slaves. For more information on the topic, see Philip D. Curtin, *The Atlantic Slave Trade,* Wisconsin University Press, cited in Manolo Garcia Florentino, *Em costas negras,* p. 59; and Thomas Skidmore, Brazil, p. 5.

7 Manolo Garcia Florentino, *Em costas negras,* p. 59.

8 Alan Manchester, *British Preeminence in Brazil,* p. 164.

9 João Luis Ribeiro Fragoso, *Homens de grossa aventura,* p. 181.

10 Manolo Garcia Florentino, *Em costas negras,* p. 146.

11 This information comes from Henry Chamberlain, *Views and Costumes.* Monetary equivalents derive from Robert Twigger, *Inflation.*

12 Manolo Garcia Florentino, *Em costas negras,* p. 125.

13 Ibid, p. 154.

14 For calculations of the mortality rate during the slave trade, see Ronaldo Vainfas, *Dicionário do Brasil colonial,* p. 556, and Manolo Garcia Florentino, *Em costas negras,* pp. 149–154.

15 Manolo Garcia Florentino, *Em costas negras,* p. 149.

16 F. O. Shyllon, *Black Slaves in Britain,* p. 184.

17 Ian Baucom, *Specters of the Atlantic.*

18 For more information on the donations and remunerations made to Dom João by slave traffickers, see Manolo Garcia Florentino, *Em costas negras,* pp. 221–222; Jurandir Malerba, *A Corte no exílio,* pp. 231–250; and João Luis Ribeiro Fragoso, *Homens de grossa aventura,* pp. 288–294.

19 Equivalents based on Robert Twigger, *Inflation.*

20 Jean Marcel Carvalho França, *Outras visões do Rio de Janeiro colonial,* p. 277.

21 Luiz dos Santos Marrocos, *Cartas,* p. 35.

22 Ibid, p. 440.

23 André João Antonil, *Cultura e opulência do Brasil por suas drogas e minas,* p. 269.

24 Almeida Prado, *Tomas Ender,* p. 34.

25 Jean Marcel Carvalho França, *Visões do Rio de Janeiro Colonial,* p. 154.

26 James Tuckey, *An Account of a Voyage,* pp. 55–56.

27 Sérgio Buarque de Holanda, *Raízes do Brasil,* p. 59.

28 Ernest Ebel, *O Rio de Janeiro e seus arredores,* p. 29.

29 John Luccock, *Notes on Rio de Janeiro*, pp. 64, 106, 201.

30 Leila Mezan Algranti, *O feitor ausente*, pp. 65–73.

31 Silvia Hunold Lara, *Campos da violência*, p. 45.

32 Ibid, pp. 73–77.

33 Cited in Eduardo Dias, *Memórias de forasteiros*, pp. 140–142.

34 James Henderson, *A History of Brazil*, p. 73.

35 Charles Boxer, *The Golden Age of Brazil*, pp. 158–59.

36 Leila Mezan Algranti, *O feitor ausente*, p. 181.

37 Francisco Gracioso and J. Roberto Whitaker Penteado, *Propaganda Brasileira*, p. 23.

38 Theodor von Leithold and Ludwig von Rango, *O Rio de Janeiro*, p. 44.

39 This estimate derives from research conducted by Silvia Hunold Lara into the registers of Vila de São Salvador dos Guaitacazes, a district in the north of the present-day state of Rio de Janeiro, in *Campos da violência*, pp. 295–322.

40 Leila Mezan Algranti, *O feitor ausente*, p. 106.

41 John Mawe, *Travels in the Interior of Brazil*, p. 224.

42 Silvia Hunold Lara, *Campos da violência*, p. 249.

43 Ronaldo Vainfas, *Dicionário do Brasil colonial*, pp. 31, 116.

44 Leila Mezan Algranti, *O feitor ausente*, p. 107.

XXI

THE TRAVELERS

1 Rubens Borba de Moraes; William Berrien, *Manual bibliográfico de estudos brasileiros*, pp. 592–627, Cited in Leonardo Dantas Silva, *Textos sobre o Recife*, at www.fundaj.gov.br.

2 Almeida Prado, *Tomas Ender*, p. 3.

3 Henry Brackenridge, *Voyage to South America*, volume 1, p. 113.

4 According to Leonardo Dantas Silva, *Textos sobre o Recife*, at www.fundaj.gov.br/docs/rec/rec02.html.

5 Luis Edmundo, *Recordações do Rio Antigo*, pp. 47–50.

6 Ibid, p. 64.

7 Such is the case with Robert Harvey, author of *Cochrane*, used as a reference here.

8 Information about Maria Graham here comes from the introduction to *Journal of a Voyage to Brazil*.

9 For more information on the life and work of Henry Koster, see Eduardo Dias, *Memórias de forasteiros*, pp. 30–50.

10 Cited in Warren Dean, *A ferro e fogo*, p. 132.

11 John Mawe, *Travels in the Interior of Brazil*, p. 189.

12 James Henderson, *A History of Brazil*, p. 76.

13 William John Burchell, *Rio de Janeiro's Most Beautiful*, p. 8.

14 Warren Dean, *A ferro e fogo*, p. 141.

15 For more information about Saint-Hilaire's voyage to São Paulo, see Roberto Pompeu de Toledo, *A capital da solidão*, pp. 269, 278.

16 Manuel de Oliveira Lima, *D. João VI no Brasil*, p. 71.

17 Alcide D'Orbigny, *Viagem pitoresca atráves do Brasil*, pp. 51–56.

XXII

NAPOLEON'S DOWNFALL

1 Cited in Charles Oman, *A History of the Peninsular War*, p. 500.

2 Charles Oman, *A History of the Peninsular War*, p. 8.

3 Patrick Wilcken, *Empire Adrift*, p. 10.

4 Maximilien Foy, *Junot's Invasion of Portugal*, p. 82.

5 According to Oman, *A History of the Peninsular War*, volume I, p. 206, some 25,000 soldiers went with Junot in the first wave in 1807, and 4,000 more went as reinforcements in 1808.

6 Maximilien Foy, *Junot's Invasion of Portugal*, p. 188.

7 Ibid, pp. 98–99.

8 Oman, *A History of the Peninsular War*, p. 106.

9 Gunther E. Rothenberg, *The Napoleonic Wars*, p. 141.

XXIII
THE REPUBLIC OF PERNAMBUCO

1 One American dollar in 1808 equals about fifteen dollars today according to the Economic History Service, a currency conversion simulator available at MeasuringWorth.com.

2 Humberto França, "Pernambuco e os Estados Unidos," in *Diário de Pernambuco,* May 2, 2006.

3 Information about the four Bonaparte sympathizers recruited in the United States comes from historian Amaro Quintas, cited by Humberto França, "Pernambuco e os Estados Unidos," in the *Diário de Pernambuco* of May 2, 2006.

4 Roderick Barman, *Brazil*, p. 61.

5 Cited by Rodolfo Garcia in the notes to Francisco Aldolfo de Varnhagen, *História geral do Brasil*, volume V, 1956, p. 150.

6 Manuel Correia de Andrade, *A Revolução Pernambucana de 1817*, pp. 4–5.

7 Francisco Aldolfo de Varnhagen, *História geral*, p. 152.

8 Cited in Eduardo Dias. *Memórias de forasteiros*, p. 41.

9 Maria Graham, *Journal of a Voyage to Brazil*, pp. 57–58.

10 Lília Schwarcz. *A longa viagem*, p. 321.

11 Humberto França. "Pernambuco e os Estados Unidos," in *Diário de Pernambuco*, May 2, 2006.

12 Like Cabugá in 1817, Manuel de Carvalho Paes de Andrade, leader of the Confederation of the Equator, went to the United States in 1824 to request support from President Monroe and for a fleet to defend the port of Recife. He returned empty-handed.

13 Henry Brackenridge, *Voyage to South America*, volume 1, p. 164.

14 Manuel Correia de Andrade, *A Revolução*, p. 19.

15 Tobias Monteiro, *História do Império*, p. 240.

16 Francisco Aldolfo de Varnhagen, *História geral*, p. 164.

17 Tobias Monteiro, citing Tollenare in *História do Império*, p. 68.

18 Manuel Correia de Andrade, *A revolução*, p. 21.

19 Oliveira Lima, *D. João VI no Brasil*, p. 17.

20 Cited by Wilson Martins in the preface to Manuel de Oliveira Lima, *D. João VI*, p. 17.

21 Lília Schwarcz, *A longa viagem*, p. 321.

22 Pernambuco paid a similar price in 1824, during the Confederation of the Equator, and lost yet another district, São Francisco, divided up between the provinces of Bahia and Minas Gerais.

XXIV

TROPICAL VERSAILLES

1 The phrase "Tropical Versailles" is used by historians such as Manuel de Oliveira Lima and Kirsten Schultz to define the period in which the court relocated to

Brazil, referring to the splendor of the royal palace built by Louis XIV on the outskirts of Paris.

2 Jurandir Malerba, *A Corte no exílio*, p. 91.

3 Ibid, p. 55. Tobias Monteiro, *História do Império*, p. 178, citing data from the *Correio Braziliense*, claims that the expenses were even greater. According to him, the ball alone cost 2 million francs.

4 One French franc in 1808 today equals 4.07 euros, according to Global Financial Data, at www.globalfinancialdata.com.

5 Tobias Monteiro, *História do Império*, p. 172.

6 Johann Moritz Rugendas, *Viagem pitoresca pelo Brasil*, p. 22.

7 Ernst Ebel, *O Rio de Janeiro*, p. 63.

8 John Luccock, *Notes on Rio de Janeiro*, p. 265.

9 Cited in Luis Edmundo, *Recordações do Rio Antigo*, p. 64.

10 Cited in Patrick Wilcken, *Empire Adrift*, p. 211.

11 The description of the preparations and the princess's arrival in Rio de Janeiro come from Jurandir Malerba, *A Corte no exílio*, p. 68.

12 Cited in Tobias Monteiro, *História do Império*, p. 183.

13 Cited in Lília Schwarcz, *A longe viagem da biblioteca*, p. 322.

14 Henry Brackenridge, *Voyage to South America*, volume 1, p. 121.

15 Lília Schwarcz, *A longe viagem da biblioteca*, p. 323.

16 Henry Brackenridge, *Voyage to South America*, pp. 149–151.

17 The description of João VI's routine comes from Pedro Calmon, *O rei do Brasil*, p. 227.

18 Tobias Monteiro, *História do Império*, p. 95.

19 Pedro Calmon, *O rei do Brasil*, p. 227.

20 Tobias Monteiro, *História do Império*, p. 96. Monteiro bases his report on the descriptions of Américo Jacobina de Lacombe, whom Almeida Prado, in *Tomas Ender*, p. 102, calls a "rumor monger" and unreliable.

XXV
PORTUGAL ABANDONED

1 Maximilien Foy, *Junot's Invasion of Portugal*, p. 57.

2 Ibid, p. 48.

3 Cited in Francisco Aldolfo de Varnhagen, *História geral do Brasil*, volume V, p. 59.

4 Luiz Norton, *A corte de Portugal no Brasil*, p. 38.

5 Maximilien Foy, *Junot's Invasion of Portugal*, p. 72. Monetary conversion based on Global Financial Data, according to which a French franc of 1808, updated for inflation, today equal 4.07 euros; see GlobalFinacialData.com.

6 Charles Oman, *A History of the Peninsular War*, p. 28.

7 Cited in Tobias Monteiro, *História do Império*, p. 188.

8 Maximilien Foy, *Junot's Invasion of Portugal*, pp. 62–64.

9 Oliveira Martins, *História de Portugal*, p. 525.

10 Ibid, p. 527.

11 Cited in Lília Schwarcz, *A longa viagem da biblioteca*, p. 223.

12 Charles Oman, *A History of the Peninsular War*, p. 207, quoting Maximilien Foy.

13 Tobias Monteiro, *História do Império*, pp. 201–202.

14 Ibid, p. 208.

15 Ibid, p. 211.

16 Maria Odila Leite da Silva Dias, *A interiorização da metrópole*, p. 16.

17 Oliveira Martins, *História de Portugal*, p. 526.

18 Manuel de Oliveira Lima, *D. João VI no Brasil*, pp. 251–252.

19 Maria Odila Leite da Silva Dias, *A interiorização da metrópole*, p. 13.

20 Ibid, p. 22.

21 Pedro Calmon, *O rei do Brasil,* p. 183.

22 Tobias Monteiro, *História do Império,* p. 241.

23 Mara Ziravello, *Brasil 500 anos,* pp. 334–335.

24 Lília Schwarcz, *A longa viagem da biblioteca,* pp. 348–349.

25 Ibid, pp. 349–350.

26 Cited by José Murilo de Carvalho, "O motivo edênico no imaginário social brasileiro," in *Revista Brasileira de Ciências Sociais,* volume 13, Number 31, October 1998.

27 Tobias Monteiro, *História do Império,* p. 281.

XXVI

THE RETURN

1 Manuel de Oliveira Lima, *D. João VI no Brasil,* p. 686.

2 Tobias Monteiro, *História do Império,* p. 294.

3 Ibid, p. 297.

4 Lília Schwarcz, *A longa viagem da biblioteca,* p. 354.

5 Thomas Skidmore, *Brazil,* p. 31.

6 Cited in José Honório Rodrigues, *Independência,* p. 44.

7 Tobias Monteiro, *História do Império,* p. 271.

8 Manuel de Oliveira Lima, *O movimento da Independência,* chapter two: "A sociedade brasileira. Nobreza e povo."

9 Maria Graham, *Journal of a Voyage to Brazil,* p. 71.

10 Pereira da Silva, *História da fundação do império,* volume 5, p. 145.

11 Oliveira Martins, *História de Portugal,* p. 532.

12 José Honório Rodrigues, *Independência,* p. 90.

13 Tobias Monteiro, *História do Império,* p. 377.

14 Oliveira Martins, *História de Portugal,* p. 538.

XXVII
A NEW BRAZIL

1 Cited in Patrick Wilcken, *Empire Adrift,* p. 257.

2 Manual de Oliveira Lima, *D. João VI no Brasil,* p. 21.

3 Wilson Martins in the preface to Manuel de Oliveira Lima, *D. João VI no Brasil,* p. 16.

4 The Brazilian delegates were elected proportionally, one for every group of 30,000 recognized inhabitants in Brazil based on the estimate at the time of the court's arrival, in Lília Schwarcz, *A Longa Viagem,* p. 362.

5 Andréa Slemian, "Outorgada sim, mas liberal," in *Revista de História* of the National Library, volume 15, December 2006, pp. 52–57.

6 Roderick Barman, *Brazil,* pp. 40–41.

7 Cited in Manuel de Oliveira Lima, *D. João VI no Brasil,* p. 56.

8 Manuel de Oliveira Lima, *D. João VI no Brasil,* p. 689.

9 Alan Manchester, *British Preeminence in Brazil,* p. 72.

10 Sérgio Buarque de Holanda, *A herança colonial—sua desagregação,* p. 13, cited in Maria Odila Leite da Silva Dias, *A interiorização da metrópole,* p. 11.

11 José Honório Rodrigues, *Independência,* p. 137.

12 Cited in Maria Odila Leite da Silva Dias, *A interiorização da metrópole,* p. 136.

13 Francisco de Sierra y Mariscal, *Idéias sobre a revolução do Brasil e suas conseqüências,* Anais da Biblioteca Nacional, Cited in Maria Odila, *A interiorização da metrópole,* p. 24.

14 José Antonio de Miranda, *Memória constitucional e política,* cited in Maria Odila Leite da Silva Dias, *A interiorização da metrópole,* pp. 135–136.

15 Cited in Maria Odila Leite da Silva Dias, *A interiorização da metrópole,* p. 137.

16 Maria Odila Leite da Silva Dias, *A interiorização da metrópole,* p. 17.

17 Ibid, p. 149.

XXVIII
THE CONVERSION OF DOS SANTOS MARROCOS

1 Luiz dos Santos Marrocos, *Cartas,* p. 434.

2 Ibid, p. 193.

3 Ibid, p. 211.

4 For more information about the original letters, see the thematic catalogs of the National Library of Ajuda, at www.ippar.pt/sites_externos/bajuda/index.htm.

5 Luiz dos Santos Marrocos, *Cartas,* p. 68.

6 Ibid, pp. 41, 112–113.

7 Ibid, p. 218.

8 Ibid, pp. 375–384.

9 Ibid, p. 218.

10 Ibid, p. 179.

11 Ibid, p. 213.

12 Rodolfo Garcia in the introduction to *Cartas,* pp. 12–13.

13 Luiz Joaquim dos Santos Marrocos, *Cartas,* p. 320.

14 Ibid, p. 369.

15 Ibid, p. 73.

16 Ibid, p. 74.

17 Lília Schwarcz, *A longa viagem da biblioteca*, p. 282.

18 Francisco Aldolfo de Varnhagen, *História geral*, volume V, p. 106.

19 Lília Schwarcz, *A longa viagem da biblioteca*, p. 400.

20 Ibid, p. 285.

21 Luiz dos Santos Marrocos, *Cartas*, pp. 375, 384.

22 Kirsten Schultz, *Tropical Versailles*, p. 78.

23 His burial is registered in volume 4 of *Assentamentos de Óbitos da Venerável Ordem Terceira dos Mínimos de São Francisco de Paula*, page 62, assentamento 218, according to Rodolfo Garcia in the introduction to *Cartas*, pp. 16–17.

XXIX

THE SECRET

1 Luiz dos Santos Marrocos, *Cartas*, pp. 249–255.

2 Ibid, p. 214.

3 Maria Graham, *Journal of a Voyage to Brazil*, p. 306.

4 The archives of the Cúria of Rio de Janeiro record the birth of two more daughters to the dos Santos Marrocos family. In this case, however, there's neither surprise nor secrecy since both were born after the interruption of the archivist's correspondence with his family in Lisbon. But as a result, historians have never been able to identify them: Both children are registered simply as Maria. One was born on March 2, 1829, and the other on July 12, 1834. On their birth certificates, their mother appears with their father's surname, as Anna Maria de Souza Marrocos. Including Joaquinna, born in 1814, Marrocos and his wife therefore had six children, not three as all prior historical accounts have reported.

Bibliography

Printed Sources

A. P. D. G. *Sketches of Portuguese life, manners, costume, and character illustrated by twenty coloured plates by A.P.D.G.* London: printed for Geo. B. Whittaker, 1826.

Abreu, Capistrano de. *Capítulos da história colonial* (sexta edição) / Prefácio e anotações de José Honório Rodrigues. Rio de Janeiro: Civilização Brasileira, 1976.

Algranti, Leila Mezan. *D. João VI: bastidores da Independência*. Rio de Janeiro: Ática, 1987.

———. *O feitor ausente: estudos sobre a escravidão urbana no Rio de Janeiro—1808–1822*. Petrópolis: Vozes, 1988.

Anderson, M. S. *The Ascendancy of Europe (1815–1914)*. Harlow, Essex: Pearson Longman, 2003.

Andrade, Manuel Correia de. *A revolução pernambucana de 1817*. São Paulo: Editora Ática, 1995.

Andrade, Manuel Correia de, Sandra Melo Cavalcanti, and Eliane Moury Fernandes (organizadores). *Formação histórica da nacionalidade brasileira—Brasil 1701–1824*. Recife: Editora Massangana, 2000.

Andrade, Santiago Silva de. "Pondo Ordem na Casa." In *Revista de História da Biblioteca Nacional do Rio de Janeiro*, 11th ed., August 2006.

Antonil, André João (João António Andreoni). *Cultura e opulência do Brasil por suas drogas e minas*. São Paulo: Companhia Editora Nacional, 1967.

Armitage, John. *The History of Brazil, from the Period of the Arrival of the Braganza Family in 1808 to the Abdication of Don Pedro the First in 1831, Compiled from State Documents and Other Original Sources Forming a Contribution to Southey's History of that Country*. London: Smith, Elder, & Co., 1836.

Aubry, Octave. *Napoléon*. Paris: Flammarion, 1961.

Azevedo, Francisca L. Nogueira de. *Carlota Joaquina na Corte do Brasil.* Rio de Janeiro: Civilização Brasileira, 2003.

Barman, Roderick. *Brazil: The Forging of a Nation, 1798–1852.* Stanford, California: Stanford University Press, 1988.

Barrow, John. *The Life and Correspondence of Admiral Sir William Sidney Smith* (two volumes). London: Richard Bentley, 1848.

Baucom, Ian. *Specters of the Atlantic.* New York: Duke University Press, 2005.

Bentley, Richard. *Memoirs of Admiral Sidney Smith.* London: K.C.B.I.&C, 1839.

Blanning, T. C. W. *The Nineteenth Century—Europe (1789–1914).* Oxford: Oxford University Press, 2000.

Bown, Stephen R. *The Age of Scurvy: How a Surgeon, a Mariner and a Gentleman Helped Britain Win the Battle of Trafalgar.* Chinchester, West Sussex: Summersdale Publishers, 2003.

Boxer, Charles. *The Golden Age of Brazil.* London: Cambridge University Press, 1962.

Brackenridge, Henry Marie. *Voyage to South America, Performed by Order of the American Government in the Years of 1817 and 1818 in the Frigate* Congress. Baltimore: published by the author; John D. Toy (printer), 1819.

Brandão, Darwin; Motta e Silva. *Cidade do Salvador—Caminho do Encantamento.* São Paulo: Companhia Editora Nacional, 1958.

Burchell, William John. *Rio de Janeiro's Most Beautiful Panorama (1825).* Rio de Janeiro: Instituto Histórico e Geográfico Brasileiro, 1966.

Burne, Jerome (editor); Legrand, Jacques (editor). *Chronicle of the World— The Ultimate Record of World History.* London: Dorling Kindersley Limited, 1996.

Caldcleugh, Alexander. *Travels in South America During the Years of 1819– 20–21; Containing an Account of the Present State of Brazil, Buenos Ayres, and Chile.* London: John Murray, 1825.

Caldeira, Jorge. *Mauá: empresário do Império*. São Paulo: Companhia das Letras, 1995.

Calmon, Pedro. *História do Brasil (volume IV)*. Rio de Janeiro: José Olympio, 1959.

———. *O rei do Brasil, vida de D. João VI*. São Paulo: Companhia Editora Nacional, 1943.

Calógeras, J. Pandiá. *Formação histórica do Brasil*. São Paulo: Companhia Editora Nacional, 1957.

Cardoso, Rafael. *Castro Maya, Colecionador de Debret*. São Paulo: Capivara; Rio de Janeiro: Museu Castro Maya, 2003.

Carvalho, José Murilo de. *O motivo edênico no imaginário social brasileiro*. Revista Brasileira de Ciências Sociais, volume 13, number 31, October 1998.

Carvalho, Marieta Pinheiro. *Uma idéia de cidade ilustrada—As transformações urbanas da nova corte portuguesa (1808–1821)*. Tese de Mestrado. Rio de Janeiro: Universidade do Estado do Rio de Janeiro (UERJ), 2003.

Cavalcanti, Nireu. *O Rio de Janeiro setecentista—a vida e a construção da cidade, da invasão francesa até a chegada da Corte*. Rio de Janeiro: Jorge Zahar Editores, 2004.

Chamberlain, Sir Henry. *Views and Costumes of the City and Neighbourhood of Rio de Janeiro, Brazil from Drawings Taken by Lieutenant Charberlain, of the Royal Artillery During the Years of 1819 and 1820*. London: Columbia Press, 1822.

Chartrand, René. *Vimeiro 1808: Wellesley's First Victory in the Peninsular War*. London: Praeger Publishers, 2001.

Cheke, Marcus. *Carlota Joaquina, Queen of Portugal*. London: Sidgwick and Jackson Limited, 1947.

Colledge, J. J. *Ships of the Royal Navy—The Complete Record of All Fighting Ships from the 15th Century to the Present*. London: Greenhill Books, 2006.

Conrad, Robert. *Tumbeiros: o tráfico de escravos para o Brasil.* São Paulo: Brasiliense, 1985.

Costa, A. Celestino da. *Lisboa, a evolução de uma cidade.* Lisboa: Câmara Municipal de Lisboa, 1951.

Cota, Francis Albert. *Polícia para quem precisa.* Article about the images of Debret and Rugendas, published in the *Revista de História* of the National Library, 14th ed., November 2006, pp. 64–68.

Cruls, Gastão. *Aparência do Rio de Janeiro.* Rio de Janeiro: José Olympio, 1952.

Dean, Warren. *A ferro e fogo: a história e a devastação da mata atlântica brasileira.* São Paulo: Companhia das Letras, 1996.

Debret, Jean-Baptiste, edited by Julio Bandeira. *Caderno de viagem.* Rio de Janeiro: Sextante, 2006.

———. *Un français à la cour du Brésil (1816–1831).* Rio de Janeiro: Museus Castro Maya/Chácara do Céu, 2000.

———. *Voyage pittoresque et historique au Brésil.* Paris: Firmin Didot, 1839.

De Oliveira Lima, Manuel. *D. João VI no Brasil* (1808), 3rd ed. Rio de Janeiro: Topbooks, 1996.

———. *O movimento da independência (1821–1822).* São Paulo: Melhora-mentos/Conselho Estadual de Cultura, 1972.

Dias, Eduardo. *Memórias de Forasteiros de aquém e além-mar—Brasil séculos XVI-XVIII e século XIX até a independência,* dois volumes. Lisboa: Livraria Clássica Editora, 1946.

Dias, Maria Odila Leite da Silva. *A Interiorização da metrópole e outros estudos.* São Paulo: Alameda Casa Editorial, 2005.

D'Orbigny, Alcide. *Viagem pitoresca através do Brasil.* Edited by Mário Guimarães Ferri. Belo Horizonte: Itatiaia; São Paulo: Edusp, 1976.

Dos Santos Marrocos, Luiz Joaquim. *Cartas de Luiz Joaquim dos Santos Marrocos, escritas do Rio de Janeiro à sua família em Lisboa, de 1811 a 1821.* Rio de Janeiro: Anais da Biblioteca Nacional, 1934.

Dumas, Alexandre. *Napoleão—uma biografia literária*. Rio de Janeiro: Jorge Zahar Editores, 2004.

Ebel, Ernst. *O Rio de Janeiro e seus arredores em 1824*. São Paulo: Editora Nacional, 1972.

Edmundo, Luiz. *A Corte de D. João VI no Rio de Janeiro*. Rio de Janeiro: Imprensa Nacional, 1939.

————. *O Rio de Janeiro no Tempo dos Vice-Reis—1763–1808*. Brasília: Senado Federal, Conselho Editorial, 2000.

————. *Recordações do Rio antigo*. Rio de Janeiro: Editora A Noite, 1950.

Ender, Thomas. *Viagem ao Brasil nas aquarelas de Thomas Ender (1817–1818)*, edited by Robert Wagner and Júlio Bandeira. Petrópolis: Kapa Editorial, 2000.

Esdaile, Charles. *The Peninsular War*. New York: Palgrave Macmillan, 2003.

Faoro, Raymundo. *Os donos do poder*. Porto Alegre: Globo; São Paulo: Edusp, 1975.

Ferguson, Niall. *Empire: How Britain Made the Modern World*. London: Penguin Books, 2004.

Ferrez, Gilberto. *As cidades de Salvador e Rio de Janeiro no Século XVIII*. Rio de Janeiro: Instituto Histórico e Geográfico Brasileiro, 1963.

Florentino, Manolo Garcia. *Em costas negras: uma história do tráfico atlântico entre a África e o Rio de Janeiro (séculos XVIII e XIX)*. Rio de Janeiro: Arquivo Nacional, 1995.

Foy, General Maximilien Sébastien. *Junot's Invasion of Portugal (1807–1808)*. Tyne and Wear: Worley Publications, 2000 (facsimile of the 1829 edition).

Fragoso, João Luís Ribeiro. *Homens de Grossa Aventura: acumulação e hierarquia na praça mercantil do Rio de Janeiro (1790–1830)*. Rio de Janeiro: Arquivo Nacional, 1992.

França, Jean Marcel Carvalho. *Visões do Rio de Janeiro colonial (1531–1800)*. Rio de Janeiro: EdUERJ; José Olympio, 1999.

França, Jean Marcel Carvalho. *Outras visões do Rio de Janeiro colonial (1582–1808)*. Rio de Janeiro: José Olympio, 2000.

Garcia, Rodolfo. *Ensaio Sobre a História Política e Administrativa do Brasil (1500–1810)*. Rio de Janeiro: José Olympio, 1956.

———. *Escritos Avulsos*. Rio de Janeiro: Biblioteca Nacional, Divisão de Publicações e Divulgação, 1973.

Gates, David. *The Spanish Ulcer: A History of the Peninsular War*. Cambridge, Massachusetts: Da Capo Press, 2001.

Glover, Gareth. *From Corunna to Waterloo—The Letters and Journals of Two Napoleonic Hussars, 1801–1816*. London: Greenhill Books, 2007.

Gracioso, Francisco, and J. Roberto Whitaker Penteado. *Propaganda brasileira*. São Paulo: ESPM; Mauro Ivan Marketing Editorial, 2004.

Graham, Maria. *Journal of a Voyage to Brazil, and Residence There, During Part of the Years 1821, 1822, 1823*. London: Longman, 1824.

Green, Vivian. *A loucura dos reis*. Rio de Janeiro: Ediouro, 2006.

Hazlewood, Nick. *The Queen's Slave Trader: Jack Hawkyns, Elizabeth I, and the Trafficking in Human Souls*. New York: Harper Collins Publishers, 2004.

Henderson, James. *A History of Brazil Comprising Its Geography, Commerce, Colonization, Aboriginal Inhabitants*. London: Longman, 1821.

Hibbert, Christopher. *George III—A Personal History*. London: Penguin Books, 1999.

Holanda, Sérgio Buarque de. *História Geral da Civilização Brasileira*. São Paulo: Difel, 1967.

———. *Raízes do Brasil*. Rio de Janeiro: José Olympio, 1987.

———. *Visão do Paraíso: os motivos edênicos no descobrimento e colonização do Brasil*. São Paulo: Companhia Editora Nacional, 1977.

Holloway, Thomas H. *Polícia no Rio de Janeiro: repressão e resistência numa cidade do século XIX*. Rio de Janeiro: Editora Fundação Getúlio Vargas, 1997.

Howarth, David. *British Sea Power: How Britain Became Sovereign of the Seas*. London: Robinson, 2003.

Karash, Mary. *A vida dos escravos no Rio de Janeiro: 1808–1850*. São Paulo: Companhia das Letras, 2000.

Kennedy, Paul. *Ascensão e queda das grandes potências— transformação econômica e conflito militar de 1500 a 2000*. Rio de Janeiro: Editora Campus, 1989.

Lacombe, Américo Jacobina. *Introdução ao estudo da história do Brasil*. São Paulo: Editora Nacional/Edusp, 1973.

Landes, David S. *Riqueza e a pobreza das nações—por que algumas são tão ricas e outras são tão pobres*. Rio de Janeiro: Editora Campus, 1998.

Lara, Silvia Hunold. *Campos da violência: escravos e senhores na capital do Rio de Janeiro 1750–1808*. Rio de Janeiro: Paz e Terra, 1988.

Lavery, Brian. *Nelson's Navy—The Ships, Men and Organization (1793–1815)*. Annapolis: Naval Institute Press, 1989.

Leithold, Teodor von, and Ludwig von Rango. *O Rio de Janeiro visto por dois prussianos em 1819*. São Paulo: Companhia Editora Nacional, 1966.

Lenharo, Alcir. *As tropas da moderação (o abastecimento da Corte na formação política do Brasil—1808–1842)*. São Paulo: Símbolo, 1979.

Lévi-Strauss, Claude. *Tristes trópicos*. São Paulo: Companhia das Letras, 1996.

Light, Kenneth H. *The Migration of the Royal Family of Portugal to Brazil in 1807/08*. Rio de Janeiro: Kenneth H. Light, 1995.

———. "Com os pés no mar." Interview in *Revista de História*, da Biblioteca Nacional, edition no. 14, November 2006, pp. 48–53.

———. "A viagem da família real para o Brasil," article for the *Tribuna de Petrópolis*, November 1997.

Lisboa, Karen Macknow. *A nova Atlântida de Spix e Martius: natureza e civilização na Viagem pelo Brasil (1817–1820)*. São Paulo: Hucitec/Fapesp, 1997.

Luccock, John. *Notas sobre o Rio de Janeiro e partes meridionais do Brasil, tomadas durante uma estada de dez anos nesse país, de 1808 a 1818*. São Paulo: Livraria Martins Fontes, 1942.

————. *Notes on Rio de Janeiro, and the Southern Parts of Brazil; Taken During a Residence of Ten Years in that Country From 1808 to 1818*. London: Printed for Samuel Lee in the Strand, 1820.

Malerba, Jurandir. *A Corte no exílio: civilização e poder no Brasil às vésperas de Independência (1808 a 1822)*. São Paulo: Companhia das Letras, 2000.

Malerba, Jurandir (editor). *A Independência brasileira—novas dimensões*. Rio de Janeiro: Editora FGV, 2006.

Manchester, Alan. *British Preeminence in Brazil: Its Rise and Decline*. Chapel Hill, N.C.: University of North Carolina Press, 1933.

Martinho, Lenira Menezes, and Riva Gorenstein. *Negociantes e caixeiros na sociedade da independência*. Rio de Janeiro: Prefeitura da Cidade do Rio de Janeiro, Coleção Biblioteca Carioca, volume 24, 1992.

Martins, Joaquim Pedro de Oliveira. *História de Portugal*. Lisboa: Guimarães e Cia. Editores, 1977.

Martins, Luciana de Lima. *O Rio de Janeiro dos viajantes—o olhar britânico (1800-1850)*. Rio de Janeiro: Jorge Zahar Editor, 2001.

Mawe, John. *Travels in the Interior of Brazil, Particularly in the Gold and Diamond Districts of That Country, by Authority of the Prince Regent of Portugal. Including A Voyage to the Rio de la Plata, and an Historical Sketch of the Revolution of Buenos Aires*. London: Longman, 1812.

Maxwell, Kenneth. *Conflicts and Conspiracies: Brazil & Portugal 1750–1808*. London: Routledge, 2004.

Mendonça, Marcos Carneiro de. *O Intendente Câmara—Manuel Ferreira Bethencourt e Sá, intendente geral das minas e dos diamantes (1764–1835)*. São Paulo: Companhia Editora Nacional, 1958.

Monteiro, Tobias. *História do Império. A elaboração da Independência (tomos 1 e 2)*, Belo Horizonte, Itatiaia; São Paulo: Edusp, 1981.

Moraes, Alexandre José de Melo. *História da transladação da corte portuguesa para o Brasil em 1807*. Rio de Janeiro: Livraria da Casa Imperial de E. Dupont, 1872.

Moraes, Rubens Borba de, and William Berrien. *Manual bibliográfico de estudos brasileiros*. Rio de Janeiro: Gráfica Editora Souza, 1949.

Norton, Luiz. *A corte de Portugal no Brasil*. São Paulo: Companhia Editora Nacional, 1938.

Novais, Fernando and Laura de Mello e Souza (editors). *História da vida privada no Brasil: cotidiano a vida privada na América portuguesa*. São Paulo: Companhia das Letras, 1997.

Novais, Fernando. *Portugal e o Brasil na crise do antigo sistema colonial (1777–1808)*. São Paulo: Hucitec, 1979.

Oman, Charles. *A History of the Peninsular War*. London: Greenhill Books, 2004.

O'Neill, Richard (consultant editor). *Patrick O'Brian's Navy—The Illustrated Companion to Jack Aubrey's World*. London: Salamander Books, 2004.

O'Neill, Thomas. *A concise and accurate account of the proceedings of the squadron under the command of admiral Sir William Sidney Smith in effecting the scape of the Royal Family of Portugal to Brazil on November, 29, 1807; and also the suffering of the royal fugitives during their voyage from Lisbon to Rio Janeiro with a variety of other interesting and authentic facts*. London: printed by J. Barfield for the author, 1810.

Peixoto, Domingos Ribeiro dos Guimarães (personal surgeon to the king). *Aos sereníssimos príncipes reais do Reino Unido de Portugal e do Brasil, e Algarves, os senhores Pedro de Alcântara e D. Carolina Jozefa Leopoldina, oferece, em sinal de gratidão, amor, respeito, e reconhecimento estes prolongamentos, ditados pela obediência, que servirão às observações, que for dando das moléstias do país, em cada trimestre*. Rio de Janeiro: Impressão Régia, 1820.

Peláez, Carlos Manuel, and Wilson Suzigan. *História Monetária do Brasil*. Brasília: Editora da UNB, 1981.

Pereira, Ângelo. *D. João VI príncipe e rei: a retirada da família real para o Brasil (1807)*. Lisboa: Empresa Nacional de Publicações, 1953.

————. *Os filhos d'El-Rei D. João VI*. Lisboa: Empresa Nacional de Publicidade, 1946.

Prado, J. F. de Almeida. *D. João VI e o início da classe dirigente no Brasil. 1815–1889*. São Paulo: Companhia Editora Nacional, 1968.

————. *Tomas Ender—pintor austríaco na corte de D. João VI no Rio de Janeiro*. São Paulo: Companhia Editora Nacional, 1955.

Presas, José. *Memórias secretas de D. Carlota Joaquina*. Rio de Janeiro: Irmãos Pongetti, 1940.

Relação das festas que se fizeram no Rio de Janeiro quando o príncipe regente N. S. e toda a sua real família chegaram pela primeira vez àquela capital, ajuntando-se algumas particularidades igualmente curiosas, e que dizem respeito ao mesmo objeto. Lisboa: Impressão Régia, 1810.

Renault, Delso. *O Rio antigo nos anúncios de jornais (1808–1850)*. Rio de Janeiro: CBBA/Propeg, 1985.

Rodrigues, José Honório. *Independência: revolução e contra-revolução*. Rio de Janeiro: Francisco Alves, 1975.

Rothenberg, Gunther E. *The Napoleonic Wars*. London: Harper Collins Publishers, 1999.

Rugendas, Johann Moritz. *Viagem pitoresca pelo Brasil (tradução da edição francesa de 1835)*. Rio de Janeiro: Revista da Semana, 1937.

Saint-Hilaire, Auguste de. *Viagem à província de São Paulo e resumo das viagens ao Brasil, província Cisplatina e Missões do Paraguai*. São Paulo: Livraria Martins Editora, 1945.

Santos, Luis Gonçalves dos. *Memórias para servir à história do reino do Brasil, divididas em três épocas da felicidade, honra, e glória; escritas na corte do Rio de Janeiro no ano de 1821, e oferecidas à S. Magestade Elrei nosso senhor D. João VI* (Tomos I e II). Lisboa: Impressão Régia, 1825.

Schultz, Kirsten. *Tropical Versailles—Empire, Monarchy, and the Portuguese Royal Court in Rio de Janeiro, 1808–1821*. New York: Routledge, 2001.

Schwarcz, Lília Mortiz. *A longa viagem da biblioteca dos reis: do terremoto de Lisboa à Independência do Brasil.* São Paulo: Companhia das Letras, 2002.

Shyllon, F. O. *Black Slaves in Britain.* London: Oxford University Press, 1974.

Silva, J. M. Pereira da. *História da fundação do império brasileiro* (seven volumes). Rio de Janeiro: B. L. Garnier, 1864.

Silva, Manuel Vieira da. *Reflexões sobre alguns dos meios propostos por mais conducentes para melhorar o clima da cidade do Rio de Janeiro.* Rio de Janeiro: Impressão Régia, 1808.

Silva, Maria Beatriz Nizza da. *Vida privada e cotidiano no Brasil.* Lisboa: Editorial Estampa, 1993.

Skidmore, Thomas. *Brazil: Five Centuries of Change.* 2nd ed. Oxford: Oxford University Press, 2010.

Soares, Carlos Eugênio Líbano. *A capoeira escrava e outras tradições rebeldes do Rio de Janeiro (1808–1850).* São Paulo: Unicamp, 2001.

Sodré, Nelson Werneck. *As razões da Independência.* Rio de Janeiro: Graphia, 2002.

————. *Formação histórica do Brasil.* Rio de Janeiro: Graphia, 2002.

Spix, Johann Baptist von, and Carl Friedrich Phillip von Martius. *Viagem pelo Brasil (1817–1820).* São Paulo: Edições Melhoramentos, 1968.

Toledo, Roberto Pompeu de. *A capital da solidão—uma história de São Paulo das origens a 1900.* Rio de Janeiro: Objetiva, 2003.

Tuckey, James. *An Account of a Voyage to Establish a Colony at Port Philip in Bass's Strait, on the Coast of New South Wales, in Her Majesty's Ship Calcutta, in the Years 1802-3-4.* London: Longman, 1805.

Vainfas, Ronaldo (editor). *Dicionário do Brasil colonial (1500–1808).* Rio de Janeiro: Objetiva, 2001.

Varnhagen, Francisco Adolfo de; with annotations by Rodolfo Garcia. *História geral do Brasil—antes de sua separação e independência de Portugal (volume V).* São Paulo: Melhoramentos, 1956.

Varnhagen, Francisco Adolfo de. *História da Independência do Brasil.* São Paulo: Melhoramentos, 1957.

Wilcken, Patrick. *Empire Adrift—The Portuguese Court in Rio de Janeiro, 1808–1821.* London: Bloomsbury, 2004.

Ziravello, Mara (editor). *Brasil 500 anos.* São Paulo: Nova Cultural, 1999.

Electronic Sources

Ackroyd, Peter. *London: The Biography—Trade and Enterprise* (audiobook). Audible, 2004.

Bergreen, Laurence. *Over the Edge of the World: Magellan's Terrifying Circumnavigation of the Globe* (audiobook). Harper Collins, 2004.

Bragg, Melvyn. *The Adventure of English: The Biography of a Language* (audiobook). BBC WW, 2005.

Bruun, Geoffrey. *The Enlightened Despots* (audiobook). Audio Connoisseur, 2005.

Correspondência de Luíz Joaquim dos Santos Marrocos para seu pai Francisco José dos Santos Marrocos. Thematic catalogue, Biblioteca Nacional da Ajuda, at www.ippar.pt/sites_externos/bajuda/index.htm.

Churchill, Winston. *The Age of Revolution: a History of the English Speaking People* (audiobook). BBC WW, 2006.

Cury, Adriano da Gama. *Correio Braziliense: ortografia e linguagem.* Site *Observatório da Imprensa,* at www.observatoriodaimprensa.com.br/artigos/alm050820032.htm.

Dicionário Histórico de Portugal, at www.arqnet.pt/dicionario.

Economic History Service, Online free converter of ancient currencies, created by professors of economics at the Universities of Illinois, in Chicago, and Miami, at http://measuringworth.com.

Fisher, H.A.L. *Napoleon* (audiobook). Audio Connoisseur, 2004.

França, Humberto. *Pernambuco e os Estados Unidos*. Article published in the *Diário de Pernambuco* on May 2, 2006, and reproduced at the site of the Fundação Joaquim Nabuco, at www.fundaj.gov.br.

Global Financial Data, paid Internet service specializing in historical records of currencies, www.globalfinancialdata.com.

Harvey, Robert. *Cochrane: The Life and Exploits of a Fighting Captain* (audiobook). Books on Tape, 2005.

Horne, Alistair. *The Age of Napoleon* (audiobook). Recorded Books, 2005.

Laquer, Thomas. *History 5—European Civilization from the Renaissance to the Present*. Podcast of 26 installments of 80 minutes each, available from the University of California, Berkeley, at http://webcast.berkeley.edu/courses/archive.php?seriesid=1906978348.

Lee, Christopher. *The Sceptred Isle: Empire* (audiobook). BBC WW, 2005.

Lima, Fernando Carlos Cerqueira, and Elisa Muller. *Moeda e Crédito no Brasil: breves reflexões sobre o primeiro Banco do Brasil (1808–1829)*. Instituto de Economia da Universidade Federal do Rio de Janeiro, at www.revistatemalivre.com/MoedaeCredito.html.

O Arquivo Nacional e a História Luso-Brasileira, at www.historiacolonial.arquivonacional.gov.br.

O exército português em finais do Antigo Regime, at www.arqnet.pt/exercito/principal.html.

Portal Arqueológico dos Pretos Novos, website with information on the Valongo market and the slave cemeteries in Rio de Janeiro, at www.pretosnovos.com.br.

Reilly, Cameron. *Napoleon 101*. Podcast about Napoeon Bonaparte consisting of 11 episodes of 90 minutes each at http://napoleon.thepodcastnetwork.com.

Rodger, Nam. *Trafalgar: The Long-Term Impact*, article for the website *British History—Empire and Sea Power*, at www.bbc.co.uk.

Silva, Leonardo Dantas. *Textos sobre o Recife*, article for the website of Fundação Joaquim Nabuco, at www.fundaj.gov.br/docs/rec/rec02.html.

Soares, Márcio de Sousa. *Médicos e mezinheiros na corte imperial: uma herança colonial.* Scientific Electronic Library Online at www.scielo.br.

Sorel, Albert. *Europe Under the Old Regime: Power, Politics, and Diplomacy in the Eighteenth Century* (audiobook). Audio Connoisseur, 2004.

Twigger, Robert. *Inflation: The Value of the Pound 1750–1998.* House of Commons Library, on the British Parliament website at www .parliament.uk/commons/lib/research/rp99/rp99-020.pdf.

Zacks, Richard. *The Pirate Coast: Thomas Jefferson, the First Marines, and the Secret Mission of 1805* (audiobook). Blackstone Audiobooks, 2005.

INDEX

Abrantes, duchess of, 22, 125, 198
ADPG (author), 141–42
advertisements, 158–59
Afonso de Albuquerque (ship), 31, 36, 52, 53, 65, 90
Age of Enlightened Despotism, 28–29
Alencastro, Luiz Felipe, 132–33
Alexander zu Wied-Neuwied, Prince, 157–58
Algranti, Leila Mezan, 164, 177, 182–83
Álvares Pereira de Melo, Miguel, 55–56
Alvas da Costa, Manoel, 94
Ancien Régime, 10
Andreoni, João Antonio, 175
animals, 133
Antonil, André João, 175
Arc de Triomphe, 214
Armitage, John, 132, 139, 154
arrest of slaves, 164–65
autos-da-fé, 25

baetas, 75
Bahia. *See* Salvador, Brazil
Bank of Brazil, 129, 134, 135, 138, 139, 232
barbers, 113
Barca, António de Araújo de Azevedo, count of, 20, 34, 52, 66–67, 122, 156

Barman, Roderick, 81, 204, 237–38
bathing, 115, 117
Beckford, William, 43
Bedford, HMS (ship), 48, 51, 52, 53, 59, 147
bells, church, 109
Beresford, William Carr, 201, 221, 225–26, 228
blackmail, literary, 129–30
Blockade, Continental, 6, 18, 145, 225
Bonaparte, Napoleon. *See* Napoleon Bonaparte
Botocudo Indians, 155
Boxer, Charles, 64, 65
Brackenridge, Henry
    Brazil, 158, 184, 187
    cannon fire, 109–10
    court, Portuguese, 141
    João VI, coronation of, 214–15, 215–16
    republicanism, 206
branding of slaves, 178, 180
Brant, Felisberto Caldeira, 153
brasileiro (Brazilian), as term, 68–69
Brazil. *See also* Rio de Janeiro; *specific towns and regions*
    administrative sectors, 135
    bathing, 117
    borders, 69

Britain, trade with, 66–67,
144–45, 147–48, 149–50
censorship, 80–81
characterization by foreign
visitors, 191–92
cheese production, 191–92
communication, 71–72, 74, 195
departure for, 31–39
diamonds, 27, 79, 185–87
dietary habits, 77–78
education, 80, 153, 192
explorers, 153
finances, 132–37, 139–40,
232–33
gold, 27, 78–79
health, public, 71
independence, 230, 238–41
indigenous people, 70, 74, 114,
142–43, 155, 194–95
industries, 152–53
intellectual life, 80–81, 192
judicial system, 148
kingdom status, 154
literacy, 71, 192
mule troopers, 75–77
Northeastern interior, 190–91
planned move to, 15–18
population, 69–71
ports, opening of, 65–67,
144–45, 147–48, 149–50
Portugal, trade with, 15–16, 227
Portuguese court in, 132–37
religious freedom, 148
roads, 153
scientific advancement, 192–95
slavery, 82, 172

smuggling, 79
Sundays and feast days, 161
transformation of, 151–61,
236–37
travelers to, 184–95
voyage to, 48–56
work ethic, 191–92
Brazilian Indians, 142–43
Britain
blockades, 6, 66–67
Brazil, Portugal court's departure
for, 37–39, 48, 50–52, 53,
54–55
Brazil, trade with, 66–67,
144–45, 147–48, 149–50
judicial system in Brazil, 148
Portugal and, 6–7, 18–19,
29–30, 147–49, 226–27
religious freedom in Brazil, 148
Royal Navy, 47–48, 101–2,
146–47
British Empire, 145
Brochado, José da Cunha, 27–28
Burchell, William, 192
burial of dead, 167, 169–70

cabinet, new, 151–52
Cabugá, 203–4, 206, 209
Cadaval, duchess of, 94
Caldcleugh, Alexander, 161
Calmon, Pedro
Brazil, 151
Carlota Joaquina, 126
court, Portuguese, 44, 131
João VI, 91, 119, 121, 123
Calógeras, Pandiá, 27, 117

Canning, George, 147
cannon fire, 109–10
capoeira, 164
Cardoso, Eliana, 26–27
cariocas. *See* Rio de Janeiro
Carlota Joaquina
　appearance, 91, 125–26,
　　131, 213
　banishment, 130–31
　Brazil, 35–36, 52, 130
　children, 128
　conspiracies and coup attempts,
　　118, 125, 126
　death, 131
　depictions of, 125
　final days, 130–31
　homage, demands for, 127
　infidelities, alleged, 128–29
　lice, 43, 91
　marriage and separation, 5, 120,
　　126, 127
　personality, 125–26
　portrait, 124
　will, 131
Carrère, J. B. F., 42–43
Castle Mountain, 167–68
Castro, Martinho de Mello e, 69
Catholic Church, 24–25
Cavalcanti, Nireu, 113
censorship, 28–29, 80–81
Chamberlain, Henry, 172, 187
cheese production, 191–92
Cochrane, Thomas, 189
Collingwood, Luke, 174
communication, 19, 61, 71–72,
　74, 195

Confederation of the Equator, 206,
　209, 237, 241
Congress (ship), 109–10, 158,
　214–15
conquest attempts, 152
conspiracies, 118, 125, 126
constitutional reforms, 230–32, 233
Continental Blockade, 6, 18,
　145, 225
Convention of Cintra, 225
Copenhagen, 6
copper warming-pans, 150
Correio Braziliense, 81, 145,
　146, 208
Cortes, 130, 189, 228, 232, 233,
　237, 239
Costigan, Arthur William, 16
Council of State (Portugal), 18, 19
coup attempts, 118, 125, 126
crime, 162, 165
Crown Manuscripts, 246
Cruz, Antonio Gonçalves, 203–4,
　206, 209

da Camara Cascudo, Luis, 189–90
da Costa, Hipólito José, 68–69, 81,
　93–94, 154, 155, 208
da Cunha, Luiz, 16
da Pina Manique, Diogo, 44
Darwin, Charles, 102
da Silva Lisboa, José, 66
dead, burial of, 167, 169–70
de Aguirre, Juan Francisco, 176
de Andrada e Silva, José Bonifácio,
　80, 239

de Assis Mascarenhas, Francisco, 152–53
de Azevedo, Joaquim, 33, 34, 135, 136–37, 233–34
de Azevedo, Madame, 135–36
Debret, Jean-Baptiste, 108, 155, 156–57, 178–79, 187, 214
de Caleppi, Lourenço, 34–35, 148
de Freycinet, Louis, 187, 188
de Freycinet, Rose, 187–88
de Jesus, Clara Maria, 182–83
de Jesus, Jorge Pardo, 182–83
de Miranda Montenegro, Caetano Pinto, 60, 207
Denmark, 6
de Oliveira, João Fernandes, 182
de Oliveira Lima, Manuel
 Brazil, 15, 69, 71, 232, 236, 238
 Carlota Joaquina, 126, 128
 Europe, 10
 João VI, 118, 123
 Pernambucan Revolt, 204, 208
 Portugal, 21, 26
 public servants, kickbacks and payments to, 134–35
 Rio de Janeiro, 104
de Sousa Coutinho, Domingos, 81, 144, 208, 224
de Sousa Coutinho, Rodrigo, 16–18, 66, 72, 80, 122, 151
diamonds, 27, 79, 185–87
Dias, Maria Odila Leite da Silva, 227, 240
dos Guimarães Peixoto, Domingos Ribeiro, 167–68

dos Santos Marrocos, Bernardina, 41, 242, 250
dos Santos Marrocos, Francisco, 40, 42, 242, 247, 250
dos Santos Marrocos, Joaquinna, 249–52
dos Santos Marrocos, Luiz
 Brazil, 159, 242–48
 career, 42
 children, 244, 249–52
 court, Portuguese, 43, 136–37
 crime, 162
 death, 248
 marriage, 244
 Portugal, invasion of, 45
 Royal Library, 40–41
 ship life, 47, 96–97
 slavery, 175, 244–45
 as source, 41–42

Ebel, Ernst, 111, 160, 176, 212
education, 80, 153, 192
Ender, Thomas, 74–75, 114, 184, 193
England. See Britain
Enlightened Despotism, Age of, 28–29
explorers, 153

Fazenda, Vieira, 121
Florentino, Manolo Garcia, 104, 172
Flyer (ship), 50, 61, 85, 87
fog, 51–52
Fontainebleau, Treaty of, 20–21
forros, 181–83

foundling wheels, 252
Foy, Maximilien, 35, 199, 222
France, 13, 18–21. *See also* French
    Revolution; Napoleon
    Bonaparte; Peninsular War
freedom, religious, 148
freed slaves, 181–83
Freemasons, 44
French Artistic Mission, 155–56,
    213, 214
French Revolution, 10–11, 12, 13,
    44, 207–8, 231
Freyre, Gilberto, 105

Gâlvea, João de Almeida de Melo e
    Castro, count of, 41–42
Gama, João de Saldanha da, 62
Gates, David, 199
George III, King, 8–9
gold, 27, 78–79
Gomes, Bernardino Antonio, 112
Gomes, Pedro, 33
Gonçalves dos Santos, Luis, 85–86,
    89, 90, 92, 93, 214
Goya, Francisco, 196, 201
Graham, Maria
    Brazil, 135–36, 188–89, 232
    foundling wheels, 252
    Pernambucan Revolt, 204
    Salvador, 63, 64–65
    slavery, 170
Great Britain. *See* Britain
Guanabara Bay, Brazil, 84–85, 86,
    87, 89–90, 109–10, 158
gunpowder, 227

Haiti, 164, 165
hand-kissing ceremony, 83, 92,
    141–42
health, public, 71
Henderson, James
    Brazil, 133, 187, 192
    court, Portuguese, 140–41, 142
    slavery, 171, 179
    violence, 165
Hibernia, HMS (ship), 37, 38,
    50, 54
Holanda, Sérgio Buarque de, 26,
    80, 139, 176, 239
housing, 87–88, 93–94, 136, 147,
    154–55
Humboldt, Alexander von, 72
hygiene, 42–43, 104–5, 115,
    117, 167

ice skates, 145, 150
indigenous people, 70, 74, 114,
    142–43, 155, 194–95
Industrial Revolution, 13, 23,
    145–46, 200
Inquisition, 25
intellectual life, 80–81, 192

João VI, king of Brazil and Portugal
    appearance, 91, 117, 118, 121
    ascension to power, 118
    bathing, 115, 117
    Brazil, departure for, 35
    Brazil, effect on, 236–37, 238
    Brazil, kingdom status for, 154
    Brazil, voyage to, 50, 52

Britain, secret agreement
  with, 19
cabinet, new, 151–52
children, 128
constitutional reforms,
  231–32, 233
coronation, 209, 210–11,
  214–16
court, new, 138–42
death, 126
depression, 118
diamond, false, 185, 187
dress, 121
fears, 115, 121
fleeing, reasons for, 5–7
France, fooling of, 19–20
habits, 121, 217–18
hand-kissing ceremony, 83, 92,
  141–42
health, 117–18
homosexual relations, 120
housing in Rio de Janeiro,
  87–88, 93
indecision, 5
legacy, 67, 83, 122–23, 236
life in Rio de Janeiro, 216–18
love life, 119–20
marriage and separation, 5, 120,
  126, 127
Napoleon Bonaparte on, 235
Pernambucan Revolt, 209
personality, 5, 118–19, 121, 125
portrait, 116
Portugal, return to, 226,
  227–34

proclamation to Brazilian
  people, 19
Salvador layover, 57–60, 62,
  65–67
territorial expansion/conquest
  attempts, 152
trellises, 154–55
Jordão, Manuel Rodrigues, 139
José, Dom, 5, 25, 118
José de Menezes, Eugênia, 119
José I, King, 8, 16, 29, 71, 83
Journal of a Voyage to Brazil
  (Graham), 189
judicial penance, 82–83
judicial system, 148
Junot, Jean-Andoche
  João VI, 119
  Peninsular War, 197–98, 200
  Portugal, 21, 22, 35, 222,
    223–24

kickbacks to public servants,
  134–35
Koster, Henry, 77, 117,
  189–91, 205

Leão, Braz Carneiro, 138
Leão, Fernando Carneiro, 129
Leão, Gertrudes Carneiro, 128–29
Lebreton, Joachim, 155, 156
Lent, 166
Leopoldina, Princess, 188, 209,
  211–12, 213–14, 229
lice, 43, 53, 91
Light, Kenneth, 38, 39, 48 58–59
Lindley, Thomas, 191

Lines of Torres Vedras, 201–2
Lisbon, 21, 22, 28, 42–43, 222–23.
   See also Portugal
literacy, 71, 192
Literary Society of Rio de Janeiro,
   80–81
Loison, General, 199
London, 145–46
Lopes, Elias Antonio, 174–75
Louis XIV, King, 9, 10
Louis XVI, King, 11, 231
Luccock, John
   Brazil, 71, 187
   court, Portuguese, 132–33,
      134–35
   palace, 212
   Rio de Janeiro, 77, 102–3,
      106–8, 112
   slavery, 176–77, 181

Madrid, Treaty of, 69
Mafra, Palace of, 5, 18, 33, 118
Magalhães, Raimundo, Jr., 131
Maler, Colonel, 94
Malerba, Jurandir
   Brazil, 155, 157
   celebrations, 211–12
   court, Portuguese, 139–40, 142
   João VI, 123
   Rio de Janeiro, 109
   Royal Pantry, 133
Manchester, Alan
   Brazil, 66, 238
   British-Portuguese treaty,
      147, 149
   court, Portuguese, 44

Portugal, invasion of, 22
   ship life, 47
   slavery, 172
manners, table, 108
Manoel, João, 194–95
manumitted slaves, 181–83
Maria I, mad Queen of Portugal
   Brazil, departure for, 36
   death, 209, 210, 230
   insanity, 4–5, 8, 9, 118
   Rio de Janeiro, arrival in, 93
   science, distrust of, 25
Marialva, marquis of, 19–20,
      211–12
Marie Antoinette, 10–11, 231
market, slave, 169–72
Martins, Oliveira, 29, 32, 42, 115,
      117–18, 234
Masonic lodges, 44
Masséna, André, 202
Mawe, John
   about, 185
   Brazil, 74, 77–78, 149–50, 155,
      191–92
   diamond, false, 185, 187
   Rio de Janeiro, 101
   slavery, 182
   smuggling, 79
meat, 108
Medusa (ship), 50, 52, 55
Minerva (ship), 49, 59, 61
Miranda, José Antonio de, 164,
      239–40
mixed porphyria, 8–9
monarchy, absolute, 4
Moniteur, Le, 32–33, 223

Monteiro, Tobias
  Brazil, 156
  gold, 27
  João VI, 7, 91, 120, 121, 122, 217, 232
  Peninsular War, 27
  Pernambucan Revolt, 207
Montigny, Grandjean de, 214, 232
moonlighting slaves, 176–77
Moore, Graham, 53
Moraes, Melo, 66
Moraes, Rubens Borba de, 184
Morro do Castelo (Castle Mountain), 167–68
Mug, Brother, 206, 209
mule troopers, 75–77
music, 157

Napoleon Bonaparte. *See also* Napoleonic wars; Peninsular War
  achievements, 13–14
  Continental Blockade, 6
  death, 235
  imprisonment, 203
  legacy, 235–36
  military genius, 11, 12–13
  power, 9–10, 18, 20
Napoleonic wars, 10, 11, 12, 13, 189, 196. *See also* Peninsular War
National Library of Rio de Janeiro, 246
neutrality, politics of, 29
New Blacks Cemetery, 169–70
news, speed of, 61

Northeastern interior of Brazil, 190–91
Norton, Luiz, 35, 93, 117

Olinda, Brazil, 204, 207
Oliveira, João Francisco de, 119
Oman, Charles, 22, 197, 224
O'Neill, Thomas, 54–55, 113
owners, slave, 175–76, 182

Palace of Mafra, 5, 18, 33, 118
Palace of Queluz, 5, 8, 33, 118
Palmela, count of, 140, 231
Pedro, prince of Beira
  appearance, 188
  birth, 128
  Brazil, 19, 67, 189, 228
  marriage, 20, 209, 211–12, 214
  rebels and, 230
Pedro Carlos, Dom, 35, 230
penance, judicial, 82–83
Peninsular War, 21–22, 197–202, 222–25, 227. *See also* Napoleonic wars
Pereira, Ângelo, 117
Pereira da Silva, J. M., 233
Pernambucan Revolt, 203–9, 237
Pimentel, Alberto, 131
pirates, 174
Plaza of Commerce massacre, 232
Pohl, Emanuel, 105
police, 163–66
Pombal, Sebastião de Carvalho e Melo, marquis of, 28–29
Pompeu de Toledo, Roberto, 74
Porto Alegre, Manuel, 121

Porto Revolution, 230, 239
ports, opening of, 65–67, 144–45, 147–48, 149–50
Portugal. *See also* Peninsular War; Portuguese ships
  Brazil, trade with, 15–16, 227
  Britain and, 6–7, 18–19, 29–30, 147–49, 226–27
  Catholic Church, 24–25
  censorship, 28–29
  constitutional reforms, 230–32, 233
  Cortes, 130, 189, 228, 232, 233, 237, 239
  Council of State, 18, 19
  decline, 23–26
  demographic resources, 24
  economy, 24, 26–27
  France, bluffing of, 18–20
  invasion of, 21–22, 197–202, 222–23
  monarchy, absolute, 4
  natural catastrophe, 28
  neutrality, politics of, 29
  reforms, 28–29
  return to, 226, 227–34
  sea power, 24
Portugal, Fernando José de, 82, 151
Portugal, Marcos Antonio, 157
Portuguese ships. *See also specific ships*
  about, 24, 46–47, 49–50
  arrival in Rio de Janeiro, 84–85, 89–92
  plans for arrival of, 85–89
post, speed of, 19

Prado, Almeida, 175
pregnancy out of wedlock, 249, 250–52
Presas, José, 129–30
Pretos Novos (New Blacks) Cemetery, 169–70
Prince of Brazil (ship), 31, 50
Princess Carlota (ship), 96–97
prostitution, 65, 75, 162, 193
public servants, kickbacks and payments to, 134–35
punishment of slaves, 164, 165, 178–79

Queen of Portugal (ship), 31, 36, 49, 52
Queluz, Palace of, 5, 8, 33, 118
Quental, Antero de, 25

Ramos, Artur, 178
Ratton, Jácome, 43
rebellions, slave, 82, 83, 164
Recife, Brazil, 203–4, 205, 207, 209
religious freedom, 148
revolts, slave, 82, 83, 164
Rio de Janeiro. *See also* Brazil
  appearance, 102, 104
  bells, church, 109
  burial of dead, 167, 169–70
  cannon fire, 109–10
  crime, 162, 165
  customs, 105–6, 163–64, 166
  dress, 105
  food, 108–9
  French influence, 159–60

health and medical care, 112–13
housing, 87–88, 93–94, 136,
   147, 154–55
manners, table, 108
meals, 106–9
meat, 108
police, 163–66
population, 103, 113, 162
as port, 101–2, 104
Portuguese ships, arrival of,
   84–85, 89–92
Portuguese ships, plans for arrival
   of, 85–89
roads, 109, 113
sanitation, 104–5, 167
slaves and slavery, 104–5,
   110–13, 164–65, 169–72,
   176, 181–83
trellises, 154–55, 163–64
violence, 165
Rio de Janeiro Gazette, 154, 158–59
Rio Grande do Sul, Brazil,
   71–72, 73
River Plate Question, 129
roads, 109, 113, 153
Rodrigues, José Honório, 233, 239
Rothenberg, Gunther, 12–13
Royal Chapel (Rio de Janeiro), 93,
   120, 157, 214, 215
Royal Library (Portugal), 39,
   40–41, 45, 96, 246
Royal Navy (Britain), 47–48,
   101–2, 146–47
Royal Pantry and Buttery (Rio de
   Janeiro), 133, 135

Royal Prince (ship), 31, 36, 38, 48,
   49, 50, 52
Rufino de Sousa Lobato,
   Francisco, 120
Rufino de Sousa Lobato, Matias
   Antonio, 120–21
Rugendas, Johann Moritz., 63,
   187, 212
runaway slaves, 180–81

Saint-Hilaire, Augustin de, 68, 78,
   187, 193
Salvador, Brazil, 57–67, 70, 245–46
sanitation, 42–43, 104–5, 167
Santa Catarina, Brazil, 73–74
São Cristovão Palace, 188, 213,
   217–18
São João Theatre, 157, 160, 165
São Paulo, Brazil, 74–75
Schultz, Kirsten, 122, 248
Schwarcz, Lília, 26, 27, 32, 45,
   117, 215
scientific advancement, 192–95
*Secret Memoirs of D. Carlota
   Joaquina, The* (Presas), 130
ship life, 46–47, 48–49, 53, 54–55,
   96–97. *See also* Portuguese
   ships; *specific ships*
shipwrecks, 173–74
Shyllon, F. O., 174
Silva, Amaro Velho da, 92, 140
Silva, Chica da, 182
slaves and slavery
   arrest of slaves, 164–65
   branding of slaves, 178, 180
   Brazil, 82, 172

Debret's documentation of, 156–57

manumitted/freed slaves, 181–83

market, slave, 169–72

moonlighting slaves, 176–77

owners, slave, 175–76, 182

price of slaves, 175, 176, 244, 245

punishment of slaves, 164, 165, 178–79

rebellions, slave, 82, 83, 164

Rio de Janeiro, 104–5, 110–13, 164–65, 169–72, 176, 181–83

runaway slaves, 180–81

statistics, 172

tigers (slaves involved in sanitation), 104–5

trafficking, slave, 172–75

Smith, Sidney

  blockade, naval, 66–67

  Brazil, 238

  Brazil, departure for, 37–38, 39

  Brazil, voyage to, 49, 50, 51

  Carlota Joaquina and, 129

  gifts to, 147

  Portugal, invasion of, 20

  Rio de Janeiro, 102

smuggling, 79

Society of English Merchants Trading in Brazil, 144–45

Souza, Anna Maria de São Thiago, 244, 249, 250, 252

Spain, 20, 200–201. *See also* Peninsular War

storm during voyage to Brazil, 50, 51–52, 57–58

Strangford, Percy Smythe, Viscount

  blockade, naval, 66–67

  Brazil, departure for, 37

  Brazil, voyage to, 49, 50

  England, return to, 51

  João and, 246

  Portugal, invasion of, 18, 20

  treaty negotiation, 147

  whipping of, 127

Sumpter, Thomas, 127

table manners, 108

Tailors' Conspiracy, 82, 83, 237

Targini, Bento Maria, 135, 136–37, 234

Taunay, Auguste, 155–56, 214

Te Deum Laudamus, 62, 65, 92

territorial expansion attempts, 152

Thiebault, Paul, 22

tigers (slaves), 104–5

timeliness, personal, 115, 117

Tiradentes, 81, 83, 231, 237

Tomas, Manuel Fernandes, 229

Tordesillas, Treaty of, 69

trafficking, slave, 172–75

travelers to Brazil, 184–95. *See also* *specific people*

Travels in Brazil (Koster), 77, 189–91

Travels in the Interior of Brazil (Mawe), 185

Trazimundo, José, 34, 38

treaties

  British-Portuguese, 147, 149

  Fontainebleau, Treaty of, 20–21

  Madrid, Treaty of, 69

Tordesillas, Treaty of, 69
Vienna, Treaty of, 152, 154
Tree Frog, Father. *See* Gonçalves dos
    Santos, Luis
trellises, 154–55, 163–64
Tuckey, James, 104, 105–6,
    175, 176
turbans, 91

United States, 203, 206
University of Coimbra, 80, 198–99
Uranie (ship), 187–88

Vainfas, Ronaldo, 182
Valongo Market, 169–72
Varnhagen, Francisco Adolfo de,
    79, 205
Viana, Paulo Fernandes, 142,
    163–68, 183, 213, 216–17
Vidigal, Miguel Nunes, 166
Vieira, José Inacio Vaz, 140
Vieira da Silva, Manuel, 167, 168
Vienna, Treaty of, 152, 154
Vienna, 211–12
Villa Nova Portugal, Thomaz,
    122, 232

violence, 165
von Leithold, Theodor, 121, 157,
    161, 181
von Martius, Karl, 75–76, 175,
    187, 193–95
von Spix, Johann Baptist, 187,
    193–95
voyage to Brazil, 48–56

Walker, James, 51, 52, 53, 59, 147
Warren, Richard, 9
Waterloo, Battle of, 14, 200, 202,
    203, 210, 225
Wellington, Arthur Wellesley, Duke
    of, 14, 200, 201, 202
wet nurses, 244–45
whipping of slaves, 164, 165,
    178–79
Wilcken, Patrick, 120
Willis, Francis, 9
woodsmen, 181
wool shawls, 145, 150
work ethic, 191–92

Zong (ship), 174

MÚSICA CUBANA

CUBANA

LOS ÚLTIMOS 50 AÑOS

TONY ÉVORA

MÚSICA CUBANA

LOS ÚLTIMOS 50 AÑOS

ALIANZA EDITORIAL

© Antonio Évora, 2003
© Alianza Editorial, S. A., Madrid, 2003
Calle Juan Ignacio Luca de Tena, 15;
28027 Madrid; teléfono 91 393 88 88
www.alianzaeditorial.es
ISBN: 84-206-2024-6
Depósito legal: M. 9.985-2003
Fotocomposición e impresión: EFCA, S. A.
Parque Industrial «Las Monjas»
28850 Torrejón de Ardoz (Madrid)
Printed in Spain

*A los creadores de música cubana de cualquier época,
tendencia o espíritu.*

*En recuerdo de mi madre Elena García Hernández (1916-2001),
a quien le habría gustado ver este libro.*

*Y a ti Carmen, porque sin tu apoyo decisivo
no lo habría podido terminar.*

Erikundis

Músicos de mi tierra
oficiantes sonoros
mensajeros de un ritmo alto y preciso.
Simples músicos,
humildes músicos que nunca dejaron de presentarse
a cumplir su trabajo de veladores
de nuestra despreocupada alegría.

Viven ahora en estas páginas
acompañándome de un lado a otro.
Solemnes en su dignidad febril,
dueños del espectáculo, donde
vestidos de sudor y sandunga
                              nos movemos
al sonar de acordes sincopados.

Oficio singular de gente
con enormes dientes blancos
y un corazón frutal.
Lean este son
bien trajeados y trajinados viajeros.
Contagiaron al mundo
confundiéndose en la noche del cinquillo.
Trastocaron el tiempo y el silencio
legendarios herederos del ron y de la guasa
con su oficio singular
y un oído sincronizado en África.
¿Quién les puso la gangarrea al cuello?

Déjenme que les levante este altar.

T. E.

AGRADECIMIENTOS

Por la ayuda recibida en distintas etapas en la
formulación de esta obra, deseo dar las gracias a las
personas que de una manera u otra contribuyeron a
alentarme. Muy especialmente al narrador Reynaldo
González, cuyos gestos son prueba del valor de una
vieja amistad; al musicógrafo Cristóbal Díaz Ayala
por la evidencia de sus excelentes libros sobre la
música cubana; a Rudy e Ivette Mangual de la revista
Latin Beat y en particular a su articulista Max
Salazar, siempre bien informado, sin olvidar el
gallardo empeño barcelonés del colombiano Enrique
Romero con su revista *El Manisero* (1993-95).
Igualmente quiero expresar mi agradecimiento a los
investigadores Nat Chediak y Philip Sweeney; a
los fotógrafos cuyas imágenes lo ilustran así como
a diversos musicólogos cubanos cuyas obras han sido
consultadas, sin olvidar algunas colaboraciones
aparecidas en la revista *Encuentro de la cultura
cubana* que se edita en Madrid. Igualmente quiero
agradecer al profesor Luis Aguilar León por
permitirme concluir esta obra con su brillante análisis
de los cubanos, así como al amigo Jordi Pujol
Baulenas, que representa los sellos discográficos
Tumbao Cuban Classics, Alma Latina y Caney, por su
colaboración en la producción del CD.

CONTENIDO

Prólogo en tiempo de bolero 13

Introducción: Moviendo el follaje rítmico 17

1. **La clave cubana** 37

   LA LUCHA CONTRA LOS NEGROS 38

   LOS GRUPOS SONEROS 40

   Un motivo rítmico obsesionante, 41. Sextetos y septetos de son, 46. Una variante poco conocida, 51.

   LA FORMACIÓN DE CONJUNTOS 54

   ¡Pelotero a la bola..!, 55. La Sonora trae su ritmo..., 60. Los «lloraos» de una trompeta, 62. Dos conjuntos Caney, 63

   LAS GRANDES ORQUESTAS 66

   El estilo Dixieland, 66. Las bandas cubanas, 67. El comerciante Cugat, 71. La orquesta espectáculo, 71.

   DÚOS, TRÍOS Y CUARTETOS 74

   Tres eran tres..., 76. Ahora a cuatro voces, 80.

2.   Guajiros y negros 83

AIRES CAMPESINOS 84

Una Guantanamera que se las trae, 91.

EL TESORO LITÚRGICO 93

El sincretismo religioso, 95. ¿En qué cree el músico cubano?, 97. Los tres tambores batá, 100. Otras músicas negras, 101.

EL COMPLEJO DE LA RUMBA 102

Suenan los cueros, 103. El baile en la rumba, 105. Timberos de siempre, 106

LOS INVESTIGADORES 111

Fernando Ortiz, 111. Lydia Cabrera, 115. Jorge e Isabel Castellanos, 117.

3.   El decenio fabuloso: 1950-60 119

Un breve recuento, 121.

EL BOLERO 125

De nuevo USA, 129. El bolero baila con otros, 130. El bolero-mambo, 134. El bolero-cha, 136. El bolero en los conjuntos, 141. En las orquestas tipo jazz band, 142. Boleros más recientes, 143.

EL ESTILO FILIN 146

EL DANZÓN MODERNO 155

Aparece el «ritmo nuevo», 157. Otras charangas de los años 50, 160.

EL NUEVO SON 162

EL MAMBO 163

Su enorme influencia, 169. La percusión en el mambo, 171.

EL CHACHACHÁ 172

Para el libro Guinness, 177.

¡A MOVER LA CINTURA! 177

Bailando en La Tropical, 178. Una noche en Tropicana, 180. Otros lugares de diversión, 183.

LA CONGA 185

LA GUARACHA 188

LAS DESCARGAS 192

LA PACHANGA 195

LA MÚSICA SINFÓNICA 196

EL CONJUNTO FOLKLÓRICO NACIONAL 216

Los mejores:

Ignacio Piñeiro, 50
Isolina Carrillo, 128
Bola de Nieve, 132
Antonio Machín, 138
Olga Guillot, 144
Benny Moré, 164
Tata Güines, 182
Celia Cruz, 191
Guillermo Barreto, 194
Paquito D'Rivera, 224
Frank Grillo *Machito,* 242
Chocolate Armenteros, 256
Armando Romeu, 320
Chucho Valdés, 329
Juan Formell, 352

Los instrumentos:

La guitarra y el tres, 44
El bongó, 59
Las claves, 86
Las congas, 99
La flauta, 158
El güiro, 174
La batería, 228
El piano, 231
El contrabajo, 260
Las pailas o timbal, 333

4. **El jazz afrocubano** 219
      «Me voy pa'Nuyó», 221. Armonías vs tambores, 222.
      INFLUENCIA DEL JAZZ EN CUBA 223
      INFLUENCIAS CUBANAS EN NORTEAMÉRICA 227
      LOS CREADORES DEL JAZZ AFROCUBANO.......................... 235

5. **Castro o *Coke*** 247
      EL ÉXODO MASIVO DE ARTISTAS.................................... 248
        El emigrado y las dos lenguas, 252. El papel de los músicos en las relaciones Cuba-USA, 252.
      CUBANOS EN LA SALSA NEOYORQUINA 253
        ¿Por qué le llamaron salsa?, 259. ¿Qué quedará de la salsa?, 261. Aparece y desaparece La Lupe, 263.
      EL SONIDO DE MIAMI 266
        La gloria de ser Gloria Estefan, 271. El fenómeno Albita, 275. Un sonero desconocido en España, 276. El son en California, 281.
      LO QUE SE TOCA EN EUROPA 282
        El sonido de París, 293.

6.   Los ritmos de la revolución   295
     APRENDIENDO MÚSICA   301
     LA NUEVA TROVA   305
     EL GRUPO DE EXPERIMENTACIÓN SONORA (GESI)   316
     EL PANORAMA SE MODERNIZA   318
     JAZZ CON FRIJOLES NEGROS   338
     EN LA ONDA DEL ROCK   340
     TROVADORES DE HOY   341

7.   Agrupaciones de los últimos años   343
     GUARAPO VS SALSA   344
     LAS BANDAS MÁS DESTACADAS   346

8.   ¿Hacia dónde se dirige la música cubana?   387
     En busca de «fulas», 392. Un buen músico en cualquier esquina, 394.
     ¿Es España un caso aislado?, 396. Un «honor» que sobra, 397.
     ¿CONOCE USTED A LOS CUBANOS?   402

Comentarios al CD   407
Bibliografía consultada   415
Índice onomástico   419

PRÓLOGO EN TIEMPO DE BOLERO

> El mundo apenas sabía bailar hasta que Cuba se estremeció con el palpitar de los tambores africanos gimiendo en la noche.
>
> LUIS AGUILAR LEÓN
> *El Nuevo Herald*, Miami,
> 10 de septiembre de 1993

Esta obra no ha sido fácil de redactar aunque reconozco que ningún libro de investigación musicológica lo es. La principal dificultad ha consistido en que el período estudiado corresponde con mi propia vida, y que cada sonido está ahí, en mi cabeza y en mi piel. Otro problema es el de escribir sobre tantas músicas que no puedo compartir con el lector; una situación tan ridícula como imposible de resolver.

Aunque el CD contiene magníficos ejemplos que cubren cabalmente este ambicioso trabajo, complementado por comentarios útiles en la pág. 405, muchas piezas que me hubiera gustado incluir se han tenido que quedar fuera. En lugar de una discografía al final, he ido añadiendo recomendaciones en el texto a medida que presentaba a los diversos grupos.

He tratado por todos los medios de informar de la manera que considero más justa, aun cuando se trata de un libro cargado de opiniones personales. Alguno pensará que juzgo demasiado fuerte a una revolución que sin duda puso al país en el mapa mundial y alcanzó extraordinarias cotas de desarrollo médico y educativo en sus primeros años. Sin embargo, me adscribo al dictado de José Martí: «No se puede dirigir un pueblo como se manda un campamento», y en mi país han dominado durante más de cuatro décadas los militares.

Por su actitud ante la vida, los músicos, en Cuba como en todas partes, son precisamente la gente más opuesta a la mentalidad castrense. La música es vuelo y libertad, deleite de la cabeza, el corazón o las caderas, tres cosas ajenas a esa voluntad empeñada en prohibir y doblegar.

He insertado aquí y allá breves descripciones sobre los instrumentos más empleados en Cuba y sus más notorios virtuosos. Enclavados en las secciones correspondientes, también aparecen músicos que considero excelentes, sin distinciones de índole política ni tendencias artísticas, una cuestión bastante difícil de establecer y que podría despertar susceptibilidades. Aprovecho para rogar a los que no aparecen mencionados, por mi propio descuido o mis limitaciones, si están vivos que me disculpen, y si alguien nota su ausencia en estas páginas, que sepa que la omisión no ha sido intencionada y que me encantaría recibir información a través de mis editores.

Los músicos se mueven alrededor de varias obsesiones. Una es que suelen hablar de música y de ligues, y sus razones tendrán para ello. Otra tiene que ver con una costumbre muy criolla de ponerle motes a la gente; de ahí los curiosos sobrenombres que desfilan por estas páginas: *Changuito, Patato, Chico, Machito, Cachao, El tosco, Guajiro, Papito, El negro, Guyún, Manteca, Bola, Mongo, Chucho, Pícolo, Rapindey, Greco, Chocolate, Angá, Gallego, Coqui, Molote, Aguaje, Chino, Bimbi, Maraca, Lilí, Bebo, Chano, Papi, Ambia, Hueso, Peruchín, Tata* y un largo etcétera. Una forma de reconocerse y de expresar la amistad, pero lo curioso es que, con el tiempo, tengo la impresión de que cada apodo ha ido adquiriendo el sonido clave del músico correspondiente, como si se le hubiera pegado a la voz o al instrumento.

Una tercera obsesión del músico cubano le impele a viajar, a conocer mundo; quizá el hecho de crecer en una isla le imprima cierta ansiedad a eso de salir del patio y demostrar lo que uno vale, como lo

ALTAR MODESTO A SANTA BÁRBARA/CHANGÓ.

hicieron los grandes en el pasado. Si aquellos viajaron mayormente por barco, los de los últimos cuarenta años quieren elevarse al cielo y cogerle unas vacaciones al comunismo. Y regresar con dólares.

La cuarta entraña el inevitable problema generacional: los músicos afinan o desafinan por coincidencias tanto como por desavenencias, y aunque coexisten en una misma finca ocupan distintas parcelas, cada vez más ricas por la sedimentación.

Como todo cubano, los músicos son superticiosos y mantienen diversas creencias que llevan con orgullo. Dicen que no creen en nada pero en realidad creen en todo; es una cuestión de ética e identidad colectiva. Y en esto no hay diferencias entre negros y blancos, ni entre la vieja guardia o los jóvenes formados por la revolución. Se trata de vestigios de una cultura y estética caribeña de los tiempos de la plantación: una forma inquietante de ser y estar siempre entre un *acá* y un *allá*.

Si este libro tiene algo de original se debe tanto a la cantidad de información que brinda como al resultado de reflexiones personales. No pretendo mayor autoridad que la que me otorga una pasión infinita por la música cubana; contagiarles ese entusiasmo es mi mayor ambición.

INTRODUCCIÓN:
MOVIENDO EL FOLLAJE RÍTMICO

> Otro don de Cuba al mundo ha sido y es su música popular. Engendro de negros y blancos: producto mulato. Mientras que el tabaco y el modo de fumarlo no fueron privativos de los aborígenes, esas músicas mulatas, que se dan en Cuba como las palmas reales, sí son creaciones exclusivas del genio de su pueblo.
>
> FERNANDO ORTIZ
> *Contrapunteo cubano del tabaco y el azúcar*
> (La Habana, 1940 / reeditado en Madrid, 1999)

Esta obra es la continuación de *Orígenes de la música cubana*, que cubre aproximadamente hasta la década de 1940, y cuya primera edición –ya agotada– apareció en 1997. Una versión revisada y aumentada de dicho libro, esta vez con un CD, saldrá al mercado muy pronto. Pero al plantearme la que lee ahora, ¿cómo iba a dejar de lado los elementos culturales y políticos que han intervenido en un período tan intenso como extenso y conflictivo, cargado de cambios drásticos? Tenía forzosamente que referirme a las ráfagas que movieron el follaje rítmico-melódico de la isla y del exilio durante las últimas décadas. Tampoco quería ni podía ignorar todo lo que ha hecho la revolución en pro o en contra de los músicos. De ahí que el lector encontrará bastante información sobre algunos momentos clave en el accidentado devenir de la revolución.

Pero hay otro aspecto clave en este libro. La inmensa masa musical al norte de la isla y las relaciones históricas de esa poderosa nación con su pequeña vecina del sur, me hicieron incluir un análisis enfocado hacia las altas y bajas de la sandunga musical y su oblicua relación con las músicas de Estados Unidos.

Un crítico ha definido el contenido de *Orígenes de la música cubana* como una historia de las relaciones Cuba-España, con el surgimiento y desarrollo de la música criolla como telón de fondo. Por supuesto, la presente obra mira en otra dirección, contribuyendo a comprender mejor ese costado importantísimo de la música cubana contemporánea relacionado con la norteamericana. Con sólo 120 km entre el rumbero David y el rockero Goliat, y con todos los medios de comunicación disponibles en ambos países alimentando tozudamente una incomunicación política que no cesa, era inevitable que así fuera.

Una parte considerable de este volumen está dedicada a lo que se ha estado haciendo en la isla en los últimos veinte años. Lo que me lleva al convencimiento de que no hay nada que envejezca más rápidamente que lo nuevo. Es arriesgado y bastante comprometedor hacer una crónica sobre lo que aún está vivo y coleando –quise decir bailando–, no sólo porque constantemente hay que actualizar la información sino porque se modifican los criterios, lo cual es mucho más difícil de ajustar; salvo que se haga un nuevo libro.

La música contemporánea de la «Perla del Caribe» aparece ante nosotros en tres grandes vertientes: la que se crea, se escucha y se baila desaforadamente en Cuba, la que se produce y disfruta en el exilio y la pequeña proporción que se conoce fuera de ambos ámbitos. Estas páginas intentan analizar las tres perspectivas, teniendo en cuenta que el humor, el doble sentido y el desplante sexual, expresados tanto en la música como en el contoneo, han sido algunos de los rasgos más auténticos y sobresalientes de la sonoridad cubana de cualquier época.

LA NUEVA ORQUESTA ARAGÓN.

¿Acaso debo afirmar que la música cubana gusta mucho en España y que este hecho ha contribuido grandemente a consolidar los lazos históricos que atan a ambas naciones? Sin embargo, el conocimiento de su potencial actual es bastante limitado, si exceptuamos las visitas anuales de algunas bandas, giras de pequeños grupos de septuagenarios, la proyección de algunas películas musicales y un documental sobre un exiliado excepcional, así como a dos conocidos cantautores que han ofrecido conciertos en este país frecuentemente. Todos han aparecido con la anuencia de la Sociedad General de Autores y Editores (SGAE), y avezados periodistas se han encargado de cubrir con acierto sus actuaciones en prensa, radio y televisión.

Quizá la nostalgia sea un lujo de países prósperos, pero es evidente que los músicos del ruido (obsesión de la mayor parte de las bandas actuales) se quedan pasmados ante la fascinación hispana por grupos típicos añejos como la Vieja Trova Santiaguera, Los Soneros de Camacho, Compay Segundo, Elíades Ochoa, o artistas del calibre de Celia Cruz, Olga Guillot o Gloria Estefan.

Hace relativamente poco que la maltrecha economía de la isla ha comenzado a organizarse para explotar un maná llovido del cielo, como ya sucedió con el turismo. De hecho, la aparición de discos en el extranjero y las actuaciones en directo en diversos países ha contribuido notablemente a atraer infinidad de turistas. Los músicos cubanos arrasan en todo el mundo, no sólo en España: en 1999 más de 6.000 salieron a conquistar 52 países, cubriendo 900 giras. La llegada a la isla de las grandes multinacionales discográficas es otro fenómeno nada desestimable; las imponentes EMI, Virgin o BMG ya han comenzado a sacarle el zumo a la caña de azúcar. Pronto le exprimirán hasta la última gota.

La mayor parte de los sellos extranjeros que llegaron a la isla en los últimos veinte años encontraron una escena musical dividida en dos grandes áreas: en primer lugar, la música tradicional, defendida y preservada por conjuntos soneros, trovadores y charangas, a menudo con una generación de nuevos músicos que mantenían los viejos nombres de las agrupaciones originales. El otro estrato musical que hallaron era sin duda más contemporáneo y excitante; conocida primero como salsa cubana o hipersalsa, fue bautizada más tarde como timba, un término de márketing que me hace recordar la acusada arbitrariedad al escoger el nombre de «salsa», también adoptado por razones de mercado por Johnny Pacheco y Jerry Masucci en Nueva York en la década de 1970.

Creo que la impresión que saca el ciudadano medio español, tanto el que ya ha visitado Cuba como el que espera disfrutar pronto de playas hermosas, un pueblo simpático y acogedor, ron de primera y sexo barato, es que aun reconociendo las estrecheces en que sobrevive la inmensa mayoría, la gente disfruta haciendo música y bailándola. Sin embargo, un observador imparcial podría concluir que si hasta hace unos cuarenta años el músico se dirigía libremente a dondequiera que reclamaran su presencia, hoy día se trata de un ansioso explotado, que habiendo firmado contrato con una empresa cubana, se apresta a cruzar el Atlántico para ganar un puñado de dólares.

UNA VECINDAD QUE NO ES UN PARAÍSO

A principios de noviembre de 1999 se celebró en Nueva York un evento revelador: «Cuba: 170 años de presencia en Estados Unidos». Organizado por la revista *Encuentro de la cultura cubana*, que se edita en Madrid, y por varias instituciones norteamericanas, la conferencia contó con el auspicio de la Fundación Ford y el apoyo del Instituto Cervantes. Este importante seminario reveló las influencias recíprocas que tan prolongado contacto ha supuesto en los terrenos de la cultura, el deporte, la política, el trabajo y la empresa. La música, sin duda el mayor aporte cubano al mundo en el ámbito de la cultura y la solidaridad, jugó un papel preponderante durante las discusiones que siguieron a las ponencias. Se reconoció el impacto de los ritmos cubanos en la corriente principal de la música norteamericana, particularmente desde la década de 1940, y se comprobó la influencia, siempre permeable y venturosa, de la música popular norteamericana en el cañaveral cubano. Se produjo así un diálogo libre y mutuamente enriquecedor, que deberá servir de ejemplo para la inevitable normalización histórica de las relaciones entre ambos países en un futuro no tan lejano como algunos pesimistas auguran.

Durante largo tiempo, la música ha sido un factor de unión, de simpatía y comprensión entre ambos países, así como de enriquecimiento recíproco para sus lenguajes y estilos respectivos. Cito al musicólogo Leonardo Acosta, curiosamente, uno de los voceros más destacados de la posición oficial del régimen:

Más allá de estas relaciones «bilaterales», nuestra música también ha sido, por una parte, una especie de *lingua franca* para los latinoamericanos y caribeños residentes en Estados Unidos, y por otra, un verdadero catalizador, un punto único de convergencia cultural y vital entre los cubanos, por encima de sus diferencias políticas, ideológicas, raciales o económicas y del país en que vivan. Porque es una parte vital de nuestro legado común y de nuestra experiencia cotidiana; porque es un espacio idóneo para el diálogo como lo ha sido y es para la experiencia compartida. Y mientras el diálogo parece casi imposible en otras áreas, en la música más bien parece no haber cesado nunca.

En el capítulo «El jazz afrocubano» se analizan estas importantes cuestiones, a sabiendas de que la vecindad con tan poderosa maquinaria conlleva toda una serie de ventajas e inconvenientes que los propios cubanos, y en este caso, los músicos creadores, tendrán que ser capaces de sobrellevar en el futuro.

HACIENDO *BUSINESS*

Por su parte, los empresarios españoles han estado aumentando su presencia en la isla a pasos agigantados con la complicidad del castrismo. No hay que asombrarse por ello: es el comportamiento propio de una economía fuerte frente a una débil. Se están posicionando para quedarse con un segmento importante del mercado cuando cambien las cosas y una avalancha de capital norteamericano vuelva a penetrar en la isla. Fidel Castro está encantado con la situación de los últimos años; aunque ya está viejo y evidencia signos de la enfermedad que lo acosa, sabe que necesita inyecciones de capital extranjero para que su aventura ideológica logre sobrevivir unos años más. De ahí que sus empresarios, en su mayoría ex militares que ahora aparecen disfrazados de seudocapitalistas, estén dispuestos a brindar todo tipo de facilidades a los inversionistas españoles en medio de una sociedad sumida en la pobreza más abyecta.

Sin embargo, no exagero al afirmar que en 1959, cuando Castro tomó el poder, la economía cubana era bastante más dinámica que la española. Más de cuatro decenios después, comercialmente hablando, la isla se encuentra a merced de un número de hispanohablantes listos y otros extranjeros advenedizos. Sería infantil echarle toda la culpa al bloqueo económico norteamericano. Castro es el verdadero bloqueo de Cuba, y mientras desgraciadamente el país se va pareciendo cada vez más a Somalia, España se acerca al modelo económico belga. No olvidemos la esencia del problema: Fidel Castro es un estratega militar nato. ¿Quién ha visto a un militar que sepa construir un destino de paz y prosperidad?

Pero en el terreno de la compra de derechos musicales y la contratación de músicos cubanos hay que aclarar varias cosas. Cualquier avis-

SECCIÓN DE TROMPETAS DE LA ORQUESTA
SABOR DE BEBO VALDÉS (1958): DOMINGO
CORBACHO, *EL NEGRO* VIVAR, *CHOCOLATE*
ARMENTEROS Y *PLATANITO* JIMÉNEZ.

pado productor de discos que al hacer negocios con la EGREM se haya aventurado a preguntar por las viejas grabaciones del trío de Servando Díaz o por las canciones de Blanca Rosa Gil –por citar dos ejemplos de probada calidad artística–, el extranjero sólo habrá encontrado un «¿De qué me estás hablando, asere?», es decir, una ignorancia total del tema. Y no es sólo porque unas directrices establecidas desde arriba hace ya mucho tiempo les impidan sacar esas grabaciones del archivo, es que simplemente las últimas generaciones de funcionarios cubanos nunca las han escuchado. Es más, los cubanos con menos de cuarenta años, que constituyen la mayoría, conocen muy poco de su propio patrimonio artístico; la ignorancia prima tanto en el empresario curioso como en las personas que lo atienden.

¿Acaso es necesario aclarar que las grabaciones de los músicos mencionados, junto a otros cientos de artistas, están proscritas del extenso catálogo musical cubano porque un día decidieron abandonar la isla? El capítulo «Castro o *Coke*» trata precisamente de este tema todavía candente.

Pero el *business* no se detiene. Veamos el siguiente ejemplo. En 1997, por primera vez en la Cuba de Fidel Castro, ocho orquestas de salsa fueron premiadas con discos de platino y oro, una fórmula de reconocimiento a las ventas hasta entonces desconocida en la isla. La iniciativa partió de Caribe Productions, empresa panameña de capital español que trabaja en la isla desde hace varios años y lleva la representación de una decena de orquestas actuales, la mayoría punteras. Caribe Productions, que está asociado con la empresa estatal RECSA, puso como requisito haber vendido más de 5.000 copias (oro) o 10.000 (platino) en la isla. En España, donde se venden 50 millones de discos al año, el disco de oro se concede cuando se llega a 50.000 y el platino a 100.000 copias. Según la empresa, en Cuba se comercializaban en 1997 unas 400.000 unidades. Uno de sus directores aseguró que «Por delante hay un futuro y un buen negocio». Lo que realmente le interesa es el mercado internacional. A mediados de ese año llegó a un acuerdo con EMI España para distribuir en todo el mundo, incluyendo a Estados Unidos, los discos de los salseros cubanos. De entonces acá, Caribe Productions se ha lanzado también a promocionar música de la trova tradicional, intérpretes de jazz afrocubano, grandes orquestas y hasta dúos noveles.

MÚSICA Y POLÍTICA

Varias veces lo advirtió el etnólogo Fernando Ortiz: la música cubana nunca ha podido separarse de los avatares políticos. La nación ha sido, durante la mayor parte del período estudiado, un conejillo de indias manipulado por un improvisado visionario. Los músicos lo han sufrido en carne propia, porque no hace tanto tiempo desde que el régimen descubrió que podía ingresar muchos dólares explotando el talento de los creadores de sabrosura. Por esa razón ahora los deja salir y entrar cuando quieran. Siempre que paguen un precio.

Sin embargo, si hacemos una comparación entre los veinte años que van de 1940 a 1960 y lo logrado musicalmente de 1960 al 2000, encontraremos un déficit muy notable en cuanto a diversidad, calidad y pujanza de lo creado, a pesar de la óptima preparación de jóvenes músicos formados bajo el período comunista. Creo que nadie lo ha logrado resumir mejor que Pancho Céspedes, el cantautor de *Vida loca*: «Me fui de Cuba porque quería que mi música trascendiera. Allí te dan las armas para que pienses, pero no salidas».

Este libro trata de demostrar –entre otras cosas– que entre 1940 y 1960 ya se encontraban establecidas casi todas las fórmulas y estilos musicales que heredó y dieron lustre a la revolución. Gran parte de los distinguidos visitantes de los primeros años creyeron que aquella maravillosa sandunga sonora era producto del cambio social, aunque por supuesto, ya hacía tiempo que estaba allí; lo que nadie habría podido imaginar es cómo se despilfarró, tergiversó o desapareció todo ese caudal musical durante los cuarenta años posteriores.

LA ISLA FRENTE AL IMPERIO

Cuba siempre ha tenido que mirar hacia el Norte para acoger la modernidad y encauzar su economía. Ya desde comienzos del siglo XIX, siendo todavía una provincia española, la isla era realmente una colonia económica de Estados Unidos, que le compraba el 90 por ciento de su producción azucarera anual, mientras que la metrópolis, situada a 9.000 km de distancia, sólo percibía el 3,7 por ciento de su factoría.

Durante la segunda mitad de dicho siglo, millares de cubanos tuvieron que establecerse en territorio anglosajón debido a sus discrepancias con el opresor régimen colonial español. Muchos contribuyeron, bien como obreros de la construcción, profesionales o torcedores de tabaco, a fomentar y a financiar el esfuerzo bélico contra España, y de paso levantaron la economía de ciudades como Tampa y Cayo Hueso, contribuyendo eficazmente a su florecimiento. El pueblito llamado Miami se asentaba entonces en una zona de pantanos pestilentes.

Ciento setenta largos años han visto pasar por tierras norteamericanas –entre otros cubanos y cubanas extraordinarios– al sacerdote exiliado Félix Varela y al boxeador Kid Chocolate, al pianista Ignacio Cervantes y al campeón internacional de ajedrez José Raúl Capablanca. En el Nueva York de 1882 publicó Cirilo Villaverde su extraordinaria novela *Cecilia Valdés,* los amores de una hermosa mulata y un blanco ricachón que resultó ser su medio hermano. Allí trabajó como periodista y mantuvo su incesante labor revolucionaria el poeta José Martí hasta su muerte en 1895 en campos cubanos. Bajo sus rascacielos, el trompeta Mario Bauzá instrumentó el jazz afrocubano entre 1932 y 1944, mientras que desde 1961 la tremenda voz de Celia Cruz ha gritado «*¡Asúuuca!*» bajo las luces de múltiples escenarios estadounidenses. Muchos otros artistas y creadores de todo tipo de música han contribuido notablemente a destacar los valores cubanos, incluyendo a Gloria Estefan, tan conocida del pueblo español.

No hay que olvidar que en Estados Unidos el adjetivo *Cuban* siempre ha tenido un vínculo semántico muy directo, como señala Gustavo Pérez Firmat en *Vidas en vilo. La cultura cubanoamericana.* En gran

EL PIANISTA IGNACIO CERVANTES.

parte de la psique yanqui sobreviven toda una serie de actividades y productos originales de la isla que no sólo producen interés o placer sino que además son estimulantes del organismo: *Cuban rum, Cuban sunshine, Cuban boxers, Cuban sugar, Cuban baseball, Cuban beaches, Cuban coffee, Cuban girls, Cuban cigars, Cuban music.* A pesar del largo divorcio transcurrido (cuarenta y dos años al momento de escribir estas páginas), el país perdura en la memoria de muchos estadounidenses como un sitio propiciatorio para dejar aflorar sin trabas todo tipo de deseos, incluyendo el haber sido en la década de 1920 una fuente de licores ilegales y base para el contrabando durante el período gansteril de la prohibición. Algo parecido ocurrió con el boxeo o con el juego de pelota, que así llamamos los cubanos a nuestra pasión por el béisbol. Los campeonatos nacionales se sucedían en el otoño y el invierno, lo cual permitía la contratación por la libre de deportistas norteamericanos que jugaban durante el verano; el fanático beisbolero se acostumbró a transitar su admiración de una figura estelar criolla o otra del Norte.

Condimento central de la industria del entretenimiento, la música ofrecía a los turistas un marco de placer ritualizado de carácter individual y colectivo, abriendo brechas hacia lo inesperado y misterioso en la noche tropical. Inevitablemente, en algún club, hotel o cabaré se ponía a prueba la consabida timidez anglosajona en la pista de baile; de ahí que, para atraerlos, a cualquier orquesta se le ocurriera comenzar *Siboney* de Lecuona con un ligero aire de fox-trot y luego introducía las claves, las maracas y el bongó, cambiándoles el ritmo cuando ya los tenían abrazados. Vaya, lo que en Cuba se conoce como «cambiando de palo pa'rumba», porque después venía un sabroso son, seguido de una sudorosa conga y un lento chachachá para reponerse. En realidad era una iniciativa inútil, porque guardando siempre la simple coreografía que ya conocían, pocas parejas lograron aprender nuevos pasos.

ACEPTAR O RECHAZAR

De una forma u otra, la mayoría de los músicos de cualquier época han estado siempre dispuestos a acoger los cambios sufridos en la música norteamericana. Unos pocos han intentado reaccionar negativamente, una actitud a menudo ambivalente que llega hasta nuestros días. Fascinados por la diversidad armónica y su riqueza instrumental, han mantenido un

MANUEL SAUMELL.

oído sintonizado en lo que acontecía en el Norte (que es como los cubanos se refieren a Estados Unidos). Veamos algunos ejemplos clave. ¿Cómo habría sido la obra del genial contradancista **Manuel Saumell** (1817-70) durante el movimiento romántico del siglo XIX, sin el aporte de su amigo Louis Moreau Gottschalk, joven pianista de Nueva Orleans que lo puso al día de lo que acontecía en el mundo? Hasta entonces, las delicadísimas formas armónicas de Saumell respondían a la influencia de Schubert. No obstante, los últimos dieciséis años de su vida estuvieron marcados por la visión de Gottschalk, el organizador de un magno concierto en 1861 con 40 pianos, en el teatro Tacón, con el acompañamiento percutivo de la sociedad de tumba francesa de Santiago de Cuba, grupo que hizo llevar con grandes esfuerzos a la capital en tiempos en que no existían los medios de transporte actuales. Este compositor –que estaba convencido del entronque musical que ya entonces existía entre Nueva Orleans y el Caribe–, no sólo dejó una estela de la sensibilidad francesa de su tiempo, provocando no pocas pequeñas revoluciones musicales durante sus estancias en la isla, sino que después se dedicó a esparcir las concepciones rítmico-melódicas cubanas en su país y en Europa.

Veamos otro ejemplo significativo: la aparición en Cuba alrededor de 1925 de varias orquestas tipo jazz band o swing band, a imitación de las que triunfaban entonces en Norteamérica (Jimmy Dorsey, Glenn Miller, Stan Kenton y otras). Este tipo de agrupación, más numerosa que los septetos, conjuntos y charangas, contaba con cuatro o cinco saxofones (dos altos, dos tenores y barítono), al menos tres trompetas y un trombón de vara, batería y percusión cubana (tumbadora y bongó), piano, contrabajo, maracas, claves y cantante. Así equipados, la capacidad sonora se enriqueció notablemente. La intención era obvia: satisfacer los gustos de la clase social más poderosa, la que comerciaba con el poderoso vecino, interpretando todo tipo de música, desde fox-trots hasta pasodobles y boleros. De todo menos danzones tocaban aquellas orquestas, porque no querían ser confundidas con una charanga u orquesta típica.

Pensando en esto de las mutuas influencias, el incontenible Gottschalk se anticipó en varios decenios al interés de George Gershwin (el autor de *Rhapsody in blue*) en la música de la isla; Gershwin visitó La Habana en 1932 y habiéndolo conocido en una emisora de radio le pidió a su modesto autor, **Ignacio Piñeiro,** los mejores compases del tema central del son *Échale salsita,* para después incorporarlos a su deslumbrante *Obertura cubana.* Poco después, en 1941, el compositor Aaron Copland recogió material para producir la versión original para dos pianos de su *Danzón cubano*; en los escasos siete minutos que dura esta partitura, Copland no reprodujo los ritmos criollos sino que captó su esencia.

EL SONERO IGNACIO PIÑEIRO (1963).

Como es sabido, la música popular norteamericana del siglo XX ha tenido su columna vertebral en el blues y el jazz. Ambos tienen sus raíces en humildes creadores afroamericanos, de ahí que a partir de la década de 1930 éstos hayan tenido la oportunidad de encontrarse a menudo en los estudios de grabación con sus primos afrocubanos; sin embargo, nunca han estado realmente juntos ni revueltos. Esta afirmación se puede comprobar en el capítulo «El jazz afrocubano». Para encontrar otras respuestas a tales situaciones de intercambio, préstamos, influencias y fusiones, sugiero ver mi ensayo *Orígenes de la música cubana.*

Son «ellos», los estadounidenses, los americanos, los gringos, los yanquis o como queramos llamarles, los que, sin pretenderlo, provocaron gran parte de las transformaciones en los formatos cubanos, desde la mencionada creación de orquestas tipo swing bands hasta la modernización, a partir de 1940, del pequeño arsenal instrumental del viejo septeto de son, convirtiéndolo en conjunto al agregarle otras trompetas, el piano y una tumbadora para sustentar el fraseo agudo del bongó. El invidente Arsenio Rodríguez fue uno de los que más insistió en esta necesidad, a sabiendas de que iba en contra de su propio instrumento, el tres, una guitarra de cuerdas metálicas que, por supuesto, no alcanzaba la sonoridad del piano aun cuando estuviera delante del único micrófono disponible en su época. En 1940, un piano vertical de calidad, *made in USA,* ya colocado en los muelles habaneros, del tipo que usaron Isolina Carrillo u Orlando de la Rosa, costaba cuarenta dólares de entonces.

Lo inaudito es que en 1994, en pleno «Período Especial» (que para el pueblo cubano se traduce en «a pasarla peor que nunca»), Adalberto Álvarez, un músico y compositor de probado talento, triunfara con una versión sonera de *Baby, te quiero a ti,* creada por el norteamericano Big Mountain. Después de decenios tratando de lavar el cerebro al pueblo inculcándole un odio desmedido contra todo lo que representa Norteamérica (rencor que no está limitado a sus gobernantes o a su sistema económico), algunos se ven forzados a retomar temas harto conocidos por la juventud a través de la onda corta y disfrazarlos con el arsenal rítmico cubano. Cuestión de poca monta cuando lo comparamos con la preocupación creciente del régimen ante la atención que recibe la música rock (considerada de siempre como un arma del imperialismo) de un inesperado segmento de la población: los hijos de los militares en el poder. Canek Sánchez Guevara, nieto de Che Guevara, es un ejemplo de esta contradicción. Símbolo de una nueva generación que quiere romper radicalmente con el comunismo, cuando fue entrevistado en 1992 el joven deseaba ser un músico de rock y emigrar. «Esta revolución está en ruinas», le comentó al periodista argentino Andrés Oppenheimer, autor de *La hora final de Castro.* Y es que el hambre vieja del «hombre nuevo» tiene muchas facetas.

ARSENIO RODRÍGUEZ Y ANTONIO ARCAÑO.

LAS PRIMERAS GRABACIONES

Desde principios del siglo XX ya estaban los músicos criollos grabando en La Habana y Nueva York. Como país productor de música excitante, la isla tuvo acceso inmediato a la industria reproductora del sonido, en comparación con otras naciones hermanas. El desarrollo tecnológico, la cercanía geográfica y el interés despertado en los primeros sellos norteamericanos por la riqueza rítmico-melódica cubana provocó un continuo ir y venir de artistas. Aunque se les pagaba muy mal y en general fueron explotados, la efectiva distribución comercial de los discos contribuyó eficazmente a sembrar la música cubana por el mundo occidental. Este importante aspecto está plenamente cubierto en el capítulo «El sonido grabado» de mi compilación *El Libro del Bolero*, publicado por esta misma editorial en 2001.

Incluso antes de la instauración de la radio en Cuba (1922), era ya considerable el flujo de música criolla que circulaba por todo el continente, especialmente alrededor de la inmensa cuenca del mar Caribe, en discos de 78 rpm. Hechos de baquelita, una mezcla de laca y polvo de roca con fibra de algodón y coloreados con negro de humo, durante largo tiempo aquellos pesados discos reinaron como únicos señores. Pero en 1948 la Columbia Records lanzó al mercado el disco de larga duración o LP *(long play)*, el llamado microsurco de 33-1/4 rpm, hecho de vinilo irrompible. Su contrapartida, el pequeño disco plástico de 45 rpm con una canción por cada lado, apareció al año siguiente promovido por la RCA Victor. Ambos formatos desplazaron a su antecesor.

¡Cuántos no recordamos la gramola de los años cincuenta! Conocida como «traganíqueles» o «vitrola» en Cuba, y «vellonera» en Puerto Rico, la máquina Wurlitzer diseñada por Paul Fuller en 1946, con sus luces de colores y adornos metálicos de fantasía y su tesoro de discos pequeños, arrebató a la juventud de la época y determinó entre la gente de barrio la adoración de ídolos menores, adaptados a su idiosincrasia.

En aquellos años cuarenta, pocos sabían que el súbito interés de los grandes sellos en producir más discos de música latina se debía a una huelga general de músicos norteamericanos en los estudios de grabación, una disputa que duró varios años. Según el musicólogo Cristóbal Díaz Ayala, el responsable de esta situación fue el dirigente sindical James C. Petrillo, cuya obstinada actitud ocasionó la desaparición de las grandes bandas norteamericanas en medio de una guerra que de Europa se había extendido al Pacífico. A consecuencia de ello, el mercado del disco creció de tal manera que propició el establecimiento de varias fábricas en La Habana.

RAPINDEY, EL PROPIETARIO DEL PALLADIUM, DIZZY GILLESPIE, *CHINO* POZO Y TITO PUENTE EN EL BONGÓ (NUEVA YORK, 1947).

INFLUENCIAS QUE SE HAN QUERIDO TAPAR

Ciertas corrientes de la música norteamericana contribuyeron inadvertidamente a echar abajo el trono que durante largo tiempo había disfrutado el bolero tradicional, en aras de una expresión armónica más rica y personalizada. Con una considerable influencia del jazz, a este tipo de canción se le llamó filin (del inglés *feeling*, sentimiento), un movimiento surgido en La Habana hacia 1950, que despertó el interés de compositores y cantautores de varias latitudes, desde el mexicano Armando Manzanero hasta el catalán Joan Manuel Serrat. En España se ha escuchado algo del filin original gracias a las visitas de los cantautores **César Portillo de la Luz** y la exquisita **Marta Valdés**, o la vocalista **Omara Portuondo**.

Aprovecharé para referirme a algo que los estudiosos de la música popular hemos lamentado: la mayor parte de los musicólogos e investigadores de la isla, muy bien preparados y con evidente talento, pero mediatizados por las restricciones impuestas por el régimen, están sumergidos en una prosa tan oscura como aburrida. Cubriéndose bajo un barniz seudomarxista, temen «meter la pata». Han dedicado cientos de páginas a tapar lo evidente: la enorme influencia norteamericana en la música cubana, y cuando tienen forzosamente que referirse a ella emplean un eufemismo, llamándola música de carácter «internacional». Rara vez han revelado el origen de las corrientes armónicas que han saturado al país de punta a punta y de género a género. Revelarlo es tabú: al imperialismo hay que odiarlo en todos los frentes.

En la Cuba amordazada no se perdona nada. Un viejo amigo, el musicógrafo Helio Orovio, publicó en 1981 su utilísimo *Diccionario de la música cubana*, esfuerzo encomiable para un autor solitario que no contó con el apoyo de un equipo asesor adecuado a las exigencias del proyecto. Pero como era de esperar, Helio se vio obligado a dejar fuera de su compilación a todo aquel que se había marchado del país; desaparecieron como por arte de magia Olga Guillot, el flautista José Antonio Fajardo, Celia Cruz, Mario Fernández Porta, el cantante Justo Betancourt y el bajista *Cachao*, entre otros talentos criollos que han triunfado plenamente en el exterior. Las críticas y protestas fueron tales que Orovio tuvo que preparar una segunda edición, publicada en 1992 (impresa en Colombia debido a las notorias deficiencias de la industria gráfica cubana), donde finalmente incorporó a los más señalados «olvidados».

Dando otro saltito en el tiempo: ¿Qué era lo que más ansiaba el gran sonero **Benny Moré** mientras se entrenaba en México con las orquestas de **Pérez Prado**, **Mariano Mercerón** y Rafael de Paz? Tener una banda en Cuba que alcanzara un sonido como la de Glenn Miller. Y lo logró a partir de 1953, sólo que él la llamaba «la tribu», por razones obvias. A menudo le salían bailes donde tenía que tocar música norteamericana toda la noche. Yo estuve en varios.

Sin embargo, si antes empleé el término rechazar es porque siempre hubo música afrocubana, ya fuese de carácter ritual o profano, que pugnó por presentar batalla a la continua invasión de temas norteameri-

PÉREZ PRADO, CREADOR DEL MAMBO.

canos, manteniéndose fiel a las raíces originales. Vaya como evidencia el complejo de la rumba (yambú, columbia y guaguancó), que se ha conservado bastante inalterable desde hace más de medio siglo y cuyos mejores representantes contemporáneos aparecen en el capítulo «Guajiros y negros».

Un ejemplo típico de la reacción ante los chorros de *ragtime, onestep* y *swing* que abrazaron entre 1926 y 1934 los jóvenes criollos de clase alta, es un sabroso son grabado en 1928 por el Sexteto Habanero, titulado *Alza los pies congo*, del tresero negro Carlos Godínez, en el cual se hace referencia a la repentina invasión en la capital del baile conocido como el charlestón

> Hay en mi Cuba un baile que se llama son
> y en el Norte hay otro que es el charlestón.
> El charlestón, el charlestón,
> no tiene comparación, cuando yo les bailo el son...

Dando otro pequeño salto llegamos hasta ese híbrido llamado jazz latino que tanto apasionó al realizador español Fernando Trueba hasta que logró celebrarlo con creces en su filme *Calle 54*. Yo prefiero llamarlo sin tapujos ni nacionalismos desmedidos por su verdadero nombre: jazz afrocubano. Aunque en dicho movimiento jazzístico participaron en distintas épocas un buen número de puertorriqueños, argentinos, dominicanos, brasileños, panameños y otros, incluyendo músicos norteamericanos de categoría, fueron los cubanos **Alberto Socarrás, Mario Bauzá, Frank Grillo** *Machito* y *Chico* **O'Farrill**, entre otros, quienes lograron incorporarlo a la riqueza espontánea del jazz. Y no caigamos en la superficialidad de creer que sólo por colocar una tumbadora tocada por Chano Pozo en 1947 junto al trompeta Dizzy Gillespie ya se formó el híbrido. De la originalidad del jazz afrocubano como corriente estética se trata ampliamente en el capítulo 4.

LA SALSA EN DISPUTA

Cuando en 1961 Castro rompió las relaciones comerciales y diplomáticas con el imperio del Norte, el régimen aprovechó para ponerle el cerrojo a la música cubana. Los otros contestaron, entre otras medidas, impiendo la entrada de músicos cubanos en su territorio, a no ser que se tratara de exiliados. Nadie habría podido sospechar entonces que diez años después el viejo son, sobre el que cabalgaba el caprichoso oricha Elegguá, iba a convertirse en la base estructural de la salsa neoyorquina. Deslumbrante y enriquecido instrumentalmente con más metales y arreglos profesionales, pero en definitiva, la misma sabrosura del son cubano. Véase el capítulo Castro o *Coke*.

JOSÉ ANTONIO FAJARDO (1919-2001).

La salsa no fue sólo un fenómeno musical. Cuando al sello Fania se le ocurrió el curioso término para promover un producto hecho en Nueva York, sólo pretendía hacer disfrutar a los millones de latinos que viven y trabajan en Norteamérica y a la vez tratar de penetrar el gigantesco mercado estadounidense, el famoso *crossover*. Sin embargo, la salsa tuvo un inusitado aspecto político para los cubanos, que no fue provocado por los músicos. Su desarrollo y éxito posterior fue atacado tanto desde la isla comunista como desde el exilio capitalista. Irritados, sintiéndose traicionados, ambos sectores se preguntaban: ¿Qué es eso de llamarle salsa al son cubano? Sin proponérselo –insisto–, la salsa se convirtió en el único tópico que ha logrado unir los criterios de ambos bandos ideológicos divididos por el Estrecho de la Florida. Por primera vez en muchos años, tanto los portavoces del régimen dictatorial de La Habana como los exaltados exiliados en Miami estuvieron de acuerdo en algo, un verdadero momento histórico que merece mayor análisis. Pero lo cierto es que la salsa no habría podido surgir sin la contribución de decenas de instrumentistas, arreglistas y vocalistas cubanos con talento, parapetados en la fría diáspora de Nueva York.

Otra contradicción curiosa. Algunos músicos que tienen éxito en la isla creen mantenerse al margen de una política de mercado que estiman tendió a encasillar a las grandes figuras de la salsa. Ellos se consideran más puros, más auténticos. «Les quitas las voces y suenan todos lo mismo, con los mismos esquemas de orquestación», afirmó Paulito (Pablo Fernández Gallo, director del grupo Paulito y su Élite) en una entrevista aparecida en la revista *El Manisero* (enero-febrero 1994), que se publica-

EL COMPOSITOR LEO BROUWER (1963).

ba en Barcelona. Y aunque llevaba algo de razón, me consta que la salsa a que él ha tenido acceso es la de los últimos estertores. Sin embargo, estimo que muchos músicos cubanos deberían estar agradecidos a los salseros neoyorquinos porque mantuvieron viva la esencia de la música cubana en el exterior durante los decenios en que Castro les impidió salir a dar batalla. Ahora se benefician de lo que sembraron otros, a pesar de que durante años la atacaron como si fuese el mismísimo demonio.

LA CREATIVIDAD PUJANTE

Y mientras la salsa triunfaba en todas partes, en la isla, durante los terribles años setenta y todavía en los ochenta, el músico cubano, si quería imponer su obra debía continuar dando testimonio, o al menos señales inequívocas, de su adhesión política a la dictadura. En cada disco había que incluir algún número donde se mencionara una frase acuñada por la revolución, o repetir lo «libre» que era aquella sociedad, o adaptar una canción de Pablo Milanés en tiempo de guaguancó, etc. Los que no lo hicieron, o aquellos cuyos mejores textos se desestimaron por considerar los comisarios políticos que podían prestarse a confusas interpretaciones, fueron gradualmente relegados.

Pero hay otro aspecto que es necesario tratar. A pesar de ser el país una fábrica de sonidos transparentes, para la mayor parte de los narradores del siglo XX, la música es algo que siempre estuvo ahí, pero no merecía demasiada consideración. Sin embargo, hace 150 años que Cuba empezó a exportar música de calidad: una amulatada habanera fue la primera en hacer las maletas. Para muchos, subrayo, raramente ha existido otro arte de valor más universal que la literatura, que sin duda ha alcanzado cotas exquisitas de creatividad literaria y poética. Tampoco los dramaturgos o los artistas plásticos le han prestado suficiente atención a la música, y aclaro que hablo en líneas generales. Afortunadamente, la cinematografía del período revolucionario ha podido recoger importantes manifestaciones en las bandas sonoras de bastantes películas y en la producción de documentales sobre músicos valiosos, aunque resulta inevitable preguntarse por qué diablos no hicieron más, porque han desaprovechado innumerables oportunidades. De hecho, el capítulo 6 examina la contribución al cine nacional realizada por Leo Brouwer, Silvio Rodríguez, Pablo Milanés y el exquisito José María Vitier, junto a otros compositores notables. Dicho capítulo presenta además un análisis crítico del quehacer de ambos cantautores dentro del movimiento de la nueva trova.

Todo dicho, y con señaladas excepciones, los músicos han tendido a ser los artistas menos propicios a instruirse y por ende, los más irresponsables, no importa de qué época hablemos, ni en qué país les tocó salir a buscar al mediodía una tienda donde comprar frijoles negros y arroz blanco. No obstante, desde mediados del siglo XIX el destino deparó a mulatos, blancos y negros la responsabilidad de practicar y dar a conocer en el mundo la creatividad más evidentemente original y pujante de la isla. Verdaderos embajadores sin nómina de su país de origen, y demasiado a menudo sufriendo miserias y penurias, pusieron a gozar a millones de personas de diversas latitudes, razas, credos y clases sociales. Personas que a su vez identificaron a Cuba como un extenso laboratorio musical donde se experimentaba con todo tipo de invenciones raras, pero sumamente vitales.

CONTRAPUNTEO Y DESPENALIZACIÓN DEL DÓLAR

En una de sus más acertadas definiciones, aparecida en *La africanía de la música folklórica de Cuba* (1950), el investigador Fernando Ortiz aseguró: «La historia de Cuba está en el humo de su tabaco y en el dulzor de su azúcar, como también está en el sandungueo de su música». Aseveración aplicable desde el siglo XVII hasta mediados de 1970, cuando las ventas mundiales de azúcar, tabaco y minerales comenzaron a ser ampliamente superadas por los créditos financieros de la antigua Unión Soviética, y posteriormente, a partir de 1990, por la descomunal entrada de dólares enviados por la comunidad cubana en el exilio para ayudar a sus familias atrapadas en la isla bajo el funesto «Período Especial». Otro truco de Castro para apoderarse de divisas. La despenalización del dólar tuvo lugar en 1993; cualquier ciudadano sorprendido con «fulas» en el bolsillo antes de esa fecha iba a parar a la cárcel. ¿Qué efecto ha tenido este cambio de política en el devenir de la música actual?

Un chiste surgido a raíz de la visita del Papa en 1998, y que pudo haber escuchado cualquier turista, insiste en que lo que hace falta en la isla es tener FE. «¿Cómo fe?», pregunta el visitante asombrado. «¡Sí, Familiares en el Extranjero!».

Los últimos cuarenta años de esta historia han visto el recrudecimiento de un régimen autoritario, represivo y dogmático que arrasó con la flora y fauna de la isla, y desmembró la vida intelectual que a trompicones había empezado a desarrollar la sociedad civil en los decenios anteriores a 1959, a pesar de gobiernos venales y de la dictadura de Batista. Desde entonces, los cubanos tenemos una enorme necesidad de recordar lo que nuestra cultura y nuestra sociedad han sufrido bajo los grandilocuentes pero desastrosos planes de desarrollo de un líder que sólo han servido para deformar la vida cotidiana y desmotivar la vigorosa creatividad del cubano. Una necesidad que probablemente nunca quede satisfecha del todo, insaciable, voraz a la hora de nombrar una y otra vez el pasado, con el consiguiente peligro de tender a idealizarlo. Historiadores, economistas y novelistas se han entregado a fondo a dicha labor y han escrito páginas imprescindibles; lo han hecho desde todas las ópticas posibles. Ahora le toca el turno a la música.

En las cinco décadas estudiadas, cada uno de los nombres en este enorme pase de lista ha hecho una contribución notable a la cultura cubana; la vocación, la sensibilidad y el trabajo diario han sido las piedras de toque de estos hombres y mujeres de la música. Ahora confío en la complicidad del lector para justificar mi propia búsqueda, que ha constituido un verdadero reto.

Tal parece como si, desde hace mucho tiempo, la creatividad musical se hubiera adaptado a los ciclos dictados por el clima: la isla reverdece bajo estaciones de sol inclemente seguidas de lluvia cálida y algún que otro terrible ciclón, con un breve pero intenso período de vientos fríos que provienen del Norte alrededor de enero y febrero, y que sacuden todo tipo de follaje. ¿Le recuerda algo?

1. LA CLAVE CUBANA

> El baile siempre fascinó a los cubanos. Lo llevan en la
> sangre española y en la africana, bien como resultado de
> la mezcla étnica o simplemente porque las barreras ten-
> dieron a desaparecer cuando de mover las caderas se tra-
> taba. Como suele decirse en la isla: «De San Antonio a
> Maisí, el que no tiene de congo tiene de carabalí», una
> irónica referencia a la posibilidad de que todo criollo
> blanco ha tenido su ramalazo de genes negros.
>
> TONY ÉVORA
> *Orígenes de la música cubana*

Hay que insistir en ello: la mejor expresión cultural de lo cubano son la
música y el baile. Lo que no he dicho es que a tono con su carácter lúdico
y tropical, ambas son exhibicionistas, densas, excesivas y hasta transgre-
soras. Llevan además una enorme carga de tristeza. No hay película o vídeo, profesional o aficionado, que tenga la capacidad de demostrar estas
propiedades si uno no está expuesto a ellas directamente. En cualquier
caso, en *Orígenes* expongo cómo a través del siglo XIX numerosos viajeros extranjeros dejaron constancia de la pasión por el baile en sus visio-
nes costumbristas. Unos fueron altamente críticos por la fama que iba ganando La Habana como ciudad demasiado alegre, otros lanzaron una
catarata de piropos a la isla.

Casi todos aquellos observadores coincidieron en varios puntos que
captaron su atención: las orquestas formadas por negros y mulatos tocando todo tipo de instrumentos, la importancia de la percusión, el carácter
antifonal de los cantos, la complejidad de los ritmos, la explícita sexualidad de los bailes y la naturaleza pública y colectiva de dichas expresiones.

¿Es acaso un estereotipo el que para muchos lo cubano es sobre
todo música, baile y ritmo? Por supuesto, se trata de una mirada superfi-

cial, pero todo estereotipo tiene su razón de ser. Debo añadir que entre los propios criollos cuando alguien muere se dice: «Fulanito cantó *El manisero*», o que cuando una persona es torpe o incapaz de ejercer alguna actividad se dice de ella que «ni canta, ni baila, ni come fruta». Entre los nacidos en la isla, el no saber bailar o cantar, o no poder llevar el ritmo con los pies, es un estigma, un defecto tan censurado como la cicatería o el olor a sudor.

El folclor local da cuenta de un rumbero famoso, conocido como «Papá Montero», a quien se le vio bailar después de muerto, suceso que dio pie a varias versiones guaracheras incluyendo *El muerto se fue de rumba*. Que un cadáver baile antes de ser enterrado cabe dentro del reino cubano de lo posible. Después de todo, en la Santería criolla es común observar cómo las presencias del más allá se manifiestan a través del baile: las deidades Elegguá, Ochún, Changó, Yemayá, Oggún, Oyá, Babalú-Ayé y otros orichas, una vez invocados, suelen descender a la tierra bailando frenéticamente al sonido de los tambores, metidos en el cuerpo de un danzante «poseído». Y no me parece casual que en el cine de los años 30 y 40 abunden versiones hollywoodenses de congas de salón, ni que Marlon Brando apareciera bailando un mambo a lo Pérez Prado en *Guys and dolls*, ni que más tarde Nat King Cole se atreviera a grabar el cha-chachá *El bodeguero* en español, ni que todavía hoy los intérpretes de jazz gusten de incluir en sus improvisaciones las once primeras notas de *El manisero*, de Moisés Simons.

Tales manifestaciones se han mantenido a través del tiempo como constantes, y las apreciaremos mejor siempre y cuando adoptemos la mirada del viajero, es decir, la mirada del de *afuera*. Si nos colocáramos *dentro*, nos interesaría más comentar el conjuro de cierta violencia que considero intrínseca a la sociedad cubana.

LA LUCHA CONTRA LOS NEGROS

En la época en que el etnólogo **Fernando Ortiz** (1881-1969) comenzaba a defender en libros y conferencias la idea de la integración de las razas, las tensiones raciales eran tremendas. En 1910 había sido aprobada la llamada Ley Morúa, que prohibía la organización de partidos políticos sobre la base de una sola raza o color. Esto hizo ilegal el Partido Independiente de Color (PIC), fundado en 1908 por Evaristo Estenoz junto a otros líderes negros; el objetivo fundamental del PIC era proteger los derechos de los cubanos de piel oscura, abandonados a su suerte después de su enorme sacrificio y contribución a la liberación del país.

A pesar de constituir más de la tercera parte de la población total de la isla, la incorporación de los negros a la vida laboral era entonces escasísima, y su representación casi inexistente en la vida política, las fuerzas armadas, el poder judicial, el servicio civil o la educación. Al no aceptar el PIC lo dispuesto por la Ley Morúa, el llamado Ejército Permanente, apoyado por varias bandas racistas, inició una brutal campaña represiva en el verano de 1912, la tristemente llamada «Guerra de las razas», en la que murieron más de 3.000 negros, especialmente en la región oriental, que fue donde se originó el son.

El miedo a la preponderancia del negro, el que había levantado la riqueza del país con el machete en la mano, fue el motor que alimentó durante largo tiempo los prejuicios raciales. De nada había servido la advertencia de José Martí: «Cubano es más que blanco, más que negro». La herida social abierta por tan horrible episodio fue superada con el tiempo, la convivencia, el deseo de olvidar y otros factores.

Sin embargo, unos diez años después de aquellas persecuciones desmadradas, Cuba comenzó a experimentar una verdadera revolución musical que, iniciándose con la popularización del son, continuó con la de la rumba, la conga y el bolero, y más tarde con la guaracha, el mambo, el chachachá y otros ritmos. Aquella lejana época de auge musical –donde proliferaron trovadores, septetos, tríos y cuartetos de mulatos, blancos y negros– fue seguida de conjuntos y orquestas, de intérpretes y grabaciones, revistas musicales, comparsas y shows de cabarés, que marcarían en adelante la idiosincrasia del cubano. Y todo esto se logró a pesar de gobiernos mediocres que saquearon sus finanzas o que entregaron el país al inversor norteamericano.

Al contribuir al acercamiento de negros y blancos, el son preparó el camino para que otros componentes culturales avanzaran lenta pero sostenidamente hacia los primeros planos de la cultura nacional. Sin embargo, el son mismo había sido objeto de discriminación, oponiéndosele la música del jazz band –sobre todo interpretando fox trots– como bailes más apropiados para los blancos. Es revelador el título de una pieza de 1924: *Mi mamá no quiere que yo baile el son*.

¿Por qué este «honor» le correspondió al son y no a los géneros de la conga, el danzón o la rumba? Porque la conga es música colectiva y ca-

DANDI NEGRO FOTOGRAFIADO EN
LOS AÑOS 30 POR EVANS.

llejera, ruido de carnaval. Requiere centenares de participantes, incluyendo gentes en las aceras, azoteas, portales, ventanas y balcones. Sin embargo, su carácter desaforado la hizo fácil víctima de periódicas prohibiciones municipales. Por su parte, el danzón parecía música de la época colonial, demasiado chapado a la antigua, cuando padres e hijos se trataban de usted; eso de detenerse en medio de una pieza para abanicarse no tenía nada que ver con conducir un nuevo Ford o irse a tomar helados con una chica. Tampoco la rumba podía llenar ese espacio; en ella hay mucho de pantomima y acrobacia, una relación íntima entre el bailador y el repiqueteo del quinto, demasiado negra y erótica. Además, ¿dónde estaban los instrumentos europeos, si todo era voces y percusión?

·Aunque la década de 1940 puede verse como un período de consolidación nacional, y a pesar de la nueva Constitución, el negro continuó siendo víctima de la segregación racial, pero no en la esfera pública, ni en la manera dominadora y generalizada de años anteriores.

Visto desde la perspectiva del siglo XXI, estoy convencido de que el principal triunfo del son fue que lo afrocubano se hiciera cubano, a pesar de que algunos negros siguieran pensando: «La vegdá que eto blanco no saben como sacá un pie».

LOS GRUPOS SONEROS

Aunque la historia lo recoge así, para mí la Cuba moderna no nació el 20 de mayo de 1902, fecha en que la bandera de Estados Unidos fue arriada de los edificios oficiales después de cuatro años de intervención militar, y la enseña de una estrella blanca dentro de un triángulo rojo junto a cinco franjas horizontales, tres azules y dos blancas, ascendió definitivamente. Los festejos estuvieron marcados por el acompasado ritmo del danzón, convertido en baile nacional con la misma pasión con que habían sido adoptados el vals vienés o el tango argentino en sus respectivos países. En realidad el siglo XX cubano comenzó dos décadas después, cuando la contagiosa música del son tomó La Habana casi por asalto. Enlazando a toda la isla a través de las bocinas de las vitrolas de manivela y de los primeros aparatos de radio, la gente se apresuró a abandonar el danzón por el nuevo ritmo. Expuesto a la comparación, el hasta entonces respetado baile nacional parecía demasiado almidonado, sus violines y su flauta ya sonaban chapados a la antigua y la modernidad exigía el ritmo que reclamaban los tiempos. Un ritmo que además incluía voces para dar rienda suelta a la expresión, porque el verdadero danzón no se cantaba.

Hay que concluir que el son no habría conquistado el país con la rapidez y la profundidad que lo hizo sin los adelantos tecnológicos que sobrevinieron después de la Primera Guerra Mundial, en particular aquéllos que generaron las industrias norteamericanas de la radio, de las grabaciones y del cine. Por paradójico que parezca, fue la modernidad creada por sesudos ingenieros de origen europeo trabajando en territorio estadounidense lo que dio paso a la música afrocubana.

Entonces era costumbre que las salas de cine proyectaran películas silentes con el acompañamiento de un pianista, y que en los entreactos presentaran música en vivo, y más tarde, al llegar el cine hablado, incorporaran espectáculos de variedades musicales. Gracias a su música y a los nuevos adelantos, el negro encontró un espacio de convivencia junto al blanco; un espacio donde, en lugar de marginársele, se le reconocía y se le aplaudía, se le buscaba y pagaba para tocar en fiestas privadas, teatros, salones de baile y cabarés.

Al recordar el súbito impacto del son, escribió Ortiz: «Los primeros sones en La Habana significaron un despertar nacionalista y democrático, en la música y en los instrumentos. Fue una conquista, una reivindicación del arte popular».

Un motivo rítmico obsesionante

El son dio lugar a muchas variantes locales para tocarlo, cantarlo y bailarlo. En su sabroso tumbaíto se definen las características esenciales de la personalidad del cubano y muy especialmente de la cubana. Desde hace casi ochenta años, el país se convirtió en una fiesta fascinante, magnificando la leyenda de gente demasiado alegre, que al sonar un tambor se transformaba en otra cosa. Quienes creen en la influencia de la temperatura sobre el carácter, podrán achacar la alegría del cubano a la benignidad del clima; otros podrán atribuirlo a la luminosidad del aire o a esa manera indolente de ver la vida.

Había germinado al oriente de la isla, una enorme región de fuerte mezcla canario/andaluza, que contó siempre con una preponderancia bantú (Congo) sobre la yoruba (Nigeria occidental). Importantes investigaciones llevadas a cabo por Danilo Orozco indican que los sones más antiguos, el nengón y el kiribá, surgieron alrededor de la Sierra Maestra y la cuenca del río Cauto, identificándolos como antecedentes de celebraciones familiares relacionadas con el complejo del son. La región de

SEXTETO OCCIDENTE DE MARÍA TERESA VERA.

Guantánamo y los territorios de Yateras y Baracoa se han señalado también como significativos debido a su proximidad a Haití. Las fiestas que organizaban los campesinos de dicha región oriental eran conocidas como «changüí», mientras que en el centro y mitad occidental de la isla se les llamó «guateques».

Aunque algunos investigadores consideran que el son llegó a La Habana en 1920, realmente se fue estableciendo mucho antes. Su expansión se debió a un hecho de carácter administrativo, la creación del Ejército Permanente antes mencionado durante el mandato de José Miguel Gómez, en cumplimiento de una resolución establecida durante la segunda intervención de tropas norteamericanas en Cuba (1906-8), enviadas para evitar una posible guerra civil entre el partido de los moderados y los liberales. Los soldados criollos fueron destinados a otras provincias con el fin de sacarlos de su población y permitirles actuar con toda severidad en zonas opuestas del país; muchos habaneros fueron destacados a la región oriental y viceversa.

Cuando los soldados santiagueros llegaron a la capital fueron alojados en el cuartel de San Ambrosio, enclavado en el populoso barrio de Jesús María, muy cerca de la bahía, mezclándose pronto con los rumberos de la zona que estaban integrados en los coros de clave, antiguas asociaciones de recreo donde grupos vocales se acompañaban de las claves, pero en cuanto se distraía la vigilancia policial sacaban los cajones para tocar rumba. También se reunían para hacer música en casas particulares y en los locales que la banda del Ejército tenía en la antigua batería de Santa Clara, en el promontorio donde ahora se levanta el Hotel Nacional, frente al malecón habanero. Otros se juntaban en el café de los Veteranos, situado en la calle Dragones. Cerca de allí funcionaban varias agrupaciones soneras, que alrededor de 1916 comenzaron a nutrirse de las peculiaridades rítmicas de los soldados orientales.

Por supuesto, la gente quería bailar y pronto aquellas pequeñas agrupaciones se convirtieron en sextetos (guitarra, tres, bajo, clave, maracas y bongó). Valga aclarar que aquellos primeros soneros se mezclaron bastante con trovadores tradicionales, y dúos y tríos de cantadores (así les llamaban) que entonces pululaban por cafés y bares, buscándose la vida. Lo que resulta sorprendente es que los instrumentos de cuerda empezaron a adoptar maneras de ejecución y concepciones interpretativas en que imitaban a los instrumentos de percusión.

En poco tiempo, los incipientes sellos norteamericanos, entusiasmados por el son y ávidos de toda suerte de mercados, llevaron a varios de los nacientes grupos a grabar en Nueva York, y así los acetatos resultantes empezaron a diseminar el nuevo género musical por todo el mundo.

En *Orígenes* presento un análisis detallado de los comienzos del son, incluyendo un estudio sobre sus instrumentos originales, tales como la botija y luego la marímbula para obtener los sonidos graves, antes de que los modestos grupos lograran hacerse de contrabajos. Otro aspecto característico del son es el uso de términos con un doble sentido, tradición que data de la época del teatro bufo del siglo anterior, con sus alegres guarachas, y que ha jugado un papel preponderante, como comenté antes, entre las principales obsesiones cubanas: el gesto lascivo y las letras picarescas. El son logró captar la dicotomía entre lo serio y el inevitable choteo criollo, dejando en una suerte de oscilación dinámica esos dos estados de una alegría elemental que lleva al cubano a pretender resolver las situaciones más difíciles entre carcajadas y comentarios irónicos aparentemente superficiales.

Cualquier son tradicional, como los que interpretan Compay Segundo, los ancianos de la Vieja Trova Santiaguera o Elíades Ochoa, revela cómo dentro de un compás de 2x4, esta música ofrece varias franjas rítmicas en continuo contraste y yuxtaposición. Se trata de un género vocal

Los instrumentos: LA GUITARRA Y EL TRES

Son varios los instrumentos de cuerda que se desarrollaron en Cuba: el laúd, el tres y el tiple, todos variantes de la guitarra española. Derivado de un instrumento persa, el laúd tomó su nombre del *ud* árabe que alcanzó su forma definitiva en el siglo XIV. Tiene cinco cuerdas dobles y una simple que es la primera; se utiliza esencialmente en la música guajira cubana como solista y como acompañante. Barbarito Torres es un virtuoso actual de este difícil instrumento.

TOCADOR DE LAÚD (1955).

El tiple, también característico de la música campesinna, es el instrumento más pequeño de cuerda en uso en Cuba y se fabrica de una sola pieza, ahuecando el tronco de un árbol al que se le adhiere una tapa de yagruma hembra. Existen tres tipos: el requinto, el doliente y el tiple con macho, que tiene una clavija en mitad del diapasón.

Entre los guitarristas de música popular que más se han destacado están Vicente González Rubiera *Guyún* (1908), quien escribió *La guitarra: su técnica y armonía*, Miguel Matamoros y Lorenzo Hierrezuelo. Casos especiales son los del extraordinario autodidacta Ñico Rojas y el filinista César Portillo de la Luz, seguidos de un sinfín de talentos. Situados a otro nivel están el profesor Isaac Nicola y su discípulo Leo Brouwer, continuadores de una escuela de la guitarra inaugurada mucho tiempo atrás por José Prudencio Mungol y ampliada por Severino López, Félix Guerrero y José Rey de la Torre, sin olvidar la contribución del español Pascual Roch y la docente Clara Romero de Nicola, que creó en 1931 la escuela de guitarra de la Sociedad Pro Arte Musical.

El tres es el instrumento de cuerdas tradicional de la música cubana y consta de tres cuerdas dobles metálicas que se afinan al unísono, dos en octava alta y la otra en re menor. Junto a otros intérpretes destacados, Isaac Oviedo, Ramón Laborit, Arsenio Rodríguez, Niño Rivera, *Papi* Oviedo y Pancho Amat han demostrado en diversas épocas su habilidad.

e instrumental con evidentes elementos de las músicas españolas y africanas, especialmente bantú, aunque ya fundidos en un estilo cubano. Su cualidad revolucionaria consiste en una estructura polirrítmica sujeta a una unidad en la cual las líneas rítmico-melódicas se entrecruzan, se persiguen, se encuentran y se separan. Mediante un diseño constante a cargo del contrabajo, ejecutado en *pizzicato* (ver pág. 260), que constituye el llamado bajo anticipado sincopado, se revela una de las principales características del genero, fijando así la primera franja de dicha base rítmico-armónica. La mayor parte de los sones actuales todavía se basan en ese quehacer del bajo.

La flexible estructura de esta música cantada y coreada liberó el movimiento de los bailadores, permitiéndoles contonearse, inventar pasos nuevos, girar, alejarse y estrecharse por tiempo indefinido. Permitió también la aparición de una cultura «blanquinegra» (adjetivo de Ortiz) que ha dominado el panorama musical cubano desde la década de 1920.

No obstante, debo insistir que tal conquista, si bien efectiva e irreversible, había sido el resultado de una larga contienda sociocultural. Los prejuicios del blanco dominante contra todo aquello que sonara a «música de color» habían sido enormes. Basta recordar que en 1884 se prohibió definitivamente la fiesta afrocubana del Día de Reyes; que en 1900, bajo el gobierno de ocupación de los Estados Unidos, la alcaldía de La Habana prohibió «el uso de tambores de origen africano en toda clase de reuniones, ya se celebren éstas en la vía pública como en el interior de los edificios». Que en 1903 quedó prohibida la sociedad secreta Abakuá, con lo cual quedaron reducidos a la clandestinidad sus tambores e *íremes*, los famosos diablitos. Que en 1913, al infiltrar las comparsas de negros los desfiles de carnaval, aquéllas habían sido suprimidas; que en 1922 una resolución del Secretario de Gobernación prohibía las fiestas y bailes ceremoniales de las creencias afrocubanas en toda la isla, «especialmente el llamado "bembé" (ver pág. 101), y cualesquiera otras ceremonias que, pugnando contra la cultura y la civilización de un pueblo, están señaladas como símbolos de barbarie y perturbadoras del orden social».

Para completar este frente racista hacía falta una campaña continua de un distinguido músico blanco, alguien que pudiera dar fe de la «pobreza musical africana» y alejar esos espíritus de las melodías de origen europeo. La arrogante burguesía criolla encontró en **Eduardo Sánchez de Fuentes** (1874-1944) el candidato ideal para representar sus prejuicios: un valioso compositor de habaneras y canciones que se jactaba de conocer el folclor como nadie, y que durante varios decenios mantuvo la tesis de que la música cubana que no fuera de origen español tenía un origen indígena. Valga aclarar que nadie sabe cómo fue la música de los indocubanos; el acelerado exterminio de la casi totalidad de la población nativa, sometida a una cruenta explotación en los lavaderos de oro y otros trabajos arduos por los colonizadores españoles, trajo como consecuencia que los posibles valores inherentes a su cultura musical no trascendieran. Por fortuna, ahí estaba el sólido Fernando Ortiz para refutar las estupideces de Sánchez de Fuentes (autor de la habanera *Tú* y de la bella canción *Corazón*). Resulta una verdadera ironía que la polémica fue enteramente recogida por el *Diario de la Marina*, el periódico de la extrema derecha.

Sextetos y septetos de son

Dentro del anterior marco histórico se desarrollaron los primeros sextetos soneros, los cuales sentaron la pauta para el devenir del nuevo género. Ya estaban lejanos los tiempos de las estudiantinas orientales, agrupaciones de fines del XIX integradas por jóvenes a menudo sólo blancos, que interpretaban guarachas, boleros y sones incipientes, y se componían por lo general de tres, marímbula, timbales o paila criolla, maracas, claves, guitarra y dos cantantes.

En distintos puntos del país se fueron formando novedosas agrupaciones soneras. Denostados por la prensa y las altas capas habaneras, los primeros grupos necesitaban ganar la aceptación de la clase dirigente para provocar posibles contratos de trabajo. Esa oportunidad surgió en 1916, cuando a un sobrino acaudalado del entonces presidente Mario García Menocal se le ocurrió seleccionar a varios músicos pertenecientes a la agrupación Los Apaches para que tocaran sones en una fiesta del exclusivo Vedado Tennis Club habanero, siempre y cuando estuvieran correctamente vestidos. De ahí en adelante, el son fue bailado por la alta sociedad habanera y la prensa se hizo eco de su sabrosura, así como lo del atuendo elegante continuó siendo característico de los soneros. Otro momento significativo tuvo lugar un año después, cuando un sexteto subió al escenario del teatro cómico Alhambra (cerrado en 1930), el más concurrido de la capital, para participar en la obrita *Las notas de mi son*, del compositor cualificado Jorge Anckermann.

Por aquellos días llegó a La Habana un representante de la RCA Victor acompañado de varios técnicos de grabaciones que se hospedaron en el hotel Inglaterra. Afortunadamente, llegaron desprovistos de prejuicios raciales, de ahí que contrataran al negro Carlos Godínez, quien todavía era soldado del Ejército Permanente, para que organizara un grupo típico y grabar sus interpretaciones. El tresero llamó al compositor Manuel Corona (guitarra y segunda voz), María Teresa Vera (voz prima y claves), Alfredo Boloña (bongó) y un mulato conocido como *Sinsonte* (tercera voz y maracas).

Ésta no fue la primera grabación realizada en Cuba, ya que el investigador Cristóbal Díaz Ayala ha podido establecer que en 1904 el pianista Antonio María Romeu había grabado varios números al frente de una pequeña orquesta de danzones.

En años posteriores siguieron otros viajes de representantes de la Victor y del sello Edison, que están reseñados en la excelente *Discografía de la música cubana, vol. 1 (1898-1925)* del fecundo musicólogo, publicada en Puerto Rico (ver direcciones para adquirirlos en la pág. XXX).

El son alcanzó su desarrollo definitivo tras la formación de dos sextetos en la capital y de un trío santiaguero que le darían popularidad universal. El primero que arrebató fue el **Sexteto Habanero**,

EL SEXTETO HABANERO (1925), CON ABELARDO BARROSO EN LAS CLAVES Y CARLOS GODÍNEZ A LA DERECHA.

fundado en 1920 por **Guillermo Castillo**, el cual realizó grabaciones en 1924 en Nueva York, participando también en la película *La puerta del infierno*. Dos años más tarde ganó el primer concurso de sones realizado en el Frontón Nuevo de La Habana. Entre sus mejores números están: *Cabo de guardia siento un tiro, Tres lindas cubanas, Eres mi lira armoniosa, Esas no son cubanas y Tribilín cantore*, grabados en Cuba entre 1925 y 1931.

Con el nombre de **Nacional** se fundó en 1927 un sexteto dirigido por el contrabajista **Ignacio Piñeiro**. Pronto partieron hacia Nueva York a grabar los siguientes números para la Columbia, que ya contaba con el sistema de grabación llamado *electrical process*, una innovación sobre el acústico: *Esas no son cubanas, Cubaneo, Fernanda, Bururún ba-*

LÁZARO HERRERA (1992)

rará, *Rosa roja, Errante por el mundo voy, ¡Mamá, se quema la Maya!, Por un beso de tu boca, Has perdido mi amor, Reliquias de amor, Yo quiero morir en Cuba, Miñaroco, Ay, Guarina, No te preocupes del mundo, Siboney, ¿Dónde vas con el rabo?, Acordes de bongó* y *¡Pepillito!* Los acompañó la excelente voz de Abelardo Barroso. A su regreso a la isla Piñeiro le agregó la trompeta de **Lázaro Herrera**, convirtiéndose en septeto. Conocido como *El pecas,* Herrera consolidó los valores armónicos del grupo y transcribió para su instrumento los sones y rumbas de Piñeiro. Fue él quien estableció el modo trompetístico tan característico del género.

Invitados a representar a Cuba en la Exposición Iberoamericana de Sevilla de 1929, el Septeto Nacional impresionó a todos. Por supuesto, la decisión de enviar un grupo sonero en lugar de una orquesta típica de danzones significó el espaldarazo definitivo para el nuevo género. Mientras que el danzón había mantenido el predominio musical desde su aparición en 1879, y se había grabado profusamente, el son estrenaba nuevas ideas. El viaje por barco empezó mal, pues Cheo Martínez, primer cantante del septeto, falleció repentinamente en altamar, siendo reemplazado por Juan de la Cruz, apoyado en el experimentado Bienvenido León. Llevaban como bongosero a Agustín Gutiérrez en lugar del *Chino* Incharte, en el tres a Francisco Solares González, más conocido como *Panchito Chevrolet,* y a Eutimio Constantín reemplazando al trovador Alberto Villalón en la guitarra.

Durante el viaje Piñeiro concibió el conocido tema *Suavecito,* motivado por una cubanita llamada Carola que había conocido al desembarcar en Nueva York para cambiar de barco, y también con la intención de grabar varios números para el sello Columbia. En Sevilla supo aprovecharlo, agregándole inspiraciones como ésta:

> Una linda sevillana
> le dijo a su maridito,
> me vuelvo loca chiquito
> por la música cubana.
> Suavecito, suavecito...

En sus actuaciones les acompañó la bailarina Urbana Troche, quien ya se encontraba en España. Al finalizar la exposición sevillana tocaron en Valladolid, Santander y Madrid, donde el septeto grabó seis sones para el sello Gramófono. Asegura el investigador Díaz Ayala:

Era evidente la preferencia del público por el son, que se convertiría en nuestro primer artículo musical de exportación por encima del danzón. En segundo lugar, el público español, y después se vería que el europeo en general, prefería el son suave, más pausado: en una palabra, el son suavecito.

El período 1930-34 representó la mejor época para el Nacional, que también fue premiado en 1933 cuando viajaron a Chicago para presentarse en la Feria Mundial «Cien años de progreso». A partir de 1935 el septeto sufrió diversos cambios, pero resurgió en 1937 y 1940 para volver a grabar. En total dejó 96 sones entre 1927-40, pero el septeto Habanero lo dejó atrás con 136 grabaciones entre 1918-48.

Otros grupos excelentes fueron el ya mencionado Occidente, de la cantadora **María Teresa Vera** (1895-1965), el sexteto Munamar, el Matancero y el de Antonio Machín, sin olvidar el del pequeñito Alfredo Boloña. Búsquese el disco *El legendario dúo de la trova cubana*, del sello Tumbao Classics, con las voces de esa mujer extraordinaria y la de Rafael Zequeira: una mezcla de canciones y sones deliciosos.

El trío que revolucionó al son fue el de Miguel Matamoros, formado en Santiago de Cuba, cuyas primeras grabaciones en 1928 en los estudios de RCA Victor de Camden, Nueva Jersey, le trajeron fama inmediata. El **trío Matamoros** permaneció unido 35 años, conformado por Siro Rodríguez en las maracas, Rafael Cueto en la guitarra acompañante y Miguel Matamoros en la guitarra puntera. Con tal limitación instrumental lograron un sello propio, alejado del tipo de son que hacían los septetos Habanero y Nacional en la capital. Como creador-recreador-intérprete, **Miguel Matamoros** (1894-1971) tomó de la melódica trovadoresca tradicio-

EL SEXTETO BOLOÑA (1923).

Los mejores: IGNACIO PIÑEIRO

EL SONERO MAYOR IGNACIO PIÑEIRO.

No es posible evitar cierta emoción al escuchar algunas de las piezas grabadas por el Septeto Nacional de Ignacio Piñeiro (1888-1969), con esas voces nasales tan empastadas, con sonido de radio antigua, que invitan a bailar. Títulos como *Marisa, ráscame aquí, Échale salsita, No juegues con los santos, En la alta sociedad y Sobre una tumba una rumba,* hablan por sí solos. Nacido en la capital, Piñeiro empezó desde muy pequeño a cantar mientras trabajaba en múltiples oficios para ayudar en la maltrecha economía familiar. A los 18 años entró en el coro de clave Timbre de oro, para continuar en Los roncos, un grupo especializado en guaguancós, luego pasó al Renacimiento. En 1926 Piñeiro era el bajista del Sexteto Occidente de la decidida María Teresa Vera, con la que viajó a Nueva York por un año; de vuelta en la isla, se independizó y fundó el Sexteto Nacional. Dos elementos le permitieron distinguirse de los demás grupos soneros y mantener el liderazgo: la originalidad de sus propias composiciones y los juegos vocales entre el tenor y el barítono. El Septeto Nacional estuvo en pie diez años y luego desapareció. Resucitó en 1954 para continuar más allá de la muerte de su fundador, dirigido primero por el trompeta Lázaro Herrera, después por el guitarrista Rafael Ortiz *Mañungo,* y más tarde por el cantante Carlos Embale (hijo), ya en pleno régimen revolucionario.

Recomiendo escuchar *Cubaneo,* un álbum del Nacional como sexteto, grabado en Nueva York entre 1927-28, del sello Tumbao Classics. Contiene algunos clásicos como *Esas no son cubanas* y *¡Mamá, se quema La Maya!*

nal un modo de hacer que tiene raíces líricas españolas pero adapta-
das y reestructuradas mediante típicos cierres de frase e inflexiones
que, junto a su forma de «cortar»
los estribillos con pequeñas frases
«montadas» e incompletas, o síla-
bas sólo sugeridas, logró imprimir
a su concepto sonero un estilo de
marchita *sui géneris*. Fue él quien
estableció el estilo del bolero-son

TRÍO MATAMOROS: MIGUEL, CUETO Y SIRO.

con los antológicos *Juramento, Promesa* y *Olvido*. Su espontaneidad y ritmo cadencioso influyó en infinidad de tríos que surgieron en los años 40 y
50, especialmente en el de Los Guaracheros de Oriente. Recomiendo los álbumes *The legendary Trío Matamoros* y *La china en la rumba*.

Después de casi veinte años como trío se convirtieron en una organización mayor, agregándole a veces una trompeta, una tumbadora y un
bajo, y llamándose consecutivamente cuarteto Maisí, septeto Matamoros,
conjunto Baconao y conjunto Matamoros. Adaptándose a los tiempos,
Miguel reconocía la necesidad de aumentar la riqueza armónica para lograr interpretar una mayor diversidad de géneros. Fue precisamente con
esta última formación con la que viajaron a México en 1945, llevando
una nueva voz de timbre muy alto que respondía al rimbombante nombre
de Bartolomé Maximiliano Moré y que pocos años después se convirtió
en un ídolo criollo: Benny Moré. Tumbao Classics publicó un disco estupendo: *Conjunto Matamoros with Benny Moré*, grabado en México entre
1945 y 1947.

Una variante poco conocida

Con un origen hacia finales del siglo XIX, que lo sitúa en una hermosa isla
con playas de arena oscura, el sucu-sucu penetró primero los oídos nacionales de forma estilizada, y por muy poco tiempo, alrededor de 1948. Varias migraciones caribeñas se asentaron en la fértil Isla de Pinos (hoy conocida como Isla de la Juventud), al sur de La Habana, a partir de 1920.
Llegaban en busca de trabajo, básicamente la limpieza y recolección de
hortalizas y cítricos como el pomelo (llamada toronja) y en labores fores-

tales. Como la pesca de esponjas y langostas también constituía uno de los renglones básicos de su economía, pronto se estableció allí una colonia japonesa de unos 200 individuos que constituyeron un importante factor de progreso; a ellos se debe el conocimiento de la «corrida» de langosta y su industrialización.

La isla estaba entonces controlada económicamente por norteamericanos que arribaron después de la debacle de 1898; en 1907 formaban el 20 por ciento de su población, calculándose que más de 5.000 adquirieron tierras en la isla y unos 2.000 se establecieron en ella, dedicándose especialmente al cultivo de cítricos. Una ardorosa campaña nacional culminó en 1925 con la ratificación por el Senado norteamericano del tratado Hay-Quesada, reconociendo la plena soberanía de Cuba sobre la isla. En 1948 sólo quedaban 150 estadounidenses.

Poco habitada, es una de las más grandes islas que forman el archipiélago cubano (en total formado por 4.010 islas, isletes y cayos) y posee los mejores mármoles del país. En el pasado también se explotaron oro y tungsteno, así como caolín, materia prima en la alfarería y la cerámica. Identificada por sus abundantes pinares, durante siglos la isla fue territorio franco para piratas y corsarios, lo cual trascendió en leyendas sobre tesoros ocultos y galeones hundidos en sus aguas; ese largo período dio lugar a que se le conociera también como la mítica Isla del Tesoro y más tarde la Isla de las Cotorras. En la segunda mitad del siglo XIX, con la intención de mantenerlos totalmente aislados, el poder colonial español la convirtió en cárcel para los revolucionarios criollos antes de deportarlos a España o a África. Allí fue a parar José Martí con 17 años, con un grillete al tobillo. Ese pasado tenebroso favoreció la erección en 1931 del llamado Presidio Modelo, gigantescas construcciones circulares en las inmediaciones de Nueva Gerona. A aquel penal fueron enviados Castro y los pocos sobrevivientes del ataque al cuartel Moncada en 1953 para cumplir una condena de quince años. Fidel gozó allí de un tratamiento especial: tomaba el sol y hacía calistenia, se adiestraba en las artes culinarias, leía sin cesar, conspiraba por correo y fumaba enormes puros. En contraposición, allí fueron hacinados y maltratados en sus celdas millares de cubanos detenidos desde el triunfo de la revolución.

Atraídos por el auge azucarero producido por la Primera Guerra Mundial, a partir de 1920 comenzó una extensa migración de trabajadores cubanos y de distintas islas del Caribe, que se mezclaron con negros norteamericanos contratados para la explotación forestal y del pomelo;

muchos llegaron para laborar en la cosecha de la caña y en la construcción de la
inmensa cárcel. Unos cantando en inglés y
otros en español, todos contribuyeron a
desarrollar un tipo de son que dieron en
llamar «sucu-sucu». La música tradicional
campesina se mezcló con viejas rumbitas
como la «caringa», el «tumbantonio», el
«calabazón» y el «cariaco»; también influyeron los sones habaneros que los rústicos
trabajadores escuchaban en la radio en sus
ratos de ocio.

EL COMPOSITOR ELISEO GRENET.

Así las cosas, cuando surgió el mambo de Pérez Prado, al compositor **Eliseo
Grenet** (1893-1950), se le ocurrió poner en
tela de juicio su cubanía y se propuso ha-
cer un ritmo que lo contrarrestara. Inspirado en viejos «golpes» que había escuchado en Isla de Pinos, se apareció con *Felipe Blanco*, un número
que inmediatamente se convirtió en un éxito entre 1948 y 1950; acostum-
brados a referencias urbanas, los citadinos vieron con simpatía un tema
campesino que hilvanaba una historia con una serpiente. Sin embargo, el
intento pronto se desvaneció porque no fue seguido de otros números de
igual impacto ni aparecieron autores que asumieran el «nuevo» ritmo.

El sucu-sucu es una música monótona, con algo de son primitivo,
poca síncopa y un palo marcando siempre el compás, mientras las semillas de las maracas llenan el espacio sonoro. A mí me recuerda mucho a
la gaita zuliana, música venezolana que surgió alrededor del lago de Maracaibo a finales del siglo XIX.

El baile responde más al estilo de lejanas islas caribeñas y consiste en
parejas entrelazadas cuyos hombros y caderas se mantienen casi sin movimiento, mientras que los pies desarrollan pasos que resultan muy difíciles
de seguir. Entre sus curiosidades instrumentales está el machete que se
raspa con un cuchillo a manera de güiro, vainas sacudidas del árbol flam-
boyán y botellas percutidas con cucharas. Esta forma sonera tiene un patrón rítmico y melódico bastante limitado que ha sido explotado por diversos grupos locales, destacándose en los últimos años el septeto La
Tumbita Criolla que dirige Ramón *Mongo* Rives; hay un disco de Virgin
que rescata algunos aspectos de esta curiosa forma del folclor sonero.

LA FORMACIÓN DE CONJUNTOS

Los conjuntos, una ampliación de los septetos de son, constituyen agrupaciones de música bailable surgidos alrededor de 1940, en gran parte gracias a las innovaciones realizadas por el tresero y compositor invidente **Arsenio Rodríguez** (1911-71). Dedicados fundamentalmente a la interpretación de boleros, sones y guarachas, los conjuntos constan de piano, contrabajo, dos o tres trompetas, guitarra, bongó, una tumbadora y tres cantantes, uno de solista y los otros en las maracas y las claves.

Conocido como el «ciego maravilloso», Arsenio se las arregló para que el piano hiciera figuraciones armónicas combinadas con arpegios y

«tumbaos», un esquema acompañante que provenía de las cuerdas del tres, con la función específica de acentuar el baile. Enseñó todos sus trucos al pianista *Lilí* Martínez Griñán (1917-90), autor de los sones *Alto Songo, se quema La Maya, Que se fuñan* y *Quimbombó*, entre otros. Con su singular estilo, *Lilí* sentó pautas en la interpretación del son al aportar elementos valiosos de la interpretación del jazz a la pianística popular cubana. Aún hoy sorprenden esos tumbaos por su vitalidad y originalidad, no sólo en Cuba sino en toda la cuenca del mar Caribe, llegando a influir en pianistas del rango del norteamericano Larry Harlow, el venezolano Enrique *Culebra* Iriarte o el extraordinario Papo Lucca, de Ponce, Puerto Rico. El veterano

LILÍ MARTÍNEZ GRIÑÁN.

Rubén González, responsable de llevar a *Lilí* al conjunto de Arsenio, hizo patente ese estilo en las teclas en el disco *Buena Vista Social Club*, la compilación de Ry Cooder aparecida en 1996 (ver pág. 372).

Para escuchar el sonido del conjunto de Arsenio Rodríguez considere *Dundunbanza*, con *Lilí* Martínez al piano, o *Chano Pozo and Arsenio Rodríguez: legendary sessions*, ambos de Tumbao Classics, que incluye varios números de *Machito*, del boricua Tito Rodríguez y de Arsenio, grabados originalmente entre 1948 y 1953.

Pronto surgieron conjuntos por toda la isla que entusiasmaron a los bailadores: el Casino, el Colonial, los Jóvenes del Cayo, Chapottín, la Sonora Matancera... El público descubría y gozaba las particularidades que los diferenciaban, vinculadas al timbre, a la «marcha» del ritmo, al repertorio que interpretaban o a la identificación de su vocalista principal. En 1960, en pleno apogeo de su popularidad nacional y continental, la Sonora Matancera, el conjunto más admirado en toda la cuenca del Caribe, marchó al exilio; con ella desaparecieron de la radio y la televisión cubana sus voces insignia: Celia Cruz, Bienvenido Granda y Celio González. Dejó una honda ausencia que ningún otro conjunto, aunque los había excelentes, consiguió llenar. Por supuesto, las grabaciones de la Sonora fueron rigurosamente prohibidas, esfumándose del tímpano cubano de un día para otro.

De entre la multitud de conjuntos que proliferaron en Cuba, he escogido a los tres más significativos, agrupaciones que abrieron nuevas brechas y que fueron muy distintas en su ejecución, a pesar de contar con la misma distribución de instrumentos.

¡Pelotero a la bola...!

El **Conjunto Casino** estuvo integrado a partir de 1950, su momento de mayor auge, por Roberto Espí (director, cantante y coro), Roberto Faz (vocalista), Agustín Ribot (guitarra y coro), Alberto Armenteros, José Gudín y Miguel Román (trompetas), Roberto Álvarez (piano), Cristóbal Dobal (contrabajo), Orlando Guzmán (bongó) y Carlos *Patato* Valdés (tumbadora).

Fundado en La Habana en 1940, el Casino fue estableciendo un estilo propio a partir de varios viajes al exterior y una gira que realizó por toda la isla en 1947. Fueron muchas las grabaciones discográficas y las actuaciones exitosas de esta agrupación. Trece años permaneció el cantante **Roberto Faz** (1914-66) con el Casino, al que se había unido en 1943. Faz había nacido en el pueblito de Regla, al otro lado de la bahía habanera, y comenzó cantando con un grupo juvenil; luego aprendió los secretos del son en dos sextetos. Se inició como profesional en 1932 con la Orquesta Continental, pasando más tarde a la Orquesta Habana, los Hermanos Palau, la Cosmopólitan (fundada en 1938 por Vicente Viana y dirigida por Humberto Suárez, durante veinte años fue la formación estable del teatro América). También trabajó con la orquesta de los hermanos LeBatard, la de Osvaldo Estivel y en el conjunto Kubavana, antes de ingresar en el Casino.

El pequeño vocalista alcanzó gran popularidad interpretando sones montunos, guarachas y boleros. Durante años el Conjunto Casino demostró su versatilidad en el programa televisivo «El Show del Mediodía» que animaba Germán Pinelli. En *Cosas del alma* y *Dueña de mi corazón*, de Pepé Delgado, Roberto Faz dejó registrada la memoria musical del momento. La melodía *Quiéreme y verás*, de José Antonio Méndez, adquirió en su voz una popularidad de gramola de bar que no alcanzó jamás el propio autor, uno de los principales creadores del estilo filin. Faz contribuyó a fijar al bolero como modalidad bailable a la vez que lo enriqueció estilísticamente. Cualquiera que escuche sus famosos mosaicos románticos (tres bolerazos en cada uno), verdaderos popurrís del conflicto amoroso, comprenderá por qué Roberto Faz se convirtió en un ídolo menor de toda una generación. También se distinguió en la guaracha, como la rápida *Pelotero a la bola*, un número que hace referencia al béisbol. En 1956 decidió separarse del Casino y formar su propia agrupación, con la que continuó deleitando al público hasta su muerte diez años después.

Era la época del «tíbiri-tábara», de «bigote e'gato», de la voz puertorriqueña de Myrta Silva con la Sonora, pero también de los abusos policiales y el latrocinio oficial. Reinaba entonces el tema *María Tripita*, guaracha de Jesús Guerra, una negra que seguramente era la «jeva» (novia) de alguien. En la calle te llamaban «monina» o «asere» (amigo), y apostaban una pecuña (peseta de veinte centavos) al 27, mientras que alguna «engañadora» (con formas artificiales) se paseaba por Prado y Neptuno, y los tambores sonaban en nerviosos bembés por las barriadas.

Otras voces que distinguieron el estilo Casino fueron la de Roberto Espí en *Luna cienfueguera* y muy especialmente la de **Orlando *Chicho* Vallejo** (1919-81) con la guajira *Alborada* y muchas otras melodías románticas. Vallejo murió, como muchos otros músicos, en el exilio de Miami, siempre considerado como uno de los más grandes vocalistas del bolero cubano. Por esta ágil agrupación también pasaron los cantantes Nelo Sosa, Orlando Contreras, *Laíto* Sureda y Fernando Álvarez, con sus brillantes interpretaciones de *Llanto de luna*, de Julio Gutiérrez, y *Cada noche que pasa* y *Humo y espuma*, de Rolando Rabí. Como representativo recomiendo el disco *Conjunto Casino: Rumba quimbumba*, grabado entre 1941 y 1946, del sello Tumbao Classics, o el posterior

EL CONJUNTO CASINO (1954) CON ROBERTO FAZ EN LAS MARACAS, ORLANDO VALLEJO EN EL GÜIRO Y *PATATO* VALDÉS EN LA TUMBADORA.

Mambo con chachachá, que produjo el mismo sello con temas recogidos entre 1953-55.

Por su calidad, fue inevitable que el Casino ejerciera cierta influencia en la cuenca del Caribe, aunque bastante menor que la popular Sonora Matancera. En Puerto Rico actuó en dos ocasiones. También viajó a Nueva York en 1953, en una presentación algo tormentosa –según señala Díaz Ayala– porque varios músicos latinos se opusieron a su presencia alegando que no estaban debidamente inscritos en la unión local para poder actuar en Manhattan. Existía entonces el temor de que los conjuntos, con un personal más reducido, compitieran con las grandes orquestas, que lógicamente tenían mayores gastos y, en consecuencia, un precio más elevado de contratación.

Del Casino surgió uno de los percusionistas más contundentes que ha dado Cuba: **Carlos *Patato* Valdés** (1926); el apodo «Patato» identifica a un hombre de baja estatura. Todavía se recuerdan sus jocosas intervenciones bailando ante las cámaras de televisión, y para él compuso Ernesto Duarte *El baile del pingüino*. Su habilidad y la callosidad de sus pequeñas manos le han permitido convertirse en uno de los mejores congueros entre los cubanos exiliados en Estados Unidos, comparable sólo a Mongo Santamaría, a Francisco Aguabella o a Julito Collazo. Ya anciano, *Patato* aparece brevemente en el filme *Calle 54* de Fernando Trueba.

Siguiendo el estilo impuesto por el Casino, sobresalieron otras agrupaciones con este tipo de formato, como las de **Nelo Sosa**, cuyo *Arrímate cariñito* es un disco con el talento añadido de los compositores Pepé Delgado y Rey Díaz Calvet, o *A burujón puñao*, cantando Orlando Vallejo. Alfonsín Quintana y **Los Jóvenes del Cayo** demostraron en *Vamos pa'la rumba* que sí sabían poner a gozar al bailador (en este disco de Tumbao aparecen las voces del puertorriqueño Daniel Santos y de Celio González). Otro destacado conjunto de aquella época fue el **Saratoga**, que contó entre sus vocalistas estelares a Ñico Membiela y a Lino Borges. El fabuloso **Senén Suárez** ganó fama con sus tumbaos pianísticos y por el contundente tema que usaba para presentar su conjunto en programas de radio; escuche *Guaguancó callejero* (Tumbao Classics) grabado a principios de los 50, donde aparecen las voces de *Laíto* Sureda y de Paulina Álvarez. Memorables fueron también el conjunto **Rumbavana**, con Raúl Planas, Orestes Macías y Fernando González. Los jóvenes de entonces considerábamos al negro **René Álvarez y su conjunto Los Astros** como uno de los mejores para dejarse la vida en la pista, de ahí que sugiera el álbum *Yumbale*, producido por el mismo sello, donde canta un Miguelito Cuní de 1950, o *Guaguancó en el solar*, que es posterior. Recuerdo a otras agrupaciones: **Musicuba**, con la potente voz de Orlando Contreras y posteriormente con José Tejedor, así como **Los Latinos**, con Ricardito Rivera y **Los Chuquis**, con Orlando Reyes. Algunos de estos conjuntos incorporaban un trombón en sus grabaciones, enriqueciendo armónicamente con una cuarta voz la sección de metales, como también agregaron una cuarta trompeta para modular el valor tímbrico y alcanzar bloques sonoros de mayor homogeneidad orquestal.

No todo sucedía en La Habana. En el interior del país también surgieron agrupaciones contundentes, como una orquesta fundada en 1932 y que estuvo sonando durante más de 25 años en la caliente Santiago de Cuba, la de **Chepín-Chovén**, que así se dieron a conocer sus directores Electo Rossell y Bernardo García Chovén; si lo que quiere es bailar no se pierda *El merenguito*, grabado a mediados de los años 40 y publicado por Tumbao Classics. *Chepín* Rossell fue el autor de la conocida guaracha *El platanal de Bartolo*, tema con que los rebeldes de Sierra Maestra

Los instrumentos: EL BONGÓ

Instrumento de percusión típicamente cubano, el bongó (acentuado en la segunda) se
compone de dos tamborcitos redondos y
unidos, de diferentes tamaños. El de menor
diámetro es el cuero macho y suena más
agudo que el otro; el bongó se sostiene entre las piernas y se toca con las yemas de los
dedos. Desarrollado a principios del siglo XX
en el contexto del son, pronto rebasó ese
marco para incorporarse a las más variadas
combinaciones instrumentales, desde los
primeros boleros hasta la salsa neoyorquina. La figuración más estable es el llamado «martilleo», que consta de ocho golpes diferentes, todos de una misma
duración, de los cuales el primero corresponde al sonido bajo (que coincide con
el cuarto tiempo del compás) y se obtiene del cuero hembra, el más grande. El
tercero y séptimo golpe del martilleo son los más agudos y se logran apretando
el cuero a todo lo largo del pulgar de una mano en tanto la yema del índice de
la otra golpea cerca del borde. Mientras las tumbadoras mantienen el ritmo, el
bongó es el encargado de hacer «cantar» a los cueros; hasta aproximadamente
1951, en que se le adaptaron tensores o llaves, había que estirar los cueros mediante el calor de un reverbero.

Un viejo proverbio advierte que «sin claves y bongó, no hay son». El
bongosero es el encargado de tocar el cencerro (también llamado gangarrea o
campana) en los montunos. En los años 40 y 50, Antolín Suárez, conocido
como *Papá Quila* fue un magnífico ejecutante. Entre los bongoseros de varios
conjuntos se estableció una competencia para destacarse de los demás a la hora
de «echar un pie»; otra buena prueba de ello es el acompañamiento rítmico en
las grabaciones del dúo Los Compadres. *Yeyito* Iglesias, el bongosero de las
descargas habaneras de *Cachao*, siempre lució su habilidad. Tanto en México
con Pérez Prado como en grabaciones de jazz afrocubano, Mongo Santamaría
(ver pág. 239) ha demostrado su virtuosismo con estos pequeños tambores. El
libro *Guía de la percusión cubana*, escrito por Osmandy Fuentes y publicado
por Tikal (Madrid), es una excelente introducción práctica a este histórico instrumento lleno de posibilidades rítmicas.

ELECTO ROSELL *CHEPÍN.*

se burlaban del temor de los soldados de Batista en 1958 (el platanal sugiere el lugar para ir a defecar).

Mientras que demasiados músicos habaneros miraban hacia lo que se potenciaba en Estados Unidos, el saxo tenor **Mariano Mercerón y sus Muchachos Pimienta,** también de Santiago, fue uno de los grupos más orientados hacia lo que se estaba haciendo en la región del Caribe sin dejar de ofrecer por ello un son de raigambre local; sacaron discos como *Negro ñañamboro* y *Yo tengo un tumbao* (en que cantan Marcelino Guerra *Rapindey* y Dominica Verges), que hoy son joyas de coleccionistas.

La Sonora trae su ritmo...

Reconocida en todo el ámbito del Caribe como el conjunto que más identificó a la música cubana durante varios decenios a través de la radio, la **Sonora Matancera** se formó originalmente en 1924 en la ciudad de Matanzas para competir con los sextetos Habanero y Boloña. Fue llamada sucesivamente Tuna Liberal, Septeto Soprano y más tarde Estudiantina Sonora Matancera, hasta que finalmente en 1932 la bautizaron como la conocemos.

La Sonora se impuso con un estilo inconfundible, con arreglos que hacían sobresalir las dos trompetas (Calixto Leicea y Pedro Knight), tocando pasajes a dos voces, con intervalos simultáneos de terceras, sextas y octavas. Entre sus dos perennes cantantes de coros predominó el timbre agudo brillante (la llamada «voz de vieja»): Rogelio Martínez, director del conjunto, marcando en una guitarra raramente audible, y Carlos Manuel Díaz Alonso, el conocido *Caíto,* en las maracas. Ambos reforzaban la base rítmico-armónica del piano (Lino Frías), el bajo (Elpidio Vázquez), la tumbadora (Ángel Alfonso Furias *Yiyo*) y la rápida percusión en las pequeñas pailas, un instrumento a medio camino entre el bongó y los timbales, tocadas con baquetas cortas de cabeza redondeada por José Ramón Chávez *Manteca,* ofreciendo un arsenal rítmico muy estable.

Su manera de acompañar los boleros y las guarachas, con las trompetas interviniendo entre frase y frase del solista, sin interferencias, mientras el resto del conjunto formaba una alfombra sonora en un segundo plano, contribuyó a cimentar interpretaciones impecables. En su etapa más brillante, mucho le debió la Sonora a los arreglos de Severino Ramos (1903-69), que aplicaba su riguroso talento a alcanzar variedad a la vez que a mantener un sonido inconfundible.

LA SONORA MATANCERA (1943): VALENTÍN CANÉ, HUMBERTO CANÉ, JOSÉ R. CHÁVEZ *MANTECA*, PABLO VÁSQUEZ *BABÚ*, CALIXTO LEICEA, CARLOS DÍAZ *CAÍTO* Y ROGELIO MARTÍNEZ.

Lino Frías, pianista autodidacta como muchos otros músicos cubanos, es el autor de *Mata siguaraya*, un número en ritmo afro que hicieron famoso las voces de Celia Cruz, Benny Moré y mucho después el venezolano Oscar D'León. El trompeta Pedro Knight, que había ingresado en 1944, se casó con Celia en 1962, y luego se retiró del conjunto en 1967. Rogelio Martínez (1906), autor de *Sunsún bambaé* y un león para los negocios, se ha mantenido como director del conjunto desde los años 20. Curiosamente, nunca logró introducir a la Sonora en el cabaré Tropicana.

Existen en el mercado varios discos que recomiendo: *Live on the radio 1952-58* del sello Harlequin, *La Sonora Matancera en Perú 1957*, con su tremendo tema *La Sonora trae un tono*, del sello Tumbao Classics, y *From Cuba to New York*, una veintena de números grabados originalmente para el sello SEECO y reeditados hace poco tiempo por el británico Charly.

En realidad son cientos los discos que han producido, popularizando a más de 60 cantantes de varios países latinoamericanos que se distinguieron con la Sonora. Una larga lista encabezada por **Celia Cruz**, quien se convirtió en la «Gran Guarachera de Cuba» dejando grabadas infinidad de guarachas debidas a autores como Pablo Cairo, José Carbó Menéndez, Alberto Caissé, Jesús Guerra, Humberto Jauma, Oscar Muñoz Bouffartique y muchos otros. Celia también grabó con la Sonora decenas de hermosos boleros, entre los que se encuentran *Tu voz*, de Ramón Cabrera, y *Lamento Jarocho,* de Agustín Lara. En distintas épocas se escucharon las voces de Daniel Santos, Myrta Silva, Bienvenido Granda, Leo Marini, Nelson Pinedo, Carlos *Argentino* Torres, Alberto Beltrán, Celio González, Vicentico Valdés, Roberto Torres y muchos otros.

Esta constelación de cantantes estelares reafirmó la importancia de la Sonora Matancera como conjunto insignia de Cuba, con inevitables imitadores dentro y fuera de la isla. En dos décadas, entre 1940 y 1960, logró establecer lo que el venezolano César Rondón, autor de *El libro de la salsa,* calificó de la «matancerización» de la música cubana en Latinoamérica; sin embargo, su ritmo no atraía a los negros, que preferían el sonido de Arsenio o del Conjunto Colonial. La Sonora Matancera se largó de Cuba en 1960 y no ha vuelto jamás. Con Nueva York como base han hecho innumerables giras por todo el continente americano, con cambios de instrumentistas y vocalistas debido a su larga trayectoria.

Los «lloraos» de una trompeta

Los logros alcanzados en el estilo interpretativo del conjunto de Arsenio Rodríguez fueron asumidos por su medio hermano, el formidable trompeta sonero **Félix Chapottín** (1909-83), quien al marchar Arsenio hacia Estados Unidos en 1949 se hizo cargo de la dirección de la agrupación. Chapottín ya había pasado por el Septeto Habanero, por el Munamar, en su primera etapa de 1930, y por otras agrupaciones de inestable duración. Su prestigio fue en ascenso cuando se unió a la agrupación del tresero invidente. Con el nuevo nombre de Félix Chapottín y sus Estrellas, a partir de sones como *El carbonero* y *Quimbombó que resbala* y empleando escalas de la época del swing (otra influencia norteamericana), Chapottín comenzó a hacer improvisaciones y solos de embocadura –influenciado por Louis Armstrong–, los famosos «lloraos» que establecieron su originalísimo estilo.

A la señal de «¡Juega *Lilí*!» aparecían los tumbaos del pianista Luis Martínez Griñán o los del tresero Arturo, mejor conocido como «alambre dulce», contribuyendo a una complicidad sonora que hizo historia, cediéndose paso entre sí para mejor disfrute de los bailadores.

Anunciar que el conjunto de Chapottín tocaba en los Jardines de La Tropical era asegurar un lleno completo, equivalente al éxito que actualmente logran Los Van Van en la misma pista. Allí desarrolló Chapottín sus interminables solos en los años 50, elevando notas altísimas a un cielo que ya presagiaba el cambio radical ocurrido en 1959. Su prestigio corrió paralelo al de su cantante, un negro de voz ronca, tocado con un sombrero pequeño, que al sonreir mostraba un enorme diente de oro y que dio en llamarse **Miguelito Cuní** (Miguel Angel Conill, 1920-84). Su voz estará siempre ligada a boleros como *Convergencia,* de Marcelino Guerra *Rapindey.* Al escucharlo, Pablo Milanés le propuso interpretarlo juntos en el Festival del Son de Guantánamo de 1980; el desaparecido pianista Emiliano Salvador realizó entonces uno de los mejores arreglos de esta pieza, a un *tempo* más vivo que lo normal, alcanzando así uno de los momentos cumbres de la música romántica.

FÉLIX CHAPOTTÍN.

Antes de unirse a Chapottín, Miguelito Cuní ya había logrado notoriedad con números del nivel de *El guayo de Catalina,* un son lento cargado de doble sentido que grabó con el conjunto de Arsenio Rodríguez. Contratado para los carnavales de Panamá, Cuní permaneció allí tres años, regresando a la isla en 1949. En 1956 acompañó a Benny Moré y su tribu a una importante gira en Venezuela, y al regresar volvió con Chapottín. También cantó con la Orquesta Novedades del pianista Bebo Valdés, uno de los mejores músicos que ha dado el país (ver pág. 231). Cuní aparece en el cortometraje cubano *Nosotros la música*, donde se aprecia su manera de decir el son. Junto a Chapottín y otros vocalistas de renombre, configuró lo que prefiero llamar el nuevo son, una línea estilística de los años 50 que finalmente pulió Benny Moré.

Dos conjuntos Caney

El cuarteto y sexteto Caney, integrados por Frank Grillo, *Machito* Johnny López, Alfredito Valdés, Manolo Suárez, Daniel Sánchez y Panchito Riset, que grabaron entre 1938 y 1941, no tienen nada que ver con las historias de dos conjuntos muy diferentes, marcados por enormes contrastes en su formación, hábitat, lanzamiento y apoyo logístico: una ha contado siempre con el apoyo oficial mientras que la otra revela la lucha permanente de un hombre por alcanzar el éxito fuera de Cuba.

En 1969, a diez años del triunfo revolucionario, se fundó en La Habana el Conjunto Caney, con el propósito de recuperar la atmósfera tímbrica establecida por la ausente Sonora Matancera, instalada en la memoria cubana a lo largo de varias décadas. Dirigida por el trompeta Benito Llanes y realzada por la experiencia de *Laíto* Sureda, quien había cantado durante años con la Sonora, esta agrupación se centró en la guaracha y el bolero. Aprovechando arreglos que Severino Ramos había

PÍO LEYVA EN SUS AÑOS MOZOS.

preparado para la Sonora Matancera meses antes de que la afamada agrupación abandonara el país, los hermanos Carlos y Benito Llanes comenzaron a formar su repertorio.

Con el conjunto Caney ha trabajado el cantante **Pío Leyva** (1915), «El montunero de Cuba», el pequeño vocalista en *Buenavista Social Club*. También trabajaron con esta agrupación la exquisita Gina León, muy popular a lo largo de los años 60 y 70, y Néstor del Castillo, heredero fiel de la saga bolerista de los años 50, marcada por las voces de Ñico Membiela y Orlando Vallejo. En ocasiones ha aparecido cantando con el Caney el director de la conocida Vieja Trova Santiaguera, **Reynaldo Hierrezuelo** (1927), así como su hermana Caridad, que también ha trabajado en España.

El conjunto Caney ha grabado profusamente, a menudo reforzado con instrumentistas de gran talla como el pianista Rolando Baró y los trompetas Jorge Varona y Elpidio Chapottín, hijo de Félix. Viajó por varios países respaldando a **Caridad Cuervo** (1956-98), guarachera de buena cepa y figura central del cabaré Tropicana durante veinticinco años. Caridad Cuervo había debutado de niña en un programa de televisión, en el que se presentó haciendo una notable imitación de Celia Cruz.

Sin embargo, anteriormente hubo otro conjunto Caney que nunca se escuchó en la isla, ni tuvo el apoyo oficial del que acabo de mencionar. Y es una historia triste porque no todos los músicos que emigraron al Norte alcanzaron el triunfo ansiado. Hablo del conjunto Caney de **Fernando Storch** (1905), surgido en Nueva York en 1933.

Storch había crecido en La Habana, donde estudió saxofón influenciado por la Orquesta de los Hermanos Palau, en una época en que los Septetos Habanero y Nacional eran los reyes de la música cubana. En 1925 el joven formó el grupo Los Gatos Locos, pero dos años más tarde decidió trasladarse a Nueva York, buscando mejores horizontes. Recogida por el musicógrafo Max Salazar y publicada en la revista *Latin beat*, que se publica en California, he aquí la vida de un músico común y sus tribulaciones en Estados Unidos.

EL CONJUNTO CANEY DE FERNANDO STORCH (A LA DERECHA).

Un amigo del Bronx le enseñó a tocar el tres en 1929, pero la dura situación económica durante la Depresión le forzó a irse a trabajar en fábricas de Delaware y Detroit. En 1930 Storch logró volver a Nueva York; pronto formó el cuarteto Borinquen con Elio Osakar en el bajo, un cubano llegado de Tampa. El grupo comenzó a actuar en modestas fiestas que se organizaban en pisos del Harlem latino, cuyos dueños alquilaban para ayudarles a pagar la renta. Fue el propietario de un restaurante quien le sugirió a Storch nombrar Caney a su agrupación, en tributo a esa zona cercana a Santiago de Cuba, famosa por la calidad de sus frutas.

Convertido en un sabroso septeto en 1939, alternaba en un club de Chicago con una orquesta norteamericana durante sus descansos de veinte minutos. Para indicar el final de su presentación, el pianista Rafael Audinot tocaba una melodía libre mientras los músicos cubanos y puertorriqueños bajaban del escenario. En 1940, *Rumba rhapsody,* melodía inventada por Audinot, vendió miles de discos de 78 rpm; fue la grabación que puso en el mapa al conjunto Caney. Más tarde, Storch tuvo que reemplazar por dos meses a su vocalista Manolo Suárez, y alguien le sugi-

rió a un joven puertorriqueño llamado Pablo Rodríguez, que había cantado con el cuarteto Mayarí de Plácido Acevedo. Pasados aquellos dos meses, Pablo Rodríguez se presentó como el principal cantante de la orquesta de Xavier Cugat, convirtiéndose más tarde en el famoso Tito
Rodríguez, que triunfó durante años con su propia orquesta en el Palladium. Definitivamente, nuestro Storch no tenía suerte.

En 1943, hastiado de Nueva York, y ya conocido como *Caney*,
Storch se mudó a la Florida donde continuó trabajando como músico. En
1957 falleció su amigo Elio Osakar. El hijo de éste, un excelente y gigantesco pianista, trabajó con el flautista Fajardo y sus Estrellas, con Willie
Bobo, Rafael Cortijo, Louie Ramírez, la Típica'73, y después fue todo un
éxito con la orquesta de Tito Puente. Se trata del teclista Sonny Bravo.

Cuando Max Salazar entrevistó a Storch *Caney* en 1974, éste se la-
mentaba amargamente de que después de treinta años trabajando como
músico no tenía nada. Había realizado más de doscientas grabaciones
para varios sellos norteamericanos y nunca recibió un dólar por derechos.

LAS GRANDES ORQUESTAS

Antes de que la Original Dixieland Jazz Band lograra que jazz fuese una
palabra familiar en los Estados Unidos y que el novelista Scott Fitzgerald
bautizara a la década de 1920 como «La era del jazz», ya un grupo de
músicos cubanos, reunidos en la calles Zanja y Santiago, lo interpretaban
en la casa del pianista Bienvenido Hernández Delgado, compositor al que
apodaban «El americano» por su afición a la música de aquel país.

El estilo Dixieland

Formado gracias a la mezcla de los diversos grupos raciales y musicales
de Nueva Orleans, el dinámico Dixieland se caracterizó por tres líneas
melódicas tocadas por una corneta (luego trompeta), un trombón y un
clarinete. Frente a estos tres instrumentos melódicos aparecieron el contrabajo (a menudo la tuba), la batería o *drums*, el banjo o la guitarra, y a
veces también el piano. Las antiguas bandas se parecían a las que actuaban en circos alrededor de 1900, con un ritmo todavía muy cercano a la
marcha europea.

Entre otros cubanos residentes, el trompeta **Manuel Pérez** (1879-1946) ya tocaba este tipo de música en 1890, y en Nueva Orleans organizó la Onward Brass Band y la Imperial Band, ejerciendo notable influencia en trompetistas locales.

Dixieland, la tierra del dixie, corrupción del vocablo francés *dix* (diez, en español), surgió alrededor de 1844 por la decisión local de agregar dicho término a los billetes de banco impresos como gesto de su independencia con respecto al resto de la Unión. El esplendor económico de Nueva Orleans, situada en el delta del río Mississippi, siempre atrajo a braceros y estibadores de diversos orígenes, que desde mucho antes exigían se les pagara en *Spanish gold*, referencia al oro extraído de yacimientos centro y suramericanos que transportaban los galeones para acuñar monedas en España desde los tiempos de Felipe II. Curiosamente, el signo del dólar surgió precisamente de la S de *Spanish*, atravesada por las dos columnas, símbolo del hijo de Carlos V, y que conserva el escudo español. La palabra proviene de *dalar*, una moneda alemana entonces en curso.

Música rápida y alegre, el jazz de Nueva Orleans, donde también surgió la interpretación «hot», no se conoció en Cuba sino en la forma convenientemente mistificada de las orquestas surgidas en Chicago a partir de 1917, ya con elementos de ragtime, two-step y otros ritmos; más tarde iría a confundirse con los primeros intentos por desarrollar un tipo de jazz con acento afrocubano. Muchos años después (1999) Jesús Alemañy logró reverdecer aquellos laureles con el álbum *¡Cubanismo! in New Orleans, Mardi Gras Mambo*, una colaboración entre su banda y músicos locales, bajo el auspicio del Ayuntamiento de Nueva Orleans.

Las bandas cubanas

Entre 1930 y 1940 se formaron excelentes orquestas en Cuba a imitación de las que triunfaban en Norteamérica. Conocidas como jazz bands, contaban con tres secciones, una de metales, generalmente con dos trompetas y un trombón, otra de cañas con tres saxos y finalmente la de percusión, piano y bajo. En 1922 **Jaime Prats** (1883-1946), autor del conocido bolero *Ausencia*, fundó la primera Cuban Jazz Band: un tipo de organización que podía cubrir el repertorio norteamericano y el español, y todo lo cubano, salvo el danzón, que evitaban para no ser identificados como una

ORQUESTA HERMANOS LEBATARD (1930).

charanga u orquesta típica. Como se trataba de agrupaciones dirigidas al mercado de clase media y alta, y para tener acceso a los clubes privados, su principal fuente de trabajo, estas orquestas solían estar integradas por músicos blancos. De vez en cuando se filtraba algún mulato, como sucedió con Miguelito Valdés, el cantante de los Hermanos Castro y después de la Casino de la Playa.

El formato del jazz band fue paulatinamente «cubanizándose», al incrementar la interpretación de ritmos bailables cubanos. De hecho, el primer intento serio de amalgamar ambas músicas se produjo en un disco de la Orquesta de los Hermanos Castro, grabado en Nueva York en 1931. Según refiere Díaz Ayala, interpretaron *Marta,* de Moisés Simons, primero en tiempo de bolero y después como fox-trot. En la otra cara del disco grabaron *Saint Louis Blues,* en cuya melodía resaltan los metales con un fondo rítmico de son, mientras el coro canta en contrapunto pasajes de *El manisero.* Fue un verdadero experimento de fusión que aparentemente no tuvo éxito en aquel momento.

Entre las más importantes orquestas de esa década hay que mencionar la del saxo alto **Germán LeBatard,** la del compositor **René Touzet,** la **Bellamar,** la mencionada **Casino de la Playa,** los **Hermanos Palau,** la del trompeta **Julio Cueva,** la de los **Hermanos Castro,** la **Riverside** y la que dirigió el guitarrista **Isidro Pérez.** Por las continuas giras internacionales que realizaban los Lecuona Cuban Boys, he colocado esta banda en otra categoría que examinaré después, ya que se pasaban años sin regresar a Cuba para recargar baterías.

Algunas orquestas que radicaban permanentemente en Estados Unidos, como las de **Don Aspiazu** (1879-1943) –de nombre Modesto–, la primera en introducir la música bailable cubana en aquel país, la de **José Curbelo** o la de **Vicente Sigler,** interpretaban sofisticadas rumbas blancas. O mejor, *rhumbas,* que era como las describían entonces los sellos discográficos norteamericanos, en la creencia de que cualquier ritmo movido provenía de la palabra *rhum* (ron). La rumba es otra cosa bien distinta, es totalmente afrocubana y no es baile de pareja abrazada (ver pág. 102). Quizá por desconocimiento o por facilismo comercial estas orquestas contribuyeron a perpetuar el error. Había otros factores, denunciados por Alejo Carpentier en su libro *La música en Cuba,* publicado en 1946:

La boga que favoreció ciertos géneros bailables cubanos a partir de 1928 hizo un daño inmenso a la música popular de la isla. Cuando los editores de Nueva York y París establecieron una demanda continuada de sones, congas y rumbas –designando cualquier cosa bajo este título–, impusieron sus leyes a los autores de una música ligera, hasta entonces llena de gracia y sabor. Exigieron sencillez en la notación, una menor complicación de ritmos, un estilo más comercial. Los arreglistas norteamericanos hicieron el resto.

Varias orquestas que contaban con músicos altamente profesionales interpretaban «rumbas» alegres que a todos gustaban. Compositores, coreógrafos, instrumentistas, cantantes y arreglistas de diversas latitudes contribuyeron a desvirtuar la esencia negra de la rumba, la suavizaron a tal grado que comenzaron a surgir verdaderos híbridos como el slow-rumba y el fox-rumba. Una excepción fue la orquesta de Alberto Socarrás que siempre buscó la fusión del jazz con los ritmos de la isla (ver pág. 236).

La superficialidad de la industria discográfica y del cine norteamericano de los años 30 y 40 tuvo mucho que ver con la identificación de Cuba con lo que llamo rumbas blancas. Para el Hollywood de entonces, los «latinos» eran una etnia ruidosa, situada en algún lugar entre México y Cuba. En muchas ocasiones fueron músicos estadounidenses los encargados de instrumentar e interpretar las composiciones cubanas, imitando un supuesto *Latin style*.

En el proceso, el famoso son-pregón *El manisero* se convirtió en 1931 en *The peanut vendor*, una adaptación edulcorada y de colores pasteles en la versión al inglés que realizó Marion Sunshine –cuñada de su autor, **Moisés Simons** (1889-1945)– ha-

DON ASPIAZU.

ORQUESTA CASINO DE LA PLAYA CON MIGUELITO VALDÉS AL CENTRO, SENTADO SOBRE UNA
TUMBADORA. SOBRE LA OTRA APARECE EL PIANISTA ANSELMO SACASAS.

ciéndola supuestamente más atractiva al oído anglosajón. La conga *Para
Vigo me voy,* de **Ernesto Lecuona** (1885-1963) devino *Say si si* en 1933.
A todo esto habría que añadir las mezclas indiscriminadas entre la música
carioca (brasileña) y los temas cubanos en multitud de filmes con profusión de rumberas blancas sacudiendo las caderas. Un verdadero rastro
musical donde reinaron la confusión y la ambigüedad, pero que divirtie-
ron a los norteamericanos.

Años después, un actor cubano que le gustaba sonar el tambor despertó un curioso interés en los habitantes de la isla en la psique yanqui, y de
paso contribuyó a aumentar el flujo de turistas. En 1951 salió al aire el programa televisivo *I love Lucy,* que llegaba a todos los confines sociales de
Estados Unidos; el santiaguero **Desi Arnaz** y Lucille Ball arrebataron a los
telespectadores hasta el último episodio rodado en 1960. A pesar de su obvio acento, el personaje Ricky Ricardo que encarnaba Arnaz ha sido quizá
el hispano de más impacto en Norteamérica (superando la imagen del *Latin
lover* Rodolfo Valentino), a pesar de que la proyección de lo cubano solía
aparecer caricaturizada o al menos condescendiente. Pero no deja de sorprender que el programa más divertido de entonces se centraba en un matrimonio «intercultural», como se diría ahora, entre una caprichosa pelirro-
ja judía y un conguero cubano (en varios programas Desi apareció tocando
el tambor en algún club) con un precario dominio de la lengua inglesa. Por
cierto, toda la música del programa provenía del pianista y compositor santiaguero **Marco Rizo**, residente en Estados Unidos desde 1940. Su Latin
Jazz Quartet ha actuado en muchos países y en 1995 sacó al mercado *Tributo a Lecuona*, veintiún temas dedicados a su maestro y mentor.

El comerciante Cugat

La orquesta de **Xavier Cugat** (1900-91) representó la mentalidad mercantilista a la perfección. Desde sus años en Hollywood hasta su larga actuación en el cabaré del hotel Waldorf Astoria de Nueva York –con un perrito chihuahua metido en el bolsillo superior de la chaqueta, sus ojillos pícaros y el sonriente bigotito–, *Cugie* orquestaba a sabiendas que no era música cubana auténtica lo que hacía, aunque estaba bien construida y elegantemente empaquetada. Se me ha argumentado, y no sin razón, que lo más importante era introducir la música cubana en los predios del swing y del jazz. Pero, ¿a qué precio? ¿Cuánto de autenticidad no se perdió en el proceso al diluir la música afrocubana?

De cara a sus compatriotas, Cugat explotó la imagen del catalán emprendedor, el que es capaz de encontrar pan bajo las piedras. En una entrevista con Terenci Moix en 1989 declaró: «Como antes había vivido en Cuba, incorporé parte de su folclor y se lo serví a los yanquis de manera que lo pudiesen bailar. ¡Estaban encantados con el invento!».

Debo subrayar que *Cugie* no fue el único culpable de sembrar esta confusión. Un buen número de músicos e intérpretes cubanos se dejaron llevar por la moda y no respetaron las enormes diferencias entre la verdadera rumba y lo que entregaban al público.

La orquesta espectáculo

En 1932 el ya afamado pianista y compositor Ernesto Lecuona organizó una orquesta que llamó Encanto, con músicos provenientes de la de los hermanos LeBatard, para hacer una extensa gira por España. Al atrapar una pulmonía en Soria, el maestro decidió regresar a La Habana, dejando a cargo de la agrupación al pianista habanero **Armando Oréfiche** (1911-2000), quien a instancias de un empresario veneciano le cambió el nombre por el de **Lecuona Cuban Boys**. Sobre la marcha, a través de actuaciones que comenzaron por la Riviera francesa, Oréfiche perfeccionó la calidad de sus músicos; tenían que dominar más de un instrumento, los saxos tocaban también los violines y así sucesivamente, incluyendo las claves, las maracas, la quijada de burro o la tumbadora. Los mejores casinos y cabarés querían escuchar a aquellos cubanos que se intercambiaban instrumentos en medio de un número y se convertían en un verdadero espectáculo, coreando juntos una pieza determinada, bailando en la pista o marcando el ritmo detrás de los atriles.

Gran trabajador, los arreglos de Oréfiche hicieron el resto. En Italia contrató al cantante Alberto Rabagliatti, a quien enseñó un español básico entre una ciudad y otra. Fueron los Lecuona Cuban Boys quienes impusieron internacionalmente la imagen del músico cubano ataviado con la colorida camisa de rumbero, con sus amplias y ondulantes mangas. Combinando la suavidad europea con la potencia rítmica cubana, recorrieron muchos países hasta que la Segunda Guerra Mundial los obligó a regresar a la isla en 1939, ya sin Rabagliatti. *Fichín*, como apodó Lecuona a Oréfiche, fue un músico talentoso y un excelente organizador; de su

LOS LECUONA CUBAN BOYS (1940).

sensibilidad brotaron algunos boleros notables como *Habana de mi amor* y *Me estoy enamorando de ti*. Compuso varias congas (que llamó rumbas) y sones, incluyendo el célebre *Mesié Julián*, un número que escribió expresamente para su amigo *Bola de Nieve*, sobrenombre de Ignacio Villa. En 1940 grabaron en La Habana antes de comenzar una extensa gira por Suramérica que culminó en 1945. Actuaron después en Estados Unidos y al concluir allí la filmación de *Costa Rica*, se produjo una división en la orquesta. Con su hermano *Chiquito*, Oréfiche formó una nueva agrupación en 1946, incorporando, entre otros, a varios instrumentistas españoles. Así surgieron los afamados **Havana Cuban Boys**, que contribuyeron grandemente a divulgar los ritmos cubanos con su atractivo espectáculo. Luego de cosechar triunfos a través de extensas temporadas en teatros, casinos y clubes de Europa y Japón, estos embajadores sin nómina regresaron a Cuba en 1960. Pero Oréfiche decidió radicarse definitivamente en España: el experimento de Castro le pareció una traición a los verdaderos anhelos del pueblo. Instalado primero en Madrid y luego en Canarias, continuó actuando como solista en Las Palmas, Suramérica y Miami. Entre los múltiples premios y condecoraciones que recibió en su larga trayectoria artística se encuentra la llave de la ciudad de Miami, en reconocimiento a su aportación a la cultura cubana en el mundo.

Sobre Armando Oréfiche escribió el poeta Gastón Baquero: «...en cuanto se sienta al piano desaparece el muy comedido y correcto señor, un poquito mayor, y surge ante los ojos y ante los oídos la música». En 1995 Oréfiche participó brillantemente en el homenaje que logré organizar en la Casa de América de Madrid con motivo del centenario del nacimiento del maestro Lecuona. Falleció a los 89 años, siempre amando a su Cuba.

EL PIANISTA ARMANDO ORÉFICHE (1992) RECIBIENDO UN GALARDÓN.

Curiosamente, la orquesta que conservó el nombre original de Lecuona Cuban Boys continuó su trayectoria internacional independiente hasta la década de 1970 en que se disolvió.

En 1932 también vino a España la **Orquesta Siboney**, dirigida por el compositor **Alfredo Brito** (1896-1954), quien a los diecisiete años ya trabajaba como flautista en la charanga típica de Antonio María Romeu. Años después, Brito viajó a Nueva York con la orquesta de Don Aspiazu tocando el saxofón; en aquella ciudad realizó un arreglo de *El manisero* con un éxito tan impresionante que la RCA Victor decidió editar un millón de discos, un verdadero récord para la época. Cuando regresó a Cuba decidió fundar la citada orquesta Siboney, con la que también actuó en Francia y Portugal. Años después, Alfredo Brito formó parte de la orquesta norteamericana de Paul Whiteman y musicalizó las películas cubanas *Rumba, Yo soy el héroe* y *Prófugos*.

Don Aspiazu, que había fundado su primera orquesta alrededor de 1925, comenzó a presentarse en el Casino Nacional de La Habana en 1929. Imaginando las posibilidades escénicas de *El manisero* para entretener a los turistas del Norte, decidió fichar a un cantante de talento que respondía al nombre de **Antonio Machín** (ver pág. 138). Vestido elegantemente, a Machín le correspondió ser el primer negro que logró actuar en el exclusivo casino; allí fue donde primero hizo sonar sus inseparables maracas. Después se cambiaba de ropa y aparecía empujando un carrito o cargando una caja con cacahuetes mientras cantaba «Maniií..., si te quieres por el pico divertir, cómprame un cucuruchito de maní...» y el público aplaudía su pintoresca presentación. Pronto la agrupación logró

ANTONIO MACHÍN (1947).

embarcarse rumbo a Nueva York, con no pocos esfuerzos para conseguir visados para tantos músicos. Debutaron en el Palace Theater en 1930 y trabajaron en otros centros nocturnos. Pero no había mucho dinero para ir de fiestas: Estados Unidos sufría las estrecheces que siguieron a la caída financiera de Wall Street en 1929. De ahí que en 1932 decidieran cruzar el Atlántico; primero tocaron en La Cabaña Cubana, un club de París con Alicia Parlá como bailarina. De allí pasaron a España, regresaron a Cuba y en 1934 fueron nuevamente contratados en Nueva York. Al terminar la temporada, Machín decidió quedarse en aquella ciudad, formando el cuarteto Machín, con el que grabó más de cincuenta números para la RCA Victor. En aquellas grabaciones participó Mario Bauzá como trompeta. Tres años después Machín sintió de nuevo la inquietud de viajar y regresó a Europa. Empezó por Londres, donde triunfó con *El lamento esclavo* de Eliseo Grenet; después pasó a París, organizando pronto una orquesta para recorrer Suecia, Dinamarca, Noruega, Alemania, Italia, Holanda y Rumanía. Pero ya era 1939 y había estallado la Segunda Guerra Mundial; Machín decidió no esperar a que los alemanes entraran en París y se trasladó a España. En *El Libro del Bolero* aparece más información sobre su trayectoria.

DÚOS, TRÍOS Y CUARTETOS

Resulta imposible incluir a todos los grupos que han cantado en y para Cuba, de ahí que los que aquí aparecen no son sino una muestra. Hacia 1941 habían surgido en La Habana notables cantantes de boleros, como Carlos Alas del Casino y Pepe Reyes, quienes competían con las voces de América Crespo, Esperanza Chediak y Hortensia de Castroverde. La soprano María Ciérvide integró un trío junto a Zoraida Marrero y Georgina Du'Bouchet, y con esta última mantuvo durante años el dúo Primavera. En la misma época aparecieron Sarita Escarpenter e Idalmi García, así como las voces masculinas de Wilfredo Fernández y Manolo Fernández, que empezó cantando tangos.

TRÍO HERMANAS LAGO.

En los años 50 se destacaron el dúo de las **Hermanas Lago**, que luego fueron tres y hasta cuatro, como en el caso de las **Hermanas Márquez**, y el dueto de las **Hermanas Martí**, depositarias de las mejores canciones de la trova tradicional. También tuvo mucha aceptación el matrimonio formado por **Olga Chorens y Tony Álvarez**, quizá por haber tenido más acceso a la televisión. Por el extraordinario ensamblaje de sus voces se distinguió el dúo **Cabrisas-Farach**, que también se marchó en 1961, y en el exilio grabó para el sello Rhumba del actor cómico Guillermo Álvarez Guedes.

Pero sin lugar a duda, los dúos que más entusiasmaron al cubano fueron los de María Teresa Vera y **Lorenzo Hierrezuelo** (1907-91), y el de **Los Compadres**, que Lorenzo formó con su compadre Francisco Repilado (1907), el conocido Compay Segundo (ver pág. 286), que ha actuado frecuentemente en España. Al separarse en 1954, después de casi cinco años juntos, Lorenzo continuó el dúo con su hermano Reynaldo, llegando a alcanzar notable celebridad por su soneo y las bromas que intercalaban en sus números. Heredero de una tradición trovadoresca familiar, Lorenzo Hierrezuelo formó parte de varios tríos y cuartetos en Santiago de Cuba y en la capital, siempre en su calidad de segunda voz y guitarra acompañante.

DÚO HERMANAS MARTÍ.

Compárese la relativa brevedad de la primera etapa de Los Compadres con los 25 años en que se escucharon las voces de María Teresa Vera y Lorenzo. Durante largas sesiones en Radio Cadena Suaritos, una de las más populares de la década de 1950, grabaron diariamente en placas de acetato, permitiéndole así a la emisora acumular suficientes discos para com-

REYNALDO Y LORENZO HIERREZUELO, LA
SEGUNDA EDICIÓN DE LOS COMPADRES.

placer peticiones. Lorenzo Hierrezuelo fue la guitarra y la segunda voz que pudo seguir la idiosincrasia única de la Vera.

Aunque en los últimos años han surgido otros dúos, quiero destacar la labor de **Postrova**, fundado en 1997 por Eduardo Sosa y Ernesto Rodríguez, aupados por su vigilante manager Salvador Palomino. Ya han actuado en España, entrelazando elementos del son, la trova, la guaracha, y por supuesto, el jazz, el blues, la música pop y hasta el rock. Aunque la propuesta del dúo es simple, el resultado no resulta simplista. Llevan la impronta santiaguera y son verdaderos perfeccionistas; descubiertos por Seju Monzón, cuentan hasta ahora con el respaldo del sello EMI-Odeon.

Tres eran tres...

Con la excepción del afamado trío Matamoros, en la extensa época de oro del bolero interpretado por tríos, no hubo en Cuba ninguno que alcanzara el prestigio de Los Panchos (creados en 1944 en Nueva York) o de Los Tres Ases. No obstante, varios tríos criollos obtuvieron cierta resonancia nacional e internacional entre 1945 y 1960, particularmente el de Servando Díaz, Taicuba, Los Guaracheros de Oriente, el Oriental, el trío La Rosa y los Hermanos Rigual. A diferencia de los mexicanos, totalmente envueltos en el bolero, estos tríos se dedicaron tanto a la canción romántica como al son y la guaracha.

Por el año 1937, **Servando Díaz** (1912-85), un trovador que tocaba muy bien la guitarra, organizó un trío con Otilio Portal, también guitarrista, y Octavio Mendoza, que hacía la segunda voz y tocaba las maracas. Realizaron numerosas actuaciones y grabaron varios discos porque se salían del estilo trillado. Conocidos como «Los trovadores sonrientes», estrenaron en Cuba el bolero *Bésame mucho*, de Chelo Velázquez, partitura que la compositora le entregó a Servando durante una gira que habían hecho por México. En Nueva York estuvieron cuatro meses en el cabaré La Conga, que animaba al piano Eliseo Grenet; también se presentaron en el hotel Waldorf Astoria, en el teatro Hispano y en los programas latinos de la NBC.

TRÍO DE SERVANDO DÍAZ (AL CENTRO).

Uno de los boleros más recordados de Servando Díaz es *Besos salvajes*, con música de E. Fontanal y versos del venezolano Rufino Blanco Fombona. El investigador Díaz Ayala asegura que este trío también destacó con el chachachá *Me lo dijo Adela*, que le representó bastantes dólares a Otilio Portal cuando llegó exiliado a Estados Unidos en 1960: el número se había convertido en *Sweet and gentle*, ganando popularidad gracias a una afamada escuela de baile.

El debut del trío **Taicuba** tuvo lugar en agosto de 1947, en un programa patrocinado por Bacardí. Interpretaron *Noche cubana*, de César Portillo de la Luz, y *No importa si mentí*, de Baz Tabrane. Ajenos al diatonismo peculiar de la trova criolla y a los efectos del requinto de la línea «panchista», el Taicuba se inclinó por los compositores del filin. Alfredo Cataneo, un bromista nato, se unió a Leyva y Tabrane para interpretar canciones cubanas y también se les recuerda por *Mi Habana*, del costarricense Ray Tico. En 1990 todavía se encontraba actuando. Verdaderos baluartes del bolero fueron infinidad de tríos surgidos durante los años 50.

El trío **La Rosa** fue quizá más conocido fuera que dentro de la isla, especialmente en Colombia y Venezuela. Surgido en Santiago de Cuba, lo integraron originalmente Juan Francisco de la Rosa, Julio León y Juan Antonio Serrano. Formado en algún momento de los años 30, en él cantó por un tiempo *Ñico Saquito* (Antonio Fernández, 1902). El estilo de este trío fue muy característico, fácilmente identificable por la cadencia bien marcada del ritmo, pero sin parecerse al tumbaíto del trío Matamoros. Gustaban de interpretar canciones y boleros de Walfrido Guevara, trovador nacido en 1916 en Santiago de Cuba; en algunas de sus grabaciones aparece la impresionante voz de Luisa María Hernández (1920), la «India de Oriente», nacida en El Cobre y trasladada después a Santiago con su familia. Esta vocalista, de timbre potente y dicción clara, es totalmente desconocida en la Cuba actual, aunque sabemos que también se trasladó a Estados Unidos alrededor de 1960. En 1999 el sello Virgin publicó doce números donde esta mujer de abolengo campesino aparece interpretando boleros melodramáticos.

Los Guaracheros de Oriente, que originalmente eran cuatro, habían perdido en 1950 al legendario *Ñico Saquito,* quien se separó del grupo durante una gira en Venezuela y luego reapareció en Cuba en 1960. Así se convirtieron en trío, pero en uno muy especial, pues su vocalista en vez de agitar las tradicionales maracas tocaba unos pequeños timbales, cosa muy difícil de lograr mientras se canta. Estuvo integrado por Florencio Santa *Pícolo* (voz segunda y guitarra), Gerardo Macías *el Chino*

LOS GUARACHEROS DE ORIENTE.

(guitarra y tercera voz) y Félix Escobar *el Gallego* (voz prima y timbales). Quizá por eso, aunque grabaron mucha música de Matamoros, se diferenciaron en el efecto total que lograban. Se mantuvieron en el favor popular durante más de un decenio y finalmente se establecieron en Puerto Rico en 1962. El sello Tumbao Classics publicó en Barcelona el estupendo disco *Adiós Compay gato,* grabado en La Habana entre 1954-55.

Otro grupo que comenzó a destacarse hacia finales de los años 40 fue el **trío Oriental,** con su director Maximiliano Sánchez *Bimbi* (1901-91), Tico Álvarez y Pedro Feliú. Formado en 1935, durante quince años viajó por varias naciones caribeñas y alcanzó a grabar más de un centenar de discos. En 1950 se establecieron en Nueva York, haciéndole la competencia a los excelentes tríos de los puertorriqueños Rafael Hernández y Pedro Flores. Allí se especializaron en guarachas de doble sentido y en boleros impresionantes como *Allí donde tú sabes,* de Luis Marquetti. Posteriormente, *Bimbi* se mudó a Puerto Rico y finalmente a Tampa, donde falleció.

Carlos, Mario y Pituko integraron el trío **Hermanos Rigual,** formado alrededor de 1944. Su calidad interpretativa estuvo bastante influida por los grupos vocales norteamericanos, armonizando las voces y usándolas en vocaliso, lo que en inglés llaman *humming,* dejando escapar por la nariz parte del aire respirado. Después de una primera visita a México en 1947, seguida de otras giras, decidieron radicarse allí definitivamente en 1958. Los Hermanos Rigual compusieron un buen número de piezas exitosas entre las que destaca el chachachá *Corazón de melón,* y el rock lento *Cuando calienta el sol,* que todavía se escucha en los veranos playeros.

El trovador **Carlos Puebla** (1917-89) era de Manzanillo, donde lo mismo «se baila el son en calzoncillo que en camisón». Antes de meterse de lleno en la música desempeñó diversos oficios, ganándose después la vida tocando en bares y restaurantes con varios tríos. Fundó Los Tradicionales en 1953. Debido a su filiación comunista, a partir de 1959 comenzó a trabajar para el Consejo Nacional de Cultura, viajando a casi todos los países latinoamericanos y algunos europeos (ver pág. 307). Alrededor de 1962 Carlos Puebla se dedicó a amenizar regularmente a la clientela de La Bodeguita del Medio; también grabó discos y fue presentado en programas de radio y televisión. Aunque solía viajar en formación de cuarteto, en la Bodeguita aparecía como trío completado por Santiago Martínez en la guitarra solista y Pedro Sosa en las maracas. Sus canciones son simples, algunas de verdadero carácter panfletista, como en *Hasta siempre Comandante* (basada en un poema de Nicolás Guillén), un número dedicado a la memoria del aguerrido argentino Ernesto Che Guevara. *La Bodeguita del Medio* es un disco grabado en vivo en 1957, en la época que el aventurero húngaro Sepy Dobronyi creó el afamado restaurante que pronto se convirtió en el principal centro de la bohemia habanera. *De Cuba traigo un cantar* (EGREM) es una colección de canciones en apoyo a la revolución. Un disco interesante fue *Este es mi pueblo. Dos etapas de Cuba* (1959), donde aparece por primera vez aquello de «...y se acabó la diversión, llegó el Comandante y mandó a parar». Afortunadamente, también contiene *Los caminos de mi Cuba,* una evocación patriótica que considero una de sus mejores creaciones.

CARLOS PUEBLA.

Ahora a cuatro voces

La influencia norteamericana se hizo sentir en el surgimiento de varios cuartetos vocales de notoriedad. Fue como una eclosión, una adaptación motivada por la aparición de grupos vocales en algunas de las mejores swing bands norteamericanas, o de cuartetos independientes al estilo de The Mills Brothers, así como otros que se presentaban en varias orquestas norteamericanas.

En 1940 surgió el del pianista **Facundo Rivero,** que tuvo como su organizadora y voz principal a la compositora Isolina Carrillo, junto a las de Joseíto Núñez, Alfredo León y Marcelino Guerra *Rapindey,* posible-

LOS RIVERO CONVERTIDOS EN TRES.

mente una de las mejores segunda voz que se escucharon en Cuba. Se dieron en llamar conjunto **Siboney** porque los acompañaba el piano, pero las voces sonaban diferentes; no se parecían en nada a otros que se habían iniciado unos años antes. Grabaron sólo cuatro números, y no alcanzaron un gran éxito porque estaban adelantados a su tiempo. Al separarse, Facundo Rivero organizó el grupo que llevó su nombre.

Más tarde se formó el cuarteto **Los Rivero**, nombre que mantuvieron después de dejar a Facundo, porque uno de sus miembros tenía el mismo apellido (Abel Rivero); originalmente eran dos voces masculinas y dos femeninas, que cantaron de todo con brillantez. Viajaron extensamente y se radicaron en España hasta su disolución en 1980.

El compositor Bobby Collazo organizó uno de voces masculinas solamente, al que bautizó **Cuarteto Antillano**, mientras que otro autor, **Orlando de la Rosa**, formó el suyo con voces mixtas. Después apareció el declamador **Luis Carbonell** con un grupo estupendo. En esta etapa los cuartetos unían el baile al canto, sobre todo en números movidos como las guarachas, convirtiéndose en pequeñas unidades coreográfico-vocales. En realidad estaban sumamente influenciados por las voces que se hicieron famosas con orquestas tipo jazz band, como Modernaire, con Glenn Miller, y los Pied Pipers con Tommy Dorsey.

En 1952 se fundó el cuarteto D'Aida que recorrió varios países regando la sabrosura y la calidez de las voces de Elena Burke, las hermanas Haydée y Omara Portuondo y Moraima Secada *La mora*, fallecida en 1989. Muy exigente, su directora, la pianista y arreglista **Aida Diestro** (1928-73), una señora muy gruesa asociada a los «muchachos del filin», que estaba dotada de un extraordinario sentido de la armonía, insistía cada día en que las chicas

EL PRIMER CUARTETO DE AIDA DIESTRO: ELENA BURKE, MORAIMA SECADA, HAYDEÉ Y OMARA PORTUONDO.

interiorizaran lo que cantaban. En los minutos que duraba una canción filin debía surgir una magia muy especial, porque creía que la interpretación de canciones románticas es un juego de verdades, no de mentiras. Muy admirado por el pueblo, el cuarteto de la «Gorda de oro» fue el primer grupo femenino que cantó a cuatro voces, con un tratamiento que correspondía a las nuevas sonoridades en la música internacional.

El importante cuarteto **Los Zafiros** aparece en el capítulo Ritmos de la revolución, pág. 297.

2. GUAJIROS Y NEGROS

> Yo soy el poeta de la rumba, soy danzón, el eco del tam-
> bor. Soy la misión de mi raíz, la historia de mi solar. Soy
> la vida que se va. Soy los colores del mazo de collares
> para que la raíz no muera. Soy ají, soy picante. ¿Soy el
> paso de Changó, el paso de Obbatalá, la risa de Yemayá,
> la valentía de Oggún, la bola o el trompo de Elegguá? Soy
> Obba, soy sire siré, soy Aberiñán y Aberisún, soy la razón
> del crucigrama, el hombre que le dio la luz a Obdebí, el
> cazador de la duda. Soy la mano de la verdad. Soy arere,
> soy conciencia. Soy Orula.
>
> ELOY MACHADO, *El Ambia*
> *Yo soy Orula*

No toda la música cubana ha disfrutado del mismo grado de popularidad. Hay todo un folclor campesino, originado en España, que apenas es
conocido fuera de la isla. Inevitablemente surge la pregunta: ¿Por qué estas tonadas guajiras no captaron la atención del mundo? Aparte de tratarse de un género no bailable, no encuentro mejor respuesta que la que
da el novelista Alejo Carpentier en *La música en Cuba*:

El guajiro ciñe su invención poética a un patrón melódico tradicional que hunde
sus raíces en el romancero hispánico, traído a la isla por los primeros colonizadores. Cuando el guajiro cubano canta, observa un tipo de melodía heredado, con la
mayor fidelidad posible. Muy poeta, el guajiro no es músico. No crea melodías.
En toda la isla canta sus décimas sobre diez o doce patrones fijos, muy semejantes
unos a otros, cuyas fuentes primeras pueden hallarse en cualquier romancero tradicional de Extremadura. En la música mulata y negra, en cambio, si el interés de
las letras suele ser muy escaso, la materia sonora es de una riqueza increíble. Por
ello se regresa siempre, tarde o temprano, a uno de sus géneros o ritmos, cuando
se pretende hacer obra de expresión nacional.

El punto guajiro ha quedado como la fuente eurocubana más claramente discernible; desde el siglo XVII aparecen menciones a este género que se acompaña tradicionalmente de guitarra, tiple, laúd, claves y güiro. El aislamiento y la conducta reservada del campesino propiciaron que, por largos años, sus elementos más importantes se conservaran casi incontaminados: arcaísmos del idioma, el uso de la décima espinela, junto a la copla, el refranero popular y los instrumentos de cuerda pulsada. Sus intérpretes efectúan controversias improvisadas, alternando los versos de la décima o tomando como pie el último lanzado para iniciar el reto o la respuesta; lo que en la isla se conoce como «repentismo».

La voz *guajiro*, que denomina al campesino cubano, proviene del siglo XVI cuando se importaron de Venezuela indios esclavizados pertenecientes a dicha tribu, justo antes de que comenzara en grande el negocio de la trata negrera.

AIRES CAMPESINOS

En el origen del punto guajiro intervinieron infinidad de cantares populares hispánicos. La migración de canarios y andaluces, que se mantuvo constante durante todo el período colonial, aportó los principales elementos nutrientes de un modo de cantar que, una vez sedimentados, conformaron aspectos de una conciencia nacional en el ámbito rural.

La investigadora María Teresa Linares ha señalado en *La música y el pueblo* que el punto guajiro tiene cercano parentesco con géneros andaluces como las peteneras, las bulerías y las seguidillas. Destaca además características notables de cantos canarios como el tono agudo y nasal, así como el empleo de inflexionales vocales algo alejadas de la afinación temperada, adornos que agregan mayor flexibilidad en la emisión del sonido.

En la poesía de la segunda mitad del siglo XIX se manifestaron dos movimientos que influyeron decisivamente en las letanías guajiras: uno marcó la vuelta a la naturaleza y a la imagen idílica del aborigen, mientras que el otro se inclinó hacia un lenguaje que aludía a las luchas por la libertad de la isla. En los cantos de campañas guerreras hubo hermosos ejemplos, así como en las respuestas que daban los soldados españoles, una controversia animada por la pasión más exacerbada. Innumerables improperios se dijeron en muchas de ellas, sobre los valientes que defendían opuestos puntos de vista.

Asombra la continua popularidad del punto guajiro en todo el ámbito nacional. Analizado históricamente, su demanda ha sido tal que Díaz Ayala considera que entre 1906 y 1907 ya se habían grabado bastantes manifestaciones:

De su inclusión hay que inferir que esta música tenía en los albores del siglo XX un arraigo en las clases económicas altas, las que contaban con capacidad económica para adquirir vitrolas y discos... No es aventurado situar el total hasta 1925 en unas 350 grabaciones.

La temática combinaba aspectos de la vega de tabaco, de los verdes campos de caña, de la fresca belleza de la mujer campesina, o recurría a descripciones de la hermosa topografía y la rica fauna, con asuntos amorosos o satíricos, e inclusive versos de protesta por el abandono económico en que se forzaba al campesino. El afán blanqueador del abolengo racista cubano estimuló este tipo de versificación para contrarrestar la presencia africana, como si todavía a las cuerdas les estuviese vedado acercarse al tambor.

ALZANDO LA CAÑA CORTADA.

Después, el auge de la radio favoreció programas en que se ofrecían cantos campesinos a tempranas horas de la mañana, cultivando una audiencia que mantenía una correspondencia copiosa y bastante ingenua con sus cantores favoritos; éstos improvisaban saludos, parabienes y una extensa gama de felicitaciones. En los años 40, la interpolación de estribillos en las décimas estimuló la identificación de algunas tonadas, como ocurrió con la *Guacanayara*, la *Tulibamba*, la *Mechita* y tantas más.

Los apelativos con que se autodenominaron algunos de los juglares campesinos tenían diversos orígenes. Algunos promocionaban la nitidez de su voz, como es el caso de «El clarín de Palatino». Otros establecieron una similitud con las aves: «El sinsonte habanero» (Liberato Gutiérrez) o «La calandria» (Nena Cruz). Los más acudían a jerarquías: «El rey de la melodía», «El cacique de Artemisa» o «El príncipe del laúd». La imitación de sonidos rurales también fue explotada por Cheo, conocido como «El hombre de los animales».

Los instrumentos: LAS CLAVES

El instrumento percutivo formado por dos palitos perfectamente redondeados, de unos 21cm de largo, ha tenido una importancia vital en el mantenimiento del cinquillo cubano. Constituyen la esencia del son y la guaracha, y también estableció el lento ritmo del bolero. Las duras claves suelen ser hechas de ácana, árbol nativo de la familia de las sapotáceas. Una se mantiene pasiva y horizontal (la hembra), sostenida por las yemas de los dedos, acostada en la mano que le hace de caja de resonancia, mientras que la otra, agarrada por la mitad (el macho), percute en el centro de la que yace inmóvil. Dejando a un lado esta descripción machista, es importante señalar que el etnólogo Fernando Ortiz estableció su origen en las clavijas que sujetaban los tablones de los antiguos barcos de madera, por lo que parecen haber surgido en las construcciones navales del puerto habanero. Allí las maderas preciosas de la isla, –caoba, cedro, majagua, quebracho, ébano, yaya–, se transformaban en buques de línea españoles. Los marineros y esclavos trabajadores las emplearon para acompañar las canciones y martinetes en boga, hasta que fueron adoptadas por el campesino rústico. En sus orígenes, pienso que la parquedad rítmica de las claves debió contrastar mucho con el repiqueteo alegre de las castañuelas. Con su usual marcado permanente (un, dos, tres—un, dos), las duras claves tienen algo de cárcel rítmica y un quejido seco, sumamente penetrante, ¡pero le han dado tremendo sabor a la música cubana! En la rumba guaguancó se atrasa ligeramente el tercer golpe, logrando así un encuadre que hace resaltar los intrincados arabescos sonoros que producan los cueros.

Aunque la expresión del canto campesino no tuvo un peso específico en el devenir de la música popular bailable, su influencia en la canción criolla y en los comienzos del son fue considerable. Tanto por la forma de tañer la guitarra como en el uso de las claves, la experiencia guajira fue aprovechada por los primeros trovadores y soneros.

El guitarrista y cantor **Guillermo Portabales** (1914-61), realmente llamado José Guillermo Quesada, falleció en el exilio en Puerto Rico, víctima de un accidente; Portabales fue de los primeros en sacar al punto de su contexto rural e inscribirlo en lo que denominó «guajira de salón», una música mecida por un aire binario muy cercano al bolero. En 1928 debutó en Cienfuegos, su ciudad natal. Llevó los aires cubanos por Puerto Rico, Venezuela, Ecuador, Colombia y Panamá, así como Estados Unidos. Formó un trío que estuvo integrado por Calixto Varela y Roberto Moya, con el cual acompañó al argentino Carlos Gardel en varias películas. Fue el autor de temas como *El carretero,* y el que sentó las bases para la posterior popularidad de Celina González en Bogotá.

EL CANTOR GUILLERMO PORTABALES.

Por su parte, el dúo de **Celina y Reutilio** (Celina González y Reutilio Domínguez) desarrolló a partir de 1948, en Radio Cadena Suaritos, un tipo de son de valores sincréticos, donde la vena campesina apareció mezclada con influencias afrocubanas, como en *A Santa Bárbara*, un número mejor conocido como *¡Que viva Changó!* o en *Flores para tu altar*, un sabroso son-pregón de July Mendoza.

Estoy convencido de que la importancia de este dueto fue bastante más significativa que lo que se creyó en su momento estelar. No sólo rompieron con la secular separación que existía entre la música guajira y la música afro, sino que también establecieron una nueva fusión donde se mantiene la décima hispánica, pero la letra se refiere a temas del patrimonio cultural-religioso heredado del continente negro. La enorme acogida que esta novedad supuso en el público estuvo aparejada por la restallante voz de Celina y el sonido producido en las cuerdas por Reutilio, que parecía provenir no de una sino de dos o más guitarras. Agréguesele el repiqueteo del bongó de Marcelo González *El blanco*, que también tocaba con la Orquesta de Julio Cueva, y ya tienen a tres músicos que, quizá sin tener suficiente conciencia de ello, subieron el son a una carreta de caña tirada por un oricha.

Asegura Raúl Fernández, ensayista y profesor de la Universidad de California, que la primera grabación de Celina y Reutilio con esa impronta fue *A Santa Bárbara*, en la cual contaron con el piano del arreglista Obdulio Morales y el bongó de un habanero conocido como *Papá Gofio*. Sobre el origen del tema, me baso en declaraciones publicadas en Puerto Rico en 1986, donde Celina relató cómo durante un sueño se le había presentado dos veces Santa Bárbara pidiéndole que le cantara, a lo que ella respondió que no podía porque no sabía cantos de Santería; argumentó que era muy joven y sólo conocía la música campesina. Entonces Santa Bárbara/Changó se echó a reir y le dijo que iba a aprender. En el segundo sueño le aseguró que si no le cantaba no triunfaría.

Celina González había conocido a Reutilio Domínguez en 1943. Cantar *Lágrimas negras* de Matamoros y enamorarse fue todo uno. Tratando de darse a conocer en Santiago de Cuba, el dueto fue ayudado por el declamador y pianista Luis Carbonell, quien logró su debut en 1947 en la CMKC, Cadena Oriental de Radio, como parte de un programa dedicado a los problemas del agro titulado «Atalaya campesina». Después se presentaron ante una multitud en el estadio de béisbol de Santiago, formando parte de un espectáculo que incluía al trío La Rosa y a la afamada

EL DÚO CELINA Y REUTILIO (1957).

Orquesta de Chepín-Chovén. Poco más tarde, el popular *Ñico Saquito* (Antonio Fernández), autor de sones como *María Cristina, Cuidadito compay gallo, Jaleo, No dejes el camino por vereda* y un prototipo de canción protesta titulado *Al vaivén de mi carreta*, los llevó a La Habana para que aparecieran en la radioemisora que había puesto de moda la música más afrocubana, presentando los fines de semana toques de tambor y cánticos a cargo de las vocalistas Merceditas Valdés, Celia Cruz y Gina Martín. Tras sus primeras presentaciones en Suaritos se convirtieron en favoritos nacionales. Era 1948.

Después aparecieron otros temas: *A la Caridad del Cobre* (Ochún, Patrona de Cuba), *A la diosa del mar* (la Virgen de Regla/Yemayá), *El 17* (dedicado a San Lázaro/Babalú-Ayé) y *El Hijo de Elegguá*. Otros números grabados pegaron igualmente: *Lágrimas negras, Me tenían amarrao con P* (Ñico Saquito), *El cuarto de Tula* (Luis Marquetti) y muchos más. En los años 50 viajaron a Nueva York, presentándose con Benny Moré; después visitaron la República Dominicana, y más tarde volvieron a Nueva York en compañía del cantante Barbarito Diez. Su prestigio era tal que aparecieron en dos largometrajes producidos en La Habana: *Rincón crio-*

llo y *Bella la salvaje*. Cantaron a menudo en la televisión y en diversas cadenas de radio; actuaron en Tropicana y en 1956 grabaron respaldados por la Orquesta Sensación. Se codearon con los principales representantes del punto guajiro: Coralia Fernández, Ramón Veloz, el *Indio Naborí*, Raúl y Radaeunda Lima, y fueron solicitados por anunciantes para grabar una variedad de *jingles* para la radio. La tonada *Yo soy el punto cubano,* compuesta por Reutilio en octavas muy sonoras, arrasó no sólo en Cuba sino en todo el Caribe: «Yo soy el punto cubano / que en la manigua vivía / cuando el mambí se batía / con el machete en la mano...»

La colaboración entre Celina y Reutilio concluyó en 1964. Reutilio falleció siete años después, y entre 1964 y 1980 Celina prosiguió su carrera como solista. Al terminar su hijo Lázaro los estudios musicales, madre e hijo se lanzaron a una nueva versión de Celina y Reutilio. Apoyándose en el programa de música campesina «Campo Alegre», ya no eran un dúo sino un conjunto moderno de música guajira y son montuno. Colombia se convirtió por aquella época en la plaza preferida para sus actuaciones. Yo la ví actuar en Bogotá en 1994 en el club Salomé de César Pagano y se ganó a la audiencia con los dos primeros números.

La incansable Celina nació en 1929 y al momento de escribir, Lázaro ya tiene 46 años. Han cantado en Europa –en Inglaterra la llaman *Queen of Cuban country music*– y en años recientes decidieron adaptar varias canciones de Silvio Rodríguez; también han colaborado con los grupos Manguaré y Adalberto Álvarez y su Son, grabando dos discos con este último timo.

En 1993 Celina González presentó *Fiesta guajira*, una selección de cuatro álbumes grabados alrededor de 1980 en los estudios de la EGREM, ya sin su esposo Reutilio, pero contando con el respaldo de las agrupaciones campesinas Palmas y Cañas y Campo Alegre; estos discos se han vendido como pan caliente en Estados Unidos y otros países. El impacto de Celina ha sido tremendo, influyendo sobre otras cantoras campesinas como la estupenda Albita Rodríguez (ver pág. 275) que triunfó plenamente en Miami. El sociólogo colombiano Alejandro Ulloa ha afirmado: «Celina es a la música guajira lo que Celia Cruz ha sido para la guaracha y el son».

Por la misma época en que surgieron Celina y Reutilio apareció en la radio habanera un parlanchín conocido por *Clavelito* (Miguel Alfonso Pozo), que explotaba un espiritismo elemental, pidiéndole a los ingenuos oyentes que colocaran un vaso lleno de agua sobre la radio para comunicarse con ellos: «Pon tu pensamiento en mí / y verás que en este momento / mi fuerza de pensamiento / ejerce el bien sobre ti...». *Clavelito* también alcanzó cierta notoriedad interpretando sones de sabor nacionalista como *Quiero un sombrero,* de Félix Cárdenas:

> Quiero un sombrero
> de guano, una bandera.
> Quiero una guayabera
> y un son para bailar...

EL JILGUERO DE CIENFUEGOS.

Otro cantante significativo, aunque no conocido fuera de Cuba como Celina, ha sido *El jilguero de Cienfuegos* (Inocente Iznaga, 1930), que aunque no poseía el pedigrí de su predecesor **Chanito Isidrón,** famoso por la *Seguidilla del café*, logró producir sones de sabor campesino con carácter urbano. Conocido por su imitación de animales domésticos, entre silbidos y una risa contagiosa, *El jilguero* exaltó la tonada, una melodía que tiene su opuesto en la controversia. Siempre logró sonar como si siguiera pegado al campo de caña, al buchito de café negro mañanero, y a menudo ha grabado cadencias reminiscentes del vallenato colombiano, como en *Caminito de Zaza,* aunque sin emplear el acordeón.

Un fenómeno de los últimos años ha sido el de Polo Montañez, un campesino sonero de voz desenfadada, oriundo de Pinar del Río, y creador también de boleros interesantes. Polo falleció a finales de 2002 en un accidente automovilístico. Mejor conocido como *guajiro natural,* debido al título de su primer disco, Polo Montañez logró ventas extraordinarias de sus dos álbumes, especialmente en Colombia. Una verdadera pérdida.

Una Guantanamera que se las trae

¿Quién no ha cantado alguna vez la guajira *Guantanamera*? El origen de la mundialmente famosa tonada ha provocado una larga batalla legal. Aparentemente fue inscrita en el Registro de la Propiedad en 1942 por el modesto cantante **Joseíto Fernández** (1908-79), quien a partir de 1939 empleaba el repetitivo estribillo en el programa radial «El suceso del día», de la CMQ, patrocinado por el jabón Crusellas; el programa duró catorce años, y el tema se difundía cinco minutos antes del final, con tal exactitud que muchos aprovechaban el momento para poner en hora sus relojes. Con sus notas de fondo, describía en décimas angustiosos melodramas pasionales o dramáticos sucesos extraídos de la crónica roja. Las décimas eran redactadas por Chanito Isidrón y cantadas por Joseíto y por La calandria. Más tarde, Coralia Fernández fue la voz femenina de *La guantanamera*. Es cierto que Joseíto Fernández grabó en 1941 con la RCA Victor un número titulado *Mi biografía*, con el subtítulo de *Guajira guantanamera*, pero es oportuno aclarar que en el registro de autor sólo aparecen ocho compases del famoso montuno, lo que confirma que la tonada era de dominio público, o sea, que pertenece al ámbito del folclor. En 1942 Joseíto cedió gentilmente su melodía, a través de la embajada de Estados Unidos en La Habana, al señor Gustavo Durán, de la Secretaría de Estado en Washington, con el objetivo de «divulgación cultural» y no con «fines lucrativos o comerciales». Para complicar aún más las cosas, en *La música en Cuba* (1946) Carpentier afirmó que los dos primeros incisos de *La guantanamera* corresponden a las del viejísimo romance de *Gerineldo*, en su versión extremeña, y que algún guajiro la habría escuchado y repetido.

Más todavía: el investigador Danilo Orozco, uno de los pocos musicólogos cubanos que ha realizado estudios de campo extensivos en la provincia más oriental, ha afirmado reiteradamente que este aire tradicional proviene por diferentes vías de una muestra anónima relacionada con el antiguo nengón oriental, precursor del son. Por su parte, el musicógrafo Helio Orovio publicó un artículo en *La Gaceta de Cuba*, órgano de la Unión de Escritores y Artistas de Cuba, N.º 15, 1993, titulado «La Guantanamera en tres tiempos», donde desarrolla otros argumentos. Finalmente, he aquí el resultado de mi propia investigación sobre la versión que todos conocemos.

Corría el verano de 1962 y el cantante norteamericano de folk Pete Seeger daba un concierto en el Woodland Camp de Nueva York, cuando escuchó a un coro juvenil dirigido por el cubano Héctor Angulo (ver pág. 211), entonces becado en la Manhattan School of Music, que interpretaba *La guantanamera*. Resulta intrigante la presencia en ese momento de un becado de la isla porque las relaciones entre Cuba y Estados Unidos habían quedado cortadas en 1961. ¿Qué hacía allí Angulo en 1962? ¿Por qué no se largó en seguida? ¿Acaso contempló alguna vez la posibilidad de quedarse en el exilio? Lo cierto es que permaneció en Nueva York entre 1959 y 1964. Todo muy curioso.

La novedad del tema no era –por supuesto– su repetitiva música, sino la inclusión de algunos de los más conocidos versos sencillos del patriota José Martí. Pete Seeger la hizo suya y un año después apareció en el mercado, atribuyéndose la versión musical del número y poniendo a Héctor Angulo como el autor de la letra. A partir de entonces, el éxito de *La guantanamera* no ha conocido fronteras ni idiomas. Más tarde, Joseíto Fernández reclamó sus derechos de autor, animado por Estela Bravo, una cineasta comunista de origen argentino-norteamericano, quien se involucró bastante en el enredo legal posterior.

EL POETA JOSÉ MARTÍ.

Aquí es donde es necesario aclarar dos puntos clave: la inclusión de los versos de Martí se debió al compositor Julián Orbón (ver pág. 207) y no a Héctor Angulo, a quien Orbón le cantó entusiasmado su versión cuando el joven era alumno suyo en la Manhattan School of Music. Por otra parte, Joseíto Fernández debía tener una cara muy dura para exigir pagos por autoría musical cuando desde 1960 Castro había borrado de un plumazo el concepto de derechos de autor. Por supuesto, se trataba de una triquiñuela del gobierno para sacarle dólares al «imperialismo» y asestarle otra «derrota moral», asunto en el que estuvo muy envuelto Ricardo Alarcón, quien entonces representaba los intereses cubanos ante Estados Unidos, y que ahora es uno de los hombres más duros del régimen después de los hermanos Castro.

En el momento más álgido del debate (1967) también estuvieron muy involucrados el compositor Rosendo Ruiz (hijo), a la sazón vicepresidente de la Sociedad Cubana de Autores Musicales (SCAM), y el también compositor Luis Yáñez, entonces responsable de la Empresa de Grabaciones y Ediciones Musicales (EGREM). Añádase a todo ésto la ironía de que el cantante Pete Seeger era de izquierdas, y un verdadero simpatizante de la revolución castrense. Aunque visitó La Habana en 1971, dudo que haya ido más allá de invitar a Joseíto Fernández a un par de mojitos en la Bodeguita del Medio.

Guantanamera significa la chica de Guantánamo, una población situada al fondo de la inmensa bahía del mismo nombre donde la armada norteamericana mantiene una base desde 1898. Como corolario a esta saga por establecer los derechos legales del número, debo agregar que en fecha tan reciente como 1999, el presidente del consejo de dirección de la Sociedad General de Autores y Editores de España (SGAE) declaró en la Feria Internacional Cubadisco'99 que la SGAE ya se había gastado medio millón de dólares en el litigio contra la empresa Folkriver, la cual capitaliza en Estados Unidos, Canadá y Australia las ganancias y usos que se generan de la tonada. Teddy Bautista aseguró en La Habana que este «no es el único caso de despojos de sus derechos a autores cubanos en Norteamérica». Que yo sepa, la maraña legal no ha sido resuelta todavía.

EL TESORO LITÚRGICO

El cubano «de pura cepa» es culturalmente un mestizo, ya sea blanco, negro, mulato o lleve algo de sangre china. En materia de creencias ese mestizaje se da en forma multiplicada en la filiación religiosa de un mismo individuo, ya que muchos que dicen ser católicos son a la vez santeros, paleros o ñáñigos, y por supuesto, espiritistas, amén de creer en el horóscopo y el calendario chino. Sin embargo, siempre son capaces de distinguir entre lo que va de un culto a otro.

Refiriéndose a la influencia católica en los cultos afrocubanos, en su monografía *Yemayá y Ochún,* la etnóloga Lydia Cabrera (cuya contribución al estudio de los valores negros aparece en la pág. 115), subrayó el papel de

Un catolicismo popular, pagano, fetichero, que a la vez que confiaba en la eficacia de las velas benditas por el cura en reliquias, medallas, escapularios y oraciones, aún confiaba más en amuletos y talismanes. Creía en el diablo, en brujas y duendes, en almas en pena y malos espíritus que, como en África, se apostaban en las encrucijadas, y en polvos, brebajes, yerbas, fumigaciones y brujerías.

Entre complejos sincretismos, originados por continuos enmarañamientos genéticos y étnicos, vino a surgir la nación cubana. Es necesario recalcar que los factores centrales de la cubanidad no son simplemente negros de África y blancos de España, revueltos y refundidos en el crisol del trópico, sino personas de muy distintas etnias, arrancadas de sus tribus y enfrentados por su esclavitud a modestos campesinos españoles, desarraigados de sus distantes aldeas, aupados de repente en un rango de amos. Ese entrecruzamiento era no sólo de blancos con características muy marcadas, sino también de inmensas naciones de negros, tan distintos unos de otros que se diferenciaban por su color y su pelo, además de por su estructura ósea. Las mezclas de africanos entre sí se convirtió en el segundo proceso de transculturación (término acuñado por Fernando Ortiz, ver pág. 111) que operó en la isla, y que no ha sido estudiado todavía con suficiente profundidad.

ESTATUILLA POPULAR DE CHANGÓ/SANTA BÁRBARA.

Las corrientes inmigratorias de la música han transcurrido en Cuba a lo largo de cauces sociales muy accidentados. Muchas melodías entraron como propias de los conquistadores y de la clase dominante; otro caudal lo aportaron los esclavos y mulatos de la masa dominada. Ortiz lo definió de manera rotunda: «Música blanca, de arriba, y música negra, de abajo».

Lo cierto es que bajo la piel del tambor se esconden muchas tragedias humanas como también infinidad de secretos sobre los orígenes de la música cubana. Para apreciar mejor su gradual formación sería necesario acudir también a los recíprocos contactos que se hacían con las músicas de España (los llamados cantes de ida y vuelta), así como con otras tierras americanas. Durante el Siglo de Oro español se hizo frecuente alusión, en las obras de algunos poetas y en entremeses representados en escena, a un grupo de antiguos sones que existían en diversos territorios americanos como los chuchumbés, paracumbés, cachumbos, gayumbos, zarambeques y otros. Por otra parte, la presencia africana en la música mestiza de México, particularmente en el son veracruzano, evidencian, junto con el huapango o son huasteco, el jarabe tapatío, el gusto y la chilena, el marcado aporte negro en un país que siempre mantuvo fuertes relaciones comerciales con las costas cubanas. Así como Cuba se convirtió en un centro de gravitación, aglutinando y exportando muchos de los estilos que enriquecieron posteriormente aspectos de la música popular latinoamericana, también recibió importantes aportes de otros territorios, incluyendo aquellos dominados por norteamericanos, franceses, ingleses y portugueses.

El sincretismo religioso

En *Orígenes* explico cómo la música negra ha estado presente tanto en el contexto religioso como en el profano, aunque es en el marco litúrgico donde se han conservado con mayor fuerza los elementos originales. Hay diversos cultos relativos a deidades (llámense orichas, vodouns, santos, etc.) que fueron llevados al Nuevo Mundo en la memoria de los esclavos; con sus incontables transformaciones a través del tiempo, dichos cultos aún se manifiestan extensivamente en Cuba, Haití, Jamaica, Trinidad y Brasil.

Entiéndase que un culto implica el reconocimiento de las divinidades originales y un sistema de creencias fundamentalmente africano, a pesar de estar adornado con vestigios del catolicismo popular. El sincretismo religioso se ha impuesto en diversos grados y aunque revela bastantes elementos de la Iglesia, no son siempre el reconocimiento de Dios o de un santo cristiano. De hecho, en el contexto afrocubano no caben deidades en tormento y sin triunfos; la crucifixión de Jesús, por ejemplo, no desempeña un papel preponderante, de ahí que su simbolismo fue transmitido a Olofi u Olodumare, el dios supremo en el panteón yoruba, que raramente interviene en los asuntos de los humanos. Esa función pertenece a los orichas.

Como resultado de un acomodo socio-histórico, el santo católico impuesto por los amos fue asimilado a la personalidad y atributos de una divinidad ancestral africana, aunque es oportuno señalar que la equivalencia exacta de santos no es en modo alguno uniforme en el continente americano.

Suele atribuirse la fuerte supervivencia del animismo yoruba en Cuba a la deficiente catequización que la Iglesia católica llevó a cabo en tiempos de la colonia, cometiéndose mucha negligencia en eso de encauzar a la población hacia una verdadera cristianización, de acuerdo con el modelo español. El espíritu supersticioso, consustancial al africano, fue encubierto bajo un barniz teológico superficial, lo que indudablemente abrió la brecha para que el esclavo pusiese en juego su poder imaginativo y barajara a su antojo sus orichas en el santoral católico.

Téngase en cuenta que las creencias de África occidental son monoteístas, de naturaleza animista, y entrañan la existencia de un panteón de deidades mayores y menores, a cada una de las cuales se rinde culto con

TOQUE PARA YEMAYÁ EN SU TEMPLO DE REGLA.

ceremonias, güemileres o bembés, ofrendas, cánticos y toques de tambor específicos. Entre los rasgos más fuertes que se practican diariamente en Cuba están el uso ritual de la sangre (sacrificios de animales), ritos de iniciación, danzas rituales con coreografía y mímica altamente simbólicas, la personificación de los orichas mediante la posesión del espíritu del iniciado, así como ofrendas de alimentos específicos y objetos afines (llamados atributos) en la adoración de los dioses. El hecho de que muchos sacerdotes de dichos cultos practiquen algún tipo de medicina tradicional hace creer que están íntimamente ligadas; después de todo, el africano llegaba a América provisto de un conocimiento profundo de la naturaleza.

Los cultos afrocubanos más significativos son el yoruba o lucumí (Regla de Ocha, más conocida como Santería), el kimbisa o mayombe de la zona del Congo (Regla de Palo Monte) y los llamados ñáñigos (la Sociedad Secreta Abakuá), que combinan sus propias creencias con prácticas incorporadas de los otros cultos.

Hay que reconocer que los sistemas religiosos de varias etnias africanas se mezclaron lo suficiente como para crear un verdadero caos, contradiciéndose unas a otras con bastante frecuencia, dentro un fabuloso mundo de leyendas. Estas historias fantásticas de los dioses, llamadas *pattakís,* fueron transferidas oralmente de generación en generación, y a menudo transcritas en modestos cuadernos llamados libretas. La mitología yoruba, que en cierta forma es comparable a la griega en riqueza filosófica y valores poéticos, constituye el único bagaje sostenible de ideas sobre la creación del mundo que ha sobrevivido entre los afrocubanos. Su importante relación con la música folclórica debido al predominio lucumí, exige un estudio particular de la Regla de Ocha.

TRES EQUIVALENCIAS ENTRE CUATRO RELIGIONES ACTIVAS EN CUBA Y EL EXILIO

Cristianismo	Regla de Ocha	Regla de Palo	Regla Abakuá
Dios	Olodumare	Nsambi	Abasí
Santa Bárbara	Changó	Nsasi o Siete Rayos	Okún
Virgen de las Mercedes	Obbatalá	Mamá Kengue o Tiembla-Tierra	Obandío

Cuando el cubano medio rinde culto a algún icono católico, en realidad su mente está más bien orientada hacia los atributos y virtudes de su homólogo africano. Y cuando al practicar sus ritos afrocubanos hace uso del agua bendita y el crucifijo, o conserva sacramentos católicos como el bautizo y la comunión, o incluso mantiene la devoción por la Semana Santa o el Día de los Fieles Difuntos, el gusto por el oro, la fastuosidad y la iconografía católicas, sencillamente está siguiendo una natural adaptación que en lo sustancial no ha cambiado nada durante siglos. Respetan el poder intrínseco de estos elementos católicos y los aplican en sus ritos sin prejuicio alguno.

Desgraciadamente, el viaje del Papa a La Habana en 1998 no incluyó el menor intento de acercamiento a los representantes de estas creencias; aunque los babalaos esperaban tener una audiencia con el Pontífice, ni uno solo pudo entrevistarse con él.

¿En qué cree el músico cubano?

Si se toman en cuenta la azarosa vida del cubano de cualquier época, no sólo bajo Castro, la precaria situación de las masas populares, la envenenada y sutil discriminación racial, la inestabilidad de la vida cotidiana, el dominante papel jugado por la cultura de la caña de azúcar con sus alternantes ciclos de trabajo y tiempo muerto, los igualmente cíclicos y destructores huracanes tropicales, los cambios de gobiernos con su secuela de desempleo para los funcionarios del partido derrotado, la alternancia de democracias corruptas y de crueles dictaduras, y un largo etcétera de incertidumbres, no será difícil comprender por qué la concepción mágico-religiosa del africano acabó por predominar en el carácter de la mayor parte del pueblo.

Es más, cuando en la isla o en Miami se dice que una persona es «hijo» o «hija» de Changó, Ochún, Yemayá, Obbatalá o Oggún, no hace falta decir más sobre su carácter y lo que cabe esperarse de ella. Asimismo, en el oricha Elegguá, un pequeño diablillo socarrón que abre y cierra los caminos según una lógica disparatada, que lo mismo dispensa el bien al malo que el mal al bueno, se encarna a cabalidad la concepción del destino del cubano. Halagar a los veleidosos orichas, consultar su voluntad mediante diversos sistemas adivinatorios, «hacerse santo» o despojarse de algún maleficio, son prácticas cotidianas en la isla, tan frecuentes como recabar el apoyo de los difuntos, proveerse de resguardos y amuletos, recurrir al poder de los *afochés* (polvos mágicos) para resolver un problema amoroso o asociarse a una secta Abakuá para asegurarse la protección física de los ekobios. Por otra parte, muchas personas creen que en el fondo son sólo formas de hacerle frente a un mundo subdesarrollado, lúdico y real-maravilloso, que carece de puntos cardinales, calificándolas como intentos esotéricos de respetar y aceptar lo impalpable, y de tratar de revertir la propia suerte.

La música popular está plagada de conceptos, ritmos y términos que denotan la influencia de estas creencias. Ignacio Piñeiro compuso algunos sones donde se advierte directamente de los sentimientos religiosos: *En la alta sociedad, No juegues con los santos* y la rumbita *Arrolla cubano,* números que la cantadora María Teresa Vera interpretó con mucha gracia con el apoyo de Lorenzo Hierrezuelo. Al cantante **Miguelito Valdés** (1916-78), que además era ñáñigo, se le conoció como *Mr. Babalú* por haber popularizado en medio mundo el afro *Babalú,* de la autora Margarita Lecuona. La voz de Miguelito Cuní cantaba aquello de *Rompe saragüey,* mientras que el dúo de Celina y Reutilio hizo famoso *¡Que viva Changó!* Lino Frías, el mejor pianista que tuvo la Sonora Matancera, fue el autor de *Mata siguaraya,* un canto que amonesta a los que intenten cortar dicha planta silvestre. Uno de los números más conocidos por infi-

Los instrumentos: LAS CONGAS

Conocidas en Cuba como tumbadoras, se tocan con ambas manos y tienen forma abarrilada; son los tambores encargados de mantener el ritmo. A principios de los años 50 empezaron a ser tensadas con llaves, ya que antes había que calentarlas al fuego, como cuando se usaban para marchas carnavalescas y se echaban al hombro. En las orquestas y conjuntos de hoy día se colocan en pareja sobre el piso o sostenidas por una base, en cuyo caso se tocan de pie. La marca de más prestigio internacional es LP (Latin Percussion). En la conga más estrecha, que hace el papel de *quinto* (el repicador en la rumba), se realizan los toques más agudos y definidos, mientras que en la de cuero de mayor diámetro se obtienen los sonidos bajos. Del golpe grave que coincide con el cuarto tiempo del compás depende el «tumbaíto» sincopado del son, la guaracha y otros géneros afines.

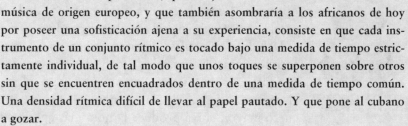

Las congas son la base de la polirritmia cubana, que encuentra su paralelo en la polifonía, sólo que en este caso, en lugar de líneas melódicas superpuestas entre sí, se trata de ejecutar varios ritmos dentro de una sola medida de tiempo. Lo que percibe el oído no entrenado es una barahúnda de ritmos «cruzados» o «atravesados». Esta polimetría, que es ajena a la música de origen europeo, y que también asombraría a los africanos de hoy por poseer una sofisticación ajena a su experiencia, consiste en que cada instrumento de un conjunto rítmico es tocado bajo una medida de tiempo estrictamente individual, de tal modo que unos toques se superponen sobre otros sin que se encuentren encuadrados dentro de una medida de tiempo común. Una densidad rítmica difícil de llevar al papel pautado. Y que pone al cubano a gozar.

nidad de criollos es El brujo de Guanabacoa, que solía cantar Abelardo Barroso: «Me boté a Guanabacoa / a casa de un babalao / pa' que mirara mi casa / y a mí que estaba salao...»

Los tres tambores batá

Son los instrumentos que se emplean en ceremonias de alto contenido espiritual y han conservado su origen, forma y poder desde hace siglos. Los batá constituyen la orquesta del templo yoruba y su función es establecer la comunicación con los orichas.

El de mayor tamaño, de voz parlante y grave es el iyá; el mediano es el itótele y el más pequeño el okónkolo; se tocan con ambas manos, colocándolos horizontalmente sobre los muslos. Los distintos planos sonoros que producen los seis parches son de una complejidad rítmica extraordinaria. Cada toque a los santos consta de varios cambios de ritmo o giros que dicta el batá iyá, con el resultado de que en un mismo toque puede

haber varios ritmos sucesivos. En los 24 toques dedicados a los orichas los expertos han llegado a identificar más de 50 ritmos distintos. Las llamadas del iyá para dirigir la atención de los otros dos tamboreros (o *olubatá*) hacia el toque que sigue en turno se hacen sumamente intrincados con los llames o murumacas.

Los batá son tambores bimembranófonos, con dos bocas de diferentes diámetros que se percuten con los dedos juntos, sin usar el pulgar. Su forma de clepsidra (como los relojes de arena) se estrecha hacia la menor abertura mientras que las proporciones entre la cintura y los extremos de la caja son vitales para obtener el sonido adecuado.

Debido a que en su interior radica una deidad o secreto llamado añá, el iyá debe ser tocado por el más virtuoso de los tres componentes y se coloca en

TAMBOR IYÁ, EL MAYOR
DE LOS TRES BATÁ.

el centro. Además de dar la nota más grave en su cuero mayor, el iyá produce la nota más aguda en su parche menor. Los tres tambores batá son objeto de ritos especiales antes de iniciarse la ceremonia de Santería, que suele comenzar con combinaciones rítmicas de carácter reposado, luego más rápido, terminando en una aceleración frenética que según Fernando Ortiz sugiere el orgasmo.

El rito ofrece una gran compensación psicológica en la suspensión de las inhibiciones, en la plena expansión de la personalidad del participante y en el alivio de sus preocupaciones reales; muchos experimentan la experiencia de un delirio místico y la consiguiente fortificación de su esperanza.

El *bembé* –una forma de definir una fiesta religiosa– se desarrolló en las zonas rurales, especialmente en Matanzas y Las Villas, posibilitando la mezcla de las lenguas yoruba, arará y otras con el español. Cuando en este tipo de fiesta se tocan los tres tambores batá se le conoce como *güemilere*. Lamentablemente, hay quienes hacen concesiones degradantes o mixtificadoras, para saciar la curiosidad de criollos o turistas, prestando poco respeto a las raíces de origen africano; en realidad, no se debería vulgarizar ofreciendo subproductos con fines mercantiles que distorsionan la verdadera esencia afrocubana.

Otras músicas negras

La música de los cultos afroides es considerada por algunos como totalmente africana, negándole el haber engrendado unas características muy criollas luego del proceso de transculturación a que estuvieron sometidos los ritmos originales al mezclarse con los modos musicales europeos.

No voy a repetir aquí todo lo que ya he explicado en *Orígenes,* valga sólo resumir que, aparte de la yoruba, está la música arará, un término genérico para definir a los esclavos provenientes de Dahomey, hoy llamado Benín. Su religión se basa en el culto al foddún o voudún, deidades bastante parecidas a las del panteón yoruba. Otro grupo importante comprende a los africanos de cultura y lengua bantú, provenientes del Congo, una inmensa región que abarcaba entre Camerún y Angola; el tambor yuka y las antiguas fiestas donde predominaba el baile de makuta identifican a los bantú en Cuba, y de su complejo cultural surgieron algunos instrumentos como la marímbula que usaron los primeros grupos soneros y que aparece descrita en la pág. 260. La marímbula está basada en la sansa o mbira del África occidental, pequeñas cajas que se sostienen entre las manos al pulsar los flejes metálicos con ambos pulgares. El tingo-talango (también conocido como tumbandera) es otro instrumento de origen bantú que posiblemente haya desaparecido por completo de la isla.

Paralela a la música que diversos grupos religiosos africanos practicaban en sus cabildos, se fueron formando en el siglo XIX otro tipo de congregaciones, llamadas abakuá o ñáñigas. Provenientes de la región

OGGÚN, EL FUERTE DUEÑO DE LOS METALES.

del Calabar, los abakuá pertenecen al complejo cultural-religioso de la nación carabalí. El baile de sus ceremonias se centra en la actuación de varios íremes o diablitos, altas figuras enmascaradas que, con su colorida vestimenta y enérgicas danzas, constituyen lo más atractivo que ha logrado preservarse del folclor afrocubano. Les acompaña el conjunto biankomeko, que está formado por cuatro tambores entre los que se encuentra el bonkó enchemiyá. Con el kuchí-yeremá, los tambores biankomé y obí-apá, el cencerro ekón y dos sonajeros llamados erikundi, se completa el conjunto musical abakuá. Un aspecto importante de la fiesta es el plante que se celebra en el cuarto de fambá, la habitación secreta donde reside el tambor sagrado ekué, oculto tras una cortina. Allí se canta wemba, que se supone relacionada con la brujería (buena o mala).

Finalmente, la música iyesá pertenece al complejo cultural yoruba y proviene de pueblos que hablan dialectos de la subfamilia kwa. Los iyesá veneran especialmente a Osaín, el guardián a la entrada de la casa, a Ochosi, el cazador, además de a Orula y a la hermosa Ochún, pero muy especialmente a Oggún, poderoso guerrero, dueño de los objetos de hierro y enemigo eterno de Changó. El instrumental rítmico iyesá consta de cuatro tambores que, aunque proyectan una sonoridad más potente que los batá, son más uniformes y menos complejos en su sincronización. Tampoco poseen la sacralidad de los batá. Los cantos aluden a una complicada mitología que tomó nuevas características en Cuba al mezclarse con la no menos compleja del catolicismo popular.

EL COMPLEJO DE LA RUMBA

Música afrocubana que carece de elementos rituales, totalmente profana y genuinamente popular, la rumba se basa sólo en voces y percusión. Tres vertientes han sobrevivido de viejas rumbas del «tiempo e'Epaña»: la campesina columbia, que es bastante rápida, el lento yambú y el urbano guaguancó, la versión más difundida. Todas tienen un carácter representativo y han absorbido parcialmente lo que de movimiento y gesto tienen las danzas consagradas a los orichas.

Proveniente de las cuarterías y sórdidos barracones de los viejos ingenios azucareros de La Habana y Matanzas, la rumba retumbó de alegría al concluir la esclavitud. Infinidad de aires rumbosos que todavía emergen aquí y allá, emanan de otros siglos, pasando de generación en generación de diversas etnias y absorbiendo en el proceso elementos del cante jondo andaluz. El gran percusionista Mongo Santamaría, asentado desde hace muchos años en Estados Unidos, considera que la rumba no es otra cosa que un negro cubano tratando de cantar flamenco; no puedo asegurar que esto sea totalmente cierto, pero sí afirmar que es un género donde la cuerda pulsada de origen español nunca formó parte del ensemble musical.

Aunque su esencia es negra, la rumba agrupa a todos los sectores de la población, convirtiéndose en una actividad colectiva en forma de ruedo donde no hay distinciones de razas ni de clases sociales, y donde los rumberos encuentran un punto de convergencia y expresión. Sin embargo, en ella encontramos plasmada toda la intensa religiosidad del negro, pero no expresada de una manera formal sino relajada, con la intención de atraer a las deidades o conjurar a sus antepasados para tratar de meterlos en su propia carne, buscando despojarlos de todo rango celestial, para tutearlos, darles aguardiente y mostrarse a sí mismos que los misterios de la vida y de la muerte son cosas de mero tránsito. Desde esta perspectiva, la rumba se convierte en una versión popular de importantes manifestaciones del panteón religioso afrocubano.

Suenan los cueros

En el largo proceso de transculturación y blanqueamiento de los antiguos tambores, éstos se convirtieron en cajones y más tarde en tumbadoras, uno de los aportes más trascendentales al patrimonio internacional según el discurso musical occidental. Fue precisamente en el contexto de la verdadera rumba y con las tumbadoras y el agudo quinto que se desarrolló al máximo una concepción politímbrica desconocida por los pueblos de origen europeo.

Para entender mejor el fenómeno de la compleja percusión cubana y la interacción entre la palabra (canto) y el tambor, donde se hallan presentes por igual el sentido y el ritmo, hay que percibirla como un resumen del equilibrio dinámico entre la realidad y la vida mismas. No exagero. En tanto que el vocalista se desgañita alabando a los grandes, relatando hechos pasados o refiriéndose irónicamente a amores perdidos, el ritmo pulsa el tiempo presente y futuro; aunque los cueros suenan a orígenes muy lejanos en realidad no es así. Es más, si el canto inmoviliza la acción en el pasado, gracias a la alquimia del movimiento y a la dinámica del arsenal sonoro, el ritmo impulsa hacia el porvenir en un jadeo que no cesa.

RUMBA COLUMBIA EN LA HABANA (1954).

Quizá otro concepto difícil de comprender para el que no sea un músico cubano o no haya aprendido a sonar los tambores en los diversos talleres que usualmente ofrecen en la isla, es que la percusión afrocubana es simultáneamente rítmica y melódica. Consiste en improvisaciones individuales y colectivas donde la unidad, destreza e imaginación de los tamboreros se pone constantemente a prueba. En cualquiera de sus formas más conocidas, la rumba ha sido siempre la gran prueba de fuego para dar oportunidad al lucimiento de los percusionistas. Los golpes han de ser duros y rapidísimos, de resonante oquedad y muy variados timbres. Las manos dibujan caprichosas notas a través de complicados arabescos sonoros, aprovechando partículas inimaginables de una semicorchea.

Observe usted a un grupo de criollos sonando una rumba de cajón, tradición que tiene su origen en la época en que no se les permitía a los esclavos construirse un verdadero tambor y tenían que limitarse a aprovechar la rústica caja donde llegaba envasado el bacalao salado o el tasajo acecinado que formaban parte de su dieta. Cuando tenían la oportunidad la desarmaban y, una vez lijadas sus tablas con piedras, la volvían a ensamblar; así conseguían los sonidos graves sobre una materia en la que un buen tocador podía producir al menos cuatro o cinco variaciones tonales básicas. También aprovecharon las cajitas donde les llegaban las velas y de ellas obtenían los sonidos agudos que corresponden hoy día al moderno quinto. Con un par de cucharas movidas constantemente golpeaban sobre cualquier superficie de madera mientras las claves mantenían el ritmo. Hoy día suelen ser tres los cajones que se emplean para tocar rumba: mientras uno mantiene el ritmo básico, el otro marca los tres golpes y un tercero despierta nuestra incredulidad con su constante repiquetear y sus no menos importantes silencios. Al musicólogo Argeliers León le gustaba contar la anécdota de un rumbero famoso de los años 40 llamado *Manano,* al que había que pagarle el taxi, además de su actuación, para transportarle sus cajones.

El baile en la rumba

Sumamente exhibicionista, en la rumba la mayor parte del lucimiento danzario corresponde a la mujer. Se cree que en sus inicios el yambú era bailado por personas de edad avanzada; quizá eso explique la lentitud de sus pasos, de una contenida sensualidad. Por contraste, en la rumba columbia –o rumba rural– a menudo sale al ruedo un hombre solo, que ejecuta inverosímiles piruetas; sus innumerables gestos miméticos pueden sugerir lo mismo un cojo que un jugador de béisbol o un ciclista, sin dejar de responder con movimientos precisos a los toques del tambor llamado quinto. También resuelve pasos acrobáticos, como ponerse un sombrero dando una voltereta o agarrar un pañuelo con la boca, bien al dar una vuelta por el suelo o en un instante en que se deja caer.

Israel Moliner Castañeda estuvo investigando la antigua rumba columbia por más de una década. Gracias a él sabemos que lo peculiar en la columbia es su carácter pugnante, primero por la oposición entre el bailador o bailadora con el tocador de quinto, después por la contienda que se establece entre los distintos danzadores concurrentes, tratando cada uno de ser el mejor, «el que más pone». Un viejo rumbero de Cárdenas, conocido por *Argó,* le afirmó que en la columbia siempre bailaban las mujeres, lo que explicaría la fama de *Aguedita,* como la conoció el pueblo de Unión de Reyes, en su calidad de pareja del famoso rumbero *Malanga*

(José Rosario Oviedo), el que provocó aquel tema de *Chano* Pozo: «Unión de Reye llora porque Malanga murió...». El uso de cuchillos es otra de las habilidades a que recurre el bailador de columbia: hay que moverlos con velocidad y virar la cabeza en sentido contrario al arma que ataca, porque los cuchillos no son cosas de juego, son brujos, «están consagrados a Sarabanda, el Oggún de la Santería».

En la modalidad guaguancó el ritmo se hace más rápido y figurativo que en el yambú. Con una coreografía rica en sugerencias eróticas, los pasos son desarticulados y la pareja lo inicia con un juego de atracción y repulsión, más de intención que de acción. Parando en seco y torciendo la cabeza con desdén, el bailador mira hacia abajo en un gesto de estupefac-

RUMBA GUAGUANCÓ (1958).

ción para seguir dando vueltas alrededor de la mujer que continúa con los movimientos de entrega y esquiva, de acercamiento y huida, hasta que el hombre, aprovechando un instante en que ella se descuida o no logra cubrirse a tiempo el sexo con su falda, mano o pañuelo, lanza un brusco movimiento pélvico hacia adelante para indicar la penetración y al que la mujer corresponde con un gesto de derrota. Es el momento que todos los presentes esperaban: el «vacunao». Los participantes lanzan gritos de alabanza, animando al hombre a tratar de «poseer» a la mujer repetidas veces. Si no lo logra, es amigablemente reemplazado por otro.

Sin embargo, en el yambú los bailadores no hacen estos gestos posesorios por lo que suele repertirse la frase: «En el yambú no se vacuna», manteniendo actitudes propias de la vejez, ejecutando movimientos con marcada dificultad y torpeza.

Timberos de siempre

Entre los quinteadores más destacados de todos los tiempos están los hermanos Orlando y Ángel Contreras *Caballerón*, *Chano* Pozo, Julio Basave

El barondó, Pedro Izquiero *Pello*, los hermanos Embale, el cuarteto Los Papines, Cándido Camero, Carlos *Patato* Valdés, Tata Güines, Mongo Santamaría, Pancho Quinto, Jesús Alfonso Miró, Justi Barreto, Armando Peraza, Félix Xiqués, Francisco Aguabella y Daniel Ponce, aunque han habido muchos otros virtuosos que no cabe mencionar aquí.

En 1952 se formó un grupo de ocho rumberos en Matanzas que pronto acaparó la atención nacional por la originalidad y nivel popular de sus temas: **Los Muñequitos de Matanzas**, llamados así por el tema de una de sus primeras grabaciones, aunque al momento de su fundación se llamaron Guaguancó Matancero. Estuvo compuesto originalmente por Florencio Calle, Gregorio Díaz, Esteban Vega, Pablo Mesa, Angel Pelladito, Ortensio Alfonso *Virulilla*, Esteban Lantric *Saldiguera* y Juan Mesa, quienes viajaban a la capital para aparecer en los Jardines de La Tropical con las voces de *Virulilla* y *Saldiguera* improvisando horrores en *El chisme de la cuchara*, *Los beodos* y el que el pueblo les impuso, *Los muñequitos*, un número grabado por el sello Puchito y que estaba basado en varios personajes de las tiras cómicas que aparecían en los periódicos dominicales. Tal fama alcanzó esta rumba, que

describía situaciones hilarantes de aquellas historietas, que decidieron cambiar el nombre del grupo porque siempre los solicitaban como Los Muñequitos de Matanzas.

Hoy día la formación cuenta con doce miembros y ha publicado dos discos con Qbadisc: *Los Muñequitos de Matanzas* y *Folklore Matancero*, originalmente grabados en La Habana en 1970, que incluye armonías del que hasta 1998 se llamó Grupo AfroCuba. El otro álbum se llama *Congo Yambumba*, con mucho sonido de chekerés. Grabado en 1983 en los estudios Siboney de Santiago de Cuba, entre varios cantos abakuá uno se encuentra con el menos probable de los temas afrocubanos: *Jingle bells*.

Los Papines, famoso cuarteto de voces y percusión fundado en La Habana en 1957 por los hermanos Luis, Alfredo, Jesús y Ricardo Abreu, suena muy diferente a Los Muñequitos. Ese mismo año apareció el disco *El vive bien,* con la aguda voz de Roberto Maza y el estupendo Grupo Folklórico dirigido por Alberto Zayas. Los Papines son un chorro de rumba con giros novedosos, que no buscan mantener ni celebrar elementos realmente folclóricos sino deslumbrar con su constante virtuosismo y alardes con los cueros. Maestros del espectáculo, han viajado profusamente desde que en 1959 aparecieron con la orquesta del Hotel Nacional bajo la dirección del trompeta Leonardo Timor.

Antes de convertirse en Los Papines, Luis, Alfredo y Jesús tocaban en diferentes agrupaciones mientras que Ricardo, el hermano mayor, tenía un grupo que llamó Papín y sus Rumberos. A partir del momento en que aparecieron con su nombre actual en el programa televisivo «Noche cubana», el cuarteto dio rienda suelta a sus fantasías percusionistas, luciéndose a menudo con la cantante **Celeste Mendoza** (1930-98), con la que grabaron varios números clave: *Papá Oggún* y *Poder mayor*. Entre sus discos recomiendo *Tambores cubanos,* de la EGREM, basado en graba-

LOS PAPINES.

ciones de hace algún tiempo, con diversas rumbas que incluyen una versión de la conga *La chambelona* (el chupachups local). En cuanto a Celeste Mendoza, Virgin publicó *La Reina del guaguancó*, una excelente compilación que incluye sones, guarachas y boleros, con la gran orquesta EGREM en 1989, con Sierra Maestra en 1990 y con Los Papines en 1996. Otra oportunidad de escuchar su voz es *Boleros con aché,* del sello español Música del Sol.

Celeste era de Santiago de Cuba pero en 1943 ya se encontraba en la capital. Eran los días del imperio de la radio y ella se presentó en un programa de aficionados cantando la guaracha de moda: *El marañón*. Obtuvo el premio, la hicieron repetir, y pronto estaba bailando rumba en el cabaré Mi Bohío. En 1956 y desde Radio Progreso, cantó con la Orquesta de Ernesto Duarte y grabó sus primeros discos; era un escándalo, sin llegar a los extremos exhibicionistas que alcanzó La Lupe años después. Le siguieron varios viajes al exterior hasta que reapareció compartiendo la escena del Alí

Bar con Benny Moré; creo que fue allí donde comenzó a ataviarse con el famoso turbante blanco de increíble altura. Continuó
introduciendo sus canciones «guaguancoseadas» (*Soy tan feliz* o *Que me castigue
Dios*) hasta que sacó un disco de sones con
el conjunto Sierra Maestra, dirigido por
Juan de Marcos González (el de Buena Vista
Social Club). En plena madurez grabó con
Los Papines y en 1994 vino a Madrid donde
se presentó con el grupo Raisón. Hacia
1996 regresó a los estudios para grabar *El
reino de la rumba* con Los Papines. Cuando

CELESTE MENDOZA.

me enteré de su solitaria muerte no pude evitar recordar aquellos versos de
una rumba: «¿Para qué tanto orgullo vano si a la tierra bajarás? / Lo más
importante de la vida es el tiempo / y a su tiempo la muerte te quita el poder...» Y realmente no supe si sólo pensaba en Celeste o también en otra
persona...

Yoruba Andabo (el amigo yoruba) es una excelente agrupación de
rumberos fundada en 1961 por varios trabajadores de los muelles habaneros, cuando se llamó Guaguancó Marítimo Portuario y contaba con la
voz de **Calixto Callava** (1930-90). Sus primeras presentaciones tuvieron
como marco los festivales organizados por la Confederación de Trabajadores de Cuba (CTC); después de muchas altas y bajas, en 1986, a instancias del poeta **Eloy Machado *El Ambia*,** fue recibido en la UNEAC
como un importante grupo folclórico de rumba. Poco después fueron invitados por Pablo Milanés a participar en el 35 Aniversario de la
EGREM, formando parte de un elenco de rumberos ya establecidos, entre
los que se encontraban Celeste Mendoza y el quintero Tata Güines. La
calidad y variedad de los guaguancós, columbias y yambús montados por
Yoruba Andabo le han valido diversos premios nacionales e internacionales; son ellos los que aparecen en el documental *Quién baila aquí (La
rumba sin lentejuelas)*. La intensa experiencia de Calixto Callava como
estibador influyó notablemente en la dirección que tomó Yoruba Andabo; sus cerca de cien composiciones lo convirtieron en una especie de cronista del puerto habanero. Y como siempre, en el solar de la Madama se
reunían los rumberos para acompañar su espíritu hacia el «campo finda»
al toque de cajones y cucharas. Llegaban los aseres del Callejón de Velas

GEOVANI Y CORO DE YORUBA ANDABO.

co en el barrio portuario de Belén con su famoso estribillo «*se está divirtiendo la gente / y a mí que me gusta el ambiente / me voy para allá*». También llegaban del Cerro con la llave que inspira la clave; de Buena Vista, donde los niches bailan en tremenda pista, y de Romerillo, donde se tiran lindos pasillos. Llegaban de La Víbora y Luyanó, de Cayo Hueso y Jesús María, Los Sitios y Guanabacoa, para implorar a Santa Bárbara Bendita que les iluminara el camino en su viaje hacia Araorúm, la tierra mítica de los rumberos.

El grupo ha encontrado en **Geovani del Pino** (coro y claves) a un gran organizador. Quizá lo mejor que ha grabado Yoruba Andabo está reunido en el disco *El callejón de los rumberos,* del sello PM Records, de Barcelona, en cuyo primer número aparece una introducción de *El Ambia,* que me he tomado la libertad de usar como exergo al capítulo 2; no se pierda una estupenda marcha Abakuá titulada *Enyenisón Enkamá* (África habla), un arreglo de Odguardo Díaz Anaya, sorprendentemente bien cantado por Román (uno de sus mejores tamboreros).

Dirigido por Amado de Jesús Dedeu Hernández, el **Conjunto Clave y Guaguancó** comenzó a destacarse en los años 80. Este rumbero, nacido en 1945, bebió de las mejores fuentes y se inició en la Santería alcanzando posteriormente el grado de babalao. En su formación contó con el apoyo en materia etnológica de Argeliers León y de Odilio Urfé, y estudió música en la Escuela de Superación Profesional Ignacio Cervantes. *Déjala en la puntica,* del sello alemán The Music Network, trae once números que incluyen variaciones sobre un mismo tema rítmico: guarapachanga, bataguacolumbia, guanbatá, guanpolirritmo y rapguaguancó.

Otro grupo reciente que me ha llamado mucho la atención por la calidad y seriedad con que abordaron su primera colección de CD, producido por Caribe Productions en 1999, es **Tambor Yoruba Abbilona**, fundado por **Dagoberto González (hijo)**. Se trata de ocho álbumes que cantan a Oyá, Obbatalá, Changó, Ochún, Aggayú, Yemayá, Elegguá, Oggún, Ochosi, Oricha Oko, Oddúa, los Ibeyis, Olókun y otros santos. Con la dirección musical de Irián López, constituyen un tesoro extraordinario en mitología, cantos y toques de batá. Los coros son fabulosos, empleando las diferentes lenguas de cada una de las formas del ciclo lucumí, mientras que los dedicados al guerrero Oggún están españolizados.

El último rumbero de calidad que quiero presentar es **Carlos Embale** (1923-98), quien se inició en el programa de radio «La Corte Suprema del Arte» hacia 1936. Fue cantante de varias agrupaciones hasta que de 1946 a 1954 estuvo en el Conjunto Matamoros reemplazando a Benny Moré; más tarde, en 1976, pasó al Septeto Nacional que había creado su protector Ignacio Piñeiro, cuyo timbre de voz emuló bastante. Director del grupo de guaguancó que llevó su nombre, Carlos Embale también grabó con el Conjunto de Guaguancó, con Los Nuevos Roncos y con Los Roncos Chiquitos. Fue amigo de algunos de los rumberos más notorios: Gonzalo Asencio *El Tío Tom*, Santo Ramírez *El Niño* y Alejandro Rodríguez *El mulatón*. El disco *Rumbero mayor*, publicado por la EGREM en 1992, recoge una selección representativa de su talento.

LOS INVESTIGADORES

Un viejo proverbio afirma que «el cubano se acuerda de Santa Bárbara cuando oye tronar». Quizá eso explique el porqué durante la segunda mitad del siglo XX se despertó una verdadera curiosidad por las creencias afrocubanas y su relación con la música. Dicho interés incluía el estudio de toda una mitología establecida alrededor de deidades como el oricha Changó, el gran guerrero yoruba, dueño del trueno, la virilidad, el fuego y los tambores, y el equivalente a Santa Bárbara en el santoral católico. ¿Cómo llegaron a difundirse estos complejos procesos, originalmente surgidos en los barracones de esclavos, en los cabildos y casas de culto, para enmascarar subrepticiamente a sus deidades bajo la advocación católica de sus amos?

Para responder a toda una serie de cuestiones relacionadas con la aportación del negro a la cultura cubana, incluyo este breve recuento de sus principales investigadores; aunque a menudo son citados en la prensa o en conferencias, poco se conoce de la obra de Fernando Ortiz, de Lydia Cabrera y de Jorge e Isabel Castellanos.

Fernando Ortiz (1881-1969), una de las grandes figuras de la cultura contemporánea en lengua española, antropólogo y etnólogo erudito, realizó una labor descomunal para el mejor conocimiento de la nacionalidad cubana. Arduo investigador y racionalista inconforme, defensor incansable del aporte africano, Ortiz fue pionero en el estudio y divulgación de la música afrocubana, vocablo que lanzó en 1906.

Halló sumas verdades al penetrar en los orígenes de esta música y su estrecha relación con los cultos religiosos. En 1936, y en medio de la indiferencia y antagonismo de la burguesía criolla, tuvo el inmenso valor de presentar su primera conferencia pública en la Universidad de La Habana: «La música religiosa de los yoruba entre los negros cubanos», ilustrada con olubatá y la voz de Merceditas Valdés. Para entonces, Ortiz ya había dedicado más de treinta años a la investigación rigurosa de la importante presencia negra. Al lector le interesará saber que los libros aquí comentados han sido editados en Madrid por Música Mundana Maqueda.

FERNANDO ORTIZ PINTADO POR JORGE ARCHE (1942).

Quisiera examinar brevemente tres obras seminales en la extensa bibliografía del sabio: *Los instrumentos de la música afrocubana*, *La africanía de la música cubana* y el extraordinario *Contrapunteo cubano del tabaco y el azúcar*. Entre 1952 y 1955, Ortiz se lanzó a producir los cinco tomos que formaron la edición original de *Los instrumentos*. Para esta ambiciosa obra organizó un trabajo original, de carácter estrictamente etnográfico, considerando y clasificando cada instrumento no sólo desde sus peculiaridades organográficas y su origen, sino que también examinó las confluencias culturales que determinaron su creación, su significación social y las peripecias que sufrieron los objetos surgidos de la imaginación africana en tierra cubana. No se limitó a catalogarlos de una manera convencional, lo cual hubiera resultado sumamente aburrido; enfocó el tema con una visión integral, rechazando simplismos y esquemas prejuiciosos.

En el capítulo X del volumen I, Ortiz reveló todo lo concerniente a los tambores de «fundamento», destacando la evolución y el poder mágico del tambor en varias culturas. Se adentró en el papel de los tambores xilofónicos y los aún más importantes tambores membranófonos en subsiguientes capítulos. No se le escapó nada, incluyendo un estudio sobre el *eribó*, un pequeño tambor que los ñáñigos nunca hacen sonar; sobre la membrana de este curioso artefacto, que tiene funciones sacramentales en la *makuba*, se deposita la cabeza del sacrificio. Colocado en el altar Abakuá, el *eribó* simboliza a Sikaneka, poderosa deidad femenina en la tradición ñáñiga. Decorado con simbólicas plumas verticales en las cuatro esquinas de la *anaforuana* dibujada en su piel de macho cabrío, el *eribó* es objeto de profunda reverencia por todos los ekobios.

Más de la mitad del volumen II está dedicada a tipos específicos de tambores, con consideraciones profundas sobre los tres tambores batá de la cultura yoruba. El resto de dicho volumen contiene información detallada sobre los instrumentos pulsativos, los fricativos, insuflativos y aeritivos.

¿Quién fue Fernando Ortiz? Hombre blanco, educado en Menorca, Madrid y Barcelona, regresó a su país de origen graduado como abogado y armado de fuertes convicciones, pero al escudriñar la vida cubana descubrió que sin el negro Cuba no sería Cuba. Logró revelar en artículos, monografías, conferencias y libros eruditos la importancia del africano en la sociedad cubana, en medio de la indiferencia de la burguesía blanca que despreciaba todo lo que tuviera que ver con el negro.

Este «ángel rebelde», que solía vestir de negro y usaba gruesas gafas, andaba con dificultad, llevando siempre consigo un bastón de carey, que también le servía para dar los tres golpes rituales a Elegguá al comenzar cualquiera de sus presentaciones públicas de los tambores afrocubanos. Fernando Ortiz se destacó como jurista, arqueólogo, lingüista e historiador. Fue también funcionario diplomático y miembro electo a la Cámara de Representantes entre 1917-27. Fundó importantes publicaciones así como sociedades de investigación del folclor musical y durante muchos años presidió la Sociedad Económica de Amigos del País, publicando desde 1910 hasta 1959 la *Revista Bimestre Cubano*, de enorme significación en la cultura nacional. Durante décadas, Ortiz fue el intelectual mejor conocido y respetado en círculos extranjeros; en 1955 se le organizó un homenaje internacional.

Recibía en su casa tanto a tamboreros y santeros como a intelectuales del patio o de ultramar, que participaban en sus habituales tertulias. Muy influido por el pensamiento de José Martí, mantenía un humor cáustico contra el oportunismo y la mojigatería. Desde su poltrona favorita, Ortiz solía lanzar audaces andanadas contra la corrupción nacional, contra los curas y la sumisión de la industria azucarera nacional a los intereses de Estados Unidos.

«Lo más expresivo de nuestra historia económica es en realidad ese contraste multiforme y persistente entre las dos producciones que han sido y son las más características de Cuba». Esta frase, escrita alrededor de 1940, está tomada de *Contrapunteo cubano del tabaco y el azúcar*, una obra clave para entender el desarrollo del país, y que muestra a un Fernando Ortiz luciendo sus mejores galas como apasionado prosista y defensor nacionalista.

Dividido en dos partes, el libro presenta una síntesis de la sociedad cubana pasada y presente (hasta 1940). La segunda parte viene en apoyo de la primera, y cubre temas específicos, elaborados con penetrante erudición. «El tabaco nace, el azúcar se hace... El tabaco es oscuro, de negro a mulato; el azúcar es clara, de mulata a blanca... El azúcar no huele; el tabaco vale por su olor y ofrece al olfato una infinidad de perfumes...»

El tabaco, que es natural de la isla, tenía un sentido sacramental de comunión que vinculaba a los aborígenes entre sí. Sin embargo, la caña de azúcar fue introducida por Colón en su segundo viaje al Caribe, sin sospechar que transplantaba las semillas de su historia económica. La mancha verde de los cañales, de los cañaduzales o de los cañamelares, se fue expandiendo sobre los antiguos cacicazgos indígenas. Usando una falsa denominación –cañaverales–, los primeros colonizadores confundieron la caña sacarífera con la ruin cañavera, que era carrizo, forraje para el ganado en España.

Cito: «La vitola es del tabaco "su figura"... En su origen ese vocablo, sacado de la jerga marinesca como muchos otros del lenguaje hispánico de América, significó el modelo por el cual en los arsenales se escantillaban las piezas para los ensambles en la arquitectura naval. Hoy día se aplica el vocablo vitola al anillo (adorno identificativo que llevan los puros)... Es un error; la vitola es la figura del tabaco puro, el anillo es sólo como su corbata de linaje». Y nos regala otro dato curioso: el sello de garantía con el escudo nacional, que todavía hoy se pega a las cajas de cigarros cubanos, fue establecido en 1931.

De los orígenes de la música cubana escribió mucho Fernando Ortiz. Diez años después de la aparición del *Contrapunteo*, se enfrascó en la publicación de libros clave para analizar el complejo panorama musical de la isla: *La africanía de la música folklórica de Cuba*, *Los bailes y el teatro de los negros en el folklore de Cuba* y *Los instrumentos de la música afrocubana*, ya comentado. *La africanía* es un libro sumamente revelador. En su primer capítulo, Ortiz desmenuzó las ilusorias teorías acerca de la música de los indocubanos y su pretendida influencia en el folclor (erróneo prejuicio que «impedía», entre muchos, el reconocimiento de las realidades étnicas de Cuba). Fue una manera de tratar de poner fin al racismo de los blancos que habían encontrado su mejor portavoz en la figura del sutil compositor Eduardo Sánchez de Fuentes, mencionado en la pág. 45.

Sin duda la obra más ardientemente defensora de los valores negros en la música folclórica de la isla, *La africanía* fue escrita con vehemencia de abogado; es posiblemente también la más claramente documentada. Fue publicada cuando el investigador tenía 69 años y había acumulado un verdadero caudal de información sobre el foclor negro a través de innumerables toques de tambor y conversaciones con tamboreros, olubatá e iyalochas.

Termino esta reseña reflexionando sobre el breve pero exigente dictamen que Fernando Ortiz legó a todo investigador: ciencia, conciencia y paciencia, porque seguramente carezco de más de una de esas cualidades.

Iniciada en el estudio del folclor africano por su cuñado Fernando Ortiz, fue **Lydia Cabrera** (1900-94) la encargada de plasmar lo fundamental en su obra cumbre, *El monte* (1954), cuyo valor se mantiene intacto como punto de partida para creyentes e investigadores. Dedicado a Ortiz, y escrito en su ya desaparecida villa Quinta San José, el libro está subtitulado *Igbó Finda. Ewe orisha. Vititi Nfinda (Notas sobre las religiones, la magia, las supersticiones y el folklore de los negros criollos y del pueblo de Cuba).*

¿Qué mejor manera de presentar su obra al lector que incluyendo aquí el testimonio de tres personas especializadas que la conocieron y admiraron profundamente? Para el voluminoso libro *Anaforuana. Ritual y símbolos de la iniciación en la sociedad secreta Abakuá* (1975), escribió el eminente sociólogo francés Roger Bastide:

El método de Lydia Cabrera es el de la no intervención. Sus libros, de cierto modo, le son dictados por negros viejos amigos y constituyen testimonios extraordinarios con su mezcla de africano y español. Son bloques de pensamiento, densos, totales, compactos, que se suceden según las leyes de la asociación y no de la lógica o del análisis. A menudo deploro que los africanistas no nos hayan dado este tipo de libros, sino aquellos en los que África está repensada a través de una mentalidad diferente, cuando no a través de una teoría académica. Necesitamos que se multipliquen estos documentos. Al etnólogo le toca interpretarlos en bruto.

Y añadía Bastide:

Nos parece que el mejor medio para un etnólogo que desee estudiar la civilización carabalí, sería el de ir a Cuba y allí hacerse iniciar primero en una agrupación de ñáñigos. Demostrando «que conoce» será recibido por sus hermanos negros de África y podrá realizar su encuesta sobre una base sólida. Este libro de Lydia Cabrera [se refiere a *Anaforuana*] le suministrará las preguntas que deberá hacer, qué terrenos explorar y el control de las informaciones que reciba.

LYDIA CABRERA E INFORMANTES (1956).

Entre 1973-75 tuve la suerte de diseñarle a Lydia tres libros clave durante los años que residió en Madrid: *La laguna sagrada de San Joaquín, Yemayá y Ochún* y el voluminoso *Anaforuana*. Fue una oportunidad única de acercarme a la tenaz investigadora y de aprender humildemente a través de largas conversaciones, siempre salpicadas de su mordaz sentido del humor entre las intervenciones de su compañera María Teresa Rojas. A punto de terminar la cubierta de *Yemayá y Ochún. Kariocha, iyálorichas y olorichas* (1974), Lydia me entregó un texto escrito por su amigo francés, el *fatumbi* Pierre Verger, que incluí en la contracubierta del libro:

Durante numerosos años, Lydia Cabrera ha recogido una documentación única de tradiciones orales africanas, fielmente conservadas en Cuba. Más que del paciente trabajo realizado por ella, y que nos da a conocer en sus obras, no es de su «trabajo» de lo que hay que hablar: es del impulso cordial hacia los africanos y sus descendientes lo que la llevó a interesarse en su estudio. No son sus libros un exponente frío y pedante de sus investigaciones, es una profunda integración espiritual en el mundo inmenso y poético de las mitologías africanas. Con *Yemayá y Ochún* nos abre un mundo encantado, el de las aguas primordiales, las saladas y dulces, puestas por los lucumís bajo la potestad de estas dos divinidades.

Me encontraba entonces en Madrid diseñando y produciendo los primeros nueve volúmenes de la *Enciclopedia de Cuba,* destinados a la comunidad en el exilio. A menudo frecuentaba la casa del poeta y periodista Gastón Baquero, quien me ayudaba a resolver muchos aspectos de mi encomienda. Mientras lo observaba teclear a toda velocidad y con sólo dos dedos en una vieja Remington, una fría mañana madrileña de 1973, Gastón me comentaba aspectos de la obra de Lydia que todavía lamento no haber grabado; terminar de redactar y salir juntos a desayunar ocurrió en un pis pas. Después usé aquel texto en la contracubierta de *La laguna sagrada de San Joaquín* (1973), obra dedicada al narrador Lino Novás Calvo, y que transcribo a continuación:

Un libro de la autora cubana Lydia Cabrera es una tentación para los interesados en el conocimiento profundo de ese poderoso ingrediente del ser americano que es el alma del negro. Quien no conozca a fondo la sensibilidad, la riqueza emotiva, el ingenio, la religiosidad sana y libre, y la imaginación fabuladora sin límites del africano transplantado al Nuevo Mundo, no puede conocer ninguna de las regiones de ese Nuevo Mundo. Estudiar deleitando al lector el aporte de lo mágico hecho por el negro a la formación de tantas naciones, pero excepcionalmente a las creadas en el Caribe, donde a la magia propia de las islas vino a sumarse la maravillada actitud del negro ante el universo, es la hermosa tarea a que ha consagrado su vida Lydia Cabrera. Desde la aparición resonante de *Cuentos negros de Cuba* (1948), hasta la emocionada narración de estos recuerdos de un viaje a la laguna sagrada de San Joaquín, un paradisíaco rincón de la isla-paraíso, Lydia Cabrera ha recorrido un vasto y fascinante territorio: el de la superviviente y viva espiritualidad de la gente africana llevada a las islas. La hazaña que realizara la autora de *El monte* al explicar, como no se había hecho jamás, la vinculación del hombre con las plantas, tiene su complemento en este análisis novelado de la actitud mágica de ese hombre ante las aguas. En todo el islario antillano, que es uno de los últimos panteones de los dioses que quedan en el mundo, y dondequiera haya gente con sensibilidad y apta para ver lo que hay debajo de un cuento graciosísimo o de una leyenda cargada de ingenua sabiduría, este libro de Lydia Cabrera ha de conmover y de fascinar. La Gran Iyalocha errante de Cuba, esa isla que ha sabido producir y exportar tanta fantasía –el humo del tabaco, la capitosidad del ron– llega en este libro a una cúspide tal de ternura y de compenetración con el alma del africano en América, que ríe riendo, llora llorando, nos entrega íntegra una espiritualidad, y nos enseña a comprender mejor a aquellos que convirtieron el dolor de sus vidas en una forma nueva y tenaz de religarse con la tierra y con el cielo.

Finalmente, quiero mencionar los cuatro volúmenes que publicaron entre 1988 y 1994, en Ediciones Universal de Miami, los investigadores **Jorge Castellanos** e **Isabel Castellanos**, binomio de padre e hija que se han dedicado durante largo tiempo al estudio de la cultura afrocubana. Los títulos comprenden: *El negro en Cuba (1492-1844), El negro en Cuba (1845-1959), Las religiones y las lenguas* y *Letras/Música/Arte.* En este cuarto y último volumen lograron establecer claramente que por su presencia decisiva el alma negra devino parte inseparable, tan inseparable como la blanca, del alma nacional.

Cuando apareció el primer tomo ambos autores recibieron merecidos elogios, entre otros de una de las personas que mejor conoció el archipiélago cubano, el historiador Leví Marrero: «...una obra notable por su organización, originalidad e información, que podemos desde ahora predecir que perdurará como un clásico en las ciencias sociales cubanas». Para el ensayista José I. Rasco, esta voluminosa obra: «...ha de ser lectura obligatoria para los que quieran investigar en el futuro sobre la transculturación étnica en nuestra patria... Mérito indiscutible de *Cultura afrocubana* es la riqueza documental que avala sus investigaciones, que indica búsqueda intensa por archivos y bibliotecas. La sobriedad corre pareja con la honestidad. El estilo, ameno y preciso».

Jorge Castellanos fue profesor de la Universidad de Oriente en Santiago de Cuba y, durante su largo exilio, alcanzó a ser profesor emérito de Marygrove College, en Detroit. Entre sus obras anteriores se encuentran *Tierra y nación* (1955), *La abolición de la esclavitud en Popayán* (Colombia, 1980), *Plácido: poeta social y político* (1984), así como numerosos ensayos y artículos literarios e históricos.

Su hija Isabel fue profesora de la Universidad del Valle en Cali, Colombia, de la Georgetown University en Washington, D.C. y es actualmente profesora de Lingüística en la Florida International University de Miami. Es autora de *Eleguá quiere tambó* (1980), *Fiestas de negros en el norte del Cauca: las adoraciones del Niño Dios* (1982), y coeditora del libro *En torno a Lydia Cabrera* (1987). También ha publicado diversos artículos sobre manifestaciones religiosas afroamericanas y acerca de las lenguas afrocubanas.

Además de los mencionados, entre otros estudiosos criollos de dentro y fuera de Cuba que han aportado valiosas experiencias y criterios sobre las religiones afrocubanas se encuentran Rómulo Lachatañeré, Juan Luis Martín, Pedro Deschamps Chapeaux, Enrique Sosa Rodríguez, Cándida Quesada, Mercedes Cros Sandoval, Walterio Carbonell, Miguel Barnet, Natalia Bolívar, Leovigildo López y Lázaro Ros, hijo de Oggún, y posiblemente el mejor *akpuón* (solista) en lengua yoruba.

3. EL DECENIO FABULOSO: 1950-60

> Esta polirritmia de planos y metros se observa no sólo
> en la música, la danza, el canto, las artes plásticas, sino
> también en la cocina –el ajiaco–, en la arquitectura, en la
> poesía, en la novela, en el teatro, en la expresión corpo-
> ral, en las creencias religiosas, en la idiosincrasia.
>
> Antonio Benítez Rojo
> *La isla que se repite*, Barcelona, 1998

No hay nada de superficilidad en el título escogido para este capítulo; lo defino así por la creatividad que se manifestó en todos los órdenes durante dicho período, no sólo por el desarrollo e intensidad que alcanzaron las actividades musicales. Fue una década en que el fenómeno sociocultural de la criollización alcanzó momentos de complejidad asombrosos. Había entonces un creciente boom turístico y se construyeron hoteles y clubes donde los músicos encontraban trabajo; a pesar de múltiples contradicciones, todo inducía a divertirse. Se confirmaba así la fama que había adquirido La Habana ante los ojos de gran parte de los viajeros que la visitaron en la segunda mitad del siglo XIX.

Sin embargo, en dicha década la sociedad vivía dos revoluciones simultáneas: una tenía que ver con las ambiciones políticas y se dirimía en las calles a tiros, mientras el campesinado sufría miseria y la mafia norteamericana imperaba en los hoteles habaneros. Pero había otra, una revolución mucho más prometedora y profunda, que avanzaba paulatinamente en la esfera de la cultura y la economía. A pesar del golpe de Estado de Fulgencio Batista (10 de marzo de 1952) y de su entrega de los negocios ilegales a los bandidos del Norte, la iniciativa y creatividad del pueblo cubano alcanzó niveles muy altos en la medicina, la arquitectura, las comunicaciones, la educación y la creatividad literaria, las artes plásticas y por supuesto, en la música. Desgraciadamente, estos avances no son suficientemente conocidos por la inmensa mayoría de hispanohablantes.

De hecho, nunca me he encontrado a un «progre» español o latinoamericano que siquiera manejara lo más elemental de la historia y la economía cubanas, más allá de los lugares comunes y las medias verdades repetidas hasta la saciedad por la maquinaria propagandística de Castro. Que supiera –y aceptara, por ejemplo– que en los años 50 Cuba ocupaba el segundo lugar entre los países hispanos en cuanto al PIB. Hasta el partido de los comunistas (Partido Socialista Popular) se vio en la necesidad de redactar una resolución, en plena dictadura de Batista, según la cual si bien había en el país una profunda crisis política, no se podía hablar de crisis económica; de hecho, mientras criticaban la acción armada de Castro en Sierra Maestra, los comunistas pactaron con Batista acogiéndose a su supuesto populismo.

Los que todavía hablan mal de la «época americana» no saben que la economía cubana de los años 50 estaba menos subordinada a la norteamericana de lo que vino a depender de la soviética veinte años después, una atadura a la que estuvo sujeta la revolución hasta el desenlace de la *perestroika* y el derrumbe del sistema comunista en la Unión Soviética (URSS) y sus satélites en 1989. Ignoran estos críticos del período anterior a Castro que tres cuartas partes de la industria azucarera estaba para entonces en manos cubanas y que uno de los mayores males de la economía, el monocultivo de la caña, resultó ser un mal menor en comparación con lo que supuso la dependencia del azúcar en la época castrista: sin azúcar, el régimen no recibía petróleo de la antigua URSS.

A pesar de lo derruida que ahora aparece La Habana (no sólo el sector más antiguo) ante los tristes ojos de nativos y turistas, la ciudad se encontraba entonces en condiciones óptimas. Un considerable número de edificios públicos y privados en varias zonas capitalinas, que todavía denotan cierta opulencia y modernidad, fueron levantados durante el período 1950-60. Obras realizadas con capital, ingenieros y arquitectos cubanos, incluyendo los túneles y el imponente conjunto, muy fotografiado, de la plaza de la revolución: Biblioteca Nacional, Teatro Nacional, varios ministerios, el monumento a Martí, etc.

En cuanto al analfabetismo, es cierto que existía, pero en menor proporción de lo que nos quieren hacer creer aquellos que se imaginan un pasado prerrevolucionario totalmente subdesarrollado. De hecho, Cuba era entonces uno de los países más alfabetizados de América, sólo adelantado por Argentina y Uruguay.

Esto no quiere decir que las cosas iban bien en el país y mucho menos que pretendo justificar la época batistiana, régimen corrupto y represivo hasta la médula. Sin duda hacía falta una revolución, y ésta se hizo realidad en enero de 1959. A pesar de pretender industrializar un país que carece de fuerza hidráulica, o entregarle la tierra a los campesinos para luego quitársela con el propósito de formar enormes granjas estatales tipo koljós soviéticos, la revolución comenzó bien, hasta que Castro dio un giro de noventa grados que apuntaba hacia la URSS. Es decir, cuando la posibilidad de desarrollar una economía agrícola diversa y establecer una industria ligera pujante fue sustituida por el marxismo utópico dentro de un capitalismo de Estado. Y en eso tuvo bastante que ver la ceguera de Einsehower, de Nixon y de los presidentes que les sucedieron, que no supieron asimilar el reclamo de un líder joven y sumamente orgulloso, renuente a claudicar en medio de una guerra fría que no parecía admitir términos medios.

Un breve recuento

El éxito alcanzado por el bolero, el danzón y el son desde la década de 1920, dentro y fuera de Cuba, había incentivado el progreso de los músicos. De ahí en adelante no se trataba tan sólo de crear nuevos géneros, sino de organizar formatos musicales diferentes y esmerar la instrumentación e interpretación de diversos estilos. A pesar de los intereses comerciales, esta gestación coincidió con un resurgir de todo lo autóctono, una necesaria vuelta a las raíces. Los tambores batá fueron sacados de los altares en los años 30, y comenzó a tratarse el folclor con la atención debida. Mucho contribuyeron a este fin la serie de conferencias ilustradas con tamboreros *olubatá* que organizara Fernando Ortiz, en que voces informadas, como la de **Merceditas Valdés** (1928-96), demostraron la riqueza intrínseca de los cánticos rituales. Paralelamente, Amadeo Roldán y Alejandro García Caturla habían iniciado una escuela nacionalista de vanguardia desde la Orquesta Filarmónica, incorporando valores rítmicos, melódicos y tímbricos a instrumentos afrocubanos. Poco después, la rumba guaguancó logró escaparse de las barriadas portuarias y andaba trastornando el mundo por los salones de Tropicana y los escenarios de lujosos hoteles.

Mientras que Antonio Arcaño marcaba el gusto de los bailadores con el nuevo danzón, el dúo de Celina y Reutilio encendía una brecha con sabor lucumí dentro de la música campesina. Sentado al piano, *Bola de Nieve* cantaba como un *crooner*, como un *diseur* francés. Varias voces y conjuntos llenaban las ondas de boleros melosos, y el dúo de las Hermanas Martí mantenía presentes ante el pueblo las mejores canciones de la trova tradicional. Por su parte, el filin continuaba ganándose adeptos en los pequeños clubes habaneros, en tanto que Pérez Prado originaba mambos estrepitosos desde México. Allí triunfaron también, en el cine y en teatros, hermosas rumberas cubanas, y pienso mayormente en Ninón Sevilla y en Rosa Carmina, entre otras. Iniciada en la «Corte Suprema del Arte» como Olga Guillot, la voz de Merceditas Valdés insistía en lo afrocubano, triunfando plenamente cuando se presentó en 1951 en la *Rapsodia negra*, dirigida por Ennrique González Mantici desde CMQ Radio. Dos años después apareció el chachachá del brazo de *La engañadora*, para contagiar al pueblo con nuevos pasos coreográficos.

LA CANTANTE MERCEDITAS VALDÉS.

Era el resultado −aclara Díaz Ayala− de un continuo proceso dialéctico de tesis, antítesis y síntesis en que surgieron ritmos y tendencias que remozaron el patrimonio musical hacia finales de los años 40 y comienzos de los 50. A pesar de la dictadura instaurada en 1952, la población prefirió asistir más que participar. No hubo ninguna huelga general, ningún movimiento masivo de resistencia, aunque por supuesto, cada vez fueron más numerosos los que reclamaban la dimisión de Batista, y apoyaban o expresaban su solidaridad con los rebeldes que peleaban desde finales de 1956 en distintas zonas montañosas de la isla.

La Habana vieja y las principales barriadas de la capital estaban entonces en todo su esplendor. Ciudad «necesaria y fatal», en palabras del poeta José Lezama Lima, desde el golpe de Estado de Batista hasta la proclamación del carácter socialista de la revolución en 1961, la capital vivió una década prodigiosa pero sangrienta, un período clave para comprender el presente cubano. Antiguo sargento autoascendido a general, Batista se convirtió en un dictador oportunista, un listillo ladrón, populista y demagogo, que en la última etapa de su control del país incrementó su carácter sanguinario.

En 1952, al arrebatarle el poder a Carlos Prío Socarrás, pocos meses antes de la celebración de elecciones, no fueron tantos los cubanos que se dieron cuenta de que una herida mortal le había sido asestada al proceso democrático y a la Constitución de 1940. Pretendiendo terminar con el latrocinio de gobiernos anteriores, Batista entronizó una corrupción aún mayor. En una Habana rutilante llena de lujo e intrigas, y de casinos dominados por mafiosos como Meyer Lansky y Santos Trafficante, los centros de placer se desplazaron de la Habana vieja a la americanizada barriada del Vedado, cuajada de hoteles de lujo y rascacielos. Pululaban los cabarés, los night clubs, los teatros y conciertos de música clásica. Todos repletos. Tropicana vivió entonces sus años estelares con las creaciones del coreógrafo Rodney. No había jineteras pero sí una zona rosa donde las putas profesionales abrazaban tanto a los nativos como a los marineros norteamericanos. Los músicos tenían trabajo y las principales ciudades no aparentaban tener problemas, a pesar de la miseria de los campos; por otra parte, apenas tuvieron efecto las explosiones de bombas y las fotos de cadáveres publicadas en una prensa libre. Mientras la televisión hacía gala de inolvidables programas musicales, con Fidel Castro alzado en Sierra Maestra, todo el mundo hablaba de revolución.

El término revolución era fascinante. Suscitaba ecos de una esperanza largo tiempo reclamada que pretendía tender un puente mágico que reivindicara el espíritu de las guerras de independencia del siglo XIX contra España, avivadas por el verbo brillante de José Martí, que nunca dejó de luchar por la revolución hasta su muerte en acción en 1895. Más reciente en la memoria popular, la lucha contra el dictador Gerardo Machado durante los años 1930-33, también convertida en revolución, destapó ansias irreprimibles de alcanzar finalmente una transformación con todas las de la ley. Sin embargo, la conspiración cuartelaria de Batista enseguida adoptó el nombre de «revolución»; entre 1952 y 1958 tuvo que enfrentar un número de ataques suicidas contra él y contra su ejército.

Entre la síncopa del mambo y las cadencias del chachachá que se escuchaban en todas las gramolas del país, seguidos de boleros de carácter arrabalero, se sucedieron varios asaltos a instalaciones militares, siendo el primero y más significativo el realizado el 26 de julio de 1953 por decenas de ilusionados jóvenes liderados por Fidel Castro Ruz, entonces un abogado de 27 años, al cuartel Moncada en Santiago de Cuba. La dura represión ordenada por Batista transformó a los asaltantes en mártires. Meses después, Castro convirtió su derrota en una victoria política gracias a un largo discurso-programa titulado «La historia me absolverá», que presentó como autodefensa en el juicio que siguió al asalto. Enviado a la cárcel por 15 años y hombre libre dos años después gracias a una generosa amnistía política de Batista (quien olvidó el viejo refrán criollo «El que no oye consejos, palos le dará la vida»), Fidel Castro se marchó a México. Allí entrenó sobre las armas a sus seguidores y organizó una «invasión» que al final consistió en 82 hombres mareados a bordo del yate *Granma,* haciendo la travesía desde el puerto de Veracruz hasta la costa sudoriental de Cuba. Era diciembre de 1956. A poco de desembarcar, el previsible desastre casi extermina a los integrantes de aquella expedición bajo las ametralladoras de los aviones del dictador. Con once compañeros supervivientes, entre los que se encontraban su hermano Raúl y Che Guevara, que iba en el contingente como médico, comenzó el mito de Fidel Castro y su guerrilla en Sierra Maestra.

Así las cosas, a algunos seguidores del régimen de Batista se les ocurrió organizar un festival titulado «50 Años de Música Cubana». Un avión de Cubana transportó a decenas de músicos de Nueva York, incluyendo a Mario Bauzá, la orquesta completa de Frank Grillo *Machito,* a Arsenio Rodríguez, *Chino* Pozo (primo del fallecido *Chano*) y a Alberto Socarrás. De España invitaron a Antonio Machín, y Miguelito Valdés voló desde México. Esperándolos en La Habana para actuar ante aquella pléyade de musicos desconocidos por las nuevas generaciones, estaban Benny Moré, Rolando Laserie y la Sonora Matancera con su cantante Celia Cruz. En ese momento se encontraba en el país Nat King Cole, buscando a Bebo Valdés para que le orquestara un álbum con boleros cubanos. Se sucedieron los encuentros, las ceremonias de premios, los conciertos, jam sessions y banquetes. Según me contó *Machito* muchos años después en Nueva York con su habitual modestia: «Fue un momento glorioso para Cuba».

Los últimos días de Batista son bastante conocidos: aterrorizado por los evidentes reveses militares, abandonó abruptamente el país la Nochevieja de 1958, y Castro y sus barbudos hicieron su entrada triunfal en La Habana, que entonces era una fiesta, el 8 de enero de 1959. Entre los números que más se escuchaban en aquellos días, pronto apareció un sonsonete de Carlos Puebla que repetía: «Y se acabó la diversión, llegó el Comandante y mandó a parar». Y todo se detuvo. Los tiempos habían cambiado, y el derrotero de la nación y su música también.

EL BOLERO

La canción romántica hecha ritmo se siguió cultivando con exquisita creatividad especialmente en el primer decenio del período estudiado. Remozado por el filin, cuyo aporte se discute más adelante, el bolero tradicional fue tratado por compositores cualificados y otros autores que, aunque autodidactas, también supieron concebir melodías inolvidables. Nuevas voces alcanzaron a interpretarlo con emoción, renovando estilos aunque siempre respetando su esencia; se hicieron aportes considerables en su ámbito temático, mejorando los aspectos melódicos, armónicos y muy especialmente su instrumentación. Entre 1950 y 1962, solistas, tríos, cuartetos, conjuntos y orquestas dejaron constancia de su pujanza como un modo de comunicación idóneo para expresar los sentimientos de la pareja, para decir el amor, la emoción del recuerdo y la ilusión del futuro.

Entre los compositores más sobresalientes de dicho período seleccionaré a **Osvaldo Farrés** (*Toda una vida, Tres palabras, Acércate más, Quizás, quizás*); **René Touzet** (*No te importe saber, Anoche aprendí, La noche de anoche*); **Adolfo Guzmán** (*No puedo ser feliz, Cuando tú me quieras, No es posible querer tanto*); **Mario Fernández Porta** (*Mentiras tuyas, Qué me importa*); **Luis Marquetti** (*Entre espumas, Plazos traicioneros, Allí donde tú sabes*); **Fernando Mulens** (*De corazón a corazón, Qué te pedí*); **Orlando de la Rosa** (*Nuestras vidas, Mi corazón es para ti*); **José Dolores Quiñones** (*Vendaval sin rumbo, Los aretes de la luna, Camarera del amor*); **Bobby Collazo** (*La última noche*); **Marcelino Guerra Rapindey** (*Convergencia, A mi manera*); **Julio Gutiérrez** (*Un poquito de tu amor, Inolvidable*); **Ernesto Duarte** (*Cómo fue, Bájate de esa nube*); **Juan Arrondo** (*Fiebre de ti, Qué pena me da*); **Ramón Cabrera** (*Tu voz*); **Pedro Vega** (*Herido de sombras, Hoy como ayer*) y **Benny Moré** (*Amor fugaz, Ahora soy tan feliz*).

Un rápido recuento arroja que la mayor parte de los boleros de estos y otros autores alcanzó la expresión de sus ideas musicales por medio de las palabras, y no como dicen algunos hoy día, por la consonancia entre las voces. Es más, se preocuparon por perfeccionar dos prácticas musicales bien diferenciadas: la primera persiguió la armonía, situada para ello en una posición de superioridad sobre las palabras. La segunda, por el contrario, buscó la perfección de la melodía, por lo que el texto se convirtió en el amo de la armonía y no en su siervo.

Las composiciones de **Osvaldo Farrés** (1902-85) siempre han sido muy cantadas en España, especialmente *Toda una vida* y *Madrecita*, en la voz del inolvidable Antonio Machín. Farrés fue un autodidacta musical que se dedicaba al dibujo publicitario; eso no evitó que se transformara en uno de los más notables autores a pesar de haber comenzado cuando ya tenía 35 años. Mucha gente conoce la anécdota de uno de sus boleros más apreciados: en 1947 la cantante mexicana Chela Campos le pidió

una canción para estrenarla, y ante las excusas y evasivas de Farrés le insistió: «Pero maestro, si con tres palabras usted hace una canción». Y el resultado fue *Tres palabras*, que con el nombre de *Without you* apareció en la película *Make mine music*. ¿Y quién no conoce *Aquellos ojos verdes,* de **Nilo Menéndez** (1902-87) o ha cantado *Mira que eres linda,* de **Julio Brito** (1908-68). Pero hay otros boleros que también se ganaron el corazón de los españoles: *Un poquito de tu amor*, de **Julio Gutiérrez** (1912-90), bolero con acento mambeado que se convirtió en un éxito desde principios de los años 50. Y cuando surgieron las *Dos gardenias,* de **Isolina Carrillo,** la gente las tenía constantemente en los labios gracias al ojo mágico de los aparatos Telefunken, Radiola o Marconi que, sintonizados en la onda media, ofrecían canciones que prendían inmediatamente.

OSVALDO FARRÉS.

La última noche, canción cumbre del siempre sonriente **Bobby Collazo** (1916-89), fue originalmente grabada por Orlando Guerra *Cascarita* en 1947 con el acompañamiento de la Orquesta Casino de la Playa. Se trata de otro bolero-mambo con arreglo del propio Pérez Prado, que le permitió a *Cascarita* lucirse, y que aquí lo conoce todo el mundo. Y debido a las frecuentes presentaciones de Olga Guillot, el público se familiarizó con algunos temas de **René Touzet** (1916) como «La noche de anoche

/ qué noche la de anoche / tantas cosas de momento sucedieron / que me confundieron...» Hace poco estaba yo esperando mi turno en una panadería madrileña cuando entró un joven de unos 26 años tarareando «Camarera, camarera / tú eres la camarera de mi amor...», del autor **José Dolores Quiñones** (1918), autor también de *Los aretes de la luna* y de *Vendaval sin rumbo*.

Entre muchos otros, todos estos boleros tuvieron en Cuba una difusión extraordinaria en la radio, la televisión y espectáculos en vivo. Las gramolas de barrio se llenaban de monedas con melodías debidas a las voces de **Vicentico Valdés, Olga Guillot, Tito Gómez, Bienvenido Granda, Orlando Vallejo, Roberto Faz, Fernando Albuerne, Lino Borges, Fernando Álvarez, Blanca Rosa Gil, Rolando Laserie** y **Orlando Contreras**, entre otros destacados cantantes.

ORLANDO CONTRERAS.

Sin embargo, a nivel internacional el bolero comenzó a sufrir a mediados de los años 60 una marcada marginación de los centros principales de explotación musical y de los focos de irradiación de los medios de comunicación en aras de la promoción, a menudo llegando a la saturación, de géneros como la balada, el rock y otros estilos híbridos. Por supuesto que la música, como todo arte, requiere de una renovación constante, no se puede vivir apegado al nostálgico pasado, eternizándolo. Pero el bolero, como pocas maneras cancioneriles, siempre ha contado con las condiciones necesarias para encontrar un espacio romántico en cada generación.

En los años 60 continuaron su carrera importantes boleristas de antaño, algunos de los cuales terminaron exiliados. Aún durante la aceleración de la penetración musical yanqui en casi todos los países del mundo, los mejores boleros cubanos continuaron siendo difundidos ampliamente en el exterior, pero casi dejaron de escucharse en la isla. Esto coincidió con la profusión de subproductos de vida efímera como el yeyé, el surf, el monkey, el shake y otros. Después, entre los años 70 y 80 surgieron nuevos valores, dispuestos a rescatar la canción romántica, pero sin el complejo vitamínico de sus predecesores, entre los que vale mencionar a **Osvaldo Rodríguez** (*El amor se acaba*), **Amaury Pérez** (*Quédate este* *bolero*), **Pablo Milanés** (*El breve espacio en que no estás*) y **Alfredo Ro-dríguez** (*Un bolerón*). No hay duda de que el género sufrió una marcada decadencia en la isla en dichos decenios tenebrosos, retomando cierta vigencia en la segunda mitad de los 80, cuando se cumplieron cien años de haberse concebido el primer bolero por el santiaguero **Pepe Sánchez** (1856-1918), y el flautista **José Loyola** logró organizar el Primer Festival del Bolero en La Habana en 1987.

El fenómeno tuvo mucho que ver con los festivales que otros países latinoamericanos organizaron para celebrarlo. Todo lo cual dio pie a un interesante *revival* que tuvo bastante que ver con el grado de saturación de las letras insulsas y prefabricadas que ofrecían infinidad de baladas y la canción rock.

En *El Libro del Bolero* presento una amplia perspectiva de la influencia del género romántico cubano en el mundo de habla hispana. Aceptando el reto artístico y fraternal que a través de varios decenios ha recibido de México, un país generador de melodías de excelente factura, en Cuba se distinguieron decenas de compositores y cantantes, músicos que vistieron de gala al bolero. Quizá sin pretenderlo, el surgimiento del estilo filin sirvió de respuesta a la avalancha de temas románticos que continuaba exportando México, cuyos creadores nunca bajaron la guardia.

Los mejores: ISOLINA CARRILLO

Entre las autoras cualificadas más elocuentes quedará por siempre Isolina Carrillo (1907-96), con *Dos gardenias*, aquel bolerazo de 1948, grabado por el puertorriqueño Daniel Santos al año siguiente, acompañado de la Sonora Matancera y que le ha dado la vuelta al mundo.

Después de Cuba, *Dos gardenias* esparció su aroma musical en México en las voces de Pedro Vargas, Toña la Negra, Jorge Negrete, María Luisa Landín y otros, convirtiéndose allí en algo parecido a un

ISOLINA CARRILLO.

himno nacional; con ese bolero ganó Isolina el premio Ariel en 1952 por mantenerse en el primer lugar dos años consecutivos. Nat King Cole también lo grabó.

¿Cómo imaginar la música cubana sin ella, sin su infatigable contribución a desarrollar nuevos talentos, sin *Sombra que besa* o *Increíble*? Isolina comenzó a componer a instancias de Amado Trinidad, propietario de la RHC Cadena Azul, una de las radios más poderosas de la época. Había empezado a trabajar allí en 1937 y era conocida como «la negrita de los 600 pesos», un sueldo considerable para la época, contratada entre otras funciones para formar artistas, entre los que se encontraron las noveles Celia Cruz y Olga Guillot. Fue precisamente esta última quien le cantó *Miedo de ti*, su primer bolero.

En 1932 Isolina Carrillo fundó las Trovadoras del Cayo, uno de los primeros septetos femeninos, donde tuvo que tocar piano, trompeta, güiro, contrabajo y hasta bongó. Cantó luego en el cuarteto Siboney de Facundo Rivero, y realizó una constante labor como pianista acompañante en el programa radial «La Corte Suprema del Arte», donde se daban oportunidades a jóvenes talentos.

Isolina fue la primera en escribir *jingles* comerciales para la radio: no le pagaban mal cuando inventaba aquello de «*Camay embellece, desde la primera pastilla...*», incluyendo cuñas musicales para Palmolive, el chocolate La Estrella, Milo, Max Factor y muchos productos más. Desde ese momento, los anuncios radiofónicos se convirtieron en otra fuente de trabajo para algunos músicos.

Le gustaba relatar que con 9 años, su padre la había sentado ante el piano de un cine y desde entonces su vida fue sólo la música. «Recuerdo que en ese tiempo en la mayoría de las casas había un piano. Donde no lo hubiera o no lo tocaran era una casa vacía, mustia», declaró mucho después. En sus últimos años se distinguió como directora de coros y trabajó como repertorista en el Instituto Cubano de Radio y Televisión. Entre las múltiples grabaciones de *Dos gardenias* debo mencionar, por supuesto, la que hiciera Antonio Machín poco antes de fallecer.

De nuevo USA

Viajero incansable, afrancesado y gay hasta la médula, en 1934 Cole Porter, evidentemente impresionado por los ritmos cubanos, recorría con dedos nerviosos la partitura ante sus ojos. Vivía entonces rodeado del art déco del lujoso hotel Waldorf Astoria. La editora musical Harm, de Nueva York, le acababa de publicar el mundialmente conocido *Begin the beguine*, melodía grabada por Xavier Cugat en 1935, que nunca fue tan famosa como la orquestación que le hiciera Artie Shaw en 1938 en tiempo de swing. Una figuración equivalente a ocho semicorcheas en cada compás, trascendiendo la tranquila armonía de la tríada con un atractivo tratamiento armónico-melódico bastaron para impresionar a autores mexicanos y cubanos, que captaron en el ritmo semitropicalizado del *beguine* el aliento del bolero. En la isla, este estilo fue ampliamente cultivado por Julio Gutiérrez, Mario Fernández Porta, Orlando de la Rosa, Candito Ruiz y Juan Bruno Tarraza.

Valga aclarar que en Hispanoamérica, durante la época de su apogeo, cualquier canción romántica de calidad fue transmutada en bolero. Así escuchamos como tales algunos tangos y valses argentinos, canciones country y varios blues. En este interesante proceso de trasvase y transfusión colaboraron compositoras del calibre de Isolina Carrillo con *Again* y *Mam'selle*, y otras no menos meritorias.

El bolero baila con otros

Si recorremos el arco de influencia del bolero, se hará evidente cómo en México se mezcló con la ranchera a mediados de los años 50, fusión que culminó en el estilo de Javier Solís y Vicente Fernández, entre otros, y las importantes creaciones de Rubén Fuentes y José Alfredo Jiménez. Y mientras se mantenía vigente en los medios latinos de Norteamérica, en España, en medio de las ilusiones que creaban entre los jóvenes los boleros interpretados por Antonio Machín, comenzaron a irrumpir otras versiones, adheridas a grupos de música pop. Ni siquiera los Beatles se vieron libres de su influjo métrico y sonoro: tengo en vídeo una grabación que realizaron los chicos de Liverpool del famoso bolero *Bésame mucho*, de Chelo Velázquez.

Mucho después, en los años 80, la llamada «salsa erótica» no fue más que el bolero arrabalero puesto en un *tempo* rápido. Es necesario considerar además las innovaciones que aportaron Yordano di Marzo y especialmente el dominicano Juan Luis Guerra con sus boleros bachata (equivalente al bolero tradicional cubano), en una época en que la voz del brasileño Roberto Carlos ocupaba la atención de muchos por su versión del bolero-balada. Más recientemente, mientras el catalán Dyango entregaba *Corazón de bolero* y Moncho (Ramón Calabuch Batista) sacó *Quédate conmigo*, un disco que incluye colaboraciones de Joan Manuel Serrat, Ketama, Mayte Martín y el guajiro cubano Elíades Ochoa, desde México el joven Luis Miguel comenzó a revivir piezas antológicas con un estilo muy atractivo.

La canción romántica originada en la isla continuó penetrando el corazón de los españoles: el espectáculo «Antología del bolero» llegó en 1993, dirigido por Rey Montesinos, bajo cuya tutela han pasado las orquestas del cabaré Tropicana y de la Radio Televisión Cubana. Recorrió medio país y en Madrid se presentó con gran éxito en el teatro Calderón, gracias a las voces de Ricardito, Magalys Gainza y María Antonieta, pero muy especialmente a la de **Luis Téllez** (1951), que sabe dar vida a sus canciones. Formado musicalmente en el ambiente familiar de su nativa Santiago, es graduado del Instituto Superior de Arte y durante años actuó en Tropicana. Téllez tuvo como mentores a los notables compositores Isolina Carrillo y Adolfo Guzmán. Ahora trabaja desde Madrid.

EL COMPOSITOR ADOLFO GUZMÁN.

El bolero reapareció también en dos películas tremendas de Pedro Almodóvar: *Tacones lejanos* y *Mujeres al borde de un ataque de nervios,* con la innconfundible voz de La Lupe entonando *Puro teatro.* Ya en 1991 la cinta mexicana *Danzón* había incluido una respetable dosis de ellos; poco después, la película venezolana *Señora Bolero* presentó un buen número. Y en *Los reyes del mambo...* se escuchó la voz de Benny Moré cantando *Cómo fue*, de Ernesto Duarte, y a Linda Ronstadt en *Perfidia* y *Frenesí,* del mexicano Alberto Domínguez, posiblemente lo mejor del filme.

El álbum *Boleros de toda una vida*, publicado en España en 1998, reveló la voz convincente del veterano **Reinaldo Creagh,** uno de los miembros de la Vieja Trova Santiaguera, que incluye el tema *No tienes*

Los mejores: BOLA DE NIEVE

Imposible hablar de la música cubana sin
pensar en Guanabacoa: un municipio tan
cercano a la capital y a la vez un reino congo en sí mismo. De sus derruidas casas sola-
riegas de rejas hasta el piso sobreviven ecos
de voces y pianos; más allá, donde el abandono actual de las calles se convierte en un
interminable bache, donde milagrosamente
permanecen en pie algunas de las modestas
viviendas de extramuros, todavía se escu-

BOLA DE NIEVE.

chan misteriosos cantos de un antiguo cabildo que insiste en seguir agarrado a
la historia. Más abajo retumban los toques de palo o una rumba de cajón.

Con pocos años de diferencia entre sus respectivos nacimientos, allí crecieron y comenzaron a hacer su música algunos de los principales artistas cubanos:
el maestro Ernesto Lecuona, la cantante Rita Montaner, los pianistas clásicos
José Echániz y los hermanos Bolet, los compositores Mario Fernández Porta,
Juan Arrondo e Ignacio Villa, cuya voz fue internacionalmente conocida como
la de *Bola de Nieve* (1911-71).

Con un estilo inconfundible y una vocecilla de tiple, su versatilidad le hizo
interpretar obras en catalán (el villancico *Lo desembre congelat*), francés (*Les
feuilles mortes*), italiano (*Monsterio de Santa Chiara*), portugúes (*Bahía* de Ary
Barroso) e inglés (*Be careful, it's my heart*, de Irving Berlin), siempre acompañado de su piano. *Bola* explicaba que al interpretar una canción ajena no la sentía así, porque la hacía suya; prueba de ello es su antológica interpretación de
La flor de la canela, de la peruana Chabuca Granda.

Camilo José Cela creía que «*Bola de Nieve* era un poeta franciscano pasado por el trópico, un espíritu delicadísimo y elemental que sonreía siempre con
dulzura»; y el poeta chileno Pablo Neruda afirmó: «Se casó con la música y vivía con ella en esa intimidad de pianos y cascabeles, tirándose por la cabeza los
teclados del cielo».

Ignacito era un niño gordo y simpático al que le pusieron el mote cuando
repartía comidas en casas de su barriada. De su madre Inés (famosa por su cocina
criolla) y de su abuela Mamaquica (criada entre antiguos esclavos congos y cara-
balíes) recibió los primeros alientos pianísticos. En realidad estudió poco su instrumento. El guitarrista *Guyún* (Vicente González Rubiera) le orientó en la busca

de un repertorio adecuado a su voz de timbre áspero; le enseñó algo de armonía y los tumbaos de los aires negros. La ayuda que le brindó Ernesto Lecuona también fue decisiva en su carrera; el maestro sabía que como él, *Bola* estaba en el vórtice de un movimiento de revalorización cultural nacido en los años 30, de una batalla por la independencia artística cuyo marco preparó el sabio Fernando Ortiz.

Años después, 1933 para ser preciso, acompañando a Rita Montaner (1900-58) en un teatro mexicano, «La Única» lo presentó públicamente con el apodo que le acompañaría el resto de su vida artística, a pesar de ser más negro que una noche sin luna. Dicen que nunca se lo perdonó.

Bola elevó el tango congo a nivel de concierto al interpretar piezas de Eliseo Grenet como *Espabílate* y la canción de cuna *Drume negrita*. Hizo famosos a *Quirino con su tres*, *Yambambó* y *Vito Manué*, tres números con sabor humorístico de Emilio Grenet, hermano del anterior. Gilberto Valdés le entregó *Baró*, lamento de un calesero africano, y los pregones *El botellero* y *Ecó*, un nombre negro para un manjar hecho de la masa del maíz, que los blancos llaman tamal y que cuando se ofrece en el altar de algún oricha se conoce como *olelé*. Del mismo autor grabó varias versiones de *Ogguere*, canción de cuna con un compás de afro muy lento.

Gran conversador, le recuerdo junto al piano, mirando de soslayo mientras se reía, ante un público que siempre lo recibía como a un hechicero que podía hacer lo que se le antojara. La noche del 21 de noviembre de 1948, en el auditorio del Carnegie Hall de Manhattan, los vítores le obligaron a salir a saludar nueve veces; la prensa neoyorquina se rindió ante aquel cubano de 37 años al que comparaban con Maurice Chevalier y Nat King Cole.

Bola de Nieve escribió canciones preciosas, incluyendo *Tú me has de querer*, *¡Ay, amor!*, *Si me pudieras querer* y *No dejes que te olvide*. Alargaba las notas, otras las dejaba en un suspenso cargado de ansiedad. En realidad, no le importaba salirse del compás: él llevaba su propio ritmo, que le servía para acentuar la emotividad de la canción.

En los años 60 grabó con notable sensibilidad *Tú no sospechas*, de la sutil autora de filin Marta Valdés. Entre otras interpretaciones antológicas se encuentran también *Corazón*, de Sánchez de Fuentes, *No te importe saber*, de René Touzet, *No puedo ser feliz*, de Adolfo Guzmán y *Tres motivos de son*, con versos de Nicolás Guillén y música de Emilio Grenet. *Bola de Nieve* falleció en México, la tierra que acogió sus primeras presentaciones profesionales, durante una gira artística. Fue un verdadero «artista mundial», como dijera en *Messié Julián*, un número escrito especialmente para él por Armando Oréfiche.

corazón, de Armando Valdespí, compositor que vivió largos años en Estados Unidos.

De la versátil Gloria Estefan, exiliada en Miami desde niña, llegaron a España a mediados de los años 90 hermosos boleros de estructura clásica cantados en su estilo pastoso y sensual. La pequeña artista tiene talento y arrastre, y es sin duda la voz cubana que más se ha escuchado en el planeta alrededor del año 2000. Entretanto, la televisión española continuó haciéndose eco del prestigio de figuras como Olga Guillot, «La reina del bolero», y apareció la voz nueva de la atractiva Lucrecia, establecida en Barcelona desde hace años. El flujo de la canción romántica no cesa: apoyado por Alejandro Sanz y Miguel Bosé, el cubano Pancho Céspedes conmovió con su álbum *Vida loca*.

El bolero-mambo

Hacia 1950 el mambo de Pérez Prado había encontrado una acogida formidable, gracias a su divulgación en la radio, el disco y el cine mexicanos. En su versión más lenta, a la manera de *Mambo en sax*, el continuo ritmo sincopado sirvió como base acompañante a nuevas obras, desplazando también esta influencia hacia la cancionística. Aprovechando la popularidad del mambo, varios compositores de talento extraordinario comenzaron a hacer piezas que reflejaron el nuevo estilo del bolero.

Entre esos creadores se destacó **Julio Gutiérrez** (1912-90), uno de los más polifacéticos músicos cubanos. Con *Un poquito de tu amor, ¿Qué es lo que pasa?* y *Así, así*, logró fijar la nueva modalidad; este prolífico autor es una de las figuras menos apreciadas en la historia de la música cubana. Debutó como pianista de la Orquesta Casino de la Playa en 1940, mientras adelantaba estudios superiores de violín y piano en el Conservatorio de La Habana; ocho años después estaba al frente de su propia formación. Comenzó entonces una gira por casi toda la América Latina y al regresar a La Habana codirigió con Pedro Jústiz *Peruchín*, el primer jam session (1956), para el sello Panart. Fue nombrado enton-

ces director musical del Canal 4 de televisión. Seleccionado por Lecuona, participó en los conciertos con varios pianos que encabezaba el propio maestro; en ellos estrenó Julio Gutiérrez sus dos canciones cumbres: *Llanto de luna*, tema con el que surgió el argentino Leo Marini como vocalista extraordinario y que también interpretó brillantemente Fernando Álvarez, e *Inolvidable*, bolero que estrenó el tenor René Cabel y que fue popularizado por el bilbaíno Gregorio Barrios y por el dúo puertorriqueño Pérez-Rodríguez. Ambas melodías fueron éxitos en la voz de Tito Rodríguez desde el Palladium de Nueva York, y volvieron a ser populares en 1992 en la interpretación de Luis Miguel.

En 1960 Julio Gutiérrez abandonó Cuba vía México, donde dirigió la revista musical del Tropicana azteca; luego se estableció en Nueva York, alternando con frecuentes actuaciones en Puerto Rico. Con el saxo tenor *Chombo* Silva grabó *Instrumentales para ti* (1968), con temas de su propia inspiración. Un par de años más tarde organizó otra descarga, *Progressive Latin*, que reunió, además de *Chombo* Silva al saxo Jesús Caunedo y al trompeta *El negro* Vivar. Durante sus últimos años estuvo amenizando el famoso Victor's Cafe de Manhattan. *Un poquito de tu amor* fue grabado por Charlie Parker en 1951; sin embargo, en una reciente reedición de sus obras en CD, las notas indican que el tema es de «autor desconocido».

En su evolución, el bolero-mambo fue asimilando también una estructura morfológica, presentando una primera parte más tranquila y como contraste una segunda sección más movida, semejante a un montuno lento. A este modelo pertenecen *Celosa*, de Juan Bruno Tarraza, *Amor sin fe*, de Benny Moré, *Camarera del amor*, de José Dolores Quiñones y otros números.

Un aspecto que merece ser destacado es que la mayoría de las obras con este énfasis fueron creadas por un solo autor, responsable tanto de la música como de la letra. La influencia del bolero-mambo llegó a extenderse hasta el estilo de los compositores más representativos de la corriente estética conocida como filin en *Y decídete mi amor*, de José Antonio Méndez, y *Eva*, del interesante guitarrista Ñico Rojas.

El bolero-mambo provocó una nueva manera de abordar la orquestación, influencia directa de lo que hacía Pérez Prado. Esta forma de arreglar un número se extendió como práctica hasta principios de los años 60, y abarca una larga lista de importantes creaciones interpretadas por cantantes famosos. Un buen ejemplo es *Como arrullo de pal-*

mas, de Ernesto Lecuona en versión de Benny Moré con su banda gigante.

El bolero-cha

Mientras el mambo reinaba a principios de los años 50, otra revolución importante se estaba gestando dentro del danzón moderno o de «nuevo ritmo». Apareció una sección cantable antes del continuo del montuno, ejecutada al unísono por dos o tres miembros del coro; esta «innovación», junto a una manera muy peculiar de rallar rítmicamente el güiro le fue abriendo el camino a un nuevo género que a partir de 1953 se denominó chachachá.

Varios compositores de boleros aprovecharon la ebullición provocada por el chachachá para lograr adaptaciones muy importantes que influyeron en su propia supervivencia como género. De los interpretados por la Orquesta América, que fue la pionera, mencionaré *Nunca*, de Guty Cárdenas, *Rival* y *Mujer*, ambos del también mexicano Agustín Lara y *Clara*, de Virgilio González. Por su parte, la contundente Orquesta Aragón continuó esa práctica y popularizó en ritmo de chachachá otros boleros antológicos: *Nosotros*, de Pedro Junco, *Amor de mis amores*, de Agustín Lara, *Silencio* y *Cuatro vidas*, del célebre puertorriqueño Rafael Hernández, y *Le dije a una rosa*, de Virgilio González, sin olvidar un bolero filin que le causó a su autora no pocos problemas con los funcionarios del régimen por estimar que se trataba de una crítica velada a la revolución: *Adiós felicidad*, de Ela O'Farrill.

Siguiendo en la línea de las charangas, por la misma época, la Orquesta Sensación contrarrestó con *Hoja seca*, de Roque Carbajo, y *Arráncame la vida*, de Agustín Lara. Las grandes orquestas también se hicieron eco de la moda, pero con arreglos sin coro de la Riverside en la voz de su cantante estelar Tito Gómez, montando números del calibre de *Vereda tropical*, del mexicano Gonzalo Curiel, y música de tres boricuas: *Bajo un palmar*, de Pedro Flores, *Ahora seremos felices*, de Rafael Hernández, y *Pobre luna*, de Bobby Capó.

Algunos boleros-cha de las charangas impusieron la novedad de evitar la aparición de la flauta, normalmente el elemento más distintivo de este tipo de agrupación, resaltando en su lugar el papel de los violines, la armonización del piano y el discreto fondo rítmico de la percusión. Cuando la Aragón presentó *No puedo vivir*, «tomaron prestado» como introducción un fragmento del *Rondó caprichoso* para violín y orquesta del francés Saint Saëns, transportado de la tonalidad en «la menor» en el original a «do menor» en la versión de la Aragón. Este lujo se lo pudieron permitir gracias a la presencia en dicha orquesta de cuerdas del calibre de Celso Valdés, Dagoberto González, Rafael Lay y el violoncellista Tomás Valdés. Un buen ejemplo de cómo se aprovechó el talento de compositores e instrumentistas dentro de las propias orquestas, fue la interpretación por Fajardo y sus Estrellas de *Si te contara*, obra antológica de su violinista principal Félix Reina, que junto a *Muñeca triste* se destaca por la complejidad del planteamiento armónico.

Buscando siempre la novedad, a Rafael Lay, violinista y director de la Orquesta Aragón, se le ocurrió luego retomar la tradición sonera de dos voces –prima y segundo– en lugar de un coro al unísono, pero siempre en ritmo de chachachá. Grabada por la RCA Victor, una de las piezas más características de esa modalidad fue *A mi manera*, un bolerazo de Marcelino Guerra *Rapindey*, interpretado en este caso por Pepe Olmos, voz prima, y el estelar Fernando Álvarez de segundo. En las actua-

RAFAEL LAY DE LA ARAGÓN.

ciones en vivo de la orquesta, la voz del segundo era entonada por Guido Sarría, el tumbador, ya que Álvarez no era integrante de la plantilla de la Aragón.

Otra ocurrencia de Lay consistió en insertar un bolero en un momento de la improvisación que solía realizar el piano a la mitad de la sección del montuno. Al insistir en este tipo de adaptación estaba aprovechando la compatibilidad y carisma escénico de sus cantantes estelares, Pepe Olmos y Felo Bacallao, a cuyas virtudes, junto a la flauta de Richard Egües, se debió durante largo tiempo la fama alcanzada por la Aragón. Del período de mayor repercusión de esta modalidad son *Ya que te vas*, de Ernestina Lecuona, *Todo me gusta de ti*, de Cuco Estévez, *Mi mejor canción* y *Novia mía*, del filinista José Antonio Méndez, *Bonita*, de Luis Arcaraz, *Muy junto al corazón*, de Rafael Ortiz *Mañungo*, *Total*, de Ricardo García Perdomo, y una melodía que estaba en boca de todos, *Canta lo sentimental*, de Urbano Gómez Montiel.

Los mejores: ANTONIO MACHÍN

El conocido cantante se encontraba trabajando en un pueblo murciano cuando súbitamente se desplomó: había pillado un gri-
pazo de aúpa. Llevado al hotel e hirviendo
de fiebre se derrumbó pesadamente en una
silla. «Es la primera vez en veinte años que
dejo sin mi actuación al público...», repetía
el cubano. Nadie podía creer que habiéndo-
se presentado como si tal cosa en la primera
parte del espectáculo, se hubiera puesto enfermo tan repentinamente, dejando al público con mal sabor de boca. Se armó una
gran algarabía; el pateo era ensordecedor.
Todos fueron hasta el hotel. Al poco, una

voz se alzó desde la calle, potente y sonora, llegando hasta la habitación del vocalista: «¡Machííín!» «¡El año próximo te haremos cantar el doble, si es que
vuelves!»

La rectitud del mulato como empresario era proverbial. Tras el éxito de
«Show 1961» presentaba todos los años un espectáculo con ese simple título,
añadiéndole el año por el que atravesaba. Siempre en la brecha, se hallaba en
plena gira por provincias con la edición de 1962; aquella noche fue una de esas
experiencias que nunca pudo olvidar.

Asociado a la historia de la canción romántica durante la dura posguerra,
Antonio Machín (1904-77) logró prolongar su éxito durante varias décadas
más; parecía como si nunca pasara de moda. Hablar en España del bolero era
hablar de Machín.

Totalmente desconocido para sus compatriotas de la segunda mitad del siglo XX, Machín se convirtió aquí en el gran embajador de la música cubana.
Había nacido en Sagua la Grande, de madre negra que tuvo dieciséis hijos; su
padre fue un campesino gallego de Orense. Empezó como muchos, cantando se-
renatas y fiestas en su pueblo, pero había heredado el tesón de su padre.

En 1926 ya estaba en La Habana, trabajando de peón de albañil, acechan-
do su oportunidad. Hizo dúo con Miguel Zaballa, un viejo trovador; aquello
sonaba bien, se le oyó en la radio y pronto lo reclutó Don Aspiazu, y fue triple

su suerte porque logró actuar en una orquesta de blancos en el Casino Nacional, el mejor cabaré de La Habana en aquella época. Allí fue donde por primera vez hizo sonar sus inseparables maracas, aunque tenía que cantar a pleno pulmón pues todavía no existían micrófonos ni amplificadores.

Durante una gira en 1929 grabó sus primeros discos en Nueva York: *Amor sincero, El berlingonero, Aquellos ojos verdes, Fuego en La Maya, Avellana y maní, Tata cuñengue, A chaper nos manda el mayoral, Un beso quisiera, No sangres corazón, A orillas del Yumurí, Cantar quise a tus ojos, Me voy a Baracoa, El camisón de Pepa* y muchos otros sones y boleros.

Desligado de la Orquesta de Aspiazu, en 1934 personificó *El manisero* en Nueva York, un número creado por Moisés Simons en 1928. Más tarde formó un trío, luego un cuarteto y hasta un sexteto después. Es un Machín joven y atrevido, y por supuesto, dándole al canuto, el que encontramos hablando hasta por los codos en una grabación de 1934 del son *Vacilando*: ¡«*Dame la mota Daniel; dame la mota, chico, para ponerme chivoncito!*» (la mota es el pitillo y chivoncito significaba entonces ponerse sabroso).

Ya había grabado más de cincuenta números para la RCA Victor antes de viajar al viejo continente en 1938. Un mes en Londres, cantando *Lamento esclavo* y *Mamá Inés* de Eliseo Grenet; luego París, donde triunfó y formó su propia orquesta, recorriendo Suecia, Dinamarca, Noruega, Alemania, Italia, Holanda y Rumanía. Un año después la guerra absorbía a Europa. Machín decidió no esperar a que los alemanes entrasen en París y se vino a España, que acababa de salir de la guerra civil, un país depauperado y donde se pasaba hambre. Fueron años muy duros para él, pero no cejó. Aquí nadie le conocía, de manera que aceptó el primer trabajo que le ofrecieron en Barcelona, en una sala llamada Shanghai, una especie de academia de baile, y en donde, mientras Machín cantaba, las chicas de alterne del local bailaban con los clientes a cambio de unos billetes que éstos adquirían previamente en taquilla. Le pagaban 25 pesetas diarias, cantidad infinitamente inferior a lo que percibía en París.

Pronto captó que lo que hacía falta eran boleros románticos para irse conquistando el cariño de la gente. De esa primera época son *Coral, Qué pasó, Un ángel fue, Rosa peregrina, Olvídame, Amor sincero, De ti me enamoré, Plegaria, Isabel, Noche azul*, de Lecuona, y otras canciones. Se unió a una compañía que hacía gira por Andalucía pero al llegar a Madrid todo resultó un fiasco. Caminando de un lado a otro en busca de trabajo, encontró la sala de fiestas Conga, pero lo rechazaron por desconocido. Se le ocurrió entonces una noche mez-

clarse con el público, subirse al escenario como si fuera un espontáneo y ponerse a cantar algunos boleros. El respetable lo aplaudió calurosamente y consiguió
el empleo por cinco duros al día. Pagaba ocho pesetas diarias en una pensión de
la calle de Espoz y Mina, cuando una noche el actor cinematográfico Fernando
Sancho *El carioco*, se ofreció a presentarlo a conocidos suyos en el Casablanca.
A partir de ese momento, contando con el respaldo de una de las orquestas más
contundentes de la época, Los Miuras de Sobré, Machín conoció lo más selecto
de los night clubs españoles hasta que finalmente, en 1942, decidió lanzarse
como solista. Un año antes había grabado sus primeros temas. Se dedicó a realizar giras con espectáculos de variedades: «Ébano y marfil», «Caras conocidas»,
«Melodías de color», «Cancionero cubano» y «Altas variedades», fueron algunas de aquellas compañías que supo organizar.

Encontró en las composiciones de Osvaldo Farrés un material idóneo.
Identificado con boleros sugerentes como *No me vayas a engañar,* dejó lo mejor de sí mismo. Su música se alimentaba desde la radio: el ojo mágico de los
aparatos Telefunken, Radiola o Marconi sintonizaba en la onda media unas
canciones que prendían en las gentes cultivadas y sin cultivar. «Con Machín
las palabras de amor fueron más fáciles y los rechazos amorosos resultaron
más difíciles», asegura el investigador José Luis Salinas. Machín no poseía una
voz potente ni un registro amplio, pero supo dosificarla con un repertorio adecuado mientras sustentaba la naturalidad en sus interpretaciones, nunca des-
provistas de emoción, pero jamás enfatizadas hasta hacerlas sensibleras o arti-
ficiosas.

Lo cierto es que España tuvo durante muchos años a un cantante muy cubano, que de una dilatada carrera internacional como sonero pasó a una extra-
ña forma de anonimato como trámite para convertirse en mito nacional. Que de
cantar: «*Yo quiero un vacilón, con una nena sabrosa, que después del vacilón,
ella se ponga melosa...*», pasó a «*Madrecita del alma querida, en mi pecho yo
llevo una flor...*». Todo un enigma.

Antonio Machín creó una escuela y alegró la vida de varias generaciones
de enamorados. Su género favorito fue cultivado después por otros intérpretes
que conformaron un bolero netamente peninsular, sin aquel ligero énfasis tropical. Murió en Madrid el 4 de agosto de 1977 y está enterrado en Sevilla, de
donde era Ángeles Rodríguez, con quien se casó en 1943. Los españoles nunca
le olvidarán.

Esta nueva forma del bolero, intercalado en medio del montuno danzonero, fue acogida por algunos autores, otros solistas y orquestas. Merecen mención *Cobarde*, de Rosendo Rosell (destacado actor cómico y periodista exiliado en Miami), en el danzón-cha *Caimitillo y marañón*, del mismo autor, interpretado por Julio Valdés con la Orquesta de Pancho *El Bravo;* también la Aragón lo montó con Felo Bacallao como solista.

El bolero en los conjuntos

Es innegable la virtud del bolero para adaptarse a los distintos formatos instrumentales y vocales de la música popular cubana. La voz ronca del sonero Abelardo Barroso destacó la presencia del bolero soneado y el bolero-son con el Septeto Habanero; el propio rumbero Carlos Embale sorprendió a muchos con sus interpretaciones cuando estuvo al frente del Septeto Nacional de Ignacio Piñeiro, y lo propio hicieron Rodolfo Marrero con el Septeto Espirituano y Humberto Rodríguez con el conjunto Los Naranjos de Cienfuegos.

Años después, como resultado de las innovaciones de **Arsenio Rodríguez** (ver pág. 54) con las armonizaciones de los metales, en su versión de tres trompetas y la acentuación metrorrítmica de la percusión, se logró una mayor diversidad tímbrica. El Conjunto Casino y la Sonora Matancera, muy distintos entre sí, demostraron a agrupaciones similares en el decenio 1950-60 las posibilidades de incrementar la comunicación obra-intérprete-receptor. En este sentido, cobraron un papel singular los arreglos imaginativos en la combinación del piano y el contrabajo, las intervenciones de los bloques armónicos y las secuencias melódicas.

El cantante **Pacho Alonso** (ver pág. 296) dejó su huella en la historia del bolero con una serie de grabaciones que contaron con el acompañamiento de Los Bocucos. Procedentes de Santiago de Cuba, aportaron boleros que agregaban una cierta vivacidad debido a la fusión con el son oriental. Entre sus mejores temas están *Necesitaste amar* y *Cada noche que estás sola*, del autor Enrique Bonne, gran amigo del vocalista, *Este sentimiento que se llama amor*, de José Antonio Méndez, *Ya tú lo verás*, de Alberto Vera y *Por mí no lo hagas*, de Luis Roja.

LA ORQUESTA RIVERSIDE DIRIGIDA POR PEDRO VILA (1947). TITO GÓMEZ EN LA TUMBADORA.

En las orquestas tipo jazz band

Como he indicado antes, las bandas cubanas tienen su origen en el jazz band norteamericano, con la diferencia de que en la sección de percusión, aparte de la batería o *drums* se incluyen instrumentos cubanos. Si entre la mayoría de los vocalistas es posible establecer una estricta delimitación entre la línea verbal y la melódica, esta última se afianzó considerablemente en los boleros difundidos por estas formidables orquestas. Tal acentuación provocó la aparición del *crooner*, un cantante lo bastante dúctil y discreto como para poder expresar la canción adaptándose a las exigencias del arreglo para una agrupación musical de envergadura.

Las orquestas que con más acierto cultivaron dicha tendencia, aparte de los Havana Cuban Boys, fueron la inolvidable Casino de la Playa, dirigida por Guillermo Portela, en la cual se iniciaron teclistas como Anselmo Sacasas, Julio Gutiérrez y Dámaso Pérez Prado, y que tuvo como intérpretes a Reinaldo Henríquez, Miguelito Valdés y Walfredo de los Reyes, entre otros, sin olvidar la de los hermanos Manuel, Antonio, Andrés y Juan Castro, con su vocalista Carlos Díaz, o Tito Gómez con la Riverside, primero bajo la batuta de Enrique González Mantici y desde 1947 dirigida por Pedro Vila.

Tito Gómez (1920), de madre madrileña y padre gallego, ha tenido una larga trayectoria al servicio del bolero. Su verdadero nombre es José Antonio Tenreiro Gómez y fue cantante estrella de la formidable Orquesta Riverside entre 1942-75. *Alma con alma*, de Juanito Márquez, y *Vereda tropical*, del mexicano Gonzalo Curiel lo identificarán por siempre como la voz que grabó más de 600 composiciones, incluyendo las que realizó con la Orquesta Jorrín en los años 80. Hombre entusiasta y honesto, Tito Gómez siempre entregó lo mejor de sí mismo.

La calidad interpretativa de las orquestas mencionadas les hicieron alcanzar fama nacional e internacional, sistematizando una nueva manera de organizar el material musical, y siempre incluyeron boleros en su repertorio. Me parece innecesario repetir la lista que aparece en la sección «Las grandes orquestas» (ver pág. 67), sólo recalcar que al aumentar la densidad y las combinaciones armónicas, las orquestas tipo jazz band extendieron las zonas de registro de sonoridades, logrando aún mayores contrastes que el conjunto. Una heredera de la complejidad tímbrica de las bandas de jazz es la actual Gran Orquesta de la Radiotelevisión Cubana, que suele acompañar a los cantantes en las vistosas galas del Festival Boleros de Oro, celebrados cada año en Cuba desde 1986. Estos festivales han servido, entre otras cosas, para lanzar varias voces nuevas como Malena Burke (hija de Elena), Annia Linares, Mirta Medina y Maggie Carlés. Por cierto, las cuatro viven en Estados Unidos desde hace pocos años. El éxodo continúa.

He aquí algunos boleros que ganaron en riqueza al ser interpretados por una banda: *¿Qué te pedí?*, de Fernando Mulens, *Mentiras tuyas*, de Mario Fernández Porta, *Ahora soy tan feliz*, de Benny Moré, *Qué pena me da*, de Juan Arrondo, *Cómo fue*, de Ernesto Duarte, *Me gustas*, de Rey Díaz Calvet, *Conversación en tiempo de bolero*, de René Touzet, y *Mi corazón y yo*, de Frank Domínguez.

Boleros más recientes

A partir de los años 70 se incorporaron otros instrumentos al formato tradicional de la llamada charanga. Las modificaciones incluyeron no sólo guitarra, bajo eléctrico y teclados electrónicos, sino también la batería del jazz band y una poderosa sección de tres trombones. Estas innovaciones surgieron a partir de la orquesta Los Van Van, fundada por el compositor, arreglista, bajista y cantante Juan Formell.

Esta formación logró un estilo innovador en la ejecución del son cubano, al que luego denominaron «songo». El bolero encontró también un

Los mejores: OLGA GUILLOT

«La Reina del Bolero» nació en Santiago de Cuba y desde muy pequeña comenzó a cantar con su hermana, ya residiendo en La Habana. Olga Guillot (1922) empezó interpretando tangos en 1938 en el famoso programa radial «La Corte Suprema del Arte». La compositora Isolina Carrillo se dedicó a pulir aquel diamante, haciéndola parte de su cuarteto Siboney en 1944 como segunda voz. Fue precisamente Facundo Rivero, el pianista del grupo, quien descubrió las posibilidades de Olga como solista y la hizo debutar en 1945 en el Zombie Club. Viajó a Nueva York al año siguiente en compañía

LA REINA DEL BOLERO (1958).

de Miguelito Valdés, actuando en teatros y cabarés y realizando sus primeras grabaciones para el sello Decca. Estrenó en 1946 *La gloria eres tú*, de José Antonio Méndez, con arreglo de Bebo Valdés, un bolero antológico que le ganó la simpatía del pueblo cubano. Más tarde obtuvo otro gran éxito con su versión de *Lluvia gris* (*Stormy weather*). Ese mismo año, la ACRI la seleccionó como la cancionera más destacada de Cuba, después de aparecer en varias emisoras de radio importantes.

En 1948 el tenor René Cabel la llevó a México y allí filmó *La Venus de fuego*, grabando también varias canciones para el sello Anfión, acompañada por la orquesta de Gonzalo Curiel. Después viajó por Centro y Suramérica, Puerto Rico y República Dominicana. En 1951 sus admiradores la hicieron la «Reina de la Radio», en un concurso patrocinado por el periódico habanero *Mañana*. El musicólogo Cristóbal Díaz Ayala asegura:

Sigue su rápida carrera ascendente, pero todavía ni ella ni nadie había logrado colocarse a la par con los cantantes masculinos, como lo habían logrado sus colegas de México.

En 1954 el productor de discos Jesús Gorís creyó en ella y le grabó varias canciones, advirtiéndole al director de la orquesta Hermanos Castro que dejara a Olga dar rienda suelta a su estilo, a su manera de decir. El resultado fue estupendo, incluyendo *Miénteme*, del mexicano Armando *Chamaco* Domínguez, que se convirtió en un *hit* extraordinario.

De ahí en adelante, todo lo que grabó Olguita se transformó en un verdadero éxito. Superó la tensión provocada por un continuo trajinar de presentaciones, giras por las Américas y muy aplaudidas actuaciones en teatros y cabarés, así como apariciones en los mejores horarios televisivos. En 1961 abandonó Cuba, donde a partir de entonces fue terminantemente prohibido escuchar su voz. Después de una estancia en Venezuela, se domicilió en México invitada por el maestro José Sabre Marroquín, tras lo cual continuó su carrera en varios países e intervino en doce películas. Fue la primera artista hispana en presentarse en el Carnegie Hall de Nueva York en 1964, y en mayo de 1965 cantó junto al trío Los Panchos y Miguelito Valdés en el teatro Paramount.

Actuó por segunda vez en Madrid en 1968 y obtuvo el premio Olé en Barcelona con el tema *Adoro*, de Manzanero. Para el sello CBS grabó en España *Me muero... me muero*, de la mexicana Lolita de la Colina. Desde entonces fue considerada como la pionera de la canción erótica. El sello Orfeón de Buenos Aires le grabó un álbum en vivo en 1978 y más tarde realizó otro en México; después volvió a la Argentina en 1980, donde grabó para el sello Interdisc, y en 1982 ofreció dos memorables recitales en el Carnegie Hall.

La larga carrera de la gesticulante, carismática y aplaudida Olga Guillot siempre contó con el asesoramiento de compositores y directores tan diestros como los hermanos Castro, Isolina Carrillo, René Touzet (con quien tuvo una hija) y Juan Bruno Tarraza, a quien le grabó *Soy tuya*.

Muy querida del público español, Olga tiene un absoluto dominio de su voz para insinuar, negar o suplicar, y una total maestría en el lenguaje del cuerpo. Con un estilo de cantar y actuar que han copiado varias vocalistas, la Guillot siempre ha sabido escoger su repertorio; cuando el bolero decayó, comenzó a incluir baladas y rock lentos en sus programas. Ha participado en un total de 16 películas y 52 discos registran su estilo característico, acumulando 20 Discos de Oro, dos de Platino y un Disco de Brillantes, así como innumerables trofeos y condecoraciones. En 1988 celebró sus Bodas de Oro con la canción romántica; ese mismo año compartió el escenario con Lucho Gatica y Roberto Ledesma en el festival «Los cien años del bolero» celebrado en República Dominicana. Olguita es infatigable y continúa cantando. En uno de sus recitales en el Palau de Barcelona recibió una merecida ovación de once minutos. Recomiendo el disco *Faltaba yo*, editado en 2001 y los dos volúmenes titulados *Olga de Cuba*.

espacio en este nuevo contexto instrumental, asumiendo una sonoridad que lo ha acercado bastante a la música de salsa neoyorquina o puertorriqueña. Por esta razón, algunas obras interpretadas por Los Van Van ofrecen una proyección más contemporánea del bolero que Formell, quizá para ser consecuente con su experimento sonero, ha denominado bolerosongo. Algunos ejemplos incluyen *Elisa* y *El tren de Jagüey*, ambos cantados por el propio director, mientras que en la interpretación del vocalista Lázaro Morúa aparecieron *Quiero que me hables de ti*, de Rafael Tortoló, y *Hoy qué quieres de mí*, de Israel Sardiñas. También surgió *Oh, no*, de Formell, con la adición de un saxofón alto, instrumento que ha sido frecuentemente incorporado en sus grabaciones.

¿Le han hecho mella estas modificaciones a la canción romántica? Yo creo que en cierto modo sí. Tanto los textos como las melodías rompieron con el predominio que ya gozaba el filin sobre el bolero tradicional. De lo que no hay duda es que se logró un estilo que lo acercó aún más al bailador contemporáneo, que no quiere saber del pasado. Sin embargo, cuando la gente va a bailar con Los Van Van, raramente interpretan boleros. Platos fuertes como *Por encima del nivel* (conocido como *Sandunguera*) o *La Habana sí*, han tendido a acaparar toda la atención, cosa que se refleja en las grabaciones que llegan a España. Quizá las baladas levemente soneadas como *Marilú* y *Yuya Martínez* representan mejor la vitalidad cancionística de esta agrupación. Ver pág. 352.

Por su parte, siguiendo la pauta marcada por el conjunto de Roberto Faz con los diversos «pegaditos» o mosaicos de boleros que impuso en el gusto popular, el conjunto Sierra Maestra arregló una secuencia como homenaje al compositor Rafael Ortiz *Mañungo*, en el estilo del bolero soneado de los antiguos septetos, pero con un concepto interpretativo más actual.

EL ESTILO FILIN

Entre 1948-50 comenzó a brotar en el cancionero romántico cubano la modalidad filin (del inglés *feeling*, sentimiento). Para la mayor parte de los jóvenes músicos que originaron este estilo, el término significó, ante todo, una manera de pensar y hacer música, de expresarse de forma diferente, de sacarle a la guitarra otros tipos de acordes. Pero la falta de divulgación y de una crítica consecuente impidió que en su momento el movimiento tuviera un cuerpo teórico de ideas o de análisis del fenómeno. De ahí que todo lo que se ha teorizado sobre el filin se haya hecho a posteriori, y quizá eso ha enturbiado un poco la visión.

No creo que sus iniciadores se propusieran romper con nada, es decir, no fueron a fundar escuela ni a buscar teoría. Eran en su mayoría gente humilde, obreros, desempleados o artesanos, mezclados con algún que otro músico profesional, pero gente de pueblo que quería hacer música de una manera distinta. Eso sí, escuchaban mucho jazz y blues y descubrieron matices que no se habían desarrollado en Cuba hasta entonces.

El filin se apoya armónicamente en las disonancias complementarias de la tónica, en las agregaciones de la dominante y en los sonidos alterados; además, la expresividad de la voz es determinante en estas piezas, donde los versos son de tono intimista y muy persuasivos. Incorporando influencias norteamericanas que ya habían asimilado elementos del impresionismo musical francés, en particular de Claude Debussy, los filinistas le imprimieron un nuevo impulso a la canción romántica.

A la vanguardia de este movimiento hay que situar a **José Antonio Méndez** (1927-89), quien en 1949 se fue a México, actuando con bastante éxito en centros nocturnos y en la radio. Abandonando la retórica amorosa del bolero tradicional, aplicó elementos clave del novedoso estilo,

JOSÉ ANTONIO MÉNDEZ (1967).

que algunos compositores mexicanos reconocieron inmediatamente como un original modo de hacer la canción sentimental. Sin proponérselo, el *King* (como le llamaron sus amigos) «exportó» a los medios musicales aztecas las nuevas ideas, repitiendo lo que había sucedido 35 años antes cuando los primeros trovadores cubanos llevaron el bolero a Yucatán. Entre sus más conocidos temas se encuentran *Si me comprendieras, Quiéreme y verás, Por nuestra cobardía, Soy tan feliz, Mi mejor canción, Ese sentimiento que se llama amor, Tú, mi adoración, Me faltabas tú* y el exquisito *Novia mía*.

José Antonio Méndez no fue rebuscado en el momento de concebir sus melodías, ni se preocupó por hacer grandes disonancias, como fue el caso de Frank Domínguez. Lo que realmente caracterizó sus canciones fue el dominio de la forma, su fluidez melódica, la coherencia del texto y su correspondencia exacta con los acentos musicales.

Salvo raras excepciones, los creadores de filin siempre escribieron las letras de sus canciones acompañados de la guitarra, contribuyendo a renovar la música sentimental en cuanto a texto, melodía y posibilidades armónicas. No sujeto al ritmo fijo del bolero con la fórmula del cinquillo, ni atrapado por las claves o el bongó, la canción ganó así en intimidad e imágenes poéticas, a la vez que permitió amplia libertad de expresión al intérprete; en muchos casos, la voz adquirió más emoción y hasta cierta teatralidad. Aquellos primeros artistas podrían haber hecho suya la frase de *Bola de Nieve*: «Yo soy la canción que canto».

Si alguien ha tenido un estilo realmente particular para decir sus canciones ese fue el *King*, desaparecido en plena madurez de su carrera artística al ser atropellado por un autobús en 1989. De naturaleza emotiva y chispeante, buscaba incesantemente una nueva forma de expresarse. El Loquibambia Swing fue uno de los grupos que empezaron a reflejar estas sonoridades y donde José Antonio Méndez tocó por primera vez con el pianista invidente Frank Emilio Flynn y la cantante Omara Portuondo, que devino una de las grandes intérpretes de la nueva modalidad.

Cuando en 1950 apareció *Contigo en la distancia*, un momento cumbre para el filin, comenzó un largo recorrido que en el caso de **César Portillo de la Luz** (1927) se concretó en composiciones como *Noche cubana, Nuestra canción, Tú, mi delirio, Canción de un festival, Perdido amor, Realidad y fantasía, Es nuestra canción, Interludio* y muchas más.

Se había estrenado en 1946, presentándose en varias emisoras de radio. Más tarde actuó en los cabarés Karachi, Chateau Piscina, El Gato Tuerto y el St. John's. Varias de las canciones de Portillo de la Luz han sido interpretadas en películas y durantes años ha trabajado como profesor de guitarra. Odilio Urfé afirmó que detrás de su obra hay una reflexión profunda sobre la vida. Por otra parte, la labor de un músico que ha luchado durante muchos años es en cierto modo cruel, porque el camino se le va estrechando; definitivamente disconforme, el compositor busca respuestas a una angustia que no cesa.

Originalmente concebido más como un modo específico de hacer canciones que un novedoso estilo músical, los iniciadores del filin querían expresar ideas o vivencias, pero a su manera, lejos del piano y otras sonoridades instrumentales dedicadas a la búsqueda de una perfección formal

envuelta en un tono manido y algo escépti-
co, que le encajaba muy bien al bolero rítmico. Los autores del filin dieron rienda
suelta al poder expresivo de la guitarra,
manteniendo la continuidad histórica de la
fecunda trova de principios del siglo XX.
Pensando en el filin no puedo evitar acor-
darme del final de un poema del argentino
Borges en el que se muestra de golpe la doble devastación del amor y de la música:
«Un símbolo, una rosa, te desgarra / y te
puede matar una guitarra». Al hacer una
nueva canción, Portillo de la Luz parece
como si tuviera una orquesta en la cabeza,
cuando todo lo que ha tenido para sugerir-

CÉSAR PORTILLO DE LA LUZ (1973).

la no son más que seis cuerdas; de ahí na-
cen sus contracantos y la atmósfera sutil que logra crear. En 1998 la Fundación Autor (SGAE) le publicó un hermoso libro.

Mientras que la mayoría de los filinistas son guitarristas, **Frank Domínguez** (1927) trabaja las teclas. Sus canciones han dado la vuelta al
mundo y su voz quebrada le ha servido como el perfecto instrumento para
contar los desvaríos del amor. Escúchese su obra romántica: *Tú me acostumbraste*, que primero le popularizó el tenor René Cabel, *Refúgiate en
mí, Pedacito de cielo, Luna sobre Matanzas, Cómo te atreves, Me recorda-
rás, Si tú quisieras* y esa joya imperecedera que es *Imágenes*, compuesta en
1959 y pronto interpretada por Pacho Alonso con su personal estilo.

Frank Domínguez conectó con el movimiento entrados los años 50 y
es posiblemente el más jazzístico de los exponentes del filin, mostrando
bastante influencia de los quintetos *cool* norteamericanos. En 1956 integró un grupo que acompañaba a César Portillo de la Luz en el cabaré
Sans Souci.

Aunque no fue nada especial cantando sus propias canciones, **Tania
Castellanos** (1920-88) escribió delicadas piezas entre las que se encuentran *Inmensa melodía, Recordaré tu boca, Canción a mi Habana, Prefiero soñar, Me encontrarás, Vuélvete a mí* y *En nosotros*.

Fue obrera metalúrgica y después textil, y desde 1939 militó en el
Partido Socialista Popular (comunista). Aunque su verdadero nombre fue
Zoila, adoptó el seudónimo Tania por razones de la lucha política como

dirigente sindical. Bastante diferente del resto de los filinistas, sus canciones tienen un elemento erótico atrapado en armonías que se asemejan en cierta forma a la obra de **Rosendo Ruiz Quevedo** (1918), un autor que ha cultivado casi todos los géneros populares, y que creó en 1945 una canción que logró mucha difusión en Cuba y en el extranjero: «Hasta mañana vida mía / qué tristeza tenerte que dejar / hasta mañana que mis labios / te puedan con un beso saludar...»

Refiriéndose a los modestos inicios del filin, Rosendo Ruiz ha relatado cómo llegó por primera vez hasta el Callejón de Hammel, donde se reunían unos jóvenes que sentían profundamente lo que estaban cantando:

Aquella casa era la de Tirso Díaz, un respetado trovador que era amigo de mi padre, y que es el padre de Angelito Díaz. Bueno, aquella noche estuvimos allí, y la siguiente, y sin darnos cuenta ya éramos parte de aquel magnífico grupo... Aquello era un taller de creación.

El filin dio lugar a varias parejas de compositores, como la de Yáñez y Gómez, pero sin duda la más admirada fue la de **Piloto y Vera**, integrada por Girardo Piloto (1929-67) y Alberto Vera (1929-96). Piloto murió con los pulmones quemados en un accidente de aviación, y su hijo se convirtió en un excelente baterista (ver pág. 368). Vera continuó componiendo, sobre todo para la vocalista Annia Linares. También ejerció como director musical del Instituto Cubano de Radio y Televisión. Sus piezas comenzaron a escucharse a mediados de la década del 50. Entre ellas destacaron *En ti y en mí, Duele, Sólo tú y yo, Ni callar ni fingir, Fidelidad, Aquí o allá, Perdóname conciencia* y *Añorado encuentro*, que grabó Vicentico Valdés en 1955 para el sello Seeco.

He aquí la opinión de José Loyola, un profesional de la música, tomado de su libro *En ritmo de bolero*:

Desde el punto de vista del análisis musical existen en el filin elementos que sobresalen comparativamente en relación con otras modalidades de la canción cubana. Como resultado de las influencias de la música de origen norteamericano, la estructura armónica es menos transparente, se hacen más complejas las funciones armónicas del acompañamiento con acordes donde proliferan los de séptima dominante, séptima disminuida, nove mayor y menor, tónica con sexta añadida, tónica con séptima, oncena, trecena y otras combinaciones intercaladas como interdominantes o dominantes auxiliares, según el centro tonal de la obra. La sucesión paralela de acordes disonantes también es muy característica.

A lo que podría definir como una segunda generación de filinistas perteneció una creadora muy especial, **Ela O'Farrill** (1930), quien estudió guitarra con Portillo de la Luz. En el período en que se afianzaba el filin, la poesía hispanoamericana había cambiado de derrotero; es el momento en que surgen la antipoesía, la poesía conversacional y la coloquial, en las cuales, presumiblemente se «pierde» la musicalidad tradicional que acerca el poema a la canción. Ela, que supo aprovechar esta circunstancia, es la autora de canciones de contenido profundo y riqueza melódico-armónicas, y desde hace muchos años radica en México. Entre sus obras más conocidas se encuentran *Cuando pasas tú* y la extraordinaria *Adiós, felicidad* (1964), que entre otros vocalistas se la cantó Olga Chorens desde el exilio: «Adiós, felicidad / casi no te conocí / pasaste sin mirarme / sin saber nada de mí...», una melodía que absurdamente le granjeó el odio del régimen castrista por convertirse en símbolo de los que no estaban de acuerdo con la abrupta dirección comunista que había tomado la revolución. Pronto Ela decidió marcharse del país.

Con la guitarra, ese mágico cofre que guarda en su entrañas múltiples acentos definidores de la historia musical de las Américas, se ha acompañado siempre **Marta Valdés** (1934), con la que para mí se cierra el concepto central del filin. Marta había estudiado Filosofía y Letras en la Universidad habanera y realizó estudios musicales con distinguidos maestros; más tarde profundizó sus conocimientos de armonía y composición con Harold Gramatges. La extraordinaria pianista Enriqueta Almanza le transcribía sus canciones cuando Marta apenas sabía dibujar las notas musicales. La autora de *Palabras* llegó al filin con mayor bagaje expresivo y cultura general, y elaborando mucho este estilo logró llevarlo a su máxima expresión.

Elena Burke le estrenó la mayoría de sus piezas, entre las que se encuentran *En la imaginación, Por si vuelves, Deja que siga sola, Palabras, No te empeñes más, Hay mil formas, Aunque no te vi llegar* y la exquisita *Tú no sospechas*, que le interpretó tantas veces *Bola de Nieve*. Recordando su difícil situación ante la mentalidad discriminatoria de los funcionarios del régimen, la propia Marta Valdés comentó en una recopilación de 1995:

Al principio fueron años de éxitos: mis canciones y boleros saltaban, tibios aún, desde mi corazón hasta las manos de arreglistas de primera como Bebo Valdés o René Hernández, para sonar en seguida en las voces de moda de Vicentico Valdés o Fernando Álvarez. Luego, en los 60, precisamente cuando empezaba a encontrar caminos que harían madurar mi pensamiento musical, la suerte me fue adversa en el campo de las grabaciones, salvo en el terreno de la música para teatro, arte que me cobijó hasta que soplaron vientos mejores, permitiéndome al menos escuchar todo lo que salía de mi cabeza, así como fortalecer el aspecto dramático de mis composiciones. En la EGREM no dejaban grabar mi música, incluso algunos intérpretes con *background* y todo fueron impedidos de hacerlo. Todavía no me explico muy bien qué pasaba conmigo.

No obstante, en 1978 fue galardonada con el gran premio del certamen «Adolfo Guzmán», en su primera emisión, por su composición *Canción eterna de la juventud*. Este importante concurso anual fue interrumpido más tarde por la torpe dirección del Instituto Cubano de Radio y Televisión, reapareciendo cerca del año 2000. Miriam Ramos le grabó en 1983 temas tildados de «difíciles» en el LP *Canción desde otro mundo*, y en 1987 apareció *Elena Burke canta a Marta Valdés*, un disco que reunió a Frank Emilio, Carlos Emilio y a Enriqueta Almanza.

La sensible Marta Valdés debutó en España en 1996: «Mi obra ha llegado con mucho retraso a la gente. Mi labor ahora es dar a oír mis canciones». Martirio le ha cantado algunas con acierto y en aquel mismo año, con Omara Portuondo, Marta subió al escenario para presentar «Ellas tienen filin». Sobre las posibilidades de las cuerdas ha declarado:

La guitarra es un universo infinito por descubrir; cada canción es un mundo, tiene que tener su arquitectura y su balance. El texto no es más importante que la música, hay que buscar incesantemente las posibilidades de la guitarra, que no tienen fin.

Por su evidente popularidad, las canciones que le ha cantado **Pablo Milanés** (1943) son las que han tenido mayor difusión. Esencialmente autodidacta, este prolífico cantautor se inició vocalizando con los cuartetos Del Rey y Los Bucaneros, pero a partir de 1964 comenzó a trabajar solo, introduciendo su propio estilo en la canción cubana, ensamblando elementos procedentes de otras músicas, incluyendo el filin. El *King* José Antonio Méndez ejerció una gran influencia en el joven Pablo, quien cursó estudios musicales bajo la guía de Federico Smith y con el brillante compositor y guitarrista Leo Brouwer. Sus letras contienen altura poética y sus melodías son muestra de una sensibilidad excepcional. Pablo Milanés es realmente un puente entre el movimiento del filin y el de la nueva trova, como se revela en la antológica *Tú, mi desengaño*. De 1965 es *Mis 22 años*, que combina dos formas expresivas diferentes: filin en la primera parte y ritmo de guajira-son en la segunda, y que determinó un vuelco en lo que se había producido hasta entonces. Milanés también ha realizado un trabajo importante de indagación y catalogación del bolero cubano, y por extensión, de muchos cantos anónimos que ha tratado de salvar del olvido. Sus versos y su música parten de ese sustrato popular que el cantautor lleva en la memoria. Sobre su fecunda actividad artística aparece más información en la sección dedicada a la nueva trova (ver pág. 314).

Como «La señora sentimiento» o «Su majestad la Burke» fue conocida **Elena Burke** (1928-2002) en la isla e Hispanoamérica; viéndola cantar era como se apreciaba mejor su desbordante cubanía y su invención rítmica. Su verdadero nombre era Romana Burgues, y de pequeña le dio por imitar a la argentina Libertad Lamarque. Debutó en 1941 en un programa de aficionados y un año después apareció en varias emisoras de radio y en los cabarés Sans Souci y el Zombie. Integró, sucesivamente, los cuartetos de Facundo Rivero, Orlando de la Rosa y D'Aida, pero en 1959 se separó del último para iniciar una brillante carrera como solista. La de Elena Burke es posiblemente la voz más identificada con el filin y ha representado a Cuba en numerosos festivales internacionales de la canción.

Bajo la influencia de vocalistas norteamericanas del calibre de Ella Fitzgerald, la Burke extremó las evidentes afinidades del filin con el blues, dándole nuevos alientos a base de transiciones bruscas y atonales, con rupturas sincopadas características del difícil estilo. Durante sus recitales, a menudo Enriqueta Almanza, su pianista acompañante, tenía que «cazarla» porque rara vez proyectó un número de la misma manera. Fue realmente una actriz de la canción, y como Olga Guillot, que también ha cantado mucho filin, tuvo ese don de emocionar a la gente.

Quizá sin ser consciente de ello, creo que Elena Burke clausuró con cierto fulgor crepuscular el itinerario de un bolero cubano ya extenuado por su propia decadencia, el hostigamiento del régimen castrista y la ingestión de conservas soviéticas. Supo resumir lo que piensa un verdadero artista sobre el fenómeno de la popularidad: «Tener siempre a alguien que piense en uno es algo que nos hace sentir el calor del pueblo».

Bastante conocida del público español, **Omara Portuondo** (1930) se inició como aficionada en la radio, a raíz de lo cual el pianista Frank Emilio Flynn la llevó a su grupo Loquibambia, que se escuchaba por la emisora Mil Diez. Más adelante se unió al espectáculo coreográfico de Alberto Alonso, a los shows de Rodney en Tropicana, al Cuarteto de Orlando de la Rosa, y también estuvo un tiempo con la orquesta femenina Anacaona, donde le enseñaron a tocar la tumbadora y se ilusionó con aprender batería. Integró el cuarteto D'Aida con su hermana Haydée durante quince años, y como solista ha ganado reconocimiento dentro y fuera de Cuba, convirtiéndose en una de las grandes de la canción filin. Aquí en España ha actuado en infinidad de ocasiones, obteniendo siempre el aplauso sincero del respetable.

MARTA VALDÉS Y OMARA PORTUONDO (1997).

Al margen de las piezas creadas para Omara por Alberto Vera, como *Lo que me queda por vivir*, están las canciones de Martín Rojas *Siempre es 26* y *Mujer del mundo tercero*, así como *Gracias a la vida*, de la chilena Violeta Parra, *Vuela pena*, de Amaury Pérez, y *La era está pariendo un corazón*, de Silvio Rodríguez, que le interpretó en 1966, posiblemente la primera grabación que se hizo de un tema del afamado cantautor.

Sobre la responsabilidad profesional del intérprete, Omara Portuondo ha enfatizado: «Nuestro trabajo consiste en transmitir ideas, mensajes, sentimientos, y si no llegan a los demás, si cantas para ti misma o para unos pocos, no cumples a plenitud el rol social que te corresponde».

Otras figuras importantes que destacaron en la interpretación del bolero en la onda del filin han sido Miguel de Gonzalo, Meme Solís, Fernando Álvarez, Marta Justiniani, Roberto Sánchez, Doris de la Torre, Amado Borcelá, *Mundito* González, Manolo del Valle, Luis García y el dúo de José Tejedor y Luis Oviedo. También han sobresalido Gina León, Maria Elena Pena, Bobby Carcassés, Miriam Ramos, Luis Téllez, Anais Abreu, Argelia Fragoso, Emilia Morales, Annia Linares, Rita Gil y Beatriz Márquez. Entre las mejores compositoras hay que destacar la labor de Teresita Fernández, que también tiene en su haber excelentes canciones infantiles: ha musicalizado el *Ismaelillo* de José Martí y las *Rondas* de la poetisa chilena Gabriela Mistral.

El filin se sigue cantando en Cuba, tanto o más que el bolero tradicional. No es un género musical en sí mismo, sino más bien una poderosa y sutil corriente musical que también empleó elementos de la trova tradicional.

Sin embargo, siempre tendió a ser un fenómeno de minorías. Si las voces de Roberto Faz o Fernando Álvarez, apoyados por agrupaciones populares como el Conjunto Casino, no hubiesen grabado en ritmo de bolero números del calibre de *Contigo en la distancia, La gloria eres tú* o *Hasta mañana, vida mía*, me atrevo a asegurar que esos importantes aciertos del filin no habrían llegado al corazón del pueblo.

Al enriquecer en los fabulosos años 50 a toda una nueva generación de creadores con armonías y acordes más amplios y ricos, el filin provocó una mayor atención al texto, dotándolo de más sinceridad y profundidad. Es más, creo que sin la experiencia del filin no se habría dado el movimiento de la nueva trova.

EL DANZÓN MODERNO

El danzón tradicional es un baile que desciende directamente de la contradanza del siglo XIX. El primer danzón reconocido como tal fue *Las alturas de Simpson* (una barriada de Matanzas), compuesto en 1877 por Miguel Faílde. Hay varias versiones sobre el origen del nombre «danzón», pero quizá la más verosímil refiere que Faílde, al alargar la duración de la danza, hasta entonces muy corta, hizo exclamar en cierta ocasión a un bailador: «Esto no es una danza, ¡es un danzón!»

El desarrollo de este género es una prueba de la continuidad histórica de la musica popular. Sus caracteres perdurables, forjados en la última etapa del período colonial, se acentuaron con la instauración de la República en 1902. Si Austria fue identificada con el vals vienés y Argentina con el tango, Cuba independiente encontró en el danzón una música que la representase con dignidad.

La pieza que fijó la forma definitiva del danzón es *El bombín de Barreto*, de José Urfé. Al aparecer en 1910 contribuyó a transformar la forma en que se bailaba este género, acentuándosele el montuno, su sección más movida; por supuesto, la picardía y el gracejo criollos se dieron cita para inventar nuevos pasos.

Notable fue también la contribución del trombonista Raimundo Valenzuela al afincamiento del danzón en aquella etapa. Pero se le ocurrió hacer instrumentaciones de fragmentos de óperas italianas como *Rigoletto*, *Tosca* o *Madame Butterfly*, «tomando prestados» pasajes y melodías pegajosas para incorporarlas indiscriminadamente a multitud de danzones. Esto tuvo lugar en una época en que el fervor del público burgués se inclinaba precisamente hacia la ópera; por carecer de un patrón melódico específico, al danzón le encajaba cuanto quisieran meterle. El resultado fue que no hubo acontecimiento durante cuarenta años que no fuese festejado por medio de un danzón. Los hubo para saludar el advenimiento de la República, de ambas guerras europeas, como *Aliados y alemanes* o *La toma de Varsovia*. Puede decirse que a partir de 1910, tanto boleros de moda como ragtimes americanos, pregones callejeros y hasta melodías chinas pasaron al danzón.

ORQUESTA DE ANTONIO MARÍA ROMEU, UNA DE LAS PRIMERAS CHARANGAS DEL SIGLO XX.

El abuso estancó su desarrollo a tal punto que cuando en 1916 visitó La Habana la primera jazz band de negros norteamericanos, fue acogida por el público con insospechadas emociones debido a la desorientación que invadía lo cubano. Afortunadamente, el son vino a poner «orden» en casa. El nuevo ritmo contribuyó pronto a la creación del danzonete, que tenía dos características novedosas: era más movido, ya que contenía elementos del son, y se cantaba. Establecido por el flautista Aniceto Díaz, el primer danzonete, titulado *Rompiendo la rutina*, fue estrenado en 1929 en el Casino Español de Matanzas. Le siguieron números como *El trigémino* y *El cocodrilo*, que lograron gran popularidad debido al inicio de la radio en octubre de 1922.

El danzón vivió años de lenta languidez hasta que al pianista Antonio María Romeu se le ocurrió incorporarle las letras de canciones y boleros, especialmente recordados en la voz de Barbarito Diez. A partir de ese momento, muchos cubanos crecieron creyendo que el danzón se cantaba.

Aparece el «ritmo nuevo»

Producto de una larga colaboración con los hermanos Israel *Cachao* y Orestes López, el contrabajista y cellista de su orquesta, el flautista **Antonio Arcaño** (1911-94), alcanzó un éxito resonante con su charanga no sólo en la radio sino también en los salones de baile más importantes, comenzando a formular el ritmo nuevo alrededor de 1940. El grandote Arcaño se había iniciado con la agrupación de Armando Valdespí y más tarde pasó a la Gris. Fundó su propia orquesta en 1937 partiendo de la estructura tradicional de la charanga (tipo de agrupación llamada también «francesa», formada por flauta, violines, piano, contrabajo, timbales y güiro, que no incluía cantantes.

Cuando grababan en Radio Cadena Suaritos se hizo famosa la voz de su director: «¿Listo Arcaño? ¡Dale Dermos!», que así se llamaba el técnico de grabaciones.

La charanga surgió en los primeros años del siglo XX como derivación de la orquesta típica (o de viento). En 1944 el ambicioso Arcaño convirtió a su charanga en una formación radiofónica,

EL FLAUTISTA ANTONIO ARCAÑO.

con una plantilla de dieciocho integrantes, iniciando trasmisiones muy escuchadas por la emisora Mil Diez.

Arcaño y sus Maravillas revolucionaron el género danzoril a base de interpretaciones novedosas y de alta calidad, y tuvo en cada instrumento al mejor músico, algunos de los cuales provenían de la Orquesta Sinfónica Nacional. Se cree que produjo más de 200 números. La suya fue la primera agrupación charanguera que incorporó la tumbadora. Su sonido se diferenciaba bastante de otra orquesta típica que le hacía la competencia, la del pianista Antonio María Romeu, quien también aumentó su plantilla, pero con instrumentos de metales; la de Arcaño era sólo de cuerdas, entre cuyos violines tocó Enrique Jorrín, el hombre que más tarde inventó el chachachá.

Los hermanos López concibieron numerosos danzones de «ritmo nuevo», verdadera revolución en la música popular cubana, que influyó en casi todas las formas posteriores. Sobre lo que ellos hacían en las cuer-

Los instrumentos: LA FLAUTA

Un instrumento clave para este tipo de música, la flauta travesera, tuvo que sufrir diversas etapas desde el establecimiento de la República en 1902 hasta el chachachá establecido por Enrique Jorrín a partir de 1953. La flauta hizo ostentación de su gallardía como instrumento clave en la sonoridad de la charanga danzonera, en contraposición a la trompeta, que le había robado al tres el papel protagonista en los septetos de son.

La tradición del siglo XIX había continuado con Roberto Ondina (1904-63), un excepcional flautista sinfónico, que realizó una valiosa labor formando algunos de los mejores ejecutantes actuales; durante largos años trabajó este virtuoso del píccolo con la Banda del Ejército. Otro distinguido flautista fue Alberto Socarrás (1908-87), quien había formado parte de la orquesta de la Familia Socarrás en Santiago de Cuba; llegado a Nueva York en 1927, se le acredita como uno de los precursores del jazz afrocubano y el haber grabado el primer solo de flauta en la historia del jazz en 1929, *Have you ever felt that way?* para el sello QRS de Clarence Williams. Socarrás fue un excelente arreglista y director de orquesta (ver pág. 236). En sus memorias, Dizzy Gillespie asegura no haber escuchado jamás un vibrato en flauta tan perfecto como el suyo.

Ese gusto del cubano bailador por escuchar registros agudos forzaba al flautista a un tipo de embocadura que creó un estilo muy sofisticado, llegando a giros que sólo la habilidad del ejecutante mantenían en el aire. La flauta actual, desde la adopción del sistema Boehm, tiene siete llaves que permiten tapar y destapar los orificios del tubo con rapidez. El instrumento sobresale en la ejecución de pasajes de velocidad: escalas, arpegios y trinos, y cubre una extensión de tres octavas en registro agudo, equivalente a la voz de soprano.

Antonio Arcaño, por su lado, y Richard Egües, de la Orquesta Aragón de Cienfuegos –sin olvidar a Efraín Loyola de la misma agrupación original– fueron buenos ejemplos de este tipo de sonido, que para muchos resultaba chillón. Sonido que reapareció más tarde en Nueva York, disfrazado de salsa, de la boca del dominicano Johnny Pacheco, después de la enorme influencia que allí ejerciera la flauta del dinámico José Antonio Fajardo en los años 60 y el continuo quehacer de Rolando Lozano, quien formó la charanga Nuevo Ritmo en Chicago y luego tocó con importantes agrupaciones. De la Orquesta Ritmo Oriental surgió Policarpo Díaz *Polo*, que después pasó al Buena Vista Social Club. Un verdadero virtuoso de la etapa revolucionaria es Orlando *Maraca* Valle (1966), miembro de Irakere desde 1988 a 1994.

das, Arcaño solía agregar un floreo de danzón sincopado con su flauta, acentuando la segunda sílaba del compás. En una entrevista de 1982 con la musicóloga Dora Ileana Torres explicó:

Orestes López incluía en la parte de piano su estilo sincopado y yo seguía esas improvisaciones haciendo filigranas con la flauta. Muy pronto la improvisación sobra la base de este estilo se generalizó en toda la orquesta, y así, sin haber creado un número específico, se comienza a tocar el ritmo nuevo. En 1940 a Orestes se le ocurre incluir en la última sección de uno de sus danzones un montuno al estilo de los que ya se venían tocando desde antes por la orquesta, escribiendo las partes fundamentales de acuerdo con la concepción del mismo, y así este danzón, cuyo título fue *Mambo*, le da nombre a lo que hace rato veníamos haciendo. Después yo le puse a este estilo ritmo nuevo.

Algunos investigadores aseguran que en 1942 la orquesta de Arcaño estrenó *Rareza de Melitón*, de *Cachao*, y que es éste el primer danzón donde aparece escrito un *tumbao* sincopado que ya Arsenio Rodríguez tocaba y le llamaba «mambo» o «candela», por lo que le atribuyen la paternidad del danzón-mambo a Israel *Cachao* y no a Orestes López.

Imposible acertar con el autor del nuevo ritmo, que se escuchó mucho durante la década 1950-60. Sin embargo, en las

ORESTES LÓPEZ.

partituras de varios danzones de *Cachao* –*Tres de café y dos de azúcar, Liceo de Peñalver, Permanganato* y *Los tres grandes*, por ejemplo–, aparece el uso frecuente de acordes disminuidos que ya eran habituales en la música norteamericana del período, así como ciertas resoluciones armónicas no clásicas, donde acordes complementarios, generalmente de séptima, sustituyen las funciones de tónica, dominante y subdominante.

También los cubanos pueden ser esnobistas. En diversas épocas, muchos han creído que lo norteamericano es lo mejor, incluyendo la música. Y digo esto porque en la segunda mitad de los años 40 Arcaño intentó detener en lo posible la avalancha de swing, fox-trots y otros ritmos que aparecían en las películas producidas en Estados Unidos. Verdadero azote sobre la música cubana, los filmes llegaban con una promoción muy poderosa y la gente pedía aquellas melodías, por lo que Arcaño se vio obligado a montar *Chatanooga Chu Chu* o temas de Tommy Dorsey y hacerles versiones que eran introducidas en los danzones en la parte melódica de los violines. Así creía mantener a raya la invasión; error craso porque en realidad sólo lograba popularizar aún más aquellos temas. Otro ejemplo de la tesis central indicada en la introducción a este libro.

Otras charangas de los años 50

FAJARDO Y SUS ESTRELLAS

Aparte de las de Arcaño y Romeu, fue la gran época para Fajardo y sus Estrellas, Sensación, Sublime, Melodías del 40, Neno González, Almendra, Cheo Belén Puig, Belisario López y las Estrellas Cubanas. Había otras, pero las citadas fueron las que marcaron toda una época. Las características muy peculiares de la Orquesta Aragón de Cienfuegos, una agrupación que impuso su patrón sonoro dentro y fuera de Cuba, se analizan en la sección dedicada al chachachá (ver pág. 172).

El flautista **José Antonio Fajardo** (1919-2001) tocó sucesivamente en las agrupaciones de René Álvarez, Armando Valdespí, Paulina Álvarez, A. M. Romeu, Neno González y Antonio Arcaño. En 1949 fundó Fajardo y sus Estrellas, un grupo con sabor dinámico. Es el autor de *Los tamalitos de Olga, Ritmo de pollo, De bala, Fajardo te pone a gozar* y muchos otros números que se escuchaban en la radio y en las gramolas de los bares. Desde 1961 radicó en Estados Unidos, donde jugó un papel preponderante justo antes del surgimiento de la salsa. Fajardo debe haber grabado más de 30 discos.

La orquesta Sensación y la Sublime continuaron tocando y grabando durante gran parte del período estudiado lo mismo que Melodías del 40, establecida en dicho año por el pianista Regino Frontela Fraga. Más antigua aún es la orquesta de Neno González, fundada en 1926 por el pianista Luis González, conocido por *Neno*, quien en la década de 1950-60 llenó de alegría los jardines de La Tropical. En sus primeros años contó con el flautista Belisario López, que después se independizó para formar su propia agrupación. La de Neno González todavía suena en La Habana bajo la dirección de Carlos González, su hijo, teniendo como eje la interpretación del chachachá, y por supuesto, con una plantilla nueva. Otra charanga memorable fue la Almendra, de Abelardito Valdés, fundada en 1940, en pleno auge del ritmo nuevo establecido por Arcaño y sus Maravillas; Valdés había sido el autor en 1938 de *Almendra*, un danzón clásico que para los cubanos es tan fundamental como el pregón *El manisero*, de Moisés Simons.

Fundada en 1934, la orquesta de Cheo Belén Puig, pianista, hijo del clarinetista del mismo nombre, se hizo muy popular en sus inicios, cuando contaba con la presencia del cantante Pablo Quevedo. En ella tocó el piano Odilio Urfé, un hombre muy delgado y gran conversador, que después se convirtió en un excelente musicógrafo. Tras la temprana muerte de Quevedo en 1936, se sucedieron los cantantes Alberto Aroche, Alfredito Valdés, Vicentico Valdés, Oscar Valdés y Paulina Álvarez. Todavía a finales de los años 50 se escuchaba esta charanga en algún baile habanero.

El flautista Belisario López formó su orquesta en 1928; entonces estaba a cargo de las teclas el notable compositor Armando Valdespí, que fue reemplazado más tarde por Facundo Rivero, compositor también y el fundador de un cuarteto que hizo historia (ver pág. 80). Belisario López ganó mucha fama por sus frecuentes apariciones en la radio hasta 1960, en que decidió abandonar el país. Un año antes, en plena euforia revolucionaria, el violinista Félix Reina había fundado la orquesta Estrellas Cubanas, con algunos músicos que procedían de la agrupación de Fajardo.

Quiero marcar los últimos compases de este rico danzón con el gran Antonio Arcaño, quien durante cinco décadas tocó la flauta brillantemente, compuso danzones, formó músicos y contribuyó a la felicidad de los bailadores. Pocos meses antes de morir en 1994, retirado y amargado porque ya no habían en Cuba charangas de calidad que interpretaran danzones, declaró en una entrevista que le realizara Luis Ríos Vega en La Habana, publicada en la revista *El Manisero* que se editaba en Barcelona:

El danzón ha decrecido mucho por falta de calidad... Si tuvieran una buena base, pero ¿quién ayuda a ese trabajo? El danzón no viaja, no se exporta, no vende. Entonces lo que hacen es crear grupos con trombones, saxofones y otros instrumentos. ¡La gente está tan saturada de música extranjera!

El nuevo son

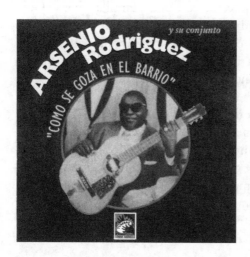

El músico que logró imprimirle un nuevo aliento al viejo son se llamó Ignacio Arsenio Travieso Scull, aunque otros aseguran que su verdadero nombre fue Ignacio Loyola Rodríguez. Al final se le conoció como **Arsenio Rodríguez**, autor del bolero *La vida es un sueño*, que conmueve por la patética declaración de que «La realidad es nacer y morir...». Cuando fundó su propio conjunto en 1940 amplió la base instrumental agregándole el piano y una tumbadora. Aunque históricamente se le acredita esta innovación, el investigador Cristóbal Díaz Ayala estima que fue el Sexteto Miquito, predecesor de lo que después se convirtió en el Conjunto Casino, a quien primero se le ocurrió incorporar el piano en 1935, tocado por un músico conocido como *El chino*.

Lo esencial es que Arsenio estableció primero un estilo de ejecutar el tres distinto al de los sextetos y septetos de son; después logró que el piano hiciera un empaste con el tres a la vez que sus figuraciones armónicas enriquecían este aspecto, además de arpegios y tumbaos. Fue Arsenio quien enseñó al teclista *Lilí* Martínez Griñán los acordes en contrapunto que él hacía en las cuerdas, estableciendo pautas no sólo en Cuba sino en todo el Caribe. La trompeta en boca de Félix Chapottín, quien logró establecer improvisaciones netamente cubanas a partir de escalas de la época del swing norteamericano, hizo el resto. Desde entonces, el género del son comenzó una evolución que para mí no ha terminado.

De origen congolés, y capaz de sonar un cuero como un percusionista profesional, Arsenio pronto adquirió renombre entre los bailadores que cada domingo acudían a La Tropical en busca del ritmo de su conjunto; durante años se le escuchó por la radio Mil Diez. En su grupo maduraron el trompeta Félix Chapottín y los vocalistas René Scull y Miguelito Cuní. *Me boté de guaño* y *Bruca maniguá*, son sones lentos firmados por Arsenio, que confirmó la voz de Miguelito Valdés como un especialista de lo afrocubano.

Su transformación del son no fue realmente un cambio de rumbo sino un desplazamiento de acentos. Músico de pueblo, Arsenio logró imprimirle una cadencia más abiertamente afrocubana en su base rítmica y lo enriqueció tímbricamente; por eso lo llamo el nuevo son. Otros músicos posteriores lograron aprovechar sus ideas con más efectividad o tuvieron mejor suerte.

Abrumado por la carencia de un clima propicio para su trabajo y buscando cura para su ceguera, Arsenio Rodríguez marchó a Nueva York en 1951, donde sostuvo un conjunto cubanísimo y contribuyó a formar a toda una serie de instrumentistas que más tarde emergieron con la salsa neoyorquina. Murió en la pobreza en la Nochevieja de 1971 en Los Ángeles, California. En la pág. 54 aparece más información sobre este singular innovador.

EL MAMBO

El creador del mambo, tal y como lo conocemos, fue **Dámaso Pérez Prado** (1916-89), un pianista singular, con un poder de síntesis muy agudo y una gran facilidad como arreglista. Hay que subrayar la verdadera dimensión de lo anterior porque el debate sobre la paternidad del mambo continúa, azuzado por desafortunadas afirmaciones surgidas a raíz de la presentación del documental *Cachao, como su ritmo no hay dos*, producido y dirigido en 1993 por el actor cubano Andy García.

No se trata de poner en tela de juicio que el bajista Orestes López (hermano de *Cachao*) escribiera en 1939 una pieza danzonera que tituló *Mambo*, hecha de violines, flauta y timbales, ni que el sonero Arsenio Rodríguez también reclamara su autoría. También sabemos que otros músicos importantes como Bebo Valdés, Andrés Echevarría, mejor conocido como el tresista Niño Rivera, y el pianista René Hernández ya venían buscando el nuevo ritmo; también Antonio Arcaño llegó a reclamar su paternidad.

Los orígenes del vocablo son bastante confusos y se pierden en el léxico de los esclavos africanos en la región del Caribe. En Haití llaman

Los mejores: BENNY MORÉ

Considerado uno de los artistas más geniales que ha producido la música popular del Caribe, por su creatividad como inspirador desenfadado de sones memorables, Benny Moré (1919-63) brilló en todos los géneros. Le dio un impulso considerable a la música bailable con los sones que Ramón Cabrera y otros realizaron para él, sumados a varios boleros de su propia autoría que crearon toda una atmósfera en aquel fabuloso momento, entre 1953 y 1963.

Oriundo de Santa Isabel de las Lajas, pueblito al que dedicó un número lento, muy sabroso de bailar, su verdadero nombre era Bartolomé Maximiliano Moré. Pasando innumerables penurias, en 1940 se trasladó a la capital donde estuvo cantando en parques y cafés, pero ya en 1945 se encontraba en México con el conjunto Cauto, de Miguel Matamoros. Fue allí donde grabó más tarde con las orquestas de Dámaso Pérez Prado, Rafael de Paz y Mariano Mercerón, entre otras, e incluso apareció en la película *Carita de cielo*, donde cantó *Por El Prado* (con la bailarina Ninón Sevilla) y *Tuñaré*, un número trepidante, anticipo de los que después hizo en Cuba, adonde regresó definitivamente en 1953.

Al coincidir con una de las estancias en la isla del saxo Mariano Mercerón y su orquesta, ambos se pusieron de acuerdo para aceptar un contrato con la Cadena Oriental de Radio para el programa «De fiesta con Bacardí», transmitido desde Santiago de Cuba; durante dos años, los futuros vocalistas Fernando Álvarez y Pacho Alonso le hicieron coro a Benny. De vuelta a la capital fue contratado por Amado Trinidad, dueño de RHC Cadena Azul, una de las radios más poderosas de la época, para tratar de hacer popular el nuevo ritmo batanga, creado por el pianista y arreglista Bebo Valdés, quien reside en Suecia desde hace muchos años. Más tarde fue llamado a Radio Progreso, haciéndose acompañar por la orquesta del compositor Ernesto Duarte. A partir de entonces, el bolero y el son cubano fueron adquiriendo un estilo nuevo, desenfadado, irrepetible para otros intérpretes.

En 1953 Benny Moré organizó su primera banda gigante, la legendaria «tribu», como le gustaba llamarla. Gracias a la amplia audiencia del programa «Cascabeles Candado» de CMQ Radio, la nueva agrupación fue conocida de inmediato en toda Cuba, y los contratos para amenizar bailes y verbenas no se hicieron esperar. Lo mismo aparecía en Radio Progreso que en el «Show del Mediodía» o el «Cabaret Regalías», del Canal 6 de televisión. La Habana era entonces una fiesta y él, el encargado de encender las luces.

Por entonces grabó, en un dúo fabuloso con el tenor mexicano Pedro Vargas, *Solamente una vez,* de Agustín Lara, *La vida es un sueño,* de Arsenio Rodríguez, y los también boleros *Perdón* y *Obsesión,* ambos del puertorriqueño Pedro Flores. Hay una anécdota muy linda que refirió Pedro Vargas, quien había quedado atónito al descubrir, tras entregarle las partituras de los temas, que el delgado Benny no sabía leer música, y que a pesar de eso, cantaba con mayor precisión y técnica que cualquier profesional de academia.

Más tarde vocalizó junto al carismático tenor venezolano Alfredo Sadel el bolero *Alma libre,* de Juan Bruno Tarraza. Todavía se recuerdan sus dúos ocasionales con Roberto Faz y la controversia sonera con Rolando Laserie en el Alí Bar Club. Y aquel otro con Paulina Álvarez, la «Emperatriz del danzonete», ante las cámaras de televisión en 1960, o el histórico con Joseíto Fernández, en un programa radial en que coincidieron, ambos improvisando alrededor de la tonada guajira *Guantanamera.*

Con su imagen de sonero mayor, resulta difícil imaginarse a Benny como un sutil creador de boleros. Sin embargo, dejó algunas piezas que él mismo interpre-

BENNY MORÉ «EL BÁRBARO DEL RITMO».

tó con afinación plena y que contribuyeron a aumentar su leyenda, especialmente *Ahora soy tan feliz, Conocí la paz, Dolor y perdón* y el bolero-cha *Mi amor fugaz,* dispersos entre unas 200 grabaciones que realizó. En ellos logró combinar una emisión clara y resonante con un fraseo donde los requiebros, las graduaciones de potencia y levedad, llegando a menudo hasta el susurro, le ganaron la admiración del público. Los sones *Manzanillo, Palma Soriano* y *Guantánamo* lo llevaron a la cima de la popularidad; la gente quería bailar y él les daba lo que querían. Basándose en los arreglos de Pedro Jústiz *Peruchín,* de Ignacio Cabrera *Cabrerita* o de Generoso *El tojo* Jiménez, la «tribu» continuó grabando para la RCA Victor y apareciendo en las fastuosos teatros habaneros Warner y América. Al escuchar hoy día cualquiera de sus sones, no deja de sorprender que puedan sonar tan actualizados: tienen armonías modernas, improvisaciones impetuosas e ingredientes jazzísticos sin dejar de ajustarse a las raíces cubanas. Con cambios ocasionales en la plantilla, los veinte miembros de la «tribu» se pasearon por todo el continente americano asombrando al público. Fue invitado especial en la entrega de los Oscar de la Academia de Hollywood en 1955 y realizó una presentación en el salón Nicola de Nueva York en el mismo año.

Desde mediados de 1954 Benny Moré comenzó a ser conocido como «El bárbaro del ritmo», sobrenombre con que lo anunciaba el locutor Ibrahím Urbino. Abría una presentación cualquiera con el son *Elige tú que canto yo*, y después seguía con los montunos *Se te cayó el tabaco* o *Qué bueno baila usted*, los afros *El tiempo de la colonia* o *Siguaraya*, guajiras como *No hay tierra como la mía*, junto a los guaguancós *Pongan atención* y *Qué sentimiento me da*, mambos lentos como *Encantado de la vida*, el changüí *Maracaibo oriental*, porros como *La múcura*, el merengue *El santo de tía Juliana*, el chachachá *Ya llegó la hora* y boleros de la importancia de *Cómo fue*, de Ernesto Duarte. Todo lo hacía bien. Menos velar por su dinero, porque ganó mucho y todo lo derrochó en francachelas. Desordenado en su vida privada, con frecuencia llegaba tarde a alguna actuación y por supuesto, con demasiadas copas. Hacia el final, de sólo oler el vaso de ron ya se sentía embriagado.

Lo que no me puedo explicar es por qué nunca grabó composiciones de personas con las que mantuvo una amistad recíproca, tales como Miguel Matamoros u Orlando de la Rosa. Por las incorporaciones que hizo del jazz, sus innovadoras inflexiones y su apego a la corriente del filin, sorprende aún más que no haya cantado obras de José Antonio Méndez o César Portillo de la Luz. Quizá rehusaba modular piezas ya estrenadas o establecidas por otros artistas.

Después del triunfo revolucionario, Benny participó en las ediciones de 1959 y 1962 del Festival de la Cultura Cubana, y actuó en el cabaré Night & Day en 1960. También se presentó en infinidad de bailes populares en varias provincias, obteniendo en 1961 resonantes éxitos en el Salón Mambí del cabaré Tropicana. Ese mismo año, en el baile público «Papel y tinta», organizado por el periódico *Revolución* y celebrado en el Parque Central habanero, tuve la increíble suerte de tocar en su banda gigante, sustituyendo al timbalero que había enfermado a última hora; no me quitó los ojos de encima en toda la noche. El espigado sonero murió de cirrosis hepática; tenía sólo 44 años. Al Benny se le podrían dedicar aquellos versos de Nicolás Guillén: «Bebedor de trago largo, / garguero de hoja de lata, / en mar de ron barco suelto, / jinete de la cumbancha...» Su última actuación fue el 16 de febrero de 1963.

mambo a las sacerdotisas del vudú, y según el etnólogo Fernando Ortiz la palabra proviene del Congo y significa conversación; lo cierto es que el término quedó flotando con diversas connotaciones en el habla caribeña. Durante su juventud, Pérez Prado escuchó a menudo aquello de que «si el mambo estaba duro era que la cosa iba mal»; no es de extrañar pues, que más de un músico popular lo emplease. El término se siguió usando por muchos años junto con «diablo» para identificar el aquelarre o clímax de los metales en el montuno de un son movido.

Lo importante es que fue Pérez Prado quien estableció el novedoso formato musical, heredero, eso sí, de una rica tradición sonera a la que el autor incorporó elementos de la música norteamericana para convertirlo en algo original y desconocido hasta enton-ces. Ello no ha impedido que algunos críti-cos continúen, en la isla y fuera de ella, considerándolo como «el malo de la pelícu-la». ¿Cuál fue el origen de toda esa envidia?

Dámaso había nacido en Matanzas, una ciudad que gozaba de cierto nivel cul-tural, y creció junto a su hermano Panta-león, también músico. Aunque provenían de un hogar humilde, Dámaso estudió pia-no clásico y órgano con Rafael Somavilla y con María Angulo, despuntando en gru-pos locales antes de irse para La Habana en 1942.

DÁMASO PÉREZ PRADO.

Tuvo que tocar mucho piano en Cuba para ganarse la vida. Cuando en 1943 se unió a la Orquesta Casino de la Playa ésta estaba dirigida por Liduvino Pereira, con su cantante Orlando Guerra *Cascarita*. El pianista ganaba 5 dólares (de entonces) por noche y otros 2 por cada arreglo mu-sical. Pero se sabía que estaba urdiendo algo nuevo. Como arreglista de éste y otros grupos musicales, así como de la obra de incipientes composi-tores, Pérez Prado alcanzó a desarrollar un sólido oficio y aprendió cómo exaltar cada instrumento. Era ambicioso e intuía que necesitaba una gran orquesta con fuertes metales para llevar a cabo el concubinato que pro-yectaba entre los ritmos afrocubanos y el jazz.

Antes de unirse a la Casino de la Playa, Pérez Prado había tocado en el cabaré El Kursaal, que quedaba por los muelles habaneros; después pasó a la orquesta del cabaret Pennsylvania en la playa de Marianao, empleando disonancias al teclado que ya anunciaban lo que se convertiría en mambo. En 1946 se independizó, organizó su propia orquesta y un año después realizó una extensa gira por Venezuela y Argentina, donde llevó a cabo sus primeras grabaciones. En 1948 fue por primera vez a México, y allí tocó el piano con varias agrupaciones.

Como en Cuba nunca le hicieron mucho caso, decidió instalarse en la capital azteca en 1949, agrupando los metales mexicanos que necesitaba, pero a los percusionistas los mandó a llamar de Cuba. Ensayó mucho y finalmente alquiló el teatro Blanquita, anunciando un espectáculo titulado «Al son del mambo». Aquella presentación se convirtió en un verdadero éxito y le dio la plataforma que necesitaba.

Había que ser muy buen instrumentista para trabajar con él, sobre todo los metales, porque les exigía muchas notas altas difíciles de alcanzar. Y empezó a lanzar una composición tras otra, grabando primero para la RCA Victor de México y luego para la de Nueva York, siempre tratando de incluir el vocablo mambo en los títulos para identificarlos. Y pegó. El «Rey del mambo» ganó mucho dinero y se hizo famoso en pocos años: *Que rico el mambo* vendió 4,5 millones de discos entre 1950-51, una cantidad extraordinaria para aquella época. Debió ser un hombre difícil, un solitario insolidario con su éxito, incluso algo mezquino con su dinero. En una entrevista realizada en 1984 se quejó amargamente de los que pretendían arrebatarle la autoría del mambo.

Lo cierto es que antes de emigrar a México, entusiasmado por los cuentos que le hiciera el cantante Kiko Mendive sobre las oportunidades de trabajo en el vecino país, Pérez Prado trató de lanzar el mambo en Cuba. Llegó a grabar un disco sencillo a manera de «demo» con su *Mambo caén* y *So caballo*, con músicos de categoría, sus amigos, que lo hicieron gratis, fascinados por los arreglos del teclista; entre ellos estaban el saxo alto Germán LeBatard, el guitarrista Vicente González Rubiera *Guyún*, el saxo barítono Osvaldo Urrutia y el contrabajista Reinaldo Mercier, pero los timoratos empresarios no se dieron cuenta de que se trataba de algo realmente innovador. El pequeño pianista estaba muy avanzado para su época. Algo parecido le sucedió al gigante Bebo Valdés con su ritmo batanga y al tresero Niño Rivera con su cubibop. Según el musicólogo Leonardo Acosta, en México Pérez Prado recibió el apoyo de la vedette Ninón Sevilla y de otros cubanos, mientras que el bongosero Clemente *Chicho* Piquero le ayudó a resolver el carné de la omnipotente Unión de Músicos Mexicanos.

Trabajó muy duro, como siempre, experimentando y desarrollando un estilo que jugaba con diferentes planos sonoros con dos registros básicos, enfrentando las agudas trompetas (que en algunas grabaciones hizo sonar contra una pared para obtener la resonancia que buscaba), al tono grave de los saxofones que llevaban la síncopa. Los primeros mambos que grabó para la RCA Victor fueron *José* y *Macamé*, muy lentos, y no pegaron como los posteriores.

Sus mambos más populares incluyen *Mambo Nº 5*, *Qué rico el mambo*, *Pianolo*, *Caballo negro*, *El ruletero*, *Lupita*, *Mambo en sax*, *La chula linda* y *Mambo Nº 8*. Grabó no sólo para la RCA sino también para Seeco, United Artists, Epic y otros sellos. En 1952, el director de orquesta Armando Romeu (ver pág. 320), sobrino del viejo pianista Antonio María Romeu, tomó un tema creado por Stan Kenton y, arreglándolo al estilo de Pérez Prado, se lo envió a México como reconocimiento por su enorme éxito. Así surgió *Mambo a la Kenton*, erróneamente atribuido a Pérez Prado. Leonardo Acosta considera que de ahí surge la confusión sobre la influencia de Stan Kenton en la obra del cubano.

Su enorme influencia

A Pérez Prado hay que analizarlo por su importante *opus mamborum*, pero también como el creador de melodías inolvidables; escuche *Cerezo rosa*, de *tempo* lento (casi un mambo caén) con la trompeta de Billy Regis suspendiendo cuatro largas notas en el espacio antes de descender en suave cadencia. Esta pieza llegó a vender casi dos millones de discos en 1955 y sirvió de tema a la película *Underwater* (1955), donde Jane Russell, acompañada de la orquesta del maestro, aparece bailándolo con sensualidad. Cosas de Hollywood.

Su celebridad se consolidó aún más con *Patricia*, con esos graves bramidos del trombón, que alcanzó ventas de cinco millones de discos gracias a la película italiana *La dolce vita* (1960), de Fellini, donde Anita Ekberg se contonea de puro gusto. Pérez Prado afirmaba sin modestia alguna que con el órgano que lleva la melodía de *Patricia*, él había introducido la música electrónica en Estados Unidos.

Prado, como le llamaban sus compañeros, siempre estuvo a la vanguardia. Eso tampoco se lo perdonaron en Cuba; es una posición incó-

moda y solitaria que pocos músicos populares han alcanzado. De pequeña estatura, vestía elegantemente, con una figura que llamaba la atención por su tipo de bigote, su grueso cuello y caída de hombros. Benny
Moré, que trabajó bastante con él, lo bautizó «el chaparrito con cara de
foca».

A partir de la locura del nuevo ritmo, con jóvenes que adquirían sus
discos antes de que los expusieran en las tiendas, otros músicos importantes empezaron a parir mambos en la isla: Bebo Valdés grabó *Rareza del
siglo* y *Güempa*; Julio Gutiérrez se apareció con *Un poquito de tu amor* y
hasta el bolerista Mario Fernández Porta aportó su mambo *Franqueza*.
Pedro Jústiz *Peruchín* sacó *Mamey colorao*, seguido de *España en llamas*
y *Semilla de marañón*.

El norteamericano Stan Kenton, que compartía el mismo interés en
las trompetas, grabó *Viva Prado!*, de Shorty Rogers, como homenaje al
«Rey del mambo». Y lo que es más importante, en México Benny Moré
grabó con Pérez Prado los temas *Anabacoa*, *Pachito e'ché*, *Rico y sabroso*, *Rabo y oreja* y otros que formaron parte del primer repertorio moderno en la voz del sonero. Fueron aquellos años muy productivos para el
Benny en México, donde aprendió a organizar una gran orquesta; después, en Cuba, haría que sus arreglistas asimilaran la dinámica del «cara
de foca». Me atrevería a asegurar que sin Pérez Prado, Benny Moré no
habría alcanzado su dimensión histórica.

Resulta aleccionador que Pérez Prado influyera sobremanera en
dos generaciones de músicos norteamericanos. Sin embargo, la película
Los reyes del mambo tocan canciones de amor, basada en la novela ho-
mónima del cubano Oscar Hijuelos, ignora totalmente al maestro, aparte de que su banda sonora no tiene nada que ver con el mambo verdadero.

La fiebre del nuevo ritmo revolucionó en cinco años el quehacer de
las mejores bandas latinas en Nueva York, incluyendo las de *Machito* y
sus AfroCubans, la de Tito Rodríguez y la de Tito Puente. Sin embargo,
en Manhattan jamás fue reconocido como el «Rey del mambo», ya que
Machito había impuesto una versión propia con los magníficos arreglos
de su pianista René Hernández. Entretanto, Gene Norman lo presentó en
Los Ángeles, donde Prado estableció una formación con músicos norteamericanos, mientras en Roma se filmaba *Mambo*, con la voz de Xiomara
Alfaro, el ballet de Catherine Dunhan y la actuación de Silvana Mangano
y Vittorio Gassman.

El mambo provocó la aparición de grandes bailarinas cubanas como las Mulatas de Fuego, de Roderico Neira *Rodney*, el genial coreógrafo durante la mejor época del cabaré Tropicana, o las Mamboletas, de Gustavo Roig. Muy difícil de bailar para la gente común, los movimientos rápidos y casi violentos del mambo le ganaron la exagerada reputación de ser un baile lascivo, un simulacro del acto sexual. Tanto fue así que en 1952 el cardenal de Lima prohibió a sus feligreses bailarlo. Cosas de la Iglesia.

Para tocar mambo hacía falta una gran orquesta con metales decididos. Para eso, los fuertes labios mexicanos resultaron los mejores; México contaba además con la rica herencia de las bandas militares que desde los tiempos del absurdo emperador austría-co Maximiliano I de Habsburgo (1863-67) habían establecido un marcado estilo de aplicar los labios a la boquilla de la trompeta. También contribuyó a difundir todo un estilo el sonido de la trompeta del Septeto Habanero en su gira mexicana de 1929. Todo eso lo descubrió Pérez Prado y lo supo explotar en los formidables solos del azteca Chilo Morán, mientras él martilleaba el teclado introduciendo los *clusters* (o racimos de notas afiladas) que son característicos del mambo.

«EL REY DEL MAMBO» EN SU MEJOR ÉPOCA.

La percusión en el mambo

Pérez Prado fue el primero en instalar la pareja de tumbadoras, una más aguda que la otra, haciendo que el bongó repiqueteara en los aquelarres, con acentos y cierres marcados por unos timbales con platillo a cargo de Aurelio Tamayo, que nunca se desorbitó pero le agregó un estilo peculiar, como sucede en la rápida versión de *Cocaleca*. ¡Que nos digan los congueros Mongo Santamaría o Modesto Durán cómo organizaba la percusión el ronco Prado! En *Caballo negro* se repite insistentemente una frase del bongó de *Chicho* Piquero que parece parida por la verdadera rumba. Aun en los mambos acelerados (que Prado denominó *batiri*) supo controlar la armonía total de los cueros.

Avanzados los años 50 el mambo se trivializó, perdiendo su frescura y Pérez Prado se dedicó a componer piezas más ambiciosas: *Voodoo Suite* (1955) en colaboración con Shorty Rogers, *Mosaico cubano* (1956), *Exotic Suite of the Americas* (1962) y su último acierto, *Concierto para bongó* (1965), rescatado por Pedro Almodóvar en el filme *Kika* (1993). También intentó duplicar, inútilmente, el éxito del mambo con la invención de otros ritmos como el suby, el pau pau, la culeta, la chunga, el mambo-twist, el rockambo y especialmente el dengue, una modalidad con elementos del mambo y de la música conga, que se afirma en un hierro percutido con dos baquetas que repiten la misma figuración durante toda la pieza.

Dámaso Pérez Prado murió en México el 13 de septiembre de 1989, seis años después que su coetáneo Frank Grillo *Machito,* el que le disputó la plaza neoyorquina del mambo. Este aspecto aparece ampliamente cubierto en el capítulo 4.

EL CHACHACHÁ

El chachachá que creó **Enrique Jorrín** (1926-1987) fue uno de los acontecimientos de mayor importancia en el ámbito musical cubano a comienzos de la década de los 50, cuando trabajaba como primer violín de la Orquesta América, agrupación formada en 1942 por Ninón Mondéjar. El género musical que vertiginosamente conectó con la atención de los bailadores pronto se puso de moda en la radio, la televisión y el disco, y logró revolucionar el quehacer de otras orquestas, las llamadas charangas de la época, y que, gracias al chachachá, volvieron a ocupar planos estelares en cuanto a demanda popular.

Jorrín había estudiado en el Conservatorio Municipal de La Habana y se inició como violinista de la Orquesta del Instituto Nacional de Música bajo la dirección de Enrique González Mantici. Posteriormente, el joven músico se vinculó a las agrupaciones danzoneras los Hermanos Contreras y a Arcaño y sus Maravillas, antes de ingresar en la América. El propio Jorrín lo explicó así al investigador Ezequiel Rodríguez:

En la época que comienzo a escribir mis primeros danzones, estaban de moda los que interpretaba la orquesta de Arcaño, llamado ritmo nuevo. La mayoría de las orquestas habían abolido los cantantes y los danzones eran netamente instrumentales, al estilo del mambo. Construí algunos danzones en los que los músicos de la orquesta hacíamos pequeños coros. Gustó al público y tomé esa vía. El danzón siempre ha sido el estilo musical que más aportaciones ha dado a los diferentes ritmos. En el danzón *Constancia* intercalé algunos montunos conocidos y la participación del público en los coros me llevó a hacer más y más danzones de ese estilo.

Cada sociedad o club que surgía pedía que se le hiciera alguna letra donde se le mencionara. De esa manera comienzan a cantar los músicos. Yo le pedía a la orquesta que todos cantaran al unísono. Así se lograban tres cosas: que se oyera la letra con más claridad, más potente, y además, se disimulara la calidad de las voces de los músicos que, en realidad, no eran cantantes. En el año 1948 cambié el estilo de una canción mexicana de Guty Cárdenas, *Nunca*. La primera parte la hice en su estilo original y la segunda tomó un sentido rítmico diferente a la melodía.

Gustó tanto al público que decidí independizar del danzón las últimas partes que yo construía, el tercer trío o montuno. Tiempo después, hacia 1951, y con la experiencia que había acumulado, vieron la luz piezas como *La engañadora*, que tiene una introducción, una parte A repetido, B y A, finalizando con una coda en forma de rumba.

Casi al principio de empezar a componer, observé los pasos de los bailadores en el danzón-mambo. Noté la dificultad en la mayoría de ellos, en especial en los ritmos sincopados. Esto se debe a que los pasos de los bailadores se producen a contratiempo. ¡Imagínense! Los bailadores a contratiempo y las melodías en

ENRIQUE JORRÍN.

forma de síncopa hacen en extremo difícil la colocación de los pasos con respecto a la música. Entonces empecé a hacer melodías con las que se pudiera bailar sin la necesidad del acompañamiento, procurando hacer las menos síncopas posibles. Con ello se desplazó el acento que se produce en la cuarta corchea, en el mambo, hacia el primer tiempo en el chachachá. Con melodías casi bailables por sí solas y el balance que surge entre melodías a tiempo y contratiempo, es que nace el chachachá.

Curiosamente, la estructura formal de *La engañadora* no se repitió en otras piezas de Jorrín, aunque su marcada y lenta cadencia señaló la esencia de lo que sería el chachachá. También es de notar que en las partes cantadas de varios números, algunos autores incorporaron rasgos estilísticos de chotis y cuplés españoles, muy de moda en Cuba en aquella época.

Enrique Jorrín permaneció en México de 1954-58; desde allí entabló una verdadera batalla con Ninón Mondéjar para dirimir quién era en verdad el rey del chachachá. Como consecuencia de la prodigalidad de ambas agrupaciones, el más perjudicado resultó ser Pérez Prado, cuyo mambo fue casi abandonado para concentrarse en el novedoso compás, que era de pareja abrazada y más fácil de bailar.

Los instrumentos: EL GÜIRO

La modesta calabaza con infinidad de surcos paralelos sobre los que se raspa firmemente con un palito ha tenido una historia singular en la música del Caribe, y particularmente en la de Cuba. Se trata de un idiófono también conocido como «guayo» o «rallador», términos que denominan además a un utensilio de cocina para rallar alimentos. Construido a partir de un fruto verde, vaciado de su pulpa y puesto a secar, que tiene forma cilíndrica alargada, algo arqueada y adelgazada hacia su extremo superior, el güiro se ejecuta normalmente por uno de los cantantes que forman el coro en las agrupaciones musicales.

Colocado en posición vertical y sostenido por dos dedos que se introducen en huecos posteriores, los sonidos que se obtienen de su raspado son bastante similares. El güiro tiene una función eminentemente rítmica, y realiza una labor de relleno continuo como las maracas, con una diferencia primordial: de la combinación y duración de los movimientos descendentes de la muñeca, que producen un sonido corto, y los movimientos ascendentes, que logran un raspado más profundo, se pueden lograr diversos acentos que pronto fueron identificados con el surgimiento del danzón hacia finales del siglo XIX. El güiro vino a suplementar el diseño rítmico de la «cáscara» o baqueteo que se hace en los costados de los timbales.

Aunque se suele emplear en otros géneros musicales, es un instrumento muy identificado con las charangas de chachachá. El término proviene precisamente del sonido de tres raspados firmes que se ejecutan en el güiro, aunque este efecto ya venía usándose ocasionalmente durante los años 40 en la interpretación del danzón moderno y en el de nuevo ritmo. Enrique Jorrín supo aprovecharlo.

El güiro tuvo que competir con las maracas, que adoptaron los primeros grupos soneros por su mayor agilidad de ejecución y por la alegría que comunican; las maracas además, provenían de los viejos tríos de trovadores santiagueros. Una versión del güiro en metal y tocado con un hierrillo había tomado cierta importancia a mediados del XIX entre los piquetes de circo y conjuntos de órgano de la zona más oriental de la isla; conocido como «guayo», este instrumento de metal es precisamente el que se emplea en el rápido merengue dominicano, mientras que en Puerto Rico usan la güira vegetal tocada con un listoncillo que lleva clavados cuatro o cinco alambres fuertes, produciendo un sonido más refinado y continuo. En Colombia toma la forma de un tubo fino y alargado, conocido como «guacharaca».

En los últimos 50 años han surgido en Cuba sorprendentes güireros, como Gustavo Tamayo (1913), quien ha sido integrante de las mejores orquestas tipo charanga y más tarde figuró en las descargas de *Cachao*, en el Quinteto de Música Moderna, bajo la dirección del pianista Frank Emilio Flynn, y en el grupo Los Amigos, de Guillermo Barreto. Otro destacado especialista de este curioso raspador es Enrique Lazaga (1939), quien estima que es más fácil hallar una aguja en un pajar que un aspirante a güirero en las aulas de un conservatorio.

Aparte de *La engañadora*, entre otros conocidos chachachás de Jorrín se encuentran *Silver Star, El alardoso, El túnel, Nada para ti, Osiris* y *Me muero*. En 1964 Jorrín realizó una gira por África y Europa con su propia orquesta; después trabajó como instrumentista y escribió las partituras para varias comedias musicales representadas en teatros habaneros.

Uno de los métodos que utilizó para reafirmar la veracidad de su autoría del género antes de irse a México fue el apoyo indiscriminado a conjuntos musicales que apenas comenzaban a destacarse. El director de uno de ellos acudió a Jorrín para pedirle ayuda; se llamaba Rafael Lay y había llegado de Cienfuegos exclusivamente con ese encargo, el cual fue fácil de conseguir: generosamente, Jorrín le entregó varios chachachás para que pudieran trabajar en su ciudad natal. La producción del grupo cienfueguero se incrementó de inmediato, pues su formato y la calidad de sus instrumentistas eran ideales para la interpretación del novedoso ritmo. Pronto estuvieron listos para registrar 35 temas originales.

Tras algunos intentos de grabación con el sello Panart, los músicos de la Aragón lograron producir en 1953 su primer disco con la RCA Victor. Cuatro temas lo conformaban: *El agua de Clavelito, Nunca, Tres lindas cubanas* y *Mentiras criollas*. Aunque se establecieron definitivamente en La Habana en 1955, ya desde 1949 actuaban ocasionalmente en la capital, alcanzando cierto prestigio en el Selva Club y en asociaciones como los Jóvenes del Vals; cuando comenzaron sus presentaciones en Radio Progreso, entonces sí que entraron por la puerta grande. Muy poco tiempo fue necesario para se convirtiera en la primera charanga de Cuba.

TOMÁS VALDÉZ, PANCHITO ARBELÁEZ Y RICHARD EGÜES DE LA ARAGÓN.

La seriedad con que la Aragón asumía los compromisos artísticos y la impresionante calidad interpretativa de su flautista **Richard Egües** (1926) le dio una fama sin precedentes, que sólo se empañó por una serie de problemas sindicales que alcanzaron a boicotear su presencia en algunos sitios. Rafael Lay había conocido en 1952 a un personaje que solucionó de plano todo el conflicto con un simple anuncio público: «De ahora en adelante, donde yo cante tocan ustedes». Era Benny Moré.

Richard Egües, uno de los más ingeniosos flautistas que ha dado Cuba, es el autor de *El bodeguero* (que cantó hasta Nat King Cole), *El Cuini, Sabrosona, Bombón chá, El cerquillo* y muchos otros. En 1984 dejó la Aragón, en el momento en que era su director, para fundar su propia orquesta, desde donde continuó haciendo sus acrobáticas improvisaciones; hace años que está solo, dedicado a la enseñanza. Por su parte, el jovial violinista **Rafael Lay** (1927-82), un jovencito de trece años cuando entró a trabajar con la Aragón en 1940, llegó a convertirse en su director a partir de 1948. Lay hizo arreglos para orquestas tipo charanga y dirigió la Orquesta Popular de Conciertos, integrada por músicos provenientes de diversas agrupaciones; fue el autor de *Cero codazos, Envidia, Charlestón-cha* y otros, así como de uno de los mejores sones de todos los tiempos: *Cienfuegos* (dedicado a la ciudad cuna de la Aragón), que le grabó

Chapottín con la voz de Miguelito Cuní y los sabios dedos de Sabino Peñalver en el contrabajo.

Para el libro Guinness

A casi medio siglo de haberse inventado el chachachá, el 23 de enero de 1994, en pleno mediodía en las Ramblas de la población catalana de Vilafranca, ocurrió un suceso destinado a convertirse en un récord del libro Guinness. Allí se dieron cita 1.290 personas para bailar una versión de la *Guantanamera* en ritmo de chachachá, interpretada por Celia Cruz en la banda sonora de la película *Los reyes del mambo tocan canciones de amor*. Al aire libre y en pleno invierno se llevó a cabo esta inusitada ocurrencia de la profesora de baile Roser Blanch Acedo. El acontecimiento fue constatado en acta por un notario, quien además de dar fe del número de participantes, incluyó en su protocolo que los bailadores gozaron este rico vacilón «con tan enorme alegría como extraordinario garbo». (Información aparecida en la revista *El Manisero*, Nº 2, abril-mayo 1994).

¡A MOVER LA CINTURA!

Ya me he referido varias veces a la pasión de los cubanos por el baile, razón de ser de gran parte de la producción musical del país. No importa de qué época se trate; ella, la criolla, más que él, buscará la forma de contonearse de la manera que mejor le sea posible, sin importar tampoco la edad ni el sitio en que suene una música sabrosona. El baile es el componente activo, la consecuencia inevitable e irreversible de esa música cuando suena y hay un cuerpo que la escucha y una banda que no ceja de comunicar sabor y vitalidad, aunque el número dure quince minutos y deje a todos agotados. Resulta impensable cualquier tipo de son cubano que no incite al baile; otra cosa es que el tema sea más o menos incitante o que los bailadores lo hagan mejor o peor. La música cubana es una síntesis de ritmo, sabor y sentimiento a través del cuerpo, es una celebración que involucra todos los sentidos del bailador, genera guiños y complicidades, trasciende la duración del número y rebasa el espacio de la sala de baile. Al igual que la música, el baile también ha evolucionado, y en muchos casos los cambios han determinado la creación, el asentamiento y hasta la desaparición de nuevos ritmos. Una profesora española de baile que conozco me comentó cierta vez: «Yo le digo a mis alumnos que si de verdad te engancha esta música, te cambia hasta la forma de caminar, porque se te mete la clave dentro y vives con ella todo el tiempo. Así es cómo te das cuenta del por qué los caribeños caminan de esa foma tan sandunguera y vacilona».

Bailando en La Tropical

Para los sectores más populares, el sitio de baile por excelencia siempre ha sido el Salón Rosado de La Tropical, una fábrica de cerveza ubicada en el sector Playa, entre las calles 41 y 46, donde se acondicionó una pista de cemento con capacidad para unas mil personas. Competía con los jardines de La Polar, otra marca de cerveza que sucumbió a la revolución. Los «lloraos» de la trompeta de Félix Chapottín y la voz de Miguelito Cuní impusieron en ambos sitios un despliegue de sones y montunos que se convirtieron en clásicos del catálogo cubano, al igual que el conjunto Casino, con Roberto Faz y Roberto Espí. Recuerdo que las agrupaciones que se presentaban eran anunciadas a la entrada del recinto en un tablero con tiza donde rezaba: «Quien triunfe en el Rosado conquista el mundo».

CARTEL ANUNCIADOR (1958).

En ambos lugares triunfaron durante muchos años las charangas de Arcaño y la Sublime, junto a la de Neno González. Ir a La Tropical un 4 de diciembre a celebrar a Changó/Santa Bárbara era como un viaje a La Meca: se bailaban sones y chachachás hasta la madrugada.

El Salón Rosado es quizá el sitio nocturno más concurrido de La Habana, y ha mantenido durante años una rivalidad con el mítico Tropicana, el sitio caro y elitista donde hace muchos años se divertía la clase pudiente y ahora van los turistas. En los últimos veinte años, esa rivalidad ha marcado definitivamente los dos tipos de público: los que pagan en dólares para ver un show musical pletórico de colorido y los que sólo van a bailar en el Rosado. Todas las noches los habaneros recorren docenas de calles a pie, en plena oscuridad por los cortes de luz, para poder disfrutar de sus orquestas en directo. No hay información oficial al respecto, ni gasolina para el transporte, pero eso poco importa.

Todo lo que interesa allí es bailar; así no se pueda consumir nada de licor, porque en la tierra del ron hay poco de beber. Sólo los turistas, a quienes en los últimos años se les ha construido un pabellón especial con atención de camareros, tienen derecho al ron en variedades tradicionales, que contrastan con los tragos que a menudo introducen clandestinamente en el Salón Rosado. Sin que muchos se den cuenta, los bailadores consumen unas bebidas llamadas «chispa e'tren», «uña e'tigre» y «azuquín», tan peligrosas que han ocasionado problemas oculares a sus bebedores habituales. No todo es alegría y buen humor en aquella pista originalmente construida en 1932: el consumo de estos mejunjes de fabricación casera provocó al comienzo de los años 90 una violencia que desencadenaban pandillas de jóvenes que encontraron allí el cuadrilátero ideal para dirimir criterios.

Es tal la pasión por el baile que el Rosado duplica a veces su capacidad cuando toca una de las orquestas preferidas. Una presentación de Los Van Van, por ejemplo, hace circular entre las barriadas habaneras aquello que se conoce en Cuba como «Radio Bemba», es decir, el comentario que va de boca en boca, pues «bemba» se refiere despectivamente a los gruesos labios del negro. Un concierto de NG La Banda o de la Orquesta Revé hace que la gente acuda sin importarle el precio del billete de entrada, ni si olvidaron inscribirse en el club de La Tropical.

No hay un solo asistente que no se sepa de memoria un número completo de sus orquestas favoritas. Paralelo a ello está el movimiento; las mujeres mueven la cintura en círculos provocadores, levantando los brazos como pidiendo clemencia al cielo por tanta sabrosura. Los turistas no salen de su asombro: la sexualidad es evidente, aunque aquellos tíos que intentan sobrepasarse pronto son rechazados picarescamente por sus compañeras con aquello de «Oye, ekobio, aquí vinimos a bailar». El cubano baila así, como si de ello dependiera la vida y eso es algo que tienen muy claro las orquestas.

Las muchachas se enloquecen con el cantante de turno y en el número final algunas suben al escenario para moverse pegadas a su ídolo. Con su impecable sombrero blanco, Pedrito Calvo, hasta hace poco el principal cantante de Los Van Van, mantiene constantes impulsos pélvicos que enloquecen a las chicas: es uno de los *sex symbols* de la isla, y en temas como *Que le den candela*, de evidentes connotaciones sexuales, el erotismo se duplica.

Antes de estos despampanantes movimientos de cintura, fue muy popular el estilo de baile llamado «casino», con una coreografía elegante que posiblemente data de los 70 y que también se baila en las discotecas de España. Los ritmos nuevos como el «charangón», extensión del nombre que le dio Revé a su orquesta por la ambigüedad de su formato que

no era charanga ni conjunto, tuvo mucho auge junto al «songo» de Los Van Van o el «rucurucu» de Irakere. Sin embargo, a pesar de la escalada de éxitos de la música cubana contemporánea, ninguna de estas variaciones del son ha podido entrar con éxito estable en Suramérica ni en Europa. Las bandas deslumbran con su fuerte y sólido sonido, pero ahí queda la cosa.

LA GRAN PASIÓN DE LOS CUBANOS.

Una noche en Tropicana

A mediados de 1952 el cabaré Tropicana era un negocio que apuntaba hacia la prosperidad. Su propietario, Martín Fox, estaba dispuesto a demostrarlo; acababa de comprar el sitio al italo-brasileño Víctor Correa, quien había construido allí un cabaré en 1940 tras adquirir la finca Villa Mina Trufín en Marianao, una extensa barriada al oeste de la capital.

Desde entonces, su pista natural, ubicada sobre un jardín, se había convertido en escenario obligado de las mejores producciones musicales. Pero a Fox le preocupaba que en la temporada invernal los fuertes vientos norteños ahuyentaban a la clientela habitual. Por esa razón contrató al arquitecto Max Borges (hijo), quien en 1953 convirtió el jardín en un moderno escenario que denominó «Salón bajo las estrellas», y además levantó otro paralelo llamado «Salón arcos de cristal». El extraordinario espacio interno se integraba dramáticamente con la frondosa naturaleza circundante por medio de arcos transparentes entre bóveda y bóveda de cemento reforzado. El original diseño daba una sensación etérea que propiciaba una noche estupenda.

Estéticamente, el nuevo Tropicana no tenía nada que envidiarle a los fastuosos escenarios de París o Las Vegas. Pero ahora había que convertir el cabaré en uno de los mejores del mundo, ofreciendo espectáculos que atrajeran a un personal dispuesto a gastarse los billetes, de lo contrario la inversión no estaría justificada. El hombre indicado para manejar la producción musical y escénica del sitio tenía que ser Roderico Neira, conocido como *Rodney*.

Bailarín y maestro de ceremonias hiperactivo, Roderico trabajaba entonces como productor de la compañía cómica de Garrido y Piñero, y ya había montado algunos números exitosos para el cabaré Sans Soucí. Además, conocía el Tropicana pues había sido asistente coreográfico del bailarín Julio Richards en el primer espectáculo que se presentó allí: *Conga pantera*, con Rita Montaner y *Bola de Nieve*. Sin duda *Rodney* tenía la capacidad y la imaginación necesaria para darle vida al sitio.

Por obra y gracia de su talento y con el apoyo financiero de Fox, grandes estrellas comenzaron a desfilar por Tropicana en revistas y shows musicales tan variados como llamativos: *Caribbean Island, Prende la vela* y *Omelenkó* en 1953; *El circo* (con trapecios y todos los hierros), *Navidad blanca* y *Prohibido en televisión* en 1954, *Carabalí* en 1955. Asegura el investigador Díaz Ayala que ese año *Rodney* se hizo cargo también de las producciones del cabaré Sans Soucí, después que fracasaran llevando coreógrafos norteamericanos para contrarrestar el exhuberante estilo de Tropicana, que siguió con *Evocación* y *En broma* (dedicado al teatro Alhambra) y *En serio* en 1956. Su ambición no conoció límites: en 1957 se le ocurrió importar bailarinas de varios países del Lejano Oriente para producir *Un paraíso del Asia* y *Chinatown*, dos fastuosos shows. Finalmente, en 1958, a punto de caer Batista, montó *Vudú ritual, This is Cuba Mister, Rumbo al Waldorf, Diosas de carne, Canciones para besar, Su Majestad la Prensa, Luisa Fernanda en chemise* y *Rodneyscope*.

Por ambos salones desfilaron infinidad de ídolos nacionales y extranjeros: Nat King Cole, Los Chavales de España, Olga Guillot, Miguelito Valdés *Mr. Babalú*, el Cuarteto Los Rivero, los bailarines Ana Gloria y Rolando, el tenor René Cabel, Xiomara Alfaro, el dúo Celina y Reutilio, el Cuarteto D'Aida, las Hermanas Lago, los Guaracheros de Oriente y el

Los mejeres: TATA GÜINES

Un ejemplo de «timbero» (otro término para el conguero) de primera clase es Tata Güines (Arístides Soto, 1930), quien suele tocar con tres congas a la vez. Mientras mantiene el ritmo con la mano izquierda, la derecha comienza a dibujar toques inimaginables, haciendo también alardes percutivos con las palmas, los dedos y hasta con las uñas. Su talento está respaldado por una larga trayectoria que incluye descargas con  Cachao y Barreto en 1957 y 1958, así como grabaciones con la banda de Chico O'Farrill. En los 70 Juan Pablo Torres lo rescató para la monumental descarga de Las Estrellas de Areíto, cuando llevaba años tocando en Tropicana rodeado de rumberas. Con un estilo que ha influido sobre otros percusionistas de dentro y fuera de Cuba, como es el caso del brillante puertorriqueño Giovannni Hidalgo, Tata Güines ha grabado Pasaporte (1994) con Miguel Angá Díaz, uno de los puntales del grupo Irakere, quien puede tocar con cinco tumbadoras afinadas.

En cierta oportunidad declaró: «Si uno trabaja con emoción y con buena técnica, todo lo consigue». Yo sospecho que se llevará a la tumba un cierto número de secretos sobre su modo de tocar. Sin perder jamás sus dotes de showman, el Tata posee un virtuosismo con los cueros que continúa desplegando en los escenarios de hoteles para turistas. También ha grabado estupendas sesiones en solitario para los discos ¡Cubanísimo! (1995) y Malembe (1996).

veloz pianista Felo Bergaza, entre otros. Le resultaba muy difícil a la competencia disputarle la supremacía al Tropicana, aunque el Montmartre, el Sans Soucí y otros locales más pequeños también alcanzaron un buen nivel de convocatoria, como cuando se abrió el hotel Capri del Vedado en 1957.

Una gigantesca orquesta dirigida por **Armando Romeu** (1911-2002) hacía las delicias de los parroquianos. Sobrino de Antonio María y padre de un notable vibrafonista, Romeu (ver pág. 320) estuvo veinticinco años al frente de aquella soberbia agrupación por la que pasaron algunos de

los mejores músicos. En 1967 fundó y dirigió la Orquesta Cubana de Música Moderna de la cual surgió Irakere.

El coreógrafo *Rodney* creó una imagen de Cuba que nos creímos hasta los cubanos. Tropicana se hizo leyenda, como el
Moulin Rouge, el Lido, las Follies Bergére
de París o el cabaré Sands de Las Vegas. A
pesar de estar marcada por la lucha clan-
destina contra Batista, fue la época que vio
el auge de los fastuosos cabarés, que hicie-

FELO BERGAZA (1957).

ron casi todo el recorrido de la década 1950-60, junto al Casino Nacional, y los escenarios de los hoteles Nacional, Riviera, Deauville, Capri y
Habana Hilton, el gigantesco edificio en la colina de L y 23 en La Rampa, convertido en Habana Libre en 1959 por obra y gracia de Castro y
que ahora está en manos de empresarios españoles.

Otros lugares de diversión

Tropicana y los cabarés mencionados no fueron los únicos centros que
convirtieron en noctámbulos a gran número de habaneros. En locales
más modestos, que por lo general contaban con dos orquestas y un espectáculo que podía tener un coro de bailarinas, una pareja nada corriente
de bailes cubanos, un trío meloso y un par de figuras de cartel, también
se pasaba una noche estupenda. Así funcionaron La Campana, el Sierra,
el Nacional Night Club, el Alí Bar, donde a menudo coincidieron Benny
Moré, Orlando Vallejo, Roberto Faz y Fernando Álvarez en un mano a
mano rumbero o cancionístico. Existía el Bambú, más tarde renombrado
Casino del Río, en la carretera que va al aeropuerto «José Martí» de
Rancho Boyeros, el Casino de Sevilla del hotel Sevilla Biltmore y el Alloy
Club, entre otros.

A pesar de su limitada capacidad, otros clubes más pequeños ofrecían también shows de calidad, como el Palete, Topeka, Silver Star, Bolero, Night & Day, Tropiranch, situado cerca de Tropicana, el Johnny 88
en las calle 13 y O en el Vedado, La Rue 19, Tango Bar Club y el
Johnny's Dream Club junto al río Almendares, donde se bebían los mejores cocteles. La zona de la playa de Marianao se colmó de pequeños ca-

barés como el Panchín, el Pennsylvania, el Southland y el Rhumba Palace. Y para terminar la noche había que ir a La Choricera: allí desplegaba su curiosa colección de artefactos percutivos el afamado *Chori* (que se llamaba Silvano Shueg), quien en sus ratos libres llenaba la ciudad de letreros hechos con tiza anunciando su modesto club. Para otros que preferían cambiar de rumbo e irse a buscar teatros del género «alegre», ahí estaban el Shanghai en la calle Zanja esquina a Rayo, o El Molino Rojo cerca de la Plaza del Mercado Único.

Valga mencionar también dos centros importantes donde se destacaron orquestas y conjuntos del interior del país: el Venecia, en Santa Clara, y el Rancho Club, de Santiago de Cuba. Aunque todo eso ha desaparecido, los cubanos de ahora bailan por igual en El Anfiteatro de Guanabacoa que en El Tropisur de Cienfuegos.

EL EXCÉNTRICO CHORI (1959).

Las sociedades privadas contribuyeron grandemente a la difusión de la música bailable. En el Centro Asturiano, el Centro Gallego, con los Naturales de Ortigueira, en el Club Candado o en el Deportivo La Estrella, en todos estos locales participaron excelentes conjuntos y grandes orquestas. Las sociedades de negros tendían a acoger las últimas novedades; recuerdo una vez que me logré colar en el famoso club Las Águilas, donde la Orquesta Aragón probaba sus nuevos números antes de lanzarlos al mercado. Increíble ambiente aportaron también las llamadas academias de baile, especialmente Marte y Belona, frente a la plaza de la Fraternidad, o el Sport Club en Prado y Neptuno, lugares donde se podía «echar un pie» mientras explotaba una bomba en alguna esquina habanera en protesta contra el gobierno de Batista.

Había de todo: desde una radio que presentaba música norteamericana del momento, muy escuchada por las clases media y alta habaneras, hasta otra que transmitía todo el tiempo en inglés, mientras que Radio Artalejo ofrecía programas de jam sessions en vivo desde finales de los años 40. Múltiples circunstancias propiciaron el desarrollo musical en el decenio 1950-60, incluyendo los avances debidos a la competencia televisiva, que en 1957 hizo que Cuba ocupase el noveno lugar mundial con 200.000 televisores. Y antes de que Fidel Castro llegara al poder dos años más tarde, ya el país disponía de cuatro canales a color.

LA CONGA

Los carnavales habaneros ofrecían cada febrero la oportunidad de seguir el paso de la conga en multitudinarias celebraciones colectivas en vísperas de Cuaresma, mientras que en Santiago de Cuba tenían lugar en julio. Originada en las festividades que efectuaban los negros esclavos, la conga nunca ha tenido rival como agitadora de masas. A su paso más popular –«uno, dos y tres, ¡fuera!»– y en medio de la algarabía de diversos tipos de tambores, trompetas, pitos, cencerros, sartenes, fotutos (caracol llamado «guamo» por los indocubanos), bombos o tambor respondedora, quijadas de burro y maracas, las diferentes comparsas salían a competir por el favor del público, organizadas en vistosas coreografías y vestuarios extravagantes.

CARNAVAL DE SANTIAGO DE CUBA.

Así como la rumba generalmente se ubica en patios e interiores, la conga es callejera y sonsacadora. Asociada a la propaganda de partidos políticos desde principios del siglo XX, se hizo burla electoral en *La chambelona,* de Rigoberto Leyva, o jocosa promoción presidencial en *La aplanadora,* de Osvaldo Farrés. Compositores refinados como Ernesto Lecuona sucumbieron a su encanto, produciendo las conocidas *Panamá* y *Para Vigo me voy*, que grabaron con éxito los Havana Cuban Boys, y recogió en 2001 el pianista Bebo Valdés, quien fuera gran amigo de Lecuona, en su álbum *El arte del sabor,* del sello Lola Records, acompañado de *Cachao* en el contrabajo y *Patato* Valdés en las congas, con la intervención de Paquito D'Rivera.

Con pasos ensayados bajo un ritmo preciso, implicación de ballet callejero, *Las jardineras* y *El alacrán* (escorpión en Cuba) fueron dos de

las más famosas, integrando a todo tipo de clase social en largos desplie-
gues callejeros:

> Oye colega no te asustes cuando veas (bis)
> Al alacrán tumbando caña (bis)
> Costumbre de mi país, mi hermano (bis)
> (coro) ¡Sí, sí, tumbando caña!

Quizá la conga más conocida sea *Una, dos y tres*, de **Rafael Ortiz
Mañungo,** quien perteneció al Septeto Nacional de Ignacio Piñeiro. Su
paso más conocido se logra al sonar un golpe fuerte del bombo, momen-

to en que los bailadores levantan ligeramente una pierna, y después de arrastrar
tres pasos más levantan la otra, marcando
el golpe con una brusca inclinación del
cuerpo en dirección opuesta a la salida de
la pierna. No sé si esta descripción valdrá
de algo, pero le aseguro al lector/a que con
dos tragos de ron dentro le saldrá mejor.

De los arrabales de extramuros, donde
ubicaron a los cabildos de los negros, surgieron las carnavalescas comparsas habaneras.
Después se organizaron por barriadas que
mantenían rivalidades exacerbadas por la
rapidez con que corría el aguardiente en las

EL MAESTRO ERNESTO LECUONA.

frescas noches de febrero. El desfile de estos
cortejos danzarios provocó en el joven **Ernesto Lecuona** una de sus más famosas composiciones para piano, escuchada por primera vez en 1912 cuando contaba sólo 17 años de edad. ¿Que cómo se titula? *La comparsa.*

Si una comparsa disponía de recursos económicos construía una carroza decorada fastuosamente; sobre ella bailaban chicas sumamente
atractivas y ligeramente vestidas, que sonreían mientras se contoneaban y
lanzaban serpentinas a los espectadores. Detrás de la carroza, vigorosos
hombres mantenían el jadeante paso mientras sostenían erectas las faro-
las colosales, polícromas y barrocas estructuras de múltiples brazos cargados de espejos y luces, que identificaban a cada comparsa. Pero, «...lle-
gó el Comandante y mandó a parar». No satisfecho con abolir la
celebración de las Navidades, Castro también ha ordenado frecuentemen-

te la cancelación de los carnavales, tanto habaneros como santiagueros, con la excusa de la zafra azucarera.

Seguramente olvidó cómo sus 165 hombres se mezclaron con los orientales durante la celebración del carnaval de Santiago de Cuba en julio de 1953, para no llamar la atención en los días anteriores al ataque al cuartel Moncada, bastión militar de Batista en aquella tierra caliente.

A la voz de «¡Abre, que viene el cocoyé!», gritado a voz en cuello por la calle de la Trocha se celebraba esta fiesta popular. En los afamados carnavales santiagueros competían la comparsa Olugo, originada en la zona de El Tivolí, y la Carabalí Izuama, que representaba a la barriada de Los Hoyos.

Al conjuro de la «corneta china», que más bien suena como un oboe de alta escala pentatónica aunque se trata de un instrumento de procedencia asiática transculturado en la música cubana, se lanzaba a la calle la muchedumbre enardecida. El tema del cocoyé fue recogido por el músico español Juan Casamitjana en 1836, quien asistía al paso de una ruidosa comparsa que lo entonaba. Anotó las coplas y los ritmos y días después la banda del Regimiento de Cataluña lo interpretó en una retreta pública, ante el escándalo de la «gente distinguida».

DESPEDIDA DEL TRÍO MATAMOROS (1960).

Este tema folclórico sufrió diversas mutaciones durante el siglo XIX, incluyendo la versión del pianista norteamericano Gottschalk, que lo llevó a un aire de danza, hasta su utilización entre 1920-30 por los compositores Amadeo Roldán y Gonzalo Roig.

Los carnavales santiagueros han provocado la aparición de no pocas canciones relacionadas con su innegable atractivo. Siempre económico y humorístico en su expresión musical, el santiaguero **Miguel Matamoros** dice en su rápida *Alegre conga*:

> Negra, oye negra,
> dame negra, pronto negra,
> mi camisa, mi corbata, mi sombrero, mi zapato colorá,
> que ya la conga va a pasá.
> (coro) Ahí va la conga, pa'rrollá...

A las congas y «arrolladoras» les fueron estilizando un buen número de formas danzarias que luego fueron usadas en varias películas cubanas, mexicanas y norteamericanas, contribuyendo así a la confusión que existe entre la rumba y la conga. El vocablo «conga» se refiere, según Ortiz, a un tambor construido de duelas, como de un metro de alto, algo abarrilado y sujeto por flejes de metal, abierto por abajo y con una membrana de piel de buey fijada por clavazón. Como sólo el fuego podía estirarle el cuero antiguamente, ¡cuántos parches no se quemaron por un desliz del tamborero! El término conga se impuso en Nueva York a partir de los años 60 para referirse a la tumbadora.

Al compositor cualificado **Eliseo Grenet** se debe la difusión de la conga callejera en Nueva York desde 1936, en el cabaré Yumurí, en pleno Broadway. En aquella fría ciudad sonaron en 1947 las tumbadoras de **Chano Pozo** para tocar be-bop con Dizzy Gillespie hasta que lo asesinaron en un bar de Harlem un año más tarde. Chano había originado la música de la comparsa «Los dandis de Belén» (o los elegantes de una populosa barriada habanera), con la ayuda de su medio hermano, el trompeta Félix Chapottín.

En pleno esplendor revolucionario la conga adquirió connotaciones políticas directas, a menudo bastante crueles con un sector de la ciudadanía, pero en otras ocasiones se convirtió en un récord histórico, como cuando Nikita Jruschov pactó con Kennedy la retirada de Cuba de los misiles (crisis de octubre de 1962), sin consultar al Máximo Líder y la gente se lanzó a cantar por las calles

> Nikita, mariquita
> lo que se da no se quita...

LA GUARACHA

La guaracha es un género muy movido y apreciado por los cubanos por su letra picaresca o burlona. Musicalmente tiende a confundirse con el nuevo son de los años 40, y no hay dudas de que una ha tomado elementos del otro y viceversa. Sin embargo, la guaracha suele ser bastante más rápida que el son y aunque hay sones con letras muy alegres, el texto de la guaracha suele ser más superficial y disparatado. Como en el son, la tumbadora marca fuertemente el cuarto tiempo del compás, aunque realiza en realidad una polirritmia sonora; el contrabajo efectúa un «tumbao» o «guajeo» tomado de la figuración rítmica enlazada del tumbador y el tres-golpes en la rumba, coincidiendo su segundo golpe de cuerda a contratiempo con el sonido grave de la tumbadora, mientras que el piano mantiene un fraseo melódico-percusivo que sirve de colchón armónico.

A mediados del siglo XIX comenzó a observarse la presencia de la guaracha en el teatro bufo habanero. Posiblemente se trataba de una forma musical deudora de la tonadilla escénica española, aunque permeada por la rumba y el inevitable choteo, ya que desde sus inicios fue portavoz del espíritu festivo y satírico del criollo. Utilizada para criticar en tono burlón a los gobernantes coloniales y a situaciones derivadas del régimen opresor, las antiguas guarachas se acompañaban de guitarras junto a sonajeros como el güiro y las maracas. Siempre han servido como crítica de costumbres o alardosas alabanzas de personajes callejeros.

Hacia finales del XIX la guaracha fue variando su esquema formal, adoptando un aire más movido y un ritmo que recurría al tradicional esquema de la habanera o ritmo tango, pero ya con el cinquillo incorporado dentro de un compás de 2x4. Se cree que la palabra significa baile, como una derivación de la palabra «guanche» o bailador. Hasta la década de 1930 fue considerado un ritmo decadente por la sociedad habanera, y en algunos casos se tomó como una simple broma o diversión.

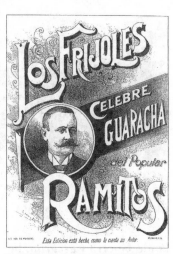

PARTITURA QUE SE CONSERVA EN EL MUSEO NACIONAL DE LA MÚSICA.

Un buen número de tríos y conjuntos impusieron este ritmo jacarandoso a partir de los años 40 y 50. He aquí una selección de guarachas que se convirtieron en verdaderos clásicos del género: *La media naranja,* de Alberto Caissé; la rapidísima *A mí qué, La bodega del ñato* y *Bigote e'gato,* de Jesús Guerra; *En el tíbiri tábara,* de Pablo Cairo; *Con la lengua afuera,* de Agustín Ribot; *El bobo de la yuca,* de Marcos Perdomo; *A romper el coco,* de Otilio Portal; *La muñeca,* de Tony Tejera; *Saoco* de Rosendo Ruiz; *Rumberito soy,* de Humberto Jauma; *Cañonazos,* de Evaristo Aparicio; *El plato roto,* de Rafael Ortiz; *A toda Cuba le gusta,* de Remberto Bécquer; *El telefonito,* de Silvestre Méndez; *Burundanga,* de

Oscar Muñóz Bouffartique, mientras José Carbó Menéndez, primer organizador de la Sociedad de Autores en el Exilio (1965) originó *Se murió
Panchita, La televisión, Cao cao maní picao* y *El baile del sillón.*

La vinculación con la rumba se hizo evidente en algunas guarachas
de Bienvenido Julián Gutiérrez. Después surgieron *La ola marina,* de Virgilio González, *Pare cochero,* de Marcelino Guerra *Rapindey,* y *Qué buena es la nochebuena,* de Walfrido Guevara.

Entrados los años 40, la guaracha se aproximó más al son bajo la
influencia del compositor e intérprete santiaguero Antonio Fernández, conocido por el sobrenombre de *Ñico Saquito.* En su larga carrera musical
este vocalista fue el fundador del quinteto Los Guaracheros de Oriente,

EL COMPOSITOR JESÚS GUERRA (GUITARRA)
QUE LLEVÓ LA GUARACHA A ALEMANIA EN LOS
AÑOS 50, CON ENRIQUETA ALMANZA AL PIANO
Y LUCY COLLANTES EN LAS MARACAS.

de quienes se separó al estallar la
revolución cubana. A Ñico Saquito se le atribuye el mérito de haber compuesto algunas de las
guarachas más alegres y humorís-
ticas que se recuerden: *María
Cristina* y *Compay gallo.* También el dúo Los Compadres –en
sus dos épocas– incluyó guarachas en su repertorio. Bandas
como los Hermanos Palau, la Casino de la Playa y la orquesta del
trompeta Julio Cueva, específica-
mente con la voz y el estilo de Or-
lando Guerra *Cascarita,* llevaron la guaracha al exterior.

Pero sin duda alguna, el conjunto que mejor supo explotar este género ha sido la Sonora Matancera, primero con las voces puertorriqueñas
de Myrta Silva y Daniel Santos, y después con la de Celia Cruz, que pronto se convirtió en «La gran guarachera de Cuba». Aunque la Sonora comenzó su larga historia interpretando sones, su verdadera especialidad
son las bulliciosas guarachas popularizadas en toda la cuenca del Caribe
por la radio cubana.

Es preciso señalar que la guaracha es el antecedente más evidente del
género rumba flamenca por su estro irónico y satírico, así como por la
velocidad de su compás. Aunque la palabra es la misma, la verdadera
rumba cubana (guaguancó, yambú y columbia) no tiene nada que ver con
este palo flamenco.

Los mejores: CELIA CRUZ

La llaman «La reina de la salsa». Una diosa negra, exótica y lejana, pero se le recibe como a una de la familia. Siempre ha tenido una voz privilegiada que sabe cuidar; una voz potente que fluye como azúcar caliente en las improvisaciones. ¿Pero qué más es Celia además de una buena voz? Puro ritmo. Sus cuerdas vocales reemplazan a las claves en el ritmo quebrado de la guaracha y en la síncopa de la sabrosura sonera. Y para quienes crean que lo de Celia Cruz con  España fue cuestión de llegar y besar el santo, debo informarles que comenzó a venir aquí desde 1970 y tuvo bastantes dificultades para triunfar; la ayudó mucho Lola Flores: todas las noches llevaba a gente para que la conocieran y la vieran cantar. Desde entonces ha actuado muchas veces más, con la Sonora Matancera, con *Machito* y con la Orquesta de Tito Puente, hasta aquella noche de 1990 en Las Ventas con Las Estrellas de la Fania, donde notó realmente el pulso de la gente.

Asegura el periodista Diego A. Manrique que la edad de Celia es un secreto. Lo que no es un secreto es el éxito alcanzado por esta señora, dueña de la música caribeña. Su carrera artística, que abarca un período de seis décadas, tuvo mucho que ver con el auge de la guaracha en Cuba y con el desarrollo de la salsa neoyorquina. La pimentosa negra no es sólo poseedora de una gran voz y figura que arrebatan en cualquier escenario, sino que su participación directa en todos los detalles de sus actuaciones y grabaciones la identifican como importante autora intelectual del impacto de su música en el mundo.

Educada en La Habana, estudió primero mecanografía y taquigrafía para alcanzar más tarde su certificado de maestra. Pero no llegó a ejercer, la música la cautivó, debutando con la Sonora Matancera el 3 de agosto de 1950. Pronto el programa de Radio Progreso donde aparecía se convirtió en uno de los favoritos de los radioescuchas. Entre sus primeras grabaciones están la guaracha *Cao, cao, maní picao*, de José Carbó Menéndez, y el afro *Mata siguaraya*, de Lino Frías.

Manifiesta reticencias a la hora de comentar sobre la situación de Cuba; realmente está harta de que le pregunten sobre Fidel Castro. «¿Por qué no le preguntan a él sobre Celia Cruz?» Todavía ofrece más de ochenta conciertos al año y recuerda –posee una memoria prodigiosa– que cantó en una película norteamericana que se rodó en Cuba en 1957, *Affair in Havana*, con Raymond Burr y John Cassavettes.

Explica Raúl Fernández, en un artículo publicado en *Encuentro de la cultura cubana*, que debido a su trepidante carrera no se casó joven. Lo hizo el 14 de julio de 1962 con Pedro Knight, el veterano trompeta de la Sonora.

Ha cantado y grabado mucho con las orquestas de Tito Puente y de Johnny Pacheco, y recuerda cómo tuvo que batallar con los directores de la Fania que no querían utilizar *Químbara*, de Junior Cepeda; su voluntad se impuso y el sabroso número (que mantiene algo del ritmo del guaguancó) se convirtió en un verdadero éxito, utilizándose después como tema de presentación en los conciertos con Las Estrellas de Fania.

Sus tacones han recorrido cientos de escenarios, plataformas que la separan del público pero también jardines desde donde ella conversa con su gente. Su carisma, su calidad de estrella y su sencillez le permiten romper las barreras del lenguaje lo mismo en el Carnegie Hall de Nueva York que en una discoteca nipona. Ha recibido infinidad de premios y homenajes, que incluyen el doctorado *honoris causa* en música otorgado por la Universidad de Yale. Celia Cruz es única y llegó a la cima hace tiempo; es también un fenómeno importante en un mundo dominado por cantantes masculinos. Y ya tiene un libro dedicado a su vida artística: después de seguirla incesantemente durante varios meses, el colombiano Umberto Valverde publicó en 1981 *Reina rumba*, una versión poética y delirante de la guarachera.

Tiempo atrás, un mulato canoso me comentaba en una esquina de Nueva Jersey: «To el que habla epañó quiere a Selia Cru». Para millones de hispanoparlantes ella es la personificación del sabor caribeño, una mujer con «*asúca*».

LAS DESCARGAS

Una descarga equivale en términos caribeños a la jam session jazzística, cuando reunidos varios músicos deciden llevar a cabo sus improvisaciones conjuntamente. Lo principal es la espontaneidad y acudir a la libre inventiva musical que emana de lo más profundo de los participantes, sin emplear arreglos preconcebidos; así se suele llegar a un clímax de máxima tensión y de explosión creativa.

La primera descarga de jazz cubano que yo recuerde la llevó a cabo el pianista Bebo Valdés en 1952 con Guillermo Barreto en la batería. Poco después, entre 1957 y 1958, *Cachao* reunió a un pequeño grupo de amigos que grabaron varias sesiones desde bien avanzada la madrugada hasta la mañana en los estudios Panart, porque todos trabajaban hasta muy tarde; una descarga tomaba unas cinco horas. Participaron los trompetas Alejandro *El negro* Vivar y Alfredo *Chocolate* Armenteros, Generoso *El tojo* Jiménez en el trombón, Niño Rivera en las cuerdas del tres, Rogelio *Yeyo* Iglesias en el bongó, con la colaboración de Gustavo Tamayo, Emilio Peñalver, su propio hermano Orestes, Barreto en los timbales y Tata Güines en las congas.

CACHAO, GUSTAVO TAMAYO, TATA GÜINES, *EL NEGRO* VIVAR, *YEYO* IGLESIAS Y GUILLERMO BARRETO (1957).

Después *Cachao* realizó varias descargas más, hasta llegar a grabar catorce LP, pero con diferentes músicos, que incluyeron a Ricardito Rivera, Armandito Armenteros, primo de *Chocolate*, *el Negro* Vivar y Los Papines. Le encantaba el estilo del tresero Isaac Oviedo, muy diferente al de Niño Rivera.

Entrevistado a mediados de los años 90 por el narrador Leonardo Padura, *Cachao* declaró:

Cuando hicimos aquellas descargas a partir de 1957, no nos estábamos fijando demasiado en el jazz, sino en la propia música cubana, en el son. Aquello fue una reunión de músicos capacitados, con ganas de hacer algunas ideas nuevas a partir de la inspiración y la improvisación.

En 1960 *Cachao* realizó *Cuban jazz* del baterista Walfredo de los Reyes y la *Descarga Nº 2* del compositor *Chico* O'Farrill. Años después, ya en el exilio, actualizó la jam session cubana con *Descarga'77*, donde le acompañaron, entre otros, Charlie Palmieri, Lino Frías, *Chocolate* Armenteros, Gonzalo Fernández, Virgilio Martí, *Papaíto* Muñoz, *Patato* Valdés, Felo Barrio, Roberto Torres, Marcelino Guerra *Rapindey* y nuevamente *El negro* Vivar, quien moriría dos años después.

Los mejores: GUILLERMO BARRETO

Luego de iniciarse con las orquestas de Obdulio Morales y los Hermanos Martínez, con sólo 18 años Guillermo Barreto (1929-91) se unió como baterista a la orquesta del cabaré Tropicana, dirigida por Armando Romeu, donde permaneció hasta 1957. Trabajó además con las orquestas del cabaré Sans Soucí y del Canal 4 de Televisión. Actuó ocasionalmente en la banda de Tommy Dorsey y acompañó a Nat King Cole en sus afamadas grabaciones de boleros y chachachás. Grabó discos con Johnny Richards y con la estupenda banda de *Chico* O'Farrill grabó en 1956 *Chico's chachachá*. Colaboró con su primo el pianista Bebo Valdés y el tumbador Rolando Alfonso en la creación del batanga, un ritmo que no llegó a pegar. En 1957 tocó los timbales en *From Havana to New York*, una descarga de Israel López *Cachao*, que fue seguida de otra con Niño Rivera, y finalmente una tercera con el flautista José Antonio Fajardo, todas para el sello Panart. Admirado por Tito Puente, con su insuperable cáscara y acertadas intervenciones, Guillermo Barreto creó toda una escuela del timbal.

En 1957 formó el Quinteto Instrumental con Orlando *Papito* Hernández (bajo), Gustavo Tamayo (güiro), Tata Güines (tumbadoras), y Frank Emilio Flynn (piano). Al abandonar el país en 1966, *Papito* fue reemplazado por Orlando López *Cachaíto*. El Quinteto comenzó entonces a darse a conocer como «Los Amigos». Un año después, Barreto y *Cachaíto* hicieron un disco de bossa nova con el violinista uruguayo Federico Britos. Más tarde tocó en la Orquesta Cubana de Música Moderna, también dirigida por Armando Romeu. Con el quinteto «Los Amigos» Barreto produjo otros dos discos, hasta que en 1991 salió al mercado un proyecto excitante que fundía el jazz con la música folclórica y popular afrocubana, con la aportación de la flautista/saxo soprano canadiense Jane Bunnett, los pianistas Frank Emilio y Gonzalito Rubalcaba, el grupo de rumba Yoruba Andabo y la cantante de temas afrocubanos Merceditas Valdés (1928-96), esposa de Barreto, entre otros. ¡Un disco estupendo!

Una vez disfruté viéndole tocar los timbales durante una de las descargas de *Cachao* alrededor de 1957: la pureza de su oído le permitía parar en seco al grupo cuando alguien desafinaba ligeramente; pero lo hacía con una sonrisa que desarmaba a cualquiera. Barreto también fue conocido como «El loro» por su tendencia a hablar demasiado.

A diferencia de las descargas de los años 50 con su enorme carga jazzística, «Los Amigos» buscaron su principal fuente de inspiración en clásicos del repertorio cubano como *Quiéreme mucho,* de Gonzalo Roig, *Marta,* de Moisés Simons, *Damisela encantadora,* de Ernesto Lecuona, *Almendra,* de Abelardito Valdés y *Tres lindas cubanas,* de Antonio María Romeu, entre otros números. Estoy totalmente de acuerdo con un comentario de Nat Chediak en su libro *Diccionario de jazz latino:* «A veces la buena música no se hace, sale».

LA PACHANGA

En medio del regocijo general ante el triunfo revolucionario de 1959, apareció un nuevo ritmo, mezcla de varias cosas, debido a un joven ambicioso llamado Claudio Cuza, que usaba el nombre artístico de Eduardo Davidson. De su remota Baracoa, al extremo oriental de la isla, se había trasladado a La Habana hacia finales de los años 50 y se ganaba la vida como escritor de programas radiales. Con su primer número, titulado precisamente *La pachanga,* obtuvo un éxito inmediato y seguidamente se grabaron otras piezas en esa línea: *Lola Catula, Agua de mar* y *La niña traviesa.* Más tarde aparecieron *Pancho calma, Sobando el son, Sabor de Cuba* y *El último bembé.* Pronto Davidson cogió las maletas y se subió al avión.

Nueva York logró apenas asimilar la avalancha de músicos e influencias que llegaban de Cuba en oleadas continuas. La pachanga, el último ritmo exportado de la isla, fue asumida por todas las big bands en su apogeo. Casi toda la música desarrollada en Manhattan y otros sectores de la Babel de Hierro entre 1960-63 llevó impreso el sello de este ritmo.

La orquesta del puertorriqueño Tito Rodríguez logró convertirse en el mejor exponente de la pachanga, a decir verdad, mejor que los grupos cubanos. El hábil cantante se vio de pronto como el líder absoluto de toda la expresión musical caribeña, utilizando la moda de la pachanga como el gancho comercial que le garantizaba los públicos mayoritarios.

Enriqueció notablemente su repertorio con boleros y sones clásicos cubanos que, al imponerse el bloqueo económico de la isla, cobraron un considerable valor evocativo. Siempre compitiendo con *Machito*, Tito Rodríguez convirtió al mambo impuesto por Pérez Prado en uno de sus fuertes. Y por encima de todo ello proyectó su voz, una voz con la suavidad necesaria para enamorar y lucir novedosa, pero con la dinámica y picardía indispensables para incitar la inevitable exhibición del público en la pista de baile.

La pachanga de Davidson comenzó a marcar su decadencia a partir de 1964, y con ella las formidables big bands que la habían apoyado. Por su parte, los salones de baile del Palladium en la calle Broadway, que habían servido de trampolín para todos los éxitos y modas, recibieron un duro golpe que le costaría el cierre definitivo del local un par de años más tarde al suspendérsele la licencia para vender licores.

Así las cosas, los AfroCubans de *Machito*, que habían sido los pioneros de todo el movimiento pachanguero, se replegaron al mundo del jazz que siempre les había garantizado la subsistencia. Tito Puente, que nunca había sido netamente jazzista, decidió quedarse a medio camino, tratando de amoldar su orquesta a los nuevos gustos que ahora caían de manera forzada, aunque siempre le surgían suntuosas fiestas privadas entre sus amistades judías. Y el público, ante la crisis de los salones grandes, tuvo que volver a los modestos locales donde una orquesta de más de doce instrumentistas apenas dejaba espacio para lucirse en el baile.

Mientras todos estos cambios tenían lugar, Nueva York continuaba atiborrándose de músicos cubanos que llegaban en busca de trabajo. Así, las emergentes charangas vieron los cielos abiertos; como eran agrupaciones pequeñas, sin mayor exigencia de sonido ni de espacio, comenzaron a proliferar, siguiendo el liderazgo de Fajardo y sus Estrellas. Y esta nueva fiebre, basada en el chachachá, duró apenas dos años. La crisis culminó en 1966, y es a partir de ese momento cuando comenzaron a surgir nuevas sonoridades que pocos años después dieron paso a la salsa.

LA MÚSICA SINFÓNICA

Durante el decenio estudiado, La Habana fue, en todos los niveles, una de las capitales musicales de América. En la actualidad es muy difícil encontrar rastros de actores y testigos de conciertos de música «culta» o «música-historia», como la llama Leo Brouwer; muchos han muerto y sobreviven pocas grabaciones. Mientras que el régimen comunista borraba deliberadamente una buena parte de ese período, algunos compositores e instrumentistas destacados, jóvenes entonces, decidieron abandonar la isla.

A pesar de la dictadura batistiana, la ciudad era hermosa y hervía de vida musical. Sin embargo, la profusión de lujo y riqueza era excesiva teniendo en cuenta la crisis que atravesaba el país. Aparte de los fastuosos shows musicales que presentaban los mejores hoteles y cabarés, las playas, el sol subtropical, el juego y la prostitución organizados eran las ofertas que más atraían al turista. La principal atracción de los hoteles que se construyeron en aquellos años –como el Havana Riviera (amueblado y decorado en el estilo que iba a caracterizar a los grandes hoteles de Las Vegas) y el Capri– eran sus casinos, hasta el punto de que ofrecían un circuito privado de televisión que les permitía a los huéspedes continuar jugando desde sus habitaciones. Y en todos estos negocios, incluyendo la impunidad para obtener drogas, dominaba la mafia norteamericana.

En verdad hacía falta una revolución que saneara al país, una revolución nacionalista y honesta, no una entrega al sistema comunista. Por eso estimo que, históricamente hablando, lo que logró Castro fue cambiarle el collar al galgo, ir de un imperialismo a otro. Pero a pesar de las transformaciones positivas de los primeros años revolucionarios, el galgo (y esto es sólo un eufemismo) se ha quedado tan mal o peor que antes, pues había puesto todas sus esperanzas en un verdadero cambio que mejorara sus condiciones de vida en todos los sentidos.

Otro fenómeno marcado por la época fueron las «crónicas sociales» que publicaban los 18 diarios habaneros anteriores a 1959. Dependiendo de cuánto se hubiera pagado por ellas, diariamente aparecían reseñas de recepciones, *cocktail parties*, banquetes y en cuanto evento social se distraía la clase adinerada, incluyendo la asistencia a conciertos y recitales. Aquellas páginas, ilustradas con abundantes fotos, cuyos pies evidenciaban el mal gusto del fatuo despliegue, eran redactadas por cronistas sociales que ejercían una considerable influencia en las redacciones de los periódicos por las conexiones que cultivaban con los más poderosos económica y políticamente del país, incluidos banqueros, industriales, ministros, senadores o generales. Aunque la mayoría de los miembros del gobierno y de las fuerzas armadas no provenían de la alta sociedad habanera, se apresuraban a alternar con ella. Nunca apareció un campesino o un negro entre tanta foto de sonrientes hombres y mujeres «de éxito». A pesar de su posición, al propio Batista, considerado mulato por la alta burguesía, le fue imposible hacerse socio del centro más exclusivo, el Havana Yatch Club. A fuerza de codearse con la *creme de l'creme* (por citar una frase salida de aquellas páginas), algunos cronistas sociales llegaron a acumular fortunas muy respetables gracias a los obsequios de quienes de ese modo agradecían la atención que se les prestaba. Era un mundo de la imagen, de la superficialidad y el esnobismo. Jamás apareció un músico en aquellas páginas.

Por contraste, desde el punto de vista educativo, el índice de alfabetización del país ocupaba entonces el cuarto puesto en Hispanoamérica después de Uruguay, Argentina y Chile. Quizá eso explique el porqué resultó bastante fácil la campaña que emprendió el régimen contra el analfabetismo en 1960. Por su parte, la medicina estaba sumamente adelantada en relación con el resto del continente; esto se debía en gran parte a la proximidad con Estados Unidos y la relativa facilidad de que gozaban los médicos para obtener el último instrumental y equipo, así como actualizar su entrenamiento en el Norte. Es más, la Escuela de Medicina de la Universidad habanera tenía ya un nivel comparable a las equivalentes del vecino yanqui. De esos adelantos y de una tradición médica que tomó 50 años en desarrollarse supo aprovecharse la revolución en su constante propaganda de los éxitos alcanzados en materia de salud pública.

¿Y la música de otro nivel que la popular? En 1950 Erich Kleiber ya había ofrecido varios conciertos y Clemens Kraus había dirigido *Tristán* de Wagner. Herbert von Karajan acababa de dirigir la Orquesta Filarmónica en la *Novena sinfonía* de Beethoven. Los principales directores se sucedían uno tras otro: Bruno Walter, Ernest Ansermet, Eugène Ormandy, Sergio Celibidache, Charles Münch, Manuel Rosenthal. Los más destacados pianistas: Horowitz, Rubinstein, Schnabel, Kempf, Arrau. Los mejores violinistas: Menuhin, Milstein, Stern. Las más grandes voces de la época: Tebaldi, Mario del Mónaco, Victoria de los Ángeles, Regina Resnik, Elisabeth Schwarzkopf. Todos pasaron por La Habana en aquel decenio portentoso.

En el corazón de la ciudad se seguían con la misma pasión los amores de *María la O*, *Amalia Batista* o *Cecilia Valdés*; el público se precipitaba para escuchar, en estas zarzuelas cubanas creadas algunos años antes, a las grandes *vedettes* Rosita Fornés, María de los Ángeles Santana o Rita Montaner, o a otras cantantes exquisitas: Esther Borja, Martha Pérez, América Crespo, Zoraida Marrero o el tenor Miguel de Grandy. La ópera había protagonizado ya veladas memorables en el teatro Auditórium, construido en 1928 gracias a una suscripción nacional promovida por la Sociedad Pro Arte Musical. Este hermoso local fue devorado por las llamas en 1977 y sólo fue restaurado y reabierto para la IX Cumbre de Jefes de Estado Iberoamericanos celebrada en La Habana en 1999.

También en 1950 se inauguró un nuevo teatro al borde del mar: acogía a 6.600 espectadores, bastante más que el Radio City de Nueva York; hablo del teatro Blanquita (el actual Karl Marx), donde se representaron durante todo el decenio las mejores revistas y los grandes espectáculos de variedades. Todo lo cual significaba trabajo para los músicos, que debido a su flexibilidad profesional, lo mismo funcionaban dentro de una orquesta de concierto que en un cabaré.

En contra de la opinión más extendida, la música cubana no se limita a la popular; en ella tienen también cabida grandes orquestas y compañías de ballet clásico. Los compositores cubanos se las habían arreglado para producir un amplio abanico de música para el intelecto, el corazón y las caderas; de ahí que en el recodo de una sinfonía de vanguardia era posible descubrir melodías afrocubanas ancladas en las

MUSEO NACIONAL DE BELLAS ARTES, DONDE SE HAN PRESENTADO GRANDES MÚSICOS.

raíces musicales de la isla. Los grandes conciertos partían regularmente de gira por provincias, incluyendo a Santiago de Cuba, que ya contaba con su propia orquesta filarmónica. Debo aclarar que algunas damas de la burguesía habanera se distinguieron por dirigir contra viento y marea varias sociedades musicales, provocando un enorme interés entre los músicos por superarse.

La televisión no se quedaba atrás. En horas de gran audiencia programas como «El Casino de la Alegría» o «Jueves de Partagás» difundieron en vivo ballets clásicos o zarzuelas como *Lola Cruz*, de Lecuona. En esa misma cadena CMQ se presentó la primera versión coreográfica de *La Rebambaramba*, de Amadeo Roldán, cuatro años antes de que entrara a formar parte del repertorio del ballet de Alicia Alonso. La música clásica se difundía a través de la radio CMZ y desde la Mil Diez, de filiación comunista. Pero los conciertos más populares eran los que patrocinaba la

General Electric en la CMBF, o los de la General Motors en la RHC, que los domingos por la mañana retransmitían a toda la isla desde el Auditórium los conciertos de la Filarmónica.

El director Erich Kleiber se interesó más por algunos compositores de raíz popular que por otros más cultos, a quienes comparaba a «vacas estériles que no daban leche». Por eso se complacía en dirigir la Filarmónica en los poemas sinfónicos de **Pablo Ruiz Castellanos** (1902-?), *Rumba en rapsodia, Río Cauto, Sinfonía heterodoxa cubana, El gran changüí* y *Monte Rus*, o en las obras afrocubanas de **Gilberto Valdés** (1905-71), *Danza de los braceros, Baró, Evocación negra, Likó-ta-irube, Sangre africana*.

En aquel decenio increíble, los compositores cualificados más populares eran **Gonzalo Roig** (1890-1970) y **Ernesto Lecuona** (1895-1963); todo el mundo conocía sus canciones y sus zarzuelas. Roig fue un ardiente defensor de García Caturla y de la música de Igor Stravinsky, de todo lo que significara vanguardia. Lecuona fue la otra gran figura legendaria de la música cubana, y valga aclarar que la obra del más grande creador de todos los tiempos no se reduce a su *Malagueña*. Denostado por el régimen comunista, se marchó del país en 1960.

Ese mismo año –apenas 23 meses desde el triunfo revolucionario– tuvo lugar el primer concierto de la Orquesta Sinfónica en el Teatro Auditórium, bajo la batuta de Enrique González Mantici, con obras del compositor Alejandro García Caturla. Desde entonces hasta la fecha, la Orquesta ha realizado más de 1.500 conciertos, desde las salas más confortables del país hasta los centros de estudios, fábricas y cooperativas agrarias, en sus giras anuales por la isla. Igualmente ha realizado numerosas grabaciones para la EGREM, el ICAIC y diversos grupos de danza y de teatro.

La Orquesta Sinfónica tenía historia: había surgido en 1922, dirigida por Gonzalo Roig. Entre sus instrumentistas de primera categoría se encontraban el violinista Virgilio Diago, el flautista Roberto Ondina y el contrabajista Fernando Anckermann. Rodrigo Prats, que entonces contaba 13 años, estaba entre los violines. Aparte del maestro Lecuona, otros notables solistas actuaron con la Sinfónica: Jorge Bolet, José Echániz, Margot de Blanck, Emilio Puyans, Marta de la Torre, Alberto Falcón, Zoila Gálvez, Alfredo Levy, Benjamín Orbón y Rita Montaner. Varios directores invitados también contribuyeron al prestigio de la incipiente orquesta: Pablo Casals, Juan Manén, Adela Verne, Julián Carrillo, Ernesto Halffter y otros.

Desde aquel 1960 revolucionario, mucho tendría que ver con la Sinfónica un talentoso joven que a los dieciséis años (1955) ya había logrado transcribir a la guitarra la *Danza del Diablito* de Amadeo Roldán. Nieto de Ernestina Lecuona –hermana mayor del maestro–, **Leo Brouwer**, cuya nota biográfica aparece más adelante, se convirtió con el triunfo revolucionario de 1959 en el más avanzado impulsor de la música nueva; para 1961 había sido nombrado director de música del Instituto Cubano del Arte e Industria Cinematográficos (ICAIC). Moviéndose alternativamente entre la tendencia aleatoria y otras formas abiertas, sin abandonar sus propias presentaciones como guitarrista, mantuvo un genuino interés en las raíces de los ritmos cubanos, componiendo un año después *Variantes* para solista percusionista. Para entonces, Brouwer era profesor de contrapunto, armonía y composición en el Conservatorio de La Habana. Sus investigaciones alrededor del jazz culminaron con la presentación de *Arioso a Charles Mingus*, escrita para quinteto de jazz y orquesta sinfónica, una obra que coincidió con la creación en 1967, gracias a sus pacientes pero firmes gestiones, de la Orquesta Cubana de Música Moderna, cuyo devenir aparece en la pag. 318.

¿De dónde provenía este amplio interés en la música contemporánea, revolucionaria en el mejor sentido, que nunca había gozado de suficientes posibilidades de divulgación? Para alcanzar una respuesta adecuada es necesario hacer un breve recuento.

En *Orígenes* explico cómo los dos primeros decenios de la Cuba republicana fueron tanto un hervidero de contradicciones y abusos sociales como también un pandemónium de ideas y desasosiegos. Esta situación de descontento popular e inquietud política animó a un pequeño pero articulado movimiento vanguardista en los años 20. Entre ellos militaban varios compositores cualificados que abrazaron un nacionalismo musical cargado de pretensiones afrocubanas, a partir de su interpretación de la obra etnológica de Fernando Ortiz. La meta consistía en equipararse a figuras como Bela Bartok y Manuel de Falla, entre los más destacados valores europeos del momento, así como los norteamericanos Aaron Copland y George Gershwin, pasando por importantes creadores contemporáneos mexicanos y brasileños como Silvestre Revueltas, Carlos Chávez y Héitor Villa-Lobos.

Concretamente, en una época en que no existía todavía la radio, era tal el hábito de la burguesía criolla de asistir a la ópera, que en 1923 el grupo vanguardista inició una campaña contra la ópera italiana. El sentido hiperbólico del cubano se manifestaba claramente: a un cierto nivel reinaba la música blanconaza, ajena al acervo cultural del país, al otro extremo dominaba la «música de las fritas», para citar el ácido comentario de un musicólogo español visitante, refiriéndose a lo que ofrecían modestos grupos de soneros en los quioscos y pequeños clubes que en los años 30 se expandieron al oeste de La Habana. Según Carpentier, al grito de «¡Abajo la lira, viva el bongó!» se defendieron los «afrocubanistas» de los «guajiristas», a raíz del escándalo que provocó el estreno en 1925 de la *Obertura sobre temas cubanos* de **Amadeo Roldán** (1900-39).

Nacido en París de padre español y madre cubana, Roldán estudió violín en el Conservatorio de Madrid; más tarde se concentró en armonía

CARICATURA DE ROLDÁN, POR MARIBONA (1927).

y composición, ganando en 1917 el premio Sarasate. A los 19 años se estableció en La Habana, adoptando la nacionalidad cubana. Nunca concibió música fácil porque era un verdadero renovador; su talento consistió en saber absorber las fuentes originales y luego presentarlas en su esencia. Roldán fue como un breve bólido luminoso en la trayectoria de la música «culta» cubana. En 1928 estrenó el ballet *La rebambaramba*, con libreto del joven escritor Alejo Carpentier, triunfo ampliado al año siguiente con el debut del ballet *El milagro de Anaquillé*, también con libreto de Carpentier. En 1931 fundó con César Pérez Sentenat la Escuela Normal de Música y dirigió más tarde el Conservatorio Municipal de La Habana, que hoy lleva su nombre. Desde 1932 y hasta su muerte por cáncer en 1939, Amadeo Roldán dirigió la Orquesta Filarmónica, reemplazando al maestro vasco Pedro Sanjuán. En el Town Hall de Nueva York estrenó en 1934 sus *Motivos de son*, dirigido por Nicolás Slonimsky, una obra que incluye la voz humana, inspirada en versos del poeta mulato Nicolás Guillén.

Hombre rebelde y sumamente activo, había adoptado una toma de conciencia artística que lo llevó a desbrozar la edulcorada apatía reinante. Roldán fue un hábil comunicador, se expresaba con una claridad que dejaba perplejos a muchos de sus oponentes. De él dijo Villa-Lobos, el famoso autor de las *Bachianas brasileiras*:

Roldán conoce la senda verdadera. No podía estar mejor orientado como músico de América. En una palabra: ve justo. Pronto llegará a la época de creación en que se dice: el folclor soy yo, y se hacen melodías más auténticas que las existentes, creándolas en pura imaginación.

Musicalmente hablando, los años 30 constituyeron una época extraordinaria. Entre la fuerza sabrosona que traía el son, el timbal del danzón que continuaba repiqueteando sobre la flauta, los boleros melosos, el tango y las canciones que ponían de moda los teatros populares y la radio, junto a las danzas para piano de Lecuona, surgieron ideas que intentaban apresar lo mejor del folclor y expresarlo con un lenguaje nuevo. Esta notabilísima tarea de expandir la música afrocubana a rangos superiores, más sofisticados y universales, correspondió no sólo a Roldán sino también a su contemporáneo **Alejandro García Caturla** (1906-40), otro compositor cualificado, blanco y con genio creativo, sin prejuicios de ningún tipo.

Multifacético, brillante, García Caturla estudió Derecho y ejerció como juez en su nativa Remedios, una adormecida ciudad del centro de la isla. En 1922 ingresó en la Universidad habanera hasta completar la carrera de leyes; simultáneamente estudió armonía, contrapunto y fuga con Pedro Sanjuán, radicado en La Habana desde 1924, quien fuera también profesor de Roldán. Su radical posición estética y su interés en el folclor afrocubano era tan definitivo que lo llevó a casarse con negras, con las que tuvo muchos hijos, algunos de los cuales se hicieron músicos. Realizó una obra más abundante y también más desordenadamente explosiva que Roldán, estrenando *La rumba* en 1933, un movimiento sinfónico con voz solista basado en un poema de José Zacarías Tallet. En 1928 y en París terminó de componer *Bembé*, obra de cámara escrita para maderas, metales y percusión, y que luego amplió para su estreno en La Habana en 1929. Se había ido a París a estudiar con Nadia Boulanger, quien más tarde declararía:

Pocas veces he tenido que vérmelas con un discípulo tan dotado... Es una fuerza de la naturaleza. Hay que dejarla que se manifieste.

Alejandro García Caturla se inició como pianista interpretando danzones y música norteamericana. Además de percusión tocaba el clarinete y el saxofón, y su voz de barítono participó en conciertos organizados por Jorge Anckermann y el maestro Ernesto Lecuona. Fue también un dedicado deportista y llegó a cultivar el periodismo como cronista cultural y crítico teatral. Su *Primera suite cubana* de 1938 es una síntesis de elementos nacionales y universales, donde combina varios géneros criollos con la acometida cromática de la poliarmonía y la polirritmia, las dos espirales de la vanguardia europea de su tiempo. Vista como un todo, su obra es bastante más barroca, más cargada orquestalmente que la de Amadeo Roldán. García Caturla fue calificado de creador sensacional por Leo Brouwer, quien lo sitúa como una de las dos figuras más grandes en América (el otro es el mexicano Silvestre Revueltas).

García Caturla tenía sólo 36 años cuando murió asesinado en su pueblo natal a manos de un criminal a quien había enviado antes a la cárcel. Sobre la descomunal labor creativa de ambos compositores escribió Carpentier en 1946:

Con su producción llena de tanteos, Roldán y Caturla liberaron a los músicos cubanos de las generaciones actuales de un buen número de angustias, reduciendo el alcance de ciertos problemas cuya solución podía haber parecido todavía extremadamente difícil hace veinte años. Por lo pronto, abrieron anchas y buenas veredas en la manigua de lo afrocubano.

La universidalidad de la obra de ambos autores es incuestionable, precisamente porque trascendieron fronteras, logrando proyectar una cubanía que fue más allá de lo puramente anecdótico o superficial. Sin embargo, hay que decir que su música no es fácilmente discernible. En realidad, su desaparición prematura les impidió madurar sus ideas y sin pretender denostar a ambiciosos autores posteriores, jamás volvió a alcanzar el país la brillantez y profundidad que ambos lograron. Ni siquiera con la creación de escuelas especializadas bajo la revolución.

A otro nivel totalmente diferente, la música que creó **Ernesto Lecuona** aportó el nuevo espíritu romántico dentro de un ámbito moderno que no corresponde en absoluto a los experimentos vanguardistas de sus contemporáneos Roldán y García Caturla. Lo que Lecuona logró con su música tampoco ha podido ser igualado: reflejar el carácter de lo cubano en su más sofisticada expresión. Supo encajar lo culto con un sabor eminentemente popular, sin caer en intelectualismos ni tampoco en soluciones fáciles.

No creo que Lecuona se haya planteado jamás narrar fidedignamente un episodio o anécdota, o tomar directamente elementos dispersos que escuchaba entre las fuentes hispana y africana que conformaron su desarrollo intelectual y estético. Sentado al piano, ante la imposibilidad ontológica de dominar la realidad, resolvió sus composiciones con gran audacia, con un estilo inigualable, limitado por las notas musicales, esas llaves exquisitas que le permitieron entrar e instalarse en el *doble* imaginativo de toda realidad. Él no pudo evitarlo: su música siempre halaga los oídos. En *Orígenes* hago un extenso análisis de la obra del maestro.

La relación que sigue de compositores, profesores y solistas comprometidos con la música sinfónica o de cámara, que se destacaron en las últimas cinco décadas, no pretende ser exhaustiva, sólo intenta dar una idea de la contribución de otro tipo de artista a la música nacional. Al informar de sus afanes experimentales, también deseo celebrar la labor de destacados intérpretes contemporáneos, teniendo en cuenta tanto a aquellos que abrazaron la revolución como a otros que alcanzaron el exilio para continuar creando buena música:

José Ardévol (1911). Compositor y profesor. Nació en Barcelona y fue iniciado en el arte musical por su padre. En 1930 se instaló en La Habana, fundando en 1934 la Orquesta de Cámara. Desde 1936 fue profesor del Conservatorio Municipal de Música y dos años después sustituyó a Amadeo Roldán en la enseñanza de composición y orquestación. Fue el organizador del Grupo de Renovación Musical, que en 1942 reunió a un número de destacados compositores jóvenes. Es el autor de aburridos artículos de crítica y evaluación musical publicados en Cuba y en el extranjero, así como del bosquejo histórico *La música*, 1969. Compuso más de cien obras, algunas grabadas en LP y escuchadas fuera de Cuba.

Carlo Borbolla (1902-90). Compositor. Nació en Manzanillo, miembro de una familia de constructores de órganos gigantes, un aspecto casi desconocido de la música popular cubana. Produjo los rollos de papel con incisiones en que se pasaba la música, generalmente danzones y sones. Autodidacta, vivió en París entre 1926-30 estudiando piano, composición y órgano. Escribió música de cámara y algunas canciones, especialmente sones que fueron editados en Francia. Escribió cinco cuadernos pedagógicos titulados *Rítmicas cubanas*.

Hilario González (1920). Compositor. Estudió música en Cuba y Venezuela, donde enseñó de 1947 a 1960, año en que regresó para ser nombrado profesor de piano en el Conservatorio Roldán. Entre 1938 y 1964 compuso preludios, sonatas, suites, así como lieds y música para ballet. Aunque su obra ha tenido poca repercusión en grabaciones, como analista ha publicado excelentes artículos sobre la música cubana.

Harold Gramatges (1918). Compositor. Estudió música en Santiago de Cuba y después en el Conservatorio Municipal de La Habana. En 1942 realizó estudios en el Berkshire Music Center bajo la dirección de Aaron Copland y Serge Koussevisky. Fue alumno de Roldán y Ardévol. En 1954 fundó la orquesta del Conservatorio Municipal de La Habana, de donde fue profesor. En 1958 obtuvo el Premio Reichold del Caribe y Centroamérica, otorgado por la Orquesta de Detroit por su *Sinfonía en mi*. Desde su fundación en 1951 hasta 1960 presidió la Sociedad Cultural Nuestro Tiempo, de orientación comunista. En los últimos cuarenta años ha viajado a diversos congresos de música. Su obra abarca composiciones para voces y orquestas, ballets, sonatas y cantatas. En 1997 recibió el Premio Iberoamericano de la Música «Tomás Luis de Victoria», la primera edición de este importante galardón español.

Antonino Hernández Lizaso (1931). Compositor y director de orquesta. Estudió piano y más tarde teoría y composición con Julián Orbón. En 1959 completó estudios en la Manhattan School of Music de Nueva York. Desde 1970 reside en Miami, compartiendo su trabajo como compositor con la dirección orquestal y la administración de programas de actividades culturales para dicha ciudad. Tiene un extenso catálogo con obras sinfónicas, una misa, sonatas, ciclos de canciones, música de cámara y una ópera. Su esposa Vivian G. Lizaso es también compositora.

Argeliers León (1918-91). Musicólogo. Doctor en pedagogía (1943), estudió en el Conservatorio Municipal de La Habana (1945) y completó su formación con Nadia Boulanger en París. En 1951 realizó estudios de posgrado en Chile. Además de su importante obra como compositor –*Sinfonía N.º 1* (1946), *Sonata para trompeta, trombón y percusión* (1944), *Quinteto para instrumentos de viento* (1969) y la cantata *Creador del hombre nuevo* (1969)– desarrolló una significativa labor como investigador y escritor. Brindó conferencias en tres continentes y contribuyó a revistas nacionales y extranjeras. Fue profesor de Arte Africano y Culturas Negras de Cuba en la Facultad de Humanidades, de la Universidad de La Habana; enseñó Musicología en la Escuela Nacional de Arte y fue director del

Departamento de Música de la Casa de las Américas y del Instituto de Etnología y Folklore de la Academia de Ciencias de Cuba. Maestro de infinidad de músicos y musicógrafos formados bajo la revolución, entre sus libros más notables se encuentran *Influencias africanas en la música de Cuba* (1959), *Música folklórica cubana* (1964) y *Del canto y el tiempo* (1974). Su viuda María Teresa Linares (1920) ha sido también una ardua investigadora de la música popular cubana, especializada en el folclor campesino.

Isaac Nicola (1916). Guitarrista. Estudió música con su madre, Clara Romero, y más tarde en París con Emilio Pujol. Hizo investigaciones en varios países sobre la vihuela y la guitarra antigua. Ofreció conciertos y conferencias en Cuba y en el extranjero. En 1951 fue nombrado profesor del Conservatorio Municipal de La Habana, del que después fue director. Presidió el Consejo Científico Técnico de la Enseñanza de la Música. Ha formado a excelentes guitarristas, entre ellos a Leo Brouwer, que hoy forman parte de la escuela cubana de guitarra. Su hermana Clara (1926) es una notable guitarrista, mientras que su hijo Noel (1946), guitarrista y cantautor, ha musicalizado poemas de José Martí y del peruano César Vallejo, y ha sido coordinador del movimiento nacional de la nueva trova.

Natalio Galán (1917-85). Compositor. Nació en Camagüey y falleció en Nueva Orleans. Autor de tendencia nacionalista, fue alumno de Luis Aguirre y en 1936 se trasladó a la capital, donde cursó estudios de composición en el Conservatorio Municipal. Fue profesor del Conservatorio Municipal habanero y colaborador de Alejo Carpentier, realizando un valioso trabajo de rescate de antiguas partituras de Esteban Salas (siglo XVIII) y otros autores para su libro *La música en Cuba* (1946). Desde 1947 residió en Estados Unidos, estudiando en la Academia Juilliard de Nueva York y con Henry Cowell. Regresó a la isla en 1959 y fue designado crítico musical del suplemento cultural «Lunes» del periódico *Revolución*. Galán compuso obras de cámara; luego estructuró *Variaciones* para pequeña orquesta, dentro del serialismo, y la ópera *Los días llenos*, con libreto de Antón Arrufat. De vuelta a Estados Unidos, residió durante varios años en Puerto Rico y colaboró conmigo en la edición de la *Enciclopedia de Cuba* en nueve volúmenes, producida en Madrid para la diáspora. Escribió dos libros: *Una historia inusitada* (1974) y *Cuba y sus sones* (1983), un original aporte al conocimiento de la música cubana, publicado por Pre-textos, de Valencia.

Julian Orbón (1925-91). Compositor. Nacido en Avilés, Asturias, aprendió música en España y desde 1932 comenzó a realizar viajes a Cuba con su padre, pianis-

JULIÁN ORBÓN.

ta concertista, hasta establecerse allí permanentemente de 1945 a 1960. En La Habana continuó sus estudios musicales, ofreciendo conciertos pianísticos. Fue miembro del Grupo de Renovación Musical. En su libro *La música en Cuba*, publicado en México en 1946, Alejo Carpentier afirmó: «Es la figura más singular y prometedora de la joven escuela cubana» (esta breve mención, que apareció en el capítulo XVIII, titulado «Estado actual de la música cubana» de la edición original, fue eliminada en ediciones posteriores hechas en Cuba a partir de 1960). Entre sus primeras obras se encuentran: *Sonata (Homenaje a Soler)*, *Tocata para piano*, *Pregón para voz e instrumentos de viento y piano*, *Quinteto para clarinete y cuarteto de cuerdas*, *Sinfonía en do mayor*, etc. En 1954 participó con sus *Tres versiones sinfónicas* en un concurso de composición en Caracas, con un jurado formado por Erich Kleiber, Adolfo Salazar, Edgar Varése y Héitor Villa-Lobos, ganando un premio compartido con el mexicano Carlos Chávez. La inclusión de algunos versos sencillos del patriota José Martí, el único elemento de interés en la conocida guajira *Guantanamera*, se debe a Orbón. En 1960 abandonó Cuba, instalándose en México como profesor del Conservatorio de Música aunque pronto se trasladó a Nueva York. Allí fue profesor del Manhattan School of Music y estrenó obras en diversas ciudades norteamericanas y españolas. Algunas están recogidas en LP y CD. En 2000 la Editorial Colibrí publicó en Madrid *En la esencia de los estilos y otros ensayos*, un libro que recoge sus pensamientos musicales.

Gilberto Valdés (1905-71). Compositor. Salvo breves lecciones que recibió del maestro Pedro Sanjuán, fue autodidacta. Introdujo la percusión afrocubana en la orquesta sinfónica con una serie de conciertos en 1937, con Rita Montaner como voz solista. Fue director musical del ballet afronorteamericano de Katherine Dunham. Algunas de sus piezas están plasmadas en LP, como *Tambó* y *Bembé*. Ya he reseñado lo mejor de su obra sinfónica. Creó también el pregón *El botellero*, y el son *Yo vengo de Jovellanos*, así como la canción de cuna *Ogguere*, que le interpretó *Bola de Nieve*. Colaboró con Fernando Ortiz en diversas investigaciones folclóricas.

Juan Blanco (1919). Compositor. Cursó estudios en el Conservatorio Municipal de La Habana. Desde la década de 1950 comenzó a crear música aleatoria, marcada por la electrónica. Inicialmente trabajó en la línea del nacionalismo, produciendo *Tríptico coral*, *Cantata de la paz*, *Elegía*, *Divertimento* y un *Quinteto* para maderas y violoncello. Fue el primero en experimentar en el campo de la música concreta y espacial con *Música de danza*, *Ensemble V*, *Texturas*, *Episodio*, *Contrapunto espacial* y *Erotofonías*. Fue director de música del Consejo Nacional de Cultura durante algunos años. Ha escrito música para cine, ballet y espectáculos al aire libre.

Aurelio de la Vega (1925). Compositor. Estudió música en La Habana y composición con Ernst Toch en California entre 1947-49. A partir de 1953 dirigió el Departamento de Música de la Universidad de Oriente y desde 1959 ha enseñado en la California State University, Northridge, de la que es *profesor emeritus*. Ha realizado incursiones en varias formas de la composición de vanguardia, pasando por el romanticismo y el posimpresionismo. Autor de *Leyenda del Ariel criollo*, de tendencia nacionalista, cultivó después la atonalidad y de 1959-70 desarrolló un estilo dodecafónico, combinándolo con formas aleatorias e incluyendo sonidos electrónicos. Más tarde reconstruyó su lenguaje para hacerlo más inteligible; a esta etapa corresponden *Madrigales*, con versos de Heberto Padilla, *Homenaje a Villa-Lobos* y las *Canciones transparentes*, obra basada en cinco poemas de José Martí, estrenada en Miami en 1995. Su música se ha tocado y grabado en América y Europa.

AURELIO DE LA VEGA.

Jorge Bolet (1914-90). Pianista. Tocó desde los seis años y a los doce ya estudiaba en el Instituto Curtis de Filadelfia. De él dijo el crítico Schonberg: «En el Curtis fue una estrella. Podía tocar cualquier cosa, leer todo, memorizar sin esfuerzo y ya tenía una técnica de nivel mundial». Después de graduarse en 1934, vino a Europa a dar una serie de conciertos. Entre 1939-42 fue jefe del Departamento de Piano del Instituto Curtis. De 1968-77 trabajó como profesor de la Universidad de Indiana. Su estilo y repertorio romántico no gozaron del favor del público entre 1940-60; sin embargo, a partir de los años 70 el interés por esta música lo colocó en los primeros planos de los concertistas mundiales. Considerado el máximo intérprete de Liszt, su repertorio cubría hasta Rachmaninoff. Interpretó la parte pianística en la película biográfica de Liszt *Song without end*. Dejó decenas de LP y CD y estuvo grabando casi hasta su muerte.

Alberto Bolet (1919). Violinista y director sinfónico. Hermano del anterior, comenzó el aprendizaje del violín y el violoncello a los siete años. Estudió en el Conservatorio Mateu de Guanabacoa y terminó sus estudios de violín a los quince años en el Conservatorio Falcón, bajo la guía de Casimiro Zertucha. Vino a Madrid para proseguir sus estudios, graduándose en el Conservatorio Nacional donde tuvo de profesor a Enrique Hernández de Arbos; más tarde pasó a París para perfeccionar su conocimiento del instrumento con Fermín Touche. Viajó por varios países europeos presentándose como violinista hasta que en 1925 se trasladó a Estados Unidos, trabajando en las orquestas sinfónicas de Detroit, Sacramento y Phoenix. En 1939 regresó a Cuba, convirtiéndose en director musical de la emisora CMZ. Tres años más tarde fue nombrado asistente de Erich Kleiber, a la sazón director de la Orquesta Filarmónica de La Habana. Ha realizado una destacada labor al frente de orquestas sinfónicas de Europa y de Estados Unidos, país donde reside.

José Echániz (1905-69). Pianista. Natural de Guanabacoa, como los hermanos Bolet. En 1920 y 1921 ofreció conciertos en el Teatro Nacional de La Habana y en el Town Hall de Nueva York. Posteriormente fue pianista acompañante de los cantantes Lucrecia Bori y el tenor Tito Schipa, en giras dentro y fuera de Estados Unidos, con los que produjo un buen número de grabaciones. En 1929 realizó giras por Francia, Holanda y España. Durante el período 1937-53 se presentó como solista de la Orquesta Filarmónica de La Habana y como director invitado de la misma; también ofreció conciertos en varias ciudades norteamericanas. Entre 1932-44 fue profesor del Conservatorio de Música de la Universidad de Decatur, Illinois. En 1944 fue nombrado profesor en la Escuela de Música de Eastman hasta su muerte. Hizo importantes grabaciones para los sellos Columbia y Westminster, cubriendo gran parte del repertorio pianístico de Albéniz y Falla, y casi todas las danzas de Lecuona.

Huberal Herrera (1929). Pianista. Nació en Mayarí, pero siendo pequeño su familia se trasladó a Güines, un pueblo de La Habana. Estudió piano con los profesores Hortensia Rojas, Arcadio Menocal, Harold Gramatges y Argeliers León, en los conservatorios Hubert de Blanck y Amadeo Roldán. Recibió clases superiores con Katia Kazandjeva, Stanislav Pochekin y Joseph Goorevich. En España tomó lecciones sobre el estilo interpretativo de la música española con Juan Bernal. Ha actuado en las mayores salas de conciertos de Cuba y ha sido invitado a tocar en calidad de solista con las orquestas sinfónicas del país, así como en espectáculos junto al eminente declamador Luis Carbonell. Ha realizado una paciente y difícil labor de recuperación de obras de Ernesto Lecuona que se consideraban perdidas, revisando y puliendo las partituras originales a partir de las propias grabaciones del maestro. En 1996 grabó la obra integral de Lecuona para la SGAE, en un álbum de tres compactos.

Juan Mercadal (1925-98). Guitarrista. Empezó a estudiar antes de los cinco años, debutando a los nueve en un concierto de la Sociedad de la Guitarra habanera. Estudió también clarinete y trompa francesa, y tocó con la orquesta Filarmónica de La Habana. En 1954 interpretó la banda sonora de la película cubana *Casta de robles*. En 1960 se radicó en Miami y en 1964 ingresó en el Departamento de Música de su Universidad, donde fundó el departamento de guitarra clásica, siendo la primera institución norteamericana en ofrecer el grado doctoral en esta materia. Viajó extensamente por Europa, Sudamérica y Estados Unidos ofreciendo conciertos. Grabó varios LP y CD.

Rey de la Torre (1917-94). Guitarrista. Comenzó sus estudios en La Habana y los continuó en España, debutando a los dieciséis años en Barcelona. Regresó a Cuba en 1934 y en 1937 embarcó hacia Estados Unidos, comenzando allí una brillante carrera. Grabó numerosos LP y estrenó trabajos dedicados a él por los maestros Julián Orbón, Joaquín Nin y José Ardévol.

Héctor Angulo (1932). Compositor. Inició estudios musicales en Santa Clara y luego en la capital, donde alcanzó el cuarto año de Arquitectura. Becado en Estados Unidos, a partir de 1959 estudió con Julián Orbón en el Manhattan School of Music y más tarde en la Juilliard School of Music de Nueva York con los maestros Giannini y Flagello. Regresó a Cuba en 1964, ingresando en el conservatorio Amadeo Roldán donde estudió con Leo Brouwer. Influenciado por Edgar Varese, escribió obras para flauta, violín y piano y para orquesta de cuerdas. Fascinado por la etnografía concibió *Sonera* (homenaje al bongó), *Son y Sonata* para piano y *Dos canciones* (sobre textos de Nicolás Guillén). Más tarde apareció *Poemas africanos*, *Ibeyí añá* (ópera de cámara para teatro guiñol), vistiendo los cantos yoruba con complejas elaboraciones armónicas.

Carlos Fariñas (1934). Compositor. Fue discípulo de Ardévol, Gramatges y Enrique González Mantici. En 1956 recibió clases de Aaron Copland en el centro musical de Berkshire, Estados Unidos. Entre 1961-63 realizó estudios en el Instituto Chaikovski de Moscú; a su regreso a Cuba trabajó como profesor y asesor musical. Fue director del Conservatorio García Caturla. Ha compuesto música para orquesta, para piano solo y para violín y violoncello, utilizando en sus composiciones elementos novedosos. Su obra *Tientos* obtuvo el premio de la Bienal de Jóvenes Compositores de París en 1970. Ha trabajado los medios electroacústicos y ha compuesto música para cine, incluyendo *Soy Cuba*. Fue director del Departamento de Música de la Biblioteca Nacional José Martí.

Leo Brouwer (1939). Guitarrista, compositor y director de orquesta. Nieto de Ernestina Lecuona, creció en una familia de músicos. Comenzó el aprendizaje de la guitarra con su padre y luego pasó a estudiar con Isaac Nicola. También fue alumno de Caridad Mezquida, Freed, Diemente, Persichetti y otros. Completó su carrera en la Escuela de Música Juilliard de Nueva York y en el Departamento de Música de la Universidad de Hartford (1959-60). Fue profesor de armonía y contrapunto en el Conservatorio Amadeo Roldán y asesor musical de la Cadena Nacional de Radio y Televisión. Estima que el festival de música «Otoño Varsoviano» de 1961 jugó un papel primordial en el desarrollo de la vanguardia cubana. Excelente guitarrista, ha ofrecido conciertos en numerosos países y ha grabado más de diez discos. Aglutinada alrededor de su obra se ha formalizado una escuela de guitarra cubana, con discípulos que han descollado dentro y fuera del país. Estilísticamente ha recorrido los caminos del serialismo, el postserialismo y el aleatorismo. Fue director y profesor del Grupo Experimental Sonoro (GESI), cuyo objetivo central fue formar creadores que hiciesen música para el cine. También ha sido director de la Orquesta Sinfónica de Córdoba.

José Luis Fajardo (1946). Pianista. Nació en Pinar del Río, en el seno de una familia que ha dado grandes músicos. Vivió en Puerto Rico y posteriormente en España, ingresando en el Real Conservatorio Superior de Música de Madrid, donde obtuvo los Premios de Honor Fin de Carrera y de Virtuosismo. Posee la medalla Lincoln-Martí (Washington, 1972), y el Primer Premio Casa de Viena (Oviedo, 1973). Al concluir sus estudios realizó oposiciones para convertirse en profesor del Real Conservatorio Superior de Música de Madrid, impartiendo clases durante nueve años; posteriormente fue nombrado profesor del Conservatorio Profesional de Música de Amaniel. Ha grabado para Radio Nacional de España, la BBC y otras entidades europeas. Grabó la integral para piano de Ernesto Lecuona en el sello Several Records. En 1993 obtuvo el premio Albéniz Institute en Nueva York. Fajardo ha brindado recitales y clases magistrales en varias ciudades españolas, europeas y en Nueva York. En 1995 participó en el homenaje a la música de Lecuona en la Casa de América de Madrid. Reside en dicha ciudad desde 1964.

Flores Chaviano (1946). Guitarrista, compositor y director. Desde hace más de dos décadas reside en España. Realizó estudios con Isaac Nicola en la Escuela Nacional de Arte, y posteriormente composición con Sergio Fernández Barroso en el Instituto Superior de Arte. Fue profesor en el Conservatorio Amadeo Roldán y en 1974 obtuvo el premio de guitarra de la Unión Nacional de Escritores y Artistas de Cuba (UNEAC). Entre sus obras de la primera época aparecen *Réquiem a un sonero* (dedicado a Miguel Matamoros), *Homenaje a Víctor Jara*, *Variaciones sobre un tema yoruba*, *Poema para flauta y guitarra*, así como música infantil. Rea-

FLORES CHAVIANO.

lizó estudios en el Real Conservatorio de Música de Madrid. En Segovia fue profesor del Conservatorio de dicha ciudad. Es director-fundador del Ensemble Ciudad de Segovia. Ha actuado en infinidad de festivales internacionales y españoles. Como compositor ha realizado obras por encargo de la Fundación Príncipe de Asturias, el Centro para la Difusión de la Música Contemporánea y Radio Nacional de España. Algunas de sus composiciones forman parte del repertorio de distinguidos guitarristas de varios países. Su catálogo abarca obras para diversos formatos instrumentales así como música electrónica y coral. Actualmente reside en Madrid.

Frank Fernández (1944). Pianista. A los cuatro años inició estudios con su madre, que continuó con Esteban Forés en Mayarí, su pueblo natal. Trasladado a la capital, fue pianista en clubes y cabarés. Ingresó en el Conservatorio Amadeo Roldán donde trabajó bajo Margot Rojas. Ganador del concurso de piano de la UNEAC, marchó becado a la Unión Soviética, donde estudió con Merchanov. Ha compuesto música coral y ha actuado como solista con la Orquesta Sinfónica Nacional; también ha trabajado como productor de grabaciones. Hombre clave del régimen, contribuyó a los planes de enseñanza pianística del Instituto Superior de Arte y se ocupó de la participación de profesores de Europa oriental. Aunque no explota su faceta de pianista de música popular, realizó brillantes solos de piano en las primeras producciones discográficas de Adalberto Álvarez y Son 14. También ha sido pianista acompañante en varias grabaciones de Silvio Rodríguez y de su hermana Anabel López.

Alberto Joya (1952). Pianista. Graduado en el Instituto Superior de Arte, cursó estudios de clavicémbalo en España con los profesores Genoveva Gálvez, Kenneth Gilbert y Pablo Cano en el Real Conservatorio Superior de Música de Madrid, y con Rafael Puyana en Compostela, y ha participado en las clases magistrales de Gustav Leonhardt. También estudió con el checo Petr Sefl. En 1968 debutó como solista en el Gran Teatro de la Habana a la edad de 16 años. Posee una amplia trayectoria de presentaciones que comprenden recitales y conciertos con diversas orquestas sinfónicas y ha realizado giras por varios países. Ha investigado la literatura pianística cubana de los siglos XIX y XX, principalmente la obra de Ignacio Cervantes, Ernesto Lecuona y Carlo Borbolla, ofreciendo conferencias y recitales especializados. En 1980 fundó el Dúo Concertante de La Habana, que se especializó en música de cámara. Estrenó en Cuba las *Sonatas y fugas* de Sebastián Albero, compositor español del siglo XVIII. En Francia ofreció una serie de conciertos en un fortepiano original de Josephus Zimmermann, construido en 1791. En 1990 obtuvo el premio Rosa Sabater de la Casa Hazen de Madrid. Posee el diploma por alta maestría artística que le otorgó la Unión de Compositores de la antigua URSS y también la orden Santa María del Rosario, su ciudad natal. En 1995 participó en el homenaje a la música de Lecuona celebrado en la Casa de América de Madrid. Reside en dicha ciudad.

Jorge Luis Prats (1956). Pianista. Comenzó a estudiar piano en 1963 en la Academia Fernández Vila con la profesora Bárbara Díaz. Ingresó en 1970 en la Escuela Nacional de Arte, trabajando bajo el cuidado de Margot Rojas hasta graduarse en 1976. Guiado por Frank Fernández continuó su formación, a la vez que ofrecía recitales en distintas salas y teatros del país. En 1977 obtuvo el primer gran premio de piano en el Concurso Margueritte Long-Jacques Thibaud de París, evento en que además recibió la distinción al Mejor Intérprete, así como el Premio Ravel. En 1979 obtuvo la medalla de oro en el Festival Musical de Laureados Katia Popová de Bulgaria.

Carlos Molina (1946). Guitarrista. Estudió en el conservatorio Hubert de Blanck y más tarde en el Amadeo Roldán. Discípulo de Isaac Nicola, recibió orientaciones de Leo Brouwer, Abel Carlevaro, Alirio Díaz y Alberto Ponce. En 1969 fue nombrado profesor del Conservatorio Amadeo Roldán; un año después obtuvo el primer lugar en el Concurso Nacional de Música. En 1979 ofreció un importante concierto en el Metropolitan Opera House de Nueva York. Fue profesor del Instituto Superior de Arte (ISA) antes de decidir quedarse en Estados Unidos, donde actualmente es profesor en la Florida International University. Ha escrito un libro sobre la historia de la guitarra en Cuba.

Sergio Barroso (1946). Pianista y compositor. Estudió en el Conservatorio Nacional y posteriormente en Praga. Aunque desde 1969 se concentró en la música electroacústica, su producción también incluye música clásica. En 1982 estudió música computerizada en la Universidad Standford de California. Sus composiciones han sido ejecutadas en tres continentes. Actualmente se le considera uno de los más importantes ejecutantes de sintetizadores en Canadá, país donde reside.

Horacio Gutiérrez (1948). Pianista. A los doce años ya era solista de la Filarmónica de La Habana. En 1962 su familia se exilió en Estados Unidos, donde continuó estudios en Los Ángeles y después se graduó en la Juilliard School of Music de Nueva York. En 1970 ganó la medalla de plata en el concurso Chaikovsky de Moscú; comenzó entonces una intensa carrera de concertista. Pianista brillante, tiene grabados varios discos de música clásica, acompañado de las más prestigiosas orquestas.

Manuel Barrueco (1952). Guitarrista. Natural de Santiago de Cuba, comenzó a estudiar música a los ocho años con Manuel Puig. Tras su exilio en Estados Unidos en 1967 continuó su formación con Juan Mercadal y Rey de la Torre. También estudió en el Conservatorio Peabody de Baltimore. Ha ofrecido recitales en varios países europeos incluyendo a España, y ha grabado importantes discos con obras clásicas, particularmente transcripciones de obras de Mozart y Bach. Ha sido profesor de guitarra en el Manhattan School of Music de Nueva York.

La falta de información y de espacio no me ha permitido incluir a todos los intérpretes y solistas de talento que han engrandecido el prestigio de Cuba en las últimas cinco décadas; que me disculpen los no citados, que afortunadamente son muchos. Sin embargo, debo mencionar a algunas pianistas que han alcanzado fama internacional: Ivette Hernández, Zenaida Manfugás, Ninowska Fernández-Brito y Numidia Vaillant, así como a las directoras de orquesta Tania León y Marlene Urbay. El respetado pianista José María Vitier (1954), uno de los pocos que han creado contradanzas contemporáneas, es el autor de las bandas sonoras de los filmes *Fresa y chocolate, El siglo de las luces y Cosas que dejé en La Habana*. Vitier considera que la música, además de un entretenimiento espectacular, es una forma de interpretar el mundo. «Le atribuyo la misma carga conceptual que tiene la literatura», ha declarado. «A mí no me preocupa tanto que no se valore la música, lo que me asusta es que se esté infravalorando al público. Como si la gente fuera tonta». De entre los músicos que escaparon del país por el puerto del Mariel en 1980 sobresale Félix Spengler, joven pianista negro que ha logrado abrirse paso en Nueva York y ha actuado en España. De la generación de cubanoamericanos –su familia emigró a Estados Unidos en 1960– surgió el pianista Santiago Rodríguez, quien a los 29 años recibió la medalla de plata en la competencia internacional Van Cliburn en Texas, y es hoy considerado uno de los mejores intérpretes del compositor ruso Serge Rachmaninov.

El Conjunto Folklórico Nacional

Fundado en 1962, el Conjunto Folklórico se constituyó para rescatar y divulgar en lo danzario y lo musical los valores imperecederos de la cultura popular y tradicional cubana; su creación fue uno de los grandes

BAILE CONGO DEL CONJUNTO FOLKLÓRICO NACIONAL.

aciertos de la primera etapa de la revolución. Entre sus objetivos estaba también la investigación y selección de aquellas expresiones cuya esencia folclórica contara con un contenido capaz de permitirles producir versiones de gran alcance estético y escénico. Aunque Rodolfo Reyes Cortés fue su cofundador, la actual dirección artística está a cargo de Teresa González, bailarina y coreógrafa reconocida como una experimentada pedagoga; el asesor folclórico continúa siendo el incansable investigador **Rogelio Martínez Furé**.

El repertorio del Conjunto Folklórico consta de más de sesenta obras que reflejan las contribuciones culturales, desde los orígenes europeos –español y francés– hasta los africanos, fundamentalmente las culturas yoruba, congo y carabalí. Ha recorrido más de cincuenta países y unas quinientas ciudades de todos los continentes, presentándose en los más prestigiosos teatros y festivales, obteniendo una extensa lista de premios importantes que son garantía del excelente trabajo de rescate y divulgación en que están comprometidos. Este nutrido colectivo, que cuenta con un cuerpo de baile y un grupo de músicos especializados, ha incorporado con los años una serie de manifestaciones culturales y religiosas de otras naciones del Caribe.

Se han presentado en España en diversas ocasiones; una de las más recientes fue durante los «Veranos de la Villa 1998», en que montaron un espectáculo que incluyó aspectos de la tumba francesa de Santiago de Cuba y música gagá de la República Do-

minicana, así como habaneras, mambos y rumbas en el Teatro de Madrid de La Vaguada, como parte de la conmemoración del centenario de la guerra hispano-cubano-americana.

De cara a los músicos y bailarines populares, aunque no siempre organizada de la forma más metódica y efectiva, el Conjunto Folklórico ha ejercido una considerable influencia en dotarlos de elementos y directrices que puedan aplicar o no en su trabajo diario.

ALICIA ALONSO.

Formada por unos sesenta bailarines y músicos, **Danza Contemporánea de Cuba**, fundada en 1959, ha sorprendido en múltiples escenarios por su alto nivel técnico y profesional. Algunos temas de su repertorio abordan las formas folclóricas enfrentadas a un lenguaje moderno, como en «Panorama de la música y la danza cubana», de Víctor Cuéllar.

Finalmente, mencionaré la ingente labor de **Alicia Alonso** (1917) al frente del Ballet Nacional de Cuba (fundado en 1959), que se ha presentado en los mejores escenarios internacionales. Con los años, al ir perdiendo algunas de sus grandes figuras por defecciones, así como a consecuencia de la ceguera y avanzada edad de su fundadora, la importancia nacional e internacional de este formidable cuerpo de ballet clásico ha disminuido considerablemente.

4. EL JAZZ AFROCUBANO

Aquí, en Estados Unidos, el jazz cubano cae dentro del cajón de sastre que se conoce hoy como jazz latino. Pero como saben bien los músicos presentes, en los años 50 surgió en La Habana un jazz cubano. El famoso Irakere de los 70 no fue un fenómeno milagroso caído del cielo. ¿Cómo podrían juntarse grandes estrellas como Paquito D'Rivera, Chucho Valdés y Arturo Sandoval en el escenario del Carnegie Hall sin que se hubiera plantado antes la semilla del jazz cubano?

ANTONIO BENÍTEZ ROJO
«Cuba en el jazz», contribución al seminario
«Cuba, 170 años de presencia en Estados Unidos»,
Nueva York, noviembre 1999

La capital del ragtime no fue Nueva Orleans sino Sedalia, al sur del estado de Missouri, donde se estableció el brillante pianista Scott Joplin. Como era música compuesta, le faltaba el rasgo decisivo del jazz: la improvisación, mas en vista de que contiene el elemento de swing, es ya costumbre incluir su aporte dentro del jazz. Música de piano del siglo XIX, pronto sus melodías sirvieron como temas para improvisaciones jazzísticas, unidas a otras influencias que han ido desde Chopin y Listz hasta la marcha y la polka, pero todo esto con la concepción rítmica de los negros. De ahí su nombre: *ragged time* = tiempo rasgado o sincopado.

Gran admirador de la música del negro nacido en Texas, el pianista habanero **Ignacio Cervantes** (1847-1905) se vio forzado a vivir largas temporadas en Estados Unidos por sus actividades contra la Corona española. En 1902, durante la Exposición Universal de Charleston, en la que participó como embajador de la música cubana, el blanco Cervantes logró conocer a Joplin, quien le mostró apuntes de su ópera *The guest of honor* que nunca se vería publicada. Ambos creadores sabían que, por origen y color de piel, pertenecían a las dos fuentes que habían formulado un sincretismo musical que revolucionó el mundo de la música popular en toda la cuenca del Caribe y en gran parte del planeta, y que precisamente se manifestaba a través de ellos en dos corrientes aparentemente opuestas.

La eclosión de los ritmos y músicas de raíz afroamericana en los años 1914-1929 coincidió en Cuba con un período de inevitables altas y bajas en lo político y una cierta prosperidad económica que permitió que las chicas de la alta sociedad pusieran de moda los afeites, el *maillot*, los cigarrillos y la música norteamericana. Era precisamente la época en que el son iba penetrando en todos los estratos sociales, teniendo que combatir con el tango y el fox-trot, que fue la carta de que se sirvió el jazz para hacer su presentación en sociedad. Ya lo había dicho en 1941 W. C. Handy, el autor del conocido *St. Louis blues*: «El jazz creció alrededor del fox-trot y todavía lo tiene como base principal». A ritmo de fox-trot tuvieron que escuchar Ignacio Piñeiro y sus compañeros del Septeto Nacional el himno oficial de la Exposición Iberoamericana de Sevilla de 1929. ¿Saben cómo se titulaba? *Sevilla, yes!*

Al fox-trot le siguió el charlestón; lo trajo a Europa Josephine Baker. Sensualidad, exotismo, champán, negritud, todo eso y mucho más significó el nuevo baile que exigía una labor agotadora. Perplejos ante tal invasión, mucho tuvieron que luchar los septetos soneros cubanos contra un ritmo que gozaba de la preferencia de los que tenían el poder para contratarlos. Además, tuvieron que enfrentar la oposición de los sindicatos de músicos de entonces, que no los admitieron en sus filas hasta aproximadamente 1935. Esta exclusión –que se prolongaba a dúos, tríos y trovadores individuales– ocasionó la pérdida de oportunidades de empleo y salarios bajos por sus actuaciones.

El desbordamiento del jazz por todo el mundo, apoyado por la industria disquera norteamericana, alcanzó tanto las costas cubanas como la lejana Argentina: la famosa orquesta de don Aspiazu grabó varios números de jazz entre 1930 y 1931, mientras que Carlos Gardel grabó muchos *shimmies* (una variante del fox-trot) antes de eternizar sus primeros tangos.

Se hablaba de jazz, o mejor, del «yas», entre platillos y el sonido de algún saxofón perdido en los vericuetos de La Habana vieja. En su acepción más generosa, el término comprendía el charlestón y el fox-trot, el shimmy, el black-bottom, el monkey-glide, el fish-walk, el one-step y el two-step, el boston, el double boston y el triple boston, el schottish americano, una variedad del bosto, el buzzard lope, el lambet walk, el jersey-bounce, el slow o balada, el turkey-trut, el horse-trut y el honey-bug, de definido carácter cómico, el stomp, el jump y el joy y el lindy-hop o jitte-

burg, el blues, el big apple, el ro-
yal-blues, la rumba-blues y el
yale-blues, una mezcla de fox-trot,
blues y tango, el schloop y otros
muchos... Lo que hizo exclamar a
un cronista español de la época:
«Al final de la (primera) guerra
europea los americanos trajeron el
jazz band y su vicio de cambiar de
baile todas las semanas».

EN LOS COMIENZOS DEL BLUES: LOS GUS
CANNON'S JUG STOMPERS (1928).

«Me voy pa'Nuyó»

Fueron causas económicas las que en los años 30 obligaron a una camada
de músicos criollos a embarcarse hacia Nueva York, que entonces gozaba
de fama como tierra acogedora de emigrantes y exiliados caribeños, nos
dice el periodista Carlos Verdecia. Conviviendo muy cerca unos de otros,
muy pronto los afroamericanos de Harlem comenzaron a pasear su curiosidad por las sesiones de música que hacían los latinos y pronto unos entraron en el campo musical de otros, no sin ciertas dificultades, como intentó explicarlo Marshall W. Stearns en su obra *La historia del jazz*:

La música cubana presentaba ciertos problemas al músico de jazz, de igual modo
que el jazz al músico cubano. El jazz emplea un patrón rítmico aparentemente
más sencillo: un golpe de marcha de 4x4. Ello hacía que el músico de jazz tuviera
dificultades para aprender a improvisar sobre el golpe de la clave. A su vez, el
músico cubano encontraba el ritmo básico del jazz muy limitante, en tanto que la
armonía le resultaba extremadamente complicada.

A diferencia de los norteamericanos, los músicos cubanos del
siglo XX siempre tuvieron metida en la cabeza la métrica asfixiante de las
claves, amén de otras diferencias marcadas por el desarrollo histórico de
ambas culturas. Curiosamente, Guillermo Barreto, un percusionista que
tocó mucho jazz, me confesó una vez que quería fundar una organización
en defensa de la clave.

No obstante, un número sustancial de músicos tenía un oído puesto
en la isla y otro en Estados Unidos. La «Voz de América» enviaba a todo

el continente un chorro diario de excelente jazz. Y no es que abandona-ran el llamado de lo telúrico, pues precisamente en esos años tiene lugar la cubanización de lo afrocubano, que culminó en la década de los 50, disponiendo el espacio para que coexistieran todas las diferencias que constituían la música cubana –el jazz incluido–, sólo que en la isla el jam session se llamó «descarga». Poco a poco se estructuró una hermandad cuyo lenguaje era hacer música de jazz; no sólo se presentaban en la isla excelentes instrumentistas norteamericanos, sino que músicos criollos que trabajaban en el Norte volaban cuando podían llevando en sus maletas lo último de lo último.

Si bien los emigrantes a Estados Unidos habían sido mayoritaria-mente europeos durante el siglo XIX y la primera mitad del XX, a partir de los años 50 la balanza se inclina hacia los latinoamericanos. Hoy se cal-cula en 40 millones la población de habla hispana, lo que en términos de mercado de consumo representa la población de España; un dato a tener en cuenta para comprender el impacto comercial que en su momento tu-vieron el mambo, el chachachá, el boogaloo (versión neoyorquina del chachachá), la bossa nova y, más tarde, la salsa y el merengue. Natural-mente, todos estos géneros jugaron su papel en el fenómeno llamado el renacimiento del jazz afrocubano.

Armonías vs tambores

Durante penosos siglos entonaron los negros sudorosos sus misteriosos cánticos en oscuros barracones mientras se repiqueteaba sobre un cajón de madera (mucho después pudieron construirse verdaderos tambores) donde les llegaba envasado el bacalao salado o el tasajo de Montevideo, con que les alimentaba el esclavista español, que de hecho tenía una idio-sincrasia completamente distinta a la del racista anglosajón, dueño de las enormes algodoneras del sur de Estados Unidos.

Entonces había en Cuba cien hombres por cada cinco mujeres blan-cas, lo que determinó que muy pronto el español dejara a un lado sus prejuicios y cohabitara con la esclava; a poco ya estaban ahí los mulatos, abriéndose un arcoiris infinito. Por su parte, el inglés pugnó por alejarse de ese deseo mientras le prohibía a sus esclavos la posibilidad de tocar un tambor porque consideraba que restaba productividad a la cosecha. Muy diferente a la actitud del peninsular, a quien le importaba un bledo que en el barracón sonaran los cajones hasta altas horas, siempre y cuando los fuertes brazos cortaran su cuota de arrobas diarias y el molino de caña diera vueltas a la mañana siguiente.

De ahí que mientras los esclavos de Norteamérica tuvieron más temprano acceso a las formas musicales europeas, armonizando a varias voces mientras atendían la cosecha de algodón, los negros cubanos se limitaron a sacarle la máxima musicalidad a sus voces y tambores. Cuando ya los negros sureños cantaban su dolor en inglés, aunque fuese un inglés basto y basado en las creencias protestantes que les inculcaban, los esclavos cubanos continuaron cantando en lenguas africanas. Pero los azarosos caminos de estos hermanos transplantados acabarían por fusionarse en un reencuentro en el que cada corriente ofreció una dinámica diferente sobre fundamentos similares.

INFLUENCIA DEL JAZZ EN CUBA

Aunque bastantes músicos criollos tocaron jazz durante años, seguían teniendo más experiencia y raíces más sólidas dentro de los parámetros de la música de la sabrosura; dichas raíces afrocubanas se evidenciaban no sólo en la percusión, también tenían mucho que ver en cómo se tocaba, en el fraseo, en el ataque y en el sentido del ritmo de los solistas, al igual que en la interpretación de pasajes enteros de una pieza jazzística.

No resulta extraño que ambas formas musicales hayan sido comparadas frecuentemente. La afinidad viene de bien atrás, mientras se forjaba el jazz y terminaba la esclavitud en Cuba. Entre 1880 y 1889 muchos negros cubanos, súbitamente libres pero sin empleo, lograron llegar a Nueva Orleans. De ahí que entre apellidos ingleses y franceses encontremos entre los primeros músicos de jazz los nombres de Lorenzo Tió, Paul Domínguez, Manuel Pérez, Willy Marrero y otros.

El novelista y musicólogo Alejo Carpentier siempre creyó que la música popular cubana era la única comparable a la vitalidad del jazz norteamericano. Además de los metales y la labor del piano y el bajo, esta afirmación tiene mucho que ver con el arsenal percutivo.

Debido a la falta de información, muchos creen que los percusionistas cubanos sólo tocan tumbadora, timbal, bongó, batá, güiro, cencerro y maracas, y que a sus colegas brasileños solamente les interesa tocar pendeiro, berimbau, cuica, surdo, a-gó-go, tamborim y reco-reco. Siguiendo

Los mejores: PAQUITO D'RIVERA

Reconocido como «El rey cubano del saxo» en cualquier capital occidental en que existan acólitos del jazz, Paquito D'Rivera (1948) es un hombre que nació para ese instrumento de viento, inventado por el belga Antoine Joseph Sax alrededor de 1890. Paquito era aún muy pequeño cuando Tito, su padre y primer maestro, encargó a un especialista francés la fabricación de un instrumento en miniatura para que el niño pudiera alcanzar la boquilla y las llaves con facilidad. De entonces a acá, partiendo de la influencia de tres maestros –Coleman Hawkins, Lester Young y Charlie Parker–, Paquito D'Rivera ha realizado una carrera extraordinaria.

Este habanero, incorregiblemente pletórico de buen humor, debutó «profesionalmente» en un saxo soprano a los seis años de edad y confirmó su vocación al escuchar repetidas veces el disco de Benny Goodman *Live at Carnegie Hall.* De adolescente se ponía al día con el programa de radio «Willis Conover's Jazz Hour» que transmitía la Voz de las Américas desde Washington. A los doce años coincidió en el Conservatorio Municipal de La Habana con un chico siete años menor que él pero dos cabezas más alto, de largas manos oscuras, también de padre músico y que se llama Chucho Valdés. En 1963 ambos participaron en la orquesta del Teatro Musical de La Habana y en 1967 ya eran miembros fundadores de la Orquesta Cubana de Música Moderna, cuya dirección D'Rivera asumió pronto.

Animados por su exitosa presentación en el Festival de Jazz de Varsovia en 1970, tres años después ambos decidieron crear el grupo Irakere con otros integrantes de la Orquesta de Música Moderna. Por aquellos días, su versión del famoso *Adagio* de Mozart se convirtió en uno de los grandes éxitos de la nueva banda: a Paquito se le ocurrió actualizarlo mediante una jocosa improvisación que trasladó al blues y al rock. Su talento para inventar pasajes no tiene límites. En 1976 grabó por primera vez en solitario con el bajo danés Orsted-Pedersen, y entre 1977 y 1979 participó con músicos norteamericanos en varios encuentros celebrados en La Habana.

En 1980 logró irse con su música a otra parte, un proyecto largamente ansiado. Vivió casi seis meses en Madrid esperando el visado para su país de destino, una época que recuerda con agrado: «De puta madre», asegura que lo pasó, en su amena biografía *Mi vida saxual.* Con la ayuda prometida del viejo trompeta Dizzy Gillespie, Paquito pudo entrar en Estados Unidos, y tan activo como

siempre, pronto fundó el grupo Havana-
New York Ensemble, que vino a cono-
cerse como «la escuelita», ya que allí se
pulieron solistas del calibre del guitarrista Fareed Haque, los pianistas Hilton
Ruiz, Michel Camilo y Danilo Pérez, el
percusionista Daniel Ponce y el trompeta Claudio Roditi, todos estrellas. Paquito D'Rivera es uno de los pocos músicos que conozco que practican el jazz
afrocubano abarcando la vasta gama de
la música hispanoamericana.

Vive en Weehawken, Nueva Jersey, al lado oeste del río Hudson, desde
donde se puede apreciar mejor la silueta de los rascacielos de Manhattan; colec-
ciona «escarabajos» Volkswagen, pasión que comparte con su hermano Enrique.
Recuerda que cuando su vuelo de Iberia se acercaba al aeropuerto J. F. Kennedy,
en el sistema de sonido de la cabina comenzó a vibrar *Let's dance*, tema musical
de la orquesta de Benny Goodman. Sólo entonces supo que había llegado.

Creo que la única fobia de Paquito D'Rivera es la solemnidad, no he conocido a músico más jocoso; sin embargo, posee un enorme tacto y total seriedad en sus compromisos. Aún cuando está concentrado en una difícil improvisación jazzística, su cuerpo se mueve constantemente, a veces se inclina tanto
que parece se va a caer, mientras del instrumento brotan ricas notas a enorme
velocidad.

De los ocho miembros de la familia del saxofón, sólo tres se suelen usar
en el Caribe: el soprano, afinado en si bemol y de tono agudo; el tenor, también
en si bemol, y el barítono, de sonido grave y afinado en mi bemol. En los grupos de jazz, el saxo es tocado por el mismo intérprete del clarinete, aunque la
historia de este último es un poco más larga. Normalmente hecho de bronce, el
saxo tiene muchas llaves y palancas, y se toca con boquilla donde va alojada
una fina caña, al igual que el clarinete.

Su afecto y admiración por Chucho Valdés lo llevó a grabar varios temas
del pianista y le dedicó *Chucho*, quizá uno de sus números más destacados. Tocando lo mismo el saxo alto que el clarinete, ha realizado excelentes dúos con
Jorge Dalto, con el conocido tango *El día que me quieras* como tema central,
con Michel Camilo en *Why not,* mientras que con las cuerdas de Haque ha gra-

bado varios valses de Antonio Lauro, y el chorinho *Segura ele* con Romero Lubambo. Más tarde, esta afinidad entre instrumentistas de primera fila se reveló
con el bolero *Como un milagro*, compartido con las teclas de Danilo Pérez. Le
siguieron interpretaciones de varias danzas de los cubanos Ignacio Cervantes y
Ernesto Lecuona, y finalmente grabó con el bajo Israel López *Cachao*, un viejo
amigo de su padre.

En 1989 Paquito D'Rivera reunió a tres generaciones de músicos cubanos
en *40 Years of Cuban Jam Sessions*, un álbum cuya ilustración para la cubierta
lo dice todo: sugiriendo el anillo de un puro aparece una tumbadora oscura con
una guitarra y un saxofón a cada lado.

Su sensibilidad, talento musical y fino humor son sólo comparables a la
modestia de su trato. No he conocido a nadie que no quiera entrañablemente a
Paquito D'Rivera. Bueno, me equivoco, hay una excepción: los esbirros musicales de Castro. En 1996 terminó de escribir un libro totalmente desenfadado, en
que se burla de todo y de todos, empezando por sí mismo; se titula *Mi vida saxual* y fue publicado por Seix Barral en 1998. Se lo recomiendo a todo el que
desee acercarse más a este genio contemporáneo y disfrutar con sus chispeantes
anécdotas.

el ejemplo de la influyente orquesta de Pérez Prado, algunos timbaleros
añadieron el bombo y el tom-tom a sus pailas. José Luis Quintana *Changuito* recuerda que «cuando Filiberto Peña tocaba con la tribu de Benny
Moré ya estaba usando un bombo».

La situación de los músicos cambió a partir de 1959 cuando –afirma
el saxo Paquito D'Rivera– «el hombre de la barba vino a liberarnos de
todas las cosas, hasta de la comida y la libertad». En 1962 Walfredo de
los Reyes decidió irse con sus baquetas para el otro lado; entre otros bateristas que siguieron la misma ruta norteña durante las últimas décadas
están Nelson *El flaco* Padrón, Ignacio Berroa, Horacio *El negro* Hernández, y Alfredo *Meyo* Martínez. Guillermo Barreto permaneció en su tierra
natal, aún a sabiendas de que el jazz equivalía a una palabra soez para el
régimen.

Enrique Pla, renombrado por su extensa labor con Irakere, se dedicó
a adaptar ciertas tradiciones percutivas de carácter afrocubano a la batería, especialmente dentro del plano jazzístico. Lo cual motivó el siguiente

comentario de *Changuito*: «Pla es un percusionista completo; el es blanco por ser blanco, pero es negro por dentro». Otro baterista prominente del período revolucionario es Daniel Díaz, integrante de la Orquesta Ritmo Oriental, que creó la «pailatería» al fusionar elementos baterísticos y timbaleros. El cronista musical Rafael Lam apuntó desde La Habana que Díaz «empleó un pedal de bombo, adaptado para pegarle al cencerro, propiciando un sonido más potente en el formato de charanga». Junto al tumbador Juan Claro *Clarito*, Díaz facilitó que la Ritmo Oriental se convirtiera en la charanga de mayor fuerza percutiva de los años 70.

INFLUENCIAS CUBANAS EN NORTEAMÉRICA

Ya he referido cómo la música afrocubana nació en las circunstancias más adversas que puedan concebirse. Quizá de ahí provenga esa fuerza que la ha hecho resistir todos los embates de la historia y la ha convertido en un paliativo para hacerle frente a los males a que ha estado sometida la nación. Como en un triste simulacro de tiempo circular, ha estado expuesta a sucesivos ciclos migratorios, es decir, a varios movimientos de diáspora y encuentros que la han debilitado en ocasiones o fortalecido en otras.

Como otras músicas de las Américas, la cubana se formó de varios encuentros seminales en que se dieron cita, sin saberlo, diversas culturas hasta entonces muy distintas entre sí. El primer encuentro se inició con los miles de españoles que abandonaron la península por un porvenir mejor, y poco más tarde con el robo y traslado de multitud de africanos, uno de los movimientos migratorios más dramáticos y extensos de los últimos siglos.

Poco se sabe de la música nacida como resultado de los continuos enfrentamientos que dieron origen a una música criolla o *créole*, que ya en el siglo XIX fue documentada tanto en Cuba y Brasil como en Yucatán, Haití y Nueva Orleans. En el caso cubano, junto al largo proceso de cristalización de incipientes estilos nacionales, ocurrió otro proceso paralelo: el éxodo de músicos, sobre todo a México y Estados Unidos, países donde comenzó a formarse una diáspora considerable.

Batallones llamados de «pardos y morenos», que habían sido enviados desde la isla a Nueva Orleans y la Florida –recuérdese que estos territorios fueron españoles entre 1762 y 1803–, participaron en la guerra de

Los instrumentos: LA BATERÍA

¿Qué tienen en común *Changuito*, el percusionista que originó el sello rítmico característico de Los Van Van, Enrique Pla de Irakere e Ignacio Berroa, el mejor baterista que pasó por el GESI? Un instrumento extraordinariamente complejo que ellos supieron adaptar a la música afrocubana pero con un oído sintonizado en el jazz.

La aparición de este equipo rítmico en Madrid hizo comentar a un conocido periodista en fecha tan lejana como 1922, cuando la batería no contaba con los adelantos actuales:

IGNACIO BERROA.

Hay un señor que, colocado un poco aparte de la orquesta, compuesta por meritísimos profesores, toca él solo quince instrumentos. ¡Quince, lector! Nuestro artista, con unos palillos de tambor, golpea en un parche, pero al mismo tiempo, con el pie izquierdo pone en marcha un pedal que hace ascender y descender un platillo sobre otro mientras que con el pedal del pie derecho golpea un bombo. Sobre éste y a sus lados aparecen enormes platillos. Estratégicamente colocados de modo que les pueda dar vida sin más que alargar la mano, hay un triángulo, una collera de cascabeles, un sonajero, unas castañuelas y una cosa que parece la caja de un dominó.

Mucho ha cambiado la batería desde los tiempos de este divertido comentario. Hoy día se le define internacionalmente como *trap drums*, y aparece atarugada de platillos, side-drums, tam-tams, timbales y hasta un bongó, cada uno con funciones y timbres específicos, que el percusionista recorre rápidamente.

La introducción del estilo be-bop en los años 50 impulsó significativamente la trayectoria de varios bateristas cubanos del calibre de Guillermo Barreto. Su destreza impresionó a numerosos músicos estadounidenses que visitaron la isla en la época precastrista. Cuando Barreto trabajó con la orquesta de los Hermanos Dorsey en Tropicana, Jimmy Dorsey se impresionó tanto que le regaló una batería.

Aparte de los cuatro virtuosos mencionados, Cuba ha contado con otros bateristas muy completos, como Walfredo de los Reyes (1933) quien tocó durante años en Tropicana bajo la dirección de Armando Romeu y acompañó a los pianistas Julio Gutiérrez y Pedro Jústiz *Peruchín* en el primer *Cuban Jam Sessions,* un disco originalmente publicado por el sello Panart en 1956. El padre de Walfredo fue un distinguido cantante, compositor y trompeta de la Orquesta Casino de la Playa, y su hijo es un vibrafonista notable. En 1977 grabó *Ecué: ritmos cubanos* con Louie Bellson en Los Ángeles. Walfredo es la primera sílaba de «Walpataca», acrónimo del cuarteto de música latina «progresiva» que también integraron Paquito D'Rivera, Tany Gil y *Cachao* en los años 80. Este gigante afable ha realizado vídeos didácticos y colaborado con *Patato* Valdés en la segunda sesión de *Ritmo y candela* (1996). Hace años que acompaña al baladista Wayne Newton en Las Vegas. *Changuito* ha señalado que «Walfredo fue el primer baterista del mundo que tocó drums y tumbadora a la vez. Cuando se habla de Walfredo hay que quitarse el sombrero».

independencia de los Estados Unidos. Al cesar el dominio español sobre la Louisiana y La Florida, muchos españoles, y un buen número de nacidos en Cuba, se quedaron a vivir en esos territorios. La continua emigración a Estados Unidos creció en la segunda mitad del XIX debido a desavenencias políticas con la Corona española y la actuación de sus representantes en la isla.

Por otra parte, la abolición efectiva de la esclavitud en la isla en 1886 motivó un impresionante éxodo de antiguos esclavos de los campos a las ciudades, donde la escasez de empleo obligó a un buen número a buscar la manera de llegar a Nueva Orleans, que desde principios del siglo XIX era el principal puerto para el comercio entre Cuba y Estados Unidos, y donde había una supuesta demanda de braceros. Junto con los núcleos que se desplazaron a aquella ciudad sureña iban bastantes músicos, como el cornetista Manuel Pérez, nacido en La Habana en 1879, que se convirtió en verdadera leyenda del dixie en Nueva Orleans.

Un modesto movimiento en dirección opuesta, pero que es imprescindible mencionar, ocurrió con el fin de la guerra hispano-cubana y la intervención norteamericana de 1898 a 1902. Muchos exiliados políticos regresaron a la isla llenos de esperanza, otros arribaron como infantería, enrolados en el ejército estadounidense. Ese fue el caso de Pedro Stacholy, un músico que había estudiado en Nueva York y que posteriormente fundó una de las primeras jazz bands cubanas de que se tiene noticias.

También desembarcaron en diversos puntos de la isla varios batallones de afronorteamericanos que pronto confraternizaron con los criollos; algunos de éstos se quedaron a vivir en Cuba, incluyendo la Isla de Pinos. Un ejemplo concreto fue el de James *Santiago* Smood, intérprete del banjo y cantante de blues, que en La Habana se hizo tresero y tocaba sones, boleros, pasodobles y polcas con un español llamado el *Gallego* Menéndez. Conocidos popularmente como «El blanco y el negro», alrededor de 1913 se les encontraba en el bodegón La Sambumbia. Smood falleció en 1929 en pleno auge del son.

Músicos cubanos fueron introduciendo sus ritmos en Estados Unidos hasta lograr que el llamado *Latin* o *Hispanic tinge* cobrara peso gradualmente en el jazz, influyendo sobre cierta parte de la cultura musical norteamericana. Mientras que algunos cubanos trataban de dominar las armonías del jazz en los predios de Harlem, otros triunfaban en ciudades tan apartadas entre sí como París, México o Buenos Aires. Poco después, en la década de 1920, comenzaron a imponer su música en Estados Unidos autores cualificados como Ernesto Lecuona, Emilio Grenet y Moisés Simons, y también se establecieron allí Vicente Sigler y Nilo Menéndez. La crítica situación económica y política de los años 30 fue otro factor que propició un nuevo éxodo de talentos a Nueva York: Alberto Socarrás, Mario Bauzá, Alberto Iznaga, Don Aspiazu, entre otros. Más tarde arribaron el actor Desi Arnaz, el pianista Anselmo Sacasas con el vocalista Miguelito Valdés *Mr. Babalú*, José Curbelo, Frank Grillo *Machito*, Rudy Calzado, Armando Valdespí, Marcelino Guerra *Rapindey*, *Chano* Pozo y finalmente Arsenio Rodríguez, ya hacia los años 50. Y sólo he nombrado a los más destacados.

ALBERTO IZNAGA.

Lleno de ambiciones, en 1929 arribó a la Babel de Hierro un violinista y clarinetista que había tocado en la Orquesta Filarmónica y en la orquesta del Teatro Nacional. Decepcionado por las pocas oportunidades en la isla para lucir su variado talento, el joven **Alberto Iznaga** (1906-95) se lanzó a probar suerte en una ciudad donde entendía que no discriminaban a los mulatos. Después de varias tenta-

Los instrumentos: EL PIANO

A partir de Ignacio Cervantes en el último tercio del siglo XIX y Ernesto Lecuona en la primera mitad del XX, el piano ha sido el instrumento favorito del músico cubano. De los talentos alrededor de 1950 también citaré a Felo Bergaza (1916-69), quien durante muchos años integró pareja con Juan Bruno Tarraza (1912); al escuchar la rapidez de Felo no puedo evitar pensar en la agilidad de Emiliano Salvador, a quien me referiré después. «El Rey del Mambo» fue otro pianista brillante: Pérez Prado realizaba *clusters* o racimos de notas con armonías poco usuales para su época. De Rubén González, el anciano que sorprendió a todos desplegando sus «tumbaos» en el filme *Buena Vista Social Club*, tengo un disco de 1953, época en que Rubén tocaba con el conjunto Kubavana de Carlos Barbería, uno de sus mejores momentos: en medio de una conga se le ocurrió hacer un solo en las teclas, situación imposible porque la conga es callejera por naturaleza, pero le agregó un color extraordinario al número.

De Chucho Valdés ya he dicho bastante, pero no de su padre, el pianista Bebo Valdés (1918), figura central de la época de oro de la música cubana. Este gigante (en ambos sentidos) comenzó en los años 40 con la orquesta del trompeta Julio Cueva, para la cual compuso el mambo *Rareza del siglo* y realizó excitantes arreglos; tanto se destacó en esa labor que pronto pasó a la emisora Mil Diez hasta 1947. Tocó durante mucho tiempo en Tropicana con la orquesta de Armando Romeu hasta que se convirtió en asesor musical del célebre cabaré; de esa etapa son los mambos *Güempa* y *Bien explicao*. Entusiasmado por la atención que cobraba el jazz afrocubano en Nueva York, el productor Norman Granz le sugirió a Bebo en 1952 la primera descarga de jazz que se grabó en la isla. Luego, con el apoyo de Benny Moré y la orquesta de Ernesto Duarte, trató de imponer su ritmo batanga, pero el intento coincidió con un momento en que arrasaba el mambo de Pérez Prado.

Bebo fue el primer y mejor maestro que ha tenido Chucho, el que le dio el aliento que ahora disfrutamos. Siempre compo-

EL GRAN PIANISTA BEBO VALDÉS (1958).

niendo y demostrando su valer, firmó para acompañar a los artistas del sello Gema, pero decepcionado con la revolución tuvo que dejar atrás a su hijo y una trayectoria profesional fascinante. Llegó a México en 1960, donde se convirtió en asesor artístico del cantante chileno Lucho Gatica. Realizó algunas grabaciones en España y desde aquí, en 1963, se unió a los Havana Cuban Boys, cumpliendo varias giras por Europa. En Estocolmo se enamoró perdidamente, decidió establecerse allí y durante más de treinta años permaneció en el más profundo anonimato, hasta que en 1994 Paquito D'Rivera lo persuadió para grabar en Alemania *Bebo rides again*, una colección de clásicos cubanos y obras nuevas de «*El caballón*», como lo llamaban afectuosamente sus muchos amigos cubanos. Una historia extraordinaria. «Como pianista –escribió Cristóbal Díaz Ayala– Bebo es elegante como Lecuona, rítmico como los danzoneros Antonio María Romeu y Cheo Belén Puig, inspirado y agresivo como los montuneros Anselmo Sacasas y *Lilí* Martínez, creativo como Frank Emilio o *Peruchín*, y tan innovador como su propio hijo Chucho».

Otros dos pianistas destacados antes de la revolución fueron Frank Emilio Flynn (1921-2001) y Pedro Jústiz *Peruchín* (1913-77). Del primero ha escrito Nat Chediak: «Para algunos es un jazzista que domina la música cubana; para otros, un pianista cubano con un sexto sentido para el jazz». El genial invidente era ambas cosas. Su gran amigo Armando Romeu aprendió braille para transcribirle el *Concierto en fa* de Gershwin, que interpretó con maestría acompañado por la Sinfónica Nacional. Frank Emilio hizo discos dedicados a Cervantes y a Lecuona. Hombre de corazón grande y noble modestia, Frank Emilio supo rescatar talentos que de otra manera habrían pasado desapercibidos, como la inclusión de dos temas del guitarrista Ñico Rojas, uno de los artífices menos conocidos del filin, en el álbum *Barbarísimo* (1996).

Por su parte, *Peruchín* dejó una impronta difícil de seguir. Afirma Chediak: «Imposible escuchar cuatro compases sin identificarle. Igual de diestro en tumbaos y montunos que en racimos y frases que trunca, como Monk, a su manera». A partir de 1950, *Peruchín* fue durante años el responsable de la brillantez de la Orquesta Riverside, haciendo también estupendas instrumentaciones para la tribu de Benny Moré. Fue el autor del bolero *Qué equivocación* y del mambo *Mamey colorao*.

En los últimos treinta años han surgido manos que lograron revelar otras facetas del instrumento de 88 teclas. Gonzalo Rubalcaba (1963), ambicioso, lanzado, a pesar de la calma que proyecta al hablar, fue un devoto de la electrónica hasta entrados los 90. Nieto e hijo de músicos notables, Rubalcaba combinó estudios de piano y percusión en la Escuela Superior de Arte. Integró la Orquesta Cubana de Música Moderna y colaboró con Todos Estrellas y Los Van Van. En 1983 realizó una gira por África y Francia con la Orquesta Aragón y más tarde creó el grupo Proyecto (ver pág. 365). En 1985 Dizzy Gillespie lo descubrió en La Habana y después se convirtió en uno de sus padrinos en el exterior; que es a donde fue a parar Rubalcaba, primero a la República Dominicana, colaborando con Juan Luis Guerra en uno de sus más acertados álbumes, y después recaló en Estados Unidos, donde actualmente reside. En 1987 produjo dos discos clave, *Inicio* y *Mi gran pasión*, en que logró actualizar el danzón sin alterar su intrínseco decoro, una vuelta a la música que prestigió a su familia pero envuelta en la panorámica del jazz.

Emiliano Salvador (1951-92), fallecido en plena madurez, fue dueño de un estilo que puso al servicio del Grupo de Experimentación Sonora del ICAIC, permaneciendo allí toda una década. Alcanzó a hacer tres discos, *Nueva visión* (1979), *Emiliano Salvador 2* (1980) y *Ayer y hoy* (1992), donde entregó su olor a tierra adentro, a su amado Puerto Padre. Sufría de insomnio pertinaz y fumaba constantemente. Mientras que algunos lo consideran heredero del legado de *Peruchín*, Chucho Valdés lo inscribe como el mejor pianista de su generación.

El nieto de *Peruchín*, de apellido Argudín, tocó con NG La Banda y contribuyó a revolucionar la pianística de los años 80, mientras que Iván González *Melón*, teclista de la banda de Isaac Delgado, rubateaba en los tumbaos.

Entre otros destacados teclistas de música bailable o de jazz afrocubano de todos los tiempos se encuentran *Lilí* Martínez Griñán, René Hernández, Paquito Hechavarría, Gabriel Hernández y Ernán López-Nussa.

tivas y tropiezos, se enteró que en «El billar de los músicos» a veces anunciaban algún trabajito. Así fue como consiguió sus primeras actuaciones con el trompeta Vicente Sigler, el primer criollo director de orquesta en la ciudad. «Sigler era una buena persona, pero nunca sabías lo que te iba a pagar», comentó años después Iznaga al cronista Max Salazar. Más tarde comenzó a hacer arreglos para el trompeta Augusto Coen y en 1938 fundó La Siboney (dos clarinetes, trompeta, piano, bajo, percusión y voz), trabajando en el cabaré La Toja. Ahí fue donde debutó en Nueva York el vocalista Frank Grillo *Machito*, aunque el grupo se disolvió en 1952 a consecuencia de la popularidad del mambo. Iznaga se unió más tarde como violinista de la charanga (la primera en territorio norteamericano) del flautista y compositor Gilberto Valdés en el club Tropicana, del Bronx; cuando éste decidió unirse al grupo de danza de Katherine Dunhan como su director musical, Iznaga quedó al frente de la charanga. Hacia 1957, el club Tropicana lo reemplazó con la agrupación que había formado el tresero Arsenio Rodríguez; Iznaga se dedicó entonces a hacer arreglos hasta que en 1974 se retiró.

El caso del pianista **José Curbelo** también es significativo. Uno de los fundadores de la Orquesta Riverside en 1938, un año después se trasladó a Nueva York donde estudió bajo la orientación de Hall Overton. Militó en la Orquesta de Xavier Cugat y en 1941 montó su propia banda, en la

EL PIANISTA JOSÉ CURBELO.

que figuraron los puertorriqueños Tito Rodríguez y Tito Puente. En 1959 la disolvió para dedicarse de lleno a empresario musical; despreciado por algunos, Curbelo se convirtió de hecho en un león para los negocios, exigiendo de los dueños de clubes y salas de baile la mejor paga y respeto para la confraternidad de músicos latinos.

Fue en Nueva York (Miami era todavía una pequeña y adormecida ciudad donde invernaban ricos septuagenarios norteamericanos) donde mejor fructificó la música afrocubana gracias a su recepción y asimilación por los puertorriqueños, que comenzaron a residir en grandes masas en el Bronx, Queens y Brooklyn a partir de 1919. También obtuvo el interés de muchos afronorteamericanos llegados a Chicago y Nueva York procedentes de los estados sureños de la Unión, así como de grupos de jóvenes judíos neoyorquinos en franca rebeldía con sus acomodados padres y con ganas de divertirse. Aunque el éxodo de cubanos comenzó a frenar hacia 1948, no evitó que un cantautor del talento de José Antonio Méndez (ver pág. 147) se fuera a México durante diez años, o que Marcelino Guerra *Rapindey* se instalara en Manhattan en 1944 y que Arsenio Rodríguez arribara poco después. Durante el decenio 1950-60, la abundancia de empleo en la isla fue tal que prácticamente se detuvo el lento movimiento de instrumentistas y vocalistas hacia Estados Unidos y otros países.

LOS CREADORES DEL JAZZ AFROCUBANO

Dos Áfricas en exilio se encontraron en el Nueva York de los años 40 para crear una veta significativa. Acreditado como el creador del jazz afrocubano, **Mario Bauzá** (1911-93) había viajado por primera vez a aquella ciudad en 1926 como clarinetista de la orquesta que Antonio María Romeu había formado para grabar un disco de danzones encargado por la RCA Victor. Bauzá se enamoró de Harlem, donde el teatro Lafayette ofrecía entonces estupendas revistas musicales, y quedó vivamente impresionado por las big bands de Tommy Dorsey y Paul Whiteman, particularmente al escuchar a su saxo Frankie Trumbauer interpretar *Rhapsody in blue* de Gershwin. El joven Mario decidió entonces adoptar ese instrumento al regresar a La Habana, y así equipado emigró definitivamente en 1930. La casualidad quiso que en el mismo barco viajaran los miembros de la orquesta de Don Aspiazu, contratados por varias semanas en el RKO Palace Theatre; en el trayecto se hizo amigo del cantante Antonio Machín, que también tenía puestas sus ilusiones en la Babel de Hierro.

GRACIELA GRILLO Y MARIO BAUZÁ.

La amistad que surgió entre ambos artistas se fortaleció aún más cuando Bauzá decidió dejar el saxo y aprendió a tocar la trompeta en sólo dos semanas para grabar con el cuarteto que rápidamente había formado Machín. Sus primeros trabajos formales fueron con las orquestas de Cass Carr, Sam Wooding y Noble Sisle, hasta que consiguió una plaza fija con esta última agrupación. En 1933 pasó a una de las mejores bandas de la época, la del batería Chick Webb, quien le enseñó a frasear en jazz (Mario Bauzá llegó a convertirse en director musical de la misma) y a finales de ese año grabó el tema más célebre de la orquesta, *Stomping at the Savoy*, que originó Edgar Sampson, saxo alto y arreglista de la formación, inspirado en la pieza *Lona* de Bauzá.

Metido en el jazz hasta la embocadura de su trompeta, fue él quien presentó a Webb a una vocalista principiante que había escuchado en el teatro Apolo: la chica, alta y delgada, se llamaba Ella Fitzgerald. Buscando otros derroteros, se integró en 1939 a la extraordinaria orquesta de Cab Calloway, y se las arregló para que éste contratase a otra figura prometedora, el trompeta John Birks (Dizzy) Gillespie.

En realidad, Bauzá no fue el único pionero que desató el interés por el estilo afrocubano entre las bandas de jazz norteamericanas. Durante los años 20 los puertorriqueños y cubanos residentes estaban maravillados por el sonido de las orquestas de Fletcher Henderson, Andy Kirk, Jimmy Lunceford, Duke Ellington y Louis Armstrong. Uno de los cubanos más aventajados en esa línea era el flautista **Alberto Socarrás** (1908-87), quien ya poseía un doctorado en música cuando dejó su país natal en 1927. Dos años después se unió a la revista musical negra Lew Leslie's

ALBERTO SOCARRÁS.

Blackbirds con el trompeta boricua Augusto Coen, donde aprendieron muchos secretos del jazz. Hacia 1934 Socarrás logró organizar una orquesta con músicos que podían manejar tanto la música afrocubana como el jazz y el blues. Se le podía escuchar en los clubes Smalls, Savoy Ballroom, Connnie's Paradise y el Cotton Club. Otras veces tocaba sones en el club Kubanacán, en el teatro Campoamor y diversos sitios donde la gente quería bailar con música que supiera a Caribe.

Sin embargo, no todos los músicos latinos podían responder a las exigencias que imponía Socarrás: en 1935 el pianista puertorriqueño Noro Morales, quien después realizó una carrera estupenda antes de morir de diabetes como sus hermanos,
se unió a su banda para dejarla más tarde porque no podía manejar las complejidades armónicas del jazz. En aquellos años de entre guerras, los bailadores latinos, mezclados con negros norteamericanos que no sabían español, pagaban 35 centavos para bailar en los matinés que organizaba el Savoy Ballroom. Después se iban al Park Palace que a partir de las 19.00 horas ofrecía guarachas, boleros y danzones. Alrededor de esa época es cuando empezó a descollar la banda AfroCubans de *Machito* con el ingenioso trompeta Mario Bauzá. Con su obra *Tanga* (1943), Mario había logrado el primer *crossover* significativo.

No obstante, otro tipo completamente distinto de *crossover* estaba teniendo lugar a mediados de los años 40 en las escuelas y calles del Harlem hispano, donde las guarachas combinadas con el Rhythm and Blues (R&B) privaban a los más jóvenes. Los blues que cantaban Nat King Cole, Billy Eckstine, The Ink Spots, The Ravens y The Orioles suavizaban en algo la dureza de las calles donde chicos norteamericanos y puertorriqueños enfrentaban sus notorias pandillas (los Turbans, Commanches, Copians, Dragons y Viceroys), tema del filme *West Side Story.*

El cronista Max Salazar, que une a su modestia y colección fotográfica un saber incalculable, reveló en un número de *Latin Beat*, cómo en 1943 *Machito* tuvo el valor de dirigirse a un grupo de estos peligrosos rivales juveniles en la sede de El Mutualista Obrero Puertorriqueño para intentar disuadirlos de que dejaran las navajas por el baloncesto o la música. Años después se descubrió que entre aquella turba se encontraban los hermanos Charlie y Eddie Palmieri, Héctor Rivera, Gilberto (Joe Cuba) Calderón, Frankie Colón, Joe Loco, Louie Ramírez y Willie (Bobo) Correa.

El interés por el blues, que había comenzado con infinidad de canciones tristes donde el negro revelaba su miserable vida, con temas que iban desde la denuncia de la más abyecta pobreza hasta el lamento de una mujer abandonada, incluían tonadas que eran verdaderas protestas contra el racismo que sufrían, pero cantadas en un argot ininteligible para los blancos, pues con su doble sentido sólo los negros podían entender aquel lenguaje críptico.

Hay otro aspecto del blues que salió a la luz en unas declaraciones muy significativas de Charlie Musselwhite en 1999, músico de armónica con más de treinta años de vida profesional: «No se menciona, pero hay mucho ritmo latino en el blues, en los temas rápidos de Muddy Waters, Jimmy Reed o Bo Diddley».

Al este de Harlem, conocido ya como «El barrio latino», siguió desarrollándose la imparable revolución musical que habían iniciado Socarrás y Bauzá. Sin embargo, durante largo tiempo se ha afirmado erróneamente que el jazz afrocubano surgió del encuentro de Gillespie con *Chano* Pozo, cuando comenzó a hablarse de un estilo «cubop». En realidad, Dizzy buscaba un percusionista cubano para su nueva banda y *Chano* le fue recomendado por Bauzá y *Machito*. **Luciano *Chano* Pozo** (1915-48) había llegado poco antes a Nueva York a instancias de Miguelito Valdés. Gillespie y *Chano* actuaron en 1947 en el Carnegie Hall interpretando la *AfroCuban Drums Suite*, y su colaboración quedó plasmada en números hoy clásicos: *Manteca* (un eufemismo para la marihuana) y *Tin Tin Deo*, ambos de *Chano*; *Algo bueno* (de *Chano* y Dizzy) y el fantástico *Cubana Be, Cubana Bop*, con una orquestación escrita por George Russell. Años después, Mario Bauzá se refirió a las dificultades que tuvo que atravesar el baterista Max Roach para adaptarse a los acentos de *Chano* en el cuero de la conga, hasta que entre ambos encontraron la solución. En su autobiografía *To Be or Not to Bop*, Dizzy Gillespie relató cómo *Chano* aprovechaba los viajes en autocar para pasarle a él una tumbadora y otra a Al McKibbon, mientras el cubano marcaba el paso: «Otro tío cogía el cencerro, y entonces descubrimos que aunque cada uno estaba haciendo una cosa distinta, aquellos ritmos se integraban para sorpresa de todos».

MARCELINO GUERRA *RAPINDEY* Y *CHANO POZO* EN NUEVA YORK (1947).

Como ya mencioné en otra parte, *Chano* Pozo fue asesinado en un bar de Harlem en 1948, al parecer por un problema de drogas con un puertorriqueño que le asestó varios balazos. Todo dicho, a pesar de su vitalidad y carisma, su contribución al jazz siempre careció de forma y estructura; por lo demás, sus temas se repiten hasta el tedio. Una lástima.

Después vinieron las grabaciones del saxo alto Charlie Parker, momento en que el jazz afrocubano pareció llegar a sus más altas cumbres, y aunque algunos críticos afirmaron entonces que se trataba de una moda pasajera, otros se dieron cuenta de que se trataba de una verdadera vuelta a las raíces africanas del género. Entre diciembre de 1948 y enero de 1949 grabaron *Okidoke*, *No noise* y *Mango mangüé*: una serie de sesiones de los AfroCubans de *Machito* con los solistas Charlie Parker, Flip Philips (saxo tenor) y Buddy Rich (batería). La sección rítmica estaba compuesta por los puertorriqueños José Mangual (bongó), Luis Miranda (tumbadora), Ubaldo Nieto (timbal), con los cubanos Roberto Rodríguez (bajo), René Hernández (piano) y el propio *Machito* (voz y maracas).

Más tarde surgieron músicos que empezaron a interpretar el jazz que hacía Charlie Parker pero manteniéndolo *cool*, es decir, relajado. La trompeta de Miles Davis vino a añadir no sólo virtuosismo sino un tono sobrio que evitaba las notas altas y favorecía un registro medio. *Keep cool!*, parecía decirle a la velocidad de fraseo de Dizzy Gillespie.

Según Max Salazar, el cantante boricua Willie Torres y el pianista Nick Jiménez fueron los primeros en 1952 en introducir letras en inglés con ritmo cubano al interpretar un arreglo de *I've got you under my skin* en una sala de baile del barrio latino. Ese mismo año Tito Puente lució sus golpes sincopados al grabar *Tonight I am in heaven*, cantado en inglés por las De Castro Sisters y editado por Tico Records.

Ya por entonces sonaban en Nueva York los cueros del percusionista **Mongo Santamaría** (1927), que había llegado en 1949. Mongo contribuyó grandemente a la evolución del jazz afrocubano; su estilo de tocar el bongó y las congas le permitió introducirse primero en las bandas de Johnny Seguí, José Luis Moneró y Gilberto Valdés, que ya contaba con cierto prestigio como compositor de temas afrocubanos. En 1953 Mongo Santamaría se unió a Tito Puente, pero en 1957 lo dejó, llevándose a Willie Bobo para formar parte del quinteto de jazz latino de Cal Tjader, que parecía más excitante; este extraordinario músico nacido en Saint Louis, de ascendencia sueca e inglesa, se convirtió en el único director no latino que continuamente grabó jazz afrocubano. Tjader había comenzado su vertiginosa carrera como baterista del trío de Dave Brubeck, pero fue en su etapa con el quinteto de George Shearing cuando consolidó su genuino interés por los ritmos de la isla; después de escuchar el nivel que alcanzaban *Machito* y Tito Puente con sus orquestas en el Palladium, grabó con su quinteto el LP *Salsa Soul*, publicado por Verve en 1964, una joya del jazz que vendió 150.000 copias porque la radio no podía resistirse a pasarlo constantemente. Y no se pierda el detalle del nombre del álbum cuando todavía no había emergido la salsa.

MONGO SANTAMARÍA.

Maestro de los golpes secos, Mongo Santamaría es sin duda el conguero que más influencia ha tenido en el desarrollo del jazz afrocubano, refiere Nat Chediak. Nacido en el barrio obrero de Jesús María, cuna de rumberos, trabajó como cartero para dedicarse a la percusión; **Cándido Camero** (1921), otro grande de las congas, le ayudaba a repartir el correo para que pudiera ensayar. Mongo logró irse a México en 1948 y allí tocó con toda libertad con la orquesta de Pérez Prado, contribuyendo a algunas grabaciones fabulosas del «Rey del mambo». En 1959, ya con ciudadanía estadounidense, visitó a su madre en La Habana y a su regreso organizó el Conjunto Manhattan con Willie Bobo, Marcelino Guerra como vocalista y el saxo José *Chombo* Silva. En 1958, Mongo y Willie volaron a San Francisco para unirse a Tjader. «Pasé tres años estupendos con Tjader, él me presentó al presidente de Fantasy Records con quien grabé *Our man in Havana, Yambú* y *Mighty Mongo*», comentó Mongo tiempo después. No obstante, fue su grabación de *Watermelon man* para el sello Battle Records, en 1963, lo que lo catapultó a la fama de costa a costa. Después vinieron sus grabaciones para *Mongo introduces La Lupe* que

CÁNDIDO CAMERO.

contiene *Besitos pa'ti, Canta bajo* y *This is my mambo*, elevando a la exuberante vocalista al estrellato. Sin embargo, cuando Mongo le habló de una gira juntos a Puerto Rico, ella le contestó que había firmado un contrato en exclusiva con Tito Puente y que su embarazo le impedía viajar por avión. *Ces't la vie!*

Pero no todo fueron amarguras. En 1977 su álbum *Amanecer* se encontraba entre los cinco contendientes al premio Grammy. «Después de cuatro nominaciones finalmente lo había ganado; alguien debe haberse fijado en lo que yo estaba haciendo», declaró Mongo modestamente.

Volviendo a Mario Bauzá, estimo que algunos investigadores no han reparado en que su óptima preparación musical fue el trampolín que le permitió asimilar y luego manejar a su antojo las armonías del jazz. Su posición anterior en Cuba como primer clarinete de la Orquesta Sinfónica a mediados de los años 20 tuvo mucho que ver con Gonzalo Roig, a la sazón su director, quien nunca escatimó esfuerzos para conseguir la calidad que buscaba, exigencias que contribuyeron a forjar el carácter del joven Mario y de toda una generación de instrumentistas.

Fue puramente casual que en 1930 Roig cruzara también en barco a Estados Unidos, al igual que Bauzá, para dirigir una serie de conciertos con las principales bandas militares norteamericanas, invitado por la Unión Panamericana para dar a conocer la riqueza rítmica de la música cubana, ya que el interés crecía en diversas áreas.

Durante su trabajo con la banda de Calloway, cuyo grito *hi de ho* marcó toda una época, Bauzá aprovechó para enseñar la rítmica cubana al baterista Cozy Cole; poco después grabó *Chili con conga*, un acercamiento del swing a los trópicos. El 3 de diciembre de 1940, convertido –sin saberlo– en su director musical por los próximos 35 años, Bauzá se lanzó a debutar con su cuñado Frank Grillo *Machito* en el Park Plaza, una sala de baile importante: aquel fue el primer concierto de los AfroCubans, la orquesta formada por el vocalista con músicos puertorriqueños y cubanos. Después pasaron al cabaré La Conga, pero debido a los estragos causados en la agrupación por la Segunda Guerra Mundial, Bauzá decidió contratar a músicos de jazz para reemplazar a los latinos que habían marchado al ejército. Este concubinato físico sentó las pautas de lo que devendría la primera orquesta de jazz afrocubano.

El tema *Tanga*, escrito por Bauzá en 1943, ha sido reconocido como el primero de ese género, que se completa con *Mambo Inn*, de finales de los 40; con ellos Bauzá consiguió nada menos que actualizar la música cubana con el jazz. Gracias a su iniciativa, nos dice Nat Chediak en su informativo *Diccionario de Jazz Latino*, desfilaron por la orquesta de *Machito* los instrumentistas Dexter Gordon, Doc Cheatham, Cannonball Adderley, Flip Phillips, Curtis Fuller, Charlie Parker, Buddy Rich, Joe Newman, Herbie Mann, Bill Taylor y el propio Gillespie. Fue también Bauzá quien persuadió al pianista René Hernández a formar parte de los AfroCubans.

Tras las embestidas del rock y la pasión por los Beatles, la orquesta quedó en franca inferioridad para sobrevivir mucho más tiempo; casi todas las grandes bandas fueron desapareciendo paulatinamente. Bauzá puso punto final a su relación musical con *Machito* cuando éste decidió reducir la formación para ir de gira por Europa en 1975. A partir de ese momento, cada cual grabó por separado para el sello Coco Records. Pero *La botánica*, título de un álbum de Bauzá, no consiguió el éxito esperado; su creador tuvo que esperar hasta 1986, cuando el pianista argentino Jorge Dalto (quien moriría un año después) le produjo *Afro-Cuban Jazz*, un álbum digno de la época de oro de los AfroCubans, con músicos de la talla de Víctor Paz, Claudio Roditi, Conrad Herwig, José Antonio Fajardo, Joe Santiago y Paquito D'Rivera, incluyendo los percusionistas Ignacio Berroa, *Patato* Valdés y Daniel Ponce, y contando con arreglos del propio Dalto, D'Rivera y Ray Santos. Casi diez años llevaba el maestro Bauzá sin pisar un estudio de grabación.

Los mejores: FRANK GRILLO *MACHITO*

Fue la figura carismática de los AfroCu-
bans, una tremenda formación, quizá la
más avanzada para su época. *Machito*
(1909-84) comenzó de percusionista y cantante en una serie de grupos habaneros, incluyendo el Septeto Nacional. Una vez en
Nueva York trabajó con la orquesta del
pianista puertorriqueño Noro Morales y
también con Xavier Cugat, quien le fue presentado por Mario Bauzá. En 1940, luego
de un par de intentos fallidos, logró formar
su primer grupo, algunos de cuyos miembros procedían de la Orquesta Siboney con
la que había estado tocando en el nuevo
Club Cuba de Manhattan. Con *Machito* de cara al público, agitando sus inseparables maracas, y Bauzá manteniendo el control instrumental al fondo, los
AfroCubans pronto se convirtieron en un verdadero éxito. Durante diez años
lucieron una sección de metales incendiarios que le dio su sonido característico.

Entre sus más conocidos vocalistas estuvo Miguelito Valdés, seguido de su
recién llegada hermana Graciela, quien se ocupaba de los lentos boleros que al
Macho nunca le interesaron. Le gustaba describir su voz como la de un borra-
cho, lo cual le vino muy bien para interpretar pimentosas guarachas. En 1946 se
completó otro elemento clave en el sonido posterior de los AfroCubans con la
llegada del brillante pianista y arreglista René Hernández (1916-77), que venía
de tocar con la Casino de la Playa y la Orquesta de Julio Cueva.

Una vez separado de Bauzá en 1975, y a pesar de que en 1982 *Machito*
obtuvo un premio Grammy por un disco grabado en Holanda, los AfroCubans
jamás recuperaron la espléndida sonoridad que alcanzaron bajo la tutela de su
cuñado.

El disco *Machito y sus AfroCubans* (Harlequin) es una fascinante colección de 22 temas, cinco grabados en vivo en 1950, incluyendo las presentaciones del conocido DJ *Symphony Sid*. Contiene además una versión corta de
Tanga, de Mario Bauzá, con solos por el propio maestro y por Zoot Sims. Lo
recomiendo de todo corazón.

En 1992 y 1993 el productor alemán Götz Wörner selló con gran estilo el legado de Bauzá: *My time is now* y *944 Columbus* se unen a la pieza de resistencia que sin duda es la *Suite Tanga*, que le montó su colega *Chico* O'Farrill con su estupenda banda. Donde hubiese cantado *Machito* escuchamos a **Rudy Calzado** (1929); Pedro *Rudy* Calzado tiene un pedigrí considerable desde que comenzó a vocalizar en Santiago de Cuba. «Yo conocí a Mario Bauzá en la década de los 60 en el Palladium cuando él dirigía la orquesta de *Machito*. Es el padre del Afrocuban jazz», le aseguró al periodista Carlos Galilea en marzo de 2000. Recordó entonces que cuando Bauzá fundó su orquesta en 1985, éste lo invitó a vivir en su casa porque los dos se habían quedado viudos. «El público conocía a *Machito* pero muy poca gente conocía a Mario. Los músicos sí, todos», afirmó. Rudy Calzado vino a España por primera vez en 1970 y trabajó en varios clubes ya desaparecidos. En 1999 produjo *A tribute to Mario Bauzá* (sello Karonte) con el apoyo artístico de Paquito D'Rivera y Jane Bunnett (saxo soprano y flauta).

Seis semanas después de terminar la última grabación Mario Bauzá murió de cáncer en el modesto piso donde residió casi medio siglo. En mérito a su labor musical se le había rendido poco año antes un merecido homenaje en el Gracie Mansion de Nueva York, donde recibió la Medalla de Honor de Arte y Cultura que anualmente otorga el alcalde de aquella ciudad. Curiosamente, el obituario publicado en *The New York Times* lo calificó de «gran músico norteamericano», supuestamente un homenaje para quien supo transformar la música cubana y la de su país adoptivo al unirlas para siempre con sus raíces africanas.

Otro artífice del jazz afrocubano ha sido **Arturo *Chico* O'Farrill** (1921), cuyo padre fue un abogado de origen irlandés establecido en La Habana. *Chico* estudió en una academia militar en Georgia antes de comenzar Derecho en la Universidad habanera, pero pronto lo dejó para dedicarse a la trompeta. Después de tocar con la banda de Armando Romeu, trató de formar grupos de jazz pero sin resultados satisfactorios; el hombre estaba demasiado adelantado a su tiempo. Buscando su destino se mudó a Nueva York a finales de los años 40 y se dedicó a hacer arreglos para las grandes orquestas; primero trabajó anónimamente en la «factoría» del arreglista Gil Fuller, hasta que logró independizarse, que fue cuando Benny Goodman le compró *Undercurrent blues*. Tan impresionado quedó el clarinetista que lo contrató por todo un año.

El contacto con Goodman le sirvió para relacionarse con Stan Kenton, uno de los directores más interesados en la música latina, para quien instrumentó el álbum *Cuban episode*, justo antes de concebir su famosa *Afro-Cuban Suite* para los AfroCubans de *Machito*, con Charlie Parker de solista. A mediados de los 50, *Chico* O'Farrill formó su propia orquesta e hizo giras por varios estados; en el Sombrero Club de Los Ángeles conoció a la cantante mexicana Lupita Valerio, quien poco después se convirtió en su mujer y representante. Volvió a La Habana entonces y participó en las descargas de *Cachao*; la terraza de su casa en El Vedado se convirtió en un sitio ideal para concebir las jam sessions que más tarde aparecieron bajo los sellos Gema, RCA Victor y Columbia. In-

EL COMPOSITOR ARTURO *CHICO* O'FARRILL.

quieto y siempre en busca de quién sabe qué, en 1957 *Chico* se instaló en México por cierto tiempo antes de regresar a Nueva York y pasarse la siguiente década instrumentando para Count Basie y Ringo Starr; también musicalizó un buen número de lucrativos mensajes publicitarios para la televisión.

Chico O'Farrill nunca ha sido un creador muy prolífico. De hecho, fue sólo en 1995 que grabó su primer álbum en treinta años, titulado *Pure emotion*, producido por Todd Barkan, que fue seguido al año siguiente por una serie de conciertos y una gira europea con una nueva orquesta, esta vez dirigida por su hijo, el pianista Arturito O'Farrill. *Heart of a legend* es una magnífica producción de 1999 en la que participaron los grandes del exilio y Juan Pablo Torres, de la isla.

La dinámica establecida por los AfroCubans de *Machito* afectó positivamente a orquestas cubanas y puertorriqueñas como las de Anselmo Sacasas, Alberto Socarrás, Pupi Campos, Johnny Rodríguez y Noro Morales. Y cosa curiosa: a pesar del fuerte elemento de jazz que la permeaba, su música sonaba más genuinamente caribeña y avanzada que la de los músicos citados. Por los AfroCubans pasaron figuras importantes, incluyendo a Tito Puente (que por entonces también tocaba el bongó) y el compositor Marcelino Guerra *Rapindey*, quien ayudó a *Machito* a formar una segunda banda debido a la creciente demanda. La voz de *Machi-*

to es inconfundible en cualquier disco: escúchense *El muerto se fue de rumba* o *Sopa de pichón* como ejemplos.

Varios músicos notables gustaban de sentarse a descargar con el ya famoso cantante, como Dizzy Gillespie y otros negros norteamericanos que propugnaban el estilo be-bop, entonces la vanguardia del jazz. Pronto se produjo el famoso «mano a mano» entre las bandas del cubano y la de Stan Kenton; de su amistad surgió el número titulado *Machito,* que después pulió Pete Rugolo, el arreglista de Kenton, seguido de la grabación de *El manisero* en que participó la sección de ritmo de los AfroCubans.

Como ya indiqué, a las orquestaciones de Bauzá se sumaron después las del brillante pianista René Hernández, que fue quien impuso en los predios de Harlem y entre puertorriqueños y dominicanos el estilo del tumbao cubano, como también lo logró el genial Anselmo Sacasas, adelantándose al concepto musical de los futuros salseros. Entretanto, Pérez Prado triunfaba con el mambo en México y en Los Ángeles. *Machito* no lo copió, más bien mantuvo su propio estilo, pero la fusión que

LA ÚLTIMA ORQUESTA DE *MACHITO.*

había logrado entre los ritmos afrocubanos y el jazz fue a influir decisivamente en el boom latino que esperaba al doblar de la esquina.

En una entrevista que logré realizarle muchos años después, el modesto *Machito* me confesó: «Charlie Parker era un genio, yo no era nada comparado con él». Eso fue lo que dijo, pero lo que yo pensaba era otra cosa.

5.   CASTRO O *COKE*

> Aunque parezca una contradicción afirmarlo, la música
> cubana aparece ahora como producto del dolor humano
> y del desarraigo.
>
> TONY ÉVORA
> *Orígenes de la música cubana*

Ya había sucedido antes con la revolución bolchevique de octubre de
1917, que originalmente puso en marcha una década prodigiosa en todos
los territorios de las artes, las letras y las ciencias rusas, antes del reflujo
estalinista y la imposición de la «dictadura del proletariado», con su persecución de disidentes. En sus inicios, también la revolución cubana supuso una enorme capacidad de convocatoria para la actividad creadora y la
industria lúdica en general. La Habana se convirtió en los años 60 en la
capital receptora de la inteligencia progresista universal y en un foco irra-
diador de una conciencia latinoamericana abierta a todas las revoluciones
posibles del espíritu y del fusil. Aparecieron nuevas publicaciones, concursos, editoriales. Importantes intelectuales de diversos países descendían
en el aeropuerto de la capital cubana mientras todo tipo de creadores hacían cola para su vuelo de salida. ¿Qué sucedió para que tantos músicos
escaparan rápidamente de aquel «paraíso»?

Con el triunfo militar de Fidel Castro en 1959 comenzaron los
problemas para muchos: el acoso a menudo terminaba en acusaciones,
encarcelamientos y condenas, sin las debidas garantías para el acusado.
En tumultuosas asambleas salieron a la luz viejos rencores, como excu-

sa para atacar a todo el que no compartiera las ideas del gobierno, cuyos hombres de confianza fueron seleccionados para apoderarse de los principales cabarés, que funcionaron a medias, «intervenidos» por el Estado, mientras que otros fueron cerrados. Todos los casinos de juego fueron clausurados y muchas gramolas de bares destruidas con el pretexto de que propendían a crear focos de prostitución y el consumo de marihuana.

EL ÉXODO MASIVO DE ARTISTAS

Fue entonces que apareció aquel estribillo de Carlos Puebla: «Y se acabó la diversión, llegó el Comandante y mandó a parar». En esa frase están encerrados los tres problemas básicos que han afectado las últimas cuatro décadas: «diversión», «Comandante» y «parar». Y mientras se acababa la «diversión», como cada año, una considerable cuota de artistas continuaba viajando por el mundo; sin embargo, en la isla comenzaba el éxodo, discreto pero imparable, de cientos de profesionales de la música.

En la Plaza de la Revolución, ante la figura del Comandante, marchaban las milicias en repetidas concentraciones y desfiles. Y cantaban; pero no cantaban congas populares como en otros tiempos, sino enardecidos himnos revolucionarios. Pocos ciudadanos vislumbraron entonces las profundas crisis a que les sometería el Comandante después de esta primera etapa de euforia e ilusiones desmedidas.

Al recrudecerse el proceso revolucionario, una situación que impidió la neutralidad o los términos medios, infinidad de instrumentistas, intérpretes y arreglistas se vieron coaccionados a tomar posiciones radicales o a hacer declaraciones en apoyo al régimen. Ya en 1959, el presidente de la Asociación de Artistas había sido expulsado sumariamente y su sucesor, que había sido elegido democráticamente por mayoría de votos, fue obligado a renunciar en una agitada asamblea. Hubo que «parar». Debido a su obvia visibilidad y nivel social, muchos músicos optaron por abandonar el país, lo que significó dejar fama, bienes materiales y familiares en la isla, para lanzarse a un mercado totalmente desconocido, mayormente dominado por el idioma inglés. ¿Qué artista en su sano juicio deja atrás la mitad de su vida profesional? Y a pesar de todo, a medida que el control de visas de salida se hacía particularmente severo, la desesperación por abandonar el infierno era mayor.

Para corroborar mi argumento y por aburrida que resulte una lectura de nombres, échele un vistazo a la siguiente selección de artistas notables que abandonaron el país en los primeros años de la revolución, o que no regresaron si es que se encontraban trabajando en el extranjero: Ernesto Lecuona, Raquel Bardisa, Celia Cruz, Renée Barrios, Fernando Albuerne, Charles Abreu, la Sonora Matancera, Xiomara Alfaro, Manolo Álvarez Mera, Blanquita Amaro, José Antonio Fajardo y sus Estrellas, Mario Fernández Porta, Olga

EL COMPOSITOR JUANITO MÁRQUEZ.

Guillot, Lolita Berrio, Xonia Benguría, Belisario López, Germán LeBatard, Martha Pérez, Zoraida Marrero, Julio Gutiérrez, Lalita Salazar, Estelita Santaló, Bobby Collazo, Rolando Laserie, Javier Dulzaides, Eduardo Davidson, Osvaldo Farrés, Rubén Ríos, las De Castro Sisters, Manolo Torrente, América Crespo, Carlos Barbería, Lina Salomé, Orlando Contreras, Roderico Neira *Rodney*, Pepé Delgado, Carlos Díaz, Ernesto Duarte, Bertha Dupuy, Servando Díaz, Bienvenido Granda, Blanca Rosa Gil, Celio González, Los Guaracheros de Oriente, Luisa María Güell, Israel López *Cachao*, La Lupe, Juanito Márquez, Ñico Membiela, Fernando Mulens, Elizabeth del Río, *El Negro* Vivar, María de los Ángeles Rabí, Bebo Valdés, Alfredo *Chocolate* Armenteros, Tata Ramos, Humberto Suárez y decenas más.

No hay duda de que los músicos que se quedaron en Cuba tenían sus razones, todas muy respetables: o bien apoyaron los primeros logros y creyeron firmemente en las promesas del gobierno revolucionario, o no querían dejar su terruño por la incertidumbre de un destino que los separaría de una madre anciana o de una hermana minusválida. Quizá otros dudaron de su capacidad artística para comenzar de nuevo a competir en otros lares menos luminosos, o tenían un hijo a punto de alcanzar la edad reglamentaria para cumplir los tres años y tres meses del servicio militar obligatorio y se resistían a dejarlo atrás. Llegada la hora, cada uno reaccionó de acuerdo a su conciencia y a sus circunstancias personales; sé de algunos que optaron por jubilarse para no tener que servir al régimen. Pero, ciertamente, la salida de tantos músicos provocó la posibilidad de que se creara un verdadero vacío en la continuidad histórico-musical.

Entre los más destacados artistas que decidieron permanecer en la isla por diversos motivos, incluyendo su avanzada edad, se encontraban Benny Moré, Félix Chapottín, Miguelito Cuní, Elena Burke, la Orquesta Aragón, Roberto Faz, José Antonio Méndez, César Portillo de la Luz, Fernando Álvarez, Antonio Arcaño, el Conjunto Casino, Celeste Mendoza, Juan Arrondo, Rosendo Ruiz Quevedo, Giraldo Piloto y Alberto Vera, Marta Valdés, Los Papines, Frank Domínguez, el cuarteto D'Aida, Ramón Veloz, Enrique Jorrín, Gonzalo Roig, Ignacio Villa *Bola de Nieve*, Felo Bergaza, Adolfo Guzmán, Esther Borja, Tito Gómez y algunos miembros de la Orquesta Riverside, Barbarito Diez, el trío Matamoros, *Lilí* Martínez Griñán, Orestes López, Celina González, Richard Egües, Tata Güines, Joseíto Fernández, Eusebio Delfín, Sindo Garay, Frank Emilio Flynn, Ñico Saquito, Niño Rivera, Rafael Lay y otros.

Ambas relaciones no aparecen aquí a modo de confrontación, porque a pesar de las envidias y las inevitables miopías mentales de algunos, en general los músicos siempre se han sentido hermanados. Esto se puede comprobar en cualquier presentación de los de la isla en el extranjero, donde un encuentro entre viejos amigos inevitablemente se convierte en una situación muy emotiva. Lamento decir que lo contrario no ha sucedido; aunque los músicos de la isla pueden salir a ganar dólares, a los de la diáspora no se les permite actuar en Cuba.

Resumiendo: una verdadera estampida de talentos cubrió la primera mitad de la década de los 60, se detuvo un poco entre 1967 y 1979 y volvió a cobrar tremenda fuerza en 1980, cuando la salida masiva por el puerto del Mariel: más de 100.000 desesperados que abordaron todo tipo de embarcaciones provenientes de marinas en la Florida, que cruzaron las corrientes del Golfo de México para recoger a familiares y amigos. Entre ciudadanos que buscaban un porvenir mejor en libertad, Castro aprovechó la oportunidad para vaciar sus cárceles de criminales, deshacerse de muchos enfermos mentales y a la vez introducir en Estados Unidos un número de agentes secretos con la misión de infiltrarse en las organizaciones del exilio, expiar sus movimientos y mantener informada a la Seguridad del Estado. Como se sabe, cada lustro, los servicios secretos norteamericanos suelen descubrir a algunos de estos agentes, que a menudo son espías dobles, pues han llegado a introducirse hasta en la CIA.

A partir de los años 90 el éxodo adquirió un nuevo impulso, con la diferencia de que ya no se trataba de la vieja guardia sino de músicos jóvenes formados por la revolución. Hoy la mayor parte de la diáspora musical no se limita a Nueva York, también está presente en Los Ángeles, San Francisco, Miami, San Juan, Caracas, México, Bogotá, Frankfurt, París, Madrid, Valencia, Bilbao y Barcelona, entre otras ciudades del mundo occidental.

Las relaciones entre el gobierno cubano y los creadores nunca han sido buenas. El llamado «caso Padilla», que estalló en 1968, determinó que infinidad de intelectuales latinoamericanos y europeos rompieran definitivamente con Castro. El poeta Heberto Padilla (1932-2000) había ganado el premio «Julián del Casal» en 1968 por su libro *Fuera del juego;* comprendiendo las amenazas que se cernían sobre la sociedad, el poeta quiso advertir de los peligros y tuvo el coraje de darlo a conocer en Cuba. Lo pagó caro. Pronto los comisarios culturales emprendieron un acoso que lo condujo a la cárcel y a una decantación pública en la propia institución que le había concedido el premio, la UNEAC. Posteriormente pudo acceder al exilio. Padilla no sólo sobresalió por la dimensión de sus textos poéticos sino también por haberse convertido en la víctima propiciatoria del régimen cuando intentó denunciar, asustado por la presión que se había ejercido contra él, las disensiones y actitudes antagónicas de otros intelectuales.

En un plano personal, aquel año 1968 marcó para mí el final de la verdadera revolución: Praga fue invadida por las fuerzas del Pacto de Varsovia (léase la URSS) y Castro se sometió a las instrucciones del Kremlin. En su infame discurso ante las cámaras de televisión, luego de muchas vueltas y revueltas para justificar lo injustificable, no sólo mintió respecto a la Primavera de Praga y a los esfuerzos de los comunistas checos para crear una sociedad más justa, sino que apoyó al tirano Ceaucescu de Rumanía (porque buscaba su petróleo) y atacó a Tito de Yugoslavia (que no tuvo vela en aquel entierro). Los veinte años que siguieron estuvieron marcados por su entrega a los designios de los soviéticos, hasta que ellos mismos le privaron de su gigantesca ayuda.

La guerra que mantiene Fidel Castro contra el libre flujo de las ideas se evidenció más recientemente en relación con Internet. Para que el lector tenga una idea del nivel represivo del régimen cubano, lo remito a un artículo del corresponsal Mauricio Vicent, publicado en *El País* (31-12-2000), titulado «Un bloqueo al gusto de Castro». Sólo 40.000 personas, de una población de 11 millones, tienen acceso a Internet, y por supuesto, con rígidas restricciones. Así entró Cuba revolucionaria en el nuevo milenio.

El emigrado y las dos lenguas

A diferencia de los músicos que han mantenido una verdadera continuidad cultural y ontológica al conservar el español en su trabajo, los que han tenido que reorientarse a través del inglés padecen la violentación del flujo vital interrumpido. Al asumir el nuevo idioma, el que le permitió ser parte del *melting pot* (cazuela de mezclas de todo tipo) norteamericano, su sensibilidad quedó invadida por la mirada y el oído del «otro», del anglosajón. En los casos individuales que he conocido de cerca, la transgresión lingüística ha precipitado algo que definiría como una ritualización de la identidad por ser músicos formados en Cuba, con problemas asociados al desarraigo: el sentimiento de pérdida y la nostalgia. La mayoría se sostiene con el apoyo de otros músicos y los recuerdos de tiempos mejores, vive la vida del barrio, manteniendo el dominó, el lenguaje criollo y sus disparates, esperando con ilusión a que cambie el sistema político para regresar.

Durante demasiado tiempo muchos músicos cubanos han vivido en el angustioso duelo de dos lenguas. Han vivido también en un universo fracturado entre la realidad tan inmediata del destierro y la realidad distante de la isla. Y en su obra algunos han podido sublimar las autenticidades históricas del espacio físico y del espacio mental; las oscilaciones entre culturas y lenguas, el pasado y el presente, la frustración y el deseo.

El papel de los músicos en las relaciones Cuba-USA

Regando simpatía y solidaridad dondequiera que han sonado sus voces o instrumentos, los músicos no han cesado nunca en la intención de tender puentes para un diálogo que parece casi imposible en otras áreas. Con una diferencia notable: los grupos de la isla actúan libremente en territorio norteamericano, llevándose dólares a casa, los llamados «fula», pero ninguna agrupación musical del exilio ha logrado pisar tierra cubana. Con la anuencia del Departamento de Estado norteamericano han visitado los Estados Unidos jazzistas y soneros de primera como los pianistas Chucho Valdés o Gonzalo Rubalcaba, Compay Segundo y grupos de renombre como los Irakere, Los Van Van, NG La Banda, la Original de Manzanillo, la Charanga Habanera, Dan Den y cantantes como Isaac Delgado, Manolín o Paulito, así como los grupos folclóricos Los Muñequitos de Matanzas, Los Papines y otros.

La música de todos ellos penetró con fuerza a partir de 1993. Alejada del público norteamericano por la hostilidad política, comenzó a escucharse a través de conciertos y grabaciones gracias a norteamericanos enamorados de la salsa que siguieron sus raíces hasta la isla. David Byrne, del grupo de rock Talking Heads, ya había demostrado su interés por los ritmos latinos en varias de sus canciones y en el disco *Rey Momo*; en los últimos años ha dado a conocer tres recopilaciones, *Cuban Classics, Dancing with the enemy* y *¡Diablo al infierno!* en su sello Luaka Bop. Cuando el vaquero Ned Sublette y Ben Socolov crearon el sello Qbadisc, sabían que por el embargo comercial sólo podían lanzar música ya grabada, y han logrado un verdadero tesoro: *Puros*, de la Orquesta Original de Manzanillo, *Rumba caliente 88/77*, de Los Muñequitos de Matanzas, *En la calle*, una recopilación de los dos primeros discos del grupo más caliente, NG La Banda. Qbadisc también reprodujo el álbum *Ancestros* del grupo Síntesis, que toma cantos yorubas y los interpreta con instrumentos electrónicos.

EL PIANISTA GONZALO RUBALCABA.

Otro sello, Institution, ofrece la combinación de Lázaro Ros, verdadera autoridad en cantos de Santería y el grupo pop Mezcla, uno de los más importantes de la isla, mientras Gonzalo Rubalcaba, el gran pianista de jazz, lanzó con el sello Messidor dos discos grabados en Alemania.

CUBANOS EN LA SALSA NEOYORQUINA

Era 1971. En la calle 52 de Nueva York, a escasos cien metros del transitado Broadway se erguía un enorme salón de baile llamado Cheetah al que semanalmente asistían jóvenes de los barrios latinos del Bronx, Queens y Brooklyn. La época de las grandes orquestas y los grandes bailes había pasado. Con el Palladium definitivamente cerrado, el dueño del Cheetah, un ambicioso negro puertorriqueño llamado Ralph Mercado, soñaba con revivir el espíritu festivo de la década anterior. El local había sido almacén, luego un gimnasio, más tarde local para maratones de baile y hasta pista de patinaje. Ralph Mercado tenía todas sus expectativas puestas en una propuesta que le había hecho el empresario discográfico Jerry Masucci (1934-97), que aunque tenía apellido de mafioso italiano, era realmente el judío dueño del naciente sello Fania Records. La intención era presentar en el Cheetah a una formidable orquesta formada por los mejores músicos del sello, la Fania All Stars, algunos de cuyos integrantes ya eran ídolos entre la comunidad latina.

Aquel caluroso 21 de agosto de 1971 el salón se atiborró de tal manera que apenas había espacio para bailar. La Fania no era sólo una agrupación de músicos con arraigo local, también representaba el encanto de una música que los cubanos exiliados llamaban son y los puertorriqueños bomba. El público provenía de los mismos barrios humildes donde vivían los músicos, y donde el escaso tiempo que podía encontrarse para el descanso estaba condicionado a disfrutar del baile. Lo que nadie pudo imaginarse entonces era que a la vuelta de dos años, y gracias al impacto inicial que produjo la presentación de las Estrellas de Fania en el Cheetah, comenzaba una revolución musical llamada salsa para aquellos jóvenes y las generaciones posteriores.

EL EMPRESARIO RALPH MERCADO.

Al margen de la modalidad boogaloo (bugalú) y las descargas jazzísticas, los cubanos que habían dejado atrás a su patria trataban a duras penas de conservar no sólo el prestigio adquirido en la isla sino también la subsistencia diaria. Para muchos se había acabado la buena música y en su lugar reinaba un desorden que utilizaba el son «como trapo de cocina», para emplear la expresión de un amigo. El propio Arsenio Rodríguez, el responsable directo de muchas de las innovaciones que años más tarde se utilizaron como bandera salsera, se vio compelido a grabar un tipo de boogaloo harto mediocre que de ninguna manera le correspondía.

Su caso se repitió bastante en Nueva York, y a pesar de las fotos a colores que los músicos enviaban a sus familiares en Cuba, de pie entre la nieve junto a un enorme coche nuevo y la imponente casa de ladrillos detrás, enfundados en un gran abrigo y siempre sonrientes, la realidad era bien distinta. La mayoría de los percusionistas emigraron rápidamente al jazz, mientras que muchos trompetas, violinistas, pianistas, saxofonistas y cantantes tuvieron que permanecer a la expectativa, ganándose la vida en otros menesteres, completamente rezagados ante la turbulencia de un son que, siendo básicamente el mismo, ya no sonaba igual.

Sin embargo, más temprano que tarde, casi todos encontraron trabajo como músicos. De entre una pléyade de instrumentistas escogeré a unos pocos para señalar su intervención en la salsa. El pianista y arreglista **Javier Vázquez** (1936), hijo de Pablo Vázquez, el contrabajista de la Sonora Matancera, realizó importantes grabaciones y tocó con varias orquestas latinas, convirtiéndose en uno de los principales instrumentistas de la salsa. El flautista **Eddie Servigón** (1940) hizo infinidad de grabaciones y fundó la Orquesta Broadway con su hermano. El cantante **Héctor Casanova** (1942) fue uno de los más destacados vocalistas del momento, figurando en la orquesta de Johnny Pacheco y grabando varios discos. Otro cantante, el matancero **Julio Betancourt** (1940), se largó de Cuba en 1964. Trabajó cinco años con la Sonora Matancera y cantó en las agrupaciones de Orlando Marín, Johnny Pacheco y Eddie Palmieri; este gran intérprete ha sido uno de los puntales de los Fania All Stars, grabando algunos de los mejores números de *Tite* Curet.

El violinista **Alfredo de la Fe** (1954) participó con Orestes Vilató y el cantante Roberto Torres en el conjunto The Latin Dimensions. Poco después tocó con Johnny Rodríguez & Friends, de cuya formación surgió la orquesta Típica'73; grabó con la Charanga'76 y con los Fania All Stars. Este gran instrumentista se fue a Colombia en 1983, donde ha continuado deleitando al público. **Orestes Vilató** (1944) comenzó a tocar sus timbales en Nueva York con la charanga de Fajardo y luego pasó a la del boricua Ray Barreto; participó en los dos primeros discos de los Fania All Stars. En 1980 se mudó a San Francisco para participar en la banda del rockero latino Carlos Santana; en 1992, la participación de Vilató en las *Master Sessions* de *Cachao* no dejó duda de que con sus impresionantes «abanicos», es uno de los grandes paileros que ha dado Cuba.

El solista **José *Chombo* Silva** (1923-95) tocaba saxo tenor y violín. Se sumó a «la tribu» de Benny Moré en 1955 y des-

ALFREDO DE LA FE.

EL TIMBALERO ORESTES VILATÓ.

pués de emigrar grabó con Cal Tjader, con *Machito* y con René Touzet. A comienzos de los 60 retomó el violín, participando en la charanga La Sabrosa, de Mongo Santamaría. Después, La Moderna de Barreto le reunió con su colega de la banda de Benny Moré, *El negro* Vivar, uno de los mejores trompetas que ha dado Cuba. En pleno crecimiento de la salsa, *Chombo* Silva grabó con los Alegre All Stars. Creo que su última gran intervención fue con Paquito D'Rivera en el disco *40 Years of Cuban Jam Sessions* (1993).

El pianista que le dio sus mejores «tumbaos» a la orquesta de Ray Barreto fue **Alfredo Valdés** hijo (1941), proveniente de una dinastía dentro de la música cubana: Alfredo, su padre, fue primera voz del Septeto Nacional de Ignacio Piñeiro; sus tíos son Oscar, veterano percusionista de Irakere, y Vicentico, el célebre vocalista de los años 50. Alfredo Valdés hizo los arreglos para las cumbias y vallenatos que grabó **Roberto Torres**, el cubano que impuso *Caballo viejo* desde su Charanga Vallenata en Miami (ver pág. 277).

Los mejores: CHOCOLATE ARMENTEROS

Verdadero puntal de la salsa neoyorquina ha sido el trompeta Alfredo *Chocolate* Armenteros (1926), que posee un sonido inconfundible y una inagotable picardía. Su currículum es uno de los más impresionantes de los músicos que optaron por el exilio: tocó primero en Cuba con el Septeto Habanero y luego con el conjunto de Arsenio Rodríguez, donde coincidió con Chapottín. En los años 50 fue trompeta de «la tribu» de su primo hermano Benny Moré y grabó para *Chico* O'Farrill y el conjunto Kubavana. Cuando emigró a Estados Unidos en 1959 intercambió improvisaciones con Doc Cheatham en la sección de metales de los AfroCubans de *Machito*, donde ocupó la silla de su compadre Mario Bauzá. Después colaboró con los hermanos Palmieri, destacándose el tema *Chocolate ice cream* para el álbum *Superimposition,* de Eddie Palmieri.

La lista de grabaciones distinguidas ocuparía varias páginas. Pero para mí su madurez en la embocadura se evidenció en los dos únicos álbumes grabados (1975 y 1976) por el Conjunto Folklórico y Experimental Nuevayorquino: *Concepts in unity* (especialmente el tema *Chocolate's guajira*) y *Lo dice todo* (en que se destaca *Cinco en uno callejero*). El primer disco de *Cachao* en el que participó *Chocolate* Armenteros se titula *Descarga'77,* aunque el siguiente encuentro entre ambos artistas se hizo esperar dieciséis años. Durante una prolongada estancia en España colaboró con *El Reverendo* Ángel Muñoz en la banda sonora de *Lulú de noche.* Siempre en la vanguardia, *Chocolate* se sumó a los empeños del productor Kip Hanrahan, con quien también se presentó en escena. Ha hecho de todo con su instrumento: llegó a grabar calypsos con el veterano jamaicano Growling Tiger y poco después alternó con un coro de caracolas bajo la batuta del trombonista Steve Turre.

En el exilio tocó unos años con la Sonora Matancera y cerca de su cincuenta aniversario grabó por primera vez en solitario: las sesiones que firmó inicialmente fueron de música tradicional para el sello SAR del cantante Roberto Torres. En los años 80 continuó haciendo descargas, demostrando su facilidad para frasear en la trompeta, algo que compartió con el difunto *El negro* Vivar. Su sonido y ataque son muy diferentes al de Arturo Sandoval, cuya trayectoria aparece en la pág. 269. Ya entradito en años, *Chocolate* continúa siendo uno de los más solicitados instrumentistas en Nueva York y en Miami. Afable y talentoso, siempre sonriente («*easy, man, easy*» diría él), es una verdadera gloria de Cuba.

La lista de los que decidieron que *Coke* (el refresco, no la cocaína) era menos dañino que sufrir bajo la férula de Castro es extensa y continúa creciendo, como el arribo del notable saxo tenor **Carlos Averhoff** (1947) quien durante una gira con el sonero Issac Delgado en 1997 decidió establecerse en Estados Unidos.

La salsa, que le debió tanto al jazz afrocubano iniciado por Bauzá y Socarrás en Nueva York como a los conjuntos que sonaban en la isla entre los años 40 y 60, se produjo dentro de un sustrato de inconformidad social que la alimentó por tiempo prolongado. No olvidemos que el decenio que se abrió en 1960 arrancó con hechos trascendentales en todos los órdenes: descolonización progresiva en Africa, recrudecimiento de la guerra en Vietnam y el enrolamiento de puertorriqueños en la misma, dramáticas protestas estudiantiles en diversas universidades norteamericanas, bloqueo comercial de los Estados Unidos a Cuba, el asesinato del presidente Kennedy y de los líderes negros Martin Luther King Jr. y Malcolm X, desarrollo de la cultura hippie junto al descomunal éxito de los Beatles, delimitación por el equilibrio nuclear de inmensas áreas de control e influencia política entre las dos grandes potencias de entonces. Y para culminar el decenio, una carrera desesperada por alcanzar el espacio sideral, con un gasto ilimitado para producir las armas más sofisticadas de destrucción. Totalmente arrinconados, los principales problemas de la humanidad sufriente tuvieron que seguir esperando soluciones radicales y permanentes.

En Nueva York entretanto se configuró un sonido cosmopolita que se desarrolló sobre la estructura básica del son cubano, mezclando elementos de la pachanga, el boogaloo, el chachachá, el shingalín, la bomba y la plena, el jazz afrocubano, el mambo, el merengue, los aportes renovadores del rock, las cadencias brasileñas y la fecunda y rica tradición del jazz norteamericano. Todo ello revuelto y envuelto en textos vibrantes y genuinos, realistas o fantásticos, que cantaban el clamor problemático de las inmensas urbes hispanoamericanas, de los desarraigados y bulliciosos vecinos de los barrios latinos de costa a costa de Norteamérica, sin olvidar por supuesto, las referencias a la mítica mulata sandunguera que en la imaginación popular siguió contoneando sus hermosas caderas por las calles del Caribe.

Alan West Durán –poeta y ensayista muy criollo a pesar del nombre–, residente en Estados Unidos, relató en un número de la revista *Encuentro* una impresionante anécdota:

Me acuerdo de un concierto de Celia Cruz con Eddie Palmieri y Tito Puente en el Boston Common. Al aire libre, en pleno verano. Estaba con miles de sillas, pero cuando la cosa se calentó de veras y Celia empezó a cantar *Bemba colorá*, la gente se botó. Empezó a bailar allí mismo donde los asientos y hasta encima de ellos, pero la policía lo prohibió. Algunos atrevidos empezamos a bailar en una pista que había no muy lejos de las sillas; allí trataron de parar la cosa también. De repente, centenares, tal vez más de mil personas estaban bailando por la pista, por los asientos, en la grama, en la calle. La policía, dándose cuenta de su tarea imposible, se rindió. La cintura pudo más que la censura.

¿Por qué le llamaron salsa?

Existen distintas versiones que podrían aclarar esta cuestión, pero como suele suceder en estos casos, nadie sabe exactamente a quién se le ocurrió el dichoso vocablo. Es cierto que desde 1929 existía un son de Ignacio Piñeiro titulado *Échale salsita*, reverenciado por los músicos caribeños. Más tarde, en los años 40, el cantante y compositor Cheo Marquetti tuvo una orquesta llamada Los Salseros, y el propio Benny Moré dejó grabado alguna vez el grito de «¡Salsa!». Por su parte, Cristóbal Díaz Ayala afirmó que en la revista cubana *Bohemia* de 11 de noviembre de 1966 había aparecido la foto de un cantante con un pie que decía: «Pedro Gómez en plena salsa...» Otros aseguran que el vocablo salsa fue difundido en los años 60 por el DJ venezolano Phidias Danilo Escalona en su programa radial «La hora del

BENNY MORÉ Y FÉLIX CHAPOTTÍN: DOS ESTILOS DIFERENTES DEL SON.

sabor, la salsa y el bembé». Todo dicho, recuerdo que en 1973 el diseñador y fotógrafo puertorriqueño Izzy Sanabria comenzó a usar el término salsa en el *Latin New York Magazine,* lo cual aprovechó Jerry Masucci para pagar por cubiertas y artículos sobre los artistas de la orquesta Fania. Dispuesto a dominar el mundillo de la música latina, Masucci firmó contratos de cinco años con sesenta músicos excepcionales, compró tiempo clave en programas de radio y produjo documentales sobre la salsa, entre otras actividades encaminadas a establecer el nuevo concepto.

El término conlleva una expresión de júbilo y había sido muy utilizado por los soneros caribeños junto a «¡fuego!», «¡sabor!», «¡agua!» o «¡azúcar!». «Estar en la salsa» siempre aludió a estar dentro y no quedar-

Los instrumentos: EL CONTRABAJO

Es el mayor y el más grave de los instrumentos cordófonos. El sonido se produce por la vibración de las cuerdas al pulsarse con las yemas de los dedos (*pizzicato*) o al ser frotadas con un arco que es más pequeño que el del violín. Los contrabajos acústicos miden casi dos metros y aunque sus antecesores se remontan al siglo XVI, hubo que esperar al XIX para que algunos compositores sinfónicos depositaran su confianza en el instrumento. Después, el jazz le brindó la oportunidad de lucirse en solitario y posibilitó la adopción de nuevas técnicas interpretativas. Unido a la banda de Duke Ellington a mediados de los 50, Charles Mingus le imprimió una intensa vehemencia a su forma de tocar, la misma que mostraba ante cualquier manifestación de racismo. Extraordinario tambien fue Ray Brown, pilar del estilo *West coast*. Años más tarde, el británico Dave Holland se convirtió en el máximo exponente del bajo eléctrico en el jazz. Cuba fue cuna de una particular saga de contrabajistas, los hermanos López, entre los que actualmente destaca *Cachaíto,* (sobrino de *Cachao)* que participó en la grabación de *Buena Vista Social Club.*

El registro grave del contrabajo –instrumento difícil de encontrar e incluso de acarrear en los montes cubanos– fue resuelto por los primeros grupos soneros a principios del siglo XX soplando primero la botija para obtener sonoridades elementales que podrían clasificarse de subdominante, dominante y tónica, y luego con la marímbula, una gran caja de madera sobre la que se sentaba el músico; en uno de sus costados se le abría un hueco, aproximadamente del diámetro del de la guitarra, y sobre él se fijaban tres varillas horizontales que sostenían varios flejes metálicos fijados verticalmente y por la presión ligeramente curvados; al pulsar dichos flejes se obtenían vibraciones profundas en la caja armónica. Como suele decirse, «el cubano le saca música a cualquier cosa».

se fuera, aunque «más salsa que pescado» aludía en Cuba a una persona alardosa que aparentaba una cosa y resultaba otra. Recuerdo que la primera vez que logré entrevistar a Tito Puente me sorprendió su obstinación; casi me echa de su casa porque defendí el vocablo. Visiblemente enfadado, me repetía en inglés y en un español aún peor que salsa era lo que él le echaba a la comida; ni siquiera prestó atención a uno de mis argumentos: «no muerdas la mano que te alimenta». El caso es que durante años el asunto se discutió acaloradamente en todos los rincones caribeños, y por supuesto, en Miami y en La Habana.

En todo esto hay una razón que para mí es central y que quizá ha pasado inadvertida. Si hubieran llamado son cubano a aquella música proveniente de los barrios latinos de Nueva York, se habría perdido la iniciativa y el elemento de novedad, el *latin tinge* (toque o sabor latino) necesario para introducirse en el mercado estadounidense. Aparte de herir susceptibilidades boricuas, llamarle son cubano habría indicado claramente que era una música originada en Cuba. Y Cuba, vista desde Nueva York en 1970, significaba Castro. ¿Acaso se le iba a hacer propaganda a Castro?

Más importante que perdernos en definiciones etimológicas es preguntarnos: ¿Qué es la salsa? Creo que comparto la siguiente opinión con muchos otros: una expresión musical movida y bailable, tan diversa y variada como el jazz, que también tuvo que padecer largos ataques y debates acerca de la validez de su término genérico. Por supuesto, cada persona tiene una versión propia de qué es la salsa y todas son respetables; pero aprovecho para recordarle al lector las interminables disquisiciones etimológicas que provocaron en Cuba la aparición del mambo, el filin y hasta la nueva trova.

¿Qué quedará de la salsa?

Considerando lo mejor de la época de oro de la salsa, que con generosidad ampliaría a todas las Nocheviejas que van de 1968 a 1982, permanecerán inolvidables, entre muchos números y derroches de creatividad, la agitación pachanguera del pianista Charlie Palmieri, el entusiasmo audaz del dominicano Johnny Pacheco, el ritmo violento y picado del pequeño estruendo causado por Joe Cuba, la contribución del ta-

lentoso Louie Ramírez, el cerebro oculto de la Fania, el humanismo rea-
lista del compositor boricua *Tite* Curet Alonso, las experiencias delirantes
de Eddie Palmieri en las teclas y el terrible dilema de Joe Bataan, deba-
tiéndose entre la basura y el soul latino.

Aunque ésta no es una historia de la salsa, debo mencionar los exce-
sos trombonísticos de Willie Colón y la voz del emisario de los tiempos
nuevos, el tempranamente desaparecido Héctor Lavoe. Las inflamadas incursiones pianísticas de Markolino *Divino* Dimond y de Papo Lucca, la
voz de Cheo Feliciano, los extraordinarios solos timbaleros del gran Tito
Puente, la poesía insurgente pero bailable del panameño Rubén Blades, la
enorme contribución de Celia Cruz con *Químbara* y muchos otros temas,
junto al aporte de la plena puertorriqueña de Rafael Cortijo y la voz de
Ismael Rivera, el inolvidable *Maelo*. También hay que mencionar el diseño tan pobre que en general tuvieron las fundas de aquellos discos de vinilo tan apetecibles.

Quedarán en la memoria colectiva los
dos discos estupendos de mediados de los
70 del Conjunto Folklórico y Experimental
Nuevayorquino, a los que ya he hecho referencia, con la trompeta experimentada de
Chocolate Armenteros, el bongó y timbales
de Manny Oquendo, el tres del también
puertorriqueño Nelson González y *Dime la
verdad*, aquel oportuno bolero-son de *Rapindey*. Por la cantidad de epítetos que se
ganó y la significación de los hechos sociales y musicales que motivó la
salsa, sorprende la desproporción entre su variada producción y la escasa
atención concedida a su estudio. Gracias a *El Libro de la Salsa* (1980), del
venezolano César Miguel Rondón, y *La Salsa* (1990), una versión más sin-
tetizada y actualizada del colombiano José Arteaga, los melómanos tenemos referencias obligadas. Más reciente y asequible, busque la *Guía esencial de la salsa* (1995), del español José Manuel Gómez, muy bien
ilustrada y publicada por Editorial La Máscara, Valencia, o la edición cubana de *Los rostros de la salsa* (1997), de Leonardo Padura.

Después de la apoteosis aparecieron formas más despersonalizadas y
extravagantes. Agotada la creatividad individual y el saqueo al añejo repertorio cubano, se impusieron los esquemas repetitivos, se olvidaron de
cantarle al barrio latino y sólo se comprometieron a penetrar el mercado

norteamericano para obtener cuantiosos dividendos en el proceso. Una crisis que terminó de remachar entre 1980-82 la invasión del merengue dominicano, con las voces de Cuco Valoy, Wilfrido Vargas y Johnny Ventura. Ya han desaparecido algunos de los pioneros, los músicos que le imprimieron a la salsa su diversidad y sabrosura. Los últimos coletazos pertenecen a una cosa gelatinosa y desteñida que se arrastra entre la pornosalsa y un tipo de balada rosa que ni siquiera canta a la conquista del otro sexo. Se nos trata de imponer un texto agresivo y repetitivo, disimulado comercialmente por buenos arreglos en los metales y el eterno martilleo del bongó.

Algunos aseguran que los puertorriqueños se apoderaron de la salsa; lo cierto es que los boricuas siempre han constituido mayoría en los barrios latinos de Nueva York y en las orquestas. En cuanto a Cuba, pienso que a los músicos de la isla se les fue el tren entre 1970 y 1982, llegaron muy tarde a un banquete al cual no habían sido invitados y tampoco irrumpieron posteriormente con el esperado torrente de renovaciones vitales. Aparecieron, eso, sí algunos números impresionantes de Los Van Van, Adalberto Álvarez y su Son, Irakere y la Orquesta Revé: *Son para un sonero, Sandunguera, Bayamo en coche, Homenaje a Chaka Zulú* y *Mas viejo que ayer más joven que mañana*. Pero todavía les quedaba competir con números como la tercera versión que grabó Tito Puente de *Qué bueno baila usted* (aquel son lento que cantó primero Benny Moré), esta vez con las improvisaciones del boricua Frankie Figueroa, dedicadas a la memoria del sonero mayor. Con las congas a cargo de *Patato* Valdés, se escuchan casi ocho minutos de una grabación poco conocida que para mí sentó un precedente difícil de igualar. Con una distinción importante: en esta versión tanto Tito como *Patato* se abstuvieron de hacer alardes percutivos, y el conjunto orquestal mantiene una equilibrada utilización de los metales sin caer en el ruido de las bandas de la isla, donde cada instrumentista pretende destacarse sobre los demás. Y ésta es una crítica que hago de corazón.

Aparece y desaparece La Lupe

Uno de los principales baluartes que encontraron algunos músicos cubanos en aquellos duros tiempos fue precisamente la orquesta de Tito Puente. «El Rey del Timbal», que a diferencia del otro puertorriqueño, Tito Rodríguez, no había disuelto su gran orquesta y que tampoco emigró al

jazz como hizo *Machito* con su banda, aceptó el reto de mantenerse a flo-
te contra viento y marea. Así grabó excelentes números con una banda
llena de veteranos instrumentistas cubanos y las voces de Celia Cruz y Vicentico Valdés. Sin embargo, fue una desenfadada cantante cubana, esca-
samente conocida en su propia tierra, la que habría de brindarle a Tito
Puente ese toque irreverente que ya parecía un enfoque obligado en la
nueva música.

La voz de **La Lupe** (1936-92) incorporó al cancionero caribeño un
canto marginal, malicioso, a veces hasta hiriente. Sin embargo, a partir de
los años 80 su desamparada vida artística se desdibujó, y fue desapareciendo gradualmente en una confusa desilusión. Aunque también se le co-

noció como la «Yiyiyi», la «Too much», o
«The Queen of Latin Soul», su nombre
original fue Guadalupe Victoria Yoli Raymond y había nacido en Santiago de Cuba.
Se preparó para maestra y en sus comienzos, según afirmó un periodista, hacía una
desmelenada imitación de Olga Guillot.
Cuando formaba parte del trío Los Tropicuba tuvo que salir del grupo por indisci-
plinada, aunque ella siempre alegó otras
razones. Sin embargo, una noche de 1960
el responsable de un cabaré habanero descubrió sus aptitudes y en poco tiempo fue
famosa; la televisión le abrió las puertas y también tuvo la oportunidad
de grabar su primer LP: *Con el diablo en el cuerpo*.

La Lupe era un verdadero espectáculo. Le encantaba salirse del camino trillado y cantar a su manera, acompañada del pianista Homero, a
quien solía pegar con un zapato; combinaba algunas manifestaciones de
mal gusto con un innegable talento como *show woman*. Su irreverente estilo levantaba ronchas, pero le creó adeptos que la siguieron a La Red,
pequeña boite de una Habana que acababa de estrenar la revolución. La
transformación de un programa nacionalista en un socialismo estilo soviético creó terribles tensiones en el país, y fue La Lupe quien mejor logró
reflejar las ganas que tenía el pueblo de gritar, de mandarlo todo al carajo, de arañarse y llorar de rabia.

Se largó de la isla en 1962 y fue a trabajar a México, de donde la
sacó el percusionista Mongo Santamaría para presentarle gente clave en

Nueva York. Con el aislamiento musical de Cuba, Manhattan se convirtió rápidamente en el escenario donde convergieron diversas migraciones de músicos cubanos, puertorriqueños y dominicanos que pusieron a gozar a los bailadores. La Lupe llegó en el momento justo: se convirtió en un puente entre una época y la otra, anticipándose a la salsa. Con ella, el poder sonoro de una gran orquesta se aproximó a los barrios latinos. Y estoy convencido de que cantando las mismas cosas con el mismo estilo pero diez años antes, habría pasado desapercibida, la gente la hubiera descartado por tratarse de una cantante chillona.

Lo cierto es que La Lupe grabó números en inglés y en español, y se presentó muchas veces con la orquesta de Tito Puente a partir de 1967, cuando todavía no se había producido el boom de la salsa. El primer LP que realizaron juntos se titula *Tito Puente swings. The exciting La Lupe sings,* que les mereció un Disco de Oro con los temas *Esas lágrimas son pocas, Going out of my head, Yesterday* y *Si vuelves tú.* Su frenesí llenó el Carnegie Hall en 1969; después se presentó en el teatro Apolo de Harlem y en el *show* de Merv Grifth, espectáculo televisivo de costa a costa, convirtiéndose en una leyenda viva de excentricidad y pasión. En

LA LUPE: UNA VIDA AGITADÍSIMA.

su repertorio llevaba entonces *Qué te pedí,* de Fernando Mulens, *La mentira,* de Angelita Rigual, *Si tú no vienes*, varios boogaloos y canciones en inglés como *Fever.*

Entre 1968-70 se apareció con tres bolerazos impactantes, creados por el puertorriqueño Catalino *Tite* Curet Alonso, que pusieron súbitamente a la mujer en un papel contestatario, acusando las veleidades masculinas con gesto inequívoco, tendencia que han seguido otras intérpretes como la mexicana Paquita la del Barrio. La Lupe recogió *La tirana* (número que inició en 1968 la carrera de *Tite* Curet por medio del productor discográfico Pancho Cristal), *Puro teatro* y *Carcajada final,* las estrujó y se las arrojó al público, con una extraordinaria capacidad escénica y una voz penetrante, como de vecina alterada por una grave discusión conyugal.

Las canciones del introvertido compositor rompieron belicosamente con el tono idílico y florido de los boleros caribeños y mexicanos de treinta años atrás, conectando con una onda revanchista que enfrentaba al oyente con el drama infecundo de una crispada relación amorosa.

Su tiempo estelar transcurrió de país en país y de escenario en escenario: televisión, cabarés de primera, hoteles de lujo. Años después, Pedro Almodóvar incluyó su inconfundible voz en la película *Mujeres al borde de un ataque de nervios*, entonando *Puro teatro*. Carmen Amaya le otorgó el calificativo de «gitana negra» y la novelista Susan Sontag llegó a definirla como «la primera punk».

La Lupe llevó una vida agitadísima, quizá demasiado violenta. Fue una de las tantas víctimas de la droga; lo tuvo todo y todo lo perdió, encadenada fanáticamente a la Santería, que la consumió. Sufrió humillaciones y tales desastres económicos que se vio forzada a vivir de la Seguridad Social para alimentar a sus dos hijos. Ya se le habían cerrado casi todas las puertas cuando el ex marido le propinó una paliza que por poco la mata. En 1984 un accidente casero le inmovilizó la columna vertebral; poco después, un incendio destruyó sus pocas posesiones. Terminó en las iglesias hispanas y calles del Bronx propagando la fe de una secta evangelista. Cantando diáfanamente y con elegancia, la feligresía religiosa pudo escucharla en Puerto Rico en varios conciertos masivos. Entonces se transformó en la reina del «God Soul». Un infarto cardíaco cerró su vida.

La Lupe seguirá por ahí, arañando angelitos blancos y angelitos negros, porque en definitiva, a pesar del angustioso desorden de su vida, dicen que en el cielo siempre habrá más alboroto por el regreso de un pecador que por la llegada de 99 justos.

EL SONIDO DE MIAMI

Una extensa comunidad de cubanos comenzó a constituirse en Miami a partir de 1960; los que llegaron niños o nacieron en esa ciudad de padres cubanos pasaron su adolescencia escuchando tanto música cubana como del resto del Caribe y, por supuesto, norteamericana.

Emilio Estefan fue de los que llegaron muy jóvenes. Mientras trabajaba para la firma Bacardí, por su definida afición a la música había fundado los Miami Latin Boys en 1974, un pequeño grupo que tocaba en bodas, despedidas de soltero, en todo tipo de fiestas donde los chicos empezaron el lento proceso de experimentar y perfeccionarse. Aunque ya existían otros grupos como Los sobrinos del Juez, fundado en 1967 en

Nueva York por Carlos Oliva, pero residente en Miami a partir del siguiente año, y las agrupaciones tipo charanga dominaban la escena, dos años más tarde Emilio tomó la decisión de convertir a su grupo en el Miami Sound Machine, siempre intentando colarse en el mercado de habla inglesa. Para 1984 lo había logrado plenamente.

Como en el caso de Nueva York, la actividad musical dependía mayormente de los instrumentistas que desertaban de la isla, aunque muy pronto las nuevas generaciones educadas sobre territorio yanqui tuvieron algo que añadir. Lo cierto es que en los últimos quince años Miami se ha convertido en un encuentro para todo tipo de experimentaciones, dando oportunidades a diversidad de talentos. Allí dejó una buena estela el vocalista colombiano Joe Arroyo con su grupo La Verdad, haciendo una mezcla de «chandé» y son cubano. Por Miami pasó hace muchos años la lambada, que iba a toda prisa, creo que de cuna boliviana y movimientos brasileños, pero afortunadamente, todo en la vida pasa. Le siguió el baile «punta» de las costas hondureñas y nicaragüenses hasta que la gente se hartó de tomar *Sopa de caracol*, tanto en Miami como en España. Como en todas partes, el bolero encontró un nicho entre las jóvenes generaciones y se hizo una norma que conocidos baladistas empezaran a cantarlos siguiendo los pasos de Luis Miguel y Linda Ronstadt; el hábil cambio estratégico de los empresarios logró que una audiencia cansada de repeticiones insulsas aceptara de buen grado una vuelta al estilo y enfoque de la música tradicional romántica.

Todo esto repercutía en aquella sociedad dinámica, joven, representativa de todas las naciones hispanoamericanas, un público ávido y exigente de otras cosas que no fueran los archiconocidos temas de la salsa, del rock y la balada. Como tampoco se perfilaban en el horizonte efectivos continuadores de Rubén Blades, Silvio Rodríguez, Oscar D'León o Pablo Milanés, por citar a cuatro artistas que por diversos motivos han suscitado actitudes extremas entre algunos cubanos de Miami, había que buscar algo nuevo, diferente. En ese momento es que la Miami Sound Machine copó el mercado.

Si los años 70 y 80 pertenecieron a la salsa de Nueva York, a partir de los 90 hay que tener en cuenta la música que se escuchó y se bailó en esa inmensa llanura pantanosa de La Florida donde se levanta la ciudad con mayor tasa de crecimiento de la región. Algunos aseguran que es una versión caribeña de Hong Kong, con la diferencia de que proliferan los coches norteamericanos y los olores a comidas de diversas naciones hispanas

CARNAVAL EN LA CALLE 8 DE MIAMI.

le hacen la boca agua a cualquiera. Mientras que en los últimos treinta años la población afronorteamericana ha permanecido casi inalterable, los anglosajones han descendido de un 82 a un 30 por ciento aproximadamente. De ahí que en algunos escaparates de la Pequeña Habana aparezca a menudo el aviso «*We speak English*». En 1960 los habitantes de origen hispano constituían el 4 por ciento de la población; para 1990 habían rebasado el 50 por ciento. Un breve recorrido por Miami mostraría tanto una exposición de cuadros de arte primitivo haitiano como música de merengue brotando de algunos establecimientos, mientras jóvenes de ascendencia cubana bailan chachachá en una terraza del South Beach. Cada marzo, cerca de un millón de personas se apretujan en la calle 8 del South West, una zona mejor conocida como la «Sauesera», para gozar del carnaval y degustar una verdadera avalancha de arepas venezolanas, tostones cubanos y chorizos españoles.

Como capital de las Américas, la ciudad atrae anualmente a miles de inmigrantes y turistas fascinados por sus posibilidades y ofertas. Sin duda alguna, el auge de Miami se debe al éxodo masivo de profesionales y empresarios cubanos que se largaron al exilio a partir de 1960. Un chiste local asegura que el día que el joven Fidel Castro comenzó a leer a Marx, la ciudad se había asegurado su futuro. Convencidos de que algún día podrán regresar a la isla, los mayores no se dejaron absorber por el famoso *melting pot* norteamericano; más bien aprendieron a manejar los negocios al estilo yanqui mientras levantaban una exitosa empalizada de habla hispana como no ha ocurrido en ninguna otra parte del inmenso país, ni siquiera en Los Ángeles. En Miami se producen lo mismo culebrones que nuevas grabaciones musicales, en todo domina el idioma español, desde la Cadena Telemundo hasta el periódico *El Nuevo Herald*.

Si lo anterior parece el panegírico de una ciudad que he visitado con frecuencia y que alberga casi el 10 por ciento de la nación cubana, una proporción nada despreciable, quiero aclarar que no todo es música y diversión. La corrupción oficial y los criminales también hacen su agosto; lo mismo pueden adquirirse rifles AK-47 que cocaína de primera con relativa facilidad; es el lado negativo de una ciudad que ha crecido desmesuradamente, y que mantiene el dudoso récord de registrar el mayor número de crímenes violentos en Estados Unidos. Filtrado entre la luz y las palmeras miamenses se esconde el odio de muchos exiliados hacia el gobierno comunista de la isla, a sólo 125 km de los cayos más sureños de la Florida. Distintos grupos extremistas se disputan la supremacía de su rencor hacia Castro, mientras que una minoría se decanta por la necesidad de dialogar para provocar cambios graduales en un régimen tan hermético como aquél.

No todos están contentos con la prosperidad de Miami: en los últimos diez años más de 140.000 anglosajones decidieron abandonar la ciudad y zonas adyacentes debido al crecimiento de los *hispanics*. Por otra parte, las continuas oleadas de inmigrantes latinoamericanos han puesto un enorme peso sobre las autoridades municipales; algunas áreas parecen ahora poblaciones del Tercer Mundo, con desarraigados viviendo bajo los puentes o en chabolas levantadas alrededor de Biscayne Bay. El futuro de Miami dependerá de la visión y sentido común de sus gobernantes; más temprano que demasiado tarde, este enorme laboratorio social que acoge a miles de personas llegadas de todas las repúblicas americanas tiene que resolver todavía las enormes contradicciones que ha provocado su acelerado crecimiento como centro financiero.

Sin embargo, el arte y la música de origen cubano gozan de un interés permanente. Hace poco, en la acera del paseo donde las estrellas dejan impresas en cemento las huellas de sus manos, el trompeta Arturo Sandoval y el conocido actor Andy García celebraban una tradición establecida desde 1984, una especie de manera oficial de honrar a las celebridades que han hecho significativos aportes a la cultura de la comunidad.

Arturo Sandoval (1949), exiliado en 1990 durante una gira por Europa –una década después que su compañero Paquito D'Rivera–, estuvo ocho años esperando la ciudadanía estadounidense, presuntamente por haber pertenecido al Partido Comunista de Cuba. Durante ese tiempo, amén de infinidad de conciertos y grabaciones estelares, Sandoval obtuvo tres premios Grammy. Este brillante instrumentista, capaz de alcanzar solos ultrarrápidos en los registros más agudos, a la manera de Freddie Hubbard o Maynard Ferguson, posee también la sensibilidad para recrearse en lentos boleros. Como muchos otros músicos de su generación, había estudiado en la Escuela Nacional de Arte, y en 1967 devino uno de los fundadores de la Orquesta Cubana de Música Moderna. Unido después a Irakere, Sandoval realizó giras internacionales e hizo contactos con músicos importantes, incluyendo a Dizzy Gillespie, el autor de *A night in Tunisia*, su primer héroe y modelo cuando era joven. Lo había conocido personalmente en 1977 durante el «desembarco jazzístico» de músicos norteamericanos en La Habana. En 1981 dejó a Irakere para formar su propio grupo, contando con el brillante pianista Hilario Durán

ARTURO SANDOVAL.

como director musical. Con Gillespie grabó *To a Finland station* en 1982, participando también en la Orquesta Naciones Unidas del propio trompeta. También dirigió varios festivales de jazz en La Habana. Más tarde compartió con sus antiguos colegas de Irakere en *Straight ahead* (1988). También destacó como solista invitado de la Orquesta Irazú en *Rumberos del Irazú* (1987) y *Homenaje a Cuba* (1989).

Tras su huida, Arturo Sandoval se instaló en Miami, donde comenzó a enseñar en la Florida State University; en 1990 grabó primero el disco *Reunión* con Paquito D'Rivera y en aquellos días (1991) también realizó la banda sonora del filme *Los reyes del mambo...* y trabajó con Emilio y Gloria Estefan en el importante álbum *Mi tierra*.

Su primer disco ya instalado en Miami lo reveló en perfecta forma, con colaboraciones de Ed Calle (antiguo miembro del Miami Sound Machine), René Luis Toledo y el conocido pianista norteamericano Chick Corea.

En escena es un consumado *showman*, cantando scat y alternando en percusión y teclados. *Tumbaíto* recoge lo mejor de su frenética energía. Con una embocadura ecléctica si las hay, desde su llegada a Estados Unidos, Sandoval ha grabado de todo un poco, incluso música clásica.

La gloria de ser Gloria Estefan

En 1994 su álbum *Mi tierra* fue el más vendido en todo el planeta (dos millones de ejemplares) y el disco extranjero con mayores ventas en España de todos los tiempos (700.000 copias). En la lista total de los discos más exigidos por el público español sólo le superan Julio Iglesias con *Raíces*, y Mecano con *Descanso dominical* y *Aidalai*. ¿Cómo se explica un éxito tan rotundo?

Gloria Estefan (1957) representa un fenómeno único que lo mismo canta en inglés que en español desde Miami, antiguo hábitat invernal de septuagenarios norteños. Su apellido de soltera es Fajardo (proviene de una familia de músicos importantes), y es un refrescante producto de la dinámica de aquella ciudad, aunque reconozco que está sostenida por fabricantes de música y espectáculo con un sesgo de bandera política. No hay duda de que su voz, dúctil y algo susurrante, se alínea en una larga tradición de la que formaron parte exquisitas vocalistas cubanas del pasado, aunque ella mantiene una dicción excelente. Esto la ha convertido en una modalidad necesaria y espléndida, lo mismo cantando boleros refinados que sones calientes. Cuenta a su favor con instrumentaciones límpidas, excelentes músicos, el adecuado uso de recursos electrónicos, los discretos textos de sus canciones y un poderoso aparato de márketing detrás de ella.

A los 18 años se unió como vocalista al grupo Miami Latin Boys, que dirigía el que posteriormente sería su esposo, Emilio Estefan, músico aficionado que toca el acordeón. A partir de 1976 el grupo se llamó Miami Sound Machine y experimentó bastante con un repertorio de soft rock y baladas en español. Gloria ha declarado:

Con la Miami Sound Machine ayudamos a restablecer la reputación de la ciudad. El cine y la televisión han difundido la idea de que Miami es sólo narcotráfico y violencia. Demostramos que también es un centro creativo importante, donde la mayoría de los latinos se dedican a trabajar honradamente.

Dr. Beat es un número en inglés de un álbum producido en 1984 y que tuvo gran éxito, no sólo en Norteamérica sino también en Europa. En 1986 lanzaron el disco *Primitive love*, del que pegaron *Bad boy* y sobre todo *Conga*, con sendos videoclips que se hicieron muy populares y que ocuparon frecuentemente los primeros lugares del *hit parade* esta-

LA EXTRAORDINARIA GLORIA
ESTEFAN.

dounidense. Paquito Hechavarría, poseedor de uno de los mejores tumbaos del exilio, es el pianista en *Conga*. Repitió con la guapa Gloria en *Oye mi canto* (1989) y en *Mi tierra* (1993). Se trataba de penetrar tanto el mercado pop de Estados Unidos (el dificilísimo *crossover* para todo artista de origen hispano) como los amplios campos de la música latinoamericana, usando a fondo la personalidad y versatilidad de la vocalista.

Si la menuda Gloria es la sensibilidad artística, Emilio es la capacidad organizativa, la visión para los negocios, el hombre que sabe sonreír y valorar el talento de los demás. La Miami Sound Machine abrió los Juegos Panamericanos de Indianápolis en 1987; dos años más tarde habían vendido más de cinco millones de discos y realizado varias giras importantes. Pero poco después, el autocar en el que viajaban los Estefan fue embestido por un camión fuera de control en una carretera nevada de Pennsylvania; su hijo Nayib se partió una clavícula, Emilio se dislocó un brazo y Gloria, quien saltaba como una cabra montesa en sus conciertos y vídeos, se rompió la espalda. «Antes del accidente, Gloria hacía 600 abdominales y corría seis kilómetros al día», explicó entonces Emilio. «Todos los días me retaba a una carrera hasta el segundo piso de la casa y siempre me ganaba». Gloria necesitó largos meses de operaciones quirúrgicas, duros ejercicios, terapia y bastante descanso, hasta que logró reincorporarse al trabajo. Una vez más, la frágil mujer demostró su firme voluntad y su capacidad de concentración.

Ganó entonces el premio «Lo Nuestro» al artista *crossover* del año que otorgan la revista *Billboard* y la cadena Univisión; millones de telespectadores en toda América y en España recibieron la sorpresa de ver a Gloria Estefan dirigirse a recibir su premio caminando desenfadadamente del brazo de Emilio.

Sus padres habían salido de La Habana cuando Gloria era apenas una criatura. Enrolado en el ejército, el padre regresó de Vietnam con el sistema nervioso envenenado por el pesticida tóxico conocido como el agente naranja; la madre trabajaba para mantener a la familia mientras

Gloria cuidaba del enfermo. En aquellos días grises, cantar con una guitarra se convirtió para la chica en una forma de desahogo. Cuando finalmente falleció, Gloria acababa de cumplir los 16 años. Lentamente, la tímida adolescente comenzó a salir del cascarón, hasta que en una boda, empujada por varias amigas, subió al escenario para cantar. El director de la banda era un joven llamado Emilio. Ahí comenzó el cuento de hadas.

ANDY GARCÍA, *CACHAO* Y EMILIO ESTEFAN.

«Yo no sabía bailar salsa», confesó la artista que tiene el don de convertir a un auditorio de holandeses o japoneses en una comparsa tropical marcando el paso de la conga. «Me crié en un ambiente musical totalmente "anglo", pero el ritmo lo traía en la sangre».

En 1991 grabaron *Into the light*, comenzando una gira por España y otros países europeos que terminó en Puerto Rico a principios de 1992. Ese mismo año, el poderoso sello Sony le produjo *Éxitos de Gloria Estefan*, donde aparecen varios números de su propia inspiración: *No será fácil* y *No me vuelvo a enamorar*.

Si entre los artistas cubanos Celia Cruz es el gran símbolo del anticastrismo, Gloria Estefan es hoy por hoy la figura más popular en el mundo. Se le agradece que no manifieste el revanchismo de tantos coetáneos de Miami; de hecho, sus opiniones sobre el futuro de la isla han resultado sorprendentemente equilibradas.

Con *Mi tierra,* que se distribuyó en 1993 –una vuelta total a la música tradicional cubana con la que ganó el premio Grammy– Gloria Estefan apareció acompañada de una constelación de grandes: *Cachao*, Paquito D'Rivera, Arturo Sandoval y Tito Puente, incluyendo al pianista Paquito Hechavarría, el de los tumbaos en *Conga* y en *Oye mi canto*. En 1995 los Estefan lanzaron otro ambicioso proyecto, *Abriendo puertas*, con un énfasis en la música colombiana, siempre contando con los arreglos del genial Juanito Márquez y empleando músicos *ad hoc*, como el acordeonista de vallenato Cocha Molina.

Ya han logrado 50 Discos de Platino y tienen en su haber, entre mu-

EL CANTANTE JON SECADA.

chos otros trofeos, la Medalla del Congreso de Estados Unidos y el título de doctor *honoris causa* conferido a Gloria por la Universidad de Miami. Pero la vida «Gloriosa» no es una vida fácil: entre su intenso trabajo de giras, ensayos y grabaciones, las secuelas del accidente y su papel de madre (además de Nayib, también tiene una hija llamada Emily), ha tenido bastantes problemas. La pareja cuenta con Crescent Moon, un estudio de grabaciones con los últimos avances tecnológicos donde trabajan sólo con los mejores ingenieros de sonido; más importante aún, han podido establecer una sofisticada organización de márketing y promoción como no la ha tenido ningún artista latinoamericano jamás. También han sido los artífices del lanzamiento de nuevos talentos, incluyendo a los conocidos Jon Secada, Ricky Martin y el debut internacional de la carismática guajira Albita Rodríguez.

Sin embargo, la sofisticación de tal aparato de producción no siempre ha cuajado: el álbum *Alma Caribeña*, aunque se vendió profusamente en 2000, no me parece estar a la altura de los anteriores, a pesar de que Gloria aparece cantando con Celia Cruz y José Feliciano, y de los extraordinarios efectos que logra en las cuerdas del cuatro el puertorriqueño Yomo Toro. La mayor parte de los números fueron escritos y arreglados por Roberto, hermano de Rubén Blades, mientras que Hernán *Teddy* Mulet mantuvo la dirección musical.

El decidido apoyo de Gloria y Emilio contra la angustia que provocó la repatriación del niño Elián González les devolvió gran parte del prestigio perdido entre los extremistas de Miami, muchos de los cuales los habían acusado en el pasado de vacilaciones ideológicas. Pero los Estefan no se pueden quejar: poseen una preciosa casa en Star Island, una isla privada, y su emporio incluye un catálogo de 3.000 canciones, varios hoteles y la pequeña cadena de restaurantes cubanos Lario. A raíz de la aparición de Gloria junto a Andy García en una película biográfica sobre Arturo Sandoval, la pareja hizo un arreglo con Universal Television Group para producir vídeos para el mercado hispano. Al momento de escribir, también tienen sobre el tapete una posible coproducción con Disney basada en sus propias vidas.

Todo dicho, es necesario subrayar que gracias a Gloria Estefan mucha gente joven de todas partes ha conocido algo de la riqueza musical cubana, gente que llena los auditorios en sus presentaciones y busca sus discos. Gloria tiene talento y arrastre, y el mérito de que sus mejores números siguen siendo una muestra exquisita de trabajo colectivo.

El fenómeno Albita

Nadie es profeta en su tierra. La cantante **Albita Rodríguez** (1962) hizo su debut discográfico en Estados Unidos en 1995 con el álbum *No se parece a nada*, tema creado por Julia Sierra, quien también fue la autora de *La esperanza* y *Bolero para nostalgiar* (en colaboración con la propia Albita). Otras piezas notables incluyen *Qué manera de quererte*, de Luis Ríos, que figuró en la película *El especialista* con Kevin Costner. Con tres temas compuestos por la propia intérprete –*Qué culpa tengo yo,*

ALBITA VIENE DE LA TIERRA.

Solo porque vivo y *Para que me beses tú*–, el disco se completó con *Mi guaguancó*, de Randall Barlow y Roberto Blades –como para no olvidar jamás sus raíces–, el son adanzonado *Un solo beso,* de Emilio Estefan, arreglado por Juanito Márquez y *Quién le prohíbe* del colombiano Estéfano Salgado.

Hija de campesinos trovadores, Albita se crió escuchando y cantando punto guajiro. En 1980 comenzó su carrera profesional, con un repertorio donde mezclaba lo tradicional con nuevas creaciones que fue haciendo sobre la marcha. Si bien había alcanzado cierta popularidad en la isla, donde llegó a cantar en el cabaré Tropicana, ha afirmado: «Ser cantante de música cubana en Cuba es la última carta de la baraja. Yo no supe lo que era tener un éxito tan rotundo hasta que fui a Colombia en 1991 para participar en el festival de salsa y jazz de Bogotá». Para los colombianos y para los propios cubanos, la voz profunda y melodramática de Albita deslumbró como una versión moderna de Celina González, muy querida en aquel país; en los años 50 Celina había impuesto en Cuba su mezcla guajiro-afrocubana con su esposo Reutilio (ver pág. 87).

En Bogotá, la pequeña y dinámica Albita grabó *Si se da la siembra* y *Cantaré*, dos discos de música tropical; con el sencillo *La parranda se canta* alcanzó considerables ventas.

Pero en Bogotá, siguiendo el acostumbrado método policial, el consulado cubano le puso inusitadas trabas a su carrera, exigiendo tener todos los detalles de lo que hacía y de cómo lo hacía para informar a La Habana. «Las cosas se pusieron muy difíciles para nosotros», explicó Albita después. La chica y sus músicos decidieron dejarse de cuentos y saltaron a Ciudad México; luego se trasladaron a Ciudad Juárez, al norte del país. En abril de 1993 el grupo atravesó a pie la frontera norteamericana y llegó a El Paso, Texas. De allí se dirigieron a Dallas y finalmente a Miami, donde fijaron su residencia.

Sus padres, Martín y Minerva, eran repentistas de punto guajiro en Las Villas, en el centro de la isla. Aunque de niña también escuchó mucho rock y funk, finalmente siguió la vena campesina heredada, aprendiendo de paso a tocar el tres. Su debut en álbum fue *Habrá música guajira,* que apareció en Cuba en 1988, convirtiéndose en un éxito para la EGREM.

Cantando en el restaurante Centro Vasco de Miami la encontró el empresario Emilio Estefan, quien poco después la contrató para su sello Crescent Moon. Siempre con su voz penetrante, cargada de reminiscencias campesinas, en 1996 Albita y su grupo lanzaron *Dicen que*, su segundo CD, y en enero de 1997 viajó a Washington para la fiesta en honor de la toma de posesión de Bill Clinton, a quien le cantó la *Guantanamera* para que el presidente bailara. Entre 1998-99 con la caída de las ventas de discos, la discográfica Sony y algunos miembros de su banda la abandonaron. Tozuda pero igualmente encantadora, la artista reapareció con el álbum *Son* en 2000, publicado por el sello Hipbop Latino de Inglaterra, que incluye una excelente versión de *El manisero.*

Un sonero desconocido en España

Willie Chirino (1947) es uno de los más distinguidos músicos de la diáspora en Miami. Su fama entre la juventud latinoamericana residente en Estados Unidos también es considerable, a tal punto que la Avenida 17 del noroeste de Miami fue renombrada en 1995 la Willie Chirino Way. En su oficina, entre discos de oro, fotos de encumbrados, medallas y premios, aparece también la inevitable carta de la Casa Blanca firmada por

Ronald Reagan. Pero no hay indicios de algún premio obtenido en España; hay que preguntarle a los empresarios y distribuidores de aquí: ¿A qué se debe que a pesar de su talento sonero Chirino sea un desconocido en este país?

Muy alto y atractivo, su nombre es Wilfredo y nació en Consolación del Sur, Pinar del Río; en 1961 su familia decidió radicarse en Miami. Toca piano, guitarra, bajo y percusión y en la escuela organizó su propio grupo. Para 1973 ya había grabado su primer LP; luego comenzó a actuar con gran éxito en teatros, plazas, radio y televisión. Ha sacado varios discos estupendos entre los que se destacan *Oxígeno*, que contó con la contribución del trompeta Arturo Sandoval; este álbum contiene el simpático *Mister, don't touch the banana*, sobre un ciudadano norteamericano que, invitado por amigos a una ceremonia de Santería, es regañado por coger un plátano del altar de Changó, todo eso dentro de un ritmo excitante. *South Beach* es otro álbum estupendo, de nuevo con la participación de Arturo Sandoval y el añadido de Albita, recién llegada entonces a Miami; incluye un tema de la autoría de Cándido Fabré y *Memorándum para un tirano*, un fuerte mensaje a Castro en tiempo de salsa ligera. El tercer disco que quiero mencionar es *Baila conmigo*, un clásico de 1997, con el tema *Bongó*, un número para agotarse bailando de gusto.

EL SONERO WILLY CHIRINO.

Su voz y el sonido de su banda lo distinguen en seguida. Ha sabido incorporar juiciosamente elementos del pop brasileño y del merengue dominicano, recordándome a veces cosas de Juan Luis Guerra y Rubén Blades. Pero Willie Chirino siempre ha demostrado ser original: sus composiciones tratan de temas muy diversos, son muy coloridas y gozan de orquestaciones excelentes, con una sección de percusión que nunca se desorbita.

El cantante **Roberto Torres** (1940) tampoco es conocido en España. Comenzó su carrera en Güines, un pueblo patatero de la provincia habanera. Cantó en varios conjuntos hasta que en 1959 se exilió en Nueva York, donde trabajó con las charangas de Fajardo y la Broadway. Más

tarde perteneció a la Sonora Matancera. Cuando decidió presentarse
como solista creó varios sellos discográficos –SAR, Guajiro y Neón–,
poco antes de instalarse en Miami a mediados de los años 80. Aparte de
sus muchas grabaciones, incluyendo homenajes a las grandes estrellas del
pasado, Roberto Torres ha producido discos para otros exiliados notorios como el percusionista *Papaíto*, el trompeta *Chocolate* Armenteros, la
fuerte vocalista Luisa María Hernández, mejor conocida como «La India
de Oriente», y Alfredo Valdés, quien fuera cantante del Septeto Nacional,
con su hijo el pianista Alfredito Valdés. Su Charanga Vallenata, una invención oportunista donde combina una flauta con el acordeón del colombiano Jesús Hernández, lo catapultó al éxito en varios países latinoa-

ALFREDO VALDÉS (PADRE).

mericanos con el tema *Caballo viejo,* del
venezolano Simón Díaz, y la hermosa historia de *Matilde Lina*, un clásico colombiano. Más tarde los Gypsy Kings modifica-
ron *Caballo viejo* para montar su *hit
Bamboleo.* Aunque problemas relaciona-
dos con el corazón lo mantuvieron un
poco más calmado en los 90, continúa
siendo una de las figuras más relevantes de
la comunidad musical de Miami y un duro
anticastrista, crítico de cualquier tipo de
acercamiento al régimen de La Habana.

Lo mejor de Roberto Torres (vols. I y
II) está lleno de sones sabrosones e incluye
canciones del boricua Rafael Hernández y
El testamento, del colombiano Rafael Escalona. En *Roberto Torres rinde homenaje
a Benny Moré* presenta música bailable de primera, un verdadero tributo
al «Bárbaro del ritmo». Con *Roberto Torres y su Charanga Vallenata*
(vols. I-III) estableció su concepción del vallenato, género colombiano
surgido en la costa Atlántica.

Asentado antes en México, después en Miami y ahora en Cancún,
Francisco *Pancho* Céspedes (1956) no puede quejarse: lo han apoyado en
su carrera Miguel Bosé y Alejandro Sanz, introduciéndolo al público español. Ya Luis Miguel, ese rey Midas del bolero, le había grabado varias
piezas cuando en 1997 Pancho participó en el Festival de la Canción de
Viña del Mar, representando a México y quedando en segundo lugar.

Desde El Candelero, el local donde solía actuar en Ciudad México, interpretaba textos melancólicos con una estructura muy moderna y una voz desgarrada. Yo tuve la oportunidad de escucharlo en 1994 en una fiesta privada y quedé muy impresionado. Se había exiliado con su madre, su mujer y su hija en 1992: «Me fui de Cuba porque quería que mi música trascendiera. Allí te dan las armas para que pienses, pero no salidas».

EL CANTAUTOR PANCHO CÉSPEDES.

Sus letras románticas, deudoras del filin, el blues y el soul, han arrebatado en España desde que publicó el álbum *Vida loca*. «Soy un bohemio empedernido que hace canciones tratando de respirarlas. Las hago para poder vivir, entenderme e inventarme», ha afirmado alguna vez. Produce boleros sensuales y emocionantes donde la palabra clave siempre es «vida»; no son melodías pegajosas, pero poseen un encanto y profundidad muy especial, particularmente en su propia voz.

Pancho Céspedes ha grabado algunas melodías de un villareño como él, que reside en México desde 1993 y que recién empieza a demostrar su valer: **Amaury Gutiérrez**. Gran admirador de Pedro Luis Ferrer y otros trovadores, este joven cantautor hace poco que sacó su segundo álbum, *Piedras y flores*.

A pesar del prestigio de que gozan entre la gente más cultivada de la ciudad, y quizá debido a la índole de los programas que montan, la pareja **Mara y Orlando** no ha trascendido de Miami. Mara Rauchman (Holguín, 1951) y Orlando González (Palma Soriano, 1952) salieron muy jóvenes de Cuba. Estos dos amantes de la canción se conocieron y se casaron en Estados Unidos, y desde los años 70 decidieron presentar anualmente varios conciertos de calidad en Miami, uno dedicado a la obra de Ernesto Lecuona y otros espectáculos donde abordan la música latina en general, siempre realzando con sus voces las canciones criollas más famosas. Después de los Festivales del Bolero organizados en Miami por el malogrado Hall Estrada en 1985 y 1987 para celebrar el centenario de la creación del género en Santiago de Cuba por Pepe Sánchez, la pareja ha puesto en marcha otros eventos importantes donde se han escuchado las voces de Tania Martí, Irene Farach, Ada Luque, Armando Te-

rrón, Olga Díaz, Martica Ruiz y Olga María. Con estos artistas ha trabajado José Antonio *Chamaco* García (1938), quien se inició con la Orquesta Hermanos Castro y más tarde fue solista en el hotel Capri y en el
cabaré Tropicana, hasta que en 1960 salió de gira hacia México, permaneciendo en Mérida durante unos diez años para luego radicarse definitivamente en Miami.

La cantante Lissette Álvarez –hija del matrimonio Olga Chorens,
excelente voz, y Tony Álvarez– comenzó adaptando el rock a un estilo
latino en Puerto Rico. Cuando años después se radicó en Miami y se
casó con Willy Chirino, decidieron mantener sus carreras artísticas sepa-
radas.

Otros desconocidos del público español son **Hansel y Raúl,** quienes
antes de largarse a Miami eran vocalistas del grupo Charanga 76 habanero, componiendo algunos de sus mejores números: *Regresarás, Wanda* y
Ku-ku-chá. Este dúo ocupó el extremo más tradicional de la salsa-pop
miamense de los años 80; varios éxitos en ese sentido los lanzaron a una
gira internacional con triunfos en Japón, Francia, Colombia y México,
así como parte de África. Hansel Martínez nació en Morón, cerca de Camagüey, y Raúl Alfonso es habanero. Hansel tuvo que separarse de su
compañero en 1988, pero volvieron a juntarse en 1996 para producir un
nuevo álbum seguido de otra gira que esta vez incluyó Suiza, Italia, Tai-
landia y las Filipinas. *Oro salsero* contiene veinte éxitos en dos CD que
incluyen *María Teresa y Danilo* y *Con la lengua afuera*. Su segundo álbum se titula *Celebrando* y contiene el éxito *Báilala pegaíta*, grabado con
una nueva charanga dirigida por el pianista Alex Arias, con Eddy *Guagua* Rivera en el bajo y Edwin Bonilla en los timbales.

La apertura en 1995 del **Café Nostalgia** de José *Pepe* Horta, antiguo
agregado cultural del gobierno cubano ante la UNESCO y ex director del
Festival Internacional de Cine que se celebra anualmente en La Habana,
ha sido celebrada por el ambiente que sugiere la decoración del local y por
proyectar documentales de los grandes músicos cubanos. Mientras que
Pepe Horta trata de facilitar la visita de músicos de la isla a su establecimiento, el pequeño grupo que entretiene a la clientela publicó un disco que
fue muy bien recibido: *Te di la vida entera,* del sello francés Naïve, que
muestra un repertorio ecléctico seleccionado por su líder, el bajista Omar
Hernández (que aunque trabajaba con diversos grupos en La Habana logró escaparse en una balsa en 1994). Aparece desde un arpa y la sección
de violines de una orquesta hasta un clásico de *Bola de Nieve: Be careful,*

it's my heart (de Irving Berlin), seguido de *Un cubano en Nueva York*, número creado por Miguel Matamoros. Entre los contribuyentes al disco está el cantante Luis Bofill, que llegó a Miami vía Alemania y luego fue reemplazado en 2000 por Nelson Trejo, antiguo miembro de la Orquesta Revé de Cuba.

La visión de Pepe Horta es establecer más sitios como el Café Nostalgia donde músicos de dentro y fuera de la isla puedan encontrarse y descargar juntos para escapar de la política que los ha mantenido divididos por décadas.

Esta sección no pretende cubrir todo lo que acontece en Miami. La búsqueda y cambios frecuentes de músicos, más los que llegan de Nueva York y otros sitios para grabaciones específicas o buscando trabajo, no cesa. Ése fue el caso del interesante disco *Mar adentro* del joven y versátil dúo **Donato y Estéfano**, publicado en 1995. Separado de Estéfano, el cantautor Donato Poveda acaba de lanzar en España su último disco, *Bohemio enamorado*.

El son en California

Aunque Nueva York y Miami se llevan la palma, usted puede encontrar músicos cubanos en cualquier ciudad de Estados Unidos. He seleccionado una agrupación de la Costa Oeste porque su repertorio es diferente y por la distancia que los separa del resto. El **Conjunto Céspedes**, que tiene su base en Oakland e irrumpió en la escena musical del exilio en 1981, se inició como un trío formado por Gladys *Bobi* Céspedes, su hermano Luis *Tati* y su sobrino Guillermo *Guille*. Debutaron en San Francisco un año después durante la celebración del ochenta aniversario del nacimiento del poeta cubano Nicolás Guillén. Esta especie de clan familiar, oriunda de El Cotorro, La Habana, se especializa en los más genuinos ritmos cubanos: guaguancó, son montuno, bolero, danzón y rumba, y abordan sus temas con líricas y arreglos propios. *Güira con son* (1984) fue su primer álbum con la ayuda de otro miembro de la familia, el percusionista Miguel Valdéz Céspedes. Para entonces el conjunto consistía de ocho músicos, entre los que se encontraban Chris Cooper (violín), Jesús Díaz (congas) y Wayne Wallace (trombón). Destaca con luz propia la voz de *Bobi*, una negra sonriente y dicharachera, quien también ejerce de compositora y codirectora del grupo. Haciéndole frente a la tradición lucumí, con muchos años como hija de

Obbatalá, la exhuberancia de *Bobi* llena todos los escenarios donde se han presentado.

En 1993 el conjunto Céspedes grabó *Una sola casa*, un pimentoso primer álbum donde contaron además con la participación de músicos de diversos orígenes, todos enamorados de una sola casa, la de la música afrocubana. Desde entonces han publicado otros CD.

LO QUE SE TOCA EN EUROPA

La música cubana siempre ha arrebatado en España, pero no sólo aquí. En París, Londres, Bonn o Bruselas pueden escucharse diversas bandas integradas por cubanos residentes en Europa, que aprovechan el interés internacional provocado por una música que no está relacionada directamente con el reclamo turístico.

No es fácil saber la cifra exacta de músicos cubanos en España, pero su presencia es contundente. Alina Puig, funcionaria del Ministerio de Cultura cubano (y «supervisora» de las giras de Compay Segundo), calcula que pueden ser más de 1.500 entre residentes y transeúntes. Madrid, Barcelona, Galicia y Canarias acogen a la mayoría. Las siguientes agrupaciones e individuos representan sólo un puñado a manera de ejemplo.

En 1993 pidieron asilo en Madrid nueve componentes de **La Familia,** una orquesta que había tenido que dejar a otros tantos miembros en Portugal. El caso recibió bastante publicidad en su día y tengo entendido que todavía están tocando en España.

Otros artistas han logrado instalarse permanentemente, como es el caso de **Lucrecia,** afincada en Barcelona desde principios de los años 90. Dotada de una hermosa voz, mucha sandunga sonera, largas piernas y las trenzas más coloridas que han visto las cámaras de televisión, Lucrecia llegó originalmente en 1992 como cantante solista del conjunto femenino Anacaona (ver pág. 323), y pocos saben que estudió piano clásico en el Conservatorio Amadeo Rol-

LA EXCITANTE LUCRECIA.

dán. Se llama Lucrecia Pérez Sáez, y pronto se convirtió en la perla negra de la salsa barcelonesa. Respaldada por un grupo que sabe seguirla sin apagarla, ha producido ya varios discos y su carrera continúa, aquí y en Cuba, desde aquel *Me debes un beso* que grabó recién instalada en España. El periodista Ricardo Aguilera considera que está tocada por el duende de la cercanía, de la facilidad de conexión con el público, por la espontaneidad y gracia que derrama en sus abarrotados conciertos. Al momento de escribir, Lucrecia ha cosechado otro gran triunfo al musicalizar el impresionante documental *Balseros*, que trata del destino de varias personas que huyeron de la isla en 1994 para lanzarse a cruzar las fuertes corrientes que separan a Cuba de la Florida. En su sexto disco, *Agua*, grabada con Dro East West, de la Warner, Lucrecia ha abordado exitosamente nuevos géneros como el acid-jazz y el tecno.

GEMA Y PÁVEL.

Al otro extremo del espectro artístico está el dúo de **Gema y Pável** (Gema Corredera y Pável Urkiza), formado en 1990, que siempre ha realizado presentaciones novedosas y que desembarcó en España con la compañía Teatro Estudio. Gema se graduó en 1982 en guitarra en la Escuela Nacional de Arte y cinco años más tarde obtuvo la licenciatura de Musicología en el Instituto Superior de Arte. Pável estudió Música en el Conservatorio Ignacio Cervantes y también es licenciado en Económicas. El sello Nubenegra de Manuel Domínguez le publicó hace algunos años *Trampas del tiempo*, donde dan cumplida cuenta de todas las influencias que han ido forjando su peculiar personalidad, desde los Beatles a Caetano Veloso, incluyendo los viejos boleros del filin, hasta el blues y la psicodelia. Si hay algo omnipresente en la grabación citada es la ciudad de La Habana, el deseo de saberla y quererla entera, liberando inquietudes cotidianas. El son *Parar de fumar* es un tema que recrea de manera humorística –y con no poca ironía– la relación hombre-voluntad por medio del daño que puede causar el tabaco. Una gira europea, dos discos más y la excelente producción de un álbum –también de Nubenegra y al que contribuyeron varios artistas españoles–

en homenaje a María Teresa Vera, avalan su labor en España. Aunque Gema y Pável se separaron al regresar a La Habana en 2000, han vuelto a juntarse en España.

Habana Abierta es un grupo de seis jóvenes que apuesta por una vanguardia muy diferente a lo que representa el Buenavista Social Club. Fueron recomendados originalmente por el dúo anterior al sello madrileño Nubenegra, que les grabó su primer disco en 1995 en La Habana, cuando actuaban bajo el nombre de Habana Oculta. Posteriormente ficharon con la multinacional BMG Ariola, que les editó su segundo álbum. Es un grupo que pugna por crear música que no esté impuesta por el todopoderoso mercado, ni por las reglas de la moda, pero sus discos no se han ofrecido en las diferentes ediciones de Cubadisco, ni se han presentado en conciertos en la isla y la televisión nacional los ha excluido. Su originalidad no es una ecuación fácil, pero ellos la resuelven por medio de la fusión integradora, aunque la tónica general apunta hacia el rock como fuerza motriz. Su último disco, *24 Horas,* es un álbum sin fisuras, una visión concebida desde Madrid.

Entre las agrupaciones bailables que suenan muy bien en diversas ciudades españolas se destaca la **Sonora Corasón,** dirigida por el teclista Juan Castillo. Formada en Cuba en 1995 con los mismos integrantes, allí trabajaron en varios centros y aparecieron en el programa televisivo «Mi salsa». En 1997 grabaron el disco *Sin brujería ni ná*, editado por la EGREM. Le siguió una gira de tres meses por el norte de España, pero regresaron en el verano de 1998 para quedarse. Han trabajado en multitud de clubes y universidades y hace poco acompañaron al conocido salsero puertorriqueño Tito Nieves en una gira por Europa.

Tres músicos que ya se conocían de su ciudad natal se unieron en Madrid en 1998 para formar el **Trío Matancero.** La vocalista Judith Rodés estudió teoría musical y ya Rubén Aguiar, guitarrista con mucho sabor a tierra adentro, comenzaba a componer cuando conoció al percusionista Osmandy Fuentes (autor de *Guía de la percusión cubana*, editorial Tikal). Durante largo tiempo trabajaron en el restaurante La Negra Tomasa de Madrid, donde ganaron muchos adeptos. Rubén Aguiar es el autor de varios temas grabados por distintas agrupaciones.

No puedo olvidar la música de otro nivel, especialmente la relacionada con el teatro lírico cubano. Entre las diversas voces criollas de gran calidad que se conocen en España, mencionaré sólo a dos, nuevamente por razones de espacio.

Alina Sánchez posee un hermoso timbre de soprano, una impecable técnica y verdadero temperamento dramático. Comenzó su carrera artística siendo alumna de la Universidad de La Habana, debutando con *Cecilia Valdés,* bajo la dirección de su autor, el maestro Gonzalo Roig. Más tarde trabajó con el maestro Rodrigo Prats. Llegó a España en 1993 como solista de la Compañía Antología de la Zarzuela (española) de José Tamayo, y se quedó. En 1998 concibió y produjo con gran acierto *María la O,* del maestro Ernesto Lecuona, en el Festival Lírico de Asturias (teatro Campoamor de Oviedo). Alina fue primera solista de la Ópera Nacional de Cuba; además de grabar varios CD, ha protagonizado cinco películas y ha cantado en el Kennedy Center y en el Roy Thompson Hall de Toronto.

La mezzosoprano **Teresa Guerra** es otra voz significativa de la Ópera Nacional que decidió residir en Madrid. Natural de Matanzas, grabó en España *El amor brujo* de Falla con la Orquesta Sinfónica de su ciudad natal, bajo la dirección de Elena Herrera. Ha actuado con éxito en el Memorial de las Américas de Brasil, en México y en España. Ambas artistas son dos baluartes de la mejor lírica cubana y en 1998 presentaron «Temas de amor y desamor» y «Ecos de La Habana colonial», este último recogido en un disco publicado por Caja Segovia.

Pasaré a referirme a lo que también sucedió en 1998, un año muy especial porque se conmemoraba el centenario de la pérdida de la isla a manos estadounidenses. Un verdadero aluvión de voces y ritmos criollos descendió sobre España en plena primavera; bajo la bandera del «Festival de las Américas» aparecieron en jornadas diferentes y en el Centro Cultural de la Villa de Madrid los artistas Amaury Pérez, el sensacional grupo Vocal Sampling, César Portillo de la Luz y Carlos Varela, Compay Segundo, Pancho Amat junto a Barbarito Torres y su Piquete, así como Chucho Valdés y algunos miembros de Irakere, con la voz de Omara Portuondo. Bajo otros promotores pero en el mismo lugar, se presentaron «La Reina del Bolero» Olga Guillot y «Los Reyes de las Canas», la popularísima Vieja Trova Santiaguera.

Aquellas presentaciones se sumaron a otras que tuvieron lugar en la Casa de América de Madrid y en la Sala Manuel de Falla de la SGAE, como parte de una estrategia mayor. La SGAE, a la cual pertenecen casi todos los artistas que salen de Cuba (calculo varios miles de miembros), fue la promotora de los más de setenta actos culturales que se integraron en el proyecto «Cuba '98: 100 años de historia y cultura». Presentado unos meses antes de la invasión primaveral, el vasto plan pretendía estrechar en este primer siglo de emancipación republicana la proximidad histórica, cultural y sentimental entre España y la isla. El programa incluyó música popular y clásica, teatro y danza, conferencias, ediciones y publicaciones, producciones discográficas y otros negocios.

«El esplendor creativo por el que atraviesa Cuba, la constatación de que las raíces y los frutos de una cultura propia han tomado cuerpo en una muy sólida cultura cubana, y el conocimiento que el resto del mundo tiene de sus artistas, ha desembocado en este proyecto de SGAE y Fundación Autor», aseguraba el material informativo distribuido por la empresa que monopoliza el quehacer artístico en España, y que tiene como filial a la Fundación Autor.

VOCAL SAMPLING.

Creo recordar que el primero en descender del avión fue **Amaury Pérez** (1953), quien se explayó en canciones cargadas de contenido poético, incluyendo varias de su disco *Amor difícil*. Amaury formó parte del núcleo de la nueva trova a partir de 1972 y después vivió varios años en México.

El fenómeno que constituye **Vocal Sampling** es para disfrutarlo en vivo. La fórmula parece fácil: una dosis bucal de ritmos y efectos percutivos a la que se añade la dinámica de animadas melodías, mientras una laringe mantiene el compás con su sonido de bajo. El resultado es sensacional (ver pág. 368).

Compay Segundo, que es muy bueno y nunca deja de sonreír, hizo lo que siempre ha hecho, y con sus tres muchachos, y en este caso con el añadido de la voz melodramática de la andaluza Martirio, ofreció una velada de sones sabrosones. Este inveterado fumador y bebedor de ron, que realmente se llama Francisco Repilado (1907), es un enorme trozo de la historia musical de la isla. A los catorce años ya acariciaba una guitarra recorriendo las mismas calles santiagueras que conocieron Sindo Garay y otros trovadores; trabajó con el Quinteto Cuban Stars dirigido por Ñico Saquito y con el Cuarteto Hatuey, antes de aprender a manejar el clarinete, instrumento que estuvo tocando doce años con el Conjunto

Matamoros. Desde 1949 formó con Lorenzo Hierrezuelo el famoso dúo Los Compadres (ver pág. 75) –cuyos sones se debían a la autoría de ambos– hasta que se pelearon en 1955 y Compay fue reemplazado por Reynaldo Hierrezuelo, diecinueve años menor que Lorenzo. Compay Segundo comenzó a tocar entonces con un grupo que él llamó Mis muchachos. Después sufrió el ostracismo y un largo período como tabaquero en la fábrica H. Upmann hasta solicitar su jubilación. Entretanto, Elíades Ochoa, que había adoptado gran parte del repertorio del compositor, lo invitó a aparecer como artista invitado en varios conciertos. En 1989 Compay Segundo contribuyó al Festival de Culturas Tradicionales Americanas, propiciado en Washington por la prestigiosa Smithsonian Institute. Le siguió otro período de abandono hasta que reapareció invitado al Primer Encuentro entre el Son y el Flamenco, celebrado a finales de julio de 1994 en Sevilla, donde fue «descubierto» por un empresario español.

Ahora su voz de barítono se acompaña de una guitarra de siete cuerdas metálicas que él llama armónico (mezcla de guitarra y tres cubano) y al que le saca filo. Y todo el mundo lo quiere escuchar; pero mejor es que no hable porque no tiene nada que decir sino tonterías y alardes de viejo verde.

Recomiendo dos álbumes: *Antología*, una selección de 34 de sus mejores éxitos, grabados en Madrid en 1995 bajo la producción de Santiago Auserón, y *Calle Salud*, grabado en 1999 en los lujosos estudios Abdala, con la participación de Charles Aznavour. Aunque es un álbum gracioso, su voz empieza a fallar, lo cual hace del disco *Antología* una mejor compra. Ambos álbumes fueron editados por el sello español Dro East West, que en 2002 sacó a la venta *Duets,* una rara mezcla donde aparecen desempolvados dúos con Elíades Ochoa, Santiago Auserón, Charles Aznavour y Pablo Milanés, ofreciendo como gancho a la africana Cesaria Évora en *Lágrimas negras,* de Matamoros, y al argelino Khaled integrado en *Saludo a Changó.*

No podría seguir hablando de cuerdas sin mencionar al tresero **Pancho Amat**, ex profesor de física (ver pág. 379), que apareció en duelo sonero con el laúd de **Barbarito Torres** y su Piquete: cuatro chicos campesinos (guitarra, tres, bajo y bongó) y una Conchita que tiene una voz tan alta como la de Celina González pero más agradable. Lo de Pancho Amat es como un reverdecer de las cuerdas (por poco escribo de las palmas), con un dominio del fraseo que lo ha convertido en uno de los mejores treseros de todos los tiempos. Por su parte, Barbarito Torres realzó la tonada campesina sonera, arrancándole al laúd rápidos arpegios del grave al agudo, y abarcando ámbitos insospechados. Al final de aquel espectáculo subió al escenario *Juan Perro*, antiguo miembro de Radio Futura, el conocido artista que tanto ha hecho por difundir la música tradicional cubana en España desde que en 1993 produjo la importante recopilación *Semilla del son*.

Como era de esperarse, lo de **Omara Portuondo** y **Chucho Valdés** fue otra cosa. Desde que en 1997 grabaron *Desafíos* para un sello español, una selección sólo para piano y voz, que por cierto no ha logrado la aceptación que se merece, estos dos señalados artistas se han encontrado raras veces. Aquella velada en el Centro Cultural de la Villa se volcaron los nuevos Irakere en una presentación de gran calidad, con el añadido gustazo de escuchar a Mayra Caridad, hermana de Chucho, una imponente voz cargada de swing y soul que deslumbró a los asistentes. Cantó un bellísimo *Cómo fue* a dúo con Omara, «La Novia del Filin», que seguramente habría conmovido a su autor, el pianista Ernesto Duarte, fallecido aquí en el exilio en 1988. Dije que eran unos nuevos Irakere porque de los fundadores sólo aparecieron el guitarrista Carlos Emilio Morales, el batería Enrique Pla y el propio director. Chucho, de quien siempre se pueden esperar nuevas concepciones, invitó a dos saxos muy jóvenes a descargar, y lo hicieron con gusto y aplomo, demostrando la calidad de la enseñanza musical en la isla. Entretanto, el hijo de Bebo Valdés inventaba secuencias apabullantes y los enormes dedos se divertían en coreografías incesantes.

Olga Guillot (ver pág. 144), enemiga acérrima del castrismo, comenzó en 1998 una minigira española en Madrid. Por supuesto, no podía faltar a esta cita con la música cubana. Coleccionista de Discos de Oro (creo que su voz ha aparecido en más de 60 discos) y creadora de una auténtica escuela interpretativa, Olga, «La Reina del Bolero», vino a celebrar sus sesenta años de carrera artística con los imborrables *Tú me acostumbraste* (que canta desde 1957), *Miénteme, Adoro, Sabor a mí* y tantas otras melodías que le han dado el prestigio de que goza en muchos países. Como en el caso de Celia Cruz, ella no piensa retirarse jamás; desde Miami o desde México continúa declarando al mundo que el trono del bolero sigue ocupado.

Y ahora pasando a las canas, nunca imaginé que mis palabras serían tan proféticas cuando presenté en 1994 por primera vez en España a aquellos ancianos; fue en la Casa de América de Madrid y ante un nutrido público. Pero cuando los cinco miembros de la **Vieja Trova Santiaguera** empezaron a sonear (con sólo cuerdas, voces, claves y maracas), no hubo cadera quieta. Los integrantes de este quinteto acumulaban toda la sabiduría de un largo batallar en memorables formaciones orientales: el Cuarteto Patria, La Estudiantina Invasora y el dúo Los Compadres. Con edades que oscilaban entre los 68 y 84 años entonces, la Vieja Trova Santiaguera estuvo integrada originalmente por la voz y claves de Reinaldo Creagh, el diabólico tres de Reynaldo Hierrezuelo, la guitarra e imprescindible segunda voz de Pancho Cobas, el contrabajo preciso del sonriente gigantón Aristóteles Limonta y las maracas del humilde Amado Machado, siempre genial en las inspiraciones vocales; se ganaron un éxito arrollador en su primer recorrido por España, Alemania y Francia. Cobas y Machado fueron reemplazados un par de años después, pero la impronta del primer grupo quedó grabada en la memoria musical española.

LA ORIGINAL VIEJA TROVA SANTIAGUERA.

Han seguido volviendo a España año tras año, realizando extensas giras en que se les cuida como oro, porque aquí adoran la música tradicional sonera, la de tierra adentro, y por supuesto, admiran la picardía y dignidad con que estos verdaderos profesionales presentan y redondean cada número. Sin embargo, al momento de redactar estas líneas recibo la noticia de su retiro definitivo después del verano 2002. Su sexto y último disco se titula *El balcón del adiós*.

Mas el peso real de esta invasión de músicos cubanos se hizo sentir aquel año 1998 en el madrileño Palacio de los Deportes con la actuación de **Team Cuba**, una gran gala con una orquesta de veinte músicos dirigida por Joaquín Betancourt. Autodefinida como «Somos lo que hay», esta agrupación se formó para deslumbrar a los españoles y dejarles entrever la potencia sonora de la isla. Contó con la participación de Juan Formell en el bajo, el cantante Isaac Delgado y el *showman* José Luis Cortés, alias *El tosco*, David Calzado, el sonero Adalberto Álvarez, Paulito y los cantantes Mayito, Aramís Galindo, Tony Calá y Michel Maza. En conjunto, son jóvenes, prepotentes e inevitables, quizá eso explique que desde las páginas del periódico habanero *El Caimán Barbudo* se les critique como música degenerada que mete demasiado ruido. Y algunos de ellos están muy irritados porque los Ry Cooder o los Santiago Auserón de este mundo se fijan únicamente en los «viejitos», dejando a un lado lo que es presente candente y turbulento en los grandes salones de baile de la isla. En resumen: Team Cuba ofreció aquel año de 1998 un espectáculo detonador con más sabor a aguarrás que a ron, con mucho movimiento escénico a lo Michael Jackson, y una música que lo mismo cabría calificarla de salsa, que de hiper-salsa o de timba. O mejor, timba heavy. ¿Por qué no?

Bajando bastantes decibelios mencionaré la participación del filinista **César Portillo de la Luz** (ver pág. 148), quien alumbró con su habitual lucidez una charla sobre la trova cubana en la Casa de América. «Canto, luego existo», fue el *motto* del genial compositor y guitarrista, al extenderse sobre aquel movimiento habanero de comienzos de los años 50 llamado filin que revolucionó al bolero. Antes de comenzar su concierto levantó su guitarra afirmando sonriente: «Yo le digo a España: mira lo que hicimos con el instrumento que nos prestaste». El autor de *Contigo en la distancia, Realidad y fantasía* y *Tú, mi delirio* recordó a su colega José Antonio Méndez, el otro gran hombre del filin, y logró intimar con los asistentes, hasta el grado de rumbear, con su parco estilo, un tema que repite: «Óyelo bien bailador, allá en New York o en París, dondequiera que estés, no podrás bailar el son como lo bailaste aquí...», su manera de recordarnos a los exiliados lo difícil que resulta vivir lejos del cañaveral, para luego machacar en el estribillo: «Para gozar el son, La Habana...».

Cuando al terminar su presentación me acerqué al viejo amigo, ambos bromeamos (la manera cubana de expresar la pesadumbre) sobre lo derruida que está La Habana. Después me dedicó su hermoso volumen *El filin*, publicado por la Fundación Autor y compilado por Radamés Giro; un recuerdo que guardaré junto a otras memorias de aquella fabulosa Habana nocturna que él tanto contribuyó a forjar y que ya no existe.

Aquella velada **Carlos Varela** (1946) no se encontraba en su mejor momento y realmente decepcionó a gran parte del público; y fue una lástima porque el cantautor tiene mucho que ofrecer. Habanero que creció escuchando rock norteamericano y las voces de Silvio y Pablo, quienes le alentaron a principios de los 80, pronto sus canciones comenzaron a llamar la atención. Después de su debut en la Cinemateca del ICAIC, su popularidad creció de tal forma que llenaba el enorme teatro Karl Marx con facilidad. Una década después abandonó sus presentaciones en solitario para formar un grupo de rock que le acompañara, dejándose el pelo largo y usando vaqueros negros, un atuendo que el régimen califica de «alternativo» y que le ocasionó algunos problemas con la policía.

Carlos Varela tiene en su haber dos álbumes: *Como los peces* (BMG, España), una mezcla de rock norteamericano y español, mezclado con suaves baladas y la contribución de artistas españoles. La influencia de la nueva trova se hace sentir en números como *Grettel*, un bello poema dedicado a su mujer; este disco apareció en Cuba cinco años más tarde, quizá por el tono de desencanto que transmite. El otro disco es *Carlos Varela en vivo* (Bis, Cuba), grabado en vivo en La Habana, con nueve largas extravagancias alrededor de sus primeros éxitos: *Guillermo Tell, Soy un gnomo, Cuchilla en la acera, Tropicollage* y *Jalisco Park*.

CONJUNTO LOS NARANJO.

Guillermo Tell describe a un padre que no comprende a su hijo, una crítica velada al «padre de la nación». Ésta y otras canciones fueron atacadas por su pesimismo y por no ser «constructivas» de cara a las dificultades del «Período Especial»; como resultado, pronto sus canciones desaparecieron de la radio. A mediados de los 90 su carrera se benefició, como la de Silvio Rodríguez, del inmenso interés de sus seguidores españoles. En 1999 Carlos Varela fue uno de los artistas que participaron del «puente musical» con artistas estadounidenses como Mick Fleetwood, Andy Summers y Burt Bacharach, quienes pasaron una semana en La Habana actuando con los cubanos.

Otras agrupaciones conocidas por un amplio sector del público español incluyen al **Conjunto Los Naranjos**, originalmente fundado en 1926 en la ciudad de Cienfuegos, que interpretan sones bastante diferentes a los que presenta el **Septeto Spirituano,** dirigido por el guitarrista

Ángel Huelga; el prestigio de este último está garantizado por contar en su repertorio con varias obras de viejos compositores de la pequeña ciudad de Sancti Spíritus, como Miguel Companioni y Rafael Gómez, mejor conocido por *Teofilito*. Ambas agrupaciones participaron en el Primer Encuentro entre el Son y el Flamenco celebrado en 1994 bajo los auspicios de la Fundación Luis Cernuda de Sevilla, donde **Faustino Oramas** *El guayabero* (1911), que es único en su género, cantó sus letanías soneras al personaje conocido como «Marieta». Este viejo y sufriente cronista de las pequeñas grandes cosas que suceden en la vida del cubano común siempre se ha mantenido en una lenta línea campesina, con una voz de un encanto especial que lo identifica como si estuviera a punto de suicidarse.

Su disco *El tren de la vida* (uno de sus temas más conocidos) fue grabado en Tenerife en 1998 por el sello Eurotropical.

El **Cuarteto Patria**, fundado en 1940 en Santiago de Cuba, es uno de los que más maestría han demostrado en elaborar complicadas improvisaciones de las cuerdas en las líneas melódicas de sones y boleros, así como en poseer una destacada voz primera. Ésta es la especialidad de **Elíades Ochoa** (1946), su director desde 1978. Trovador y poeta con imaginación para versos humorísticos y pasionales, Ochoa sabe mantener la frescura de los viejos sones y ha sido propuesto varias veces para el premio Grammy. Desde los once años comenzó a cantar en los bares de Santiago de Cuba y también se ganaba la vida limpiando zapatos; es totalmente autodidacta, como tantos otros trovadores y juglares. En los años 60 tocó con el Quinteto de la Trova y en el Septeto Típico Oriental. Con Humberto Ochoa en la guitarra segunda, Armando Machado en el bajo acústico y Joaquín Solórzano en el bongó, el Cuarteto Patria maneja un repertorio de números creados por grandes del pasado: Miguel Matamoros, Manuel Corona, Lorenzo Hierrezuelo, Compay Segundo, Ñico Saquito y Luis Marquetti. Preguntado si es real el personaje de su número *Píntate los labios, María*, aseguró que no sabía la respuesta ya que se trataba de un arreglo de Roberto Faz que escuchaba en la década del 60 y que le gustaba mucho. Al parecer, tras la muerte de Faz también «enterraron» a María hasta que a Elíades Ochoa se le ocurrió reponerlo, insertándole *Amor de hombre*.

En 1994 el sello Nubenegra le publicó al Cuarteto Patria *A una coqueta*, un excelente álbum que luego editó Corasón de México, junto a *¡Se soltó el león!*. Gracias a su participación en **Buena Vista Social Club,** Elíades Ochoa ha recibido el merecido premio a su trabajo. *Sublime ilusión*, un disco grabado en California y editado por Virgin, incluye varios boleros famosos (abarca desde *Chan Chán*, de Compay Segundo, hasta *Siboney*, de Lecuona) y cuenta con la contribución de Ry Cooder, Charlie Musselwhite en la armónica y David Hidalgo en la guitarra, mientras que la voz del guajiro Ochoa se eleva sobre su instrumento de ocho cuerdas. Musselwhite añadió bellas estrofas de blues en inglés, mientras los cubanos cantaban los estribillos originales y la doliente armónica encajaba como un guante.

El sonido de París

Con bien asentadas raíces en la música tradicional cubana, el pianista **Alfredo Rodríguez** (1936) estudió en los años 60 en Nueva York, participando en importantes sesiones de música latina. *Ready for Freddy* (1976), un álbum del conguero *Patato* Valdés, fue su carta de presentación en el competitivo ambiente musical de Manhattan. Después, en *Sonido sólido* (1983) su piano aparece envuelto entre las congas de *Patato* y de *Totico* Arango. Ecléctico por naturaleza, no dudó en agregarle una trompeta al formato de charanga típica.

Poco más tarde se trasladó a París –su actual base de operaciones– convirtiéndose en el mejor embajador del jazz afrocubano. En el álbum *Monsieur Oh La La* (1985) reveló su intensa relación con el danzón, rindiendo el primero de varios homenajes a su ídolo, el pianista Pedro Jústiz *Peruchín*. Su charanga cuenta ahora con el apoyo del saxo barítono Mario Rivera. En 1991 y 1993 grabó *La fiesta del timbalero* y *Boleros* con la Orquesta Irazú, del chileno Raúl Gutiérrez Villanueva. Una extensa gira europea con *Patato* Valdés dio lugar al disco *Cuba-New York-París: Absolutely live* (1992).

Para Yoya (1992) fue el cuarto trabajo discográfico de Alfredo Rodríguez y quizá el más versátil, metiéndose de lleno en el cañaveral cubano. Grabado en un estudio de París, el bravo pianista contó con la colaboración de importantes músicos cubanos y de otras nacionalidades, entre los que destacan la guitarra de Pedro Jústiz (hijo de *Peruchín*), Aramís Castellanos, Paul Taylor, Lisa Graham, Mike Charropin, Ian Dean, ¡y hasta la voz de Pedrito Calvo, el antiguo cantante de Los Van Van! Ya había advertido de su eclecticismo.

Después fue más alla en *Cuba linda* (1996), un excelente intento de reconciliar el piano con esquemas folclóricos, y donde Rodríguez reproduce con exactitud algunas de las más conocidas frases logradas por *Peruchín* en las teclas. Su evidente agilidad (en eso me recuerda a Felo Bergaza) se destapó en las descargas *Cubanismo* (1996) y *Malembe* (1997), que produjo con el trompetista Jesús Alemañy en Cuba.

6.   LOS RITMOS DE LA REVOLUCIÓN

> La gente quería salsa brava, ver al cantante entregándose
> de verdad, oír un buen solo, escuchar letras que le hablen
> de la vida, todo lo que la salsa le dio desde un principio.
>
> ADALBERTO ÁLVAREZ
> (Entrevista con Leonardo Padura, 1992)

La primera década después del triunfo revolucionario de 1959 mantuvo a la música cubana moviéndose en dos direcciones casi paralelas: la preservación y el redescubrimiento de las mejores tradiciones, y desde otra perspectiva, un ansia de experimentación en todos los niveles, incluyendo la inmediata incorporación de tendencias de vanguardia.

Aunque muchos casinos y cabarés habían sido cerrados con la llegada de los barbudos, el pueblo se las arregló para seguir bailando. El chachachá era todavía inmensamente popular, y con él tuvo que competir la pachanga, un ritmo creado precisamente en 1959 por **Eduardo Davidson**, que metió en su equipaje cuando salió exiliado hacia Nueva York. Un par de años después, Che Guevara aseguraba que lo de Cuba era «un socialismo con pachanga», queriendo subrayar el carácter festivo que aportaría al fallido experimento sociopolítico de pretensiones mundiales el espíritu alegre y burbujeante de los cubanos.

Fue una época saturada de «nuevos» ritmos, cuando la posibilidad de exportarlos ya había desaparecido del todo. Dos de los que lograron imponerse nacionalmente fueron el mozambique de **Pello el Afrokán** (Pedro Izquierdo) y el pilón de **Pacho Alonso**. El primero consistía en una

EDUARDO DAVIDSON.

masiva presentación de congas basadas en tradiciones santiagueras, con una sección de metales y un coro contestando al solista. Algunos de los números de Pello, especialmente *María Caracoles*, sobrevivieron a través de la década del 60, a tal punto que en Nueva York el pianista boricua Eddie Palmieri llegó a grabar una excelente versión que ya anticipaba la tendencia en que se formularía la salsa.

El pilón tenía más sustancia que el mozambique. Inicialmente basado en los movimientos que hacen las africanas para machacar los granos en un enorme mortero, pronto derivó en nuevos pasos, bien alejados del chachachá. Su creador fue **Pacho Alonso** (1928-82), un brillante cantante santiaguero que se hizo un favorito durante los primeros carnavales de la era revolucionaria con temas como *Rico pilón*. Caracterizado por un golpe del timbal en el tercer tiempo de cada compás, el ritmo pilón se debió a la estrecha asociación del carismático Pacho con el compositor Enrique Bonne, otro santiaguero que había trabajado con cincuenta tamboreros al formar los Tambores de Oriente. Pacho Alonso viajó a Francia en 1962, y señalando claramente la dirección en que se movería la incipiente revolución, actuó también en Checoslovaquia y en la Unión Soviética. Los integrantes de su grupo Los Bocucos fueron los primeros intérpretes de música popular cubana que tuvieron el honor de tocar en la Sala Chaikovski de Moscú. El cantante de Los Bocucos era un joven sonero oriental, muy delgado, de nombre Ibrahim Ferrer (ver pág. 376), quien fue fotografiado en 1962 estrechando la mano del capitán ruso del crucero *Aurora*. Era la época de la crisis de los misiles (octubre 1962), cuando el presidente Kennedy y Jhruschov tuvieron al mundo temblando debido al ultimátum americano sobre la inmediata retirada de los cohetes soviéticos instalados en Cuba.

Esta explosión de «nuevos ritmos» correspondió con la etapa de aislamiento político del país y algunas de aquellas combinaciones rítmicas que tuvieron éxito en el ámbito nacional no trascendieron internacionalmente. No es posible negar que hubo una búsqueda en este sentido, pero se anduvo por caminos ya trillados, con desplazamientos más o menos notables de acentos en los que el nuevo montaje no justificaba la denominación de nuevo ritmo y mucho menos de nuevo género.

EL SANTIAGUERO PACHO ALONSO.

El ritmo pilón duró unos pocos años mientras que Pacho Alonso buscaba otras posibilidades hasta dar con el upa-upa, que coincidió con la popularidad del mozambique. A su repentina muerte en 1982 su hijo siguió sus pasos, reorganizando la banda ahora bautizada **Pachito Alonso y sus Kini Kini**. Más tarde decidió relanzar el pilón, inspirado en la popularidad internacional momentáneamente alcanzada por la lambada. Otro ritmo que acaparó bastante la atención popular fue el pa'cá del guitarrista **Juanito Márquez**, con *Pituka la bella, Arrímate pa'cá, Cuidao con la vela* y *Tengo ahora una chiquita*.

Entre otros artistas que se disputaban los mejores escenarios en aquellos primeros años revolucionarios estaban la Orquesta de Jorrín, el versátil cantante *Bola de Nieve*, los filinistas César Portillo de la Luz y Elena Burke, y Los Papines en los cueros. Sin embargo, fue un cuarteto vocal muy influenciado por Los Platters, Los Ink Spots, Frankie Lymon y Los Teenagers, quienes pronto acapararon la atención. **Los Zafiros** marcaron toda una época con sus suaves interpretaciones de filin, calypsos, baladas y rumbas; la incorporación de una guitarra eléctrica, tocada primero por Oscar Aguirre y un año después por Manuel Galván, sugería un nuevo sonido para combatir la beatlemanía. Curiosamente, en cierta oportunidad el cuarteto actuó en la sala Olympia de París inmediatamente después de los Beatles.

Influenciados por la brillantez del cuarteto D'Aida y los argentinos que formaron Los Cinco Latinos de Estela Raval, los Zafiros se originaron en la barriada de Cayo Hueso en 1962, con el objetivo de crear un cuarteto moderno de armonías vocales que mantuviera un repertorio muy amplio. Sólo uno de sus miembros tenía experiencia profesional por haber cantado en el cuarteto de Facundo Rivero, me refiero a Miguel Cancio. Los otros miembros eran Eduardo *El chino* Hernández, un instructor de judo que hacía de tenor, la voz aguda de Leoncio *Kike* Morúa, empleado en una empresa de coches de alquiler, e Ignacio Elejalde, que había sido bailarín antes de poner su voz de falseto al servicio del nuevo cuarteto. Los asesoró el compositor Néstor Milí (1910-67) (autor de *La caminadora, El yerberito, Despacito* y *Sólo tengo un amor*), quien los pulió hasta obtener una verdadera sincronización de voces y baile.

Su primer disco, con música de Milí, causó sensación. Antes de terminar el año le habían robado el show al gran Benny Moré en el cabaré del Habana Libre, y constantemente recibían ofertas de otros cabarés y canales de televisión. Para 1965 estaban al frente del Grand Music Hall de Cuba, que viajó por la Europa comunista y concluyó con el concierto en el Olympia. El regreso a la isla, sin embargo, estuvo marcado por continuas desavenencias entre los cuatro jóvenes, que para entonces consumían grandes cantidades de alcohol. Pronto se cancelaron contratos y Los Zafiros vivieron una década lucrativa pero frustrante, trabajando en el mismo cabaré antes de separarse. Elejalde, su voz principal, falleció en 1981 a los 39 años.

EL CUARTETO LOS ZAFIROS (1963).

El sello World Circuit editó *Bossa cubana*, una estupenda compilación de blues y calientes efectos vocales, con la guitarra de Galván marcando casi guturalmente. Un renovado interés en Los Zafiros se debió a la película *Zafiros, locura azul*, dirigida por Manuel Herrera y producida por Hugo Miguel Cancio, hijo de uno de sus integrantes, quien escapó de Cuba vía Mariel en 1980. Filmada en la isla en 1997 con capital norteamericano, se convirtió en un culto en La Habana, provocando la creación de grupos como Los Nuevos Zafiros y Los Zafiritos.

A partir de 1960 la vida de los músicos había cambiado, con la consecuencia de un imparable éxodo de artistas. Sin embargo, si muchos músicos confirmaron por experiencia propia que el nuevo régimen era un obstáculo para sus carreras, otros tantos lo apoyaron. Ese fue el caso del trompeta y director de orquesta Julio Cueva o la estrella del filin José Antonio Méndez, quien se apresuró a regresar de México en 1959. La popular Orquesta Aragón fue de las primeras en anunciar que se quedaría en el país.

La revolución pronto empezó a ejercer cambios sustanciales en las condiciones de trabajo de los músicos, así como en verificar el contenido ideológico de sus creaciones y presentaciones. Para empezar, el grupo de empresarios que regenteaba la industria lúdica, que conocían perfectamente las características nacionales, fue reemplazado por funcionarios del Estado con poca o ninguna experiencia en el sector. Los equipos, masters y archivos de los sellos discográficos fueron confiscados, poniendo todas las facilidades industriales bajo el control de una nueva entidad, la Empresa de Grabaciones y Ediciones Musicales (EGREM). La familia Sabat, propietaria de Panart, el sello más importante, había tomado la precaución de enviar copias de sus masters a Nueva York antes de exiliarse. Los nuevos funcionarios encargaron papel barato de China para las etiquetas de los discos de vinilo, pero como el deficiente pegamento chino no resistía el calor hacía que los discos se combaran. Por su parte, la cera traída de Polonia rompió varias prensas por su mala calidad. Al momento de escribir, la EGREM todavía utiliza los estudios Panart –tan machacados y dilapidados como los vetustos coches norteamericanos sobrevivientes de los años 50– para grabaciones esporádicas o para alquilárselos a productores extranjeros.

La situación se hizo desesperante. Una banda importante tenía que esperar más de un año para grabar un álbum, y como la política oficial insistía en producir todo tipo de música, sin importar criterios como la popularidad o el índice de ventas, la banda tenía que aguardar quizá otro año para que la EGREM editara su trabajo. La razón de las demoras se debía no sólo a la ineficacia del sistema, tenía mucho que ver con las sospechas del régimen a que el grupo grabado no regresara al país después de alguna gira o que algunos de sus miembros terminaran en Miami. A menudo no había pasta para producir vinilos, o se había acabado el cartón para las fundas. Las tiendas no podían ordenar los discos que consideraban más importantes, sino simplemente esperar a que la distribución centralizada le llevara los títulos que quisiera.

Los artistas cubanos no tenían ningún control sobre las ventas, ni nadie que les indicara cuándo recibirían sus derechos, que en realidad nunca se les abonaban. La EGREM instituyó una gama de premios casi kafkiana: entregaba un «disco platino» a sus creadores sin que éstos recibieran ningún estímulo económico. Un «número uno» no tenía nada que ver con las ventas, sino en una impresión subjetiva de la reacción de la audiencia.

Entretanto, los cubanos no eran inmunes a lo que sucedía en el mundo. La radio WQAM de Miami, que era escuchada por sus programas de rock, provocó la creación de grupos clandestinos como Los Kent, Los Gnomos, Los Jets y Los Hanks, que tocaban en fiestas particulares; como acontecía en los países tras el Telón de Acero, el rock era visto como una desviación ideológica, como un movimiento musical promovido por la CIA. Ser homosexual o tener el pelo largo se convirtió en un pasaporte directo a uno de los campos de trabajo forzado. Habría que esperar hasta 1970 para que Almas Vertiginosas, un grupo cubano de rock, participara brevemente en los carnavales habaneros de ese año.

Tanto las estaciones de radio como los canales de televisión fueron nacionalizados y el contenido de sus programas totalmente modificado. Los músicos se convirtieron en empleados del Estado, percibiendo un salario fijo de entre 200 y 300 pesos al mes. Eran evaluados periódicamente con una calificación de A para un virtuoso hasta descender a F. Otros tuvieron que firmar contratos indefinidos con una de las «empresas» (identificadas con los nombres de figuras como Ignacio Piñeiro o Adolfo Guzmán), a las que todos tenían que reportar y pertenecer. Estas empresas eran las encargadas de autorizar cualquier viaje al exterior y obtener las visas necesarias, incluso tenían el poder para cambiar grupos o formar otros nuevos. Por otra parte, raramente alguien se quedaba sin trabajo, y la condena por reiteradas malas actuaciones significaba el ingreso en cualquiera de las crecientes escuelas de música que ofrecían una educación libre.

Uno de los cambios fundamentales del nuevo sistema fue romper los lazos entre la demanda de actuaciones o la venta de discos y el éxito artístico. Bajo el modelo cubano, los músicos reciben sus sueldos modestos y son requeridos a actuar regularmente, sin considerar realmente si existe o no demanda para su tipo de música.

Sin embargo, el caudal creativo es tal que la música prosperó, a pesar de tantas ausencias notables. El empleo masivo combinado con la indiferencia ante las reglas del mercado, por ejemplo, hizo que decenas de trovadores y soneros provinciales, algunos de dudosa calidad y otros excelentes, siguieran actuando. El autoaislamiento de Cuba se intensificó en la década de los 70, a raíz de un terrible Congreso de Cultura; comenzaban los verdaderos años grises. Es una verdadera ironía que el encerramiento provocado por un nacionalismo exacerbado contribuyera a la preservación de elementos musicales que de otra forma quizá se habrían perdido. Además, con las evidentes mejoras en la atención médica y el ejercicio colectivo, la revolución logró que los músicos vivieran hasta una ancianidad activa, de ahí la vitalidad demostrada por los viejos soneros redescubiertos por el público europeo en los años 90.

APRENDIENDO MÚSICA

La transformación social ocurrida en Cuba produjo un vuelco hacia nuevas directrices educacionales que abarcaron todos los tipos y niveles de enseñanza, incluida la artística. Las primeras Escuelas de Instructores de Arte surgieron en 1961 y un año después se creó la Escuela Nacional de Arte (ENA), un plan pedagógico de proyección nacional. Las extraordinarias cinco Escuelas de Arte de Cubanacán (nombre indígena de la isla, que sustituyó a la zona conocida como Country Club) fueron diseñadas por el arquitecto Ricardo Porro y dos colegas italianos, Roberto Gottardi y Vittorio Garratti, sobre 150 hectáreas de campos de golf, con la misión de construir una ciudad artística para cubrir pintura, escultura, teatro, música, danza moderna y ballet. Aquellos atractivos edificios constituyeron –porque actualmente están destruidos por el abandono– lo más atrevido que logró la revolución arquitectónicamente. Otros edificios de los antiguos clubes de la burguesía fueron aprovechados, formando un inmenso complejo. A pesar de una serie de errores y las estrecheses económicas que siempre ha sufrido el país, se logró desarrollar gradualmente un sistema de enseñanza artística con una red de centros en toda la isla.

Un país no se hace ron sonoro de la noche a la mañana. Desde el siglo XIX se había forjado una tradición musical excelente como podrá comprobar cualquiera que lea mi libro *Orígenes*. Hubo virtuosos de todos los tonos posibles de la piel, desde el contradancista Saumell a los violinistas negros Claudio Brindis de Salas y José White, artistas de fama internacional en su época, o desde Cervantes y Lecuona en las teclas hasta los creadores de canciones imperecederas de principios del XX.

Como ocurrió con los deportes, otra área con un historial respetable en el país, y por tanto, destinada a recabar prestigio y mantener viva la propaganda de éxitos revolucionarios a nivel internacional, el régimen se dio muy pronto cuenta de que tenía que buscar posibles talentos artísticos en la fértil cantera nacional; a ese fin se establecieron las Escuelas Vocacionales de Arte (EVA), centros de nivel elemental en que los jóvenes reciben la enseñanza general hasta el noveno grado; según la selección hecha previamente (mientras más inmaduros mejor) cursan música, artes plásticas, danza o ballet. Entre 1977 y 1985 se instalaron este tipo de escuelas en nueve provincias, algunas con capacidad para régimen de internado, lo que posibilitó la incorporación de niños y jóvenes de las zonas más apartadas, evitando que cientos de posibles talentos se perdieran por falta de condiciones y oportunidades de desarrollo.

Estructurada en tres niveles, al concluir la enseñanza musical a nivel medio-superior el egresado es ya un profesional y puede incorporarse a la esfera laboral. Los estudios de licenciatura se realizan en el Instituto Superior de Arte (ISA) creado en 1976; es importante señalar que se accede a cada nivel mediante rigurosas pruebas de ingreso. En el ISA se imparten las mismas especialidades que en el nivel medio, sumándose dirección de orquesta, musicología y composición. Todas las carreras tienen una duración de cinco años. Según sus estatutos, el ISA, que ya cuenta con filiales en tres provincias con capacidad de internado, debe promover cursos de posgrado y proyectos de investigación científica para profesores y egresados, cosa muy difícil de alcanzar dadas las limitaciones de carácter práctico que sufre el país y la desconfianza que permea todas sus actividades.

De gran importancia fue el sistema que se adoptó para la enseñanza de la guitarra –un privilegio en Hispanoamérica–, que partiendo de la escuela de Tárrega incluye lectura a primera vista, armonía, música de cámara, contrapunto, instrumentación, formas musicales, historia de la música, piano complementario y otras asignaturas. El resultado en los últimos 40 años incluye el mismo número de concertistas de alto nivel y alrededor de 300 obras para el instrumento. Por supuesto, algunos de dichos concertistas y autores ya no viven en Cuba.

Por su parte, muchos viejos músicos, en su mayoría autodidactas, tuvieron que asistir a las Escuelas de Superación Profesional (ESP), planteles creados para capacitar y titular a gente que en su momento no había podido acceder a las escuelas vocacionales o profesionales.

Aunque se supone que el apoyo logístico para una estructura educacional tan formidable debía provenir de la Editora Musical de Cuba (ya desaparecida), publicando obras destinadas a la enseñanza, partituras, metodologías y libros de texto, la realidad fue bien distinta. Todos los egresados con quienes he conversado largamente denunciaron la carencia total de partituras en sus cursos; entraba el profesor, repartía un número de obras extranjeras, ordenando acto seguido que las copiaran, única manera de que tuvieran algún material de enseñanza. Los libros de texto –cuando aparecían– eran copias «fusiladas» de ediciones españolas e inglesas. Sin embargo, en una página de la publicación *Sonoridad cubana*, Nº. 9, 1990, me encontré una lista de quince partituras –¡sólo quince!–, anunciada como «una variada colección para estudiantes o profesionales». De ese número sólo una correspondía a un músico anterior a la revolución: *Dos danzas* (para guitarra), de Ernesto Lecuona.

A través del Instituto Cubano de la Música, durante años en manos de Alicia Perea, antigua profesora de piano ascendida a directora por obra y gracia de sus conexiones con figuras del Comité Central del Partido Comunista, el Estado cubano tuvo buen cuidado de establecer una serie de perfiles ocupacionales, diseñados de acuerdo a las necesidades específicas y a sus ambiciones de largo alcance. De ellos se derivan los planes de estudio, haciendo explícitos los presupuestos artísticos, estéticos y culturales que requiere la formación del músico profesional. Todo esto plantea un constante rehacer de los planes de estudio, supuestamente para incorporar y evaluar las experiencias más novedosas. Con la necesidad de dólares que tiene el Estado, es obvio concluir que las modificaciones van dirigidas a lo que triunfa en el exterior, a los tipos de música más exportables. Luego de una breve estancia en París, la Sra. Perea se dedica ahora a promover su actividad como concertista.

Al momento de escribir me entero de la posible apertura de una escuela para la formación de tríos en Guantánamo, que sería la primera del país; el propósito básico es formar en esa modalidad a las nuevas generaciones en vista de que casi todos los jóvenes quieren meterse en la timba, que es lo que está ahora de moda, y ven a los tríos –aunque éstos se encuentran entre los que más triunfan en Europa, junto a cuartetos y quintetos de cuerdas– como una cosa del pasado.

No obstante, para mí constituye un hermoso ejemplo la gratuidad de la enseñanza musical, garantizando el acceso de jóvenes de cualquier origen con talento artístico. La libertad estética es otra cosa, ya que está condicionada a los intereses políticos del régimen: «Con la revolución todo, contra la revolución, nada» ha sido el motto durante decenios. ¿Y quién decide una cosa o la otra? Durante años persiguieron a los jóvenes que trataban de hacer música popular, llegando a echar de las escuelas al que tocara un son al piano; sólo podían hacerlo clandestinamente.

Otro aspecto importante es la supuesta inclusión de obras cubanas y latinoamericanas en los programas de exámenes, buscando preservar las tradiciones musicales y crear una conciencia de hermandad continental. En la realidad no siempre es así: la obra de Lecuona (el más importante músico cubano) no se enseña ni se estimula su estudio porque el maestro abandonó el país en 1960; aplique el lector esta limitación a las docenas de creadores que se marcharon del país, pero que ya habían sentado las pautas de los frutos que se recogen ahora. Se mantiene a los jóvenes de espaldas a los que les precedieron y como la revolución insiste constantemente en que todo lo anterior a su triunfo es deleznable, usted me dirá. La formación siempre ha consistido en mucha música clásica europea –en el supuesto de que ya los jóvenes irán recogiendo las esencias cubanas a través de lo que escuchan en la radio y en la televisión–, pero esta academización de la enseñanza obedeció tanto a los «lazos fraternales» establecidos hasta 1990 con los países de Europa oriental como al número considerable de instrumentistas rusos, alemanes del este, húngaros, etc., que se sentaron junto a los cubanos en las orquestas sinfónicas del país. Especialmente útiles fueron sus enseñanzas en la sección de cuerdas (violines, viola, cello, contrabajo), bajo la anuencia del pianista Frank Fernández.

FRANK FERNÁNDEZ.

Aunque era mal visto practicar deportes porque podrían dañarse las manos, todos tenían que cumplir con temporadas de tres meses seguidos en lo que se llamó eufemísticamente la «escuela al campo». Conozco a algunos músicos que fueron enviados a limpiar enormes extensiones de marabú (una gran planta seca sumamente espinosa) en la Sierra del Escambray, destrozándose las manos en el empeño, bajo la insistencia de que «los músicos tienen que adquirir conciencia política». Muy útil resultó en toda esa presión un personaje llamado Mario Hidalgo, ya fallecido. Antiguo tripulante del yate *Granma* y preso por Batista desde su desembarco en diciembre de 1956 hasta el triunfo de la revolución, este señor –puesto al frente de la ENA por el propio Fidel Castro– se dedicó a perseguir implacablemente a los jóvenes músicos, buscando homosexuales para humillarlos delante de sus compañeros y sacarlos de la enseñanza. Otra que hizo estragos es Berta Serguera, hermana del peligroso *Papito* Serguera (ver pág. 315), que expulsaba a cualquier alumno sorprendido tocando jazz.

Tengo entendido que a partir de 1995, el vínculo de la enseñanza con la música popular comenzó a mejorar con la creación de los Talleres de Música Popular. Sin embargo, la incorporación de compositores e intérpretes de prestigio es siempre una preocupación, evitando a aquellos artistas que el régimen mantiene en su lista negra, por estar tildados de «desviación ideológica» o por evidenciar tendencias sexuales opuestas al machismo manifiesto del régimen.

Aunque los chicos toman por hecho la garantía de empleo como músico profesional, los dos primeros años de trabajo del recién egresado se limitan a realizar «servicios sociales», otro eufemismo para conducirlos por los senderos estipulados por el Partido Comunista. Como en cualquier otro aspecto de la enseñanza, en el sector musical se busca formar a jóvenes de ambos sexos que sean igualmente aptos profesional y políticamente (lo que quiere decir que hayan sido Pioneros –organización infantil– y miembros de la Asociación de Jóvenes Comunistas, etc.). A los estudiantes se les promete la participación en festivales y concursos nacionales e internacionales, ofertas que siempre están condicionadas a su lealtad al sistema. La presión ideológica nunca cesa en Cuba: si no han dado claras señales de su adhesión, no hay participación.

Un caso concreto de limitación ideológica lo constituyen los Encuentros Latinoamericanos de Enseñanza Artística, que se realizan desde 1986 con una periodicidad bienal y donde el Estado cubano invita a acólitos de su ideología para que confirmen la pobreza de la enseñanza en sus respectivos países y continúen persuadiendo a los jóvenes e inexpertos criollos que viven en el mejor país del mundo para realizarse como músicos.

La cantera no cesa y ya el país cuenta entre 13.000 y 15.000 músicos profesionales, todos dispuestos a lanzarse a buscar «fulas» en el exterior.

LA NUEVA TROVA

La nueva trova fue el primer movimiento musical que devino directamente asociado –política y culturalmente– con la revolución. Siempre acompañada de la guitarra, fue consecuencia de una inquietud mucho más amplia que buscaba desarrollar las formas tradicionales con elementos innovadores tomados del jazz y el uso de instrumentos electrónicos, pero con un evidente contenido de protesta social, lo que en Estados Unidos se llamó *protest song*. Fue tal la diversidad y dispersión de las obras creadas a partir de 1960 –tanto en Norte como en Suramérica– que no resulta fácil delimitar fechas que enmarquen ese proceso de búsqueda de nuevos derroteros estilísticos. Lo cierto es que dio lugar al surgimiento de una relación de hermandad y de mutuas influencias que fue crucial para alimentar una de las tendencias más significativas de la música cubana contemporánea. Es más, no hay duda de que la nueva trova cubana le debe mucho –estilística y conceptualmente– a los artistas rebeldes suramericanos, así como a creadores norteamericanos, franceses, ingleses, italianos y españoles.

Como consecuencia del despertar político motivado por la agudización de los conflictos sociales, en la década de 1950 ya había surgido en el extremo de Suramérica el germen de lo que posteriormente se denominó nueva canción o canción protesta latinoamericana. Este género ha tenido varios nombres, pero el de «canciones de lucha y esperanza» me parece el más apto. Llamarlo «canción política» resulta demasiado restringido, mientras que hablar de «canción comprometida» lo habría relacionado con un movimiento poético identificado como tal. De hecho, hoy día se le conoce también como «el nuevo canto latinoamericano».

El folclor musical de varios países del Cono Sur, saqueado tanto por mezquinos intereses disqueros locales como por algunos compositores «cultos» que lo manipulaban para crear obras de síntesis, cobró un nuevo sentido como arma de denuncia social. Aparecieron solistas y grupos jóvenes de notable calidad que elaboraron el folclor con sofisticación, como la chilena Violeta Parra, una de las primeras en componer canciones de contenido político relacionadas con la explotación del campesinado y los mineros de su país. Más tarde se destacaron Isabel y Ángel Parra junto a Víctor Jara, asesinado por los esbirros de Pinochet en 1973, así como los grupos Inti-Illimani y Quilapayún.

En Argentina y Uruguay la denuncia partió de la música urbana como principal nutriente, dando rotunda respuesta a la brutal represión gubernamental. Asi emergieron, entre otros cantautores, Atahualpa Yupanqui y Mercedes Sosa en Buenos Aires, comprometidos desde hacía tiempo con la lucha política, mientras que Daniel Viglietti, Alfredo Zitarrosa y Los Olimareños cantaron desde Montevideo. Tania Libertad surgió en México casi al mismo tiempo que Judith Reyes y Los Folkloristas, con Gloria Marín en Venezuela y Alejandro Gómez en Perú, los hermanos Carlos y Luis Enrique Mejía Godoy en Nicaragua, Patricio Manns en Chile, el Conjunto Cantaclaro y el Cuarteto Cedrón de Argentina, el grupo Jatari del Ecuador y varios más.

Este movimiento de rebeldía coincidió con una renovación sorprendente del samba: la bossa nova. Música urbana, lanzada en 1958 a partir del álbum *Canción del amor demás* de Alizete Cardoso, el guitarrista

Joao Gilberto presentó un nuevo tipo de síncopa que devendría característica del promisorio estilo. Un año después, con *Desafinado*, el mismo músico empleó el término «bossa nova» por primera vez. Para 1962, con la música cubana encerrada en la isla, la bossa, gran deudora del jazz, llegó a Estados Unidos donde encontró hábiles promotores.

Entre 1960 y 1974, la mayor parte de los artistas arriba mencionados abundaron en tonadas repetitivas referidas a las luchas de liberación, principalmente dirigidas contra la guerra en Vietnam y en apoyo a Cuba comunista, en un tono épico disfrazado de elementos folclóricos locales. Cantos que llevaron al primer Encuentro de la Canción Protesta, celebrado bajo los auspicios de la Casa de las Américas de La Habana (29 de julio al 10 de agosto de 1967). Entre los norteamericanos se hallaban presentes Julius Lester, Irwin Silber y Barbara Dane, los británicos Ewan MacColl y Peggy Seeger (nacida en USA, hermana de Pete), los italianos Ivan Della Mea y Elena Morandi, con Luis Cilia de Portugal y el valenciano Raimón.

Un temprano equivalente cubano de lo que significó la iniciativa suramericana fue Carlos Puebla (ver pág. 79), cantor de tendencia comunista que se dedicó a glosar los logros de la incipiente revolución. Convertido de la noche a la mañana en el embajador musical del gobierno, Puebla recorrió casi todas las naciones americanas regando sus sones, a veces solo y o en formación de cuarteto. Gran parte de su música consistía en panfletos propagandísticos mezclados con números divertidos, menos cargados de «mensaje», y siempre dentro del conocido tumbaíto criollo. Su audiencia recibía encantada aquellas noticias de la isla, supuestamente rodeada de enemigos por todas partes, canciones envueltas en los ritmos tradicionales que hacían reconocible al país de origen desde cualquier escenario. Carlos Puebla era entonces el único músico en quien el régimen confiaba para representarlo plenamente; pero ya tenía sus años y había que buscarle un reemplazo novedoso, a tono con la imagen cultural que Castro buscaba para prestigiar su revolución y ganarse el corazón de millones de seguidores centro y suramericanos.

Una mezcla de coincidencia, intereses musicales similares y oportunismo hizo que los jóvenes Silvio Rodríguez y Pablo Milanés se conocieran en 1968 gracias a la vocalista Omara Portuondo, quien los presentó en un estudio de televisión donde se pasaron varias horas cantándose sus canciones. En aquel momento no tenían idea de que ambos se convertirían pronto en cofundadores del movimiento de la nueva trova cubana, aportando su indudable talento a este cambio drástico del bolero tradicional. Y es realmente simbólico que haya sido una excelente intérprete de filin quien pusiera en contacto a ambos músicos, porque la nueva lírica que revitalizó la canción cubana y la catapultó nuevamente al plano internacional tenía bastante de filin en sus inicios.

Un análisis objetivo revela que Silvio y Pablo han tenido la dicha de hacer su propia revolución con sus composiciones, y reconocen que fue el pueblo español quien primero les tributó su simpatía y reconocimiento, y quien contribuyó a proyectar su música. En medio de la transición a la democracia, los jóvenes de aquí se identificaron con unos códigos que sonaban a esperanza; desde entonces, mucha gente sigue siendo sus incondicionales. Apareciendo solos con sus guitarras o acompañados de AfroCuba o Irakere, esa meca del espectáculo que es México también acogió y difundió a la nueva trova sin prejuicio alguno.

PABLO MILANÉS (1967).

Como sus colegas del Cono Sur, Silvio y Pablo han cantado a la América de los hambrientos y explotados, de los oprimidos o encarcelados, de los desaparecidos y masacrados, desde una Cuba «asediada por el imperialismo». Pero mientras aquellos hicieron de la irreverencia y de la sátira armas musicales para atacar a diestra y siniestra, nuestros cantautores han logrado expresar sus ideas sin recabar en las evidentes contradicciones sociales que prevalecen en su propio país. Maestros ilusionistas, han hecho creer a millares de admiradores que sus canciones se vierten desde un lugar donde la justicia social está firmemente implantada. Sin embargo, parece innecesario afirmar que tienen mucho talento.

Silvio Rodríguez (1946) comenzó a cantar piezas originales, frescas y de calidad temática y melódica en 1967, poco antes de su estreno en el Palacio de Bellas Artes, durante un recital organizado por un periódico en honor de la cantautora de filin Teresita Fernández. En agosto de ese mismo año se celebró el Primer Encuentro de la Canción Protesta en la Casa de las Américas de La Habana, en el que Silvio no participó porque aún no era conocido. Poco después comenzó a escucharse su voz en la radio, mientras hacía sus primeras apariciones en televisión y centros culturales. Pronto se sumó a los jóvenes cantautores que se reunían periódicamente en la Casa de las Américas: entre ellos estaban Pablo Milanés y **Noel Nicola** (1946), hijo del profesor de guitarra Isaac Nicola, quien fuera maestro de Leo Brouwer.

Ya desde el cambio político en 1959 Silvio se había unido a la Juventud Socialista (comunista) de su pueblo, San Antonio de los Baños, y en 1960 se integró en la Asociación de Jóvenes Rebeldes. Como muchos otros jóvenes, creyó ciegamente en Castro. Creció aceptando el dogma de que ser revolucionario era ser fidelista; y ser fidelista era repetir a pies juntillas el discurso del comandante, apoderarse de sus palabras y devolvérselas con la fidelidad de un disco.

Durante el bachillerato conoció a **Vicente Feliú** (1947), quien más tarde se convirtió en otro de los máximos exponentes de la nueva trova. En 1960 el gobierno declaró la guerra contra el analfabetismo: las escuelas cesaron su actividad durante un año y Silvio Rodríguez fue uno de los 100.000 jóvenes que se sumaron a las brigadas de maestros improvisados que convivieron entre 6 y 10 meses con familias campesinas.

A los 16 años entró a trabajar en la revista *Mella*, órgano propagandístico de la Unión de Jóvenes Comunistas. Sumamente delgado y ya con poco pelo, usaba entonces unas gafas enormes. Un compañero le enseñó los primeros acordes en la guitarra mientras escribía poemas y enviaba colaboraciones a otras revistas. Comenzó a estudiar arte y poco después pintó un Fidel Castro a tamaño natural y vestido de verde olivo en la cocina de su casa; su obsesión era tal que llegó incluso a tallar la efigie del máximo líder en madera. Por la misma época estudió piano hasta que en 1964 tuvo que abandonarlo todo para incorporarse al ejército, cumpliendo su servicio de tres años y tres meses. Para él constituía un honor estar en las fuerzas armadas, pero después de varios fracasos durante el entrenamiento dada su débil constitución física, fue enviado a la revista *Venceremos*, instalada en un campamento militar. En aquella época, y para no aburrirse, comenzó a hacer canciones de temática amorosa y de tono marcadamente pesimista.

Aceptado ya como hombre de confianza del régimen, en 1965 pasó a la revista *Verde Olivo*, órgano oficial del ejército, donde permaneció hasta terminar su servicio militar. En las aburridas noches de guardia recurría a la guitarra y con ella expresaba sus sentimientos. «Ya está el flaco jodiendo con su guitarrita», solían comentar otros reclutas. Sin embargo, comenzó a participar en actividades culturales en otras unidades militares y en festivales de aficionados de las Fuerzas Armadas Revolucionarias.

Una noche, el director de la revista leyó unos poemas de Silvio y comprendió que el chico tenía talento. Le prestó algunos libros que impresionaron al sensible adolescente, quien descubrió que podía haber poesía en cualquier tema o lugar, el problema residía en encontrarla. Conoció entonces a Emilia, una joven con inquietudes artísticas y literarias, un primer amor que le dio a leer al peruano César Vallejo, cuya poesía ocuparía posteriormente una dimensión decisiva en sus canciones. Entretanto, iba adquiriendo mayor destreza con la guitarra y hacía incursiones en ritmos de bolero, calypso y rock.

Aunque sus primeras referencias eran las de la música popular bailable, carecía de influencias concretas. Le gustaba Charles Aznavour porque tenía otra dinámica diferente a la de los temas manidos que diariamente escuchaba. También se enamoró de los Beatles. Durante un permiso descubrió en su casa un viejo disco de Sindo Garay. «De pronto oí sonoridades que tenían que ver con mis sonoridades», declaró más tarde. Otra importante sorpresa fue descubrir que Vicente Feliú también había aprendido a tocar la guitarra y concebía textos con una perspectiva nueva, arrinconando los esterotipos machistas y cantándole a la mujer desde un sentimiento compartido e igualitario. Sin embargo, en lugar de relacionarse con otros músicos, a Silvio Rodríguez le encantaba vincularse a jóvenes poetas y narradores. «Había un sentido crítico y me sugerían lo que era mejor; eso me permitió adiestrarme, ver la canción con una óptica poética», explicó posteriormente.

Más tarde conoció al pianista **Mario Romeu** (1924), que impresionado por las canciones que le escuchó, le invitó a una prueba de grabación en el Instituto Cubano de Radio y Televisión.

Cuando le dieron de baja en el ejército se encontró desconcertado: tenía una vida con múltiples caminos por delante, casi cien canciones y 20 años de edad. Mario Romeu logró presentarlo entonces en el programa televisivo «Música y estrellas». Nervioso, con mucho miedo escénico y calzado con sus queridas botas militares, hizo penetrar a los espectadores en la dimensión cósmica que había imaginado en sus canciones, un mundo surrealista, seductor y misterioso, preludio de lo que sería una nueva forma de cantarle al amor y a los sueños.

Cuando murió Che Guevara en Bolivia en octubre de 1967, Silvio se encontraba en la playa de Varadero realizando actuaciones en el marco

del Festival de la Canción. Allí entró en contacto directo con el jazz a través del grupo Sonorama 6, al cual pertenecían **Martín Rojas** (1944) y
Eduardo Ramos (1946). Fueron ellos quienes lo introdujeron a la música
brasileña. Se le abrieron más perspectivas aún por la influencia del rock y
por el descubrimiento de la creatividad de los españoles Joan Manuel Serrat, Raimón y Luis Eduardo Aute.

Más tarde condujo el programa dominical televisivo «Mientras tanto», el cual definió años después como «la primera trinchera que tuve
para arrojar mis canciones». Y es que en su combativo corazón siempre
ha conservado la pasión por lo militar. La realidad es que olvidaba el
guión en el plató y se ponía muy nervioso.

En febrero de 1968 Silvio, Pablo y Noel ofrecieron su primer recital
conjunto en la Casa de las Américas. No tenían ni idea de que estaban
propiciando un movimiento artístico que se llamaría la nueva trova, porque aún no se le había dado ese nombre. El autor de *Mientras tanto, El
barquero, La víspera de siempre, La canción de la trova, Hay un grupo
que dice, La era está pariendo un corazón, Canción del elegido, El Mayor, Rabo de nube, En el claro de la luna, Sueño con serpientes, Te doy
una canción, Unicornio, Óleo de mujer con sombrero, Ojalá* y muchas
obras más, ha afirmado que

Mi canto no pudo haber surgido sin esta revolución que lo sustenta y anima, y
porque, gracias a ella, en el terreno artístico e ideológico puedo proponer mejores
cosas que las que sustenta un mundo decadente.

La voz de Silvio Rodríguez no es cálida ni particularmente seducto-
ra, sino más bien aguda, de un timbre casi metálico y bastante frágil. Al
escucharlo, uno llega a temer que en cualquier momento se le quiebre, y
ese riesgo forma parte de su peculiar atractivo. Es un verdadero poeta de
la segunda mitad del siglo XX; quizá el secreto resida en que siempre ha
logrado trasmitir una gran franqueza, un no aparentar lo que no es, pero
sin adoptar una actitud subversiva ni siquiera ligeramente crítica del régimen. No obstante, su contribución comenzó siendo una bocanada de aire
fresco en un ámbito como el lúdico, por lo común tan especulativo como
artificial. «Silvio Rodríguez es un poeta que canta», ha afirmado alguna
vez el escritor uruguayo Mario Benedetti.

A lo largo de su estancia en el Grupo de Experimentación Sonora (al
que me referiré más adelante), musicalizó varías películas, como *Testimo-*

nio, de Rogelio París, *Nombre de guerra: Miguel Enríquez,* de Patricio Castilla, y *Nace una comunidad,* de Víctor Casaus.

Lo que es cuestionable ha sido su silencio ante la zozobra a que ha estado sometido el pueblo cubano durante más de cuatro décadas bajo el castrismo. Mientras que sus amigos de vanguardia denunciaban los atropellos y la ausencia de libertad en Suramérica, Silvio y Pablo cerraron los ojos ante el aparato de intimidación totalitaria de un régimen incapaz de satisfacer las necesidades más perentorias del pueblo cubano. Comulgando con la generación del entusiasmo, siguieron suscritos a los primeros avances positivos de la revolución. No han sido críticos en su propio patio. Pero ni Pablo ni Silvio son profetas: un profeta es el que ve y dice la verdad.

SARA GONZÁLEZ.

En diciembre de 1972 se creó oficialmente en Manzanillo, Oriente, el movimiento de la nueva trova, auspiciado por la Unión de Jóvenes Comunistas con el objetivo de «orientar» a los cientos de jóvenes que habían comenzado a expresarse por su cuenta bajo la influencia de Silvio, Pablo y otros cantautores. La decisión había surgido a raíz de un opresivo Primer Congreso Nacional de Educación y Cultura, celebrado poco antes en La Habana, en que se declaró: «El arte es un arma revolucionaria».

Una veintena de cantautores se reunieron en Manzanillo. Actualizando la época de los viejos trovadores y de los filinistas, todos tenían en común el instrumento transportable que les permitía los mejores recursos rítmicos, armónicos y melódicos: la guitarra. Ilusionados por la oportunidad de no encasillarse en un estilo, género o ritmo determinado, los jóvenes artistas asumieron una conciencia política cargada de autocrítica, que aunque hacía continuas alusiones al propio trovador, integraba elementos de la vida cotidiana que se transformaban en pequeñas epopeyas fundidas con el amor y la lucha revolucionaria. Pero sin tocar ningún tema realmente escabroso para el régimen. Como excepción, Noel Nicola logró producir algunas piezas críticas, sin bien limitadas a sátiras contra la burocracia, los convencionalismos o el machismo.

Quiero dejar aclarado que Silvio y Pablo contribuyen religiosamente con los ingresos de sus giras y las cuantiosas ventas de discos a mantener los Estudios de Grabaciones y Ediciones Musicales, la omnipotente EGREM. Arropada por el Instituto de la Música, que a su vez depende del Ministerio de Cultura, la EGREM es un organismo estatal surgido en 1964 tras la nacionalización del sello Panart, la primera discográfica cubana cuyo quehacer se remonta a 1943. La EGREM contribuye con el 20 por ciento de sus ingresos al presupuesto nacional. Lleva a cabo la producción de discos y casetes a través de varios sellos, fabrica instrumentos musicales, edita partituras y libros de música, y organiza las presentaciones públicas de más de 200 agrupaciones artísticas y solistas. Un verdadero negocio.

Con los años y el desgaste, el movimiento de la nueva canción latinoamericana ha tendido a institucionalizarse, pero seguirá teniendo presencia mientras haya opresión política y económica. Ya no suenan tanto los nombres de Sara González y Noel Nicola y los de otros fundadores de la versión cubana. Nicola, que fue de los primeros en componer «canciones arenga» cuando todavía trabajaba en el Instituto de Etnología y Folclor bajo el magisterio de Argeliers León, había formado antes parte de un grupo de seis jóvenes fascinados por la invasión del rock, la balada italiana estilo Fausto Papeti, la canción francesa y por supuesto, los Beatles. En el GESI aprendió bastante, pero su humildad le hizo abandonar la avidez de los escenarios –propia de sus colegas– para convertirse en promotor cultural. No obstante, Noel Nicola ha realizado una importante labor al musicalizar canciones para niños, de ahí sus discos *Tricolor* y *Papaloteros*.

Quedan Pablo y Silvio, aunque han surgido otras figuras que han hecho una crítica más o menos velada al sistema, como Pedro Luis Ferrer y Carlos Varela, y hasta una tercera generación de nuevos troveros, como Gema y Pável, envueltos en una onda más existencialista, y que prohijaron a su vez a una camada de jóvenes enmarcados ahora bajo el nombre Habana Abierta (ver pág. 284).

El caso de **Pedro Luis Ferrer** (1953) es también interesante. Aprendió por sí mismo a tocar la guitarra y el tres, y al trasladarse a la capital en 1969 comenzó a asociarse con Carlos Alfonso, el líder del grupo Síntesis. Después de trabajar con Los Dada, un grupo similar de fusión, Pedro Luis comenzó a aparecer como cantautor; su originalidad y cantar nasal pronto atrajeron la atención, llegando a publicar tres LP y realizar una gira europea en 1974. Algunos de sus temas, especialmente *Inseminación artifical*, en que se burla oblicuamente de los experimentos realizados por el propio Comandante en Jefe, le granjearon la enemistad del régimen, hasta que en 1985, al regreso de una gira al Perú –y tengo entendido que debido a declaraciones alabando a Celia Cruz– fue interrogado y durante casi diez años le fue prohibido actuar en el país ni salir al extranjero. En 1994 Pedro Luis Ferrer se trasladó a Miami y en 1999 publicó un nuevo disco que pertenece al sello estadounidense Havana Caliente. Ahora trabaja con un grupo de ocho músicos que incluye a su hija Lena como vocalista y percusionista.

Aunque muchos así lo creen, el cantautor **Pablo Milanés** (1943) nunca ha sido el *alter ego* de Silvio Rodríguez. De hecho, se formó mucho antes, desde que siendo muy joven y extremadamente delgado le dejaba oír sus obras a Aida Diestro, la gorda que formó el cuarteto de voces femeninas más importante de Cuba, convirtiéndose en su chico mimado. Mucho ha llovido desde que su madre lo sorprendió, con sólo cinco años, cantando entero y sin desafinar *Juan Charrasqueado*, un popular corrido mexicano, y comprendió que su hijo iba a ser cantante. Están sus labores como tipógrafo, su debut profesional con el Cuarteto del Rey, con el que desarrolló el oficio de vocalista que más tarde aplicó a su Cuarteto Los Bucaneros, después vino el encuentro con el filin y su antológica canción *Mis veintidós años* (una balada filinesca que pronto da paso a una guajira-son de tema filosófico), los vínculos con Silvio, Noel, Martín y los avatares con el Grupo de Experimentación Sonora, sin olvidar las presentaciones en la Casa de las Américas en presencia de Haydée Santamaría, directora de dicha institución y heroína del Moncada y Sierra Maestra, quien lo cobijó hasta suicidarse en 1984. Están su experiencia chilena, así como los éxitos en España, México, Brasil, Venezuela y Argentina.

Pero sobre todo, me pregunto si para Pablo Milanés ha llovido lo suficiente como para olvidar cuando lo internaron a la fuerza durante casi un año en una de las prisiones rurales llamadas Unidades Militares de Apoyo a la Producción (UMAP) en la remota provincia de Camagüey, porque los miembros del Comité de Defensa de la Revolución (CDR) de su calle decidieron que de algún modo oblicuo sus canciones ocultaban contrarrevolución, mariconería o ambas cosas a la vez. O sencillamente por vivir la *dolce vita* y no tener un trabajo fijo. ¿Acaso no cantaba en el Cuarteto Del Rey? Porque ya sabían los del CDR que aquellos jóvenes negros pertenecían a una iglesia de Adventistas del Séptimo Día, a quienes la revolución les había declarado la guerra junto a otras organizaciones religiosas.

Mientras se reponía de un intento de suicidio, Pablo compuso *Mis veintidós años*. Lo sacaron de aquella prisión para lavarle el cerebro, lo casaron con la hija de un capitán de la Seguridad del Estado y lo encerraron a vivir en un edificio del Vedado. Hasta que cedió y resucitó como el Pablo Milanés que hoy conocemos. Terminó ofreciendo su enorme talento a sus propios verdugos.

El saxo Paquito D'Rivera ha revelado en sus memorias que al encontrárselo una noche aprovechó para preguntarle por qué hacía tanto tiempo que no lo veía en televisión. «No, mulato, no más televisión pa'mí», le contestó Pablo. «Coño, cada vez que llevo una canción nueva tienen que oirla primero *Papito*, los "segurosos" de la comisión de ética revolucionaria, el Partido, me hacen cambiar pedazos de los textos, que si se puede malinterpretar esto o lo otro. No y no. ¡Pal carajo con *Papito* y su televisión!». *Papito* era el comandante Jorge Serguera, puesto al frente del Instituto Cubano de Radio y Televisión porque en Cuba siempre se las han arreglado para enviar a los organismos culturales a los tíos que menos saben del tema y que carecen de sensibilidad. Pero estos acosadores de artistas son incondicionales del Máximo Líder.

A diferencia de Silvio, Pablo Milanés ha cantado música de otros autores y además ha compuesto *Tú mi desengaño, Estás lejos, Para vivir, Su nombre puede ponerse en verso, A Santiago, La vida no vale nada, Hombre que vas creciendo, Los caminos, Años, El breve espacio en que no estás* (inspirada en la actriz Lilí Rentería Llerena), *Defiende el amor que te enseñó, Proposiciones, Quiero ser de nuevo el que te amó, Yolanda* (Yolanda Benet, madre de sus tres hijas mayores, su esposa entre 1969-73), entre muchas otras canciones. Su música ha recorrido el mundo en la voz de varios intérpretes; sus letras contienen frases de altura poética y sus melodías son muestra de una sensibilidad excepcional; se le reconoce también su actividad en establecer fuertes lazos con la música de Brasil.

A partir de una gira por Argentina en 1984 comenzó a disfrutar de mayor popularidad entre los propios cubanos, aunque ya una década antes era capaz de colmar estadios en otros países, con gente dispuesta a cantar al unísono todo su repertorio, cumpliéndose aquello de «ver para creer». Sobre esta evidente contradicción, Pablo ha declarado:

No es un secreto que hemos crecido en la preferencia nacional de afuera hacia adentro. De inicio, trascendimos a Europa en especial, con amplia difusión en España, luego de 1976 con la apertura democrática. Después llegamos a varios países de América y en la actualidad (1987) convocamos una buena cantidad de público en Cuba.

Al igual que Silvio, Pablo ha «disparado» infinidad de balas invisibles en sus canciones, esgrimiendo un fantasmal machete aguerrido y otros mitos guerrilleros cubanos, así como la queja por la pérdida del Chile de Allende, que rompió los planes de Fidel Castro para el Cono Sur. Temas que siempre ha logrado disfrazar con instrumentaciones estupendas, en que a menudo aparece el tumbao criollo, como en la canción a su hija Haydée.

EL GRUPO DE EXPERIMENTACIÓN SONORA

En junio de 1969, al terminar su servicio militar, Pablo pasó a trabajar al Instituto Cubano del Arte e Industria Cinematográficos (ICAIC), junto con Silvio, Noel Nicola y Eduardo Ramos. Allí integró el Grupo de Experimentación Sonora (GESI), que se formó a instancias de Alfredo Guevara, amigo íntimo de Castro y entonces director del ICAIC, con la intención de crear una nueva cultura sonora acorde con la política. Años más tarde se incorporaron Sara González y Amaury Pérez, mientras que Vicente Feliú sólo pasó esporádicamente por los estudios. También participaron originalmente los instrumentistas Sergio Vitier (guitarra), Leonardo Acosta (saxo alto, fliscornio, flauta) y tres jóvenes graduados de la Escuela Nacional de Arte: Pablo Menéndez (guitarra), Leoginaldo Pimentel (batería) y Emiliano Salvador (piano). En distintos momentos colaboraron Genaro García Caturla (flauta), Lucas de la Guardia (clarinete), Amado del Rosario (oboe), Norberto Carrillo (percusión) y Carlos Averhoff y Manuel Valera (saxos).

EL CANTAUTOR AMAURY PÉREZ.

Las materias impartidas incluían solfeo con Juan Elósegui, armonía a cargo de Federico Smith, electroacústica por el ingeniero de sonido Jerónimo Labrada. **Leo Brouwer,** compositor, director y guitarrista de fama internacional, enseñaba morfología, orquestación y estética musical, y les inició además, en palabras de Silvio, en «una materia un poco que él inventa y que pudiera ser quizás la ética del arte, ya que es demasiado general para denominarla».

Los objetivos del GESI buscaban renovar la música popular, recuperando sus raíces más auténticas, el estudio de las diferentes técnicas de composición y realización, y la elaboración de música para cine. Leo Brouwer planteó las siguientes líneas de trabajo: la música pop actual / elementos esenciales de la música cubana / la canción actual y su fuerza de comunicación social / el fenómeno beat en la música pop / la relación musical entre Brasil y Cuba / los formatos de sonoridad / el arte trascendente / el arte momentáneo / la experimentación electrónica aplicada a la música popular / el jazz / el arte abierto, el happening (arte casual) y su posible cohesión social.

Hacia 1973 la labor del GESI se caracterizó por una mayor proyección hacia los recitales en vivo y por la grabación de seis LP representativos de su quehacer, aparte de algunas grabaciones compartidas con figuras y grupos destacados. También promovió giras a otras provincias, así como recitales en escuelas y fábricas, ante unidades militares y en la sala de la Cinemateca del ICAIC.

EL PIANISTA EMILIANO SALVADOR.

La película *La primera carga al machete*, dirigida por Manuel Octavio Gómez, musicalizada por Leo Brouwer, fue el primer filme que utilizó canciones de los jóvenes trovadores, en este caso de Pablo Milanés: melodías de la vieja y la nueva trova caminaron de la mano en esta reconstrucción de la memoria histórica.

En los años en que participó en el GESI, Pablo Milanés creó todo tipo de temas y géneros, como el guaguancó *Los caminos* o *Su nombre puede ponerse en verso*, dedicado al líder vietnamita Ho Chi Min, con texto de Félix Pita Rodríguez. También compuso la *Canción del constructor*, *América: tu distancia* y *Éramos*, sobre un texto de José Martí. El propio Silvio ha declarado: «Conocer a Pablo era conocer una maravilla, y oírlo cantar era recibir lecciones de musicalidad por sus composiciones y por la manera de cantarlas».

Era tan prolífico produciendo canciones, conciertos y partituras para filmes y cadenas de televisión extranjeras, que con tales ingresos logró persuadir al Jefe Máximo de crear la Fundación Pablo Milanés en 1993 para fomentar la creatividad entre músicos jóvenes y encaminar varios proyectos: el sello discográfico PM Records, la editorial PM, la revista *Proposiciones*, la productora de vídeo PM, el centro de información cultural PM informática y la Casa de la Nacionalidad. Era la primera vez que se creaba una entidad cubana de carácter civil, no gubernamental, autónoma y sin fines de lucro. Poco más tarde fueron súbitamente cerrados, como toda iniciativa individual en la isla, por orden del mismo que la había autorizado. Todo este embrollo fue seguido de un empeoramiento en la ya delicada salud del famoso cantautor.

Quizá el movimiento de la nueva trova no ha significado una renovación literaria en sí mismo, sin que este juicio obste para afirmar que existen en su seno auténticos poetas. Los textos de Pablo y Silvio, particularmente los del primero, suelen mantener una discreta rima, preferentemente asonante, que crea esa recurrencia sonora indispensable para la canción. Por lo demás, sus versos más románticos narran, dialogan, deslizan la ironía, obligan a reflexionar sobre lo que estaba ante nuestros ojos y en nuestros corazones, y que de tanto mirarlo y vivirlo no lo apreciábamos.

EL PANORAMA SE MODERNIZA

Un momento clave en el desarrollo jazzístico en la isla fue la creación de la **Orquesta Cubana de Música Moderna**, sorpresivamente autorizada en abril de 1967. El director designado fue el saxo **Armando Romeu**, perteneciente a una prestigiosa familia de músicos. Romeu había organizado su primera orquesta tipo jazz band en 1933, con la que hizo una extensa gira por Suramérica. En 1942 creó su mejor formación: la orquesta del cabaré Tropicana. Era simpatizante de la revolución y tenía el prestigio indudable de haber dirigido dicha orquesta sin interrupción durante 25 años. De la generosidad profesional de Armando Romeu se han dicho muchas cosas, pero quiero dejar aquí constancia de que aprendió a escribir música en el sistema Braille sólo para ayudar a su amigo, el brillante pianista Frank Emilio Flynn. Como asistente de dirección nombraron al pianista y arreglista **Rafael Somavilla** (1927-80); este admirable artista poseía unos conocimientos y un talento nato para orquestar y arreglar las más difíciles melodías.

La decisión de formar la orquesta significó un cambio radical en la política del régimen sobre una música hasta entonces perseguida o cuando menos mal vista por extranjerizante. Pronto aparecieron instrumentos y enseres importados: guitarras y bajos eléctricos, amplificadores, baterías americanas, saxofones Selmer, una organeta Farisa italiana, boquillas y otros accesorios indispensables para los músicos. Por órdenes superiores sacaron de sus centros de trabajo a gente clave para el proyecto: Orlando López *Cachaíto*, Linares y Luis Escalante fueron llamados de la Sinfónica, Chucho Valdés y el guitarrista Carlos Emilio del Teatro Musical, Andrés Castro y Guillermo Barreto de las orquestas de televisión, y un largo etcétera que incluía a Arturo Sandoval. Paquito D'Rivera, que a la sazón cumplía el servicio militar obligatorio, fue relevado de su unidad.

La orquesta debutó en Guane, un pueblito olvidado, al extremo más occidental de la isla, y llegó a grabar dos discos para el sello cubano Areíto. Después se organizaron giras por todo el país, incluyendo conciertos tumultuarios en los teatros Amadeo Roldán y Karl Marx de la capital, donde la gente se mataba por entrar y disfrutar de la interpretación de canciones de los Beatles, Ray Charles y otros artistas extranjeros.

La Orquesta de Música Moderna participó en la feria mundial Expo'67 de Montreal, Canadá, sin la contribución de tres músicos importantes que a última hora no pudieron acceder al avión por decisión del resentido **Manuel Duchesne Cuzán** (1932), director titular de la Orquesta Sinfónica Nacional y, desgraciadamente, persona muy influyente en la política cultural del país. Tampoco fueron a Montreal Chucho Valdés, Paquito D'Rivera, Carlos Emilio, Orlando López *Cachaíto* ni Enrique Pla, en preparación a una presentación muy especial en el Festival Jazz-Jamboree de Varsovia, Polonia, como el Quinteto Cubano de Jazz.

El entusiasmo suscitado por la creación de la orquesta declinó notablemente cuando empezaron a acompañar a cantantes pop y a tocar en *shows* de variedades. Lo de Montreal seguramente demostró las dificultades de viajar con una plantilla tan numerosa. Cuando en 1968 se formó una especie de Music Hall de Cuba, con Pacho Alonso, Los Bucaneros, Carlos Puebla y la Orquesta Aragón entre otros, se hizo una selección de sólo nueve músicos para acompañar el *show* que los llevaría de gira por varios «países amigos», como llamaban los jerarcas políticos a Alemania del Este, Bulgaria, Rumanía, Checoslovaquia, Hungría

Los mejores: ARMANDO ROMEU

Director de numerosas agrupaciones musicales, orquestador, compositor, saxo y flautista, incursionó en casi todos los géneros musicales cubanos y en la música norteamericana; bajo su orientación se formaron varias generaciones de instrumentistas excelentes. Una trayectoria de más de medio siglo acredita a este pionero del jazz en Cuba en la década de 1920. Armando Romeu (1911-2002) es uno de los pocos latinos que aparece en la *Enciclopedia del jazz* del crítico británico Leonard Feather.

Miembro de una prominente familia de músicos (sobrino del pianista danzonero Antonio María Romeu), Armando fue instruido por su padre y a los ocho años integraba la Banda Municipal de Regla. Estudió flauta con Alfredo Brito y a menudo practicaba con Antonio Arcaño (ver pág. 157). Pero en 1924 su carrera dio un vuelco cuando, tocando en el Jockey Club, su grupo alternaba con la banda del norteamericanno Ted Naddy. Después de comprarle el saxo a un músico de la orquesta comenzó a trabajar con este instrumento en el cine Céspedes junto al pianista Nacho Alemany.

Yo había adquirido la escuela norteamericana de jazz y pronto me adapté al género. Y empecé a tocar en bailes con las primeras orquestas que iban apareciendo en Cuba. Muchos directores venían durante el verano a contratar músicos jazzistas porque eran muy buenos lectores.

Los primeros saxos que se destacaron fueron Germán LeBatard (que tocaba en el hotel Almendares), Luis López Viana (en el hotel Sevilla) y Armando Romeu en el Casino Nacional; a menudo se reunían con otros músicos para realizar las primeras jam sessions. Siempre consideró que su estadía en el Nacional con la orquesta del estadounidense Earl Carpenter constituyó una «experiencia esencial» en su carrera.

Estudioso y dedicado, solía detenerse a diario junto a la casa en que el joven pianista José Echániz estudiaba el repertorio clásico. Curiosamente, el flautista Belisario López (ver págs. 160-161) le enseñó historia y Amadeo Roldán (ver pág. 202) matemáticas. Por aquellos años conoció al impresionante mexicano Julián Carrillo, iniciador del tipo de composición que utiliza cuartos de tono, y a quien se le conoce como el «inventor del sonido 13». Gran emprendedor en el campo de la radio, que iniciaba su ascendente marcha, Armando trabajó con su padre en la emisora PWX; después instaló una fábrica de rollos de pianola junto a su hermano Antonio María.

Cuando aparecieron las primeras jazz band entre 1925-30, los Hermanos Curbelo, Hermanos Palau, Los Diplomáticos de Maya, Hermanos Castro y otras, Romeu tocó con casi todas ellas; también trabajó en el teatro Payret con Ernesto Lecuona.

La creación de la Orquesta Siboney de Alfredo Brito en 1930 le permitió tocar en el aristocrático Country Club. Dos años después, esta agrupación comenzó una exitosa gira por Europa como parte de un espectáculo cubano-español. Al regresar a La Habana decidió abandonar la Siboney para formar su propia orquesta, que debutó en el cabaré Eden Concert (luego llamado Zombie Club, y situado frente al Hotel Plaza). Aquellos años 30 era la época de las balaceras entre los jóvenes revolucionarios y los «porristas» del dictador Gerardo Machado. La situación económica obligó a Romeu a disolver esa primera orquesta; pero pronto organizó otra y con ella actuó en 1936 en el Hotel Nacional, seguido de una gira por Suramérica. En Chile, luego de familiarizarse con el espectáculo de Carmen Amaya y sus Gitanos, escribió *Momento español*.

De vuelta en Cuba se unió a la Casino de la Playa, donde conoció a uno de los mejores saxos criollos, Gustavo Mas (1918-2001), quien años después tocó con la banda de Woody Herman. En 1940 formó la Orquesta Bellamar con el trompeta Luis Escalante, trabajando en el Sans Souci hasta que el lujoso cabaré cerró en los años de la Segunda Guerra Mundial y la Bellamar se desintegró. Después de tocar en diversas agrupaciones y componer música para espectáculos teatrales, el infatigable Armando Romeu logró formar una nueva orquesta. Eso fue en 1942, y esta vez logró permanecer al frente de ella durante 25 años en el cabaré Tropicana. Los mejores músicos del momento desfilaron por aquella agrupación ejemplar, contando con arreglos del propio Armando, de *Chico* O'Farrill, de Roberto Sánchez Ferrer, de *Peruchín* y de Bebo Valdés, pero también con las transcripciones que hacía Armando, directamente de los discos, de arreglos de las orquestas de Duke Ellington, Stan Kenton, Woody Herman, Tommy Dorsey, Ted Heath, Ray Anthony y Dizzy Gillespie.

Entre sus composiciones más conocidas sobrevivirán con toda seguridad *Mambo a la Kenton* (grabado por Pérez Prado), *Mocambo* y *Bob City*.

y la antigua URSS. La fundación de Irakere en 1973 representó un duro golpe a los adocenados del régimen.

¿Qué razón política animó realmente la creación de aquella orquesta de jazz contemporáneo? Me lo pregunto porque hasta ese momento escuchar o cantar canciones extranjeras podía causarle duras sanciones a cualquier ciudadano. El súbito interés en el jazz llegó a alentar la formación de agrupaciones similares en provincias. Creo que la razón fue la presión de Leo Brouwer, a la sazón uno de los pocos músicos cualificados que viajaba mucho y regresaba cargado de impresiones, grabaciones nuevas y partituras. Brouwer logró persuadir a los zares de la música que había que batir a los norteamericanos en su propio terreno y que, además, el jazz era producto de los negros, no de los blancos imperialistas. Explicó que el momento era el correcto, ¿acaso no contaba ya el país con un grupo de profesionales capaces de producir un jazz de primera clase? Logró salirse con la suya porque, además, él amaba el jazz. Sin embargo, el permiso oficial para formar esta orquesta quedará para mí como un misterio, nunca podré explicármelo del todo.

Aquellos años marcaron también el surgimiento de grupos estimulados por la nueva trova y la fusión experimental. Uno de los primeros fue el **Grupo Manguaré**, creado en 1971, cuyo repertorio incluía elementos folclóricos andinos, así como la asimilación del charango y el cuatro venezolano. La labor del Grupo Manguaré estuvo muy influida por el desarrollo del movimiento de la nueva canción en Chile, Argentina y Uruguay, que como ya he indicado antes, tuvo un peso considerable en la aparición de la nueva trova cubana.

Al año siguiente apareció el **Grupo Moncada** (nombre del cuartel en Santiago de Cuba atacado por Castro y sus seguidores el 26 de julio de 1953), que ha tendido a conciliar los textos y melodías de la nueva trova con los ritmos tradicionales afrocubanos y la instrumentación del rock más progresivo. Formado por estudiantes universitarios, debutó en 1972 y continúan trabajando la línea de la canción política y folclórica latinoamericana. Quizá se consideran los herederos del panfletismo musical del guitarrista Carlos Puebla, aunque el resultado musical es bien diferente.

Es importante incluir aquí a dos agrupaciones que ejercieron un papel señalado en el mantenimiento del son tradicional: el Rumbavana y la Anacaona. Poco conocido fuera de Cuba, el **Conjunto Rumbavana**, fundado en 1956 por el percusionista Ricardo Ferro, llenó un importante espacio durante las difíciles décadas del 70 y 80. Entre sus tres trompetas tocó el *Guajiro* Mirabal y entre sus tempranos vocalistas destacaron Raúl Planas y el bolerista Lino Borges. En 1967, con el arribo del pianista Joseíto González como director, el conjunto avanzó notablemente, no sólo reforzando su repertorio sino también dando cabida a autores noveles como Adalberto Álvarez, quien más tarde sería muy significativo en el devenir del son. Alguna vez experimentaron con guitarras eléctricas, mas el Rumbavana se mantuvo abrazado al son, al mambo y la guaracha. Aunque no lograron participar del boom musical de los 90, su existencia y popularidad contribuyó efectivamente a la subsiguiente aceptación de Adalberto Álvarez y Son 14, así como a las creaciones de Cándido Fabré. Algunos atribuyen el origen de la «timba» a este formidable conjunto, cuyo disco *Lo que le trae Rumbavana* es una colección de grabaciones de los años 70 y 80 publicada por el sello francés Declic: una excelente manera de acercarse al tumbao del son.

También establecida desde mucho antes del triunfo revolucionario, la estupenda **Orquesta Anacaona**, formada por mujeres, se originó como septeto en 1932, integrado mayormente por las hermanas Castro Zadarriaga, dirigidas por Concepción, la mayor, quien había aprendido piano, guitarra y saxofón. No obstante, varios hombres tuvieron que ver con su desarrollo estilístico: Alberto Socarrás en 1938 y más tarde Rafael Lay, el violinista que después dirigiría la Orquesta Aragón de Cienfuegos, así como su flautista Richard Egües. Gracias a la versatilidad de sus miembros, Anacaona siempre supo abordar un repertorio muy variado; establecidas en el café al aire libre del hotel Pasaje, casi frente al Capitolio Nacional habanero, contaban entonces con la voz de Graciela Grillo, hermana de *Machito*, quien más tarde se trasladó a Nueva York para unirse a su banda. Mucho después, en 1987, con sus integrantes originales ya jubilados y contando con la dirección de la bajista Georgia Aguirre, quien se había unido a la orquesta con su hermana Doris en 1983, remozaron su repertorio con la ayuda de la pianista Jannysett MacPherson Zapata, cubriendo de merengue a timba. Aquí, en España, siempre han cosechado notables éxitos.

En 1998 la Anacaona realizó en París la música para la obra teatral de Molière, *Le Bourgeois Gentilhomme*, un concepto atrevido del director Jerome Savary, y posteriormente aparecieron en un álbum con el sello francés Lusafrica. *Lo que tú esperabas*, grabado en La Habana en 2000, incluye colaboraciones de Richard Egües, Raúl Planas y varios saxos liderados por Ernesto Varona. El sonido dominante es una mezcla de temas románticos y sones debidos a Ignacio Piñeiro, Mario Bauzá y Marcelino Guerra *Rapindey,* así como otros de Juan Formell y Manolito Simonet. Un corto número en aire de merengue, titulado *Il fait trop beau pour travailler,* del jazzista francés Claude Bolling, completa este variado disco.

Así las cosas, en 1973, irrumpió en la escena el que devendría el más famoso e influyente de todos los grupos de jazz afrocubano: **Irakere**, la creación de Chucho Valdés (ver pág. 329), hijo del también pianista y director de orquesta exiliado Bebo Valdés. Pero si cuento cómo surgió realmente su núcleo principal algunos pensarán que he estado bebiendo: Irakere se gestó a partir del grupo seleccionado para amenizar las presen-

IRAKERE Y CHUCHO VALDÉS.

taciones del Circo de Moscú, otro deseo del Gran Jefe: tener un circo soviético haciendo giras por todo el país.

Desde sus comienzos, Irakere reflejó los gustos eclécticos de su fundador: la polirrítmica afrocubana mezclada con deconstrucciones de boleros y sones clásicos, incluyendo pasajes de obras de Mozart o el aprovechamiento de elementos clave del rock, todo mezclado con extraordinarios solos del propio Chucho y los metales de Paquito D'Rivera y Arturo Sandoval. Combinando guitarra y bajo eléctrico con las congas, la dominante tendencia a un jazz de vanguardia fue atemperada por un sólido interés en ritmos dancísticos autóctonos. Inmensamente popular en la isla, Irakere pronto impresionó favorablemente a los asistentes a festivales de jazz en Escandinavia, Italia, Alemania y finalmente Estados Unidos, donde el grupo tocó en 1978 en el Carnegie Hall de Nueva York.

Su enorme éxito no sólo estableció el escenario en que se movería el jazz afrocubano de los 80 y 90, sino que también aseguró la creación de otros grupos con diversas búsquedas. Ése fue el caso de **Tema IV** (Ele Valdés, Silvia Acea, Eliseo Pino y Carlos Alfonso), que fue el primero en emplear sintetizadores en el país y adoptar las técnicas occidentales de actuación en el escenario. Este grupo luego se metamorfoseó en **Síntesis** en 1976, bajo la dirección de Carlos Alfonso, con obvias referencias de Pink

Floyd y de los británicos Emerson, Lake & Palmer. Síntesis se integró al espectro musical en uno de los primeros festivales de la nueva trova celebrado en Varadero a finales de 1976, y su primera formación contaba con compositores de la talla de José María Vitier y Mike Porcel. Inicialmente emplearon versos del poeta chileno Pablo Neruda y canciones de Amaury Pérez, así como de Silvio Rodríguez, cuyos poemas formaron la base del álbum *El hombre extraño*, publicado en 1992. Con elementos del rap, de guaguancó y de rock, han montado también temas de Carlos Varela y de Donato Poveda.

Adoptando una línea más definida dentro del mundo religioso afrocubano, el disco *Ancestros*, grabado en 1987 y publicado en CD por Qbadisc en 1992, y con arreglos de jazz, samba, funk y la nueva trova, está dedicado a varias deidades del panteón lucumí. Sus dos volúmenes presentan una extraordinaria fusión de cánticos rituales envueltos en sonido electrónico sin alterar su pureza, por algo contó con el asesoramiento de Lázaro Ros. Después de grabar *Ancestros* y durante una gira por España, el percusionista Frank Padilla decidió quedarse a vivir aquí.

PRIMER FORMATO DE SÍNTESIS.

En su disco *Orishas*, Alonso logró evocadores juegos vocales con las antiguas oraciones religiosas gracias a la vocalista Ele Valdés, el percusionista Fidel García, el teclista Equis Alfonso y el guitarrista rastafari Víctor Navarrete, y la totalidad de sus recursos electrónicos. El director de Síntesis ha asegurado que su grupo tiene adquirido «un compromiso generacional, cultural y étnico». Han participado en importantes festivales como el Pop Komm en Alemania, African Market Place en Los Ángeles, el Cervantino en México, el Festival Rock de Río de Janeiro, el Pirineos Sur, así como en señalados eventos jazzísticos. Magic Music les publicó el álbum *Ancestros II* en 1994, y tienen otros en su haber. Como en el caso de otros grupos cubanos de éxito, la modernización le permite hoy día a Síntesis contar con su propio mánager, asistente de producción y técnico de sonido; un contrato discográfico con el sello brasileño Velas les ha asegurado la distribución de su música por toda la América Latina y los Estados Unidos. Por Síntesis han pasado personalidades como Amaury Pérez, Pablo Menéndez, Gonzalo Rubalcaba, Ernán López-Nussa, Jorge

CARLOS ALFONSO, LÍDER DE SÍNTESIS

Aragón y Lucía Huergo, entre otros, que aportaron su talento a la consolidación del proyecto. Al celebrar sus 25 años de triunfos durante Cubadisco 2001, sigue siendo una de las agrupaciones más sorprendentes del pentagrama sonoro de la isla.

Otra pequeña agrupación que emergió en 1985 fue **Mezcla,** entregada por entero a la fusión de rock moderno con el tratamiento instrumental de ritmos tradicionales; a menudo trabaja en una corriente parecida a la de Síntesis, también con la orientación y participación del experto Lázaro Ros. Son los casos de otros grupos como Arte Vivo, Septiembre 5, Los Magnéticos, El Grupo Láser de Bayamo, Monte de Espuma, bajo la dirección de Mario Daly (ya desaparecido) y la cantante Tanya Rodríguez, que después se separó del grupo y continuó como solista, Edesio Alejandro y su Banda de Mákina, que sigue la línea implantada por el británico Elton Jones, y el cantante Laronte, quien sigue los pasos de Michael Jackson.

Curiosamente, el talentoso líder de Mezcla nació en Oakland, California, y se trasladó a La Habana en 1966, donde estudió música. Pablo Menéndez estuvo ligado al GESI y a los creadores de la nueva trova antes de incorporarse a Síntesis como guitarrista. Ya había tocado con el grupo de jazz Sonido Contemporáneo antes de fundar Mezcla. Este grupo fue el precursor del interés de la nueva trova en el rock, y su canción *Nacimos del fuego* logró una enorme popularidad aunque desconozco por qué el álbum de donde provenía nunca vio la luz. Sin embargo, los miembros de Mezcla tienen un valor añadido: a raíz de sus conciertos en la Costa Oeste de Estados Unidos, y en vista de las dificultades confrontadas por los músicos cubanos para obtener visas del Departamento de Estado, lograron crear un fuerte *lobby* de opinión pública que fue decisivo para la posterior entrada al país de otros artistas de la isla.

A pesar de la atracción de Irakere con números como *Bacalao con pan*, le fue difícil eclipsar la popularidad de **Los Van Van**, las grandes estrellas de la música bailable, cuyos objetivos estaban más dentro del pop que en el jazz. Su director, el bajista Juan Formell (ver pág. 352), provenía de la orquesta de Elio Revé, un timbalero nacido en 1930 y ya fallecido.

Cuando Formell creó Los Van Van aplicó la misma fórmula que había establecido en sus dos años de colaboración con Revé: un formato con guitarra y bajo eléctricos, y una batería con todos los hierros, aunados a su formidable intuición para resolver letras con sabor popular. Su primer

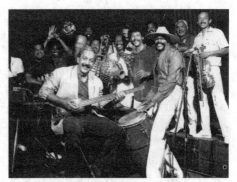

LOS VAN VAN DE JUAN FORMELL.

gran éxito fue *Marilú*, un híbrido con obvias tendencias de rock tropicalizado, característico del momento, que le sirvió para establecer definitivamente lo que intentó hacer cuando pertenecía a la orquesta de Revé. El fichaje del percusionista José Luis Quintana *Changuito* fue el paso clave en la creación del **songo,** un nuevo ritmo con complejos golpes sincopados en la batería y en las congas. Por muchos años, el songo se convirtió en el principal caballo de batalla de Los Van Van e influyó en el trabajo del grupo Batacumbele de Puerto Rico.

Fue una época marcada por una intensificación en el autoaislamiento del régimen castrista, que mantenía una fuerte presencia policial en la isla, tomando medidas drásticas como excusa ante una hipotética invasión de marines yanquis. Uno de sus principales medios de control fue el recrudecimiento de las actividades de los Comités de Defensa de la Revolución, establecidos en 1961 en cada calle del país para denunciar a cualquier sospechoso o desafecto al régimen.

Para amargar aún más la situación, la «Ofensiva revolucionaria» de 1968, que terminó con todo negocio particular, bien fuera un zapatero o un vendedor de helados, también afectó a la mayoría de los clubes y cabarés. Los conciertos fueron severamente reducidos y miles de bailarinas, músicos y todo tipo de artistas se vieron súbitamente en la calle.

Incluso en esa etapa tan angustiosa México se las arregló para mantener sus relaciones con Cuba, aún cuando los gobiernos de los demás países latinoamericanos le habían dado la espalda. Mi impresión es que reciprocaba la decisión de Castro de no retirar a sus atletas durante las Olimpiadas de 1968 en México, a pesar del asesinato de cientos de jóvenes mexicanos en la plaza de Tlatelolco, a punto de comenzar los Juegos.

De hecho, Fidel Castro no dijo jamás una palabra sobre aquel crimen porque entonces no le convenían sus principios, sino ganar medallas para su campaña propagandística.

España, que comenzaba a estructurar la democracia tras la muerte del dictador Franco en 1975, siempre ha acogido a músicos cubanos y también sirvió de lanzamiento internacional a los cantautores Silvio Rodríguez, Pablito Milanés y Sara González. Otros artistas eran enviados a donde mejor le conviniera al régimen políticamente: orquestas importantes como la de Jorrín y la Aragón visitaron Tanzania, el Congo, Guinea y Mali, lo que provocó que importantes músicos africanos viajaran a Cuba más tarde, estrechando los lazos ancestrales.

Hacia finales de los 70 el presidente Jimmy Carter trató inútilmente de acercarse a Castro de diversas formas, llegando a permitir conciertos ocasionales de artistas norteamericanos en la isla. El más espectacular de todos fue el originado por la empresa norteamericana Carras, una línea de cruceros caribeños que en abril de 1977 desembarcó a músicos del calibre de Dizzy Gillespie, Earl Hines, Stan Getz, Ry Cooder y el conguero Ray Mantilla en el puerto de La Habana. Durante 36 horas extenuantes, los estadounidenses ofrecieron conciertos y descargaron con Chucho Valdés, Arturo Sandoval, Paquito D'Rivera, Los Papines y otros. Interesado en los asuntos musicales del patio, Ry Cooder se dedicó a localizar a Miguel Ojeda, un virtuoso del laúd que alguna vez había escuchado en grabaciones. Todos estos artistas se volverían a encontrar años más tarde en circunstancias dramáticamente diferentes.

Lo de la línea Carras fue pura chiripa: no habiendo podido vender suficientes pasajes para un crucero a Montego Bay y Nassau (en el que estaban programados para actuar Dizzy Gillespie, Lionel Hampton, Roberta Flack, Joe Williams y Earl *Fatha* Hines), se enteraron esa misma semana del súbito cambio en la política del presidente Carter; inmediatamente ofrecieron su «Crucero cubano». A Gillespie y a Hines no les molestó el cambio de ruta, pero Hampton, Flack y Williams se negaron, creyendo que aparecer en La Habana afectaría sus carreras. El compositor David Amram llamó a un amigo de la línea Carras para ofrecer su participación mientras que Jerry Masucci ofreció enviar a las Fania All Stars. Dos semanas más tarde llegó la aprobación oficial cubana y la banda de Amram fue seleccionada.

Los mejores: CHUCHO VALDÉS

Desde su inicio en 1973, Irakere ha ocupado un lugar cimero. En su mejor época estuvo formado por los saxos Germán Velasco y Carlos Averhoff, los trompetas Arturo Sandoval y Jorge Varona, en la guitarra eléctrica Carlos Emilio, bajo eléctrico Carlos del Puerto, batería Enrique Pla, los percusionistas Jorge Alfonso y Carlos Barbón, Oscar Valdés cantante y percusión, y Jesús *Chucho* Valdés (1941) piano, órgano y director.

En su *Diccionario del jazz latino*, Nat Chediak recoge una anécdota preciosa que le contó *Cachao*: Bebo Valdés, famoso pianista, compositor y director de orquesta y padre de Chucho, le hizo escuchar de espaldas a «un joven pianista norteamericano recién llegado a La Habana». Era Chucho a los cuatro años de edad, a quien su padre aconsejó aprender a tocar música cubana primero y luego jazz, sin mezclarlos antes de dominar ambos. «Se formó armónicamente escuchando a Bebo hasta la madrugada», recordó en su día el timbalero Guillermo Barreto, primo segundo de Chucho, cuyo patio lindaba con el de los Valdés.

Para el lector que no tenga nada de Chucho Valdés en solitario le recomiendo *Lucumí,* del sello Messidor, posiblemente su obra maestra, un disco grabado en noviembre de 1986. Reproduzco un comentario certero de Chediak:

Él no lo sabe, pero es el nexo entre el sabor de sus maestros y el afán técnico de los virtuosos de su generación. A partir de Chucho será difícil obviar el carácter «olímpico» del nuevo jazz cubano. Esta sesión demuestra la vigencia del «deleite» en toda música, incluso el jazz. Advertencia: estar expuesto a ella induce a euforia. La identidad afro se logra a base de ritmo, sin más percusión que la de un piano.

A los seis años de edad Chucho aprendió solfeo con Oscar Muñóz Bouffartique, notorio compositor de guarachas, y a los dieciséis debutó como pianista de la célebre orquesta Sabor de Cuba que dirigía su padre, con la que acompañó durante tres años a importantes cantantes de la época como

Rolando Laserie, Fernando Álvarez y Pío Leyva. En 1963 integró con Paquito D'Rivera la orquesta del Teatro Musical de La Habana. Tengo entendido que la primera vez que Paquito se asombró al ver a Chucho tocar el piano fue en 1961 durante las jam sessions que se organizaban los domingos en el restaurante Havana 1900, un local en el centro de la capital, donde años antes el Club Cubano de Jazz había presentado a Zoot Sims, el trío de Sara Vaughan, Stan Getz y a otros jazzistas norteamericanos; algunos tomaban el vuelo de menos de una hora desde Miami para compartir con los cubanos. Chucho tenía entonces veinte años y Paquito trece. El local fue cerrado con el triunfo de la revolución, pero 38 años después encontró su sucedáneo en La Zorra y el Cuervo, un antiguo club de filin en El Vedado.

En 1967 Chucho fue invitado a formar parte de la Orquesta Cubana de Música Moderna dirigida por Armando Romeu. Después del éxito alcanzado en el Festival de Jazz de Varsovia en 1970, decidió reclutar a varios de los principales solistas de la orquesta de Romeu para crear Irakere.

Es evidente que Chucho no necesita a Irakere para expresarse a fondo. Por otra parte, desconozco las razones personales que pueda tener el genial pianista para permanecer en Cuba. Pero me consta que cuando un artista cubano de envergadura viaja al exterior no deja atrás a familiares sino a rehenes. Al respecto, dice Paquito D'Rivera en *Mi vida saxual*:

En los treinta y tantos años que han pasado desde que conocí a mi amigo Chucho, jamás supe lo que realmente estaba pensando, y que por lo general, lo que dice que piensa hacer resulta muchas veces algo bien diferente a lo que realmente hace.

Chucho ya ha realizado bastantes grabaciones acompañado y en solitario, tanto en Cuba como en Estados Unidos. Se ha codeado con los mejores jazzistas de ambos países y algunos europeos de alto nivel. Y tuvo un emotivo encuentro con su padre en 1996 con motivo de la filmación de *Calle 54*, de Fernando Trueba, donde aparecen a cuatro manos interpretando *La comparsa*, de Ernesto Lecuona. Como dice un viejísimo son cubano: «*Cada uno se defiende como puede, y de su cuero hace un bongó...*»

El excelente pianista Andy Narell ha indicado:

Irakere fue el primer grupo cubano que grabó en Estados Unidos en 1979 y es muy difícil expresar el impacto que hizo ese álbum entre aquellos que estamos interesados en la música afrocaribeña. El grupo poseía un poder explosivo. Su nivel de oficio musical y las composiciones se ganaron el respeto inmediato y una admiración con casi un sobrecogimiento. Desde entonces hemos podido escuchar más sus grabaciones, pero aún hay que viajar fuera del país para verlos en vivo. Dos veces tuve la oportunidad de escucharlos cuando tocamos en el mismo festival de Curaçao, y estaban que «echaban candela». Pude sentarme a tocar con ellos, lo que fue una experiencia inolvidable.

¿Por qué es Chucho Valdés un caso único? Porque antes de ingresar en el Conservatorio Municipal de La Habana ya había bebido tanto de los jazzistas norteamericanos de los años 40 y 50 como de su padre Bebo, figura central de la época de oro de la música cubana, y exiliado en Suecia desde 1962. Chucho también escuchó mucho a Lecuona y a otros creadores cubanos que después le fueron vedados a los músicos formados por la revolución.

Durante un viaje de intercambio cultural en 1995 se dio el gustazo de rearmar la orquesta de *Machito* en Nueva York y tocar su música con el apoyo de Papo Vázquez, Dave Valentín, Mario Rivera, Carlos Emilio Morales, Carlos del Puerto y el puertorriqueño Giovanni Hidalgo en los cueros. Antes había ofrecido una inolvidable jam session en el teatro del Bronx Lebanon Hospital. Más tarde, el alcalde de San Francisco le entregó las llaves de la ciudad en reconocimiento a sus aportes a la cultura universal, y en Los Ángeles encabezó un «All Stars» con Justo Almarío, Alex Acuña y Luis Conte, extraordinario conguero cubano exiliado desde hace tiempo, quien suele acompañar a figuras del prestigio de Madonna y Julio Iglesias.

En dicha gira de varios meses por Estados Unidos, Chucho Valdés hizo de todo, incluyendo una sólida conferencia que cubrió desde Chopin y Debussy hasta Cervantes y Lecuona, y descargar ante estudiantes de un High School de Hollywood.

Elió Revé (1930-1997), percusionista guantanamero, fue el responsable de popularizar su versión del son changüí en los tiempos actuales, labor que mantiene su hijo después de la trágica muerte de su padre. Surgida alrededor de 1956, su charanga alcanzó súbita popularidad diez años después debido a los arreglos y creaciones innovadoras de un contrabajista que había fichado poco antes y cuyo nombre le revolvía el estómago a pesar de la importante contribución que realizó en favor de su agrupación: Juan Formell.

Uno de los veinticuatro hijos de una familia de recogedores de café en las montañas, Elio se mezcló pronto con los soneros Julián Venao, Negra con Pelo, Mongolo, Felipe Radical y Cuatro Filos, personajes locales que lo introdujeron al viejo son changüí tocado con tres, marímbula, bongó y maracas. Trabajó en diversos oficios, desde cortador de caña a ferrocarrilero, mientras comenzaba a desenvolverse con los timbales (pailas en Cuba). Entonces andaba muy metido en asuntos de Santería y llegó a bailar con la tumba francesa de Santiago de Cuba. Luego se trasladó a La Habana donde ganó experiencia tocando en las charangas de Cheo Belén Puig y la Orquesta Almendra antes de independizarse.

Cuando Formell lo dejó se llevó a algunos de sus músicos para fun-

ELIO REVÉ.

dar Los Van Van. Hombre corpulento y chillón, Elio Revé decidió entonces hacer algunos cambios en su plantilla, incluyendo un trío de tambores batá dirigidos por su hermano Odelquis; también fichó al tresero *Papi* Oviedo y pudo encontrar en el cantante *Padrino* Rafael la «voz de vieja» que buscaba para rememorar a los viejos soneros de antaño. En 1986 la **Orquesta Revé** o el Charangón, como prefería llamarla, sacó los discos *La explosión del momento* (Real World) y *Rumberos latinoamericanos*, que alcanzaron ventas considerables. Contratado por WOMAD después, recorrió varios festivales musicales europeos, derrochando energía sabrosona con su música. Sin embargo, creo que su mayor habilidad no fue como percusionista porque en ese aspecto no podía impresionar a nadie, sino en su insistencia en revitalizar el son changüí unido a un curioso talento para rodearse de buenos músicos que contribuyeron a realzar su agrupación.

Su fama duró menos de una década: en 1997 un coche lo mató mientras se encontraba junto al autocar de la banda. Su hijo, un excelente teclista, continúa al frente del Charangón y con los mismos gritos viscerales del viejo Elio, como si estuviera cortando un campo de caña él solo. Otros discos de la Revé son *Tributo al maestro,* una compilación de la EGREM, y *Changüí en la casa de Nora*, un álbum grabado en 1999 ya bajo la nueva dirección.

Los instrumentos: LAS PAILAS O TIMBAL

Consta de dos tambores redondos de un diámetro ligeramente diferente. Ambas estructuras metálicas (abiertas por abajo) se colocan sobre un trípode, acompañado por dos cencerros de tamaños y timbres diferentes, y ocasionalmente por un platillo. El timbalero lo toca de pie y usa baquetas de madera sin cabeza. Proviene de los grandes *timpanis* de la música sinfónica, hechos de cobre, que en Cuba se denominaron pailas al fabricarlas de menor diámetro y ser usadas tanto por murgas callejeras en el siglo XIX como por las primeras orquestas típicas de danzones; entonces tenían el fondo cerrado y redondeado.

Entre los timbaleros que más se han destacado está Ulpiano Díaz (Pinar del Río, 1920), que trabajó con diversas charangas, entre ellas las de Félix González, Tata Alfonso, Arcaño y sus Maravillas, Fajardo y sus Estrellas y Estrellas Cubanas. Díaz aportó una nueva línea en la ejecución del instrumento; fue el primer timbalero contratado en Nueva York por una banda de jazz afrocubano, en la cual mantuvo su estilo cadencioso y moderado, típico del danzón, donde no se solía repetir un golpe o dejar en el aire una resonancia. Sus golpes secos se opusieron abiertamente a la vía marcada por el puertorriqueño Tito Puente (nacido en Nueva York), considerado «El rey del timbal», quien impuso un estilo acelerado y con solos llenos de repiqueteos a modo de redoblante. Entre ambas variantes se encuentra la escuela que estableció Guillermo Barreto, que como baterista consumado le dio un carácter más lírico al timbal. El efecto de «abanico» característico del nuevo danzón y luego del chachachá al comenzar una nueva sección de la pieza se logra con un primer golpe seco, inmediatamente seguido de un rápido redoble. Aparte de diversos golpes directos, también se logran fuertes efectos al hacer coincidir el borde metálico con el cuero o plástico. El exiliado Orestes Vilató (Camagüey, 1944) es otro verdadero virtuoso del timbal; ha tocado con las mejores agrupaciones, incluyendo la Fania All Stars y la banda del rockero latino Carlos Santana. En 1992 la participación de Vilató durante las *Master Sessions* de *Cachao* no dejó duda de que se encuentra entre los más grandes paileros que ha dado Cuba y uno de los pocos que se atrevieron a desafiar a Tito Puente en una presentación pública.

JUAN PABLO TORRES.

En 1979 se autorizó la visita a Cuba de la Fania All-Stars, la mejor banda del movimiento salsero neoyorquino (ver pág. 254). El evento atrajo a un buen número de músicos interesados en descubrir la razón de ser de una nueva marca de música que estaba mayormente basada en el son cubano. Pocos meses después, Cuba respondió con la creación de **Las Estrellas de Areíto,** bajo la dirección de Juan Pablo Torres, quienes grabaron una serie de temas tradicionales muy bien orquestados, en contraste con lo que Los Van Van y Mezcla brindaban al público.

El verdadero instigador de Las Estrellas de Areíto fue Raúl Diomandé, un productor de Costa de Marfil que insistió en la inclusión de determinados músicos conocidos en África para ampliar las posibilidades de exportación. Así fueron seleccionados el cantante Rafael Bacallao y el flautista Richard Egües junto al violinista Rafael Lay (quien murió cuatro años después). Entre los diez vocalistas estaba el viejo sonero Miguelito Cuní, y en la sección de trompetas descollaba Félix Chapottín. Otros muy conocidos eran el tresero Niño Rivera y el conguero Tata Güines. La suma de más de cuarenta profesionales incluyó al pianista Rubén González, al timbalero Amadito Valdés, los trompetas Arturo Sandoval y *Guajiro* Mirabal y el saxo Paquito D'Rivera, quien gozaba de la mayor popularidad.

Las partituras de Teresa García Caturla y del propio Juan Pablo Torres estimularon el nivel de las improvisaciones de tanto talento reunido en los estudios. El resultado para el mercado europeo fue *Los héroes,* editado por World Circuit en dos compactos, con un excelente libreto. Lamentablemente, a pesar de su excelencia, el proyecto no tuvo éxito en su momento debido a la pobre calidad de la producción y distribución que son endémicas en Cuba. Aunque una versión reducida de aquel batallón de músicos visitó Venezuela, donde el disco de vinilo se vendió bastante, el trabajo tuvo que esperar otros veinte años para que fuera digitalizado y la música llegara a un público internacional.

Los que sí tuvieron un éxito tremendo desde su aparición fueron **Adalberto Álvarez y Son 14,** agrupación con ese número de músicos que su director, nacido en Camagüey, tuvo que formar en Santiago de Cuba en 1977 después de atravesar un terrible período lidiando con la burocracia oficial. Cansado de que otros tocaran sus composiciones, el activo músico, que originalmente quiso ser piloto de aviación y finalmente logró estudiar en la Escuela Nacional de Arte, se ha convertido en uno de los mejores soneros de los últimos veinte años. Al escucharlos, el pianista Frank Fernández se apresuró a recomendar a la EGREM que los grabara sin demora. Cuando cualquier fan de la salsa de Nueva York, San Juan o Cali de visita en la isla preguntaba quién era el equivalente cubano de Oscar D'León o José Alberto *El canario,* la respuesta señalaba a Adalberto Álvarez. Su primer vinilo, titulado *A Bayamo en coche*, se convirtió en un éxito inmediato y fue adoptado por Willy Chirino en Miami y por Juan Luis Guerra en Santo Domingo.

EL SONERO ADALBERTO ÁLVAREZ.

Aún considerando las composiciones y arreglos de su director, Son 14 se destacó también por su cantante Eduardo *Tiburón* Morales, un sonero carismático, pegado a la tierra. Durante quince años alegraron infinidad de plazas y fiestas, incluyendo un estadio de Caracas que casi se desborda con 70.000 personas. En 1984, Adalberto dejó al grupo santiaguero y se trasladó a la capital donde formó **Adalberto y su Son**, manteniendo las principales características de Son 14 más el añadido del tres de Pancho Amat. Los vocalistas Félix Baloy y posteriormente Jorge Luis Rojas *Rojitas*, junto al juego entre los poderosos metales y tumbaos del tres y el teclado, lo convirtieron en «El caballero del son», una referencia a su dignidad personal y a temas que evitan el sensacionalismo de otras bandas. En 1991 *¿Y qué tú quieres que te den?* fue el álbum del año en Cuba, grabado en el desaparecido sello PM de Pablo Milanés. Recomiendo los compactos *Son 14 with Adalberto Alvarez* y *La máquina musical, 20th Anniversary*, ambos editados por Tumi, así como *Jugando con candela* que sacó el sello Havana Caliente de Estados Unidos.

Entretanto, Son 14 siguió su propio rumbo y aunque la vieja magia ya no existía, poco a poco fueron levantando presión sin el aporte de su

TIBURÓN MORALES.

antiguo director. Para mí sigue siendo uno de los pocos conjuntos de la era revolucionaria –junto al matancero Yaguarimú– que han demostrado habilidad para refinar y expandir la tradición sonera; escuche *Luces de mi Santiago* o *Agua que cae del cielo* (que incluye toques de batá y efectos de vientos tropicales) como muestra de lo que afirmo. *Tiburón* Morales mantiene su carisma de tierra adentro, y le sigue cantando a los personajes que ya había inmortalizado: «Señora Elvira» (una manera de burlarse de un amigo que siempre lo estaba pinchando), «Rosa Zayas» (la mamá de Adalberto Álvarez, una gran señora) y «Pedro el Cojo» (personaje mítico santiaguero al que le han cantado desde Los Compadres hasta Pacho Alonso).

A mediados de los años 90, Adalberto Álvarez fichó a Aramís Galindo como vocalista, y a su propia hija Dorgeris en el piano. Adalberto y su Son esperaron el 2000 en Los Ángeles, tocando en una enorme fiesta organizada por Vanity Fair después de la ceremonia del Oscar, con Robert de Niro, Madonna y Mónica Lewinsky echando un pie con su sabrosa música.

El deshielo iniciado por el presidente Jimmy Carter no duró mucho. En 1978, cuando la Orquesta Aragón reciprocaba el acercamiento anterior con presentaciones en Estados Unidos, dos de sus tres actuaciones contratadas con el Lincoln Center de Manhattan tuvieron que ser canceladas tras el estallido de una bomba que destruyó la sala después de su primera presentación. Poco después tuvo lugar un exilio memorable, el del saxo Paquito D'Rivera, ayudado por Dizzy Gillespie. Paquito devino uno de los críticos más agudos del sistema porque conocía perfectamente la organización y fines de la política musical del régimen de Castro. En 1981, cuando apareció la primera edición del importante *Diccionario de la Música Cubana* de Helio Orovio, muchos descubrimos con horror que infinidad de artistas prominentes no habían sido incluidos, incluyendo a Paquito y a la gran Celia Cruz.

A través de los 80 la música de Los Van Van y los conciertos de Irakere continuaron dominando la imagen internacional de la isla. Sin embargo, comenzaba a perfilarse un renovado interés en el son tradicional.

Cientos de tríos y cuartetos soneros –envejecidos pero disfrutando de un salario– todavía operaban esporádicamente en todo el país.

Entretanto, en la Universidad de La Habana un grupo de estudiantes de ingeniería que incluía a Juan de Marcos González, guitarrista aficionado y tocador de tres, y a un joven trompeta llamado Jesús Alemañy, se sintieron más atraídos por el sonido de los antiguos septetos que por la avalancha de jazz, songo, nueva trova y música andina que constantemente escuchaban en radio o televisión. En 1976 decidieron formar el grupo **Sierra Maestra**, empleando al principio sólo instrumentos acústicos para recrear los viejos estilos. Este conjunto devino extremadamente popular al modernizar gradualmente sus composiciones. Años después, De Marcos creó el **Buena Vista Social Club** mientras que Alemañy fundó la igualmente exitosa banda **Cubanismo**.

GRUPO SIERRA MAESTRA (1977).

Todo esto coincidió con la aparición en La Habana del venezolano Oscar D'León, cuyas atractivas actuaciones contribuyeron a galvanizar el interés por el son en un sector importante de la gente más joven, que ya seguía la labor del excelente grupo Excorde. Los Van Van, siempre alertas a lo que pide el ambiente, contestaron con números más cadenciosos como *Sandunguera* y el *Baile del buey cansado*. Entretanto, para sorpresa de todos, las puertas de los salones de La Tropical volvieron a abrirse en 1986 para dar paso a la muchedumbre enardecida por bailar con un nuevo grupo, muy dinámico y coherente: **NG La Banda**, cuyas siglas significan Nueva Generación.

Sin embargo, el colapso del bloque soviético y la suspensión de la gigantesca ayuda que Cuba recibía año tras año, agravaron las actividades musicales en la isla. El país había perdido el 85 por ciento de su comercio exterior, y casi todo el abastecimiento de petróleo barato. Castro declaró en 1990 un austero programa como medida de emergencia para hacerle frente a la nueva situación: comenzaba el llamado «Período Especial» que ya dura doce años al momento de escribir.

JAZZ CON FRIJOLES NEGROS

Las estrictas giras de intercambios culturales organizadas a través del Departamento de Estado del coloso del Norte y los organismos que rigen la música en Cuba han permitido en varias ocasiones que importantes jazzistas norteamericanos fueran presentados en La Habana. La ironía es que la Ley Torricelli, aprobada por el gobierno de Estados Unidos para apretar aún más a la isla, sirvió para suavizar el bloqueo en lo referente a los intercambios culturales y artísticos; un pequeño resquicio en su articulado bastó para concluir 35 años de incomunicación impuesta

WYNTON MARSALIS EN CUBA (1997).

por la política. En este sentido, fue especialmente memorable el XVI Festival Jazz Plaza celebrado en 1996, en el que el trompeta Roy Hargrove y su quinteto, y el saxo Steve Coleman y su grupo compartieron intensas sesiones con Gato Gótico, de Islas Canarias. También participaron Jane Bunnett y Hugh Fraser de Canadá, la agrupación Fra Fra Sound de Holanda, pero natural de Surinam, y el JazzProject del puertorriqueño Humberto Ramírez; éstas fueron algunas de las figuras que dejaron una intensa impresión en el público conocedor.

Desde La Habana comentó de forma optimista el corresponsal de *El País* Mauricio Vicent: «Las tumbadoras, teclados y metales de los músicos cubanos han comenzado a derretir el hielo del bloqueo por la costura del jazz». Se hizo coincidir aquel festival de ocho días con la presentación de un pobre carnaval habanero, cancelado hasta entonces por mandato de Castro.

Al plantel visitante se unió una renovación de Los Amigos, pilar del movimiento jazzístico en los años 60: el percusionista *Changuito*, el tumbador Miguel *Angá* Díaz y el flautista Orlando *Maraca* Valle se sumaron al legendario pianista Frank Emilio Flynn, el único sobreviviente de Los Amigos pero fallecido en 2001. Como era de esperar, el plato fuerte fue Irakere. Una vez más Chucho Valdés desbordó su pianismo insuperable, con César López en el saxo alto, Carlos del Puerto al bajo, Enrique Pla ante la batería y el también veterano Carlos Emilio en la guitarra eléctrica. A ellos se sumaron nuevos rostros en viento, percusión y voces.

La actuación de los norteamericanos fue en reciprocidad al recorrido que realizó el gigantón pianista por Estados Unidos en el último trimestre de 1995, y que tenía como antecedentes añejas incursiones, un lejano Grammy y algún que otro disco. Organizada sólo como una gira de intercambio cultural y para dar clases magistrales y conferencias en la escuela de música Juilliard de Nueva York y la Berklee de Boston, la larga visita le permitió una

EL GENIAL FRANK EMILIO FLYNN.

puesta al día en el panorama jazzístico y la oportunidad de demostrar su nivel. En las aulas en las que alguna vez soñó poder estudiar, tocó Chucho Valdés acompañado del bajo Carlos del Puerto y el guitarrista Carlos Emilio. Pero cada noche en Nueva York se encaminaba al club Bradley, donde suelen reunirse los músicos de jazz al terminar su trabajo; allí escuchó a varios pianistas, algunos nuevos y otros ya conocidos. En una oportunidad quiso comprobar en qué punto se encontraba en la escala internacional, y cuando le pidieron acompañar al saxo Gary Bartz en un piano al que sólo pueden acceder los consagrados, según el testamento dejado por el saxo Paul Desmond, Chucho hizo gala de su versatilidad y capacidad improvisatoria.

Tuvo que volver dos días después, para que la dueña del club tuviera tiempo de avisar a los que no lo habían escuchado. «Toqué y fue escandoloso; la señora me quería contratar por un mes, pero mi visa era sólo de intercambio cultural y no pude hacer el trabajo», declaró Chucho más tarde. Luego apareció una crónica en *Newsweek* comparándolo con Tommy Flanagan y Kenny Barron, los dos más admirados en el ránking del piano ese año. Para Chucho, ésa fue la confirmación de que no andaba lejos de la actualidad jazzística.

En la historia del desarrollo del jazz en Cuba habrá que tener siempre en cuenta los esfuerzos de una serie de músicos casi olvidados, que van desde el trombonista *Pucho* **Escalante** hasta el acordeonista/pianista **Felipe Dulzaides** (1917-91), infatigable promotor del género en la isla. Durante un cuarto de siglo, en su grupo se formaron importantes músicos mientras vendía productos farmacéuticos o administraba una fábrica de chocolates. Por cuenta propia creó en 1956 el cuarteto vocal Los Armónicos, que pronto se convirtió en una versión tropicalizada del quinteto de

George Shearing. Poco antes de morir, asegura Nat Chediak, le rindieron homenaje en el X Festival Jazz Plaza de La Habana, en cuya ocasión afirmó Dulzaides: «El jazz en Cuba se ha abierto paso y no hay quien lo detenga».

Esto lo podría haber afirmado también el saxo **Gustavo Mas**, fallecido en 2001 sin jamás recibir el reconocimiento que merecía. Nacido en Holguín, logró dominar el estilo del cool jazz de los años 50, cuando residía la mayor parte del tiempo en Estados Unidos. Mas realizó un aporte estupendo en el Club Cubano de Jazz hasta principios de los 60, cuando ya había asimilado el novedoso lenguaje de John Coltrane.

Otro luchador de siempre por celebrar la fusión de los ritmos criollos con el blues y el jazz es **Bobby Carcassés** (1938), un multiinstrumentalista y cantante de todo un poco: son, scat, afro, bolero... En *La esquina del Afrojazz*, publicado por Areíto/EGREM/RMM en 1989, le dedicó *Emiliano 1* al pianista Emiliano Salvador, a cuyo debut discográfico contribuyó (Nueva Visión, 1979). Bobby Carcassés, que posee tanto talento como poca suerte, trabajó durante años en el Teatro Musical de La Habana; quizá de ahí le venga su habilidad para la danza y la pantomima en sus actuaciones. Entre sus obras más notables figura *Blues-guaguancó*.

EN LA ONDA DEL ROCK

La invasión del fenómeno rock ha cautivado a los más jóvenes con una fuerza incontenible, forzando todo un movimiento que se consolidó realmente a mediados de los terribles años 70, quizá como una reacción ante la intolerancia de las autoridades cubanas.

Uno de los grupos más destacados de aquellos inicios fue **Los Dadas**. Algunos trataron de incorporar elementos de la música criolla, cada uno a su manera. Desde 1966 el grupo rockero de **Osvaldo Rodríguez y los 5UA** comenzó a cultivar textos alusivos a temas del acontecer popular, pero con una interpretación basada en el más auténtico estilo de rock. Su tema *Quiero tomarme contigo una taza de té* comienza con una especie de hard rock mezclado con blues que después pasa a ritmo de chachachá. Incluso integraron el bolero al contexto sonoro y estilístico del rock, todos creados por Osvaldo Rodríguez. En *Si es hora de acabar*, de Manuel Ornellas, en la voz de Bertha Ripes, una de las fundadoras del grupo, lograron una compleja armonización que unida a los sonidos electrónicos de los instrumentos otorga a la pieza un valor sonoro impresionante. Rodríguez después se separó de los 5UA y formó otro grupo, continuando la línea de boleros fusionados con el mundo sonoro del rock; a esa etapa corresponden *El amor se acaba* y *De lo simple a lo profundo*, donde mantiene una tendencia musical algo melancólica, empleando el tradicional modo menor del género del bolero con las estridencias del rock más vanguardista. Tildados de ofrecer música extranjerizante, estos grupos tuvieron que hilar muy fino para no terminar en la cárcel. Por supuesto, nunca les permitieron referirse a los verdaderos problemas de la sociedad cubana, razón que determinó que Rodríguez se escapara finalmente del país en 1994.

TROVADORES DE HOY

Como en el resto del libro, es imposible incluir a todos los que han ido surgiendo. Sin embargo, entre los nuevos talentos que puede enarbolar el país con orgullo se encuentra **Liuba María Hevia** (1964), quien trata de renovar la música guajira desde una óptica de trovadora. Visitó España en 1997 para promover *Alguien me espera*, el tercer disco de su carrera, donde aparece una canción de Sara González, fundadora de la nueva trova y varios temas de la poetisa Alda Elva, así como el son *Guitarra febril*, un homenaje a su instrumento. Hevia también compone música infantil y aunque está por la recuperación de las músicas ancestrales, no cree en planteamientos puristas a la hora de expresarse. «El folclor, si no se transforma, si no se le da aire, se convierte en una pieza de museo», ha expresado. De ahí la aparición de su segundo disco, *Habaneras en el tiempo*, una sugerencia de la musicóloga María Teresa Linares, quien había recopilado algunas habaneras de tradición oral; a la joven trovadora se le ocurrió integrar esas piezas de autores anónimos con temas de Silvio Rodríguez, María Teresa Vera, Miguel Matamoros y el español Carlos Cano. Editado por el Instituto Cubano de Radio y Televisión, nadie recuerda cuándo fue la última vez que en Cuba se grabó un disco completo de habaneras.

Liuba María Hevia sabe decir las canciones que interpreta y tiene recursos para cualquier situación. Hace unos años, durante la presentación del sello Eurotropical en el teatro Karl Marx habanero, fue capaz de embelesar a un público sediento de salsa dura. Premio Distinción por la Cultura Nacional, proviene de la generación que creció escuchando a Silvio y a Pablo, quien hizo posible su primer disco *Coloreando la esperanza*.

La Familia Valera Miranda comenzó a llamar la atención alrededor de 1983 cuando el musicólogo Danilo Orozco los descubrió y grabó durante sus extensas investigaciones sobre los orígenes del son; una década después, sellos discográficos franceses y británicos recogieron su fascinante cuerpo de melodías y la igualmente impresionante historia de esta familia. Con ramales que trazan su genealogía hasta dos siglos atrás, los Valera Miranda vivieron disueltos en pequeños terruños a lo largo del valle del río Cauto en Oriente. Félix y su mujer Carmen viven desde hace años en Santiago de Cuba, donde mantienen un pequeño arsenal de guitarras, tres, cuatro, contrabajo acústico, bongó, claves, sus voces y las de sus hijos. El repertorio es tradicional y lo apoya la habilidad en el cuatro de Enrique *Quique* Valera, quien también suele tocar con el grupo de salsa Los Karachi de Santiago. El disco *Music from Oriente de Cuba* (sello Nimbus) recoge una grabación hecha en 1994 con el acompañamiento de cuerdas metálicas y voces de trovadores de recia raigambre. Cinco años después, Danilo Orozco volvió al estudio de grabación con La Familia, acompañado de Antoine Chao, hermano del compositor Manu Chao, para producir *A Cutiño*, un álbum que incluye cantos más arcaicos como los *nengones*, considerados los predecesores del son.

Muy diferente a los anteriores, **3 de La Habana** es un trío de voces armónicas formado por Germán David Pinelli, Ana María Páez y su hijo Ari Pinelli. Combina hábilmente temas tradicionales con piezas del talante de *Capricho* (adaptación vocal de una composición francesa del siglo XIX para violín y piano) y canciones ya olvidadas de Sindo Garay y Miguel Matamoros, así como otras nuevas de Tony Pinelli, autor de *La ciudad y el llanto*, que describe críticamente cómo La Habana se ha convertido en el Bangkok del Caribe.

Al grabar un par de canciones nostálgicas del exiliado miamense Willy Chirino (ver pág. 276), 3 de La Habana dio testimonio del continuo contacto entre las dos capitales cubanas, ignorando así las manipulaciones ideológicas sostenidas por iracundos demagogos a ambos lados del Estrecho de la Florida. Las voces del trío se combinan felizmente con las cuerdas del violinista Lázaro Dagoberto González y el tresero Efraín Ríos.

7. AGRUPACIONES DE LOS ÚLTIMOS AÑOS

Hoy, principalmente, en La Habana, se baila de forma muy peculiar. En los primeros minutos de la pieza los pasos son de casino: la pareja se mantiene unida con una marcha de vueltas y jalones que requieren destreza. De pronto, bajo la invitación del tumbao que propician piano, bajo, percusión y metales, se realiza un brusco vuelco rítmico que obliga a los bailadores a separarse. Las mujeres comienzan a mover la cintura en círculos frenéticos, con los brazo en alto y acentuando su aire provocativo; los varones aceptan el reto y se pegan a ellas (imitando al «vacunao» del guaguancó) en franca proposición erótica. Cada quien con sus habilidades pélvicas desata su exhibicionismo mezclando diferentes pasos; la muchedumbre se contagia hasta llegar al «tongoneo», es decir, al «despelote» total.

CARLOS OLIVARES BARÓ
«Ni salsa ni son, baila con timba»,
revista *Encuentro* N° 23, invierno de 2001-2002

El término salsa sigue siendo un aguijón clavado en el cuero de la fiel tumbadora cubana. Mi impresión es que existe una confusión colectiva entre algunos músicos de la isla, producto de no haber tenido la oportunidad de escucharla en su mejor momento y de haber reaccionado muy tarde a sus evidentes logros. Además, los músicos cubanos siempre han insistido en comparar la salsa con lo que ellos hacen en la isla, aferrándose a las obvias diferencias entre ambos centros irradiadores de ron sonoro. Cuando quisieron actuar ya la salsa había entrado en su período decadente: se habían saltado un momento estelar de producciones con mucho de música cubana y otros elementos caribeños, interpretadas por músicos neoyorquinos muy influenciados por el contacto directo con el jazz moderno. ¿En qué residen estas diferencias?

GUARAPO VS SALSA

Aclarando que «guarapo» es el zumo de la caña de azúcar, quiero incidir sobre tres factores que a mi modo de ver decidieron las diferencias básicas entre lo que se hacía en Cuba y lo que nacía en Nueva York. Primero, la distancia geográfica impuso obvias modificaciones más el hecho de haberse cerrado el grifo cubano. Segundo, muchos músicos latinos crecidos en los barrios de Nueva York, o los que continuaban llegando en busca del éxito estuvieron expuestos al contacto directo con el jazz moderno y otras músicas norteamericanas; se trataba de gente que venía de escuchar y bailar otras cosas como la bomba, la plena, el merengue, la cumbia, la bossa nova, el tamborito panameño, etc. Finalmente, bastantes versiones de temas cubanos que se desarrollaron en Nueva York entre 1960 y 1970 fueron robadas del repertorio criollo sin pagar derechos, de ahí las siglas que vemos en muchos discos: D.R., que indican «Derechos Reservados», una manera de eludir el nombre de los autores y de advertir el pago si apareciese una reclamación posterior ¿Pero acaso Castro no había abierto la brecha al eliminar los derechos de autor al comienzo de la revolución?

Esto de las diferencias es algo curioso. Durante largo tiempo se aceptaron las notables divergencias entre las músicas creadas en Santiago de Cuba y las formuladas en La Habana. Como ejemplo propongo el concepto de son que siempre mantuvo el trío Matamoros, que no se parece en nada al que desarrolló Ignacio Piñeiro con su Septeto Nacional en la capital, a pesar de ser contemporáneos. ¿Cómo es posible entonces que los musicógrafos y periodistas cubanos no hayan tenido en cuenta las enormes diferencias entre lo que se hacía en Cuba y lo que se logró durante la etapa culminante de la salsa neoyorquina? La salsa, a pesar de sus altas y bajas, contribuyó a ampliar las posibilidades sonoras de la sabrosura que se practicaba en la isla. Trataré de explicarlo por bloques de instrumentos:

PERCUSIÓN. En este aspecto destacaron Tito Puente, Nicky Marrero, Orestes Vilató, Manny Oquendo y otros, que lograron darle preponderancia al timbal en Nueva York, liberándolo de la sumisión a que siempre estuvo sometido entre las charangas dedicadas al danzón y al chachachá. Otra: los mejores congueros de la salsa, Ray Barretto, Cándido Camero, *Patato* Valdés o Mongo Santamaría, que solían tocar con tres tumbadoras a la vez, hicieron un aporte magnífico que, con algunas excepciones, no se practicaba regularmente en Cuba. En la salsa, hasta el bongó se hizo más abierto y sonoro, sin embargo, las claves desaparecieron.

PATATO Y CHANGUITO.

PIANO Y BAJO. Otra diferencia tiene que ver con los cambios ocurridos en Nueva York al bajo y el piano, que siempre habían estado amarrados al diseño melódico-percutivo de los ricos tumbaos criollos. Partiendo de esa base, los pianistas Paquito Hechavarría, los hermanos Palmieri, Rafael Ithier y Papo Lucca lograron ampliar su marco de referencia, enriqueciéndola a menudo con diferentes elementos absorbidos del jazz y de la plena puertorriqueña; ésa fue precisamente una de sus más significativas contribuciones. En cuanto al contrabajo acústico, invito a cualquiera a que escuche lo que alcanzó Andy González, puertorriqueño nacido en el Bronx, un músico que trabajó con las mejores bandas, desde Eddie Palmieri hasta Fort Apache (y que aparece en el documental *Calle 54* de Fernando Trueba), pasando por el Conjunto Libre del percusionista Manny Oquendo. Andy, que había escuchado lo mejor de la música cubana grabada en los años 40 y 50, se dio cuenta a tiempo de lo que estaba pasando en la isla (ver el libro *Salsiology* de Vernon W. Boggs); así me lo hizo ver en una entrevista. Su contribución en los dos álbumes del Conjunto Folklórico y Experimental Nuevayorquino (1975 y 1976) lo establecieron como uno de los bajistas más significativos de la mejor salsa.

METALES. Cuando examinan el fraseo de las trompetas en la salsa, los críticos cubanos encuentran que su dicción es claramente jazzeada, que matizan con leyes distintas a las que siempre rigieron los conjuntos tradicionales cubanos. ¿Y qué esperaban? ¿Más de lo mismo? Al llegar a los trombones hay que hablar de una verdadera revolución salsera, pues raramente se usó en Cuba ese instrumento con un papel tan preponderante. Como ejemplo sugiero que el lector escuche lo que logró Reinaldo Jorge en *Contrabando*, un curioso número del CD *Rubén blades y Son del solar*, que trata de un indio que vende artículos de todo tipo desde su canoa. No olvido a los grandes del trombón en Cuba, especialmente a **Leopoldo *Pucho* Escalante** (1919), el que tuvo la osadía de organizar un noneto de jazz cuando la música norteamericana estaba prácticamente proscrita (como música del enemigo) en la isla. Después –ironías de la vida– fue miembro fundador de la Orquesta Cubana de Música Moder-

na. *Pucho* Escalante es otro que no aparece mencionado en el *Diccionario* de Orovio, pero Luis, su hermano trompeta sí.

Negándose a aceptar el hecho irrefutable de la contribución salsera al son, algunos pretenden limitar sus antecedentes a las orquestaciones realizadas por Pedro Jústiz *Peruchín* y Generoso Jiménez para importantes números de la orquesta gigante de Benny Moré. Sin embargo, ahora tenemos que el *sonos* y el estilo característicos de la salsa fueron asumidos por la casi totalidad de las agrupaciones cubanas de música bailable, pero llamándola **hipersalsa**, con excepción de aquellos conjuntos que se mantuvieron en la línea más tradicional del son.

No pretendo sugerir ni por un momento que, oída en su conjunto, la instrumentación en la salsa fuera mejor o más figurativa que lo que se hacía o se hace actualmente en Cuba, sino recalcar las contradicciones y tergiversaciones en que se desenvuelven las cosas en la isla, sometidos los músicos a una constante presión «desde arriba» y al poco acceso que han tenido a lo que pasaba en el resto del mundo. El siguiente argumento empujará aún más el aguijón clavado en el cuero de la tumbadora: estimo que si no hubiera sido por la salsa neoyorquina, la música de la isla habría caído posiblemente en el mimetismo, la uniformidad, el esquematismo y el epigonismo, tan dañinos en la esfera del arte musical.

Creo que todos estamos de acuerdo en que si no hubiera sido por el son cubano no habría surgido la salsa neoyorquina. Pero visto desde la orilla opuesta, si no hubiera sido por la salsa, ¿de qué se habría retroalimentado la música bailable cubana de los últimos veine años?

LAS BANDAS MÁS DESTACADAS

A partir de 1990 en que el régimen estableció el duro «Período Especial», el país cayó verticalmente en una mezcla de apatía y desilusión. Las estanterías vacías de las tiendas y las largas colas para alcanzar artículos de primera necesidad se convirtieron en norma. Los discos también se buscaban como oro molido: la EGREM, que llegó a publicar hasta cien títulos nuevos al año a mediados de los 80, tuvo verdaderas dificultades en lanzar una docena de álbumes en 1991. Los cortes de electricidad se sucedían uno tras otro, y la gasolina era casi inexistente. Excepto en los hoteles para turistas, la vida nocturna se vio reducida drásticamente. No obstante, en los Jardines de La Tropical todavía sonaban las mejores bandas, pero el ron sólo iba a parar a gargantas extranjeras, mientras los nativos tenían que limitarse a beber una horrible cocción de color marrón que con ironía bautizaron «vino espumoso». Chicas desesperadas practicaban una prostitución todavía bastante discreta, y al ciudadano que sorprendían con dólares encima lo esperaba la cárcel, aunque sólo con dólares se podía comprar en las tiendas reservadas a turistas y diplomáticos.

Para los músicos, una gira al extranjero equivalía a que le tocara la lotería (inexistente en la isla), no porque su minúsculo salario en pesos fuera a ser incrementado, cosa que habría ayudado en algo a sus familias, sino por la esperanza de, haciendo sacrificios, ahorrar algunos de los dólares diarios de caché, y quizá poder vender algunas cajas de puros Cohiba extraídos de contrabando. Las bandas cubanas cobraban entonces sólo una fracción del caché ingresado por un grupo norteamericano, colombiano o puertorriqueño, y los músicos estaban siempre dispuestos a tocar en lugares que no estaban incluidos dentro de la gira, por menos dinero aún. Lo importante era regresar a casa con «fulas».

Las cosas se veían bastante feas para la música cubana en 1991. Sin embargo, ya cercanos al 2000 la situación había cambiado notablemente, como una reminiscencia de la década de 1950. El turismo aumentaba continuamente, llegando a alcanzar la cifra de 600.000 visitantes entre 1988 y 1993. La mayor parte de estos extranjeros eran jóvenes, con una evidente curiosidad cultural; se encontraban en casa de la peonza y querían bailar y pasarlo bien. La música cubana comenzaba a fascinar a nuevas audiencias, abriendo horizontes no sólo a latinos amantes de la salsa sino también a europeos y hasta japoneses.

La aparición de discos en el extranjero contribuyó notablemente a atraer infinidad de turistas. He aquí algunos de los que más penetraron el mercado. En Gran Bretaña el sello Earthworks publicó en 1985 *Viva el ritmo!*, una compilación de números de Irakere, Son 14, Los Van Van y otros, con licencia de la EGREM. Comenzando en 1987, el sello World Circuit terminó vendiendo en 1999 cuatro millones de compactos de *Fiesta guajira,* de Celina González. Entretanto, en España, Nuevos Medios sacó a Benny Moré y a *Bola de Nieve* en 1989, mientras que en Estados Unidos el sello Blue Note contrató al brillante pianista Gonzalo Rubalcaba en 1995, burlando el bloqueo oficial sobre artistas cubanos al transferirle toda la responsabilidad a su subsidiaria japonesa, la cual a su vez dio el permiso para las grabaciones a su sede central en Nueva York.

La mayor parte de las discográficas extranjeras que llegaron a la isla encontraron una escena musical dividida en dos grandes áreas: en primer lugar, la música tradicional preservada por conjuntos soneros, trovadores y charangas, a menudo con nuevos músicos que mantenían los viejos nombres de las agrupaciones originales; consideradas de poco interés por los responsables culturales cubanos, estos grupos habían ganado gran arraigo fuera de Cuba. No hay que olvidar que en 1989, Compay Segundo y Elíades Ochoa viajaron a Washington para aparecer en el prestigioso Smithsonian Institute. Ese mismo año, la Orquesta Revé, muy popular entre los bailadores por su ritmo de son changüí, realizó una extensa gira por Europa a través del festival WOMAD; casi no logran salir de la isla porque los burócratas continuaban insistiendo –hasta el último momento– con los organizadores del evento que una banda progresiva como Irakere o Síntesis sería más apropiada que un grupo de negros soneros.

Es importante señalar que el público que asiste a los festivales WOMAD está compuesto principalmente por gente de clase media con un promedio de menos de cuarenta años; pronto estos espectadores comenzaron a mirar hacia Cuba como un verdadero tesoro de música fascinante.

El otro estrato musical era sin duda más contemporáneo y excitante. Fue bautizada más tarde como «timba», un término de márketing que me hace recordar la acusada arbitrariedad al escoger el nombre de «salsa», también adoptado por razones de mercado por Pacheco y Masucci en 1970 en Nueva York. En La Habana, este tipo de música también es conocida como «salsa cubana» o «hipersalsa».

Al presentar un resumen de las principales bandas e individuos que han descollado en los últimos años, no puedo olvidar la definición que me hizo un músico joven recién llegado. Allí hay tres tipos de música actualmente: una dice «incorpórate y baila»; la otra sugiere: «escucha y desnúdate», mientras que la última toma una intención irónica: «recuerda y no jodas más».

La timba es una música fuerte, dinámica, compleja, ruidosa, saltarina, llena de frases callejeras. Uno de sus más brillantes exponentes es **NG La Banda,** el grupo fundado en 1988 por **José Luis Cortés,** flautista y cantante nacido en 1953 en Santa Clara, que había comenzado su carrera como cofundador de Los Van Van antes de unirse a Irakere. Los músicos provenían de la banda de Pachito Alonso, de Irakere, de la Orquesta de la Radiotelevisión Cubana y de la del cabaré Tropicana. Las trompetas y saxofones de NG La Banda, conocidos localmente como «los metales del terror», se hicieron famosos por sus cierres abruptos y cambios constantes, características que contribuyeron a identificar a la timba. Cortés y su vocalista estelar, Tony Calá, presentaban números cargados de lenguaje barriobajero, a menudo interrumpidos por secciones de rap, dirigidos a jovencitos desarraigados en las barriadas, sin oportunidades de realizar sus vidas. De las piezas más ligeras y románticas se encargaba entonces Isaac Delgado.

MIEMBROS DE NG LA BANDA.

La búsqueda de un nuevo modo de sonar los ritmos cubanos venía gestándose desde el 85, un empeño en alcanzar una fusión que asumiera la contemporaneidad sin caer en lo estrictamente comercial. Organizados en abril de 1988 bajo el nombre de Nueva Generación La Banda, se juntaron Cortés y Germán Velasco en el clarinete y saxo, Elpidio Chapottín y José Miguel Greco en la trompeta y el saxo Carlos Averhoff. La percusión estaba a cargo de Barbarito Argudín, Gerardo Piloto y Víctor Valdés. Su dominio escénico, el desenvolvimiento espontáneo y atrevido, la inspiración en el soneo y los movimientos corporales desinhibidos lograron cautivar a los espectadores inmediatamente.

Pronto montaron números que expresaban el clamor de sectores de la población abandonados a su suerte, como en la rumba *Los Sitios entero,* incluyendo una denuncia sobre la profusión de jineteras en *La bruja.* Otros temas favoritos de NG La Banda son los que introducen aspectos de la Santería, como en *Santa palabra* y *Papá Changó.*

Por la «dureza» de la mayor parte de su repertorio, José Luis Cortés confirmó el apodo de «*El tosco*» que se había ganado en sus días estudiantiles. La banda pronto experimentó fuertes críticas del régimen, incluyendo una total censura radial para algunos de sus números. Sin embargo, los bailadores la adoraban, en parte porque lucían atractivas botas y boinas, un vestuario brillante y collares de oro. El número *Échale limón*, que en Cuba quiere decir que se vayan al diablo, se convirtió en una coreografía específica conocida como «limón», que arrebató a mucha gente. Hacia 1995 nuevos grupos comenzaron a rivalizar con NG La Banda, incluyendo a dos antiguos miembros, Isaac Delgado y Giraldo Piloto, su baterista. Para entonces habían grabado con la cantante **Malena Burke**, hija de Elena Burke, que tiene talento propio. El debut de la vocalista **Osdalgia**, un descubrimiento del año 2000, condujo a un álbum producido por el propio José Luis Cortés.

Issac Delgado

Otra Idea

Por su parte, «El chévere de la salsa», el impecable **Isaac Delgado**, nacido en 1962, fue señalado como un posible éxito internacional para representar a Cuba en el ámbito salsa/timba. Sin embargo, Isaac tomó otra dirección, concentrándose en un tipo de salsa romántica con toques de bolero y algo de la nueva trova, de ahí que su repertorio incluya canciones de Pablo Milanés y Pedro Luis Ferrer. Isaac tenía sólo 16 años cuando tuvo la suerte de que el pianista Gonzalo Rubalcaba lo escogiera como vocalista para su banda **Proyecto**. Allí se quedó dos años, aunque conservó una gran amistad con Rubalcaba, quien siguió arreglándole números nuevos, incluso después de convertirse en una estrella internacional del jazz.

En los años 80, Isaac Delgado había trabajado con el grupo **Galaxia** y con la banda de **Pachito Alonso** antes de unirse a NG La Banda. Cuando decidió abandonarla en 1992 y formar su propia agrupación, se llevó con él al percusionista y compositor Giraldo Piloto (su padre, fallecido en un accidente aéreo en 1967, había compuesto bellos boleros tipo filin en compañía de Alberto Vera). Hombre ambicioso y un vocalista nada común, Isaac Delgado grabó dos álbumes estupendos en Venezuela: *Dando la hora*, para el sello PM de Pablo Milanés, y *Con ganas*, que le publicó

Qbadisc, una discográfica independiente de Nueva York. También actuó bastante tiempo en España y en la discoteca Azúcar de Cancún, México.

Pero en 1994, cuando Giraldo Piloto lo dejó para formar su propia banda de timba fuerte, Isaac Delgado se arriesgó a coquetear con la censura en *El año que viene*, sugiriendo la necesidad de cambios para mejorar al país. Inevitablemente, después de haber sido un éxito televisivo, el número jamás se escuchó en la radio cubana; el lector sacará sus propias conclusiones. Dos años después, Issac Delgado fue el elegante presentador del documental *Yo soy del son a la salsa*, un impresionante esfuerzo por abarcar a los mejores artistas latinoamericanos dentro de un contexto histórico, producido por el empresario dominicano Ralph Mercado en Nueva York, con guión del novelista Leonardo Padura y dirigido por Rigoberto López (ambos residentes en la isla).

Isaac se situó a la vanguardia de los artistas cubanos que intentaban penetrar el mercado estadounidense; firmó con RMM, el sello de Ralph Mercado, y produjo *Otra idea*, un álbum que revela elementos de pop y salsa, a pesar de su declarada meta de hacer de la timba un éxito internacional. Incontenible y afortunado, fue el primer artista de la isla en actuar en 1998 en el Onyx Club de Miami, en medio de las protestas de los extremistas anticastristas. Pero en 2000 rompió su contrato con RMM, aduciendo que su trabajo no recibía adecuada promoción. La empresa contestó, y esto no lo he podido corroborar

EL VOCALISTA ISAAC DELGADO.

(aunque lo dudo), que lo tenían que dejar ir porque su principal estrella, la incomparable Celia Cruz, se negaba a compartir un sello discográfico con un cubano procastrista.

Inmutable y decidido, Isaac Delgado logró conseguir apoyo financiero entre varios inversionistas extranjeros para grabar un nuevo álbum en los recién estrenados estudios Abdala de La Habana, otra vez con el apoyo artístico de Gonzalo Rubalcaba. El disco fue lanzado por Ahí-Namá, un sello independiente de California. «El chévere de la salsa» se situaba nuevamente a la cabeza de otros artistas cubanos.

Los mejores: JUAN FORMELL

La orquesta Los Van Van surgió entre 1969 y 1970, y desde entonces ha ocupa-
do un lugar prominente en la vanguardia de la música bailable. La idea fue de
Juan Formell (1942), quien en 1959 se había unido a la Banda de la Policía Na-
cional Revolucionaria como contrabajista. Después pasó a los grupos de Pedro
Jústiz *Peruchín* y de Guillermo Rubalcaba, director de la charanga típica del
Ministerio de Cultura, hasta ingresar en la orquesta del cabaré Caribe del hotel
Habana Libre. Debido a un serio problema laboral se vio forzado a agarrar lo
primero que se le presentó: una agrupación muy ruidosa de segunda categoría.
Poco más de un año le bastó a Formell para reformar con sus arreglos y cambios de instrumentos el estilo de charanga de la Orquesta Revé, pero incontables choques con su director, el percusionista Elio Revé, lo disuadieron a fundar
su propia banda. Músico de obvias inquietudes musicales y políticas, todavía algunos lo recuerdan en las noches bohemias de los años 60 descargando con una
guitarra en La Rampa. Ya entonces se advertía en él una intención de renovar el
género cancionístico, sugiriendo una zona de intereses más allá del filin, enmar-
cada en una cierta sonoridad sonera.

En 1969 la isla vivía un momento peculiar. Todos los recursos humanos y
técnicos del país habían sido dirigidos a los preparativos de una supuesta zafra
supergigante, la cosecha azucarera más grande de todos los tiempos: diez millones de toneladas en 1970. Comprometido hasta el cuello con su quijotesco plan,
Fidel Castro eliminó a los pocos que se atrevieron a hacerle ver tamaña locura.
Ése fue el caso del teniente Orlando Borrego, entonces al frente del Ministerio
del Azúcar. Borrego provenía de las filas guerrilleras formadas por Che Guevara, muerto dos años antes en Bolivia. Por supuesto, Castro no lo consideraba
uno de sus incondicionales.

En prensa, radio, televisión, vallas y posters se repetía la obsesiva consigna
«Los diez millones van», una referencia a la meta fijada. Pronto la propaganda
del Partido apareció con la frase «De que van, van». De ahí tomó Formell el
nombre para su proyecto, en la seguridad de que su orquesta iría adelante. Y tenía razón. Sin embargo, Castro no alcanzó su absurda meta: a pesar del esfuerzo
descomunal que absorbió a todo el país –en detrimento de otras producciones
necesarias–, se lograron poco más de ocho millones de toneladas de oro blanco.

Fue la dirección del Consejo Nacional de Cultura la que apoyó a Formell
a conformar su agrupación, a la que se unieron inicialmente varios músicos de

la de Revé, impresionados por su quehacer. Aupada por el régimen, la orquesta comenzó a ser seguida por la afición a través de la radio; pronto no había baile público en que no fueran aclamados. La leyenda de su sonido nuevo se confirmó cuando fueron incluidos en una delegación artística oficial que actuó en Perú para halagar a los dirigentes militares de entonces, amigos de Fidel, que habían asestado un golpe de Estado al gobierno constituido democráticamente.

¿Cómo se convirtieron Los Van Van en un gran acontecimiento? En aquellos tiempos parecía que se había olvidado la tradición sonera. Dejando aparte el exilio de músicos importantes y otros factores como la irrupción de la era del pop, el rock y la pasión por los Beatles, sumado a una falta de fe en los objetivos de la revolución, hizo que buena parte de la juventud sintonizara con lo que le llegaba del Norte y de España, despreciando como algo fuera de moda el bailar con charangas o conjuntos tradicionales. El son, el bolero, el chachachá y la guaracha habían sido metidos en el trastero. Los intentos de presentar ritmos que pegaran habían sido efímeros, desde el mozambique de Pello el Afrokán, que impusieron hasta el agotamiento, hasta el ritmo pa'cá de Juanito Márquez, pasando por el pilón del binomio Pacho Alonso/Enrique Bonne.

Así las cosas, no le fue muy difícil al ambicioso Formell conseguir que su grupo encabezara una puesta al día de la música popular bailable, en la que también desempeñaron un papel importante agrupaciones como Rumbavana, Los Reyes 73 y muy especialmente la Ritmo Oriental, entre otras.

Había que inventar algo nuevo. El caballo de batalla de Los Van Van fue el songo, un modo de hacer en el que el color orquestal y el diseño de la percusión prestaron el elemento novedoso, y a la vez, una inequívoca señal de continuidad sonera mezclada con música beat norteamericana. Mientras que en Nueva York triunfaba la salsa, Formell conquistaba en Cuba el espacio del bailador con el songo, apoyado en las coreografías del llamado estilo casino, que aunque originadas mucho antes, ahora se avenían a la perfección a su propuesta. El songo consiste en una repetición de breves frases musicales provocadas por los violines o las dos flautas, mientras el coro repite insistentemente una o pocas palabras sugerentes («*Candela, que le den candela*»), entre improvisaciones sagaces del cantante (Pedrito Calvo) que culminan en bruscos cierres donde la batería/timbales acentúa el ritmo, seguido de un solo por uno de los trombones. El ritmo es lento, a veces da la impresión de quedarse ligeramente detrás del compás. Muy sabroso de bailar. Un teclado electrónico y el bajo eléctrico de Formell hicieron el resto. En 1997 declaró al diario *Clarín* de Buenos Aires:

> Yo me fijo en lo que la gente habla; no hago más que crónicas de un país que tiene un desarrollo bien complejo y muchas cosas que contar. De una anécdota o de una situación que está ocurriendo a nivel nacional surge el comentario, bien sea sobre algo positivo, simpático o de lo que sea. Sobre todo, siempre en broma.

Quizá porque no cursó en ningún conservatorio, Formell no se parece a nadie tocando el bajo, instrumento que cobró relieve en el jazz y el rock, y que tiene mucho que ver con el estilo sonoro de la agrupación. Admirador del pianista Gonzalo Rubalcaba, también ha expresado su fascinación por el percusionista José Luis *Changuito* Quintana, quien permaneció casi 25 años con él y tuvo mucho que ver con el impulso que cobró el songo. *Changuito* fue el primero en incorporar los timbales a la batería y fue sustituido por Samuel, hijo del director.

Formell tiene otro hijo que es cantautor y, aparentemente, las relaciones entre ambos nunca han sido satisfactorias. Después de varios incidentes con el régimen, el joven decidió largarse; se llama Juan Carlos (1964) y aprendió guitarra y contrabajo. En una gira con el conjunto Rumbavana se quedó en México, entrando más tarde a Estados Unidos como un clásico espalda mojada. En 1999 sacó su primer álbum, *Songs from a little blue house* (sello Wicklow/BMG), trece canciones envueltas en la imaginería del agua. *Las calles del paraíso* es el título de su segundo CD, en que Juan Carlos trasciende la rutina convencional, y lo convierte en uno de los mejores músicos de la nueva generación en el exilio.

Los Van Van tiene más de treinta años de existencia y consiste de quince músicos, algunos ya cubiertos de canas. Favoritos de la audiencia, el mérito principal corresponde al propio Formell, aunque el pianista César Pedroso y el cantante Pedrito Calvo (el del sombrero), aportaron alguno que otro tema. Integrante desde 1974, ya Pedrito no está con Formell, se separó en noviembre de 2000, poco después de una gira por Argentina y Uruguay. En los primeros años montaron piezas de Evaristo Aparicio, Alina Torres, Enrique Bonne y Rodolfo

Cárdenas, precisamente el autor de *Que le den candela*, que no eran miembros de la orquesta.

El mensaje de algunos números es claramente propagandístico o absurdamente optimista. A pesar de la evidente ruina en que se encuentra la capital, en *La Habana sí* se insiste en que «*La Habana entera quiere ser la capital más bella de América Latina...*». Un bonito deseo pero la realidad es bien distinta.

Formell reconoce que si hubiera tenido acceso a los avances tecnológicos podría haber prescindido de algunos músicos y hacer más rentable la orquesta, pero el sistema en que viven le permite darse el lujo de mantener los que quiera. El Estado paga y sus músicos gozan de un status especial. Cuba no aplica los conceptos de rentabilidad de los países capitalistas, donde para competir el director tiene que ingeniárselas en cómo mantener o reducir la plantilla. En este sentido, me permito recordarle a Formell y a otros responsables de bandas un viejo proverbio afrocubano: «Algún día la araña tendrá que pagar alquiler».

Los Van Van han viajado por muchos países regando sabrosura. Ostentan cuatro premios EGREM, cinco Girasoles de la revista *Opina*, y entre 1995-98 fue la formación cubana que apareció con mayor frecuencia en las listas de éxitos de la revista *Latin Beat* de Los Ángeles. Han aparecido en los filmes cubanos *Los pájaros tirándole a la escopeta*, *Se permuta* y *En tres y dos*, y cuando se estrenó en La Habana el documental cubano-norteamericano *Yo soy del son a la salsa*, hizo bailar al público asistente desde la pantalla. En 1999 fueron galardonados con el codiciado premio Grammy por el disco *Van Van is here* (Havana Caliente).

El formato instrumental logra un timbre muy especial que los hace fácilmente identificables. La introducción de los trombones a la charanga fue una excelente idea, así como el papel de la batería respaldando el buen trabajo de las congas, mientras los cantantes siempre han sabido dar fuste para encaminar la melodía.

Con los años, el sonido de la orquesta ha acentuado su potencia dentro de lo que el propio Formell, bastante gastado por ingerir sustancias nocivas, ha llamado «timba» y que se aprecia en el documental de Liliana Mazure y Aaron Vega, el cumplir la orquesta 30 años. La timba es francamente estridente, ruidosa; por lo demás, sus músicos tocan muy fuerte y el aquelarre que se forma es de cuidado. Suenan como si todos quisieran sobresalir a la vez. ¿Por qué será que mientras más difícil se pone la vida del cubano más aumentan los decibelios?

Paulito y su Élite lleva ese nombre porque su fundador, Pablo Fernández Gallo, tuvo que darse a conocer como Paulito porque en Cuba «Pablito» ya tenía dueño. Habanero nacido en 1963, estudió diseño industrial antes de aprender a tocar el clarinete. Se convirtió en cantante cuando se dio cuenta de que jamás podría obtener en Cuba un instrumento de calidad. Paulito es uno de los jóvenes que transformaron la escena musical en los 90; el hombre delgado, de movimientos sinuosos, que promocionaba la cerveza Cristal y las playas de Varadero en videoclips que se veían en las pantallas televisivas de los hoteles para turistas y en el nuevo aeropuerto José Martí.

Sus números son un verdadero rastro musical: un poco de jazz mezclado con algo de rock, merengue, bomba, son, guaguancó, lo que sea, un cóctel que lleva de todo un poco. Lo que a menudo provoca que su música pase de la fusión a la confusión en cuestión de segundos. Paulito proyecta un perfil que corresponde al de algunos músicos de hoy: lo arriesga todo con la evidente intención de asaltar el mercado internacional.

Cansado de hacer coros en el conjunto sonero de Adalberto Álvarez, quien lo había llamado en 1986, Paulito se integró al nuevo grupo **Dan Den** de Juan Carlos Alfonso, antes de pasar a **Opus 13**, una banda de jazz-rock progresivo, en la línea de Irakere, pero que no logró conectar con el gran público, quizá porque a sus textos –tal y como están las cosas– les faltaba algo de picardía para agarrar al bailador. Los dejó para formar su propia banda en 1992, logrando un éxito inmediato con *Tú no me calculas*. El estilo de Paulito me recuerda en algo el de Isaac Delgado, quizá por aquello de ligero, romántico y no demasiado frenético al interpretar timba. Sin embargo, en los últimos años ha tendido a comenzar con piezas de salsa suave en cuyo desenlace él suele romper con todo, como sucede en el tema señalado. Con Dan Den había destilado una obvia capacidad para la improvisación sonera, y esto le permitió una excelente base para competir con Cándido Fabré, el santiaguero que tenía al son cogido por el mango ante las cámaras de la televisión cubana; igualmente desarrolló una cierta rivalidad con Manolín, «El médico de la salsa».

Después de lanzar un CD con un sello español, en 1996 Paulito firmó con Nueva Fania, una empresa de Jerry Masucci, el padrino de la salsa neoyorquina, pero como le sucedió a Issac Delgado con RMM, después se quejó de que no lo promocionaban debidamente. El nuevo siglo lo encontró de pionero en el concepto de *joint ventures* entre artistas del patio y el Estado cubano, financiando de su propio bolsillo un proyecto con la EGREM para producir un nuevo álbum, *Una vez más por amor,* ecléctica mezcla de salsa romántica, timba suave y pop tropical que incluye un tango de Carlos Gardel con el apoyo del teclado.

Ya he mencionado varias veces a **Manolín, el médico de la salsa.** Su verdadero nombre es Manuel González Hernández y comenzó muy temprano con su hermano mayor al formar una banda de adolescentes, aunque no se dedicó a la música como carrera hasta que terminó sus estudios médicos en 1992. Los asiduos al cabaré del hotel Capri fueron los primeros en verlo actuar; con presentaciones bien recibidas desde aquel escenario, ahí comenzó a ser invitado para abrir conciertos de Los Van Van y NG La Banda en centros clave como el Palacio de la Salsa y el Café Cantante. Aunque a sus rivales siempre les pareció un tío curioso, apareciendo en la televisión vestido de blanco y con un estetoscopio, rápidamente comenzó a ganarles en popularidad. Creo que su secreto reside en las letras de sus canciones, en su evidente carisma, más que en su voz. Como autor ha demostrado habilidad para generar frases que toman por asalto la imaginación popular. Contando con el teclado de su arreglista Luis Bu Pascual, sus números aparecen vestidos con una curiosa mezcla de timba y funk, que le permitió vender suficientes copias de su primer álbum, *Una aventura loca,* el cual le proporcionó la envidiable suma de $4.000, nada inestimable para un cantante que debutó en 1994. Aquel primer disco fue seguido de *Para mi gente,* producido por el sello español Caribe, que vendió aún más ejemplares por la inclusión de *Arriba de la bola,* un éxito que inmediatamente fue aprovechado por el gobierno para usarlo en videoclips propagandísticos.

Pero en Cuba el apoyo oficial no suele durar mucho. Durante aproximadamente un año, Manolín fue el músico mimado del régimen, mas las autoridades pronto le dieron la espalda cuando sacó *Tengo amigos en Miami,* un número que fue terminantemente prohibido en las ondas nacionales. Invitado a participar en un homenaje a NG La Banda, tuvo la idea de interpretar una canción que invita a la reconciliación entre los cubanos de ambos lados: «Viva la paz en nombre de los espíritus / pido una tregua para esta larga guerra / pido cordura / que se contagien de mi sabrosura...», es parte de la letra que también pide «un puente de mangas largas / para que la gente de Miami venga / y la gente de La Habana vaya...» El periódico oficial *Granma* procedió a regañarlo: «Lo que va

MANOLÍN «EL MÉDICO DE LA
SALSA».

más allá de la música resulta en su caso inadmisible, cuando se sabe muy bien –y en él no es una actitud ingenua– cuán turbia y tensa es la relación por parte de quienes atentan allá contra nuestra identidad y nuestra cultura». A lo que respondió valientemente el médico salsero: «Como artista tengo el derecho y la obligación de reflejar la realidad de mi tiempo y lo hago desde mi punto de vista, que no será perfecto, pero es el mío. Los cubanos de Miami también existen».

Para complicar más las cosas, Manolín comenzó a pasar largas temporadas en Miami, que allí aprovecharon para reportar que había decidido abandonar el país. Sin embargo, él lo negó todo, aduciendo que se encontraba buscando trabajo y un nuevo sello discográfico que respondiera a sus planes. Entre 1998 y 1999, Manolín y su banda actuaron con bastante éxito en los clubes Amnesia y Starfish de Miami, pero pronto surgieron acaloradas discusiones con sus músicos debido a la mala calidad del alojamiento en que se les mantenía; después no se pusieron de acuerdo sobre el caché recibido, mientras que su sello español se negó a dejarlo ir. Lo del representante español lo puedo entender, pero en la actitud de sus compañeros músicos puedo entrever el largo brazo de la Seguridad del Estado poniendo presión al colectivo. «Le hicieron un número 8» se suele decir en Cuba. Como resultado, a finales del 2000 Manolín se había separado de su banda y de regreso en La Habana tuvo que pedirle a Paulito que le cediera músicos para cumplir algunas actuaciones; poco después desapareció nuevamente, creo que a México.

De todas las bandas de la generación de la timba, **Bamboleo**, casi un recién llegado, es quizá la agrupación que ofrece la música más variada, inventiva y sin fórmulas preconcebidas. Fue fundada por **Lázaro Valdés,** un teclista y arreglista fuera de serie que puede mostrar un pedigrí impecable: el abuelo Oscar había sido percusionista de la Orquesta Cubana de Música Moderna; Vicentico, su tío abuelo, muerto en el exilio, fue una de las mejores voces del bolero, y su padre tocó el piano con Benny Moré, mientras que su tío Oscar era cantante y tocador de batá de Irakere. Lázaro Valdés había aprendido violín y piano en la Escuela Nacional de Arte, y trabajó con el jazzista Bobby Carcassés, así como con el cantautor Amaury Pérez. Su carrera antes de crear Bamboleo incluía cinco años como pianista de Pachito Alonso y sus Kini Kini.

Bamboleo surgió como resultado de un intento de crear un grupo muy diferente. El sello español Caribe le había pedido a Valdés que formara una banda para acompañar a un grupo de bailarinas, basadas en las famosas Mulatas de Fuego de los años 50. Las audiciones no arrojaron suficientes chicas con la calidad requerida y el proyecto fue abandonado, dejando a Lázaro con un núcleo de músicos y un definitivo interés en emplear cantantes femeninas. Se le ocurrió entonces reclutar a Vannia Borges, que había trabajado con el cuarteto femenino D'Capo, y que por entonces actuaba con Pachito Alonso. Después conoció a Haila Monpié, una bailarina de cabaré. Entonces agregó un dúo de cantantes masculinos: Rafael y Alejandro Leberra; los cuatro serían respaldados por una banda de nueve miembros que incluía dos saxos y una trompeta.

Debutaron en febrero de 1995 y pronto tuvieron éxito. Esto se debió a la dinámica de sus presentaciones y a arreglos con personalidad propia, sin olvidar la astuta imagen que Lázaro Valdés le creó al grupo: las cabezas rapadas de ambas chicas sorprendió a muchos cubanos, que encontraron la innovación extremadamente moderna y atrevida. Otro aspecto de la imagen tuvo que ver con las cubiertas de los discos, diseñadas por la empresa norteamericana Ahí-Namá, que se veían excitantes y modernas, contrastando notablemente con los diseños concebidos en La Habana. Tengo entendido que lo de las cabezas afeitadas se debió a un accidente: Vannia Borges había posado como modelo para la cubierta de un disco del grupo AfroCuba, donde mostraba la palabra Cuba afeitada en su pelo, y la única manera de borrarlo era raparle toda la cabeza. Valdés se dio cuenta de que era un *look* distinto y diferente, y logró convencer a Haila Monpié de que hiciera lo mismo.

Yo no me parezco a nadie fue el segundo álbum de Bamboleo, con nueve números debidos al compositor Leonel Limonta, que entonces también era el representante del grupo. Desde los compases iniciales del asalto que acometen los metales en el primer surco, la música se sale del promedio producido por otras bandas de timba, debido también a los irresistibles tumbaos del piano.

Dan Den, una de las agrupaciones más modernas centradas en la salsa sonera en lugar de la estridente timba, fue fundada por el pianista **Juan Carlos Alfonso**, un fan del rock en su juventud, transformado después en salsero bajo la influencia de las bandas en que participó. Nacido en el habanero pueblo de Bejucal en 1963, de padre músico, Juan Carlos y su hermana María de los Ángeles (quien también ha seguido una carrera musical), estudiaron con un maestro prominente en su pueblo natal. Después de graduarse en el Conservatorio Alejandro García Caturla, comenzó una década muy intensa como pianista y teclista del Conjunto Colonial dirigido por Nelo Sosa, un veterano de la década de los 50. Más tarde, Juan Carlos pasó a la Orquesta Sensación, otra agrupación de larga existencia, hasta que finalmente, en 1984, se unió al Charangón de Revé. Ésta estaba entonces a punto de alcanzar notoriedad con su versión revitalizada del son changüí, y la influencia en las teclas de Juan Carlos, más sus arreglos originales, se convirtieron en una parte vital del destino del grupo. Casi sin quererlo, también logró fama como autor de canciones: *Yo sé que tú sabes que yo sé*, constituyó uno de los más grandes éxitos de la Revé junto a *Más joven que mañana*.

Decidido a crear su propia agrupación, dejó a Revé en 1998. El nombre Dan Den es onomatopéyico, y tengo entendido que se debe al sonido acompasado que hacen los cencerros en las comparsas carnavalescas de su nativo Bejucal. Allí fue precisamente donde debutaron, contagiando la fiesta de alegría con sus tres trombones, que llenaron el espacio en el mejor estilo neoyorquino, bien apoyados por el piano y el bajo. Dan Den pronto ganó fama en México y Colombia, países que recorrieron en una extensa gira en 1992. Un año después, ganaron el premio a «La mejor banda tropical», en la Feria de Cali, la capital salsera de Colombia. El álbum *Salsa en Ataré* fue lanzado en 1997, con ocho números de Juan Carlos y uno de Mo Fini, propietaria del sello Tumi. Profundos trombones, timbales de primera, un bajo que se las arregla para combinar lo mejor de la salsa con rápidos vuelos sobre territorio timbero, y todo amarrado por unas teclas excepcionales. Atarés es una barriada popular de La Habana, muy cercana al fondo de la bahía.

La banda que estaba en los labios de todos en 1997, debido en parte a la controversia surgida a raíz de la acusación oficial de representar actos obscenos en público, era la **Charanga Habanera**, una agrupación que comenzó su vida en 1988 como una orquesta tipo charanga (violín, flauta, bajo, piano y percusión). Dirigida por **David Calzado,** violinista con un pasado tradicional, el grupo se dedicó originalmente a un repertorio de chachachás y salsa ligera. David nació en 1960 y proviene de una familia musical: su abuelo había sido trovador en las calles de Santiago de Cuba, y su padre Sergio era miembro de la Orquesta Estrellas Cubanas. Luego de graduarse en la Escuela Nacional de Arte en 1978 se pasó diez años acumulando experiencia en diversos roles musicales. Tocó con su padre y en la Orquesta Ritmo Oriental, pero también arregló y produjo discos para la EGREM, terminando como primer violín de la orquesta de Tropicana. Una noche de 1988 se le acercó el empresario del Casino Riviera Francesa, del Sporting Club de Mónaco, que buscaba una banda tipo charanga para actuar en la tempora-da veraniega. Calzado se apresu-ró a formar un grupo idóneo y obtuvo trabajo en Europa duran-te cinco años; en Mónaco acom-pañaron a estrellas como Whitney Houston, Barry White y Charles Aznavour, mientras David obser-vaba los trucos europeos del ne-gocio del espectáculo. Hasta la fecha, la Charanga Habanera ha hecho siete discos con distintos sellos: EGREM, Magic Music,

LA CHARANGA HABANERA.

Universal y Géminis, pero la etapa dorada fue con Magic Music y Francis Cabezas, con quienes se consolidó la carrera del grupo. El primer disco, *Me sube la fiebre*, los colocó en el mercado, y aunque *Hey you, loca* se realizó con rigor y está muy bien logrado, no fue el más popular. Dura-mente criticado por el gobierno, *Pa'que se entere La Habana* (1995) es el cuarto y quizá su mejor disco con los temas *Superturística,* sobre las chi-cas que buscan la amistad de los extranjeros, y *El temba,* el caso de una cubana que renuncia al amor por la comodidad de juntarse con un caba-llero de edad madura pero con solvencia económica. La cubierta del disco llamó mucho la atención por mostrar la imagen irreverente de Benjamín Franklin, uno de los padres fundadores de la Unión norteamericana –am-pliada de un billete de 100 dólares– transformado en pirata.

En 1993 David Calzado remozó la Charanga Habanera, reduciendo los violines y agregándole metales; adquirió un nuevo repertorio y arreglos extravagantes de timba saltarina. Vistió a los músicos de amplias camisetas tipo hip-hop y coloridas chaquetas estilo africanas; también se esmeró en montar coreografías con elementos de breakdance y demostraciones de nuevos pasos. La «pelota», en particular, tenía aspectos de carácter onanístico. Todo esto logró, junto a letras sexualmente explícitas, una enorme atención por parte del público, pero también dejó un flanco abierto para ser duramente atacado.

Así las cosas, el 29 de julio de 1997 la Charanga actuaba en un concierto al aire libre cerca del malecón habanero dentro de los actos del Festival de la Juventud. Se presentaron con su exuberancia habitual ante un público cifrado en 100.000 jóvenes, y el concierto terminó sin incidentes.

DAVID CALZADO.

El problema es que se emitió una hora después por uno de los dos canales de la televisión, provocando el inevitable choque entre la realidad de la calle y la Cuba oficial: la procacidad en textos y gestos desencadenó el escándalo, el peloteo de responsabilidades y el palo consiguiente. David Calzado se defendió alegando que el doble sentido había sido una norma de la música popular desde los días de Miguel Matamoros; argumentación que no logró impedir que a la Charanga le fuera negado actuar en público o viajar al extranjero durante seis meses, incluyendo el bloqueo de su música en los medios cubanos. En el 2000, al concluir su participación en un concierto de Team Cuba en Francia, la Charanga Habanera se dispersó. Algunos instrumentistas permanecieron unidos, rebautizándose más tarde como la Charanga Forever (para siempre), mientras que Calzado conservó el nombre de Charanga Habanera y formó otra agrupación muy diferente, que incluye a Yulién Oviedo, un chico de 15 años entonces, y un verdadero prodigio en los timbales.

Un rápido examen de 1994, año clave para la música popular, arroja un incesante movimiento. A pesar de separaciones, apariciones de nuevas orquestas, algunos números que fueron mal difundidos y otros que llevaban letras pobres o elementales, hubo cambios significativos en varias agrupaciones, como en la de Isaac Delgado, lo cual no afectó para que ese año llegara a colocarse entre las cinco más favoritas del país. Adalberto Álvarez tuvo que preparar nuevamente otro cantante porque se le desprendió *Rojitas*, y con su versión sonera del tema norteamericano de Big Mountain, *Baby, te quiero a ti*, se mantuvo en la «pelea», logrando ser de los primeros. ¿Recuerda lo que dije en la introducción sobre la influencia yanqui?

En 1994 Félix Santiago se desprendió de Dan Den y formó su propia orquesta, pero al mismo tiempo Los Van Van retumbaron con «*Mándalo y ven*», el estribillo de *Gallina vieja*, logrando mantenerse en la cúspide de la popularidad. Por su parte, Paulito y su Élite mantuvo un buen nivel de temas viejos y nuevos que lo llevaron al primer lugar en una encuesta nacional llevada a cabo por el programa radial «Visión», situándose como una de las figuras más carismáticas de la música actual. Esta agrupación lanzó al año siguiente un nuevo disco con el tema *El cacharrero* y un popurrí de éxitos de Benny Moré.

EN EL PALACIO DE LA SALSA.

La Charanga Habanera le siguió muy de cerca con *Hey you, loca*, y fue junto a las dos anteriores la orquesta de las multitudes con un sonido fuerte y pegajoso. El Palacio de la Salsa, la vieja Tropical y otros centros de distracción se llenaron cuando tocaba la Charanga. Por su parte, Pachito y sus Kini Kini lograron buena puntuación con su versión de *Locos de amor*, mientras el grupo Yumurí mantuvo bailando al público con *Quítate tú*. Entre las voces femeninas, Lucrecia (que reside en Barcelona) se mantuvo en la radio nacional hasta finales de año con sus temas *Me quito la...* y *Me debes un beso*.

Aunque Cándido Fabré, el líder vocal de la Original de Manzanillo, decidió montar su propia orquesta, en poco tiempo su director Pachi Naranjo recompuso el repertorio y mantuvo a toda la región oriental en movimiento con piezas como *Patica de chivo*. Por otro lado, NG La Banda y la Orquesta Revé presentaron títulos que tuvieron su público, al igual que Manolín, «El médico de la salsa», y Los Surik, que a pesar de vivir tan lejos de la capital se hicieron sentir con *A ése le llaman parejero* y *Lo que cae es candela*.

A finales del año en cuestión se celebró en el Salón Rosado de La Tropical el Primer Festival de Soneras de Cuba, con la participación de nueve agrupaciones femeninas de la isla, que presentaron un espectáculo bajo la dirección musical de José Luis Cortés, líder de NG La Banda. El evento fue concebido como una coproducción entre las firmas Artex de Cuba y Network de Alemania para la realización de un disco grabado en vivo. Cuatro horas de música caliente hicieron vibrar a los más de 4.000 espectadores que asistieron a este gigantesco bailable, donde las muchachas se lucieron como verdaderas estrellas del ritmo y el goce caribeño.

Manolito y su Trabuco podría describirse como una agrupación de timba que se mantiene atada al son y la guaracha. Se destaca de las demás no sólo por su sonido y repertorio, sino también porque lo dirige un tresero:

Manuel Simonet. Nacido en Camagüey, aprendió los secretos del tres observando cómo tocaba un tío suyo, aficionado al instrumento de las seis cuerdas metálicas. Una vez dominado, se concentró en la guitarra y el contrabajo; después tomó clases para poder tocar también el piano. Aunque finalmente estudiaría ingeniería, a los 14 años ya había formado su primer grupo, el Conjunto Safari, de donde salieron músicos que después trabajaron con Irakere, con la Orquesta Revé y con el propio Trabuco. La música hizo que se perdiera un ingeniero porque una vez graduado fue reclutado por la Orquesta Maravillas de Florida, una vieja charanga basada en el pueblo de Florida, provincia de Camagüey. Cinco años tocó con la Maravillas, terminando como su director; había adquirido una considerable reputación por sus arreglos innovativos, adaptando efectos de los metales para su sección de violines y también creando canciones para la orquesta.

En 1993 Manuel Simonet formó el Trabuco, alterando sustancialmente el formato de la charanga tradicional al mezclar un violín, un cello y una flauta con dos trompetas y dos trombones. Con el disco *Para que baile Cuba* acaparó la atención nacional por bastante tiempo, en particular el número *La boda de Belén*, acerca de una fiesta extravagante que tuvo a media isla bailándolo al terminar el milenio. Bastante diferentes a los de las demás bandas, algunos temas aparecen como guajiras, guaguancó-sones, sones montunos y salsa, mucha salsa buena. En este disco aparece un viejo número de Ignacio Piñeiro, así como dos debidos a César Pedroso, de Los Van Van, una marcada influencia en la vida profesional de Manolito.

Creo que gran parte del atractivo de Manolito y su Trabuco tiene bastante que ver con la simplicidad de sus presentaciones, sobre todo al compararlas con las de otras bandas de timba. Entre las piezas que han causado furor están *La parranda* y *Caballo grande*. En consecuencia, la banda firmó un contrato en 2000 con Eurotropical, el sello español con más intereses en el país. Varias canciones de Manuel Simonet han pasado a otros repertorios, como el del puertorriqueño Víctor Manuelle, quien hizo de *El águila* un éxito internacional.

Un joven pianista con verdaderas raíces en el instrumento de las 88 teclas vino a deslumbrar a todos como el virtuoso más cotizado de su generación. Proviene de una familia de músicos populares y creció entre danzones, guarachas, mambos y sones. Me refiero al extraordinario **Gonzalo Rubalcaba** (1963). Escúchelo descargar en *Por eso yo soy cubano*, publicado en España por Eurotropical, o en *Mi gran pasión* (1987), compuesto de danzones y un homenaje personal a Chaikosvski, puesto a la venta por el sello alemán Messidor, y se dará cuenta de que me quedo corto en elogios. Es el único que podría ponerse a la altura de Chucho Valdés, aunque reconoce que la excelencia del gigante de Irakere lo marcó bastante en su juventud.

El abuelo Jacobo fue el autor del danzón antológico *El cadete constitucional* y su padre Guillermo es director y pianista de la Charanga Típica de Concierto. Aunque sus tres hijos se volcaron por la música, uno de ellos se resistió bastante a sentarse al piano; su pasión estaba entonces en la percusión. A los cuatro años Gonzalito ya tocaba güiro, claves, maracas, bongó, cencerro y cuanto pudiera producir ritmo. Dos años después se enredó con una tumbadora, timbales y batería, sin imaginar que en los conservatorios no existían cátedras de percusión y que tendría que matricular piano. Curiosamente, cuando rindió el examen de aptitudes para el conservatorio fue suspendido por considerarlo «antirrítmico». Una segunda prueba logró resultados satisfactorios.

Gonzalito recuerda que su primer año de estudios fue caótico; el piano no le interesaba para nada. Le parecía muy complejo y no demostraba avances. Dos dedicadas maestras lograron definirlo en aquella difícil etapa: Teresita Valiente y Silvia Echeverría. Cuando le aseguraron que podía tomar percusión como estudio complementario comenzó a entender mejor el instrumento.

Egresado de la Escuela Nacional de Arte, en seguida comenzó una carrera vertiginosa en los años 80. Tocó con la Orquesta Cubana de Música Moderna y con Los Van Van, hizo una gira por África con la Orquesta Aragón y más tarde formó su propio grupo **Proyecto**, un excelente septeto que contó inicialmente con algunos miembros de la charanga de su padre. Una noche de 1985 en que Dizzy Gillespie lo escuchó tocar en el bar del Hotel Nacional durante el Festival de Jazz de La Habana, comentó que era el mejor pianista que había oído en años, y lo invitó a unirse a su grupo a la noche siguiente. Un año después, Rubalcaba cono-

RUBALCABA ES CONSIDERADO UNO
DE LOS MEJORES DEL CARIBE.

ció al famoso bajista Charlie Haden, quien logró que lo invitaran a la edición de 1989 del Festival de Jazz de Montreal. Inmediatamente, el sello Blue Note le extendió un contrato usando su filial japonesa para burlar la legislación estadounidense con respecto a Cuba. Sin embargo, doy crédito a los funcionarios del gobierno cubano que vieron en él a una estrella potencial y permitieron que obtuviera residencia en Estados Unidos sin menoscabo de frecuentes viajes a la isla. Gonzalo Rubalcaba primero se trasladó a la República Dominicana en 1992, donde había grabado con Juan Luis Guerra dos años antes el álbum *Ojalá que llueva café*. En 1993 llegó a USA por primera vez para asistir a los funerales de Dizzy Gillespie, y más tarde ofreció un concierto en el Lincoln Center, impresionando a las autoridades de ambos países al negarse rotundamente a hablar de política. No obstante, su debut en Miami atrajo airadas protestas de varios grupos de exiliados.

Su estilo es ecléctico; lo mismo si actúa en solitario, en trío o con pequeños grupos, sus dedos fluyen entre un vanguardismo muy personal y una muy criolla y desenfadada manera barroca de incorporar temas de danzones, de filin e incluso de algunos números de los Beatles.

Al observar el panorama de la música bailable, no es difícil identificar a un hombre solitario que mantuvo el sonido de la charanga tradicional en el favor del público oriental a través de los 90. **Cándido Fabré**, sonero y compositor de Manzanillo, está metido en la música desde la niñez; comenzó a cantar en fiestas locales a los 13 años, y a los 19 era miembro de El Combo Samurai, el cual dejó en 1983 para unirse a la Orquesta Original de Manzanillo. Había cumplido así un entrenamiento riguroso.

Aunque de puro sabor regional, la Original siempre ha sido una charanga respetada, compuesta de músicos profesionales que han logrado pulir un repertorio cargado de sones y chachachás. Mantienen un sonido tradicional, y se las han arreglado para atraer una audiencia juvenil y obtener a la vez trabajo en la radio y televisión nacionales. Cándido Fabré ha logrado desarrollar una habilidad impresionante para la improvisación. Una amiga de mis largos años en Inglaterra, la musicóloga Lucy Durán, me contó que cuando visitó Manzanillo para investigar sobre la Original, en una actuación oportuna, Fabré la asombró al improvisar un número entero describiendo todos los detalles de su viaje y sus conversaciones. El sonero posee también talento para componer no sólo sones y boleros sino hasta merengues; cuenta con un evidente carisma y huele a son oriental. Es suya la banda sonora de la película *Las edades de Lulú,* de Bigas Lunas. Yo lo vi por primera vez en 1994, durante un festival de música caribeña en Cartagena de Indias, Colombia, y aunque aquella noche estaba bas-

EL SONERO CÁNDIDO FABRÉ.

tante afónico, logró que el público congregado en la plaza de toros disfrutara bailando su larga intervención. Apareció con su propia banda, formada en 1993 por catorce instrumentistas, al estilo de la Original.

Entre los tres discos que ha grabado en el extranjero, recomiendo *La Habana quiere guarachar contigo,* del sello británico Tumi; con una mayoría de números dedicados al tema del baile, hay uno en que descarga amistosamente, pero con desenfado, al mencionar a los líderes de bandas rivales, desde Paulito a David Calzado. En el cuarto surco sorprende un ritmo con algo de soca y merengue, dos géneros caribeños que suelen aparecer en la música que hace Cándido Fabré. A mediados de los 90, este ingenioso sonero ya había escrito cientos de números, y estrellas del calibre de Celia Cruz, Oscar D'León, Willy Chirino y José Alberto *El canario*, que admiran su incansable creatividad, han grabado algunos de ellos.

Antes he mencionado a varios músicos que responden a importantes dinastías. Ése es el caso de Giraldo Piloto, no sólo por su padre, autor de bellas melodías, sino también por su tío, el timbalero Guillermo Barreto (ver pág. 194). **Giraldo Piloto y Klimax** han recorrido un interesante camino desde que se crearon en 1995. Sus trece miembros incluyen un piano y un teclado electrónico, dos trompetas, un saxo tenor y un trombón, y el propio Piloto en la batería, que interpretan mayormente sus composiciones, números románticos con un fuerte acento sexual, en un estilo que comienza suave y progresa a arreglos más complejos con armonías jazzísticas que concluyen en un aporreado final de timba. Su primer álbum, *Mira si te gusta*, del sello Manzana, fue un éxito inmediato; el segundo, *Juego de manos*, vendió más de 100.000 copias en Europa, convirtiendo al grupo en el más accesible fuera de la isla.

Giraldo Piloto se graduó en composición, arreglos y percusión en 1980, comenzando su carrera profesional como baterista en Tropicana. Fue uno de los fundadores en 1988 de NG La Banda, donde jugó un papel significativo no solo como percusionista sino también como autor y orquestador. Se le considera el cerebro detrás del disco *En la calle* (1990), que fijó la dirección en que se movería la timba. Dos años después dejó la NG para unirse a la nueva banda de Isaac Delgado, al que también apoyó como director de sonido en el álbum *Con ganas* (1994). *Mira si te gusta* es característico de su frenesí timbero: una historia que revela la infravida de un barrio, con un coro que no cesa de palpitar de lo rápido que interviene y una siempre presente percusión dominante, duras trompetas con pasajes angulares y un teclado que, de estar metido en el jazz hasta el cuello, de pronto se transforma en un clásico tumbao. El tema central termina exhortando a la gente a olvidarse de todas sus penurias y ponerse a bailar.

GIRALDO PILOTO.

Vocal Sampling es otra cosa, no necesariamente como lo han descrito, «los seis

Bobby McFerrins cubanos». Es el grupo más inusual dentro del panorama de los últimos años, simulando el sonido de toda una banda, percusión incluida, sólo con sus voces, palmas y bocas infladas. No hay duda de que están tan influenciados por McFerrin como por Los Zafiros (ver pág. 297). Se estrenaron en el Aula Magna de la Universidad de La Habana en 1989, y descubiertos por Poney Gross de ZigZag Productions, llamaron la atención de Peter Gabriel, quien les grabó algunos números, uno de los cuales apareció en la recopilación *Luaka Bop* de David Byrne: *¡Diablo al infierno!*

Los periodistas europeos siempre se asombran de la versatilidad de Vocal Sampling: «¡No es posible, deben tener algún disco detrás que complementa sus sonidos!». En su álbum *De vacaciones*, del sello East-West World, se vieron obligados a explicar que no habían utilizado instrumento alguno durante las grabaciones. Estos seis malabaristas de la boca logran extraordinarios efectos del bajo y de la percusión mientras mantienen una calidad melódica muy alta. Sus primeros miembros eran estudiantes de la Escuela Nacional de Arte en los años 80; se empezaron a agrupar informalmente después de clases, bajo la iniciativa de René Baños, un enamorado de los *crooners* de la escuela de Frank Sinatra y del doo-wop, con una mezcla de temas cubanos y de gospel. Tuvieron suerte. En 1990, durante un viaje de investigación sobre la percusión cubana, el director de un festival musical belga los escuchó accidentalmente, se convirtió en su representante y resolvió la primera gira del grupo en Europa, donde fueron contratados por WOMAD.

Tres veces han coincidido en escenarios con Bobby McFerrin; la primera vez los invitó a improvisar con él. «Nos íbamos pasando el micrófono como niños que se lanzan una pelota». En otra ocasión, al finalizar un concierto en 1995 en Nueva York se les apareció en el camerino Paul Simon: «Nos dijo que nuestro espectáculo era el mejor que había visto en quince años».

Para 1993 ya habían grabado un álbum en Alemania que adquirió el sello norteamericano Sire y fue puesto a la venta en 1995. Ese mismo año debutaron en USA, con visas aprobadas a regañadientes por el Departamento de Estado bajo la insistencia de la Sociedad A Cappella del país. Después de una extensa gira por diversas ciudades, siempre cosechando aplausos interminables, Vocal Sampling sufrió una transformación, incorporando nuevos miembros con entrenamiento vocal y añadiendo otros números a su repertorio, que incluye algunos del propio René Baños. El grupo está integrado actualmente por Baños, Abel Sanabria (el experto en percusión), Oscar Porro (especialista en los efectos del bajo) y Reinaldo Santer, Jorge Núñez y Renato Mora, compartiendo un sinfín de instrumentos. *Live in Berlin* es un disco grabado en vivo en Alemania en 1998, durante el Festival Heimatklänge. Escuchar a Vocal Sampling siempre es un deleite, pero pasada la impresión del obvio virtuosismo queda la pregunta: ¿sobrevivirá un grupo *a capella* de estas características dentro de la actual jungla sonora?

LOS JÓVENES CLÁSICOS DEL SON.

Creados en 1994, los **Jóvenes Clásicos del Son** revitalizaron el bonito trabajo que venía realizando el conjunto Sierra Maestra. Tres años después fueron seleccionados como «El Mejor Grupo Cubano del Año» durante los premios anuales de la EGREM. Su director y fundador es **Ernesto Reyes Proenza**, un bajista que tocó con Cándido Fabré. Reyes proyectaba un grupo más reducido que el de Fabré, con la intención de desarrollar un repertorio de sones clásicos capaces de incorporar nuevas armonías. Finalmente optó por el formato del septeto. Sergio Pereda Rodríguez fue el primero que se le unió: un ingeniero y percusionista con una década de experiencia detrás de él, habiendo recorrido la antigua Unión Soviética con un grupo llamado Muralla; después formó parte de Vocal Sampling. Con Pereda en el bongó y segunda voz, los Jóvenes Clásicos ficharon al habanero Pedro Lugo como vocalista. Juan Manuel Hernández *Lolo* tomó posesión de las congas. Tres músicos santiagueros completaron el equipo: Carlos Manuel Céspedes, guitarrista interesado en la nueva trova, César Hechavarría en el tres, quien ha tocado frecuentemente con el Cuarteto Patria, y Raudel Marzal, un trompeta entrenado con dos grupos de Santiago: el Septeto Turquino y la Sonora la Calle. Su disco *Fruta bomba* (papaya) fue publicado en 1997 por el sello Tumi; contiene un atractivo y lúcido ramillete de sones para paladares atragantados con tanta timba. Cándido Fabré contribuyó con dos números, incluyendo *Ya se durmió la guitarra*; también aparece un dueto al estilo de Los Compadres en *La flor y la hoja seca*, y nuevas composiciones de David Álvarez, un interesante compositor cuyos pasos habrá que seguir atentamente.

Mientras que algunos egresados de Irakere se metieron de lleno en la timba, otros siguieron portando la llama del jazz afrocubano. Uno de estos últimos ha sido **Orlando *Maraca* Valle,** el mejor flautista contemporáneo de la isla. Nacido en La Habana en 1966, *Maraca* es uno de cinco hermanos músicos. Moisés, el mayor, conocido como *Yumurí,* que devino un cantante popular, me contó que su padre pretendía disuadirlos de dedicarse a la música, pero que en el caso de *Maraca,* cuando éste le reveló que quería ser jugador de béisbol, el viejo se inclinó por la música.

Orlando *Maraca* Valle estudió en el Instituto Superior de Arte y también se entrenó con Rafael Carrusco, el flautista de Gonzalito Rubalcaba. Después tomó lecciones con Raúl Valdés, flautista de la Orquesta Sinfónica Nacional. Comenzó a trabajar con el grupo de Bobby Carcassés, el conocido cantante y multiinstrumentalista de jazz, con quien visitó Panamá en 1987. Después se unió al grupo del pianista Emiliano Salvador, reconocido después de muerto como uno de los más grandes nombres del jazz criollo; tal es su admiración por el malogrado pianista que nombró a su primer grupo Otra Visión en homenaje al Nueva Visión de Salvador.

ORLANDO *MARACA* VALLE.

Fichado por Irakere en 1988 para sustituir a José Luis Cortés, *Maraca* disfrutó de seis años con ellos antes de crear su propio grupo. *Pasaporte* fue el título de su primer álbum, con el veterano Tata Güines en el agudo quinto, apoyado por las congas de Miguel *Angá* Díaz. Le siguió *Fórmula Uno,* un disco en solitario con Chucho Valdés y Richard Egües como invitados. En 1996 creó el mencionado **Otra Visión,** una alternativa que ofrecía un repertorio de todos los géneros musicales, muy diferente a la uniformidad de la timba. En *Havana calling* empleó a varios antiguos miembros de Irakere, mientras que en *Sonando* mezcló estilos tan disímiles como los de Compay Segundo, Pío Leyva, Barbarito Torres y Los Muñequitos de Matanzas (posiblemente el mejor *ensemble* rumbero).

Además de dirigir su propio grupo, Orlando *Maraca* Valle aceptó varias ofertas individuales, formando parte de la banda Cubanismo de Jesús Alemañy en giras internacionales, así como dirigiendo la grabación habanera del álbum *Café Atlántico* de la cantante Cesaria Évora, de Cabo Verde. También participó en discos de Frank Emilio Flynn y de Orlando Poleo. Hacia finales de los 90 *Maraca* se instaló en París, donde se casó con la flautista Céline Chauveau, quien fuera su alumna y después segunda flauta, productora y representante de Otra Visión.

Descarga total, producido por Warner Jazz, de Gran Bretaña, está cargado de energía y calidad y tiene de todo menos jazz puro. Intervinieron el timbalero *Changuito*, el tresero Pancho Amat, su hermano *Yumurí* como vocalista y la sección de cuerdas del cabaré Tropicana combinada con la Orquesta Sinfónica Nacional. El resultado es variado y bien escogido, incluyendo un danzón y *La pelea*, uno de las mejores incorporaciones de rap al son. *Pa'gozar pilón*, un número ideal para dejarse uno la vida en la pista, es una de las mejores versiones del ritmo pilón en disco.

Uno de los más grandes éxitos de finales del siglo XX es sin duda ***Buena Vista Social Club,*** un álbum imprescindible en todos los sentidos, realizado por artistas reunidos por primera vez, con un tema central cuyo autor permanece siendo un desconocido, dedicado a una institución bailable desaparecida hace mucho tiempo, en un país que lo ha olvidado todo. En una escena de la película de Wim Wenders, aparece Compay Segundo con su chaqueta *tweed* y su sombrero de Panamá, sentado en el asiento trasero de un elegante convertible norteamericano de los años 50, buscando el club, para ser informado por varios vecinos que el sitio ya no existe.

El título fue escogido por Nick Gold, el joven propietario de la empresa World Circuit, uno de los tres sellos detrás del disco aparecido en 1997. El segundo elemento clave fue el guitarrista Ry Cooder. Sus experiencias anteriores con la música latina habían estado limitadas a músicos del estilo Tex-Mex en los años 70, y su interés particular en la música cubana se nutrió de casetes que le regalaban amigos entrañables como Chris Strachwitz, el fundador en los años 60 de Arhoolie Records.

Ry Cooder ya conocía La Habana de cuando formó parte de los músicos que en 1977, y con Dizzy Gillespie a la cabeza, abrieron una puerta fresca al jazz para los cubanos, y en un segundo viaje (1996) cuando grabó con el grupo irlandés Chieftains para el álbum *Santiago,* del gaitero gallego Carlos Núñez. El aglutinador del disco *Buena Vista* fue **Juan de Marcos González**, que solía tocar el tres con el grupo Sierra Maestra; a él se deben la selección y localización de los instrumentistas y vocalistas. También el aliento y la pasión.

Aunque en las grabaciones participaron un total de veinte artistas, incluyendo al propio Cooder y su hijo Joachim, insertado en la banda sin ton ni son, un pequeño núcleo de seis músicos veteranos pasaron a alcanzar fama internacional. Entre éstos se encuentran los cantantes Ibrahim Ferrer y Omara Portuondo (ver pág. 154), así como Compay Segundo y Elíades Ochoa (ver págs. 286 y 291). Otros dos músicos de primera categoría lograron añadir una nueva dimensión a sus ya sólidas carreras: el bajista Orlando *Cachaíto* López y el trompeta Luis Manuel *Guajiro* Mirabal Vázquez.

JUAN DE MARCOS GONZÁLEZ Y PÍO LEYVA.

Cachaíto es hijo de Orestes López, fallecido, hombre de las cuerdas gruesas como su hermano Israel *Cachao*, quien vive en Miami. Nacido en 1933, *Cachaíto* pasó casi medio siglo tocando en diversas agrupaciones, como la Charanga Armonía de René Hernández, antes de integrarse sucesivamente a Arcaño y sus Maravillas, la Orquesta Riverside y la Charanga Rubalcaba. También fue bajista de la Orquesta Sinfónica Nacional a partir de 1960, e integró seis años después la Orquesta Cubana de Música Moderna. Es profesor del Conservatorio Guillermo Tomás y ha actuado como especialista en los comités de evaluación de orquestas populares ante el Ministerio de Cultura. Después del éxito de *Buena Vista* y el subsiguiente álbum *Afro-Cuban All Stars*, *Cachaíto* formó parte de las bandas itinerantes de Ibrahim Ferrer y Omara Portuondo.

Por su parte, el trompeta *Guajiro* Mirabal, que no aparece en la segunda edición del *Diccionario de la Música Cubana* de Helio Orovio a pesar de una distinguida carrera profesional, nació en 1933; su padre fue director de la banda municipal de Melena del Sur. Desde los 18 años comenzó a tocar con el Conjunto Rumbavana y otras agrupaciones antes de unirse a la Orquesta Cubana de Música Moderna. Pasó largos períodos en la orquesta del cabaré Tropicana bajo la dirección de Armando Romeu y más tarde del trombonista y arreglista Demetrio Muñiz, quien también figura en el disco *Buena Vista*. *Guajiro* Mirabal, que es profesor de trompeta, y miembro de la principal banda de las Fuerzas Armadas, trabajó una larga temporada en Venezuela contratado por Oscar D'León.

Aunque los veinte artistas sólo se reunieron para hacer el disco *Buena Vista*, la frase «Buena Vista Social Club presenta a...» ha sido usada para introducir a algunas de sus estrellas ante el público. El enorme éxito del disco, que ha vendido más de 4 millones de copias, pasó casi inadvertido en la Cuba oficial, y sólo fue lanzado al mercado local cuatro años después de que el resto del mundo lo disfrutara.

Con **Afro-Cuban All Stars**, Juan de Marcos quiso aprovechar la fama alcanzada por *Buena Vista Social Club*. Este brillante aglutinador de talentos nació en La Habana en 1954 en el seno de una familia musical; como su padre era miembro de la sociedad secreta Abakuá Íreme Ita Ipó, **Juan de Marcos** creció entre cánticos religiosos, mucha rumba y rock británico y norteamericano. Un cóctel nada despreciable que lo persuadió a graduarse de ingeniero hidráulico. Pero en 1978 se entregó por entero a la música, esencialmente a la sabrosura del son tradicional, formando el conjunto Sierra Maestra que condujo por más de quince años.

GUAJIRO MIRABAL.

Cuando en 1994 el Sierra Maestra firmó contrato con el sello World Circuit, De Marcos comenzó un tipo de asociación que lo llevó a la creación del proyecto *Buena Vista*. La gran ilusión de este emprendedor artista siempre había sido la creación de una banda gigante que recuperara los grandes nombres del pasado, algunos deambulando sin trabajo, otros ya retirados, para producir grabaciones con lo mejor del repertorio de los años 40 y 50. El personal del primer disco de Afro-Cuban se juntó con el de *Buena Vista*: entre los veinticuatro vocalistas e instrumentistas estaban Ibrahim Ferrer, Rubén González, *Cachaíto* López, *Guajiro* Mirabal y el maestro del laúd, Barbarito Torres. Otros músicos importantes incluyeron al trombonista Demetrio Muñiz, el trompeta Luis Alemañy, tío de Jesús, el del conjunto Sierra Maestra, así como el conguero *Angá* Díaz. Junto a Ibrahim Ferrer, a De Marcos se le ocurrió poner a Pío Leyva (1917), cuya voz sonera y jacarandosa había trabajado en los años 50 con bandas que incluyeron la Orquesta Riverside y más tarde el Conjunto Caney. Pío

Leyva (ver pág. 64) es el autor de *Francis-co Guayabal*, un son que Benny Moré hizo famoso en su día.

Raúl Planas, otro vocalista de rai-gambre nacido en 1933, había cantado con la Sonora Matancera y con el Con-junto Rumbavana, mientras que Manuel Licea, conocido de toda la vida como *Puntillita* (ambos ya fallecidos) represen-taba el más popular de los cantantes de *Buena Vista* con la excepción de Omara Portuondo. Nacido en 1927, *Puntillita* ha-bía actuado con la orquesta de Julio Cue-va y con la Sonora Matancera, llegando a ser estrella de cabaré y de la televisión, pero había decidido jubilarse a principios de los 80. El cuarto cantante contratado fue Félix Baloy, un sonero de calidad naci-

PUNTILLITA (1953).

do en 1944, fraguado en las bandas de Elio Revé y de Adalberto Álva-rez, entre otras.

El éxito del disco *Afro-Cuban All Stars* llevó al grupo a una gira in-ternacional, y finalmente a la producción de *Distinto, diferente*, lanzado en 1999. Esta vez la lista de artistas aumentó a casi cincuenta, incluyendo importantes nombres, como *Maraca* Valle en la flauta, Rubén González, David Alfaro, Guillermo Rubalcaba y el invidente Frank Emilio Flynn en el piano. Ángel Terry, percusionista de tambores rituales Abakuá, es quien marca los ritmos en *Warariansa*, un tributo al padre de De Marcos. Son de notar las contribuciones del bolerista Lino Borges y del popular Pedrito Calvo, sin olvidar las oportunas intervenciones de Teresita García Caturla.

Un número que sorprende por su contenido es *Reconciliación*, tim-ba-son de Juan de Marcos y Lázaro Villa, que aborda el problema de la separación actual del pueblo cubano. Vea los siguientes fragmentos:

> Si te creo enemigo, ¿qué yo gano?
> ¿Qué ganas al mirarme con recelo?
> Si nacimos bajo este mismo cielo,
> si queremos seguir siendo cubanos.

Basta de odio, ¡no más odio entre hermanos!
Nos lo pide la tierra en que nacimos.
Que para hacerla próspera vivimos
con el orgullo de sentirnos cubanos...

Este nuevo álbum buscó sincronizar el viejo son con un repertorio que incluye arreglos de timba y números de la pluma del propio De Marcos. Sin embargo, pienso que el disco *A toda Cuba le gusta* es aún mejor, quizá por la ecléctica selección de sones, guaguancós y guarachas, así como por la inclusión de una rareza para los oídos actuales: el mozambique *María Caracoles* (ritmo surgido a principios de los años 60), cantado por Ibrahim Ferrer. Todos estos éxitos transformaron a Juan de Marcos en un verdadero personaje del mundillo musical cubano y de los circuitos internacionales. Como resultado, se mudó a una nueva casa cerca de las playas al este de La Habana, donde estableció un pequeño estudio de grabación y su propia empresa de producciones.

Afortunadamente, **Ibrahim Ferrer** fue desenchufado de una jubilación paupérrima para participar en *Buena Vista Social Club*. De Marcos se lo había encontrado accidentalmente el verano anterior, participando en los carnavales habaneros; conocía bien su trayectoria, incluyendo su estupendo papel como cantante de Pacho Alonso y sus Bocucos (ver pág. 296). Ya pasados los ochenta, pero todavía firme y ocurrente, el delgado vocalista no podía creer su suerte: de nuevo estaría delante de un gran colectivo de brillantes músicos; estaba a punto de pasar del anonimato total a un reclamo internacional.

Ferrer (otro ausente del *Diccionario* de Orovio) nació en 1927 en el pueblo de San Luis, cerca de Santiago de Cuba. Huérfano de madre a los 12 años trabajó como vendedor ambulante y después como carpintero y estibador de los muelles. Comenzó a cantar a los 18 con Los Jóvenes del Son de un primo suyo, y así pasó por varios grupos, hasta que fue fichado en 1955 por la Orquesta Chepín-Chovén (ver pág. 58). Radicado en la capital desde 1961, grabó con Los Bocucos cuando estaban en su mayor gloria, pero años después no encontró suficiente trabajo, sobreviviendo en casa de diversos nietos en la barriada de Cayo Hueso y terminando con una pequeña pensión estatal que lograba mejorar limpiando zapatos. Su papel en *Buena Vista*, el dúo con Omara (una escena clave del filme de Wim Wenders) y la subsiguiente gira lo catapultaron al reconocimiento de todos. Había esperado sesenta largos años para lograr grabar su propio álbum, que le dirigió Ry Cooder en 1999, instrumentado por Juan de Marcos, Demetrio Muñiz y otro octogenario, el trombonista Generoso *El tojo* Jiménez, quien había hecho varios arreglos al sonero mayor Benny Moré. Hay que escuchar a Ibrahim Ferrer en *Herido de sombras*, de Pedro Vega, y en *Silencio*, del puertorriqueño Rafael Her-

EL CANTANTE IBRAHIM FERRER.

nández. Omara Portuondo y Teresa García Caturla le hicieron dúos impresionantes, mientras que Manuel Galván, el antiguo guitarrista de Los Zafiros, demostró lo que se hacía con las cuerdas eléctricas en los años 60. Para un vocalista especializado en mantener excitados a los bailadores en la pista, Ibrahim sorprendió a todos con sus interpretaciones románticas.

El pianista **Rubén González** representa otro gran músico desempolvado del pasado, otro anciano jubilado, que no esperaba el éxito a estas alturas. Afortunadamente, Ry Cooder había escuchado su quehacer en viejos discos de vinilo, tocando con orquestas del nivel de los Hermanos Castro y los conjuntos de Arsenio Rodríguez y de Senén Suárez. Rubén estaba encantado de volver a mover las artríticas manos sobre las teclas. No sé de dónde saca su energía, pero puede tocar sin parar; tengo entendido que solía llegar a las sesiones de grabación primero que nadie para sentarse a practicar; cuando le aseguraron que haría un primer álbum en solitario lo logró en sólo dos días. Poco después estaba de gira por las mejores salas de concierto del mundo, rodeado de un coro de críticos de jazz que se despepitaban en aclamarlo. No sé qué disco recomendar, si *Introducing Rubén González* (1996) o *Chanchullo,* ambos editados por World Circuit. Su última grabación antes de aparecer en *Buena Vista* había sido con Las Estrellas de Areíto en 1979 (ver pág. 334).

Nacido en Santa Clara en 1919, Rubén se graduó en el conservatorio de Cienfuegos, donde estudió con una maestra que lo marcaría para siempre, Amparo Riso, porque lo hizo trabajar mucho. Pero no quiso convertirse en pianista de concierto, a él sólo le interesaba el son. Aunque ambicionaba hacerse médico y alcanzó a terminar la carrera, Santa Cecilia, la bella patrona de los músicos, lo engatusó. Decidió mudarse a La Habana en 1941, cuando el ambiente musical estaba en su apogeo. Se ga-

naba poco entonces pero lo hacían por amor. El propio Rubén lo ha declarado: «Las bases de todo lo bueno que se oye ahora en Cuba vienen de
aquel período brillante».

Este hombre dulce y modesto fue quien introdujo a *Lilí* Martínez
Griñán al conjunto de Arsenio Rodríguez en los años 40, porque debía
partir hacia Panamá con el conjunto Las Estrellas Negras. Pensándolo
bien, me doy cuenta de que ha tocado con casi todos los músicos importantes de la isla. Gran amigo de *Peruchín*, otro bastión de los tumbaos
criollos, Rubén González se unió a la charanga de Enrique Jorrín, el creador del chachachá, permaneciendo con ella casi treinta años y convirtiéndose en su director tras la muerte del violinista. Pero dirigir no le gustó;

RUBÉN GONZÁLEZ.

demasiado papeleo y complicaciones. Lo
suyo era tocar y volver a casa.

Su estilo es fluido y elegante, se le reconoce en seguida; puede hacer todas las
piruetas que quiera alrededor de un tema,
pero sin abandonarlo jamás. Es un verdadero artesano del tumbao criollo. Quizá el
disco *Chanchullo* es más excitante, especialmente *La guajira* de Choco, que incluye
un brillante solo del tres de *Papi* Oviedo.

Aseguraba el viejo trovador Sindo Garay
que el tres se había originado en Baracoa,
al extremo oriental de la isla. A esta derivación de las cuerdas españolas le correspondía puntear los motivos en el son tradicional, acompañando la línea
del canto, mientras la guitarra sostenía un permanente patrón rayado que
ajustaba el ritmo. Totalmente asociado con los inicios del son, el tres se
llama así porque consta de tres cuerdas dobles de acero, afinadas al unísono, dos en octava alta y la otra una octava más baja. Se suele tocar con
púa de carey (tortuga nativa) y ha sido también un instrumento muy ligado al punto guajiro (ver pág. 44).

A través de todo el siglo XX grandes treseros brindaron su creatividad intuitiva al desarrollo de un estilo propio, autodidacta en su dominio, pero exigente de una amplia capacidad de improvisación. Sin embargo, las disquisiciones sobre las diversas maneras de afinarlo parecen no
terminar nunca.

Pancho Amat es uno de los más destacados treseros actuales. Nació en Güira de Melena en 1950 en una familia muy humilde (su padre vendía carbón vegetal por las calles). Sin embargo, el decidido Pancho quiso hacerse maestro y a este fin estudió matemáticas y educación, pero al mismo tiempo tomaba lecciones de guitarra clásica en el Conservatorio Ignacio Cervantes.

En los años 60 estuvo muy enrollado con el movimiento de la nueva trova, y estoy convencido de que fue él quien acuñó ese término. Durante una visita a Chile quedó fascinado con el charango, la pequeña guitarra andina que solía hacerse del cuerpo del armadillo; por supuesto, aprendió a tocarlo en seguida. En 1971 se unió a Manguaré, y durante los doce años con dicho grupo se convirtió en su director; con ellos recorrió gran parte de Latinoamérica y Europa. Su aprendizaje clásico en las cuerdas y el prestigio cultural aportado por la nueva trova le permitieron convertir al tres en un instrumento de concierto, tan importante como la guitarra. A mediados de los años 90, Pancho Amat ya había trabajado con los mejores artistas, incluyendo la Orquesta Sinfónica Nacional, el Conjunto Folklórico Nacional, el guitarrista Leo Brouwer, Pablo Milanés, Silvio Rodríguez, así como el flautista Richard Egües y otros miembros de la Orquesta Aragón.

En 1995 apareció *Son por tres*, un álbum en solitario, mientras recorría medio mundo con Cubanismo, tocando con los irlandeses Chieftains o con Ry Cooder, o actuando como invitado de los cantantes Joaquín Sabina y Santiago Auserón *Juan Perro*, un gran amante del son cubano.

En 2000 apareció el álbum *De San Antonio a Maisí*, acompañado de un nuevo grupo llamado El Cabildo del Son; Auserón canta *Al vaivén de mi carreta* y Silvio Rodríguez insistió en recrear *La cocainómana*, un añejo son de Miguel Matamoros, que el cantautor consideró particularmente relevante para los tiempos presentes. El resultado es una producción de calidad del sello español Resistencia, que incluye un son de 1932 de Miguel Matamoros sobre una chica llamada Celina que le mete a la cocaína.

El estilo de Pancho Amat se diferencia bastante del de **Papi** Oviedo, el otro tresero que me interesa comentar. Se llama Gilberto Oviedo la Portilla y es hijo de Isaac Oviedo, uno de los mejores treseros que ha dado el país, quien dejó su nativa Matanzas en 1926 para instalarse en la capital. Apodado *Papi*, Oviedo hijo nació en 1937 y comenzó su vida musical tocando congas. Pronto las dejó para concentrarse en el tres, que de algo le viene al galgo. Tocó con diversos grupos, incluyendo la orquesta del gran bolerista Orlando Contreras (ver pág. 127). Entre 1952 y 1968 *Papi* Oviedo tocó con el Conjunto Típico Habanero de Manuel Furé, con la agrupación de Enrique Pérez y con el conjunto de Chapottín hijo.

En 1980 fue fichado por Elio Revé, quien estaba reformando su charanga, cosa que llamó mucho la atención, eso de tener a un tresero en tal formato, pero el nuevo ingrediente resultó vital. Quince años después *Papi* Oviedo dejó a Revé para formar su propio grupo con el que sacó su primer disco, *Encuentro entre soneros* (1996), con las voces de Cristina Azcuy, Miguel Martínez y Osvaldo Montalvo, un especialista de la guajira. En este disco se escucha su poderosa simplicidad e intensidad rítmica,

EL TRESERO *PAPI* OVIEDO.

un juego de cuerdas muy distinto al de Pancho Amat. Un par de sones de la autoría de su padre y una curiosa interpretación de *Chan chán* de Compay Segundo completan otras atracciones del álbum. Ya cercano al 2000, Oviedo se unió a la banda que acompañó a Omara Portuondo en su extensa gira. También ha hecho música de fusión con Papá Noel, el cantante y guitarrista congolés.

El otro miembro del Sierra Maestra que emergió con evidente fuerza sonera en los 70, contribuyendo a la internacionalización de la música cubana dos décadas después es **Jesús Alemañy,** cuya trayectoria es similar a la de su colega Juan de Marcos. Nacido en 1952 en Guanabacoa, aprendió trompeta en el Conservatorio Guillermo Tomás y fue reclutado por el Sierra Maestra en 1978, poco después de la creación del grupo. Junto a sus compañeros, Alemañy comenzó a investigar las raíces del son, lo cual lo condujo hasta los miembros sobrevivientes del viejo Septeto Nacional de Piñeiro; pronto se encontró tomando lecciones del trompeta Lázaro Herrera *El pecas* (ver pág. 48), el hombre que fijó todo un estilo sonero.

A través de dos décadas, Alemañy viajó con el Sierra Maestra como único metal del grupo. También trabajó en la orquesta de Tropicana, donde ya tocaba su tío Luis Alemañy y de cuando en cuando participó en el grupo Proyecto, de Gonzalo Rubalcaba. De todas estas experiencias adquirió una enorme facilidad para la improvisación y para acentuar los valores melódicos, dos roles que raramente se ven en un mismo trompeta.

Jesús Alemañy se casó con la musicóloga británica Lucy Durán en 1994 y se instaló en Londres, donde trabajó con músicos latinos como el timbalero colombiano Roberto Pla. En 1996, y con el apoyo del sello Hannibal, regresó a La Habana para grabar un álbum con un objetivo muy parecido al que sostenía Juan de Marcos con el Afro-Cuban All Stars: recrear los estilos clásicos del son, renovando el repertorio de las décadas 1940 y 1950, pero aprovechando las modernas técnicas de grabación. Su principal colaborador fue el pianista Alfredo Rodríguez (ver pág. 292), que había tocado con la Sonora Matancera y que emigró a Estados Unidos en 1960, trabajó luego con los grandes de la salsa y finalmente se instaló en París en 1983.

La orquesta que formó Alemañy para las grabaciones se componía de algunos conocidos y otros jóvenes que pronto serán figuras importantes. El disco fue bautizado *Cubanismo* por Joe Boyd, el dueño de Hannibal, quien pensó que el nombre era claro y memorable para la mayoría que sabe poco o nada de la música cubana. Básicamente instrumental, lleno de ritmo y fabulosos solos de los metales, *Cubanismo* vendió 100.000 copias sólo en Estados Unidos. También se han vendido bien los dos discos que le siguieron: *Malembe* y *Re-encarnación*.

JESÚS ALEMAÑY.

Las giras que emprendió la banda Cubanismo tuvieron el mismo éxito. Su primer concierto tuvo lugar en 1997 en Nueva Orleans, convirtiéndose pronto en la vanguardia del considerable número de músicos cubanos actualmente tocando en Estados Unidos. Combinando los conciertos con talleres, demostraciones en escuelas y conferencias, lograron cumplir con el requisito de «intercambio cultural» de la legislación vigente para lograr y renovar sus visas. Como resultado se pasaron casi la mitad de 1999 presentándose en varias ciudades. También lograron el patrocinio oficial del Ayuntamiento de Nueva Orleans para grabar el álbum *Mardi Gras Mambo*, una colaboración entre Cubanismo y músicos locales que

fraternalmente reexaminaron las viejas conexiones entre aquella ciudad y
La Habana: el son y el mambo se dieron allí la mano con el blues, el soul
y el rock.

Entretanto, en La Habana seguía dominando la timba. El término no era
nuevo. Aparte de indicar guayaba, como en «pan con timba», había sido
usado anteriormente por diversos grupos para destacar la sección de ritmo, o para indicar una fiesta. Además, timbero denota un tamborero de
rumba. Posiblemente originado en el contexto de la rumba columbia, el
vocablo estuvo en boca de todos alrededor de 1948, cuando el puertorriqueño Daniel Santos grabó con la Sonora Matancera una guaracha de
Pablo Cairo precisamente titulada *Pa'la timba* que repetía:

> Los tambores, mi Yemayá, se entonan (bis)
> (coro) Oh, mi, oh, ma, pa'la timba...

Como «La banda que manda», se autopromovían los componentes
de **NG La Banda**, que pronto tuvo una docena de seguidores, aunque variando considerablemente su propio tipo de música. Un buen ejemplo es
La Charanga Habanera, una vieja agrupación con formato de orquesta típica o charanga, que David Calzado supo reactivar con los elementos de
la «timba», acelerando los efectos en el teclado y fuertes golpes del pedal
en el bombo de la batería, pero agregando lo que devino la marca reconocible del grupo: pasos acrobáticos por el grupo de cantantes que no ce-
saban en inventar coreografías sumamente sugestivas.

Así las cosas, a medida que estas bandas se hicieron más populares, el público desarrolló nuevos pasos con su música; se trataba esencialmente de una fresca versión de los contoneos cubanos de la década
del 60, sumados a los avances pélvicos que había instituido desde el escenario la Orquesta Revé en los 80. Estos movimientos incluían una
alocada batida de hombros y caderas llamado «tembleque» cuando las
orquestas caían en el largo montuno instrumental. Con el desarrollo de
la «timba» y el «despelote», el baile se alejaba cada vez más del modo
de bailar –bastante más controlado– identificado con la salsa que hacían las bandas puertorriqueñas o colombianas, la misma distancia que
se apreciaba en las continuas vueltas y giros que daba la pareja con el
estilo casino, y que identificaba a la generación bailadora que se identificó con Los Van Van.

El investigador Carlos Olivares baró, residente en México, considera que la timba es el fenómeno musical cubano más importante de fines del siglo XX, y que a pesar de los escépticos se abre paso igual que sus hermanos de décadas anteriores.

Por su parte, Helio Orovio ha apuntado que «Revé, Chucho Valdés, Formell y Adalberto Álvarez son las cuatro patas de la mesa musical que sostiene al movimiento timbero».Quizá la característica fundamental de la timba sea precisamente ese aire de afrosantería mezclado con son y rap, desde una acelerada «moña» pianística (herencia de *Peruchín* y de Paquito Hechavarría), en una línea melódico/armónica alternada con propuestas jazzeadas de saxos, trompetas y trombones.

Las orquestas timberas poseen singularidades que las caracterizan entre sí, de ahí que se podría trazar la siguiente clasificación: timberos/guaracheros/bravos: Paulito y su Élite, Manolito y su Trabuco, y Revé y su Charangón. Después agregaría los timberos/charangueros: Los Van Van y La Charanga Habanera, seguidos de los timberos/funky/jazzistas: NG La Banda y Bamboleo, para concluir con los timberos/soneros: Pachito Alonso, Adalberto Álvarez, Dan Den e Isaac Delgado. Algunas agrupaciones latinoamericanas empiezan a imitarlos, aunque con reservas.

Además del tipo de música y pasos de baile, la timba se distingue por sus letras agresivas, cínicas, cargadas del argot relacionado con el continuo trasiego de compra-venta-tengo-que-resolver de la vida urbana, totalmente ininteligible para el que no sea cubano citadino. Cuando los sellos discográficos internacionales comenzaron a fijarse en la timba, la impenetrabilidad de sus textos y los excesivamente largos números, cargados de solos ruidosos de diferentes instrumentos, fueron considerados como verdaderas desventajas para su comercialización en el mundo industrializado. La radio cubana, que carece de anuncios, podía darse el lujo de emitir números de entre 6 a 16 minutos de duración, pero el mundo capitalista dictaba 4 minutos como máximo, de manera que Manolín e Isaac Delgado pronto comenzaron a tratar de recortar sus versiones para discos.

Paralelo al auge de la timba emergió un sector de gente nueva haciendo **rap** o **hip-hop** a lo cubano. Mientras que sus hermanos y hermanas mayores escuchaban a Celia Cruz, a Willy Chirino o a Gloria Estefan en la radio de onda corta emitida desde Miami, los habaneros más jóvenes sintonizaban las estaciones de rap, e incluso, cuando las condiciones atmosféricas lo permitían, trataban de captar programas televisivos como «Soul Train», que les llegaba desde la Florida, con exhibiciones de Public Enemy o de Grand Master Flash, así como *breakdancers* dándose gusto. Pronto los criollos comenzaron a seguir a los puertorriqueños y otros jóvenes latinos al crear su propia versión del rap.

La nueva locura se introdujo en Cuba poco antes de 1980 a través de dichas emisiones y por discos que entraban de manera individual; hoy día hay más de 400 grupos. Por otra parte, la popularidad alcanzada en la isla por las películas *Flashdance* y *Mentes peligrosas*, contribuyó significativamente a la asimilación del nuevo género como una forma de expresión y de protesta de una generación hastiada del proceso revolucionario. Grupos de jóvenes –fundamentalmente negros, quizá en alusión al movimiento originario y por constituir los más damnificados de la población por las estrecheses impuestas por el «Período Especial»– comenzaron a manifestarse en parques y esquinas de las barriadas más populares, particularmente en La Habana, Villa Clara y Santiago de Cuba.

La tendencia general es hacia un rap duro, cáustico, ríspido, tipo *underground,* con temas que abordan ácidos problemas sociales. Musicalmente se caracteriza por el ostinato monótono del bajo, y en cuanto a las letras, apréciese la siguiente:

> Revolución
> no me la aprietes más
> que yo sigo aquí.
> No me la aprietes más,
> déjame vivir...

Al momento de escribir, el Festival de Rap en Alamar, una urbanización junto a la costa, muy cercana a la capital, ya ha realizado siete ediciones, siempre en el mes de agosto, el más cruel; nuclea las principales agrupaciones del país con un espíritu competitivo y suele incluir un evento teórico. A estos festivales asisten raperos de diversos países, además de periodistas y estudiosos del género, lo cual ha contribuido a la difusión incipiente del rap criollo en el extranjero.

Lo cubano está en los temas y en las realidades sociales que aborda, haciendo una crítica obvia que es tolerada a regañadientes por el régimen que lo manipula como una válvula de escape para los jóvenes. Otro elemento a tener en cuenta es la intertextualidad de las letras, ya que a me-

nudo incorporan pasajes textuales y musicales de piezas reconocibles de la música
popular, como se puede apreciar en el tema
537 Cuba del grupo Orishas, residente en
París.

El disco *Orishas a lo cubano*, el primer
rap criollo que se abrió paso en Europa, se
logró gracias a la combinación de dos raperos habaneros y un trío de cubano-fran-
ceses que habían estado trabajando en dis-
tintos medios musicales por algunos años. Los habaneros eran Yothuel y
Ruzzo, dos miembros de Amenaza, uno de los líderes en la primera ola de
rap cubano. En 1998, ayudados por un programa de intercambio bajo los
auspicios de la organización cultural cubana Hermanos Sáenz, ambos
chicos arribaron a París (el tercer miembro del trío llegó vía Noruega).
Comenzaron a buscar lugares de hip-hop con los que pudieran conectarse
y pronto entraron en un club donde trabajaba el DJ Niko, un joven criollo muy comprometido con lo último que pasaba en la ciudad.

Niko, Ruzzo y Yothuel fueron contactados por otro cubano basado
en Paris, el DJ Liván, quien había trabajado para Radio Nova desde su
arribo en 1995 y había comenzado a presentar noches latinas en un disco. Liván había participado en el álbum *Sargento García*, que incluye un
número de rap titulado *Afrocuban orishas underground*. El último miembro del grupo que se convirtió en **Orishas** fue Roldán, un cantante y guitarrista clásico que había estudiado música en la Universidad de La Habana y trabajó como como profesor de música por seis años, tocando en
hoteles con un grupo tradicional llamado Ricosón. Dándose cuenta de
que en Cuba siempre estaría limitado, Roldán logró llegar a París, donde
se unió a un grupo similar llamado Sabor de son.

La casete «demo» que produjeron persuadió al sello EMI a apoyar-
los, y en 1999 todos regresaron a La Habana para grabar ejemplos de
música de Santería y otros materiales. De vuelta en París, conectaron con
varios profesionales: *Angá* Díaz, que entonces se encontraba allí, puso sus
congas y otras percusiones mientras que músicos franceses agregaron las
cuerdas, el piano y algo de metales. Con la programación de Niko y el
colombiano Mario Rodríguez encargado de la mezcla final, el álbum
Orishas a lo cubano salió a la luz.

Hay gente que tiene suerte. Ése es el caso de **Carlos Manuel**, que se ha convertido en la nueva sensación de la vida nocturna habanera. Nacido en 1974 en la capital, adquirió sus primeras influencias musicales de sus padres, él tocaba la guitarra y ella cantaba en un coro. Acostumbrado a escuchar música romántica en la radio, como muchos jóvenes de su generación, más tarde se entusiasmó con Silvio Rodríguez y Pablo Milanés. Pronto tomó sus primeros pasos como cantante profesional al unirse al grupo de nueva trova Mayohuacán. Con ellos experimentó la aprobación del público cuando su versión de *Carapacho pa'la jicotea*, de Pedro Luis Ferrer, se convirtió en un éxito. En 1996 le propusieron cantar con Guayacán, una excelente y versátil banda colombiana de salsa, pero en

CARLOS MANUEL.

el último minuto se decidió por Irakere, con quienes pasó un año en giras internacionales que incluyó una temporada en el club Ronnie Scott de Londres y presentaciones en el Festival Playboy de Hollywood.

Carlos Manuel aprovechó estas oportunidades para ahorrar dinero y adquirir un sintetizador Roland de segunda mano y después un teclado electrónico. Ya cercano al 2000 se decidió a formar su propia banda: **Carlos Manuel y su clan**, apareciendo cada viernes en el Café Cantante y los domingos en el Havana Café. Su grabación de *Soy malo cantidad*, un híbrido mitad timba mitad vaya-usted-a-saber-qué-cosa, apareció en octubre 2000, pegó y lo convirtió temporalmente en el cantante número uno de la isla. Aunque sus grabaciones no aparecen en disco sino que son diseminadas directamente del máster a la radio, hacia finales de ese año había firmado con el sello británico Palm Pictures.

Ignoro cuánto durará esta nueva «figura» de la música cubana. *Soy malo cantidad* me dejó lelo. Es un ejercicio en música pop que mezcla timba frenética con hábiles pinceladas de baladas románticas y algunos elementos de rap, rock y hasta reggae jamaicano. Hay momentos en que la banda consigue convencernos con ritmos salseros, y las letras, especialmente si usted está en posición de saber qué diablos está sucediendo en La Habana actualmente, son vagamente entretenidas.

8. ¿HACIA DÓNDE SE DIRIGE LA MÚSICA CUBANA?

> La vida debe vivirse hacia adelante,
> pero sólo se comprende
> mirando hacia atrás.
>
> SÖREN KIERKEGAARD

Ya quisiera yo tener la respuesta, pero mi bola de cristal sólo refleja confusión y un sálvese-quien-pueda ante la inminente debacle. Aunque el poder de la música no es de índole política, suele revelar con bastante claridad los altibajos y contradicciones inherentes al sistema; es un hecho que bajo la revolución, música y política han estado ligadas condicionalmente. Y todo parece estar supeditado a la supervivencia o no del régimen –tal y como está establecido– tras la desaparición de Castro.

En la Cuba del siglo XXI existe una fuerte contradicción: las tesis de la revolución están agotadas desde hace rato, pero la música evidencia una pujanza extraordinaria. ¿Sabrán los músicos reorientarse una vez que sean totalmente libres? ¿No se quedarán algunos añorando los viejos tiempos en que se podían recostar al sistema «para ir tirando»? Actualmente, un buen número de músicos están envueltos en el mundo de la competitividad; se hacen de un nombre en la isla para ganar prestigio y lograr los permisos de salida, y pronto aparece un empresario extranjero dispuesto a sacarlos al exterior. ¡Manía eterna de un país que tiene que depender de alguien de afuera para que descubra el talento de sus hijos!

La situación actual es crítica y bastante confusa. Hay intérpretes con capacidad para dirigir y orquestar que se consideran a sí mismos subutilizados. Por otra parte, la falta de instrumentos de calidad plantea el exigirle a una agrupación que le «preste» a otra, o el joven músico tiene que conformarse con «heredar» un trasto inadecuado. A menudo hay discrepancias con el nivel técnico o con el tipo de disciplina que impone el director, así como múltiples inconformidades con los funcionarios empresariales por programaciones erradas o por falta de éstas, asignación de equipamiento, la casi total ausencia de locales de ensayo, facilidades de viajes al extranjero... Ahora buscan la cadena que se perdió hace más de cuarenta años: el nexo creación-interpretación-grabación-difusión, para que se proyecte en toda su plenitud. Más tarde o más temprano tendrán que volver a los lazos entre la demanda de actuaciones combinada con la venta de discos (en cifras reales, no manipuladas), y el éxito artístico.

Soy un historiador más que un vaticinador –y mucho menos un especulador–, sin embargo, existen varios indicadores significativos. Al considerar todos y cada uno de estos puntos a manera de discusión, habrá que tener en cuenta lo importante que es y será la confrontación con luminarias internacionales, y el hecho de que actualmente existen magníficos instrumentistas pero no productores avezados. Veamos:

• Las principales agrupaciones tienen ahora patente de corso para organizar contactos con empresarios extranjeros y manejar sus propios asuntos. En realidad, son los que ponen la banda sonora a un país traumatizado, convirtiéndose en malabaristas del dólar.

Se produce una música popular que no se plantea el menor compromiso con el futuro, que se fundamenta en pocos elementos de fácil reconocimiento y aceptación popular, como para no turbar la capacidad intelectiva. Pero en justicia, ésto no es nuevo. La diferencia –si es que hubiera alguna– está en que se esperaba algo más de músicos con disciplina formativa, supuestamente armados de otros mundos teóricos que los de generaciones anteriores a la revolución. Mi opinión es que uno de los problemas que más frena la innovación es limitarse a creer que los parámetros fundamentales de la música no pueden ser sustituidos, como supeditar los ritmos afrocubanos a los elementos armónicos y formales, o considerar que en música hay aspectos más importantes que otros, sin olvidar la chabacanería y la repetición de las mismas fórmulas. Aquí reside el arte del verdadero creador, algo que no puede ser enseñado, ni siquiera sugerido.

• El boom actual de la música cubana puede resultar contraproducente; ¿qué pasará cuando desaparezcan los viejitos o las transnacionales se cansen de explotar ese filón?

• Prevalece una tendencia a sobrevalorar la técnica y la velocidad, y una preferencia unilateral por los tiempos vivos –que son más fáciles de tocar que los números lentos– quizá como consecuencia del marcado interés en satisfacer a los bailadores. Esta locura por el baile de un sector de la población, ¿representa acaso una actitud escapista ante un sistema que le niega todo lo demás?

• La hipersalsa ha tenido una saturación por más de diez años en los que hubo de todo. Hay bandas que se beneficiaron enormemente con el boom de lo bailable, pero llega un momento en que tanto el público como los músicos se agotan y eso tiene efectos negativos para todos. Y buscar nuevos temas que peguen para mantenerse cerca del gusto popular no es fácil.

• Existen muchos músicos jóvenes bien preparados pero que no tienen posibilidades de desarrollarse dentro del país. Me atrevo a asegurar que una buena parte de los mejores talentos viven sumidos en un medioexilio, esperando a ver qué pasará. Me vuelve a la mente aquella frase tremenda del cantautor Pancho Céspedes: «Me fui de Cuba porque quería que mi música trascendiera. Allí te dan las armas para que pienses, pero no salidas».

No hay que olvidar a los artistas que abandonaron el país. Aunque las principales figuras de la diáspora pertenecen a otras generaciones, lo del exilio nunca es reductible a problemas colectivos (aunque los hubiere), sino a conjuntos de individualidades muy dispersas entre sí, algunas excepcionales.

• La nueva trova está totalmente desarticulada. A partir de 1987 cada cual empezó a buscar su propio derrotero y aunque hubo intentos de resucitarla, la burocracia de siempre lo apagó todo. Ahora cada cual resuelve por su lado, llámese Silvio, Pablo, Santiago, Gerardo, Frank o Carlos.

Los músicos de la isla viven cercados por una revolución frustrada que todavía intenta mantenerlos atados. Un ejemplo clásico de la sempiterna desconfianza del régimen hacia los artistas fue el cierre de la Fundación Pablo Milanés, que examino en la pág. 318, a pesar de tratarse de un hombre Fuerte del régimen. La utopía y el desencanto se han juntado cuando el deber de la música es decir NO –como toda actividad intelectual–, pero al músico se le exige decir que SÍ.

• Las dinastías musicales han sido, son y serán sumamente significativas para el país: los Valdés, los Romeu, los Rubalcaba, los López, los Formell, otra vez los Valdés (el del grupo Bamboleo), los Piloto, los Oviedo, Alemañy, Calzado y Alfonso, para citar sólo algunos. A no ser que se interrumpa el flujo por continuas deserciones.

• Importantes artistas latinoamericanos han señalado que ya los cubanos no hacen música compacta, que están muy influidos por la música norteamericana, que le están metiendo mucho funk a lo que antes era el son, y que también se está empleando demasiado el virtuosismo de cada uno de los miembros de cualquier agrupación, con el resultado de mucho ruido porque todos quieren lucirse a la vez.

«Esta música no funciona con arreglo a las normas internacionales del márketing musical», aseguró en 1998 el periodista Diego A. Manrique. «Una jugada complicada. En América domina la estereotipada salsa romántica; en Europa prefieren el son añejo. Y la salsa cubana tiende a lo indómito: sus temas, incluso en disco, son muy largos. El lenguaje es bien cubano y rebosa guiños, citas, putaditas que no se entienden fuera». Gran parte de la música actual es difícilmente exportable, por la extensa duración de sus temas, y por sus ininteligibles y orgullosos localismos (interminables estribillos, referencias a los barrios, uso de jerga callejera, ideología pragmática cargada de incitaciones al público que corresponde con bailes altamente lascivos). En otro comentario, el mismo crítico indica: «Los dólares y el desenfreno desencadenaron el fervor del público mientras los cantantes popularizaban "peligrosos" latiguillos.»

Las leyes básicas de la tecnología de las multipistas en una grabación actual exigen que el orquestador o arreglista forme un verdadero equipo con el director musical y su solista, el técnico grabador y el productor. Es imprescindible conocer bien el número, la personalidad del solista, el carácter de la letra o la función (bailable o no) de las secciones instrumentales, etc. En el caso cubano observo una debilidad de la sección rítmica que no cambia ni refresca apoyos, *breaks*, ponches e incluso compases completos. La grabación permite la transformación de algunos clichés (una expresión demasiado repetida), pero raramente la eliminación de ellos, porque es innegable que los clichés forman parte del código de lenguaje del mensaje concreto. Hace falta recordar un viejo axioma medieval que dio origen al contrapunto de Palestrina: «Cuando una parte de las voces se mueve, la otra queda quieta y viceversa».

ZENAIDA CASTRO ROMEU.

• A pesar de algunas bandas de calidad (Las Canelas, Son Damas, Azúcar, Almendra y la ya reseñada Anacaona, entre otras), veo pocas mujeres dedicadas profesionalmente a la música popular, aunque se suponía que bajo la revolución se lograría una verdadera apertura para ellas. Una excepción a otro nivel son los casos de la compositora y directora Tania León o la labor de Zenaida Castro Romeu al frente de la Camerata Romeu, grupo de cuerdas femenino que ya acumula importantes premios.

• El jazz mantiene una puerta abierta para algunos, aunque se revela cierta pobreza armónica, que proviene de convertir en fórmulas lo que fue una necesidad expresiva en los grandes creadores del modalismo y el free jazz como John Coltrane o Charlie Mingus. Aún reconociendo que actualmente coexisten cerca de diez tendencias en el jazz internacional, con una especie de neo-bop como elemento dominante, así como varios tipos de música de fusión, queda por ver si La Habana podrá convertirse y mantenerse como la capital del Latin jazz, el que a través de estas páginas he definido como jazz afrocubano.

• Desde hace algún tiempo, grupos de artistas cubanos y españoles –entre los que se hallan Joan Manuel Serrat, Víctor Manuel y el argentino Fito Páez– han grabado discos para recabar fondos a favor de las escuelas de música. Hace falta de todo: cuerdas, clavijas, arcos, pianos, boquillas para los saxos, partituras, papel pautado, instrumentos de todo tipo. «El talento, con recursos, se hace más llevadero», aseguró Vicente Feliú.

• Según las estadísticas del Instituto Cubano de la Música y el Sindicato de Trabajadores de la Cultura, hay casi 15.000 músicos profesionales. Y todos quieren lo mismo.

LA PASIÓN POR EL BAILE NO CONOCE
FRONTERAS.

En busca de «fulas»

Huir o salir para sobrevivir: *that's the question*. En realidad hay tantos músicos en activo fuera como dentro del país. De los mencionados en los últimos capítulos, poco más de una docena de grupos actúa de forma estable en su patria, los demás tienen que buscarse la vida fuera. Sin embargo, los que lo consiguen no lo tienen fácil.

Debo denunciar que los músicos siempre han sido explotados y robados por otros músicos, por sus propios directores musicales, por los sellos discográficos, por las casas editoriales, por sus representantes y empresarios de conciertos, actuaciones y espectáculos, y por otras entidades comerciales. Muchos autores han trabajado «por amor al arte», sin recibir tipo alguno de reconocimiento por su talento y su aportación a la industria. ¡Cuántos artistas han confiado sus destinos a agentes sin escrúpulos que los han esquilmado!

La situación de los músicos que están comprometidos con Artex, una agencia artística cubana, es característica de la Cuba de hoy. La empresa se mueve ahora bajo una estrategia que podría concretarse así: «Hay que cuidar al músico porque ingresa dólares al país». Por su parte, el músico necesita dólares desesperadamente para mantener a su familia, por lo que está dispuesto a entregarle un fuerte porcentaje al gobierno. Artex sólo le entrega un tanto por ciento al artista, una fracción de lo ganado. ¡Vaya negocio!

Las siguientes palabras de Marianela Dufflar, representante y directora artística de Artex, son definitorias:

Durante mucho tiempo hemos estado improvisando en materia de negocios, no éramos duchos en ello porque no había posibilidad de negociar. Desde la despenalización del dólar (1993) ha habido un período de aprendizaje y ya tenemos un nivel de experiencia en los mecanismos contractuales del mercado capitalista.

Es decir, ahora el régimen quiere darse el lujo de pretender jugar al capitalismo, pero sin quitarle la garra de encima al artista. Muchos músicos que salen contratados desde Cuba a través de Artex u otras empresas suelen viajar acompañados en sus giras por un «seguroso», un agente de la Seguridad del Estado disfrazado de funcionario cultural. Esta denuncia fue publicada en *El País* el 26 de agosto de 1995, en un artículo firmado por Ricardo Cantalapiedra. «Los artistas están sometidos a control obsesivo y burocracia patológica», afirmó el periodista. Este anacronismo totalitario provoca rubor y crispación entre los empresarios y representantes artísticos españoles, algunos de los cuales simpatizan todavía con Castro. Un agente de espectáculos muy relacionado desde hace tiempo con los ambientes cubanos le comentó a Cantalapiedra: «El régimen considera que quien sale al extranjero está expuesto a la contaminación capitalista».

En sus giras, la mayoría opta por el silencio cuando se les pregunta por la situación política del país; ni una broma, ni un chiste; de todo lo demás hablan con fluidez y gran sentido del humor. Este mutismo tiene una explicación: cualquier palabra o insinuación puede ser utilizada en su contra, convirtiéndose en diversos inconvenientes –como no dejarle volver a salir del país– al regresar a La Habana. Como le sucedió a Pedro Luis Ferrer (ver pág. 314) y a otros.

Una evidencia del valor intrínsico de la música en eso de crear opinión pública fue la sensibilidad que destapó la salsa a ambos lados del Estrecho de la Florida; lo que me hace repetir aquel apotegma (no recuerdo de quién): «Cualquier pueblo defiende más su música que sus leyes». A pesar de los iracundos demagogos a ambos extremos del espectro político, los músicos siguen montando números originados de un lado u otro, lo que me hace sentirme optimista. Pero cada vez que uno de la isla trata de acercarse de alguna forma a los de Miami el régimen los castiga.

Sin embargo, la gente ha aprendido a circunnavegar las limitaciones que les imponen. Más que socialismo, en la isla siempre ha prevalecido el «sociolismo», que en lenguaje local quiere decir el amiguismo cómplice; para sobrevivir, muchos han tenido que hacer un arte de la picaresca, aún temiendo las consecuencias a que les somete la omnipresente policía y los «segurosos» vestidos de civiles.

A principios de los 90 los cubanos se las apañaron para aguantar estoicamente apagones de seis, ocho o diez horas diarias. También les tocó idear platos a base de picadillo de cáscara de plátano, o hacer desodorante casero con bicarbonato y leche de magnesio. Después de doce años bajo el «Período Especial», la creciente crisis con su subida de precios en los mercados en dólares ha sido un duro golpe para la gente. Los apagones han vuelto a castigar sin piedad dos o tres veces por semana. Lo inmediato –informó el 6 de julio de 2002 Mauricio Vicent desde La Habana– ha sido la aparición de revendedores de velas. Un pregonero anunciaba: «Aquí, aquí. Velas pa'l apagón y lindano pa'la picazón» (el lindano se utiliza para combatir los piojos y la sarna, dos lacras que han aumentado en los últimos tiempos). Doce años después de la caída de Europa del Este, cuando la isla perdió el 85 por ciento de sus mercados y el PIB descendió un 35 por ciento, de nuevo la consigna de los cubanos es –incluyendo a los músicos– «resolver o morir».

Quedan una serie de temas que invitan a reflexionar. ¿Logrará la música cubana convertirse en la principal alternativa al rock en todo el planeta? Algunos piensan que lo que el guitarrista mexicano Carlos Santana hizo con el rock le correspondía haberlo conseguido a los cubanos. Pero ya he indicado que el rock es anatema para el régimen. ¿No hará falta precisamente que otras manifestaciones tengan un espacio acomodado al estilo cubano? Dizzy Gillespie creía firmemente que algún día la música del hemisferio occidental se uniría, una idea provocativa pero nada deleznable.

Gracias a la música cubana, el Caribe empieza ahora en los barrios de Nueva York y acaba más abajo de Valparaíso, sin mencionar a los europeos, africanos y asiáticos que ya la están disfrutando a plenitud. Estoy convencido de que el futuro de esa música tendrá mucho que ver con el pasado, con las eternas raíces, pero evitando el facilismo y la comercialización excesiva.

Los principales musicólogos criollos no discutirán lo anterior; no suelen tomar riesgos y aventurar posibles direcciones. Imbuidos de concepciones marxista-leninistas (para usar su autodenominación oficialista), consideran que su metodología es única en el mundo. Por lo general manejan una prosa bastante aburrida y elitista, sofocada bajo unas directrices muy concretas. ¡Una verdadera lástima porque hay gente de mucho valer entre los investigadores de la isla!

Un buen músico en cualquier esquina

Como ya he indicado, desde principios de los años 90 Cuba ha sido destino preferente de cazatalentos de diversos países, incluyendo algunos empresarios estadounidenses, a pesar de la absurda ley Helms-Burton. Ellos saben que el «cocodrilo verde» contiene una de las mayores reservas musicales del planeta y que el llamado «Período Especial» ha reducido la producción discográfica a la mínima actividad, dejando a la intemperie a un considerable número de artistas. La mayor parte de estos buscadores de oro sonoro se quedan en La Habana o quizá alcancen a andar por las calles de Santiago de Cuba. El resto del país permanece relativamente virgen, esperando al mejor postor o impostor. Sin embargo, sé de alguno que se lanzó a investigar el efecto de la efervescente salsa capitalina en el resto del país, decidiendo que valía la pena armarse de gasolina y paciencia y explorar el interior. Tras pactar una jugosa transacción con el Instituto Cubano de la Música, o sus representantes, su equipo realizó audiciones en varias ciudades de la isla, grabando en audio y vídeo cerca de doscientos grupos y solistas que respondieron a la convocatoria publicada. No faltó por supuesto el tradicional listillo criollo: algún burócrata quiso colar a familiares o amigos sin mucho talento. Sin embargo, la cosecha reveló suficiente material artístico para producir cuarenta o cincuenta discos. Así funcionan los cazatalentos ambiciosos.

Esta experiencia destapó varias verdades. *Primera:* en Cuba no han existido nunca barreras entre la música popular y la «culta», el músico se ha movido indistintamente entre una y otra sin prejuicio de ningún tipo. *Segunda:* La terrible escasez de instrumentos, especialmente pianos y cuerdas, ha hecho surgir un número de agrupaciones vocales escandalosamente asombrosas. *Tercera:* El país ofrece más variedad musical que la implacable hipersalsa o timba que domina la radio nacional y las pistas de baile donde se contonean los turistas. *Cuarta:* Cualquier pueblo del interior de la isla cuenta con más de una orquesta, tan potentes como las que arrasan en La Habana, y a un costo ridículo para su contratación. El fenómeno tiene una explicación: los músicos necesitan dólares desesperadamente para sobrevivir, sobre todo en provincias, donde no surgen tantas oportunidades como en la capital. Pero deben compatibilizar su urgencia con la estructura burocrática de los organismos gubernamentales que exigen comercializar su arte, pero que no se distinguen por su eficacia.

¿Es España un caso aislado?

¿Por qué gustan más los viejitos que toda esa barahúnda timbo/salsera? Aparte de los elevados costes para organizar una gira provechosa a toda una banda, ¿no resulta curioso que los que triunfan en España suelen ser artistas veteranos que interpretan temas compuestos en la época prerrevolucionaria? Es evidente que en los últimos años las compañias disqueras han preferido apostar más por la música tradicional, seguros de unas ventas mínimas, que por la música de baile que es para bailar y no para escuchar en el teatro o en casa.

Lo que es de extrañar es lo que tardó en ser reconocida, sobre todo si la comparamos con la brasileña, que lleva mucho más tiempo difundiéndose y cuenta con un buen número de seguidores en España. Dejando a un lado a Celia, a Gloria, Pablo o Silvio, la presencia habitual de músicos cubanos en los escenarios del viejo continente es relativamente reciente.

INTEGRANTES Y AMIGOS DE NG LA BANDA
(1993).

Si se observan las programaciones de festivales de auténtico prestigio, como puede ser el de Pirineos Sur, hasta 1995 no habían contratado a ningún grupo cubano. En las tres primeras ediciones de La Mar de Músicas de Cartagena, la presencia criolla ascendió a ocho grupos. En el Mercat de la Música Viva de Vic, de entre centenares de artistas que suelen participar, sólo un puñado son cubanos. En la super feria de festivales, el WOMEX, su edición de 1995 se redujo a NG La Banda, sin que en los años posteriores la oferta haya aumentado significativamente.

Las diversas formas de difusión se limitan a una mínima expresión, sobre todo si las comparamos con la calidad de composiciones y artistas disponibles. La doble moral o el doble juego parecen dominar la escena; por un lado algunos empresarios hacen «el paripé», acudiendo a la isla y denunciando «la situación tan injusta que sufren», por otro, continúan apoyando a la música pop y rock por encima de cualquier otra, a pesar de ser totalmente ajenas a las raíces hispanas y a las corrientes culturales que unen a España con América Latina.

Fue tan poderosa, tan sistemática y universal la primera imagen que creó la revolución, que a pesar de sus incumplidas promesas una buena parte del pueblo español ha tardado largo tiempo en corregir el imaginario que sostenía del castrismo. Entretanto, en la isla siguen prevaleciendo dos problemas gravísimos: la necesidad de proteínas diarias y la persecución por parte del régimen autoritario de la disidencia. Al cabo de tantos decenios de racionamiento estricto la gente tiene hambre no ya de productos que le permitan sobrevivir sino de todo lo que imagina y desea; han llegado al desencanto de desencantarse de todo y no hablan de otro sueño que la huida, a pesar de que cada día el periódico y la televisión les pintan un panorama dantesco de la situación económica en otros países. Con la música del decenio 1950-60 ha sucedido algo parecido a la comida: no se sabe lo que es comer si no se ha comido antes de la revolución.

Cito un par de chistes crueles que Manuel Vázquez Montalbán se apresuró a incluir en su voluminoso análisis Y *Dios entró en La Habana*:

«¿En qué se parece una nevera cubana y un coco? En que los dos nada más que tienen agua», era quizá el chiste más inocente sobre las hambres del «Período Especial», y el más cruel hacía referencia al zoo donde se contaba que habían ido sustituyendo los letreros: «Prohibido dar comida a los animales... Prohibido comerse la comida de los animales... Prohibido comerse a los animales».

Un «honor» que sobra

El período estudiado en este trabajo me recuerda bastante el siglo XIX, en que se fundaron los principales géneros músicales de la isla. Aquella estuvo muy lejos de ser una etapa idílica para la creatividad músical: conspiraciones, guerras, latigazos, arrestos y exilios se sucedían. La dureza de los capitanes generales y sus secuaces se cebaba precisamente entre las jóvenes generaciones, por lo que aparecieron infinidad de canciones habaneras y guarachas que reflejaban las quejas sobre deportados y presos políticos.

En esa desazón vivía La Habana de mediados del siglo XIX, inquieta por las relaciones entre la isla y los Estados Unidos, especialmente por los posibles efectos entre los negros criollos debido a la Guerra de Secesión norteamericana (1861-65), que enfrentó a hermanos por el grave problema de la esclavitud. Por aquel entonces, el asturiano Antonio de las Ba-

rras y Prado captó magistralmente la fuerte influencia del vecino poderoso en las cuestiones cubanas:

Aquí se ha inoculado, más que en ninguna otra parte de la América española, el
go-ahead o espíritu progresivo de los Estados Unidos, con quienes está muy en
contacto por sus relaciones intelectuales y mercantiles; y como esta nación es, sin
disputa, la más adelantada del mundo, por esto es por lo que Cuba, cuyas necesidades han ido creciendo al par que su riqueza fabulosa, se sirve para todas esas
necesidades de los procedimientos más nuevos e ingeniosos, mecánicos e industriales, y de todos los ramos culturales y científicos.

Ese espíritu progresivo ha sido machacado y tergiversado durante
más de cuarenta años; Castro se ha empecinado en destruir la capacidad
empresarial del cubano medio. Sin embargo, es de notar que el comercio
en grandes superficies nació en Cuba y que uno de sus creadores, el también asturiano Pepín Fernández, trajo a España. ¿Acaso se puede olvidar
que en 1959 (cuando Castro llegó al poder) la isla tenía una renta per cá-
pita de 500 dólares, cuando en España apenas se llegaba a los 300?

Mientras que el régimen continúe tercamente repitiendo que detrás
de todo disidente está la CIA, y no acepte el hecho de que en la raíz de
toda disidencia hay un déficit obvio del sistema, seguirá prevaleciendo
uno de sus más crueles juegos: la persecución de los que claman por los
derechos humanos. No existe otro tipo de remedio para la crisis de las libertades públicas en el país de los cubanos que el instaurar un estado de
derecho civilizado como fórmula de gobierno. No hay la menor posibilidad de que una ideología basada en el odio y en el exterminio de clases o
sectores sociales –demonizados oficialmente– pueda algún día respetar los
derechos humanos del pueblo.

La historia musical de Cuba no se ha detenido con la revolución
–como muchos quisieran creer–, sino que ha adquirido mayor complejidad. Al comenzar el siglo XXI, Cuba tiene el «honor» de ser a la vez la
gran reserva de la humanidad en cuanto a música con sandunga, y el con-
trovertido hecho de mantenerse como el último bastión comunista de Occidente. Cabe preguntarse sin prejuicio alguno: ¿Qué rumbo habría tomado la música cubana si no se hubiese tenido que cantar en 1959 aquel
sonsonete de Carlos Puebla?: «Y se acabó la diversión, llegó el Comandante y mandó a parar». Que cada cual haga la interpretación que quiera
de esa pregunta, que es tan honesta como cualquiera otra. ¿No es acaso

una verdadera ironía que tal parece que el país ha dado una vuelta en redondo? El propio trovador tenía otro son, concebido en la misma época del anterior y le aseguro que de mejor calidad musical, donde repetía: «Los caminos de mi Cuba, nunca van a dónde deben...», pero que la revolución pronto hizo desaparecer.

TROVADORES SANTIAGUEROS.

Es evidente que el «hombre nuevo» que anunciaba el Che se ha retrasado bastante; después de cuarenta años llega con hambre y bailando timba, como la jinetera no es precisamente la «mujer nueva» que soñó el argentino. ¿Cómo habría reaccionado un resucitado Guevara ante los efectos desmoralizadores de la dolarización de la economía, la creciente desigualdad social, la frustración de una juventud sin horizontes, el drama de los profesionales forzados a dejar sus carreras para ser «meseros» o taxistas y ganarse alguna propina en dólares, la prostitución asociada al turismo, los sueños rotos de campesinos hambrientos, los apagones constantes, la aparición de las drogas y el auge de la delincuencia?

Me preocupa especialmente la situación actual de los negros, un importante sector de la población que al no recibir dólares de familiares en el exterior sufre más que otros la crudeza económica del país. ¿Acaso esta discriminación no constituye otra forma de terrorismo como el que tuvieron que sufrir en 1912 tantos luchadores?, cosa que denuncio en la pág. 38. ¿Se ha preguntado alguien el contrasentido de que una población negra y mulata que llega al 63 por ciento (con sus diferentes matices) se haya convertido en una mayoría invisible? Esta discriminación es real y se puede observar hasta en la composición de los cuadros dirigentes de la revolución. Más del 85 por ciento de los miembros del Buró Político del Comité Central del Partido Comunista son blancos; el Consejo de Estado está constituido en un 98 por ciento de blancos; los miembros del Consejo de Ministros son todos, excepto uno, blancos; la inmensa mayoría de los ejecutivos y directores de empresas también lo son, mientras que los barrios marginales son habitados mayoritariamente por negros, que también constituyen el grueso de la población penal.

Creo en la integración de las razas y en la libertad como no dominación, como ausencia de servidumbre, partiendo del principio de que la libertad real no la garantiza tampoco el todopoderoso mercado, sino la continua acción política velando por el bienestar de los más débiles a través de las instituciones y normas colectivas. En mi experiencia es bastante fácil ser bueno, lo difícil es ser justo. Alguien debe empezar a perdonar.

Cuba sólo puede ofrecer mano de obra barata y algunos recursos naturales. Si el actual gobierno ha logrado evitar los casos de pobreza extrema, ha sido al costo de repartir la pobreza. Si ha logrado mantener los servicios sociales, ha sido a expensas de los salarios extremadamente bajos que paga. Si ha alcanzado algunos repuestos económicos en los últimos años, ha sido a expensas de la reducción del consumo personal y de la sobre-explotación de una fuerza de trabajo sin amparo gremial consistente.

A pesar del rencor, del miedo y la apatía que prevalecen en la sociedad actual, será necesario hacer un lugar para los músicos que tuvieron que abandonar el país y labrarse un porvenir en el extranjero con su talento, aunque pagando un precio muy alto por su libertad, o para los que crecieron en otras tierras y aprendieron a tocar un instrumento. Reencontrarse y mantener su propia identidad entre el maremágnum de sonidos que hoy pueblan el mundo occidental es uno de los peligros en que se verán envueltos los músicos y artistas cubanos el día de la reconciliación. Habrá que evitar a toda costa la destrucción posterior de la cultura nacional en la forma de una brutal penetración foránea, impulsando nuevos géneros musicales, nuevas ideas, dando oportunidades a los que buscan su propia expresión. Aunque la música popular se mueve dentro de una cultura de lo efímero, es posible alentar una visión musical de futuro, no solamente por una cuestión de sensibilidad sino porque crea economía.

Cuando termine la larga noche del totalitarismo, la música será con toda seguridad uno de los puentes más sólidos y gratos para el abrazo definitivo de un mismo pueblo que tiene tanto de cautivo como de cautivador. Pienso que en ese fontanar de música está una de las claves de la futura reconciliación, porque está grabada en el alma de todos los cubanos y porque no sigue banderas ni se adscribe a ningún partido. Aunque reconozco que no será fácil: no habrá reconciliación si a la intolerancia de un lado responde la excomunión del otro.

Tengo confianza en la determinación de la gente joven con ideas y buenas intenciones a ambos lados de la actual división ideológica; creo en ellas no sólo por lo que están haciendo sino por lo que piensan y quieren hacer. Al pueblo cubano siempre lo ha salvado su capital afectivo, su espontánea bondad, su inalienable confianza en las relaciones humanas. Quizá se trate de una manera preindustrial de sentir o de haberse detenido en el tiempo, instalado el país en una modernidad cuya truncada presencia no ha logrado destruir del todo la intimidad ni los vínculos de afecto.

De ahí que a ambos extremos ideológico-territoriales existan criterios muy firmes de hermandad; después de todo, lo que moldeó a tantos músicos de la isla no fueron los discursos del líder –a quien la mayoría considera un loco– como tampoco han sido los cuentos de papá y mamá para los que crecieron en el destierro. Fue el hecho, por un lado, de vivir en un país tan complejo como Cuba, que induce a reflexionar, a ser sensatos y mantener un sentimiento comunitario como no se acostumbra en el mundo occidental, y por el otro, el sentirse desarraigados, desterrados de un estilo de vida que ha obligado a muchos a valorar las cosas de forma distinta.

Termino este libro al cumplirse los primeros cien años de la fundación de la República de Cuba (mayo de 1902), un proyecto de nación que la revolución se ha encargado de vilipendiar hasta la saciedad. Sin embargo, si algo debemos agradecer los de mi generación (y otras anteriores) al derrotero que tomó el régimen castrista es el habernos enseñado a valorar la Cuba que perdimos, un país paradójico, difícil, defectuoso, pienso que a medio hacer –«frustrado en lo esencial político», decía Lezama Lima–, pero vital y en ascenso, del que nadie quería emigrar y en el que casi todos los que llegaban querían quedarse. El paredón de fusilamiento, el racionamiento perpetuo, el retroceso económico, el pensamiento único, la prensa cautiva, las pandillas parapoliciales disfrazadas de «pueblo indignado», la multiplicación de las cárceles, los actos de repudio, el drama del exilio y el holocausto de los balseros vinieron después. Y todo éso lo han sufrido los músicos.

Tengo suficiente esperanza en los que luchan por los derechos humanos dentro de Cuba. Y como estimo que la democracia sólo puede entenderse como el derecho a ejercer la oposición, quiero referirme finalmente al importante caso del Proyecto Varela: 11.020 firmas de cubanos valerosos –incluyendo todos sus datos personales– apoyaron una propuesta legislativa, amparados en el artículo 88 de la Constitución socialista de 1976 (que exige 10.000 firmas), para presentar ante la Asamblea Nacional del Poder Popular una iniciativa de ley que propone, en esencia, un

referéndum nacional en el que se consulte a todos los ciudadanos si están
o no de acuerdo con las siguientes demandas:

1. Amnistía general para presos políticos de conciencia.
2. Apertura de la pequeña y mediana empresa privada nacional.
3. Una reforma legislativa que garantice las libertades de expresión
    y asociación.
4. Revisión y cambio de la ley electoral orientándola al pluralismo
    político, y
5. Elecciones libres en un plazo de nueve meses.

La reacción del régimen momificado no se hizo esperar. Anunció a
los cuatro vientos su verdadero propósito de eternizarse en el poder, dejando claro que no desea reformarse, y que los caminos para un cambio
pacífico se han clausurado «legalmente» para siempre. En resumen: el actual sistema político cubano no es reformable porque los pocos que de-
tentan el poder real no están dispuestos siquiera a honrar su propia Constitución.

Fuera de Cuba destrozada, vivimos en la época de la imagen y del
sonido, aunque a menudo importe bastante poco lo que haya detrás de
ese sonido. Ahora con un ProTools (herramienta informática musical) se
puede afinar o corregir la voz de un cantante en un estudio de grabación;
ha llegado el momento que con las grabaciones pasa lo que con la cocina
china: es preciso no presenciar las manipulaciones previas. Por otra parte,
a las discográficas sólo parecen interesarles los clónicos que funcionen;
no tienen tiempo de pararse a escuchar. Las multinacionales tienen tal nivel de gastos e inversiones que asistimos a la mayor malversación de fondos de artistas. ¿Llegaremos a cantar con Celia Cruz aquello de «no hay
cama pa'tanta gente»? Predecir es muy difícil, sobre todo el futuro.

Después de todo lo que he escrito, sólo me queda aceptar que la verdadera riqueza de la sonoridad cubana permanecerá siendo un enigma
inaccesible a las palabras. Algunos incluso creen que es mejor que su
fama. Por eso reconozco que los historiadores de la música deberíamos
cerrar el negocio; mientras el mundo se abre, la historia se cierra. Y no
quedan herramientas para ver el futuro; aunque es muy fácil realmente.
Sólo hacen falta paz y buena música.

¿CONOCE USTED A LOS CUBANOS?

Terminaré con un escrito revelador reproducido por cortesía de su autor, el profesor jubilado Luis Aguilar León, residente en Miami. Aparecido originalmente en su libro *Reflexiones sobre Cuba y su futuro*, se titula «He aquí que el profeta habla de los cubanos».

«Desde una roca en el puerto, el profeta contemplaba la blanca vela de la nave que a su tierra había de llevarlo. Una mezcla de tristeza y alegría inundaba su alma. Por nueve años sus sabias y amorosas palabras se habían derramado sobre la población de Elmira. Su amor lo ataba a esa gente, pero el deber lo llamaba a su patria. Había llegado la hora de partir. Atenuábase su melancolía pensando que sus perdurables consejos llenarían el vacío de su ausencia.

»Entonces, un político de Elmira se le acercó y le dijo: "Maestro, háblanos de los cubanos"».

El Profeta recogió en un puño su alba túnica y dijo: «Los cubanos están entre vosotros, pero no son como vosotros. No intentéis conocerlos porque su alma vive en el mundo impenetrable del dualismo. Los cubanos beben de una misma copa la alegría y la amargura. Hacen música de su llanto y se ríen con su música. Los cubanos toman en serio los chistes y tornan lo serio en chiste. Y ellos mismos no se conocen.

Nunca subestiméis a los cubanos. El brazo derecho de San Pedro es un cubano, y el mejor consejero del Diablo es también cubano. Cuba no ha dado ni un santo ni un hereje. Pero los cubanos santifican entre los heréticos y heretizan entre los santos. Su espíritu es universal e irreverente. Los cubanos creen simultáneamente en el Dios de los católicos, en Changó, en la charada y en los horóscopos. Tratan a los dioses de tú y los regañan cuando no los complacen. No creen en nadie y creen en todo. Y ni renuncian a sus ilusiones, ni aprenden de las desilusiones.

No discutáis con ellos jamás. Los cubanos nacen con sabiduría inmanente. No necesitan leer, todo lo saben. No necesitan viajar, todo lo han visto. Los cubanos son

CREENCIAS DEL PUEBLO CUBANO.

el pueblo elegido... por ellos mismos. Y se pasean entre los demás pueblos como el espíritu se pasea sobre las aguas.

Los cubanos se caracterizan individualmente por su simpatía e inteligencia, y en grupos por su gritería y apasionamiento. Cada uno lleva la chispa del genio, y los genios no se llevan bien entre sí. De ahí que reunir a los cubanos es fácil, unirlos imposible. Un cubano es capaz de lograr todo en este mundo menos el aplauso de otros cubanos.

No les habléis de lógica. La lógica implica razonamiento y mesura, y los cubanos son hiperbólicos y desmesurados. Si os invitan a un restaurante, os invitan a comer no al mejor restaurante del pueblo, sino "al mejor restaurante del mundo". Cuando discuten, no dicen "no estoy de acuerdo con usted", dicen "Usted está total y absolutamente equivocado".

Tienen una tendencia antropofágica. "Se la comió" es una expresión de admiración, "comerse" un cable señal de situación crítica y llamarle a alguien "¡comemierda!" es su más usual y lacerante insulto. Tienen voluntad piromaníaca, "ser la candela" es ser cumbre. Y aman tanto las contradicciones que llaman a las mujeres hermosas "monstruos" y a los eruditos "bárbaros". Y cuando se les pide un favor no dicen "sí" o "no", sino que afirman "sí, cómo que no".

Los cubanos intuyen las soluciones antes de conocer los problemas. De ahí que para ellos "nunca hay problema". Y se sienten tan grandes que a todo el mundo le dicen "chico". Pero ellos no se achican ante nadie. Si se les lleva al estudio de un famoso pintor, se limitan a comentar "a mí no me dio por pintar". Y van al médico, no a preguntarle qué tienen, sino a informarle lo que ellos saben que tienen.

Usan los diminutivos con ternura, pero también con voluntad de achicar al prójimo. Así, piden "un favorcito", ofrecen una "tacita de café", visitan "por un ratico" y de los postres sólo aceptan "un pedacitico". Pero también a quien se hizo construir una mansión le celebran la "casita", o el "carrito" que tiene a quien compró un Mercedes Benz. Como llamar "Herodes" a un médico de niños; "cocktail de guisasos" a un tipo no simpático o "cuchara" a un presidente que ni pincha ni corta.

Cuando visité su Isla me admiraba su sabiduría instantánea y colectiva. Cualquier cubano se consideraba capaz de liquidar al comunismo o al capitalismo, enderezar a la América Latina, erradicar el hambre en África y enseñar filosofía a los alemanes. No permiten que nadie opine sobre Cuba, pero el ser cubano les autoriza a dar su opinión sobre todos los países y generalizar sobre todo el mundo. Y se asombran de que los extranjeros no comprendan cuán sencillas y evidentes son sus fórmulas. Así, viven entre vosotros y viajan por el mundo pero siguen siendo ellos la medida de todos los pueblos. Y no entienden por qué la gente no es como ellos».

Había llegado la nave al muelle. Alrededor del Profeta se arremolinaba la multitud transida de dolor. El Profeta tornose hacia ella como queriendo hablar, pero la emoción le ahogaba la voz. Hubo un largo minuto de conmovido silencio. De pronto se oyó la voz del timonel de la nave: 'Decídase, mi hermano, dése un sabanaso y súbase, que ya ando con el *schedul* retrasao'.

El Profeta se volvió hacia la multitud, hizo un gesto de resignación y lentamente abordó la nave. Acto seguido, el timonel cubano puso proa al horizonte.»

Aché.

¿Dónde obtener libros que no se distribuyen en España?

PUERTO RICO

Para las obras de Cristóbal Díaz Ayala (ver Bibliografía): Fundación Musicalia, P.O. Box. 190613, San Juan, Puerto Rico 00919-0613.
Tel: 1-787-727 4168/Fax: 727 7037.

MIAMI

Para los cuatro volúmenes de Jorge e Isabel Castellanos (ver Bibliografía): Ediciones Universal, 3090 SW 8 St, Miami, Fl 33135, USA.
Tel: 1-305-642 3234/Fax: 642 7978.
Esta librería también tiene los libros de Lydia Cabrera y los de Cristóbal Díaz Ayala. Quizá pueda conseguirle *El libro de la salsa* (Caracas, 1980) de César Miguel Rondón, y *La salsa* (Bogotá, 1990), de José Arteaga.

CUBA

Para *Los rostros de la salsa* (Ediciones Unión, 1997), de Leonardo Padura, o para *Panorama de la música popular cubana* (2.ª edición, 1998), selección de Radamés Giro, o el *Diccionario de la música cubana* (2.ª edición, 1992), de Helio Orovio, dirigirse a Editorial Letras Cubanas, Palacio del Segundo Cabo, O'Reilly 4, esq. a Tacón, La Habana. Es muy posible que también puedan suministrar el importante libro de Leonardo Acosta: *Raíces del jazz latino,* Barranquilla (Col.), 2001.

ESPAÑA

La editorial Música Mundana Maqueda de Madrid ha reeditado varias obras clave de Fernando Ortiz.

COMENTARIOS A LA SELECCIÓN DEL CD

La cantidad de música estupenda producida durante el largo período comprendido en esta obra ha impedido que todos los estilos y tendencias quedaran equitativamente representados en el compacto. Por otra parte, he seleccionado números poco conocidos, representativos de los principales géneros, evitando incluir a aquellos artistas y agrupaciones cuya música está actualmente a la venta en excelentes grabaciones o que visitan el país con bastante frecuencia.

1. **VOY PA' MAYARÍ**, de Compay Segundo. Canta el autor.
    Abren las cuerdas del tres y entra una trompeta con sordina para dar pie a la introducción en pleno goce sonero. El rápido número nombra a varios poblados orientales: Mayarí, Guisa, Jagua, donde se divierten los mozos «tacos» (elegantes). Después entra el solo de cuerdas del Compay (que originalmente tocaba el clarinete), cuando todavía era conocido como Francisco Repilado (ver pág. 286). El sobrenombre surgió cuando le hacía segunda voz a Lorenzo Hierrezuelo en la primera versión del dúo Los Compadres.

2. **ELIGE TÚ, QUE CANTO YO,** de Joseíto Fernández. Canta Benny Moré.

Un número en la mejor tradición sonera del «Bárbaro del Ritmo» (ver pág. 164), con el respaldo de su propia «tribu», la orquesta gigante que lo elevó a la fama en toda Cuba y otros países. Unos acordes del trombón de Generoso *El Tojo* Jiménez dan pie al aquelarre de las trompetas, entre las que se encontraba *Chocolate* Armenteros (ver pág. 256). Se dice que este número surgió a raíz de una controversia con Rolando Laserie, que se había proclamado mejor que Benny cantando guaguancó.

3. **EL BRUJO DE GUANABACOA,** de Hermenegildo Cárdenas. Trío de Servando Díaz.

La historia tiene lugar en Guanabacoa, un municipio de La Habana y tierra de importantes babalaos (sacerdotes de la santería). Durante la consulta éste le dice que «estaba salao», que tenía mala suerte. De ahí el dinero y los animales que le pide para el sacrificio de la sangre. Los siete pedazos de coco se refieren al tablero de Orula, según la posición en que caigan el babalao le dirá la «letra» que indican los santos. Changó y Yemayá son dos deidades u orichas de la cultura yoruba; uno simboliza la virilidad y el trueno, mientras que la segunda es la madre de las aguas.

Conocidos como «Los trovadores sonrientes» y formado en La Habana en 1937 por el cantor y guitarrista Servando Díaz (ver pág. 76) junto a Otilio Portal y Octavio Mendoza, este trío grabó infinidad de discos, interpretando mayormente guarachas y boleros que llevaron con éxito a varios países. Salieron de Cuba en 1960 y se establecieron en Puerto Rico, donde su fundador falleció en 1985.

4. **A MI MANERA,** de Marcelino Guerra *Rapindey.*

Primera grabación (1943) de este bolero antológico, donde el compositor hace la segunda voz, con el respaldo de la orquesta del saxo Mariano Mercerón y sus Muchachos Pimienta, una formidable agrupación de Santiago de Cuba. La letra es de Panchito Calvo, un veterinario que nunca quiso se supiera que era de su autoría. Como novedad, en esta versión el bolero se convierte en un son cadencioso, con un solo de piano que no tiene nada que envidiarle a otros momentos estelares de la música bailable cubana. En esta sección se escucha claramente el marcado de las claves.

5.   **AL COMPÁS DEL MAMBO,** de Dámaso Pérez Prado. Orquesta del autor.

El pequeño pianista tuvo que irse con su mambo a México en 1949 para triunfar porque en Cuba nunca le hicieron mucho caso. *Que rico el mambo* ya había alcanzado ventas de 4,5 millones de discos entre 1950-51, cuando Pérez Prado trató de emular esas cifras con esta composición (ver pág. 163). Había que ser muy buen instrumentista para trabajar con él, sobre todo los metales, porque les exigía muchas notas altas difíciles de alcanzar. Esta grabación tiene al gran Mongo Santamaría en las congas (ver pág. 239).

6.   **PERMANGANATO,** de Israel López *Cachao*. Orquesta de Antonio Arcaño.

Un típico danzón del estilo «ritmo nuevo», que se escuchaba a menudo en la radio en la década de 1940. La flauta del gigantesco Arcaño (ver pág. 157) domina el número, creado por el contrabajista *Cachao*, que muchos años después y desde el exilio ha continuado produciendo música estupenda. En esta grabación participó su hermano Orestes López en el cello. En la segunda parte entra una cadencia que ya anuncia el futuro ritmo del chachachá mientras Arcaño improvisa y aparece el piano de Jesús López antes de caer en un «abanico» de los timbales, dando la señal a los bailadores que llegó el momento cumbre para dejarse la vida en la pista.

7.   **MI LINDO YAMBÚ,** del Conjunto Casino.

Aunque el yambú es una de las vertientes de la rumba, este son no tiene nada de rumba, sólo lo celebra. Las voces de Roberto Faz, Roberto Espí y Agustín Ribot identificaron a esta agrupación, que gozó de gran prestigio en la década de 1950 (ver pág. 55). La frase «en el yambú no se vacuna» indica que en este tipo de rumba no se hacen los movimientos pélvicos característicos del guaguancó.

8.   **BONCÓ.** Canta Celia Cruz con la Sonora Matancera.

Típica guaracha rápida, sonsacadora, de ritmo abierto, que caracterizó a este estupendo conjunto (ver pág. 60). Como siempre, Celia es vivaz en la improvisación, con esa voz con sabor a pueblo que todavía mantiene intacta (ver pág. 191). Esta grabación de 1953 tiene un solo de congas ¡que vale un Congo!, mientras el cencerro mantiene un mismo golpe a partir del estribillo. El solo de trompeta es también excelente, y seguramente se debe a Calixto Leicea.

9.   **MIS MARACAS CUBANAS,** de Lorenzo Hierrezuelo. Dúo Los Compadres.

La segunda versión de Los Compadres la formaron Lorenzo y Reynaldo Hierrezuelo. Ambos hermanos se divertían inventando este tipo de son, siempre destacando algún valor nacional, en este caso las modestas maracas, que con su alegría han llenado los valores tímbrico-rítmicos de la música cubana. Los comentarios intercalados ambientan el número, aunque nadie se encontraba presente durante la grabación. Reynaldo (que fuera líder de la Vieja Trova Santiaguera) siempre ha sido muy hábil haciendo efectos de clave con la lengua o imitando una flauta con su silbido.

10.   **SOY HIJO DE SIBONEY,** de Guillermo Portabales. Canta el autor.

Los siboneyes fueron los indígenas que habitaron la mitad occidental de la isla. La voz y la guitarra de Portabales (ver pág. 86), un trovador conocido como el creador de la «guajira de salón», da aquí fe de un orgullo nacionalista tardío, con aire campesino. En este suave son lo acompaña al piano el puertorriqueño Noro Morales.

11.   **UNA RUMBA EN LA BODEGA,** de Alberto Zayas. Canta Roberto Maza.

Rápido guaguancó que empieza con el típico la-la-leo y el sonar de tres tambores que mantienen valores rítmicos muy diferentes, especialmente el quinto, de sonido agudo y seco, que es el que se escucha repiquetear. El tema relata que estaban sonando una rumba en una bodega –que en Cuba indica un bar, que también vende alimentos–, cuando los sorprende un policía y les apaga la vitrola (gramola), pero tras la insistencia de los músicos, éste les permite continuar divirtiéndose. Una oportunidad para apreciar la verdadera rumba cubana, que no tiene nada que ver con la flamenca o la catalana. Ver pág. 102.

12.   **SI ME COMPRENDIERAS,** de José Antonio Méndez. Canta el autor.

Bolero estilo filin (del inglés *feeling*, sentimiento), de uno de los iniciadores de este importante movimiento cancionístico surgido en La Habana hacia finales de los años 40. La canción es preciosa, con una rareza: la inclusión de un piano en un grupo de cantautores que adoptaron la guitarra como su mejor acompañante. José Antonio Méndez, autor de *Novia mía, Quiéreme y verás, Tú, mi adoración* y otros temas, vivió casi diez años en México y regresó a la isla al triunfo de la revolución en 1959. Ver pág. 147.

13. CIENFUEGOS, de Víctor Lay. Conjunto de Félix Chapottín.

Uno de los mejores sones que cantó Miguelito Cuní con el apoyo de la trompeta de Félix Chapottín (ver pág. 62). Preste atención a los «lloraos» de este brillante instrumentista (que grabó este número con el respaldo de otras dos trompetas), ni tampoco se pierda el cambio al montuno cuando el contrabajista Sabino Peñalver introduce una figuración original, que mantiene durante el resto de la pieza. Luego, al grito de «Juega, Lilí» se destaca el piano de *Lilí* Martínez Griñán. Cienfuegos es una hermosa ciudad al sur de la isla, la patria chica de Marcelino Guerra *Rapindey*.

14. DESCARGA CUBANA, de Tumbao All-Stars.

Mientras la flauta revolotea, el piano va marcando un compás que no cesa, con el insuperable Tata Güines en las congas (ver pág. 182). Después, con la complicidad del contrabajo, Chucho Valdés (ver pág. 329) comienza a divertirse, moviendo sus enormes dedos cual si fueran bailarinas contoneándose sobre el teclado. El líder de Irakere se lo juega todo en este número que simplemente salió así, sin ensayo, como las mejores descargas que este grupo grabó en 1996. Vuelve la flauta del veterano Richard Egües (que durante largo tiempo trabajó con la Orquesta Aragón), para llevarnos hacia nuevos repiqueteos del Tata, que se apoya en el juego del contrabajo de Orlando López *Cachaíto* (sobrino de *Cachao*) para lucir su estilo único.

15. QUE VIVA CHANGÓ, de Celina y Reutilio. Interpretado por los autores.

Con este rápido son el dúo de Celina González y Reutilio Domínguez (ver pág. 87) rompió en la década de 1950 con la secular separación que existía entre la música guajira y la afrocubana. Sorprendieron a todos subiendo el son a una carreta de caña tirada por un oricha yoruba, Changó, poderoso guerrero, dueño del fuego, la virilidad, la música y el baile, sincretizado con Santa Bárbara en el panteón católico (ver pág. 93).

16. TANGÁ, de Mario Bauzá. Interpretado por *Machito* y sus AfroCubans.

Una hermosa demostración de jazz afrocubano, lo que en Estados Unidos se conoce como Latin jazz, con los AfroCubans de Frank Grillo *Machito* (ver pág. 242) luciendo sus mejores galas en esta grabación en directo de 1951. En este CD del sello Tumbao Cuban Classics, el batería juega alrededor del golpe de la clave en tanto las congas no se desorbitan y el piano de René Hernández inventa acordes precisos, mientras la trompeta de Mario Bauzá (ver pág. 235) –uno de los padres de esta importante tendencia del jazz contemporáneo– nos deja escuchar algunos de sus mejores momentos. Contiene un fabuloso solo del trompeta Bobby Woodlen y otro del saxo Zoot Sims.

17. BAILA JOSÉ RAMÓN, de Enrique Bonne. Canta Pacho Alonso.

El pilón fue uno de los primeros ritmos que surgieron con el triunfo de la revolución, junto a la pachanga, el mozambique y el pa'cá, originados por otros músicos. Impuesto durante los carnavales de aquella primera etapa, su creador fue Pacho Alonso (ver pág. 295), un brillante cantante santiaguero, en estrecha asociación con el compositor Enrique Bonne. El ritmo pilón duró unos pocos años mientras que Pacho buscaba otras posibilidades novedosas. A su repentina muerte en 1982 su hijo siguió sus pasos, con una banda bautizada Pachito Alonso y sus Kini Kini (ver pág. 363).

18. AGUANTA AHÍ, de René Álvarez. Interpretado por el autor.

Un ejemplo del tipo de música que se bailó en Cuba durante décadas, en este caso del conjunto de René Álvarez, una agrupación que amenizaba numerosos bailes populares. El número trata de defender la posición del género del son como la música más característica del pueblo cubano ante la intención de algunos de soslayarlo. En esta grabación de 1987 se distingue claramente el sonido de las cuerdas metálicas del tres en las manos de Gerardo Llorente. El solo de bongó de Guillermo Romero es un verdadero clásico del instrumento (ver pág. 59), y hay que dispensar los errores de dicción de René.

19. NOCHE CUBANA, de César Portillo de la Luz. Canta Omara Portuondo.

Elegante versión de una hermosa composición por uno de los iniciadores del bolero filin, grabado cuando la voz de la elegante Omara Portuondo (ver pág. 154) era más dulce, y sin duda más sexy. El gran guitarrista que es Portillo de la Luz ha creado otras melodías memorables: *Tú, mi delirio, Realidad y fantasía, Canción de un festival* y muchas más. Ver pág. 148.

20. GUAJEO DE SAXOS, de E. Peñalver. Descarga dirigida por *Cachao*.

Grabado en La Habana en 1957, esta descarga contó con el aporte de *El negro* Vivar en la trompeta, Guillermo Barreto (ver pág. 194) en las pailas, Gustavo Tamayo en el güiro, Tata Güines en las tumbadoras, Rogelio *Yeyo* Iglesias en el bongó, Israel López *Cachao* en el bajo acústico, y los saxos Emilio Peñalver y Virgilio Lisama. Entrevistado hace pocos años, el gran *Cachao* comentó: «Cuando hicimos aquellas descargas a partir de 1957, no nos estábamos fijando demasiado en el jazz, sino en la propia música cubana, en el son. Aquello fue una reunión de músicos capacitados, con ganas de hacer algunas ideas nuevas a partir de la inspiración y la improvisación». Ver pág. 192.

21. ESTOY MATIZANDO, de Bebo Valdés. Interpretado por el autor.

Nacido en 1918, padre de Chucho y figura central durante la época de oro de la música cubana, Bebo Valdés (ver pág. 231) fue durante años el pianista y asesor musical de la orquesta de Armando Romeu en el cabaré Tropicana. En 1952 grabó la primera descarga de jazz cubano en la isla, y con su Orquesta Sabor ocupó los principales centros de diversión. Bebo abandonó Cuba en 1960 y conoció a su segunda mujer en Estocolmo en 1963. Allí estuvo más de treinta años hasta que Paquito D'Rivera (ver pág. 224) lo invitó a grabar un nuevo disco en Alemania. De él ha escrito Cristóbal Díaz Ayala: «Como pianista, Bebo es elegante como Lecuona, rítmico como los danzoneros Antonio María Romeu y Cheo Belén Puig, inspirado y agresivo como los montuneros Anselmo Sacasas y *Lilí* Martínez, creativo como Frank Emilio o *Peruchín*, y tan innovador como su propio hijo Chucho».

BIBLIOGRAFÍA CONSULTADA

ACOSTA, Leonardo, *Música y descolonización*, La Habana, 1982.
  Del tambor al sintetizador, La Habana, 1983.
  Elige tú, que canto yo, La Habana, 1993.
  Raíces del jazz latino. Un siglo de jazz en Cuba, Barranquilla, 2001.
ALÉN, Olavo, *Géneros musicales de Cuba*, San Juan, 1992.
ARTEAGA, José, *Música del Caribe*, Bogotá, 1994.

BARNET, Miguel, *Cultos afrocubanos*, La Habana, 1995.
BERGEROT, Frank y MERLÍN, Arnaud, *The story of jazz. Bop and beyond*, New
  York, 1993.
BLANCO, Jesús, *80 Años del son y soneros en el Caribe*, Caracas, 1992.
BOGGS, Vernon W., *Salsiology. Afro-Cuban music and the evolution of salsa in
  New York City*, New York, 1992.
BOLÍVAR Aróstegui, Natalia, *Opolopo owó*, La Habana, 1994.
BROUWER, Leo, *La música, lo cubano y la innovación*, La Habana, 1989.

CABRERA, Lydia, *El monte*, La Habana, 1954.
  La sociedad secreta abakuá, La Habana, 1958.
  La laguna sagrada de San Joaquín, Madrid, 1973.

Yemayá y Ochún, Madrid, 1974.

Anaforuana. Ritual y símbolos de la iniciación en la sociedad secreta Abakuá, Madrid, 1975.

CARPENTIER, Alejo, *La música en Cuba*, La Habana, 1988.

CASTELLANOS, Jorge e Isabel, *Cultura afrocubana* (4 vols.), Miami, 1988-1994.

CHEDIAK, Nat, *Diccionario de jazz latino*, Madrid, 1998.

CONTRERAS, Félix, *Porque tienen filin*, Santiago de Cuba, 1989.

La música cubana: una cuestión personal, La Habana, 1999.

CROS SANDOVAL, Mercedes, *La religión afrocubana*, Madrid, 1975.

DE LA FUENTE, Alejandro, *Una nación para todos. Raza, desigualdad y política en Cuba, 1900-2000*, Madrid, 2000.

D'RIVERA, Paquito, *Mi vida saxual*, Seix Barral, 2000.

DEPESTRE, Leonardo, *Cuatro músicos de una villa*, La Habana, 1990.

DÍAZ AYALA, Cristóbal, *Música cubana del areyto a la nueva trova*, San Juan, 1981.

Discografía de la música cubana, vol. 1/1898 a 1925, San Juan, 1994.

Cuando salí de La Habana. 1898-1997: Cien años de música cubana por el mundo, San Juan, 1998.

ELI RODRÍGUEZ, Victoria, y GÓMEZ GARCÍA, Zoila, *Haciendo música cubana*, La Habana, 1989.

Enciclopedia de Cuba (9 volúmenes), Madrid, 1975.

ÉVORA, Tony, *Orígenes de la música cubana*, Madrid, 1997.

El Libro del Bolero, Madrid, 2001.

Orígenes de la música cubana (2.ª edición), Madrid, 2003.

FRANCO, José Luciano, *Folklore criollo y afrocubano*, La Habana, 1959.

GALÁN, Natalio, *Cuba y sus sones*, Valencia, 1983.

GARCÍA Martínez, José María, *Del fox-trot al jazz flamenco*, Madrid, 1996.

GIRO, Radamés (selección), *El mambo*, La Habana, 1993.

(sel. y prólogo), *Panorama de la música popular cubana*, La Habana, 1995.

César Portillo de la Luz. El filin, Madrid, 1998.

GÓMEZ, José Manuel, *Guía esencial de la salsa*, Valencia, 1995.

GÓMEZ, Zoila, *Amadeo Roldán*, La Habana, 1977.

Musicología en Latinoamérica, La Habana, 1985.

GONZÁLEZ, Hilario, *Manuel Saumell / Contradanzas*, La Habana, 1981.

GOTTSCHALK, Louis Moreau, *Notes of a pianist*, New York, 1964.

KINKLE, Roger D., *The complete encyclopaedia of popular music and jazz 1900-50*, 4 volumes), Connecticut, 1974.

LARKIN, Colin, *The Guinness who's who of jazz*, Middlesex, 1995.
LEÓN, Argeliers, *El patrimonio musical cubano*, La Habana, 1952.
   Presencia del africano en la cultura cubana, Las Vilas, 1972.
   Del canto y el tiempo, La Habana, 1974.
LINARES, María Teresa, *La música y el pueblo*, La Habana, 1968.
   La música popular, La Habana, 1970.
LINARES, María Teresa, y NÚÑEZ, Faustino, *La música entre Cuba y España*, Madrid, 1998.
LOYOLA Fernández, José, *En ritmo de bolero*, La Habana, 1997.

MARTÍNEZ Furé, Rogelio, *Diálogos imaginarios*, La Habana, 1979.
MARTÍNEZ, Mayra A., *Cubanos en la música*, La Habana, 1993.
MOORE, Robin D., *Música y mestizaje. Revolución artística y cambio social en La Habana, 1920-1940*, Madrid, 2002.
MORA Ayora, Antonio, *De orilla a orilla*, Vitoria-Gasteiz, 1993.

NÚÑEZ, M. V. y GUNTÍN, R., *Salsa Caribe y otras músicas antillanas*, Madrid, 1992.

OPPENHEIMER, Andrés, *La hora final de Castro*.
ORBÓN, Julián, *En la esencia de los estilos y otros ensayos*, Madrid, 2000.
OROZCO, Danilo, «*El son ¿ritmo, baile o reflejo de la personalidad cultural cubana?*», (material mimeografiado), Guantánamo, 1980.
OROVIO, Helio, *Música por el Caribe*, Santiago de Cuba, 1990.
   Diccionario de la música cubana, La Habana, 1992.
ORTIZ, Fernando, *Los instrumentos de la música afrocubana* (2 vols.), Madrid, 1996.
   La africanía de la música folklórica de Cuba, Madrid, 1998.
   Los bailes y el teatro de los negros en el folklore de Cuba, Madrid, 1998.
   Contrapunteo cubano del tabaco y el azúcar, Madrid, 1999.

PADURA Fuentes, Leonardo, *Los rostros de la salsa*, La Habana, 1997.
PARDO, José Ramón, *El canto popular. Folk y nueva canción*, Madrid, 1981.
PATTERSON, Enrique, "Cuba: discursos sobre la identidad", (*Encuentro* Nº 2, Madrid, 1996.
PÉREZ Firmat, Gustavo, *Vidas en vilo. La cultura cubanoamericana*, Madrid, 2000.
PÉREZ Perazzo, A., *Ritmo afrohispano antillano 1865-1965*, Caracas, 1988.
PIERRE-CHARLES, G., *El Caribe contemporáneo*, México, 1983.

Revista *El Manisero*, (varios números), Barcelona, 1993-95.
Revista *Encuentro de la cultura cubana* (Nº 1-24), Madrid, 1996-2002.

Revista *Latin Beat* (varios números), Los Ángeles, 1995-2002.

Revista *Salsa cubana* (varios números), La Habana, 1995-2002.

ROBERTS, John Storm, *The Latin tinge*, New York, 1985.

RODRÍGUEZ, Ezequiel, *Iconografía del danzón*, La Habana, 1967.

RONDÓN, César Miguel, *El libro de la salsa*, Caracas, 1980.

SALAZAR, Adolfo, *La música como proceso histórico de su invención*, México, 1953

SALINAS, José Luis, *Jazz, flamenco, tango. Las orillas de un ancho río*, Madrid, 1994.

SCHNNEIDER, Marius, "Ritmo" (en *Enciclopedia Salvat de la música*), Barcelona, 1967.

SLONIMSKY, Nicolás, *Music of Latin America*, Nueva York, 1946.

SOSA Rodríguez, Enrique, *Los ñáñigos*, La Habana, 1982.

STEARNS, Marshall W., *La historia del jazz*, La Habana, 1966.

STORM Roberts, John, *The Latin tinge*, Nueva York, 1979.

SWEENEY, Philip, *The rough guide to Cuban music*, Londres, 2001.

ULLOA, Alejandro, *La salsa en Cali*, Cali, 1992.

URFÉ, Odilio, *Síntesis histórica del danzón*, La Habana, (s.f.)

VÁZQUEZ MONTALBÁN, Manuel, *Y Dios entró en la Habana*, Madrid, 1998.

ÍNDICE ONOMÁSTICO

Abbilona, Tambor Yoruba 110
Abreu, Anais 154
Abreu, Charles 249
Acea, Silvia 324
Acevedo, Plácido 66
Acosta, Leonardo 20, 168, 169, 316
Acuña, Alex 331
Adderley, Cannonball, 241
Aguabella, Francisco 58, 107
Aguiar, Rubén 284
Aguilar León, Luis 399
Aguilera, Ricardo 283
Aguirre, Georgia y Doris 323
Aguirre, Oscar 297
Alarcón, Ricardo 92
Alas del Castino, Carlos 74
Albuerne, Fernando 127, 249
Alejandro, Edesio 326
Alemany, Nacho 320
Alemañy, Jesús 67, 294, 337, 371, **380**
Alemañy, Luis 374, 380
Alfaro, David 375

Alfaro, Xiomara 170, 181, 249
Alfonso, Ortensio *Virulilla* 107
Alfonso, Carlos 313, 324
Alfonso, Equis 325
Alfonso, Jorge 329
Alfonso, Juan Carlos 356, 360
Alfonso, María de los Ángeles 360
Alfonso, Rolando 194
Almanza, Enriqueta 151, 152, 153
Almarío, Justo 331
Almas Vertiginosas, grupo 300
Almendra (orq. femenina) 389
Almodóvar, Pedro 131, 172, 266
Alonso, Alberto 154
Alonso, Alicia 199, 217
Alonso, Pachito 297, 383
Alonso, Pacho 141, 164, 295, **296**, 319, 353, 376
Álvarez Guedes, Guillermo 75
Álvarez Mera, Manolo 249
Álvarez, Adalberto 27, 89, 323, 335, 336, 356, 363, 383

Álvarez, David 370
Álvarez, Dorgeris 336
Álvarez, Fernando 56, 127, 135, 137, 152, 154, 155, 164, 183, 250, 330
Álvarez, Paulina 58, 161, 165
Álvarez, René 58
Álvarez, Roberto 55
Álvarez, Tico, 78
Álvarez, Tony 75
Allende, Salvador 316
Amaro, Blanquita 249
Amat, Pancho 44, 285, 287, 335, 372, **379**, 380
Amaya, Carmen 266, 321
Amigos, Los 175, 194, 338
Amram, David 328
Ana Gloria y Rolando 181
Anckermann, Fernando 200
Anckermann, Jorge 46, 204
Angulo, Héctor 92, 211
Angulo, María 167
Ansermet, Ernest 198
Anthony, Ray 321
Aparicio, Evaristo 189, 354
Aragón, Jorge 325
Arango, *Totico* 293
Arbeláez, Panchito
Arcaño, Antonio 122, **157**, 158, 159, 161, 163, 250, 320
Arcaraz, Luis 137
Ardévol, José 205
Argudín, Barbarito 233
Argudín (nieto de *Peruchín*) 233
Arias, Alex 280
Armenteros, Alfredo *Chocolate* 193, 249, **256**, 257, 262, 278
Armenteros, Alberto 55
Armenteros, Armandito 193
Armstrong, Louis 62
Arnaz, Desi 70, 230
Aroche, Alberto 161
Arrau, Claudio 198
Arrondo, Juan 125, 132, 143, 250
Arroyo, Joe 267
Arte Vivo, grupo 326
Arteaga, José 262
Asencio, Gonzalo *El tío Tom* 111

Aspiazu, Modesto *Don* 139, 230
Atahualpa Yupanqui 306
Audinot, Rafael 65
Auserón, Santiago *Juan Perro* 286, 287, 288, 289, 379
Aute, Luis Eduardo 311
Averhoff, Carlos 257, 316, 329, 349
Azcuy, Cristina 380
Aznavour, Charles 287, 310, 361
Azúcar (orq. femenina) 389

Bacallao, Felo 137, 141
Bacallao, Rafael 334
Bacharach, Burt 291
Baker, Josephine 220
Baloy, Félix 335, 375
Ball, Lucille 70
Ballet Nacional de Cuba 217
Bamboleo, grupo 358, 383
Baños, René 369, 370
Baquero, Gastón 73, 116, 117
Barbería, Carlos 231, 149
Barbería, Luis Alberto 284
Barbón, Carlos 329
Bardisa, Raquel 249
Barkam, Todd 244
Barlow, Randall 275
Barnet, Miguel 118
Baró, Rolando 64
Barreto, Guillermo 175, 182, 192, **194**, 195, 221, 226, 228, 319, 329, 333, 368, 344
Barreto, Justi 107
Barretto, Ray 255, 256
Barrio, Felo 194
Barrios, Gregorio 135
Barrios, Renée 249
Barron, Kenny 339
Barroso, Abelardo 48, 99, 141
Barroso, Ary 132
Barroso, Sergio 215
Barrueco, Manuel 215
Bartok, Bela 201
Bartz, Gary 339
Basave, Julio *El barondó* 107
Basie, Count 244
Bastide, Roger 115, 116

Bataan, Joe 262
Batacumbele, grupo 327
Batista, Fulgencio 60, 119, 120, 122, 123, 124, 183, 184, 187, 198
Bautista, Teddy 93
Bauzá, Mario 23, 31, 74, 124, 230, 235, 236, 237, 240, 241, 242, 243, 245, 256, 258, 324
Beatles, Los 130, 241, 283, 310, 313, 319, 353, 366
Bécquer, Remberto 189
Beltrán, Alberto 62
Bellson, Louie 229
Benedetti, Mario 311
Benet, Yolanda 315
Benguría, Xonia 249
Bergaza, Felo 182, 231, 250, 294
Berlin, Irving 132, 281
Berrio, Lolita 249
Berroa, Ignacio 226, 228, 241
Betancourt, Joaquín 289
Betancourt, Julio 255
Betancourt, Justo 30
Big Mountain 27
Blades, Roberto 274, 275
Blades, Rubén 262, 267, 277
Blanco, Juan 208
Blanco Fombona, Rufino 77
Blanch Acedo, Roser 177
Bofill, Luis 281
Boggs, Vernon W. 345
Bola de Nieve (Ignacio Villa) 72, 122, 132, 133, 148, 151, 181, 250, 280, 297, 348
Bolet, Alberto 132, 210
Bolet, Jorge 132, 200, 209
Bolívar, Natalia 118
Boloña, Alfredo 47, 49
Bolling, Claude 324
Bonilla, Edwin 280
Bonne, Enrique 141, 296, 353, 354
Borbolla, Carlo 205
Borbolla, familia 90
Borcelá, Amado 154
Borges (hijo), Max 180
Borges, Jorge Luis 149
Borges, Lino 58, 127, 323, 375
Borges, Vannia 359

Borja, Esther 198, 250
Borrego, Orlando 352
Bosé, Miguel 134, 278
Boulanger, Nadia 203
Boyd, Joe 381
Brando, Marlon 38
Bravo, Estela 92
Bravo, Sonny 66
Brindis de Salas, Claudio 301
Brito, Alfredo 73, 320
Brito, Julio 126
Britos, Federico 194
Brouwer, Leo 33, 44, 153, 197, 201, 212, 309, 316, 317, 322, 355, 379
Brown, Ray 260
Brubeck, Dave 239
Bu Pascual, Luis 357
Bunnett, Jane 194, 243, 338
Burke, Elena 151, 153, 250, 297, 350
Burke, Malena 143, 350
Burr, Raymond 192
Byrne, David 253, 369

Caballero, Ihosvani Vanito 284
Cabel, René 135, 144, 181
Cabrera, Ignacio Cabrerita 165
Cabrera, Lydia 93, 115, 116, 117
Cabrera, Ramón 61, 125, 164
Cabrisas-Farach, dúo 75
Cairo, Pablo 61, 189, 382
Caissé, Alberto 61, 189
Calá, Tony 289, 349
Calvo, Pedrito 180, 293, 354, 375
Calzado, David 289, 361, 362, 367, 382
Calzado, Rudy 230, 243
Calzado, Sergio 361
Callava, Calixto 109
Calle, Ed 270
Calle, Florencio 107
Calloway, Cab 236, 241
Camerata Romeu 389
Camero, Cándido 239, 344
Camilo, Michel, 225
Campos, Pupi 244
Campos, Chela 126
Cancio, Hugo Miguel 298
Cancio, Miguel 297

Canela, Las (orq. femenina) 389
Cano, Carlos 341
Cantaclaro, conjunto 306
Cantalapiedra, Ricardo 391
Capablanca, José Raúl 23
Cappó, Bobby 136
Carbajo, Roque 136
Carbó Menéndez, José 61, 190, 191
Carbonell, Luis 88
Carbonell, Walterio 118
Carcassés, Bobby 154, 340, 359, 371
Cárdenas, Félix 90
Cárdenas, Guty 136, 173
Cárdenas, Rodolfo 355
Cardoso, Alizete 306
Carlés, Maggie 143
Carlos Manuel y su Clan 385, 386
Carlos V 67
Carlos, Roberto 130
Carmina, Rosa 122
Carpenter, Earl 320
Carpentier, Alejo 69, 83, 91, 202
Carr, Cass 235
Carrillo, Isolina 27, 80, 126, **128**, **129**, 131, 144, 145,
Carrillo, Julián 200
Carrillo, Norberto 316
Carrusco, Rafael 371
Carter, Jimmy 328, 336
Casals, Pablo 200
Casamitjana, Juan 187
Casanova, Héctor 255
Casaus, Víctor 312
Cassavettes, John 192
Castellanos, Aramís 293
Castellanos, Isabel **117**, 118
Castellanos, Jorge **117**, 118
Castellanos, Tania 149
Castilla, Patricio 312
Castillo, Guillermo 47
Castillo, Juan 284
Castro Romeu, Zenaida 389
Castro Zadarriaga, Concepción 323
Castro, Andrés 319
Castro, Fidel 21, 52, 92, 120, 121, 123, 124, 183, 185, 186, 192, 226, 247, 250, 251, 261, 268, 277, 304, 309, 314, 315,

316, 318, 322, 324, 327, 328, 336, 337, 338, 352, 353, 387, 391
Castro, Raúl 124
Cataneo, Alfredo 77
Caunedo, Jesús 135
Ceaucescu, Nicolae 251
Cedrón, cuarteto 306
Cela, Camilo José 132
Celibidache, Sergio 198
Celina y Reutilio 87, 98, 122, 181
Cepeda, Junior 192
Cervantes, Ignacio 23, 219, 226, 231, 232, 301, 331
Céspedes, Carlos Manuel 370
Céspedes, Francisco *Pancho* 22, 134, **278**, 279, 389
Céspedes, Gladys *Bobi* 281
Céspedes, Guillermo 281
Céspedes, Luis 281
Ciérvide, María 74
Cilia, Luis 307
Cinco Latinos, Los 297
Claro, Juan *Clarito* 227
Clavelito (Miguel Alfonso Pozo) 89, 90
Clinton, Bill 276
Cobas, Pancho 289
Coen, Augusto 233, 236
Cole, Cozy 241
Cole, Nat King 38, 124, 129, 133, 176, 181, 194, 237
Coleman, Steve 338
Colón, Frankie 237
Colón, Willie 262
Coltrane, John 340, 390
Collazo, Bobby 125, 126, 249
Collazo, Julito 58
Combo Samurai 367
Compadres, Los (dúo) 59, 75, 286, 289
Companioni, Miguel 291
Compay Segundo (Francisco Repilado) 43, 75, 252, 285, 286, 287, 293 348, 371, 372, 380
Conjunto Adalberto Álvarez y Son 14 323, 334, 348
Conjunto Adalberto y su Son 263, 335, 375
Conjunto Baconao 51
Conjunto Caney 64, 65, 374

Conjunto Casino 55, 56, 57, 141, 155, 162, 178, 250
Conjunto Céspedes 281
Conjunto Clave y Guaguancó 110
Conjunto Colonial 55, 62, 360
Conjunto Chapottín y sus Estrellas 55, 62, 380
Conjunto de Arsenio Rodríguez 256, 377, 378
Conjunto de Enrique Pérez 380
Conjunto de Nelo Sosa 58
Conjunto de René Álvarez 58, 160
Conjunto de Senén Suárez 377
Conjunto Estudiantina Invasora 289
Conjunto Excorde 337
Conjunto Folklórico Nacional 216, 217, 379
Conjunto Folklórico y Experimental Nuevayorquino 257, 262, 345
Conjunto Jóvenes Clásicos del Son 370
Conjunto Jóvenes del Cayo 55, 58
Conjunto Kubavana 56, 231, 256
Conjunto Las Estrellas Negras 378
Conjunto Los Astros 58
Conjunto Los Bocucos 141, 376
Conjunto Los Chuquis 58
Conjunto Los Jóvenes del Son 376
Conjunto Los Latinos 58
Conjunto Los Naranjos 141, 291
Conjunto Los Nuevos Roncos 111
Conjunto Los Roncos Chiquitos 111
Conjunto Manguaré 89
Conjunto Matamoros 51, 111, 286
Conjunto Musicuba 58
Conjunto Raisón 109
Conjunto Rumbavana 58, 322, 323, 353, 373, 375
Conjunto Safari 364
Conjunto Saratoga 58
Conjunto Siboney 80
Conjunto Sierra Maestra 108, 109, 146, 337, 374, 380
Conjunto Sonora Corasón 284
Conjunto Sonora Matancera 55, 56, **60**, 61, 62, 64, 124, 128, 141, 190, 191, 249, 255, 257, 278, 375, 381, 382
Conjunto Típico Habanero 380

Conjunto Yaguarimú 336
Constantín, Eutimio 48
Conte, Luis 331
Contreras, Ángel y Orlando 106
Contreras, Orlando 56, 58, 127, 249, 380
Cooder, Joachim 373
Cooder, Ry 289, 293, 328, 372, 373, 377, 379
Copland, Aaron 26, 201
Corbacho, Domingo
Corea, Chick 270
Corona, Manuel 47, 292
Correa, Willie *Bobo* 66, 239, 240, 237
Correa, Víctor 180
Cortés, José Luis *El tosco* 289, 349, 350, 364, 371
Cortijo, Rafael 66, 262
Costner, Kevin 275
Creagh, Reinaldo 131, 288
Crespo, América 74, 199, 249
Cristal, Pancho 265
Cros Sandoval, Mercedes 118
Cruz, Celia 23, 30, 55, 61, 64, 88, 124, 129, 177, 190, **191**, 192, 249, 258, 262, 264, 273, 274, 288, 314, 336, 351, 368, 383, 399
Cuarteto Antillano 80
Cuarteto D'Aida 81, 153, 154, 181, 297
Cuarteto D'Capo 359
Cuarteto de Facundo Rivero 153, 297
Cuarteto Hatuey 286
Cuarteto Los Rivero 80, 181
Cuarteto de Luis Carbonell 80
Cuarteto Maisí 51
Cuarteto de Orlando de la Rosa 80, 153, 154
Cuarteto Del Rey 152, 314
Cuarteto Los Armónicos 339
Cuarteto Los Bucaneros 152, 314, 319
Cuarteto Los Guaracheros de Oriente 181, 249
Cuarteto Patria 289, 292, 370
Cuarteto Siboney 80
Cuarteto y Sexteto Caney 63
Cuéllar, Víctor 217
Cuervo, Caridad 64
Cueto, Rafael 49

Cueva, Julio 298
Cugat, Xavier 71, 130, 234, 242
Cuní, Miguelito 58, **63**, 98, 163, 177, 178, 250, 334
Curbelo, José 230, 234
Curiel, Gonzalo 136, 143, 144

Chaikovsky, P. I. 365
Chao, Antoine 342
Chao, Manu 342
Chapottín, Elpidio 64, 349
Chapottín, Félix **62**, 162, 163, 177, 178, 250, 256, 334
Charanga Armonía 373
Charanga Broadway 277
Charanga Forever 362
Charanga Habanera **360**, 361, 362, 383
Charanga Hermanos Contreras
Charanga La Moderna 256
Charanga La Sabrosa 256
Charanga Rubalcaba 373
Charanga'76 255
Charanga Vallenata 256, 278
Charles, Ray 319
Charropin, Mike 293
Chauveau, Céline 372
Chavales de España (orquesta), Los 181
Chávez, José Ramón *Manteca* 60
Chávez, Carlos 201
Chaviano, Flores 213
Che Guevara, Ernesto 27, 124, 295, 310, 352, 397
Cheatham, Doc 241, 256
Chediak, Esperanza 74
Chediak, Nat 195, 232, 239, 241, 329, 340
Chevalier, Maurice 133
Chieftains, The 372, 379
Chirino, Willie **276**, 277, 335, 342, 368, 383
Chopin, Frederic 331
Chorens, Olga 75
Chori (Silvano Shueg) 184

Dada, Los 340
Danza Contemporánea de Cuba 217
D'Rivera, Enrique 225
D'Rivera, Paquito 185, **224**, 225, 226, 229,

232, 241, 243, 256, 269, 270, 273, 315, 319, 324, 328, 330, 334, 336
D'León, Oscar 61, 267, 335, 337, 368, 373
D'Rivera, Tito 224
Dalto, Jorge 225, 241
Daly, Mario 326
Dan Den, Grupo 252, 356, **360**, 363, 383
Dane, Barbara 307
Davidson, Eduardo (Claudio Cuza) 195, 196, 249, 295
Davis, Miles 238
De Blanck, Margot 200
De Castro Sisters 239, 249
De Castroverde, Hortensia 74
De Falla, Manuel 201
De Gonzalo, Miguel 154
De Grandy, Miguel 199
De la Colina, Lolita 145
De la Cruz, Juan 48
De la Fe, Alfredo 255
De la Guardia, Lucas 316
De la Rosa, Juan Francisco 77
De la Rosa, Orlando 27, 125, 130, 166
De la Torre, Doris 154
De la Torre, Marta 200
De la Torre, Rey 211
De la Vega, Aurelio 209
De las Barras y Prado, Antonio 396
De los Ángeles, Victoria 198
De los Reyes, Walfredo 142, 229
De los Reyes, Walfredo (baterista) 193, 226, 228
De Marcos González, Juan 109, 337, 372, **374**, 375, 376, 377, 380, 381
De Niro, Robert 336
De Paz, Rafael 30, 164
Dean, Ian 293
Debussy, Claude 147, 331
Dedeu Hernández, Amado de Jesús 110
Del Castillo, Néstor 64
Del Mónaco, Mario 198
Del Pino, Geovani 110
Del Puerto, Carlos 329, 331, 338, 339
Del Río, Elizabeth 249
Del Rosario, Amado 316
Del Valle, Manolo 154
Del Valle, Pepe 284

Delfín, Eusebio 250
Delgado, Isaac 233, 252, 257, 289, 350, 351, 356, 363, 368, 383
Delgado, Pepé 56, 58, 249
Della Mea, Ivan 307
Deschamps Chapeaux, Pedro 118
Desmond, Paul 339
Di Marzo, Yordano 130
Diago, Virgilio 200
Díaz Alonso, Carlos M. *Caíto* 60
Díaz Anaya, Odguardo 110
Díaz, Miguel *Angá* 182, 338, 371, 374, 385
Díaz Ayala, Cristóbal 28, 47, 49, 57, 68, 77, 85, 122, 144, 162, 181, 232, 259
Díaz Calvet, Rey 58, 143
Díaz, Policarpo *Polo* 158
Díaz, Angelito 150
Díaz, Aniceto 156
Díaz, Carlos 142, 249
Díaz, Daniel 227
Díaz, Gregorio 107
Díaz, Olga 280
Díaz, Servando 21, 249
Díaz, Simón 278
Díaz, Tirso 150
Díaz, Ulpiano 333
Diddley, Bo 237
Diestro, Aida 314
Diez, Barbarito 88, 156
Dimond, Markolino *Divino* 262
Diomandé, Raúl 334
Dobal, Cristóbal 55
Dobronyi, Sepy 79
Domínguez, Armando *Chamaco* 145
Domínguez, Alberto131
Domínguez, Frank 143, 148, **149**, 250
Domínguez, Lázaro 89
Domínguez, Manuel 283
Domínguez, Paul 223
Domínguez, Reutilio **87**, 88, 89, 275
Donato y Estéfano 281
Dorsey, Jimmy 25, 228
Dorsey, Tommy 160, 194, 228, 235, 321
Du'Bouchet Georgina 74
Duarte, Ernesto 57, 125, 131, 143, 164, 166, 249, 288
Duchesne Cuzán, Manuel 319

Dufflar, Marianela 391
Dulzaides, Felipe 339
Dulzaides, Javier 249
Dunhan, Catherine 170
Dupuy, Bertha 249
Durán, Gustavo 91
Durán, Hilario 270
Durán, Lucy 367, 381
Durán, Modesto 171
Dyango 131

Eckstine, Billy 237
Echániz, José 132, 200, 210, 320
Echeverría, Silvia 365
EGREM 21, 93, 108, 109, 111, 152, 200, 276, 284, 299, 313, 332, 335, 340, 346, 348, 355, 357, 361, 370
Egües, Richard 137, 158, **176**, 250, 323, 334, 371, 379
Eisenhower, Ike 121
Ekberg, Anita 169
Elejalde, Ignacio 297, 298
Ellington, Duke 236, 260, 321
Elósegui, Juan 316
Elva, Alda 341
Embale, Carlos 50, **111**, 141
Emerson, Lake & Palmer 325
Escalante, Leopoldo *Pucho* 339, 345, 346
Escalante, Luis 319, 321
Escalona, Phidias Danilo 259
Escalona, Rafael 278
Escarpenter, Sarita 74
Escobar, Félix *El gallego* 78
Espí, Roberto 55, 56, 178
Estefan, Emilio 266, 267, 268, 270, 271, 272, 273, 274, 275, 276
Estefan, Gloria 134, 270, **271**, 272, 273, 274, 275, 383
Estenoz, Evaristo 38
Estévez, Cuco 137
Estrada, Hall 279
Évora, Cesaria 287, 372

Fabré, Cándido 277, 3,23, 356, 363, **367**, 370
Faílde, Miguel 155
Fajardo, José Antonio 30, 158, **160**, 194, 241, 255

Fajardo, José Luis 212
Falcón, Alberto 200
Familia, La (orquesta) 282
Fández, Gonzalo
Farach, Irene 279
Fariñas, Carlos 211
Farrés, Osvaldo 125, **126**, 140, 185
Faz, Roberto 55, 56, 127, 146, 155, 165, 178, 183, 250, 292
Feather, Leonard 320
Feliciano, Cheo 262
Feliciano, José 274
Felipe II 67
Feliú, Pedro 78
Feliú, Vicente 309, 310, 316
Fellini, Federico 169
Ferguson, Maynard 270
Fernández Porta, Mario 30, 125, 130, 132, 143, 170, 249
Fernández, Coralia 89, 91
Fernández, Frank 213, 304, 335
Fernández, Joseíto **91**, 92, 93, 165, 250
Fernández, Manolo 75
Fernández, Pepín 396
Fernández, Raúl 87, 192
Fernández, Teresita 154, 308
Fernández, Vicente 130
Fernández, Wilfredo 75
Fernández-Brito, Ninowska 215
Ferrer, Ibrahim 296, 373, 374, **376**
Ferrer, Lena 314
Ferrer, Pedro Luis 279, **313**, 314, 350, 386
Ferro, Ricardo 322
Figueroa, Frankie 263
Fini, Mo 360
Fitzgerald, Ella 153,
Fitzgerald, Scott 66
Flack, Roberta 328
Flanagan, Tommy 339
Fleetwood, Mick 291
Flores, Lola 191
Flores, Pedro 78, 136, 165
Flynn, Frank Emilio 148, 152, 154, 175, 194, 232, 250, 318, 338, 372, 375
Folkloristas, Los 306
Fonda, Jane 280
Fontanal, E. 77

Formell, Juan 143, 146, 289, 324, 327, 331, 332, **352**, 353, 354, 355, 383
Formell, Juan Carlos 354
Formell, Samuel 354
Fornés, Rosita 198
Fox, Martín 180
Fra Fra Sound 338
Fragoso, Argelia 154
Franco, Francisco 328
Franklin, Benjamín 361
Fraser, Hugh 338
Frías, Lino 60, 61, 98, 191, 193
Frontela Frag, Regino 160
Fuentes, Osmandy 59, 284
Fuentes, Rubén 130
Fuller, Curtis 241
Fuller, Gil 243
Fuller, Paul 28
Furé, Manuel 380
Furias, Ángel Alfonso *Yiyo* 60

Gabriel, Peter 369
Gainza, Magalyis 131
Galán, Natalio 207
Galaxia, grupo 350
Galilea, Carlos 243
Galindo, Aramís 289, 336
Galván, Manuel 297, 298, 377
Gálvez, Zoila 200
Garay, Sindo 250, 286, 310, 342, 378
García Caturla, Alejandro 121, 200, **203**, 204
García Caturla, Genaro 316
García Caturla, Teresa 334, 375, 377
García, José Antonio *Chamaco* 280
García Chovén, Bernardo 58
García Menocal, Mario 46
García Perdomo, Ricardo 137
García, Andy 163, 269, 274
García, Fidel 325
García, Idalmi 74
García, Luis 154
Gardel, Carlos 87, 356
Garratti, Vittorio 301
Garrido y Piñero 181
Gassman, Vittorio 170
Gatica, Lucho 145, 232
Gato Gótico 338

Gema y Pável 283, 284, 313
Gershwin, George 26, 201, 232, 235
GESI 228, 233, 311, 314, 317, 326
Getz, Stan 328, 330
Gil, Blanca Rosa 21, 127, 249
Gil, Rita 154
Gil, Tany 229
Gilberto, Joao 307
Gillespie, Dizzy 31, 158, 188, 224, 233, 236, 237, 238, 239, 241, 245, 270, 321, 328, 336, 366, 372, 392
Giro, Radamés 290
Gnomos, Los 299
Godínez, Carlos 31, 47, 220
Gold, Nick 372
Gómez Montiel, Urbano 137
Gómez, Rafael *Teofilito* 291
Gómez, Alejandro 306
Gómez, José Manuel 262
Gómez, José Miguel 42
Gómez, Manuel Octavio 317
Gómez, Pedro 259
Gómez, Rolando 150
Gómez, Tito 127, 136, **142**, 250
González, Dagoberto 137
González (hijo), Dagoberto 110
González, Marcelo *El blanco* 87
González Mantici, Enrique 122, 142, 172, 200
González, Iván *Melón* 233
González Rubiera, Vicente *Guyún* 44, 132, 168
González, Andy 345
González, Carlos 160
González, Celina **87**, 88, 89, 250, 275, 287, 348
González, Celio 55, 58, 62, 249
González, Elián 206
González, Fernando 58
González, Hilario 206
González, Joseíto 323
González, Lázaro Dagoberto 342
González, Luis *Neno* 160
González, Nelson 262
González, Rubén 231, 334, 374, 375, **377**, 378
González, Sara 313, 316, 328, 341

González, Teresa 216
González, Virgilio 136, 190
Goodman, Benny 224, 225, 243, 244
Gordon, Dexter 241
Gorís, Jesús 144
Gottardi, Roberto 301
Gottschalk, Louis Moreau 25, 26, 187
Graham, Lisa 293
Gramatges, Harold 151, 206
Gran Wyoming 22
Grand Master Flash 383
Granda, Bienvenido 55, 62, 127, 249
Granda, Chabuca 132
Granz, Norman 231
Greco, José Miguel 349
Grenet, Eliseo 53, 74, 76, 133, 139, 188
Grenet, Emilio 133, 230
Grifth, Merv 265
Grillo, Frank *Machito* 63, 124, 170, 172, 196, 230, 233, 237, 2388, 239, 241, **242**, 243, 244, 245, 264, 323, 331
Grillo, Graciela 242, 323
Gross, Poney 369
Guayacán, banda 386
Gudín, José 55
Güell, Luisa María 249
Guerra, Orlando *Cascarita* 126, 167, 190
Guerra, Marcelino *Rapindey* 60, 63, 80, 125, 137, 190, 194, 230, 234, 240, 244, 262, 324
Guerra, Jesús 56, 61, 189
Guerra, Juan Luis 130, 233, 277, 335, 366
Guerra, Teresa 285
Guerrero, Félix 44
Guevara, Alfredo 316
Guevara, Walfrido 77, 190
Guillén, Nicolás 79, 133, 166, 281
Guillot, Olga 30, 122, 126, 127, 129, 134, **144, 145**, 153, 181, 249, 264, 285, 288
Gutiérrez Villanueva, Raúl 293
Gutiérrez, Agustín 48
Gutiérrez, Alejandro 284
Gutiérrez, Amaury 279
Gutiérrez, Bienvenido Julián 190
Gutiérrez, Horacio 215
Gutiérrez, Julio 56, 125, 126, 130, **134, 135**, 142, 170, 229, 249

Guzmán, Adolfo 125, 131, 133, 250
Guzmán, Orlando 55
Gypsy Kings 278

Habana Abierta 284
Haden, Charlie 366
Halffter, Ernesto 200
Hampton, Lionel 328
Handy, W. C. 220
Hanks, Los 299
Hanrahan, Kip 257
Hansel y Raúl 280
Haque, Fareed 225
Hargrove, Roy 338
Harlow, Larry 54
Hawkins, Coleman 224
Heath, Ted 321
Hechavarría, César 370
Hechavarría, Paquito 233, 272, 273, 345, 383
Henderson, Fletcher 236
Henríquez, Reinaldo 142
Herman, Woody 321
Hermanas Lago, dúo 75, 181
Hermanas Márquez, dúo 75
Hermanas Martí, dúo 75, 122
Hernández Delgado, Bienvenido 66
Hernández, Eduardo El chino 297
Hernández, Horacio El negro 226
Hernández Lizaso, Antonino 206
Hernández, Juan Manuel Lolo 370
Hernández, Orlando Papito 194
Hernández, Gabriel 233
Hernández, Ivette 215
Hernández, Jesús 278
Hernández, Omar 280
Hernández, Rafael 78, 136, 278, 377
Hernández, René 152, 163, 170, 233, 238, 242, 245, 373
Herrera, Huberal 210
Herrera, Lázaro 48, 50, 380
Herrera, Manuel 298
Herwig, Conrad 241
Hevia, Liuba María 341
Hidalgo, David 293
Hidalgo, Giovanni 182, 331
Hidalgo, Mario 304

Hierrezuelo, Caridad 64
Hierrezuelo, Lorenzo 44, **75**, 76, 98, 286, 292
Hierrezuelo, Reynaldo 64, 75, 287, 289
Hijuelos, Oscar 170
Hines, Earl Fatha 328
Ho Chi Min 317
Holland, Dave 260
Horowitz 198
Horta, José Pepe 280, 281
Houston, Whitney 361
Hubbard, Freddie 270
Huelga, Ángel 291
Huergo, Lucía 326

ICAIC 200, 316
Iglesias, Julio 271, 331
Iglesias, Rogelio Yeyo 59, 193
Incharte, Chino 48
India de Oriente (Luisa Mª Hernández) 77, 278
Indio Naborí 89
Ink Spots, The 297
Inti-Illimani 306
Iriarte, Enrique Culebra 54
Isidrón, Chanito 90, 91
Ithier, Rafael 345
Iznaga, Alberto 230, 234
Izquierdo, Pedro Pello 107, 295, 353

Jackson, Michael 290, 326
Jara, Víctor 306
Jatari, grupo 306
Jauma, Humberto 189
Jets, Los 299
Jilguero de Cienfuegos (Inocente Iznaga) 90
Jiménez, Generoso El tojo 165, 193, 346, 377
Jiménez, José Alfredo 130
Jiménez, Nick 239
Joe Cuba (Gilberto Calderón) 237, 261
Jones, Elton 326
Joplin, Scott 219
Jorge, Reinaldo 345
Jorrín, Enrique 157, 158, **172**, 173, 174
José Alberto El canario 335, 368
Joya, Alberto 214

Jhruschov, Nikita 188, 296
Junco, Pedro 136
Justiniani, Marta 154
Jústiz, Pedro *Peruchín* 134, 165, 170, 229, 232, 293, 321, 346, 352, 378, 383
Jústiz, Pedro (hijo) 293

Karachi, Los 342
Kempf (pianista) 198
Kennedy, John F. 188, 258, 296
Kent, Los 299
Kenton, Stan 25, 169, 170, 244, 245, 321
Ketama 131
Khaled 287
Kid Chocolate 23
King, Martin Luther 258
Kirk, Andy 236
Kleiber, Erich 198, 200
Klimax (ver Giraldo Piloto) 368
Knight, Pedro 60, 61, 192
Kraus, Clemens 198

La del Barrio, Paquita 265
La Lupe 131, 249, **264**, 265, 266
La Verdad, Grupo 267
Laborit, Ramón 44
Labrada, Jerónimo 316
Lachatañeré, Rómulo 118
Laíto Sureda 56, 58, 64
Lam, Rafael 227
Lamarque, Libertad 153
Landín, María Luisa 128
Lansky, Meyer 123
Lantric, Esteban *Saldiguera* 107
Lara, Agustín 62, 136, 165
Laronte (cantante) 326
Larramendi, Boris 284
Láser de Bayamo, grupo 326
Laserie, Rolando 124, 127, 165, 249, 330
Lauro, Antonio 226
Lavoe, Héctor 262
Lay, Rafael 137, 175, **176**, 250, 323, 334
Lazaga, Enrique 175
LeBatard, Germán 168, 249, 320
Leberra, Rafael y Alejandro 359
Lecuona, Ernestina 137, 201
Lecuona, Ernesto 24, 73, 132, 136, 139, 185, 186, 195, 199, 200, 203, **204**, 205, 226, 230, 231, 232, 249, 279, 292, 301, 303, 321, 330, 331, 354
Lecuona, Margarita 98
Ledesma, Roberto 145
Leicea, Calixto 60
León, Alfredo 80
León, Argeliers 105, 110, 206, 313
León, Bienvenido 48
León, Gina 64, 154
León, Julio 77
León, Tania 215
Leslie, Lew 236
Lester, Julius 307
Levy, Alfredo 200
Lewinsky, Mónica 336
Leyva, Pío 64, 330, 371, 374
Leyva, Rigoberto 185
Lezama Lima, José 122
Libertad, Tania 306
Licea, Manuel *Puntillita* 375
Lima, Radaeunda 89
Lima, Raúl 89
Limonta, Aristóteles 289
Limonta, Leonel 359
Linares, Annnia 143, 150, 154
Linares, María Teresa 84, 341
Loco, Joe 237
López, Belisario 160, 161, 249, 320
López, Orlando *Cachaíto* 194, 260, 319, 373, 374
López, Israel *Cachao* 30, 59, 157, 159, 163, 175, 182, 185, 193, 194, 226, 229, 244, 249, 255, 257, 260, 273, 329, 333, 373
López Viana, Luis 320
López, César 338
López, Irián 110
López, Johnny 63
López, Leovigildo 118
López, Orestes 157, 159, 163, 193, 250, 260, 373
López, Rigoberto 351
López, Severino 44
López-Nussa, Ernán 233, 325
Loyola Fernández, José 128, 150
Loyola, Efraín 158

Lozano, Rolando 158
Lubambo, Romero 226
Lucca, Papo 54, 262, 345
Lucrecia 134, 282, 283, 363
Lugo, Pedro 370
Luis Miguel 131, 135, 267, 268
Lunas, Bigas 367
Lunceford, Jimmy 236
Luque, Ada 279
Lymon, Frankie 297
Llanes, Benito 64
Llanes, Carlos 64

MacColl, Ewan 307
Macías, Gerardo El chino 78
Macías, Orestes 58
MacPherson Zapata, Jannysett 323
Machado, Eloy El Ambia 109
Machado, Amado 289
Machado, Armando 292
Machado, Gerardo 123, 321
Machín, Antonio 49, 73, 74, 124, 126, 129, 130, **138**, 139, 140, 235
Madonna 331, 336
Magnéticos, grupo Los 326
Mákina, grupo 326
Malanga (José Rosario Oviedo)
Malcolm X 258
Manén, Juan 200
Manfugás, Zenaida 215
Mangano, Silvana 170
Mangual, José 238
Manguaré, grupo 322, 379
Mann, Herbie 241
Manns, Patricio 306
Manolín (Manuel González Hernández El médico de la salsa) 252, 356, **357**, 358, 363, 383
Manolito y su Trabuco **364**, 365, 383
Manrique, Diego A. 191, 389
Mantilla, Ray 328
Manzanero, Armando 29, 145
Mara y Orlando 279
María Antonieta 131
María, Olga 280
Marín, Gloria 306
Marín, Orlando 255

Marini, Leo 62, 135
Marquetti, Cheo 259
Marquetti, Luis 78, 88, 125, 292
Márquez, Beatriz 154
Márquez, Juanito 143, 249, 273, 275, 297, 353
Marrero, Leví 118
Marrero, Nicky 344
Marrero, Rodolfo 141
Marrero, Willy 223
Marrero, Zoraida 74, 199, 249
Martí, José 23, 39, 52, 113, 123, 155, 317
Martí, Tania 279
Martí, Virgilio 194
Martín, Gina 88
Martín, Juan Luis 118
Martín, Mayte 131
Martin, Ricky 274
Martínez Furé, Rogelio 216
Martínez Griñán, Lilí 54, 62, 162, 232, 233, 250, 378
Martínez, Alfredo Meyo 226
Martínez, Cheo 48
Martínez, Miguel 380
Martínez, Rogelio 60, 61
Martínez, Santiago 79
Martirio 152
Marx, Karl 268
Marzal, Raudel 370
Mas, Gustavo 321, 340
Masucci, Jerry 254, 259, 328, 356
Matamoros, Miguel 44, 49, 78, 88, 164, 166, 187, 281, 292, 341, 342, 362, 379
Mayito (cantante) 289
Mayohuacán, grupo 386
Maza, Michel 289
Maza, Roberto 108
Mazure, Liliana 355
McFerrins, Bobby 369
McKibbon, Al 238
Medina, José Luis 284
Medina, Mirta 143
Mejía Godoy, Carlos y Luis Enrique 306
Membiela, Ñico 58, 64, 249
Méndez, José Antonio 135, 137, 141, 144, **147**, 148, 152, 166, 234, 250, 290, 298
Méndez, Silvestre 189

Mendive, Kiko 168
Mendoza, Celeste **108**, 109, 250
Mendoza, July 87
Mendoza, Octavio 76
Menéndez, *Gallego* 230
Menéndez, Nilo 230
Menéndez, Pablo 316, 325, 326
Menuhin, Yejudi 198
Mercadal, Juan 211
Mercado, Ralph 253, 254, 351
Mercerón, Mariano 30, 164
Mercier, Reinaldo 168
Mesa, Juan 107
Mesa, Pablo 107
Mezcla, Grupo 253, ,326, 334
Miami Latin Boys 266, 271
Miami Sound Machine 267, 271, 272
Milanés, Haydée 316
Milanés, Pablo 29, 33, 63, 109, 128, 152,
153, 267, 287, 307, 308, 309, 311, 312,
314, 315, 316, 317, 318, 328, 335, 341,
350, 379, 385
Milí, Néstor 298
Milstein (violinista) 198
Miller, Glenn 25, 30
Mills Brothers, The 80
Mingus, Charlie 260, 390
Mirabal, Luis Manuel *Guajiro* 323, 334,
373, 374
Miranda, Carmen 342
Miranda, Luis 238
Miró, Jesús Alfonso 107
Mistral, Gabriela 155
Modernaire 80
Moix, Terenci 71
Molina, Carlos 214
Molina, Cocha 273
Moliner Castañeda, Israel 105
Moncada, grupo 322
Moncho (Ramón Calabuch Batista) 131
Mondéjar, Ninón 172, 174
Moneró, José Luis 239
Monk, Telonius 232
Monpié, Haila 359
Montalvo, Osvaldo 380
Montaner, Rita 132, 133, 181, 198, 200
Montañez, Polo, 90

Monte de Espuma, grupo 326
Montesinos, Rey 131
Monzón, Seju 22, 76
Mora, Renato 370
Morales, Eduardo *Tiburón* 335, 336
Morales, Carlos Emilio 152, 288, 319, 329,
331, 338, 339
Morales, Emilia 154
Morales, Noro 236, 242
Morales, Obdulio 87
Morán, Chilo 171
Morandi, Elena 307
Moré, Benny 30, 51, 61, 63, 88, 109, 111, 124,
125, 131, 135, 136, 143, **164**, 165, 166,
170, 176, 183, 226, 231, 232, 250, 255,
256, 259, 263, 298, 348, 363, 375, 377
Morúa, Leoncio *Kike* 297
Morúa, Lázaro 146
Moya, Roberto 87
Mozart, W. A. 324
Mulens, Fernando 125, 143, 249, 265
Mulet, Hernán *Teddy* 274
Münch, Charles 198
Mundito González 154
Muñequitos de Matanzas, Los 107, 252,
253, 371
Mungol, José Prudencio 44
Muñiz, Demetrio 373, 374, 377
Muñoz Bouffartique, Oscar 61, 190, 329
Muñóz, Ángel *El Reverendo* 257
Muñoz, *Papaíto* 194, 278
Musselwhite, Charlie 237, 293
Muralla, grupo 370

Naddy, Ted 320
Naranjo, Mayelín 35
Naranjo, Pachi 363
Narell, Andy 330
Navarrete, Víctor 325
Negrete, Jorge 128
Neira, Roderico *Rodney* 123, 154, 171,
181, 249
Neruda, Pablo 132, 325
Newman, Joe 241
Newton, Wayne 229
Nicola, Isaac 44, 207, 309
Nicola, Noel 309, 311, 312, 313, 316

Nieto, Ubaldo 238
Nieves, Tito 284
Niño Rivera (Andrés Echevarría) 44, 163, 168, 193, 194, 250, 334
Nixon, Richard 121
Norman, Gene 170
Novás Calvo, Lino 117
Nueva Visión, grupo 340
Nuevos Zafiros, Los 298
Núñez, Carlos 372
Núñez, Jorge 370
Núñez, Joseíto 80

Ñico Saquito (Antonio Fernández) 77, 78, 88, 190, 250, 286, 292

O'Farrill, Arturo Chico 31, 182, 194, 243, 244, 256, 321
O'Farrill, Arturito 244
O'Farrill, Ela 136, 151
Ochoa, Elíades 43, 131, 286, 287, 292, 293, 348
Ochoa, Humberto 292
Ochoa, Kelvis 284
Ojeda, Miguel 328
Olga María 280
Olimareños, Los 306
Oliva, Carlos 267
Olivares Baró, Carlos 383
Olmos, Pepe 137
Ondina, Roberto 158, 200
Oppenheimer, Andrés 27
Opus 13, grupo 356
Oquendo, Manny 262, 344, 345
Oramas, Faustino El guayabero 291
Orbón, Benjamín 200
Orbón, Julián 92, 207
Oréfiche, Armando 71, 72, 73, 133
Orioles, The 237
Orishas (Niko, Ruzzo, Yothuel y Roldán) 384, 385
Ormandy, Eugène 198
Ornellas, Manuel 340
Orovio, Helio 30, 91, 336, 373, 376, 383
Orozco, Danilo 42, 91, 342
Orquesta Afro-Cuban All Stars 374, 381
Orquesta Alegre All Stars 256

Orquesta AfroCubans (de Machito) 241, 242, 244, 245, 256
Orquesta Almendra 160, 161, 332
Orquesta América 136, 172
Orquesta Anacaona 154, 322, 323
Orquesta Aragón de Cienfuegos 137, 141, 160, 176, 184, 233, 250, 298, 319, 323, 328, 336, 366, 379
Orquesta Arcaño y sus Maravillas 157, 160, 161, 172, 178, 333, 373
Orquesta Bellamar 68, 321
Orquesta Buena Vista Social Club 337
Orquesta Casino de la Playa 68, 126, 134, 142, 167, 190, 229, 242, 321
Orquesta Continental 55
Orquesta Cosmopólitan 55
Orquesta Chepín-Chovén 58, 88, 376
Orquesta Cubana de Música Moderna 194, 201, 224, 233, 270, 318, 319, 330, 345, 358, 366, 373
Orquesta Cubanismo 337, 371, 381
Orquesta de Alberto Socarrás 69, 244
Orquesta de Anselmo Sacasas 244
Orquesta de Antonio Mª Romeu 160
Orquesta de Armando Valdespí 157, 160
Orquesta de Belisario López 160
Orquesta de Cheo Belén Puig 160, 161, 332
Orquesta de Don Aspiazu 68, 73
Orquesta de Ernesto Duarte 108, 231
Orquesta de Félix González 333
Orquesta de Isidro Pérez 68
Orquesta de Johnny Pacheco 192, 255
Orquesta de Johnny Rodríguez 244, 255
Orquesta de José Curbelo 68
Orquesta de Julio Cueva 68, 87, 190, 231, 242
Orquesta de Mariano Mercerón y sus Muchachos Pimienta 60
Orquesta de Neno González 160, 178
Orquesta de Noro Morales 244
Orquesta de Pancho el Bravo 141
Orquesta de Paulina Álvarez 160
Orquesta de Pupi Campos 244
Orquesta de Ray Barreto 256
Orquesta de René Touzet 68, 2,56
Orquesta de Tata Alfonso 333
Orquesta de Tito Puente 191, 192

Orquesta de Vicente Sigler 68
Orquesta del Teatro Musical de La Habana 224, 330, 340
Orquesta Estrellas Cubanas 160, 161, 333, 361
Orquesta Estrellas de Areíto 182, 334, 377
Orquesta Fajardo y sus Estrellas 66, 137, 160, 196, 249, 277, 333
Orquesta Fania All Stars 328, 333, 334
Orquesta Gris 157
Orquesta Habana 55
Orquesta Havana Cuban Boys 72, 142, 232
Orquesta Hermanos Castro 68, 142, 144, 145, 280, 321, 377
Orquesta Hermanos Contreras 172
Orquesta Hermanos Curbelo 321
Orquesta Hermanos LeBatard
Orquesta Hermanos Martínez 194
Orquesta Hermanos Palau 55, 65, 190, 321
Orquesta Irakere 180, 226, 228, 252, 263, 270, 285, 288, 322, 324, 326, 330, 336, 338, 348, 349, 364, 371
Orquesta Irazú 270, 293
Orquesta Jorrín 143, 297, 328
Orquesta La Charanga Habanera 252, 382
Orquesta La Familia 282
Orquesta Las Estrellas de Fania 191, 255
Orquesta Lecuona Cuban Boys 68, 71, 72, 73
Orquesta Los Bocucos 296
Orquesta Los Diplomáticos de Maya 321
Orquesta Los Miuras de Sobré 140
Orquesta Los Reyes'73 353
Orquesta Los Van Van 62, 143, 146, 179, 180, 228, 233, 252, 263, 293, 326, 327, 332, 334, 336, 337, 348, 349, 352, 353, 354, 355, 357, 363, 366, 382, 383
Orquesta Maravillas de Florida 364
Orquesta Melodías del 40 160
Orquesta Naciones Unidas 270
Orquesta NG La Banda 179, 252, 253, 337, 349, 350, 357, 363, 364, 368, 382, 383, 394
Orquesta Novedades 63
Orquesta Obdulio Morales 194
Orquesta Original de Manzanillo 252, 253, 363, 367

Orquesta Osvaldo Estivel 56
Orquesta Pachito Alonso y sus Kini Kini 349, 350, 359, 363
Orquesta Popular de Conciertos 176
Orquesta Radiotelevisión Cubana 143, 349
Orquesta Revé 179, 263, 281, 327, 348, 352, 353, 360, 363, 364, 375, 382, 383
Orquesta Ritmo Oriental 353, 361
Orquesta Riverside 68, 136, 142, 143, 232, 234, 250, 373, 374
Orquesta Sabor de Cuba 329
Orquesta Sensación 89, 136, 160, 360
Orquesta Siboney 73, 321
Orquesta Sinfónica Nacional 372, 373, 379
Orquesta Sublime 160, 178
Orquesta Team Cuba 290, 362
Orquesta Típica'73 66, 255
Orquesta Todos Estrellas 233
Ortiz Rafael, *Mañungo* 50, 137, 146, 186, 189
Ortiz, Fernando 17, 22, 34, 38, 41, 86, 94, 100, 111, 112, 113, 115, 121, 132, 167, 188, 201
Osakar, Elio 65, 66
Osdalgia (cantante) 350
Otra Visión, grupo 371, 372
Overton, Hall 234
Oviedo, Gilberto *Papi* 44, 332, 378, 379, 380
Oviedo, Isaac 44, 193, 379
Oviedo, Luis 154
Oviedo, Yulién 362

Pacheco, Johnny 158, 261
Padilla, Frank 325
Padilla, Heberto 251
Padrón, Nelson *El flaco* 226
Padura, Leonardo 193, 262
Páez, Ana María 342
Páez, Fito 390
Pagano, César 89
Palmieri, Charlie 193, 237, 256, 261, 345
Palmieri, Eddie 237, 256, 257, 258, 262, 296, 345
Palomino, Salvador 76
Pancho Quinto 107
Papá Noel 380

Papeti, Fausto 313
Papines, Los **107**, 108, 193, 250, 252, 297, 328
París, Rogelio 312
Parker, Charlie 224, 238, 241, 244, 245
Parlá, Alicia 74
Parra, Isabel y Ángel 306
Parra, Violeta 306
Paulito (Pablo Fernández Gallo) 32, 252, 289, 356, 358, 367
Paulito y su Élite 356, 363, 383
Paz, Víctor 241
Pedersen, Orsted 224
Pedroso, César 354
Pelladito, Ángel 107
Pello el Afrokán (Pedro Izquierdo) 295
Pena, María Elena 154
Peña, Filiberto 226
Peñalver, Emilio 193
Peñalver, Sabino 177
Peraza, Armando 107
Perdomo, Marcos 189
Perea, Alicia 303
Pereda Rodríguez, Sergio 370
Pereira, Liduvino 167
Pérez Prado, Dámaso 30, 38, 59, 122, 126, 134, 135, 142, **163**, 164, 167, 168, 169, 170, 171, 172, 174, 196, 226, 231, 240, 245, 321
Pérez Prado, Pantaleón 167
Pérez Sentenat, César 202
Pérez, Amaury 127, 285, 286, 316, 325, 359
Pérez, Danilo 225, 226
Pérez, Manuel 67, 223
Pérez, Martha 198, 249
Pérez-Rodríguez, dúo 135
Petrillo, James C. 28
Phillips, Flip 238, 241
Pied Pipers 80
Piloto, Giraldo (padre) 150
Piloto, Giraldo 250, 349, 350, 351, 368
Pimentel, Leoginaldo 316
Pinedo, Nelson 62
Pinelli, Ari 342
Pinelli, Germán 56
Pinelli, Germán David 342

Pinelli, Tony 342
Pink Floyd 324
Pino, Eliseo 324
Pinochet, Augusto 306
Piñeiro, Ignacio 26, 47, 48, **50**, 98, 111, 141, 220, 256, 259, 324, 344, 365, 380
Piquero, Clemente *Chicho* 168, 171
Pita Rodríguez, Félix 317
Pla, Enrique 226, 227, 228, 288, 319, 329, 338
Pla, Roberto 381
Planas, Raúl 58, 323, 375
Platters, Los 297
Poleo, Orlando 372
Ponce, Daniel 107, 225, 241
Porcel, Mike 325
Porro, Oscar 370
Porro, Ricardo 301
Portabales, Guillermo 86
Portal, Otilio 76, 77, 189
Portela, Guillermo 142
Porter, Cole 129
Portillo de la Luz, César 29, 44, 77, **148**, 149, 151, 166, 250, 285, 290, 297
Portuondo, Haydée 154
Portuondo, Omara 29, 148, 152, **154**, 285, 288, 307, 373, 375, 376, 377, 380
Poveda, Donato 281, 325
Pozo, Chano 31, 106, 124, 188, 230, **237**, 238
Pozo, Chino 124
Prats, Jaime 67
Prats, Jorge Luis 214
Prats, Rodrigo 200, 285
Primavera, dúo 74
Prío Socarrás, Carlos 123
Proyecto, Grupo 233, 350, 366, 380
Public Enemy 383
Puebla, Carlos **79**, 124, 248, 307, 319, 322, 397
Puente, Tito 66, 170, 194, 196, 234, 239, 240, 244, 258, 260, 262, 263, 265, 273, 333, 344
Puig, Alina 282
Puig, Cheo Belén 232
Puyans, Emilio 200

Quesada, Cándida 118
Quevedo, Pablo 161
Quilapayún 306
Quintana, José Luis *Changuito* 226, 227, 228, 229, 327, 354, 372
Quintana, Alfonsín 58
Quinteto de la Trova 292
Quinteto de Música Moderna 175
Quinteto Instrumental 194
Quiñones, José Dolores 125, 127, 135

Rabagliatti, Alberto 72
Rabí, María de los Ángeles 249
Rabí, Rolando 56
Rachmaninov, Serge 216
Raimón 307, 311
Ramírez, Santo *El niño* 111
Ramírez, Humberto 338
Ramírez, Louie 66, 237, 262
Ramos, Eduardo 311, 316
Ramos, Miriam 152, 154
Ramos, Severino 61, 64
Ramos, Tata 249
Rasco, José I. 118
Raval, Estela 297
Ravens, The 237
Reagan, Ronald 277
Reed, Jimmy 237
Regis, Billy 169
Reina, Félix 137, 161
Rentería Llerena, Lilí 315
Resnik, Regina 198
Revé, Elio 331, 352, 380, 383
Revé, Odelquis 332
Revueltas, Silvestre 201
Rey de la Torre, José 44
Reyes Cortés, Rodolfo 216
Reyes Proenza, Ernesto 370
Reyes, Judith 306
Reyes, Orlando 58
Reyes, Pepe 74
Ribot, Agustín 55, 189
Rich, Buddy 238, 241
Richards, Johnny 194
Richards, Julio 181
Rigual, Angelita 265
Ríos Vega, Luis 161

Ríos, Efraín 342
Ríos, Luis 275
Ríos, Rubén 249
Ripes, Bertha 340
Riset, Panchito 63
Riso, Amparo 377
Rivera, Eddy *Guagua* 280
Rivera, Ismael *Maelo* 262
Rivera, Héctor 237
Rivera, Mario 293, 331
Rivera, Ricardito 58, 193
Rivero, Abel 80
Rivero, Facundo **80**, 129, 144, 161
Rives, Ramón *Mongo* 53
Rizo, Marco 70
Roach, Max 238
Roch, Pascual 44
Rodés, Judith 284
Roditi, Claudio 225, 241
Rodríguez, Alejandro *El mulatón* 111
Rodríguez, Albita 89, 274, **275**, 276, 277
Rodríguez, Alfredo 128, 293, 294, 381
Rodríguez, Ángeles 140
Rodríguez, Arsenio 26, 44, 54, 62, 63, 124, 159, **162**, 163, 165, 230, 234, 254
Rodríguez, Ernesto 76
Rodríguez, Ezequiel 172
Rodríguez, Humberto 141
Rodríguez, Mario 385
Rodríguez, Osvaldo 127, 340, 341
Rodríguez, Pablo 66
Rodríguez, Roberto 238
Rodríguez, Santiago 216
Rodríguez, Silvio 33, 89, 154, 267, 291, 307, **308**, 309, 310, 311, 312, 314, 316, 317, 318, 325, 328, 341, 379, 385
Rodríguez, Siro 49
Rodríguez, Tanya 326
Rodríguez, Tito 54, 66, 135, 170, 195, 196, 234, 263
Rogers, Shorty 172
Roig, Gonzalo 187, 195, 200, 240, 250
Roig, Gustavo 171
Roja, Luis 141
Rojas, Jorge Luis *Rojitas* 335
Rojas, María Teresa 116
Rojas, Martín 311, 314

Rojas, Ñico 44, 135
Roldán, Amadeo 121, 187, 199, 201, **202**, 203, 320
Román, Miguel 55
Romero de Nicola, Clara 44
Romeu, Antonio Mª 47, 156, 157, 169, 182, 195, 232, 235, 320
Romeu, Armando 169, 182, 194, 229, 231, 232, 318, **320**, 321, 373
Romeu, Mario 310
Rondón, César Miguel 62, 262
Ronstadt, Linda 131, 267
Ros, Lázaro 118, 253, 325, 326
Rosell, Rosendo 141
Rosenthal, Manuel 198
Rossell, Electo *Chepín* 58
Rubalcaba, Gonzalo 194, 232, 233, 251, 253, 325, 348, 350, 351, 354, **365**, 366, 371, 380,
Rubalcaba, Guillermo 352, 365, 375
Rubalcaba, Jacobo 365
Rubinstein, Arthur 198
Rugolo, Pete 245
Ruiz Castellanos, Pablo 200
Ruiz Quevedo, Rosendo 92, **150**, 189, 250
Ruiz, Cándido 130
Ruiz, Hilton 225
Ruiz, Martica 280
Russell, George 238
Russell, Jane 169

Sabat, familia 299
Sabina, Joaquín 379
Sabre Marroquín, José 145
Sacasas, Anselmo 142, 230, 232, 245
Sadel, Alfredo 165
Saint Saëns, Camile 137
Salazar, Lalita 249
Salazar, Max 65, 66, 233, 237, 239
Salgado, Estéfano 275
Salinas, José Luis 140
Salomé, Lina 249
Salvador, Emiliano 63, 231, 233, 316, 340, 371
Sampson, Edgar 235
Sanabria, Abel 370
Sanabria, Izzy 259

Sánchez, Alina 285
Sánchez *Bimbi*, Maximiliano 78
Sánchez de Fuentes, Eduardo 45, 46, 115, 133
Sánchez Ferrer, Roberto 321
Sánchez Guevara, Canek 27
Sánchez, Daniel 63
Sánchez, Pepe 128, 279
Sánchez, Roberto 154
Sancho, Fernando *El carioco* 140
Sandoval, Arturo 257, **269**, 270, 273, 274, 277, 319, 324, 328, 329, 334
Sanjuán, Pedro 202, 203
Santa, Florencio *Pícolo* 78
Santaló, Estelita 249
Santamaría, Haydée 314
Santamaría, Mongo 58, 59, 103, 107, 171, **239**, 240, 264, 344
Santana, Carlos 255, 333, 392
Santana, María de los Ángeles 198
Santer, Reinaldo 370
Santiago, Félix 363
Santiago, Joe 241
Santos, Daniel 58, 62, 128, 190, 382
Santos, Ray 241
Sanz, Alejandro 134, 278
Sardiñas, Israel 146
Sarría, Guido 137
Saumell, Manuel 25
Savary, Jerome 323
Sax, Antoine Joseph 224
Scull, René 163
Schnabel (pianista) 198
Schubert, Franz 25
Schwarzkopf, Elisabeth 198
Secada, Jon 274
Secada, Moraima 81
Seeger, Peggy 307
Seeger, Pete 91, 93
Seguí, Johnny 239
Septeto Boloña 60
Septeto Espirituano 141, 291
Septeto Habanero **47**, 49, 60, 62, 65, 141, 256
Septeto Matamoros 51
Septeto Miquito 162
Septeto Munamar 62
Septeto Nacional **47**, 48, 49, 65, 111, 141, 220, 242, 256, 278, 344, 380

Sexteto Occidente 49
Septeto Típico Oriental 292
Septeto Trovadoras del Cayo 129
Septeto Turquino 370
Septiembre 5 326
Serguera, Jorge *Papito* 315
Serrano, Juan Antonio 77
Serrat, Joan Manuel 29, 131, 311, 390
Servigón, Eddie 255
Sevilla, Ninón 122, 164, 168
SGAE 18, 93, 149, 211, 285
Shaw, Artie 130
Shearing, George 340
Sierra, Julia, 275
Sigler, Vicente 230, 233
Silber, Irwin 307
Silva, José *Chombo* 135, 240, 255, 256
Silva, Myrta 56, 62, 190
Simon, Paul 369
Simonet, Manuel 324, 364, 365
Simons, Moisés 38, 68, 139, 195, 230
Sims, Zoot 242, 330
Síntesis, grupo 253, 313, 324, 325, 326
Sisle, Noble 235
Slonimsky, Nicolás 202
Smith, Federico 153, 316
Smood, James *Santiago* 230
Sobrinos del Juez, Los 266
Socarrás, Alberto 31, 124, 158, 230, 236, 237, 258, 323
Socolov, Ben 253
Solares González, Francisco 48
Solís, Javier 130
Solís, Meme 154
Solórzano, Joaquín 292
Somavilla, Rafael 167, 318
Son Damas (orq. femenina) 389
Sonora La Calle 370
Sonorama 6, grupo 311
Sontag, Susan 266
Sosa Rodríguez, Enrique 118
Sosa, Eduardo 76
Sosa, Mercedes 306
Sosa, Nelo 56
Sosa, Pedro 79
Spengler, Félix 215
Stacholy, Pedro 229

Starr, Ringo 244
Stearns, Marshall W. 221
Stern (violinista) 198
Storch, Fernando 65, 66
Strachwitz, Chris 372
Stravinsky, Igor 200
Suárez, Antolín *Papá Quila* 59
Suárez, Humberto 55, 249
Suárez, Manolo 63, 65
Suárez, Senén 58
Sublette, Ned 253
Summers, Andy 291
Sunshine, Marion 69
Symphony Sid 242

Tabrane, Baz 77
Talking Heads 253
Tallet, José Zacarías 203
Tamayo, Aurelio 171
Tamayo, Gustavo 175, 193, 194
Tarraza, Juan Bruno 130, 135, 145, 165, 231
Tárrega, Francisco 302
Tata Güines (Arístides Soto) 197, 109, 182, 193, 194, 250, 334, 371
Taylor, Bill 241
Taylor, Paul 293
Tebaldi, Renata 198
Teenagers, Los 297
Tejedor, José 58, 154
Tejera, Tony 189
Téllez, Luis **131**, 154
Tema IV, grupo 324
Terrón, Armando 279
Terry, Ángel 375
Tico, Ray 77
Tiger, Growling 257
Timor, Leonardo 108
Tió, Lorenzo 223
Tite Curet Alonso, Catalino 262, 265
Tito, Josip Broz 251
Tjader, Cal 239, 240, 256
Toledo, René Luis 270
Toña la Negra 128
Toro, Yomo 274
Torrente, Manolo 249
Torres, Carlos *Argentino* 62

Torres, Alina 354
Torres, Barbarito 44, 285, 287, 371, 374
Torres, Dora Ileana 159
Torres, Juan Pablo 182, 244, 334
Torres, Roberto 62, 194, 255, 256, 257, 277, 278
Torres, Willie 239
Tortoló, Rafael 146
Touzet, René 125, 126, 133, 143, 145
Trafficante, Santos 123
Trejo, Nelson 281
Tres de La Habana 342
Trinidad, Amado 129, 164
Trío Hermanos Rigual 76, 78
Trío La Rosa 76, 77, 88
Trío Los Guaracheros de Oriente 76, 78
Trío Los Panchos 76, 145
Trío Los Tradicionales 79
Trío Los Tres Ases 76
Trío Matamoros 49, 76, 77, 250, 344
Trío Matancero 284
Trío Oriental 76, 78
Trío Servando Díaz 76
Trío Taicuba 76, 77
Trío Tropicuba
Troche, Urbana 49
Trueba, Fernando 31, 58, 330, 345
Trumbauer, Frankie 235
Turre, Steve 257

Ulloa, Alejandro 89
UNEAC 91, 109, 213, 251
Urbay, Marlene 215
Urbino, Ibrahím 166
Urfé, José 155
Urfé, Odilio 110, 148, 161
Urrutia, Osvaldo 168

Vaillant, Numidia 215
Valdés, Abelardito 161, 195
Valdés, Alfredito 63, 161, 256, 278
Valdés, Alfredo 256, 278
Valdés, Amadito 334
Valdés, Bebo 63, 124, 144, 152, 163, 168, 170, 164, 185, 193, 194, 231, 249, 288, 321, 324, 329, 331
Valdés, Celso 137

Valdés, Chucho 224, 225, 231, 233, 252, 285, 288, 319, 324, 328, 329, 330, 331, 338, 339, 365, 371, 383
Valdés, Ele 324, 325
Valdés, Gilberto 133, 200, 208, 234, 239
Valdés, Julio 141
Valdés, Lázaro 358, 359
Valdés, Marta 29, 133, 151, 152, 250
Valdés, Mayra Caridad 288
Valdés, Merceditas 88, 112, 121, 122, 194
Valdés, Miguelito Mr. Babalú 68, 98, 124, 142, 144, 145, 163, 181, 230, 237, 242
Valdés, Oscar 161, 256, 329, 359
Valdés, Oscar (de Irakere) 359
Valdés, Carlos Patato 55, 57, 107, 185, 194, 229, 241, 263, 293, 344
Valdés, Raúl 371
Valdés, Tomás 137
Valdés, Vicentico 62, 127, 150, 152, 161, 256, 264, 358
Valdés, Víctor 349
Valdespí, Armando 131, 161, 230
Valdéz Céspedes, Miguel 281
Valentín, Dave 331
Valentino, Rodolfo 70
Valenzuela, Raimundo 156
Valera, Enrique Quique 342
Valera, Félix 342
Valera, Manuel 316
Valera Miranda, familia 342
Valerio, Lupita 244
Valiente, Teresita 365
Valoy, Cuco 263
Valverde, Umberto 192
Valle, Orlando Maraca 158, 338, 371, 372, 375
Valle, Moisés Yumurí 371, 372
Vallejo, Orlando Chicho 56, 58, 64, 127, 183
Vallejo, César 310
Varela, Calixto 87
Varela, Carlos 285, 291, 313, 325
Varela, Félix 23
Vargas, Pedro 128, 165
Vargas, Wilfrido 263
Varona, Ernesto 323

Varona, Jorge 64, 329
Vaughan, Sara 330
Vázquez Montalbán, Manuel 395
Vázquez, Elpidio 60
Vázquez, Javier 255
Vázquez, Pablo 255
Vázquez, Papo 331
Vega, Aaron 355
Vega, Esteban 107
Vega, Pedro 125, 377
Velasco, Germán 329, 349
Velázquez, Chelo 76, 130
Veloso, Caetano 283
Veloz, Ramón 89, 250
Ventura, Johnny 263
Vera, Alberto 141, **150**, 154, 250
Vera, María Teresa 47, 49, 50, 75, 98, 341
Verdecia, Carlos 221
Verger, Pierre 116
Verges, Dominica 60
Verne, Adela 200
Viana, Vicente 55
Vicent, Mauricio 251, 338
Víctor Manuel 390
Víctor Manuelle 365
Vieja Trova Santiaguera 35, 43, 64, 285, **288**, 289
Viglietti, Daniel 306
Vila, Pedro 142
Vilató, Orestes 255, 333, 344
Villa, Lázaro 375
Villa-Lobos, Héitor 201, 203
Villalón, Alberto 48
Villalón, Andy 284

Villaverde, Cirilo 23
Vitier, José María 325
Vitier, Sergio 316
Vivar, Alejandro *El negro* 135, 193, 194, 249, 256, 257
Vocal Sampling 286, **368**, 369, 370
Von Karajan, Herbert 198

Walter, Bruno 198
Water, Muddy 237
Webb, Chick 235
Wenders, Wim 372, 376
West Durán, Alan 258
White, Barry 361
White, José 301
Whiteman, Paul 73, 235
Williams, Clarence 158
Williams, Joe 328
Wooding, Sam 235
Wörner, Götz 243
Xiqués, Félix 107

Yáñez y Gómez 150
Yañez, Luis 93, 150
Yoruba Andabo **109**, 110, 194
Young, Lester 224
Yumurí, grupo 363

Zaballa, Miguel 138
Zafiritos, Los 298
Zafiros, Los **297**, 298, 369, 377
Zayas, Alberto 108
Zequeira, Rafael 49
Zitarrosa, Alfredo 306